Volvo S60
Owners Workshop Manual

Martynn Randall

Models covered

(4793 - 320)

S60 Saloon, including special/limited editions

Petrol: 2.0 litre (1984cc), 2.3 litre (2319cc), 2.4 litre (2401cc & 2435cc) & 2.5 litre (2521cc)
Turbo-Diesel: 2.4/2.5 litre (2401cc)

Does NOT cover bi-fuel or AWD models, or S60R

© Haynes Publishing 2009

ABCDE
FGHIJ
KLMNO
PQRS

A book in the **Haynes Owners Workshop Manual Series**

ISBN **978 1 84425 793 5**

British Library Cataloguing in Publication Data
A catalogue record for this book is available from the British Library.

Printed in the USA

Haynes Publishing
Sparkford, Yeovil,

Haynes North America, Inc
861 Lawrence Drive, Newbury Park, California 91320, USA

Haynes Publishing Nordiska AB
Box 1504, 751 45 UPPSALA, Sverige

Contents

LIVING WITH YOUR VOLVO S60

Contents

REPAIRS & OVERHAUL

Engine and associated systems

Transmission

Brakes and suspension

Body equipment

Wiring diagrams

REFERENCE

Index

The Volvo S60 Saloon was introduced in 2001, and shares similar running gear and appearance with the larger S80 model. The stylish, 5-door, front-wheel drive models were given a 'soft' facelift in 2004, including minor changes to the front and rear bumpers, and some aspects of the interior.

The petrol engines are all fuel-injected, in-line, five-cylinder units of 1984 cc, 2319 cc, 2401 cc, 2435 cc or 2521 cc displacement. Both normally-aspirated and turbocharged versions are available. The engines feature a comprehensive engine management system with extensive emission control equipment. Although only one diesel engine was available, the turbocharged, direct-injection D5244T five-cylinder was uprated and modified for the 2005 model year. These improvements were mostly concerned with reducing emissions, and included the fitment of a particle filter to the exhaust system.

Transmissions are either 5- or 6-speed manual, or 5- or 6-speed automatic with computer control. The automatic transmission features mode control selection, allowing the driver to alter the transmission characteristics to suit normal or winter driving requirements.

Braking is by discs all round, the handbrake acting on drums incorporated in the rear brake discs. Anti-lock braking (ABS) and power-assisted steering is standard on all models. All models are equipped with independent front and rear suspension

A wide range of standard and optional equipment is available within the range to suit virtually all tastes. As with all Volvo models, safety features are of paramount importance, and the Supplemental Restraint System and Side Impact Protection System offer an exceptional level of driver and passenger protection throughout the vehicle.

Provided that regular servicing is carried out in accordance with the manufacturer's recommendations, the Volvo S60 will provide the enviable reliability for which this marque is famous. Despite the engine's complexity, the engine compartment is relatively spacious, and most of the items requiring frequent attention are easily accessible.

Your Volvo manual

The aim of this manual is to help you get the best value from your vehicle. It can do so in several ways. It can help you decide what work must be done (even should you choose to get it done by a garage). It will also provide information on routine maintenance and servicing, and give a logical course of action and diagnosis when random faults occur. However, it is hoped that you will use the manual by tackling the work yourself. On simpler jobs it may even be quicker than booking the car into a garage and going there twice, to leave and collect it. Perhaps most important, a lot of money can be saved by avoiding the costs a garage must charge to cover its labour and overheads.

The manual has drawings and descriptions to show the function of the various components so that their layout can be understood. Tasks are described and photographed in a clear step-by-step sequence. The illustrations are numbered by the Section number and paragraph number to which they relate – if there is more than one illustration per paragraph, the sequence is denoted alphabetically.

References to the 'left' or 'right' of the vehicle are in the sense of a person in the driver's seat, facing forwards.

Acknowledgements

Thanks are due to Draper Tools Limited, who provided some of the workshop tools, and to all those people at Sparkford who helped in the production of this manual.

We take great pride in the accuracy of information given in this manual, but vehicle manufacturers make alterations and design changes during the production run of a particular vehicle of which they do not inform us. No liability can be accepted by the authors or publishers for loss, damage or injury caused by any errors in, or omissions from the information given.

Working on your car can be dangerous. This page shows just some of the potential risks and hazards, with the aim of creating a safety-conscious attitude.

General hazards

Scalding

• Don't remove the radiator or expansion tank cap while the engine is hot.
• Engine oil, automatic transmission fluid or power steering fluid may also be dangerously hot if the engine has recently been running.

Burning

• Beware of burns from the exhaust system and from any part of the engine. Brake discs and drums can also be extremely hot immediately after use.

Crushing

• When working under or near a raised vehicle, always supplement the jack with axle stands, or use drive-on ramps. *Never venture under a car which is only supported by a jack.*
• Take care if loosening or tightening high-torque nuts when the vehicle is on stands. Initial loosening and final tightening should be done with the wheels on the ground.

Fire

• Fuel is highly flammable; fuel vapour is explosive.
• Don't let fuel spill onto a hot engine.
• Do not smoke or allow naked lights (including pilot lights) anywhere near a vehicle being worked on. Also beware of creating sparks (electrically or by use of tools).
• Fuel vapour is heavier than air, so don't work on the fuel system with the vehicle over an inspection pit.
• Another cause of fire is an electrical overload or short-circuit. Take care when repairing or modifying the vehicle wiring.
• Keep a fire extinguisher handy, of a type suitable for use on fuel and electrical fires.

Electric shock

• Ignition HT voltage can be dangerous, especially to people with heart problems or a pacemaker. Don't work on or near the ignition system with the engine running or the ignition switched on.

• Mains voltage is also dangerous. Make sure that any mains-operated equipment is correctly earthed. Mains power points should be protected by a residual current device (RCD) circuit breaker.

Fume or gas intoxication

• Exhaust fumes are poisonous; they often contain carbon monoxide, which is rapidly fatal if inhaled. Never run the engine in a confined space such as a garage with the doors shut.
• Fuel vapour is also poisonous, as are the vapours from some cleaning solvents and paint thinners.

Poisonous or irritant substances

• Avoid skin contact with battery acid and with any fuel, fluid or lubricant, especially antifreeze, brake hydraulic fluid and Diesel fuel. Don't syphon them by mouth. If such a substance is swallowed or gets into the eyes, seek medical advice.
• Prolonged contact with used engine oil can cause skin cancer. Wear gloves or use a barrier cream if necessary. Change out of oil-soaked clothes and do not keep oily rags in your pocket.
• Air conditioning refrigerant forms a poisonous gas if exposed to a naked flame (including a cigarette). It can also cause skin burns on contact.

Asbestos

• Asbestos dust can cause cancer if inhaled or swallowed. Asbestos may be found in gaskets and in brake and clutch linings. When dealing with such components it is safest to assume that they contain asbestos.

Special hazards

Hydrofluoric acid

• This extremely corrosive acid is formed when certain types of synthetic rubber, found in some O-rings, oil seals, fuel hoses etc, are exposed to temperatures above 400°C. The rubber changes into a charred or sticky substance containing the acid. *Once formed, the acid remains dangerous for years. If it gets onto the skin, it may be necessary to amputate the limb concerned.*
• When dealing with a vehicle which has suffered a fire, or with components salvaged from such a vehicle, wear protective gloves and discard them after use.

The battery

• Batteries contain sulphuric acid, which attacks clothing, eyes and skin. Take care when topping-up or carrying the battery.
• The hydrogen gas given off by the battery is highly explosive. Never cause a spark or allow a naked light nearby. Be careful when connecting and disconnecting battery chargers or jump leads.

Air bags

• Air bags can cause injury if they go off accidentally. Take care when removing the steering wheel and/or facia. Special storage instructions may apply.

Diesel injection equipment

• Diesel injection pumps supply fuel at very high pressure. Take care when working on the fuel injectors and fuel pipes.

⚠ *Warning: Never expose the hands, face or any other part of the body to injector spray; the fuel can penetrate the skin with potentially fatal results.*

Remember...

DO

• Do use eye protection when using power tools, and when working under the vehicle.

• Do wear gloves or use barrier cream to protect your hands when necessary.

• Do get someone to check periodically that all is well when working alone on the vehicle.

• Do keep loose clothing and long hair well out of the way of moving mechanical parts.

• Do remove rings, wristwatch etc, before working on the vehicle – especially the electrical system.

• Do ensure that any lifting or jacking equipment has a safe working load rating adequate for the job.

DON'T

• Don't attempt to lift a heavy component which may be beyond your capability – get assistance.

• Don't rush to finish a job, or take unverified short cuts.

• Don't use ill-fitting tools which may slip and cause injury.

• Don't leave tools or parts lying around where someone can trip over them. Mop up oil and fuel spills at once.

• Don't allow children or pets to play in or near a vehicle being worked on.

The following pages are intended to help in dealing with common roadside emergencies and breakdowns. You will find more detailed fault finding information at the back of the manual, and repair information in the main chapters.

If your car won't start and the starter motor doesn't turn

☐ If it's a model with automatic transmission, make sure the selector is in P or N.
☐ Lift the luggage compartment floor and make sure that the battery terminals are clean and tight.
☐ Switch on the headlights and try to start the engine. If the headlights go very dim when you're trying to start, the battery is probably flat. Get out of trouble by jump starting (see next page) using a friend's car.

If your car won't start even though the starter motor turns as normal

☐ Is there fuel in the tank?
☐ Is there moisture on electrical components under the bonnet? Switch off the ignition, then wipe off any obvious dampness with a dry cloth. Spray a water-repellent aerosol product (WD-40 or equivalent) on ignition and fuel system electrical connectors like those shown in the photos. (Note that diesel engines don't usually suffer from damp).

A Check the mass airflow sensor or inlet air temperature sensor wiring connector for security.

B Check the security of the battery positive connection at the fuse/relay box.

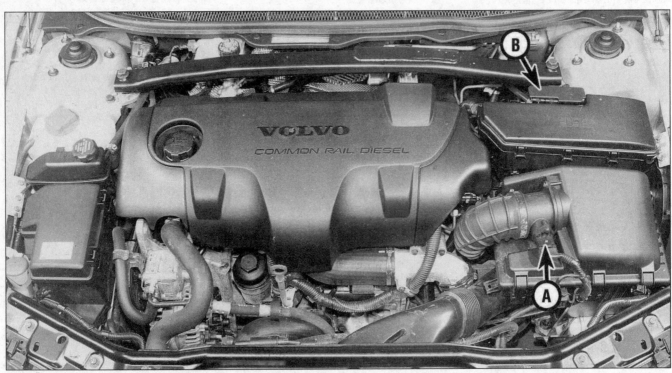

Check that electrical connections are secure (with the ignition switched off) and spray them with a water-dispersant spray like WD-40 if you suspect a problem due to damp

Jump starting

When jump-starting a car using a booster battery, observe the following precautions:

✔ Before connecting the booster battery, make sure that the ignition is switched off.

✔ Ensure that all electrical equipment (lights, heater, wipers, etc) is switched off.

✔ Take note of any special precautions printed on the battery case.

✔ Make sure that the booster battery is the same voltage as the discharged one in the vehicle.

✔ If the battery is being jump-started from the battery in another vehicle, the two vehicles MUST NOT TOUCH each other.

✔ Make sure that the transmission is in neutral (or PARK, in the case of automatic transmission).

HAYNES HINT

Jump starting will get you out of trouble, but you must correct whatever made the battery go flat in the first place. There are three possibilities:

1 *The battery has been drained by repeated attempts to start, or by leaving the lights on.*

2 *The charging system is not working properly (alternator drivebelt slack or broken, alternator wiring fault or alternator itself faulty).*

3 *The battery itself is at fault (electrolyte low, or battery worn out).*

1 Lift the cover from the jumpstart terminal (+) on the left-hand side of the engine compartment in front of the suspension turret, and connect the red lead to the terminal.

2 Connect the other end of the red lead to the positive (+) terminal of the booster battery.

3 Connect one end of black jump lead to the negative (-) terminal of the booster battery.

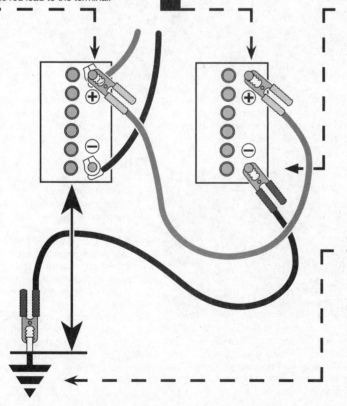

4 Connect the other end of the black jump lead to a bolt or bracket on the engine block on the vehicle to be started.

5 Make sure that the jump leads will not come into contact with the cooling fan, drivebelts or other moving parts on the engine.

6 Start the engine, then with the engine running at fast idle speed disconnect the jump leads in the reverse order of connection.

Wheel changing

⚠️ *Warning: Do not change a wheel in a situation where you risk being hit by other traffic. On busy roads, try to stop in a lay-by or a gateway. Be wary of passing traffic while changing the wheel – it is easy to become distracted by the job in hand.*

Preparation

- ☐ When a puncture occurs, stop as soon as it is safe to do so.
- ☐ Park on firm level ground, if possible, and well out of the way of other traffic.
- ☐ Use hazard warning lights if necessary.

- ☐ If you have one, use a warning triangle to alert other drivers of your presence.
- ☐ Apply the handbrake and engage first or reverse gear (or Park on models with automatic transmission).

- ☐ Chock the wheel diagonally opposite the one being removed – a couple of large stones will do for this.
- ☐ If the ground is soft, use a flat piece of wood to spread the load under the jack.

Changing the wheel

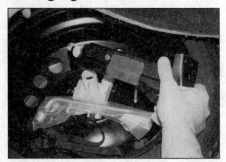

1 The spare wheel and tools are stored in the luggage compartment under the carpet. Release the restraining straps, remove the wheelbrace and jack . . .

2 . . . then unscrew the spare wheel retainer from the centre of the wheel.

3 Slacken each wheel bolt by a half turn, using the wheelbrace. If the bolts are too tight, DON'T stand on the brace to undo them – call for assistance.

4 On models with alloy wheels, a Volvo socket may be needed to remove the security bolt – the socket should be in the glovebox or toolkit.

5 Engage the jack head with the reinforced bracket located in the middle of the sill on each side of the car (don't jack the vehicle at any other point of the sill).

6 Turn the handle clockwise until the wheel is raised clear of the ground, then unscrew the wheel bolts and remove the wheel.

7 Fit the spare wheel, noting that there is a special locating peg (arrowed) on the wheel hub, which must fit through the hole in the temporary spare wheel, or into the space inside the wheel hub on regular roadwheels.

8 Fit and screw in the bolts. Lightly tighten the bolts with the wheelbrace, then lower the vehicle to the ground. Securely tighten the wheel bolts, then refit the wheel trim or hub cap, as applicable. The wheel bolts should be slackened and retightened to the correct torque (140 Nm/103 lbf ft) at the earliest possible opportunity.

Finally...

- ☐ Remove the wheel chocks.
- ☐ Stow the jack and tools back in the car.
- ☐ Check the tyre pressure on the wheel just fitted. If it is low, or if you don't have a pressure gauge with you, drive slowly to the nearest garage and inflate the tyre to the right pressure. In the case of the space-saver spare wheel, this pressure is much higher than for a normal tyre.
- ☐ Have the damaged tyre or wheel repaired as soon as possible.

Note: *Some models are supplied with a 'space-saver' spare wheel, the tyre being narrower than standard, and marked TEMPORARY USE ONLY. This spare wheel **must** be replaced with a standard wheel as soon as possible. Drive with particular care, especially through corners and when braking – Volvo recommend a maximum speed of 50 mph when the special spare wheel is in use.*

Identifying leaks

Puddles on the garage floor or drive, or obvious wetness under the bonnet or underneath the car, suggest a leak that needs investigating. It can sometimes be difficult to decide where the leak is coming from, especially if the engine bay is very dirty already. Leaking oil or fluid can also be blown rearwards by the passage of air under the car, giving a false impression of where the problem lies.

 Warning: Most automotive oils and fluids are poisonous. Wash them off skin, and change out of contaminated clothing, without delay.

 HAYNES HiNT *The smell of a fluid leaking from the car may provide a clue to what's leaking. Some fluids are distinctively coloured. It may help to clean the car carefully and to park it over some clean paper overnight as an aid to locating the source of the leak.*
Remember that some leaks may only occur while the engine is running.

Sump oil

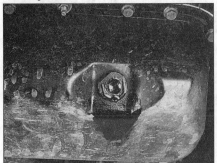

Engine oil may leak from the drain plug...

Oil from filter

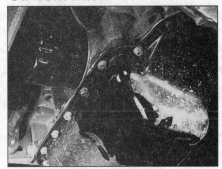

...or from the base of the oil filter.

Gearbox oil

Gearbox oil can leak from the seals at the inboard ends of the driveshafts.

Antifreeze

Leaking antifreeze often leaves a crystalline deposit like this.

Brake fluid

A leak occurring at a wheel is almost certainly brake fluid.

Power steering fluid

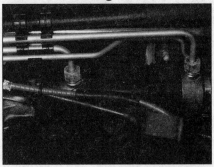

Power steering fluid may leak from the pipe connectors on the steering rack.

Towing

When all else fails, you may find yourself having to get a tow home – or of course you may be helping somebody else. Long-distance recovery should only be done by a garage or breakdown service. For shorter distances, DIY towing using another car is easy enough, but observe the following points:

☐ Use a proper tow-rope – they are not expensive. The vehicle being towed must display an ON TOW sign in its rear window.

☐ Always turn the ignition key to the 'On' position when the vehicle is being towed, so that the steering lock is released, and the direction indicator and brake lights work.

☐ A towing eye is provided below each bumper. The front towing eye is hidden behind a cover panel below the right-hand end of the front bumper **(see illustration)**.

☐ Before being towed, release the handbrake and select neutral on the transmission. Automatic transmission models should not be towed for more than 50 miles at a maximum speed of 50 mph.

☐ Note that greater-than-usual pedal pressure will be required to operate the brakes, since the vacuum servo unit is only operational with the engine running.

☐ Because the power steering will not be operational, greater-than-usual steering effort will be required.

☐ Make sure that both drivers know the route before setting off.

☐ The driver of the car being towed must keep the tow-rope taut at all times to avoid snatching.

☐ Only drive at moderate speeds and keep the distance towed to a minimum. Drive smoothly and allow plenty of time for slowing down at junctions.

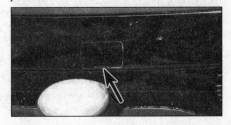

Introduction

There are some very simple checks which need only take a few minutes to carry out, but which could save you a lot of inconvenience and expense.

These *Weekly checks* require no great skill or special tools, and the small amount of time they take to perform could prove to be very well spent, for example:

☐ Keeping an eye on tyre condition and pressures, will not only help to stop them wearing out prematurely, but could also save your life.

☐ Many breakdowns are caused by electrical problems. Battery-related faults are particularly common, and a quick check on a regular basis will often prevent the majority of these.

☐ If your car develops a brake fluid leak, the first time you might know about it is when your brakes don't work properly. Checking the level regularly will give advance warning of this kind of problem.

☐ If the oil or coolant levels run low, the cost of repairing any engine damage will be far greater than fixing the leak, for example.

Underbonnet check points

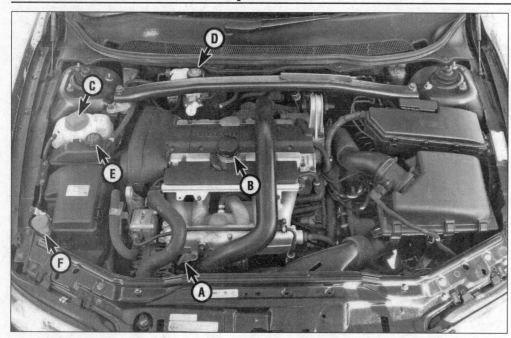

◄ 2.0 litre petrol engine (others similar)

A *Engine oil level dipstick*

B *Engine oil filler cap*

C *Coolant expansion tank*

D *Brake fluid reservoir*

E *Power steering fluid reservoir*

F *Screen washer fluid reservoir*

◄ 2.4 litre diesel engine

A *Engine oil level dipstick*

B *Engine oil filler cap*

C *Coolant expansion tank*

D *Brake fluid reservoir*

E *Power steering fluid reservoir*

F *Screen washer fluid reservoir*

Engine oil level

Before you start
✔ Make sure that the car is on level ground.
✔ Check the oil level before the car is driven, or at least 5 minutes after the engine has been switched off.

 HAYNES HiNT *If the oil is checked immediately after driving the vehicle, some of the oil will remain in the upper engine components, resulting in an inaccurate reading on the dipstick.*

The correct oil
Modern engines place great demands on their oil. It is very important that the correct oil for your car is used (see *Lubricants and fluids*).

Car care
● If you have to add oil frequently, you should check whether you have any oil leaks. Place some clean paper under the car overnight, and check for stains in the morning. If there are no leaks, then the engine may be burning oil, or the oil may only be leaking when the engine is running.
● Always maintain the level between the upper and lower dipstick marks. If the level is too low, severe engine damage may occur. Oil seal failure may result if the engine is overfilled by adding too much oil.

1 The dipstick top is brightly coloured for easy identification (see *Underbonnet check points* for exact location). Withdraw the dipstick.

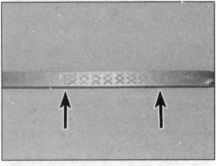

3 Note the oil level on the end of the dipstick, which should be in the hatched area between the upper (MAX) mark and lower (MIN) mark. Approximately 1.2 litres of oil will raise the level from the lower mark to the upper mark.

2 Using a clean rag or paper towel remove all oil from the dipstick. Insert the clean dipstick into the tube as far as it will go, then withdraw it again.

4 Oil is added through the filler cap. Unscrew the cap and top-up the level; a funnel may help to reduce spillage. Add the oil slowly, checking the level on the dipstick often. Don't overfill (see *Car care*).

Coolant level

⚠ *Warning: Do not attempt to remove the expansion tank pressure cap when the engine is hot, as there is a very great risk of scalding. Do not leave open containers of coolant about, as it is poisonous.*

Car care
● With a sealed-type cooling system, adding coolant should not be necessary on a regular basis. If frequent topping-up is required, it is likely there is a leak. Check the radiator, all hoses and joint faces for signs of staining or wetness, and rectify as necessary.

● It is important that antifreeze is used in the cooling system all year round, not just during the winter months. Don't top up with water alone, as the antifreeze will become diluted.

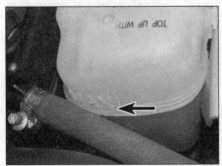

1 The coolant reservoir is located on the right-hand inner wing. The coolant level is visible through the reservoir body. The coolant level varies with engine temperature. When cold, the coolant level should be between the MAX and MIN marks. When the engine is hot, the level may rise slightly above the MAX mark.

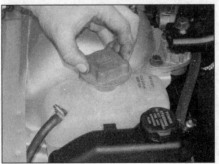

2 If topping-up is necessary, wait until the engine is cold. Slowly unscrew the expansion tank cap, to release any pressure present in the cooling system, and remove it.

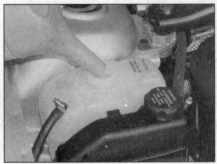

3 Add a mixture of water and antifreeze to the expansion tank until the coolant is at the correct level. Refit the cap and tighten it securely.

Brake and clutch fluid level

 Warning: Brake fluid can harm your eyes and damage painted surfaces, so use extreme caution when handling and pouring it. Do not use fluid which has been standing open for some time, as it absorbs moisture from the air, which can cause a dangerous loss of braking effectiveness.

Before you start

✔ Make sure that the car is on level ground.

 The fluid level in the reservoir will drop slightly as the brake pads wear down, but the fluid level must never be allowed to drop below the MIN mark.

Safety first!

● If the reservoir requires repeated topping-up, this is an indication of a fluid leak somewhere in the system, which should be investigated immediately.

● If a leak is suspected, the car should not be driven until the braking system has been checked. Never take any risks where brakes are concerned.

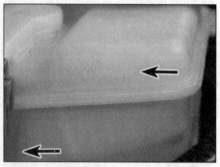

1 The MAX and MIN marks are indicated on the reservoir. The fluid level must be kept between the marks at all times.

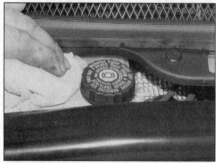

2 If topping-up is necessary, first wipe clean the area around the filler cap to prevent dirt entering the hydraulic system. Unscrew the reservoir cap and carefully lift it out of position. Inspect the reservoir, if the fluid is dirty, the hydraulic system should be drained and refilled (see Chapter 1A or 1B).

3 Carefully add fluid, taking care not to spill it onto the surrounding components. Use only the specified fluid; mixing different types can cause damage to the system. After topping-up to the correct level, securely refit the cap and wipe off any spilt fluid. Reconnect the fluid level wiring connector.

Power steering fluid level

Before you start

✔ Make sure that the car is on level ground.
✔ Set the steering wheel straight-ahead.
✔ The engine should be turned off.

 For the check to be accurate, the steering must not be turned once the engine has been stopped.

Safety first!

● The need for frequent topping-up indicates a leak, which should be investigated immediately.

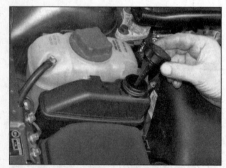

1 On early models, the reservoir is mounted on the right-hand front of the engine, while later models have the reservoir on the right-hand inner wing, in front of the cooling system expansion tank. Wipe clean the area around the reservoir filler neck, and unscrew the filler cap/dipstick from the reservoir.

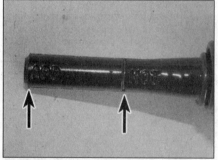

2 Dip the fluid with the reservoir cap/dipstick by screwing it fully back into place. When the engine is cold, the fluid level should be between the ADD mark and the COLD mark; when hot it should be between the ADD and HOT marks. Top-up when the level is at the ADD mark.

3 When topping-up, use the specified type of fluid – do not overfill the reservoir. When the level is correct, securely refit the cap.

Battery

Caution: Before carrying out any work on the vehicle battery, read the precautions given in 'Safety first!' at the start of this manual.

✔ Make sure that the battery tray is in good condition, and that the clamp is tight. Corrosion on the tray, retaining clamp and the battery itself can be removed with a solution of water and baking soda. Thoroughly rinse all cleaned areas with water. Any metal parts damaged by corrosion should be covered with a zinc-based primer, then painted.

✔ Periodically (approximately every three months), check the charge condition of the battery as described in Chapter 5A.

✔ On batteries which are not of the maintenance-free type, periodically check the electrolyte level in the battery – see Chapter 1A or 1B.

✔ If the battery is flat, and you need to jump start your vehicle, see *Roadside Repairs*.

Battery corrosion can be kept to a minimum by applying a layer of petroleum jelly to the clamps and terminals after they are reconnected.

1 The battery is located under the luggage compartment floor. Models up to 2004 model year have a large cover over the battery, whereas models from 2004 model year have a small cover over the battery positive terminal – lift the floor covering, remove the tool tray (where fitted) . . .

2 . . . undo the nuts/bolt (arrowed) and remove the battery retaining bracket, followed by the plastic cover over the battery. The exterior of the battery should be inspected periodically for damage such as a cracked case or cover.

3 Check the tightness of battery clamps to ensure good electrical connections. You should not be able to move them. Also check each cable for cracks and frayed conductors.

4 If corrosion (white, fluffy deposits) is evident, remove the cables from the battery terminals, clean them with a small wire brush, then refit them. Automotive stores sell a tool for cleaning the battery post . . .

5 . . . as well as the battery cable clamps

Screen washer fluid level

● On models so equipped, the screenwasher fluid is also used to clean the headlights.

● Screenwash additives not only keep the windscreen clean during bad weather, they also prevent the washer system freezing in cold weather – which is when you are likely to need it most. Don't top-up using plain water, as the screenwash will become diluted, and will freeze in cold weather.

Caution: On no account use engine coolant antifreeze in the screen washer system – this may damage the paintwork.

1 The washer fluid reservoir filler is located at the front right-hand side of the engine compartment (the reservoir itself is actually located under the car).

2 Release the cap and observe the level in the reservoir by looking down the filler neck. When topping-up the reservoir, a screenwash additive should be added in the quantities recommended on the bottle.

Tyre condition and pressure

It is very important that tyres are in good condition, and at the correct pressure - having a tyre failure at any speed is highly dangerous. Tyre wear is influenced by driving style - harsh braking and acceleration, or fast cornering, will all produce more rapid tyre wear. As a general rule, the front tyres wear out faster than the rears. Interchanging the tyres from front to rear ("rotating" the tyres) may result in more even wear. However, if this is completely effective, you may have the expense of replacing all four tyres at once! Remove any nails or stones embedded in the tread before they penetrate the tyre to cause deflation. If removal of a nail does reveal that the tyre has been punctured, refit the nail so that its point of penetration is marked. Then immediately change the wheel, and have the tyre repaired by a tyre dealer.

Regularly check the tyres for damage in the form of cuts or bulges, especially in the sidewalls. Periodically remove the wheels, and clean any dirt or mud from the inside and outside surfaces. Examine the wheel rims for signs of rusting, corrosion or other damage. Light alloy wheels are easily damaged by "kerbing" whilst parking; steel wheels may also become dented or buckled. A new wheel is very often the only way to overcome severe damage.

New tyres should be balanced when they are fitted, but it may become necessary to re-balance them as they wear, or if the balance weights fitted to the wheel rim should fall off. Unbalanced tyres will wear more quickly, as will the steering and suspension components. Wheel imbalance is normally signified by vibration, particularly at a certain speed (typically around 50 mph). If this vibration is felt only through the steering, then it is likely that just the front wheels need balancing. If, however, the vibration is felt through the whole car, the rear wheels could be out of balance. Wheel balancing should be carried out by a tyre dealer or garage.

1 *Tread Depth - visual check*
   The original tyres have tread wear safety bands (B), which will appear when the tread depth reaches approximately 1.6 mm. The band positions are indicated by a triangular mark on the tyre sidewall (A).

2 *Tread Depth - manual check*
   Alternatively, tread wear can be monitored with a simple, inexpensive device known as a tread depth indicator gauge.

3 *Tyre Pressure Check*
   Check the tyre pressures regularly with the tyres cold. Do not adjust the tyre pressures immediately after the vehicle has been used, or an inaccurate setting will result.

Tyre tread wear patterns

Shoulder Wear

Underinflation (wear on both sides)
Under-inflation will cause overheating of the tyre, because the tyre will flex too much, and the tread will not sit correctly on the road surface. This will cause a loss of grip and excessive wear, not to mention the danger of sudden tyre failure due to heat build-up.
Check and adjust pressures
Incorrect wheel camber (wear on one side)
Repair or renew suspension parts
Hard cornering
Reduce speed!

Centre Wear

Overinflation
Over-inflation will cause rapid wear of the centre part of the tyre tread, coupled with reduced grip, harsher ride, and the danger of shock damage occurring in the tyre casing.
Check and adjust pressures

If you sometimes have to inflate your car's tyres to the higher pressures specified for maximum load or sustained high speed, don't forget to reduce the pressures to normal afterwards.

Uneven Wear

Front tyres may wear unevenly as a result of wheel misalignment. Most tyre dealers and garages can check and adjust the wheel alignment (or "tracking") for a modest charge.
Incorrect camber or castor
Repair or renew suspension parts
Malfunctioning suspension
Repair or renew suspension parts
Unbalanced wheel
Balance tyres
Incorrect toe setting
Adjust front wheel alignment
Note: *The feathered edge of the tread which typifies toe wear is best checked by feel.*

Wiper blades

Note: *Fitting details for wiper blades vary according to model, and according to whether genuine Volvo wiper blades have been fitted. Use the procedures and illustrations shown as a guide for your car.*

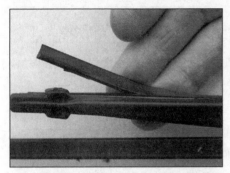

1 Check the condition of the wiper blades; if they are cracked or show any signs of deterioration, or if the glass swept area is smeared, renew them. Wiper blades should be renewed annually.

2 Two different types of wiper blades may be fitted. On the first type, pull the arm fully away from the glass until it locks. Swivel the blade through 90°, press the locking tab (arrowed) with your fingers and slide the blade out of the arm's hooked end. On the second type, pull the arm fully away from the glass until it locks, then squeeze together the retaining clips and pull them away from the blade, then slide the blade from the end of the arm.

3 Don't forget to check the headlight wiper blades as well. To remove the blade, lift the arm and simply pull the blade out of the arm fitting. Push the blade firmly home to refit.

Bulbs and fuses

✔ Check all external lights and the horn. Refer to the appropriate Sections of Chapter 12 for details if any of the circuits are found to be inoperative.

✔ Visually check all accessible wiring connectors, harnesses and retaining clips for security, and for signs of chafing or damage.

HAYNES HiNT *If you need to check your brake lights and indicators unaided, back up to a wall or garage door and operate the lights. The reflected light should show if they are working properly.*

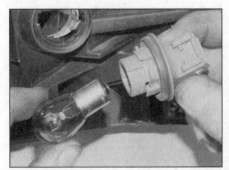

1 If a single indicator light, stop-light or headlight has failed, it is likely that a bulb has blown and will need to be renewed. Refer to Chapter 12 for details. If both stop-lights have failed, it is possible that the stop-light switch is faulty (see Chapter 9).

2 If more than one indicator light or headlight has failed, it is likely that either a fuse has blown or that there is a fault in the circuit (see Chapter 12). The fuses are located in the fusebox situated in the engine compartment on the passenger's side. Additional fuses are located in a fusebox under a plastic cover at the end of the facia, and in the luggage compartment behind the side panel trim on the left-hand side.

3 To renew a blown fuse, simply pull it out using the plastic tweezers provided. Fit a new fuse of the same rating (see Chapter 12). If the fuse blows again, it is important that you find out why – a complete checking procedure is given in Chapter 12.

Lubricants and fluids

Engine . . . . Most models have a decal in the engine compartment which details the engine oil specification. Where no decal is fitted, use multigrade engine oil, viscosity SAE 0W/30 to ACEA A5/B5

Cooling system . . . . Volvo coolant

Manual transmission . . . . Volvo synthetic gearbox oil (MTF 97309) 1161745*

Automatic transmission . . . . Volvo synthetic gearbox oil (JWS 3309) 1161540*

Braking system . . . . Brake and clutch fluid to DOT 4+

Power steering . . . . Volvo power steering fluid (WSS M2C204-A) 1161529* (Dexron III can be used for topping up)

Consult a Volvo dealer or specialist for latest recommendation

Tyre pressures

Refer to the tyre pressure sticker on the inside of the fuel filler flap (vehicles up to and including 2006 model year), or on the pillar of the driver's door aperture (vehicles from 2007 model year). Pressures apply only to original-equipment tyres, and may vary if other makes or type is fitted; check with the tyre manufacturer or supplier for correct pressures if necessary.

Chapter 1 Part A:
Routine maintenance and servicing – petrol models

Contents

Degrees of difficulty

Easy, suitable for novice with little experience	**Fairly easy,** suitable for beginner with some experience	**Fairly difficult,** suitable for competent DIY mechanic	**Difficult,** suitable for experienced DIY mechanic	**Very difficult,** suitable for expert DIY or professional

Lubricants and fluids
Refer to end of *Weekly checks* on page 0•16

Capacities

Engine oil
Drain and refill including filter change:
    Engines with oil level sensor............................... 5.5 litres
    Engines without oil level sensor .... 5.8 litres

Cooling system
With turbo.. 8.8 litres
Without turbo .... 8.0 litres

Fuel tank
All models... 70 litres (approximately)

Cooling system

Specified antifreeze mixture................................. 50% antifreeze/50% water
Note: *Refer to Chapter 3 for further details.*

Ignition system

Spark plugs:	Type	Electrode gap
Turbocharged engines	Bosch FR 7 DPP 10	0.7 mm
Non-turbocharged engines...............................	Bosch FGR 7 DQE 0	1.2 mm

Brakes

Brake pad minimum lining thickness .... 2.0 mm
Handbrake lever travel after adjustment .... 2 to 5 clicks

Remote control battery

Type .... CR 2032 3V

Tyres

Tyre pressures .... See the sticker on the inside of the fuel filler flap/driver's door aperture pillar

Torque wrench settings

	Nm	lbf ft
Automatic transmission drain/filler plugs......................	35	26
Automatic transmission level plug (6-speed only)	8	6
Auxiliary drivebelt tensioner	20	15
Engine oil drain plug......................................	35	26
Ignition coil...	10	7
Oil filter cover	25	18
Roadwheel bolts...	140	103
Spark plugs	30	22

The maintenance intervals in this manual are provided with the assumption that you, not the dealer, will be carrying out the work. These are the average maintenance intervals recommended by the manufacturer for vehicles driven daily under normal conditions. Obviously some variation of these intervals may be expected depending on territory of use, and conditions encountered. If you wish to keep your vehicle in peak condition at all times, you may wish to perform some of these procedures more often. We encourage frequent maintenance because it enhances the efficiency, performance and resale value of your vehicle.

When the vehicle is new, it should be serviced by a dealer service department (or other workshop recognised by the vehicle manufacturer as providing the same standard of service) in order to preserve the warranty.

The vehicle manufacturer may reject warranty claims if you are unable to prove that servicing has been carried out as and when specified, using only original equipment parts or parts certified to be of equivalent quality.

If the vehicle is driven in dusty areas, used to tow a trailer, driven frequently at slow speeds (idling in traffic) or on short journeys, more frequent maintenance intervals are recommended.

Every 250 miles or weekly
- [ ] Refer to Weekly checks.

Every 9000 miles or 12 months, whichever comes first
- [ ] Renew the engine oil and filter (Section 3).

Note: *Although Volvo recommend that the engine oil and filter are changed at 18 000 miles or every 12 months, frequent oil and filter changes are good for the engine. We therefore recommend changing the oil at the mileage specified here.*

Every 18 000 miles or 12 months, whichever comes first
- [ ] Check the condition of the brake pads (Section 4).
- [ ] Thoroughly inspect the engine compartment for fluid leaks (Section 5).
- [ ] Check the condition and security of the steering and suspension components (Section 6).
- [ ] Check the condition of the driveshaft gaiters (Section 7).
- [ ] Inspect the clutch hydraulic components (Section 8).
- [ ] Renew the pollen filter (Section 9).
- [ ] Check the battery electrolyte level (Section 10).
- [ ] Inspect the underbody, brake hydraulic pipes and hoses, and fuel lines (Section 11).
- [ ] Check the condition and security of the exhaust system (Section 12).
- [ ] Check the handbrake adjustment (Section 13).
- [ ] Check the condition of the seat belts (Section 14).
- [ ] Lubricate the locks and hinges (Section 15).
- [ ] Check the headlight beam alignment (Section 16).
- [ ] Check the coolant antifreeze concentration (Section 17).
- [ ] Reset the service reminder indicator (Section 18).
- [ ] Road test (Section 19).
- [ ] Check the operation of the air conditioning system (Section 20).
- [ ] Renew the remote control battery (Section 21).

Every 36 000 miles or 2 years, whichever comes first
In addition to the items listed above, carry out the following:
- [ ] Renew the air cleaner element (Section 22).
- [ ] Renew the spark plugs (Section 23).
- [ ] Check the automatic transmission fluid level (Section 24).

Every 108 000 miles or 6 years, whichever comes first
In addition to the items listed above, carry out the following:
- [ ] Renew the fuel filter (Section 25).
- [ ] Check and clean the crankcase ventilation system – turbocharged engines only (Section 26).

Every 108 000 miles or 10 years, whichever comes first
In addition to the items listed above, carry out the following:
- [ ] Renew the timing belt and tensioner (Section 27).

Note: *It is recommended that this interval is reduced on vehicles which are subjected to intensive use, ie, mainly short journeys or a lot of stop-start driving. The actual belt renewal interval is very much up to the individual owner, but bear in mind that severe engine damage will result if the belt breaks.*
- [ ] Renew the auxiliary drivebelt (Section 28).

Every 2 years, regardless of mileage
- [ ] Renew the brake fluid (Section 29).

Every 3 years, regardless of mileage
- [ ] Renew the coolant (Section 30).

Note: *This work is not included in the Volvo schedule, and should not be required if the recommended Volvo antifreeze/inhibitor is used.*

Underbonnet view of a 2.0 litre petrol model (other models similar)

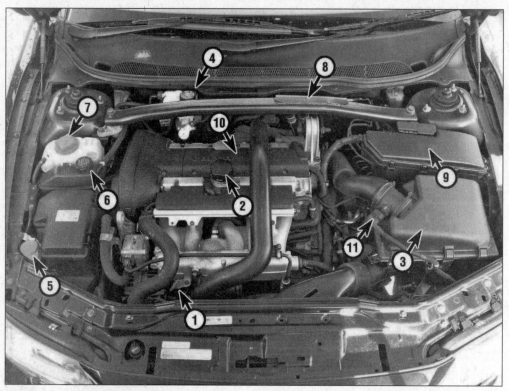

1 Oil level dipstick
2 Oil filler cap
3 Air filter cover
4 Brake and clutch fluid reservoir
5 Washer reservoir filler cap
6 Power steering fluid reservoir
7 Coolant expansion tank
8 Engine cross-stay
9 Fuse/relay box
10 Spark plug/ignition coils cover
11 Mass airflow meter

Front underbody view

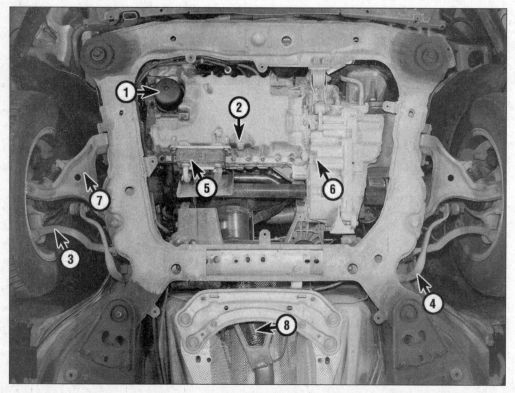

1 Oil filter
2 Engine oil sump drain plug
3 Steering track rod
4 Anti-roll bar
5 Engine oil cooler
6 Automatic gearbox fluid drain plug
7 Lower control arm
8 Exhaust pipe flexible section

Rear underbody view

1 Fuel filter
2 Suspension tie-rod
3 Trailing arm
4 Coil spring
5 Handbrake cable
6 Fuel tank
7 Lower control arm
8 Rear exhaust silencer

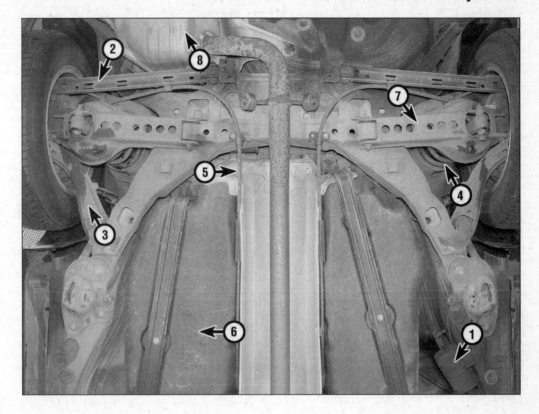

Maintenance procedures

1 Introduction

This Chapter is designed to help the home mechanic maintain his/her vehicle for safety, economy, long life and peak performance.

This Chapter contains a master maintenance schedule, followed by Sections dealing specifically with each task in the schedule. Visual checks, adjustments, component renewal and other helpful items are included. Refer to the accompanying illustrations of the engine compartment and the underside of the vehicle for the locations of the various components.

Servicing your vehicle in accordance with the mileage/time maintenance schedule and the following Sections will provide a planned maintenance programme, which should result in a long and reliable service life. This is a comprehensive plan, so maintaining some items but not others at the specified service intervals will not produce the same results.

As you service your vehicle, you will discover that many of the procedures can – and should – be grouped together, because of the particular procedure being performed, or because of the close proximity of two otherwise-unrelated components to one another. For example, if the vehicle is raised for any reason, the exhaust should be inspected at the same time as the suspension and steering components.

The first step of this maintenance programme is to prepare yourself before the actual work begins. Read through all the Sections relevant to the work to be carried out, then make a list and gather together all the parts and tools required. If a problem is encountered, seek advice from a parts specialist or a dealer service department.

Service interval display

All models are equipped with a service interval display indicator in the instrument panel. When a predetermined mileage, time period, or number of hours of engine operation has elapsed since the display was last reset, the service light will illuminate, providing a handy reminder of when the next service is required.

The display should not necessarily be used as a definitive guide to the servicing needs of your Volvo, but it is useful as a reminder to ensure that servicing is not accidentally overlooked. Owners of older cars, or those covering a small annual mileage, may feel inclined to service their car more often, in which case the service interval display is perhaps less relevant.

2 Regular maintenance

1 If, from the time the vehicle is new, the routine maintenance schedule is followed closely, and frequent checks are made of fluid levels and high-wear items, as suggested throughout this manual, the engine will be kept in relatively good running condition, and the need for additional work will be minimised.

2 It is possible that there will be some times when the engine is running poorly due to the lack of regular maintenance. This is even more likely if a used vehicle, which has not received regular and frequent maintenance checks, is purchased. In such cases, additional work may need to be carried out, outside of the regular maintenance intervals.

3 If engine wear is suspected, a compression test (refer to Part A of Chapter 2) will provide valuable information regarding the overall performance of the main internal components. Such a test can be used as a basis to decide on the extent of the work to be carried out. If, for example, a compression test indicates serious internal engine wear, conventional maintenance as described in this Chapter will not greatly improve the performance of

the engine, and may prove a waste of time and money, unless extensive overhaul work (Chapter 2C) is carried out first.

4 The following series of operations are those often required to improve the performance of a generally poor-running engine:

Primary operations

a) *Clean, inspect and test the battery (See Weekly checks and Section 10).*

b) *Check all the engine-related fluids (See Weekly checks).*

c) *Renew the auxiliary drivebelt (Section 28).*

d) *Renew the spark plugs (Section 23).*

e) *Check the condition of the air cleaner filter element and renew if necessary (Section 22).*

f) *Renew the fuel filter (Section 25).*

g) *Check the condition of all hoses, and check for fluid leaks (Section 5).*

Secondary operations

5 If the above operations do not prove fully effective, carry out the following operations: All the items listed under *Primary operations*, plus the following:

a) *Check the charging system (Chapter 5A).*

b) *Check the ignition system (Chapter 5B).*

c) *Check the fuel system (Chapter 4A).*

Every 9000 miles or 12 months

3 Engine oil and filter renewal

 Frequent oil changes are the best preventative maintenance the home mechanic can give the engine, because ageing oil becomes diluted and contaminated, which leads to premature engine wear.

1 Make sure that you have all the necessary tools before you begin this procedure. You should also have plenty of rags or newspapers handy, for mopping-up any spills. The oil should preferably be changed when the engine is still fully warmed-up to normal operating temperature, just after a run; warm oil and sludge will flow out more easily. Take care, however, not to touch the exhaust or any other hot parts of the engine when working under the vehicle. To avoid any possibility of

scalding, and to protect yourself from possible skin irritants and other harmful contaminants in used engine oils, it is advisable to wear gloves when carrying out this work.

2 Access to the underside of the vehicle is greatly improved if the vehicle can be lifted on a hoist, driven onto ramps, or supported by axle stands (see *Jacking and vehicle support*). Whichever method is chosen, make sure that the vehicle remains level, or if it is at an angle, that the drain point is at the lowest point. Release the screws and remove the engine undershield for access to the sump and filter **(see illustration)**.

3 Position the draining container under the drain plug, and unscrew the plug **(see illustration)**. If possible, try to keep the plug pressed into the sump while unscrewing it by hand the last couple of turns.

 As the drain plug releases from the threads, move it away sharply, so the stream of oil issuing from the sump runs into the container, not up your sleeve.

4 Allow the oil to drain into the container, and check the condition of the plug's sealing washer; renew it if worn or damaged.

5 Allow some time for the old oil to drain, noting that it may be necessary to reposition the container as the oil flow slows to a trickle; when the oil has completely drained, wipe clean the drain plug and its threads in the sump and refit the plug, tightening it to the specified torque.

6 The oil filter is located at the base of the sump on the front right-hand side.

7 Reposition the draining container under the oil filter then, using a suitable filter removal tool if necessary, slacken the filter initially, then unscrew it by hand the rest of the way; be prepared for some oil spillage **(see illustration)**. Empty the oil in the old filter into the container and pull the old filter element from the filter cover. Discard the filter cover O-ring seal, a new one must be fitted.

8 Using a clean, lint-free rag, wipe clean the cylinder block around the filter mounting.

9 Apply a light coating of clean engine oil to the new O-ring seal and fit it to the filter

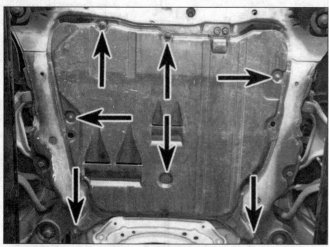

3.2 Undo the screws (arrowed) and remove the engine undershield

3.3 Undo the engine oil drain plug (arrowed)

3.7 Slacken the filter cover (arrowed) with a suitable removal tool

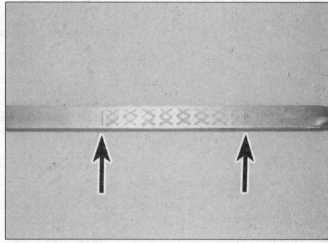

3.11 The maximum and minimum level markings (arrowed) are at the end of the hatched section on the dipstick

cover. Insert the filter element into the cover, then screw the filter cover into position on the engine until it seats, then tighten it to the specified torque.

10 Remove the old oil and all tools from under the vehicle, then lower the vehicle to the ground.

11 Remove the dipstick and the oil filler cap from the engine. Fill the engine with oil, using the correct grade and type of oil (see *Specifications*). Pour in half the specified

quantity of oil first, then wait a few minutes for the oil to run to the sump. Continue adding oil a small quantity at a time, until the level is up to the lower mark on the dipstick **(see illustration)**. Adding approximately 1.2 litres will raise the level to the upper mark on the dipstick.

12 Start the engine. The oil pressure warning light will take a few seconds to go out while the new filter fills with oil; do not race the engine while the light is on. Run the engine

for a few minutes, while checking for leaks around the oil filter seal and the drain plug. Refit the engine undershield.

13 Switch off the engine, and wait a few minutes for the oil to settle in the sump once more. With the new oil circulated and the filter now completely full, recheck the level on the dipstick, and add more oil as necessary.

14 Dispose of the used engine oil safely and in accordance with environmental regulations (see *General repair procedures*).

Every 18 000 miles or 12 months

4 Brake pad wear check

1 Jack up the front or rear of the vehicle in turn, and support it on axle stands (see *Jacking and vehicle support*).

2 For better access to the brake calipers, remove the roadwheels.

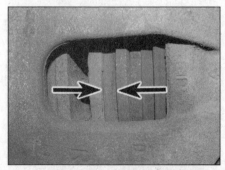

4.3 Check the thickness of the brake pad friction material (arrowed) through the inspection window in the caliper

3 Look through the inspection window in the caliper, and check that the thickness of the friction lining material on each of the pads is not less than the recommended minimum thickness given in the *Specifications* **(see illustration)**. If any one of the brake pads has worn down to, or below, the specified limit, *all four* pads at that end of the car must be renewed as a set (ie, all the front pads or all the rear pads).

4 For a comprehensive check, the brake pads should be removed and cleaned. The operation of the brake calipers can then be checked, and the brake discs can be fully examined. Refer to Chapter 9 for details.

5 Underbonnet check for fluid leaks and hose condition

Caution: Renewal of air conditioning hoses must be left to a dealer service department or air conditioning specialist who has the equipment to depressurise the system safely. Never remove air conditioning components or hoses until the system has been depressurised.

General

1 High temperatures in the engine compartment can cause the deterioration of the rubber and plastic hoses used for engine, accessory and emission systems operation. Periodic inspection should be made for cracks, loose clamps, material hardening and leaks.

2 Carefully check the large top and bottom radiator hoses **(see illustration)**, along with the other smaller-diameter cooling system

5.2 Check all hose connections for tightness and signs of leakage

A leak in the cooling system will usually show up as white- or antifreeze-coloured deposits on the areas adjoining the leak.

hoses and metal pipes; do not forget the heater hoses/pipes which run from the engine to the bulkhead **(see Haynes Hint)**. Inspect each hose along its entire length, renewing any that are cracked, swollen or shows signs of deterioration. Cracks may become more apparent if the hose is squeezed.

3 Make sure that all hose connections are tight. If the spring clamps that are used to secure some of the hoses appear to be slackening, they should be updated with screw-type clips to prevent the possibility of leaks.

4 Some other hoses are secured to their fittings with screw-type clips. Where screw-type clips are used, check to be sure they haven't slackened, allowing the hose to leak. If clamps or screw-type clips aren't used, make sure the hose has not expanded and/or hardened where it slips over the fitting, allowing it to leak.

5 Check all fluid reservoirs, filler caps, drain plugs and fittings, etc, looking for any signs of leakage of oil, transmission and/or brake hydraulic fluid, coolant and power steering fluid. If the vehicle is regularly parked in the same place, close inspection of the ground underneath will soon show any leaks; ignore the puddle of water which will be left if the air conditioning system is in use. As soon as a leak is detected, its source must be traced and rectified. Where oil has been leaking for some time, it is usually necessary to use a

steam cleaner, pressure washer or similar, to clean away the accumulated dirt, so that the exact source of the leak can be identified.

Vacuum hoses

6 It's quite common for vacuum hoses, especially those in the emissions system, to be numbered or colour-coded, or to be identified by coloured stripes moulded into them. Various systems require hoses with different wall thicknesses, collapse resistance and temperature resistance. When renewing hoses, be sure the new ones are made of the same material.

7 Often the only effective way to check a hose is to remove it completely from the vehicle. If more than one hose is removed, be sure to label the hoses and fittings to ensure correct installation.

8 When checking vacuum hoses, be sure to include any plastic T-fittings in the check. Inspect the fittings for cracks, and check the hose where it fits over the fitting for distortion, which could cause leakage.

9 A small piece of vacuum hose can be used as a stethoscope to detect vacuum leaks. Hold one end of the hose to your ear, and probe around vacuum hoses and fittings, listening for the hissing sound characteristic of a vacuum leak.

⚠️ *Warning: When probing with the vacuum hose stethoscope, be very careful not to come into contact with moving engine components such as the auxiliary drivebelt, radiator electric cooling fan, etc.*

Fuel hoses

⚠️ *Warning: Before carrying out the following operation, refer to the precautions given in Safety first! at the beginning of this manual, and follow them implicitly. Petrol is a highly dangerous and volatile liquid, and the precautions necessary when handling it cannot be overstressed.*

10 Check all fuel hoses for deterioration and chafing. Check especially for cracks in areas where the hose bends, and also just before fittings, such as where a hose attaches to the fuel filter.

11 High-quality fuel line, usually identified by the word Fluoroelastomer printed on the hose, should be used for fuel line renewal. Never, under any circumstances, use un-reinforced vacuum line, clear plastic tubing or water hose for fuel lines.

12 Spring-type clamps are commonly used on fuel lines. These clamps often lose their tension over a period of time, and can be 'sprung' during removal. Update all spring-type clamps with screw clips whenever a hose is renewed.

13 If a fuel leak is suspected, remember that any leak will be more obvious with the system at full pressure, such as when the engine is running, or shortly after switching off.

Metal lines

14 Sections of metal piping are often used for fuel line between the fuel filter and the engine. Check carefully to be sure the piping has not been bent or crimped, and that cracks have not started in the line.

15 If a section of metal fuel line must be renewed, only seamless steel piping should be used, since copper and aluminium piping don't have the strength necessary to withstand normal engine vibration.

16 Check the metal brake lines where they enter the master cylinder and ABS hydraulic unit for cracks in the lines or loose fittings **(see illustration)**. Any sign of brake fluid leakage calls for an immediate and thorough inspection of the brake system.

6	**Steering and suspension check**	

Front suspension and steering

1 Apply the handbrake, then jack up the front of the vehicle and support it on axle stands (see *Jacking and vehicle support*).

2 Visually inspect the balljoint dust covers and the steering gear gaiters for splits, chafing or deterioration **(see illustration)**. Any wear of these components will cause loss of lubricant, together with dirt and water entry, resulting in rapid deterioration of the balljoints or steering gear.

3 Check the power steering fluid hoses for chafing or deterioration, and the pipe and hose unions for fluid leaks. Also check for signs of fluid leakage under pressure from the steering gear rubber gaiters, which would indicate failed fluid seals within the steering gear.

4 Check for signs of fluid leakage around the suspension strut body, or from the rubber boot around the piston rod (where fitted). Should any fluid be noticed, the shock absorber is defective internally, and renewal is necessary.

5 Grasp the roadwheel at the 12 o'clock and 6 o'clock positions, and try to rock it **(see illustration)**. Very slight free play may be felt, but if the movement is appreciable, further investigation is necessary to determine the

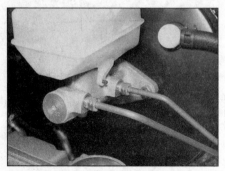

5.16 Check the metal brake pipes

6.2 Check the condition of the steering rack rubber gaiters

source. Continue rocking the wheel while an assistant depresses the footbrake. If the movement is now eliminated or significantly reduced, it is likely that the wheel bearings are at fault. If the free play is still evident with the footbrake depressed, then there is wear in the suspension joints or mountings.

6 Now grasp the wheel at the 9 o'clock and 3 o'clock positions, and try to rock it as before. Any movement felt now may again be caused by wear in the wheel bearings or the steering track rod end balljoints. If the outer track rod end is worn, the visual movement will be obvious. If the inner joint is suspect, it can be felt by placing a hand over the rack-and-pinion rubber gaiter, and gripping the track rod. If the wheel is now rocked, movement will be felt at the inner joint if wear has taken place.

7 Using a large screwdriver or flat bar, check for wear in the suspension mounting bushes by levering between the relevant suspension component and its attachment point. Some movement is to be expected as the mountings are made of rubber, but excessive wear should be obvious. Also check the condition of any visible rubber bushes, looking for splits, cracks or contamination of the rubber.

8 With the vehicle standing on its wheels, have an assistant turn the steering wheel back-and-forth, about an eighth of a turn each way. There should be very little, if any, lost movement between the steering wheel and roadwheels. If this is not the case, closely observe the joints and mountings previously described, but in addition, check the steering column universal joints for wear, and also check the rack-and-pinion steering gear itself.

9 The efficiency of the shock absorber may be checked by bouncing the car at each front corner. Generally speaking, the body will return to its normal position and stop after being depressed. If it rises and returns on a rebound, the shock absorber is probably suspect. Examine also the shock absorber upper and lower mountings for any signs of wear or fluid leakage.

Rear suspension

10 Chock the front wheels, then raise the rear of the vehicle and support it on axle stands (see *Jacking and vehicle support*).

11 Check the rear hub bearings for wear,

6.5 Check for wear in the wheel bearing by grasping the wheel and trying to rock it

using the method described for the front hub bearings (paragraph 5).

12 Using a large screwdriver or flat bar, check for wear in the suspension mounting bushes by levering between the relevant suspension component and its attachment point. Some movement is to be expected as the mountings are made of rubber, but excessive wear should be obvious. Check the condition of the shock absorbers as described previously.

7 Driveshaft gaiter check

1 With the vehicle raised and securely supported on axle stands (see *Jacking and vehicle support*), turn the steering onto full lock, then slowly rotate the roadwheel. Inspect the condition of the outer constant velocity (CV) joint rubber gaiters, squeezing the gaiters to open out the folds **(see illustration)**. Check for signs of cracking, splits or deterioration of the rubber, which may allow the grease to escape, and lead to water and grit entry into the joint. Also check the security and condition of the retaining clips. Repeat these checks on the inner CV joints. If any damage or deterioration is found, the gaiters should be renewed as described in Chapter 8.

2 At the same time, check the general condition of the CV joints themselves by first holding the driveshaft and attempting to rotate the wheel. Repeat this check by holding the inner joint and attempting to rotate the driveshaft. Any appreciable movement indicates wear in the

7.1 Inspect the condition of the driveshaft gaiters

joints, wear in the driveshaft splines, or a loose driveshaft retaining nut.

8 Clutch hydraulic check

1 Check that the clutch pedal moves smoothly and easily through its full travel, and that the clutch itself functions correctly, with no trace of slip or drag.

2 Undo the two screws and remove the lower facia panel (above the pedals) for access to the clutch pedal, and apply a few drops of light oil to the pedal pivot. Refit the panel.

3 From within the engine compartment, check the condition of the fluid lines and hoses.

9 Pollen filter renewal

1 Undo the two screws and remove the lower facia panel from above the passenger's footwell **(see illustration)**.

2 Undo the four screws, remove the cover and pull the pollen filter downwards from the heater housing **(see illustrations)**.

3 Note there are two possible locations in the heater housing for the pollen filter. Standard filters slide up into the narrower of the two slots in the housing, whilst multifilters (vehicles with an air quality sensor) slide up into the wider of the slots. **Note:** *Under no circumstances should both a standard and multifilter be fitted together.*

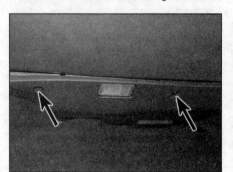

9.1 Undo the two screws (arrowed) and remove the lower facia panel

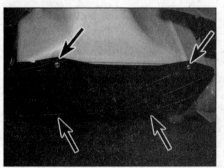

9.2a Undo the four screws (arrowed), and remove the cover . . .

9.2b . . . then slide the pollen filter downwards

10.4 Unscrew the plastic caps (arrowed) to check the electrolyte level

4 Slide the appropriate filter into place, then refit the cover and tighten the retaining screws securely.

5 Refit the lower facia panel.

10 Battery electrolyte level check

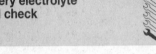

Warning: The electrolyte inside a battery is diluted acid – it is a good idea to wear suitable rubber gloves. When topping-up, don't overfill the cells so that the electrolyte overflows. In the event of any spillage, rinse the electrolyte off without delay. Refit the cell covers and rinse the battery with copious quantities of clean water. Don't attempt to syphon out any excess electrolyte.

1 The battery is located under the flooring in the luggage compartment. Lift up the flooring, and where applicable, unclip the cover from the battery.

2 Some models covered by this manual may be fitted with a maintenance-free battery as standard equipment, or may have had one fitted. If the battery in your vehicle is marked Freedom, Maintenance-Free or similar, no electrolyte level checking is required (the battery is often completely sealed, preventing any topping-up).

3 Batteries which do require their electrolyte level to be checked can be recognised by the presence of removable covers over the six battery cells – the battery casing is also

12.2 Make sure the rubber exhaust mountings are in good condition

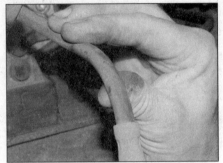

11.5 Check the condition of the rubber brake hoses by bending them slightly and looking for cracks

sometimes translucent, so that the electrolyte level can be more easily checked. One of the project vehicles seen in our workshop had a battery marked 'maintenance-free', which still had removable cell caps – in this case, check the electrolyte level as described, but consult a Volvo dealer if topping-up appears to be required.

4 Remove the cell caps or covers, and either look down inside the battery to see the level web, or check the level using any markings provided on the battery casing **(see illustration)**. The electrolyte should cover the battery plates by approximately 15 mm.

5 If necessary, top-up a little at a time with distilled (deionised) water until the level in all six cells is correct – don't fill the cells up to the brim. Wipe up any spillage, then refit the cell covers.

6 Further information on the battery, charging and jump starting can be found at the start of this manual and in Chapter 5A.

11 Underbody and fuel/brake line check

1 With the vehicle raised and supported on axle stands (see *Jacking and vehicle support*), or over an inspection pit, thoroughly inspect the underbody and wheel arches for signs of damage and corrosion. In particular, examine the bottom of the side sills, and any concealed areas where mud can collect.

2 Where corrosion and rust is evident, press and tap firmly on the panel with a screwdriver, and check for any serious corrosion which would necessitate repairs. If the panel is not seriously corroded, clean away the rust, and apply a new coating of underseal. Refer to Chapter 11 for more details of body repairs.

3 At the same time, inspect the treated lower body panels for stone damage and general condition.

4 Inspect all of the fuel and brake lines on the underbody for damage, rust, corrosion and leakage. Also make sure that they are correctly supported in their clips. Where applicable, check the PVC coating on the lines for damage.

5 Inspect the flexible brake hoses in the

vicinity of the front calipers and rear axle, where they are subjected to most movement **(see illustration)**. Bend them between the fingers (but do not actually bend them double, or the casing may be damaged) and check that this does not reveal previously-hidden cracks, cuts or splits.

12 Exhaust system check

1 With the engine cold (at least three hours after the vehicle has been driven), check the complete exhaust system, from its starting point at the engine to the end of the tailpipe. Ideally, this should be done on a hoist, where unrestricted access is available; if a hoist is not available, raise and support the vehicle on axle stands (see *Jacking and vehicle support*).

2 Check the pipes and connections for evidence of leaks, severe corrosion, or damage. Make sure that all brackets and rubber mountings are in good condition, and tight; if any of the mountings are to be renewed, ensure that the new ones are of the correct type **(see illustration)**. Leakage at any of the joints or in other parts of the system will usually show up as a black sooty stain in the vicinity of the leak.

3 At the same time, inspect the underside of the body for holes, corrosion, open seams, etc, which may allow exhaust gases to enter the passenger compartment. Seal all body openings with silicone or body putty, with due consideration given to the heat generated by the exhaust system and gases.

4 Rattles and other noises can often be traced to the exhaust system, especially the rubber mountings. Try to move the system, silencer(s) and catalytic converter. If any components can touch the body or suspension parts, secure the exhaust system with new mountings.

13 Handbrake check and adjustment

In service, the handbrake should be fully applied within approximately 5 clicks of the handbrake lever ratchet. Adjustment will be necessary periodically to compensate for lining wear and cable stretch. Refer to Chapter 9 for the full adjustment procedure.

14 Seat belt check

1 Check the seat belts for satisfactory operation and condition. Inspect the webbing for fraying and cuts. Check that they retract smoothly and without binding into their reels.

2 Check the seat belt mountings, ensuring that all the bolts are securely tightened.

15 Door, boot and bonnet check and lubrication

1 Check that the doors, bonnet and boot lid close securely. Check that the bonnet safety catch operates correctly. Check the operation of the door check straps.
2 Lubricate the hinges, door check straps, the striker plates and the bonnet catch sparingly with a little oil or grease **(see illustration)**.
3 If any of the doors or bonnet do not close effectively, or appear not to be flush with the surrounding panels, carry out the relevant adjustment procedures contained in Chapter 11.

16 Headlight beam alignment check

Accurate adjustment of the headlight beam is only possible using optical beam-setting equipment, and this work should therefore be carried out by a Volvo dealer or service station with the necessary facilities.

Basic adjustments can be carried out in an emergency, and further details are given in Chapter 12.

17 Coolant antifreeze concentration check

1 The cooling system should be filled with the recommended antifreeze and corrosion protection fluid. Over a period of time, the concentration of fluid may be reduced due to topping-up (this can be avoided by topping-up with the correct antifreeze mixture) or fluid loss. If loss of coolant has been evident, it is important to make the necessary repair before adding fresh fluid. The exact mixture of antifreeze-to-water which you should use depends on the relative weather conditions. The mixture should contain at least 40% antifreeze, but not more than 70%. Consult the mixture ratio chart on the antifreeze container before adding coolant. Hydrometers are available at most automotive accessory shops to test the coolant. Use antifreeze which meets the vehicle manufacturer's specifications.
2 With the engine cold, carefully remove the cap from the expansion tank. If the engine is not completely cold, place a cloth rag over the cap before removing it, and remove it slowly to allow any pressure to escape.
3 Antifreeze checkers are available from car accessory shops. Draw some coolant from the expansion tank and observe how many plastic balls are floating in the checker **(see illustration)**. Usually, 2 or 3 balls must be floating for the correct concentration of antifreeze, but follow the manufacturer's instructions.

4 If the concentration is incorrect, it will be necessary to either withdraw some coolant and add antifreeze, or alternatively drain the old coolant and add fresh coolant of the correct concentration.

18 Service reminder indicator – resetting

2001 model year

1 Turn the ignition switch to position I.
2 Press and hold the mileage trip reset button, then turn the ignition switch to position II.
3 Service reminder indicator starts to flash after the button has been pressed for approx 10 seconds. Release the button within 5 seconds. An audible signal will be given when the reset is complete.

From 2002 model year

4 Turn the ignition switch to position I.
5 Press and hold the mileage trip reset button, then turn the ignition switch to position II within 2 seconds.
6 Hold the reset button in until the indicator has been reset. On models from 2003, a yellow light in the cluster will illuminate when the button is to be released. Release the reset button within 4 seconds. An audible signal will be given when the reset is complete.

19 Road test

Braking system

1 Make sure that the vehicle does not pull to one side when braking, and that the wheels do not lock when braking hard.
2 Check that there is no vibration through the steering when braking. Note that, under heavy braking, some vibration may be felt through the brake pedal – this is a normal feature of the Anti-lock Braking System (ABS) operation, and does not normally indicate a fault.
3 Check that the handbrake operates correctly, without excessive movement of the lever, and that it holds the vehicle stationary on a slope.
4 With the engine switched off, test the operation of the brake servo unit as follows. Depress the footbrake four or five times to exhaust the vacuum, then start the engine. As the engine starts, there should be a noticeable give in the brake pedal as vacuum builds-up. Allow the engine to run for at least two minutes, and then switch it off. If the brake pedal is now depressed again, it should be possible to detect a hiss from the servo as the pedal is depressed. After about four or five applications, no further hissing should be heard, and the pedal should feel considerably harder.

15.2 Lubricate the door hinges

Steering and suspension

5 Check for any abnormalities in the steering, suspension, handling or road feel.
6 Drive the vehicle, and check that there are no unusual vibrations or noises.
7 Check that the steering feels positive, with no excessive sloppiness or roughness, and check for any suspension noises when cornering and driving over bumps.

Drivetrain

8 Check the performance of the engine, transmission and driveline.
9 Check that the engine starts correctly, both when cold and hot.
10 Listen for any unusual noises from the engine and transmission.
11 Make sure that the engine runs smoothly when idling, and that there is no hesitation when accelerating.
12 On manual transmission models, check that all gears can be engaged smoothly without noise, and that the gear lever action is smooth and not abnormally vague or notchy.
13 On automatic transmission models, make sure that the drive seems smooth without jerks or engine speed flare-ups. Check that all the gear positions can be selected with the vehicle at rest.

Clutch

14 Check that the clutch pedal moves smoothly and easily through its full travel, and that the clutch itself functions correctly, with no trace of slip or drag. If the movement is uneven or stiff in places, check the system components with reference to Chapter 6.

17.3 Use a hydrometer to check the antifreeze strength

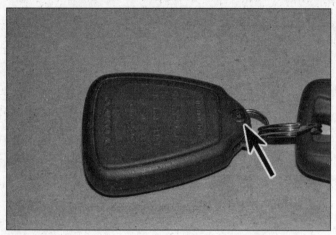

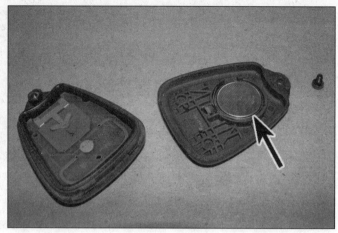

21.1 Undo the Torx bolt (arrowed) and remove the cover

21.2 The battery (arrowed) fits with the positive side facing down in the cover

Instruments and electrical equipment

15 Check the operation of all instruments and electrical equipment.

16 Make sure that all instruments read correctly, and switch on all electrical equipment in turn, to check that it functions properly.

20 Air conditioning system check

 Warning: The air conditioning system is under high pressure. Do not loosen any fittings or remove any components until after the system has been discharged. Air conditioning refrigerant must be properly discharged into an approved type of container, at a dealer service department or an automotive air conditioning repair facility capable of handling the refrigerant safely. Always wear eye protection when disconnecting air conditioning system fittings.

1 The following maintenance checks should be performed on a regular basis, to ensure that the system continues to operate at peak efficiency:

  a) *Check the auxiliary drivebelt. If it's worn or deteriorated, renew it (see Section 28).*
  b) *Check the system hoses. Look for cracks,*

  bubbles, hard spots and deterioration. Inspect the hoses and all fittings for oil bubbles and seepage. If there's any evidence of wear, damage or leaks, renew the hose(s).
  c) *Inspect the condenser fins for leaves, insects and other debris. Use a 'fin comb' or compressed air to clean the condenser.*

 Warning: Wear eye protection when using compressed air.

  d) *Check that the drain tube from the front of the evaporator is clear – note that it is normal to have clear fluid (water) dripping from this while the system is in operation, to the extent that quite a large puddle can be left under the vehicle when it is parked.*

2 It's a good idea to operate the system for about 30 minutes at least once a month, particularly during the winter. Long term non-use can cause hardening, and subsequent failure, of the seals.

3 Because of the complexity of the air conditioning system and the special equipment necessary to service it, in-depth repairs are not included in this manual, apart from those procedures covered in Chapter 3.

4 The most common cause of poor cooling is simply a low system refrigerant charge. If a noticeable drop in cool air output occurs, the following quick check will help you determine if the refrigerant level is low.

5 Warm the engine up to normal operating temperature.

6 Place the air conditioning temperature selector at the coldest setting, and put the blower at the highest setting. Open the doors – to make sure the air conditioning system doesn't cycle off as soon as it cools the passenger compartment.

7 With the compressor engaged – the clutch will make an audible click, and the centre of the clutch will rotate – feel the inlet and outlet pipes at the compressor. One side should be cold, and one hot. If there's no perceptible difference between the two pipes, there's something wrong with the compressor or the system. It might be a low charge – it might be something else. Take the vehicle to a dealer service department or an automotive air conditioning specialist.

21 Remote control battery renewal

Up to 2003 model year

1 Undo the bolt and remove the cover from the remote control **(see illustration)**.

2 Remove the battery from the cover, noting its orientation – negative side up **(see illustration)**. Avoid touching the battery and contacts with bare fingers.

3 Fit the new battery into the cover (negative side up), then refit the cover and tighten the bolt.

From 2004 model year

4 Use a small, flat-bladed screwdriver to gently prise up the rear edge of the cover on the remote **(see illustration)**. Remove the cover.

5 Remove the battery from the control, noting its orientation – positive side up **(see illustration)**. Avoid touching the battery and contacts with bare fingers.

6 Fit the new battery into the control (positive side up), then refit the cover, ensuring the rubber seal is correctly fitted.

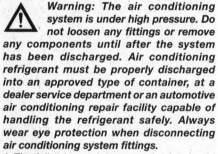

21.4 Prise up the plastic cover

21.5 Fit the battery with the positive side facing upwards

22.1 Depress the clip and disconnect the airflow meter wiring plug

22.2a Release the air filter cover clips . . .

22.2b . . . then lift the cover and remove the filter element

Every 36 000 miles or 2 years

22 Air cleaner element renewal

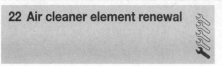

1 Disconnect the mass airflow meter wiring plug – located on the air filter cover **(see illustration)**.
2 Release the clips lift the cover upwards sufficiently to gain access, and remove the air cleaner element **(see illustrations)**.
3 If greater access is required, the cover can be removed as described in Chapter 4A.

23.2 Typical spark plug removal tools

4 Wipe clean inside the housing and cover with a cloth. Be careful not to sweep debris into the air inlet.
5 Fit the new element, making sure it is the right way up. Press the seal on the rim of the element into the groove on the housing.
6 Refit the cover and secure it with the clips. Note that the rear of the cover can be difficult to refit. Take care to endure the three 'hinges' locate correctly in the air cleaner housing.

23 Spark plug renewal

1 It is vital for the correct running, full performance and proper economy of the engine that the spark plugs perform with maximum efficiency. The most important factor in ensuring this is that the plugs fitted are appropriate for the engine (a suitable type is specified at the beginning of this Chapter). If this type is used and the engine is in good condition, the spark plugs should not need attention between scheduled renewal intervals. Spark plug cleaning is rarely necessary, and should not be attempted unless specialised

equipment is available, as damage can easily be caused to the firing ends.
2 Spark plug removal and refitting requires a spark plug socket, with an extension which can be turned by a ratchet handle or similar. This socket is lined with a rubber sleeve, to protect the porcelain insulator of the spark plug, and to hold the plug while you insert it into the spark plug hole. Depending on the type of spark plug to be fitted, you may also need a wire-type feeler blade, to check and adjust the spark plug electrode gap. A torque wrench will be needed to tighten the new plugs to the specified torque **(see illustration)**.
3 On turbocharged engines, release the clamps and remove the charge air hose from the turbocharger to the intercooler (over the top of the engine).
4 Remove the two screws, and release the two spring clips securing the timing belt upper cover, and unclip the cover from the spark plug cover in the centre of the cylinder head **(see illustration)**.
5 Remove the six screws securing the spark plug cover, and lift the cover away for access to the ignition coils **(see illustration)**.
6 Starting at the coil nearest the timing belt, disconnect the wiring plug from the coil (see

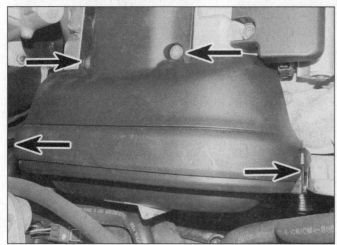

23.4 Release the two clips (arrowed), then undo the two screws (arrowed) and remove the timing belt upper cover

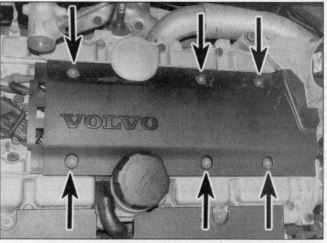

23.5 Undo the six screws (arrowed) and remove the cover

23.6 Depress the clip (arrowed) and disconnect the ignition coil wiring plug

23.7 Pull the coil and HT cap out of the cylinder head

23.13 Adjust the spark plug electrode gap

illustration). It is safest to work on one coil at a time. However, if the coils and their wiring plugs are marked for position, all five could be removed at once.

7 Unscrew the coil retaining bolt, then pull the coil and HT cap out of the recess in the cylinder head (see illustration).

8 Unscrew the spark plugs, ensuring that the socket is kept in alignment with each plug – if the socket is forcibly moved to either side, the porcelain top of the plug may be broken off. If any undue difficulty is encountered when unscrewing any of the spark plugs, carefully check the cylinder head threads and sealing surfaces for signs of wear, excessive corrosion or damage; if any of these conditions is found, seek the advice of a dealer as to the best method of repair.

9 As each plug is removed, examine it as follows – this will give a good indication of the condition of the engine. If the insulator nose of the spark plug is clean and white, with no deposits, this is indicative of a weak mixture.

10 If the tip and insulator nose are covered with hard black-looking deposits, then this is indicative that the mixture is too rich. Should

the plug be black and oily, then it is likely that the engine is fairly worn, as well as the mixture being too rich.

11 If the insulator nose is covered with light tan to greyish-brown deposits, then the mixture is correct, and it is likely that the engine is in good condition.

12 The spark plug electrode gap is of considerable importance as, if it is too large or too small, the size of the spark and its efficiency will be seriously impaired. However, several models covered by this manual use spark plugs with multiple earth electrodes – unless there is clear information to the contrary, *no attempt should be made to adjust the plug gap on a spark plug with more than one earth electrode.*

13 To set the electrode gap on plugs with one earth electrode, measure the gap with a feeler blade or adjusting tool, and then bend open, or closed, the outer plug electrode until the specified gap is achieved (see illustration). The centre electrode should never be bent, as this may crack the insulation and cause plug failure, if nothing worse. If the outer electrode is not exactly over the centre electrode, bend it gently to align them.

14 Before fitting the spark plugs, check that the threaded connector sleeves at the top of the plugs are tight, and that the plug exterior surfaces and threads are clean.

15 On installing the spark plugs, first check that the cylinder head thread and sealing surface are as clean as possible; use a clean rag wrapped around a paintbrush to wipe clean the sealing surface. Ensure that the spark plug threads are clean and dry, then screw them in by hand where possible. Take extra care to enter the plug threads correctly (see Tool Tip).

16 When each spark plug is started correctly on its threads, screw it down until it just seats lightly, then tighten it to the specified torque wrench setting.

17 Align the coil with the mounting bolt hole, then push it down firmly onto the spark plug. Tighten the retaining bolt to the specified torque.

18 Press the wiring plug until it can be heard to 'click' into place.

19 The remainder of refitting is a reversal of removal. Reconnect the wiring plugs to the

coils, ensuring that each one is refitted to its original location.

24 Automatic transmission fluid level check

Fluid level check

1 The level of the automatic transmission fluid should be carefully maintained. Low fluid level can lead to slipping or loss of drive, while overfilling can cause foaming, loss of fluid and transmission damage.

2 Ideally, the transmission fluid level should be checked when the transmission is hot – 80°C for 5-speed transmissions, and 50 to 60°C for 6-speed transmissions.

5-speed transmissions

3 Park the vehicle on level ground, firmly apply the handbrake, and start the engine. While the engine is idling, depress the brake pedal and move the selector lever through all gear positions (pausing in each position for at least 3 seconds), returning finally to the P position.

4 Wait two minutes then, with the engine still idling, remove the dipstick (yellow handle) from its tube which is located at the front of the transmission (see illustration). Note the condition and colour of the fluid on the dipstick.

5 Wipe the fluid from the dipstick with a clean rag, and re-insert it into the filler tube until the cap seats.

6 Pull the dipstick out again, and note the fluid level. The level should be between the MIN and MAX marks, on the side of the

24.4 Automatic transmission fluid level dipstick (arrowed)

TOOL TIP

It is often difficult to insert spark plugs into their holes without cross-threading them. To avoid this possibility, fit a short length of 8 mm diameter rubber/plastic hose over the end of the spark plug. The flexible hose acts as a universal joint to help align the plug with the plug hole. Should the plug begin to cross-thread then the hose will slip on the spark plug, preventing thread damage to the cylinder head.

dipstick marked HOT **(see illustration)**. If the level is on the MIN mark, stop the engine, and add the specified automatic transmission fluid through the dipstick tube, using a clean funnel if necessary. It is important not to introduce dirt into the transmission when topping-up.

7 Add the fluid a little at a time, and keep checking the level as previously described until it is correct. The difference between the MIN and MAX marks on the dipstick is approximately 0.5 litre.

8 If the vehicle has not been driven and the engine and transmission are cold, carry out the procedures in paragraphs 3 to 7, but use the marks of the dipstick marked COLD. It is, however, preferable to check the level when the transmission is hot, as a more accurate reading will be obtained.

6-speed transmissions

9 Park the vehicle on level ground, firmly apply the handbrake, and remove the engine transmission undershield.

10 Remove the air cleaner housing as described in Chapter 4A.

11 Clean the area on the top of the transmission around the filler plug, then using a T55 Torx bit, unscrew the filler plug **(see illustration 24.34)**.

12 Position the end of a hose in the filler aperture, and attach a funnel to the other end. Temporarily refit the air cleaner housing.

13 Start the engine. While the engine is idling, depress the brake pedal and move the selector lever through all gear positions (pausing in each position for 2 seconds), returning finally to the P position.

14 With the engine still running, unscrew the level plug from the centre of the transmission drain plug using a T40 Torx bit **(see illustration 24.30)**. If no fluid emerges from the level aperture, add specified fluid through the funnel and hose until it does emerge. Refit the level plug and tighten it to the specified torque, using a new sealing washer.

15 Stop the engine, remove the air cleaner housing, and tighten the fluid filler plug to the specified torque, using a new sealing washer.

16 Refit the air cleaner housing as described in Chapter 4A, then refit the engine/transmission undershield.

All transmissions

17 The need for regular topping-up of the transmission fluid indicates a leak, which should be found and rectified without delay.

18 The condition of the fluid should also be checked along with the level. If the fluid at the end of the dipstick is black or a dark reddish-brown colour, or if it has a burned smell, the fluid should be changed. If you are in doubt about the condition of the fluid, purchase some new fluid, and compare the two for colour and smell.

19 If the car is used regularly for short trips, taxi work, or does a lot of towing, the transmission fluid should be renewed on a regular basis. Likewise, if a high mileage has been completed, or the history of the car is

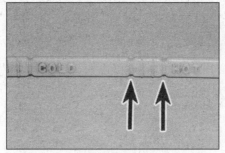

24.6 With the transmission hot, the fluid level should be between the marks arrowed

unknown, it might be worth renewing the fluid for peace of mind. Normally, however, renewal of the fluid is not a service requirement.

Fluid renewal

Note: *The automatic transmission fluid does not normally require changing. It's only necessary on vehicles which are used predominantly for towing or as taxis.*

20 Ideally, the transmission fluid level should be drained when the transmission is hot (at its normal operating temperature). If the vehicle has just been driven for about 30 minutes, and the transmission is hot. Note that on 6-speed transmissions, the fluid temperature must not be allowed to exceed 60°C, or an incorrect fluid level will result.

21 Jack up the front and rear of the vehicle and support it securely on axle stands (see *Jacking and vehicle support*). The vehicle should be level.

22 Release the screws and remove the engine undershield **(see illustration 3.2)**.

5-speed transmission

23 Position a container beneath the transmission and unscrew the drain plug **(see illustration)**. Discard the drain plug sealing washer, a new one must be fitted.

24 If required, detach the oil cooler hoses from the transmission and allow the fluid in the cooler and pipes to drain into the container.

25 Refit the drain plug with a new sealing washer, and tighten it to the specified torque. Refit the engine undershield, and lower the vehicle to the ground.

26 Ensure the handbrake is fully applied and the selector lever is in position P.

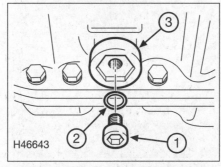

24.30 Transmission level plug (1), drain plug (2) and sealing washer (3)

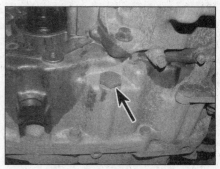

24.23 Unscrew the automatic transmission fluid drain plug (arrowed)

27 Pull out the fluid level dipstick, and with the aid of a funnel, pour approximately 2.0 litres of new fluid down through the dipstick guide tube **(see illustration 24.4)**.

28 Start the engine and allow it to idle for a few seconds, then turn it off, and add another 2.0 litre of fluid.

29 Start the engine, allow it to idle, then move the selector lever through all positions, pausing for at least 3 seconds in each position. Insert and remove the fluid level dipstick and check the level. With the transmission warm, the temperature of the fluid should be approaching 80°C. At this temperature the fluid level should be upto the mark adjacent to the 'Hot' marked on the dipstick. Add fluid as necessary. After adding fluid, move the selector lever through all positions, pausing for at least 3 seconds in each position as previously described.

6-speed transmission

30 Position a container beneath the transmission and unscrew the level plug from the centre of the drain plug using a T40 Torx bit **(see illustration)**.

31 Unscrew the drain plug from the transmission and allow the fluid to drain. Refit the drain plug with a new seal and tighten it to the specified torque.

32 Refit the level plug, but only finger-tighten it at this stage.

33 Remove the air cleaner housing as described in Chapter 4A.

34 Clean the area on the top of the transmission around the filler plug, then using a T55 Torx bit, unscrew the filler plug **(see illustration)**.

24.34 Transmission filler plug (arrowed)

35 Disconnect the fluid return hose from the cooler adjacent to the radiator, and attach a length of clear hose to the cooler outlet. Volvo special tool No 999 7363 may be available for this purpose. Place the end of the hose into a container.

36 Using a funnel, add 4.0 litres of the specified fluid into the transmission casing through the filler hole.

37 Fully apply the handbrake, and check the selector lever is in position P.

38 Start the engine, and allow it to idle. Shift through all the selector positions, pausing for 2 seconds at each position. Switch the engine off when air bubbles are visible in the clear hose attached to the cooler.

39 Add 2.0 litres of the specified fluid, then start the engine again and allow it to idle. Switch the engine off when air bubbles are visible in the clear hose.

40 Add 2.0 litres of the specified fluid, then start the engine again and allow it to idle. Switch the engine off when air bubbles are visible in the clear hose.

41 Disconnect the clear hose from the cooler, and reconnect the fluid return hose.

42 Unscrew the level plug from the centre of the drain plug, and add fluid through the filler hole until it begins to run out of the level plug hole. Refit the level and filler plugs and tighten them to their specified torques.

43 Refit the air cleaner housing.

All transmissions

Note: *If the 'Gearbox oil change' indicator illuminates, this can only be reset using dedicated Volvo test equipment. Entrust this task to a Volvo dealer or suitably-equipped specialist.*

Every 108 000 miles or 6 years

25 Fuel filter renewal

⚠️ *Warning: Before carrying out the following operation, refer to the precautions given in Safety first! at the beginning of this manual, and follow them implicitly. Petrol is a highly dangerous and volatile liquid, and the precautions necessary when handling it cannot be overstressed.*

1 The fuel filter is located under the rear of the car, just forward of the fuel tank **(see illustration)**.

2 Raise the rear of the vehicle on ramps or drive it over a pit (see *Jacking and vehicle support*).

3 Thoroughly clean the area around the fuel pipe couplings at each end of the filter, then cover both with absorbent rags.

4 The fuel pressure must now be relieved before disconnecting the fuel pipe connections (refer to Chapter 4A, Section 1). To do this, a valve similar to a tyre valve is fitted in the fuel line supplying the filter **(see illustration)**.

Unscrew the valve cap, then position a container or wad of absorbent rag under the valve. Turn your head to one side to avoid any fuel spray, then depress the valve stem for a few seconds to release the initial spurt of fuel. Refit the valve cap on completion.

5 Disconnect the quick-release couplings by depressing the release button on the coupling **(see illustration)**. Be prepared for fuel spillage as the couplings are released.

6 Plug the couplings after disconnection to prevent further loss of fuel.

7 Undo the filter mounting strap retaining bolt and remove the filter.

8 Fit the new filter, making sure it is the same way round as the old one. Observe the arrow on the new filter showing the direction of fuel flow **(see illustration)**.

9 Secure the filter with the mounting strap, then push the fuel pipe couplings back on the filter outlets.

10 Run the engine and check that there are no leaks.

⚠️ *Warning: Dispose of the old filter safely; it will be highly flammable, and may explode if thrown on a fire.*

25.1 The fuel filter is under the right-hand side of the vehicle, just in front of the fuel tank

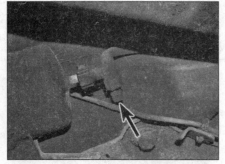

25.4 Undo the valve cap (arrowed) and depress the valve stem to relieve the fuel pressure

25.5 Depress the coupling release button (arrowed)

25.8 Observe the arrow on the filter (arrowed) indicating the direction of flow

26 Crankcase ventilation system oil trap cleaning – turbocharged models only

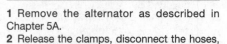

1 Remove the alternator as described in Chapter 5A.

2 Release the clamps, disconnect the hoses, then undo the bolts and remove the oil trap.

3 Use degreaser or methylated spirits to wash through the oil trap.

4 Refit the oil trap to the cylinder block and tighten the retaining screws securely.

5 Check the condition of the various connecting hoses, and renew as necessary.

6 Reconnected the hoses to the oil trap.

7 Refit the alternator as described in Chapter 5A.

28.2a Undo the 2 nuts (arrowed) and remove the metal plate

28.2b Fold the wheel arch liner forwards to access the belt lower run

Every 108 000 miles or 10 years

27 Timing belt and tensioner renewal

Refer to Chapter 2A.

28 Auxiliary drivebelt renewal

1 The auxiliary drivebelt transmits power from the crankshaft pulley to the alternator, steering pump and air conditioning compressor (as applicable).
2 Although not strictly necessary, access to the lower belt run is easier through the right-hand wheel arch. Loosen the right-hand front wheel bolts, then jack up and support the front of the car on axle stands. Remove the roadwheel, then remove the two plastic nuts, remove the metal plate and fold forward the inner wheel arch panel to give access to the crankshaft pulley (see illustrations).
3 Before removing the old belt, note its fitted routing around all pulleys.
4 The correct drivebelt tension is continually maintained by an automatic adjuster and tensioner assembly. This device is bolted to

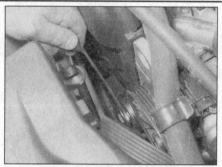

28.5 Using a spanner on the tensioner nut, rotate the tensioner clockwise

the front of the engine, and incorporates a spring-loaded idler pulley.
5 Use a screwdriver to prise off the plastic cap (where fitted), then using a spanner on the tensioner nut, rotate the tensioner clockwise, thereby relieving the belt tension. Slip the belt off all the pulleys, then release the tensioner and remove the belt (see illustration).
6 Check the tensioner and idler pulleys for any roughness or damage. Renew as necessary.
7 Fit the new belt loosely over the pulleys and the tensioner wheel, ensuring that it is properly seated – leave the belt off the top (power steering pump) pulley, however (see illustration).

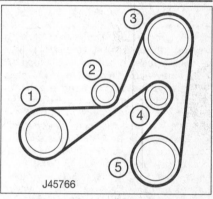

J45766

28.7 Auxiliary drivebelt routing

1 Crankshaft pulley
2 Tensioner pulley
3 Power steering pump pulley
4 Alternator pulley
5 Air conditioning compressor pulley

8 Rotate the tensioner clockwise, then work the drivebelt over the top pulley. Release the tensioner, which will now automatically take up the adjustment.
9 If removed, refit the inner wheel arch panel, then refit the wheel and lower the car to the ground. Tighten the wheel bolts to the specified torque.

Every 2 years, regardless of mileage

29 Brake fluid renewal

> **Warning: Brake hydraulic fluid can harm your eyes and damage painted surfaces, so use extreme caution when handling and pouring it. Do not use fluid that has been standing**

open for some time as it absorbs moisture from the air. Excess moisture can cause a dangerous loss of braking effectiveness.

The procedure is similar to that for the bleeding of the hydraulic system as described in Chapter 9, except that the brake fluid reservoir should be emptied by syphoning, and allowance should be made for the old fluid to be removed from the circuit when bleeding a section of the circuit.

Since the clutch hydraulic system uses the same fluid and reservoir as the braking system, it will probably be necessary to bleed the clutch system also (see Chapter 6).

HAYNES HINT

Old hydraulic fluid is invariably much darker in colour than the new, making it easy to distinguish between the two.

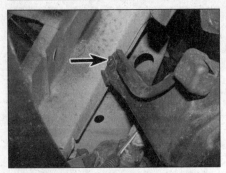

30.3a Undo the screw at each end of the radiator undertray (arrowed – viewed through the wheel arch) . . .

30.3b . . . then release the undertray retaining clips (arrowed – shown with the bumper removed for clarity)

30.4 Radiator drain tap and bottom hose clamp (arrowed)

Every 3 years, regardless of mileage

30 Coolant renewal

⚠️ *Warning: Wait until the engine is cold before starting this procedure. Do not allow antifreeze to come into contact with your skin, or with painted surfaces of the vehicle. Rinse off spills immediately with plenty of water. Never leave antifreeze lying around in an open container, or in a puddle in the driveway or on the garage floor. Children and pets are attracted by its sweet smell, but antifreeze can be fatal if ingested.*

Note: *If genuine Volvo coolant has been continuously maintained in the system in the specified ratio, then coolant renewal will not normally be necessary. However, to be absolutely sure about the integrity of the antifreeze and anti-corrosion properties of the coolant, periodic renewal is to be recommended.*

Coolant draining

1 To drain the system, first remove the expansion tank filler cap (see *Weekly checks*).
2 If the additional working clearance is required, raise the front of the vehicle and support it securely on axle stands (see *Jacking and vehicle support*).

30.5 Cylinder block drain tap is located just above the right-hand intermediate driveshaft (arrowed – viewed from the rear-underside of the engine)

3 Undo the screw at each end of the radiator undertray, then using a long screwdriver to depress the clip each side and pull the undertray to the rear and remove it **(see illustrations)**. Undo the screws and remove the engine undershield, then place a large drain tray underneath the radiator.
4 Slacken the drain tap at the bottom left-hand corner of the radiator and allow the coolant to drain into the tray. If no drain tap is fitted, carefully loosen the clamp and disconnect the radiator bottom hose **(see illustration)**.
5 When the radiator has drained, move the tray to the rear right-hand side of the engine and unscrew the cylinder block drain tap (where fitted) **(see illustration)**.

System flushing

6 With time, the cooling system may gradually lose its efficiency, as the radiator core becomes choked with rust, scale deposits from the water, and other sediment. This is especially likely if an inferior grade of antifreeze has been used. To minimise this, as well as using only the specified type of antifreeze and clean soft water, the system should be flushed as follows whenever any part of it is disturbed, and/or when the coolant is renewed.
7 With the coolant drained, close the drain taps and refill the system with fresh water. Refit the expansion tank filler cap, start the engine and warm it up to normal operating temperature, then stop it and (after allowing it to cool down completely) drain the system again. Repeat as necessary until only clean water can be seen to emerge, then refill finally with the specified coolant mixture.
8 If only clean, soft water and good-quality antifreeze has been used, and the coolant has been renewed at the specified intervals, the above procedure will be sufficient to keep the system clean for a considerable length of time. If, however, the system has been neglected, a more thorough operation will be required, as follows.
9 First drain the coolant, then disconnect the radiator top and bottom hoses. Insert a garden hose into the top hose, and allow

water to circulate through the radiator until it runs clean from the bottom outlet.
10 To flush the engine, remove the thermostat (see Chapter 3), insert the garden hose into the thermostat housing, and allow water to circulate until it runs clear from the bottom hose. If, after a reasonable period, the water still does not run clear, the radiator should be flushed with a good proprietary cleaning agent.
11 In severe cases of contamination, reverse-flushing of the radiator may be necessary. To do this, remove the radiator (see Chapter 3), invert it, and insert the garden hose into the bottom outlet. Continue flushing until clear water runs from the top hose outlet. A similar procedure can be used to flush the heater matrix.
12 The use of chemical cleaners should be necessary only as a last resort. Normally, use of the correct coolant will prevent excessive contamination of the system.

Coolant filling

13 With the cooling system drained and flushed, ensure that all disturbed components or hose unions are correctly fitted, and that the two drain taps are securely tightened. Refit the engine undershields removed for access. If it was raised, lower the vehicle to the ground.
14 Prepare a sufficient quantity of the specified coolant mixture (see *Specifications*); allow for a surplus, so as to have a reserve supply for topping-up.
15 Slowly fill the system through the expansion tank; since the tank is the highest point in the system, all the air in the system should be displaced into the tank by the rising liquid. Slow pouring reduces the possibility of air being trapped and forming airlocks. It helps also, if the large radiator hoses are gently squeezed during the filling procedure.
16 Continue filling until the coolant level reaches the expansion tank MAX level line, then wait for a few minutes. During this time, continue to squeeze the radiator hoses. When the level stops falling, top-up to the MAX level and refit the expansion tank cap.
17 Start the engine and run it at idle speed,

until it has warmed-up to normal operating temperature. If the level in the expansion tank drops significantly, top-up to the MAX level line, to minimise the amount of air circulating in the system.

18 Stop the engine, allow it to cool down *completely* (overnight, if possible), then remove the expansion tank filler cap and top-up the tank to the MAX level line. Refit the filler cap, tightening it securely, and wash off any spilt coolant from the engine compartment and bodywork.

19 After refilling, always check carefully all components of the system (but especially any unions disturbed during draining and flushing) for signs of coolant leaks. Fresh antifreeze has a searching action, which will rapidly expose any weak points in the system.

Airlocks

20 If, after draining and refilling the system, symptoms of overheating are found which did not occur previously, then the fault is almost certainly due to trapped air at some point in the system, causing an airlock and restricting the flow of coolant; usually, the air is trapped because the system was refilled too quickly.

21 If an airlock is suspected, first try gently squeezing all visible coolant hoses. A coolant hose which is full of air feels quite different to one full of coolant, when squeezed. After refilling the system, most airlocks will clear once the system has cooled, and been topped-up.

22 While the engine is running at operating temperature, switch on the heater and heater fan, and check for heat output. Provided there is sufficient coolant in the system, lack of heat output could be due to an airlock in the system.

23 Airlocks can have more serious effects than simply reducing heater output – a severe airlock could reduce coolant flow around the engine. Check that the radiator top hose is hot when the engine is at operating temperature – a top hose which stays cold could be the result of an airlock (or a non-opening thermostat).

24 If the problem persists, stop the engine and allow it to cool down **completely**, before unscrewing the expansion tank filler cap or disconnecting hoses to bleed out the trapped air. In the worst case, the system will have to be at least partially drained (this time, the coolant can be saved for re-use) and flushed to clear the problem.

Notes

Chapter 1 Part B:
Routine maintenance and servicing – diesel models

Contents

Degrees of difficulty

| Easy, suitable for novice with little experience | Fairly easy, suitable for beginner with some experience | Fairly difficult, suitable for competent DIY mechanic | Difficult, suitable for experienced DIY mechanic | Very difficult, suitable for expert DIY or professional |

Lubricants and fluids

Refer to end of *Weekly checks* on page 0•16

Capacities

Engine oil
Drain and refill including filter change . . . . 6.5 litres
Cooling system
All models . . . . 12.5 litres
Fuel tank
All models . . . . 70 litres (approximately)

Cooling system

Specified antifreeze mixture . . . . 50% antifreeze/50% water
Note: *Refer to Chapter 3 for further details.*

Brakes

Brake pad minimum lining thickness . . . . 2.0 mm
Handbrake lever travel after adjustment . . . . 2 to 5 clicks

Remote control battery

Type . . . . CR 2032 3V

Tyres

Tyre pressures . . . . See the sticker on the inside of the fuel filler flap/driver's door aperture
pillar

Torque wrench settings

	Nm	lbf ft
Automatic transmission drain/filler plugs	35	26
Automatic transmission level plug (6-speed only)	8	6
Auxiliary drivebelt tensioner	20	15
Engine oil drain plug	35	26
Oil filter cover	25	18
Roadwheel bolts	140	103

The maintenance intervals in this manual are provided with the assumption that you, not the dealer, will be carrying out the work. These are the average maintenance intervals recommended by the manufacturer for vehicles driven daily under normal conditions. Obviously some variation of these intervals may be expected depending on territory of use, and conditions encountered. If you wish to keep your vehicle in peak condition at all times, you may wish to perform some of these procedures more often. We encourage frequent maintenance because it enhances the efficiency, performance and resale value of your vehicle.

When the vehicle is new, it should be serviced by a dealer service department (or other workshop recognised by the vehicle manufacturer as providing the same standard of service) in order to preserve the warranty.

The vehicle manufacturer may reject warranty claims if you are unable to prove that servicing has been carried out as and when specified, using only original equipment parts or parts certified to be of equivalent quality.

If the vehicle is driven in dusty areas, used to tow a trailer, driven frequently at slow speeds (idling in traffic) or on short journeys, more frequent maintenance intervals are recommended.

Every 250 miles or weekly
- [ ] Refer to *Weekly checks*.

Every 9000 miles or 12 months, whichever comes first
- [ ] Renew the engine oil and filter (Section 3).

Note: *Although Volvo recommend that the engine oil and filter are changed at 18 000 miles or every 12 months, frequent oil and filter changes are good for the engine. We therefore recommend changing the oil at the mileage specified here.*

Every 18 000 miles or 12 months, whichever comes first
Note: *Up to and including 2005 model year this interval was 12 000 miles or 12 months.*
- [ ] Check the condition of the brake pads (Section 4).
- [ ] Thoroughly inspect the engine compartment for fluid leaks (Section 5).
- [ ] Check the condition and security of the steering and suspension components (Section 6).
- [ ] Check the condition of the driveshaft gaiters (Section 7).
- [ ] Inspect the clutch hydraulic components (Section 8).
- [ ] Renew the pollen filter (Section 9).
- [ ] Check the battery electrolyte level (Section 10).
- [ ] Inspect the underbody, brake hydraulic pipes and hoses, and fuel lines (Section 11).
- [ ] Check the condition and security of the exhaust system (Section 12).
- [ ] Check the handbrake adjustment (Section 13).
- [ ] Check the condition of the seat belts (Section 14).
- [ ] Lubricate the locks and hinges (Section 15).
- [ ] Check the headlight beam alignment (Section 16).
- [ ] Check the coolant antifreeze concentration (Section 17).
- [ ] Reset the service reminder indicator (Section 18).
- [ ] Road test (Section 19).
- [ ] Check the operation of the air conditioning system (Section 20).
- [ ] Drain fuel filter of water (Section 21).
- [ ] Renew the remote control battery (Section 22).

Every 36 000 miles or 2 years, whichever comes first
Note: *Up to and including 2005 model year this interval was 24 000 miles or 2 years.*
In addition to the items listed above, carry out the following:
- [ ] Renew the air cleaner element (Section 23).
- [ ] Check the automatic transmission fluid level (Section 24).
- [ ] Renew the fuel filter (Section 25).

Every 90 000 miles or 5 years, whichever comes first
Note: *Up to and including 2005 model year this interval was 96 000 miles or 8 years.*
In addition to the items listed above, carry out the following:
- [ ] Renew the timing belt and tensioner (Section 26).

Note: *It is recommended that this interval is reduced on vehicles which are subjected to intensive use, ie, mainly short journeys or a lot of stop-start driving. The actual belt renewal interval is very much up to the individual owner, but bear in mind that severe engine damage will result if the belt breaks.*
- [ ] Renew the auxiliary drivebelt (Section 27).

Every 2 years, regardless of mileage
- [ ] Renew the brake fluid (Section 28).

Every 3 years, regardless of mileage
- [ ] Renew the coolant (Section 28).

Note: *This work is not included in the Volvo schedule, and should not be required if the recommended Volvo antifreeze/inhibitor is used.*

Underbonnet view (D5244T engine)

1 Engine oil filler cap
2 Engine oil level dipstick
3 Air filter
4 Brake and clutch fluid
   reservoir
5 Oil filter cover
6 Coolant expansion tank
7 Washer fluid reservoir
8 Engine electrical box
9 ECM box
10 Power steering fluid
   reservoir
11 Engine cross-stay

Front underbody view

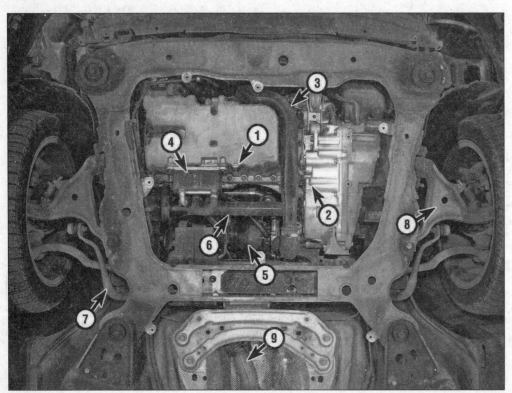

1 Engine oil (sump) drain
   plug
2 Automatic transmission
   drain plug
3 Air charge pipe
4 Oil cooler
5 Turbocharger
6 Driveshaft
7 Anti-roll bar
8 Control arm
9 Front exhaust pipe

1 Fuel tank
2 Exhaust tail box
3 Rear anti-roll bar
4 Handbrake cable
5 Trailing arm
6 Tie-rod
7 Lower control arm
8 Shock absorber lower
  mounting
9 Fuel filter

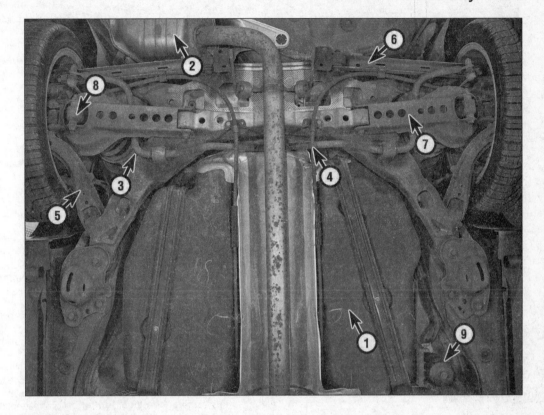

Maintenance procedures

1 Introduction

This Chapter is designed to help the home mechanic maintain his/her vehicle for safety, economy, long life and peak performance.

This Chapter contains a master maintenance schedule, followed by Sections dealing specifically with each task in the schedule. Visual checks, adjustments, component renewal and other helpful items are included. Refer to the accompanying illustrations of the engine compartment and the underside of the vehicle for the locations of the various components.

Servicing your vehicle in accordance with the mileage/time maintenance schedule and the following Sections will provide a planned maintenance programme, which should result in a long and reliable service life. This is a comprehensive plan, so maintaining some items but not others at the specified service intervals will not produce the same results.

As you service your vehicle, you will discover that many of the procedures can – and should – be grouped together, because of the particular procedure being performed, or because of the close proximity of two otherwise-unrelated components to

one another. For example, if the vehicle is raised for any reason, the exhaust should be inspected at the same time as the suspension and steering components.

The first step of this maintenance programme is to prepare yourself before the actual work begins. Read through all the Sections relevant to the work to be carried out, then make a list and gather together all the parts and tools required. If a problem is encountered, seek advice from a parts specialist or a dealer service department.

Service interval display

All models are equipped with a service interval display indicator in the instrument panel. When a predetermined mileage, time period, or number of hours of engine operation has elapsed since the display was last reset, the service light will illuminate, providing a handy reminder of when the next service is required.

The display should not necessarily be used as a definitive guide to the servicing needs of your Volvo, but it is useful as a reminder to ensure that servicing is not accidentally overlooked. Owners of older cars, or those covering a small annual mileage, may feel inclined to service their car more often, in which case the service interval display is perhaps less relevant.

2 Regular maintenance

1 If, from the time the vehicle is new, the routine maintenance schedule is followed closely, and frequent checks are made of fluid levels and high-wear items, as suggested throughout this manual, the engine will be kept in relatively good running condition, and the need for additional work will be minimised.

2 It is possible that there will be some times when the engine is running poorly due to the lack of regular maintenance. This is even more likely if a used vehicle, which has not received regular and frequent maintenance checks, is purchased. In such cases, additional work may need to be carried out, outside of the regular maintenance intervals.

3 If engine wear is suspected, a compression test (refer to Chapter 2B) will provide valuable information regarding the overall performance of the main internal components. Such a test can be used as a basis to decide on the extent of the work to be carried out. If, for example, a compression test indicates serious internal engine wear, conventional maintenance as described in this Chapter will not greatly improve the performance of the engine, and may prove a waste of time and money, unless extensive overhaul work (Chapter 2C) is carried out first.

4 The following series of operations are those often required to improve the performance of a generally poor-running engine:

Primary operations

a) Clean, inspect and test the battery (See Weekly checks and Section 10).

b) Check all the engine-related fluids (See Weekly checks).

c) Renew the auxiliary drivebelt (Section 27).

d) Check the condition of the air cleaner filter element and renew if necessary (Section 23).

e) Renew the fuel filter (Section 25).

f) Check the condition of all hoses, and check for fluid leaks (Section 5).

Secondary operations

5 If the above operations do not prove fully effective, carry out the following operations: All the items listed under *Primary operations*, plus the following:

a) Check the charging system (Chapter 5A).

b) Check the preheating system (Chapter 5A).

c) Check the fuel system (Chapter 4B).

Every 9000 miles or 12 months

3 Engine oil and filter renewal

> **HAYNES HINT** *Frequent oil changes are the best preventative maintenance the home mechanic can give the engine, because ageing oil becomes diluted and contaminated, which leads to premature engine wear.*

1 Make sure that you have all the necessary tools before you begin this procedure. You should also have plenty of rags or newspapers handy, for mopping-up any spills. The oil should preferably be changed when the engine is still fully warmed-up to normal operating temperature, just after a run; warm oil and sludge will flow out more easily. Take care, however, not to touch the exhaust or any other hot parts of the engine when working under the vehicle. To avoid any possibility of scalding, and to protect yourself from possible skin irritants and other harmful contaminants in used engine oils, it is advisable to wear gloves when carrying out this work.

2 Access to the underside of the vehicle is greatly improved if the vehicle can be lifted on a hoist, driven onto ramps, or supported by axle stands (see *Jacking and vehicle support*). Whichever method is chosen, make sure that the vehicle remains level, or if it is at an angle, that the drain point is at the lowest point. Release the screws and remove the engine undershield for access to the sump and drain plug **(see illustration)**.

3 Position the draining container under the drain plug, and unscrew the plug **(see illustration)**. If possible, try to keep the plug pressed into the sump while unscrewing it by hand the last couple of turns.

> **HAYNES HINT** *As the drain plug releases from the threads, move it away sharply, so the stream of oil issuing from the sump runs into the container, not up your sleeve.*

4 Allow the oil to drain into the container, and discard the drain plug sealing washer. A new one must be fitted.

5 Allow some time for the old oil to drain, noting that it may be necessary to reposition the container as the oil flow slows to a trickle; when the oil has completely drained, wipe clean the drain plug and its threads in the sump and refit the plug with a new sealing washer **(see illustration)**, tightening it to the specified torque.

6 The oil filter is located at the front side of the engine, accessible from above. Pull the plastic cover over the engine straight up to release it from the mountings.

7 Using a 36 mm socket or adjustable spanner, undo the filter cover and remove it, followed by the old filter element **(see illustrations)**. Discard the filter cover O-ring seal, a new one must be fitted.

8 Using a clean, lint-free rag, wipe clean the inside of the filter housing and cover.

9 Apply a light coating of clean engine oil to the new O-ring seal and fit it to the filter cover **(see illustration)**. Insert the filter element into the cover, then screw the filter cover

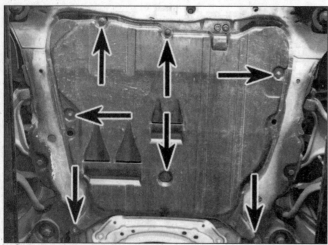

3.2 Undo the screws and remove the engine undershield (arrowed)

3.3 Unscrew the sump plug (arrowed)

3.5 Refit the plug with a new sealing washer

3.7a Unscrew the filter cover . . .

3.7b . . . and withdraw the filter element

3.9 Fit the new O-ring seal to the filter cover

3.11a Unscrew the oil filler cap

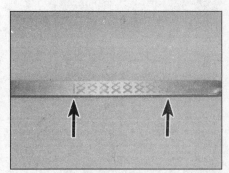

3.11b Maximum and minimum markings on the dipstick (arrowed)

into position on the engine until it seats, then tighten it to the specified torque.

10 Remove the old oil and all tools from under the vehicle, then lower the vehicle to the ground.

11 Remove the dipstick and the oil filler cap from the engine. Fill the engine with oil, using the correct grade and type of oil (see *Specifications*). Pour in half the specified quantity of oil first, then wait a few minutes

for the oil to run to the sump. Continue adding oil a small quantity at a time, until the level is up to the lower mark on the dipstick. Adding approximately 1.2 litres will raise the level to the upper mark on the dipstick **(see illustrations)**.

12 Start the engine. The oil pressure warning light will take a few seconds to go out while the new filter fills with oil; do not race the engine while the light is on. Run the engine for a few minutes, while checking for leaks

around the oil filter seal and the drain plug. Refit the engine undershield.

13 Switch off the engine, and wait a few minutes for the oil to settle in the sump once more. With the new oil circulated and the filter now completely full, recheck the level on the dipstick, and add more oil as necessary.

14 Dispose of the used engine oil safely and in accordance with environmental regulations (see *General repair procedures*).

Every 18 000 miles or 12 months

4 Brake pad wear check

1 Jack up the front or rear of the vehicle in turn, and support it on axle stands (see *Jacking and vehicle support*).

2 For better access to the brake calipers, remove the roadwheels.

3 Look through the inspection window in the caliper, and check that the thickness of the

friction lining material on each of the pads is not less than the recommended minimum thickness given in the *Specifications* **(see illustration)**. If any one of the brake pads has worn down to, or below, the specified limit, *all four* pads at that end of the car must be renewed as a set (ie all the front pads or all the rear pads).

4 For a comprehensive check, the brake pads should be removed and cleaned. The operation of the brake calipers can then be checked, and the brake discs can be fully examined. Refer to Chapter 9 for details.

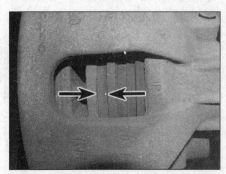

4.3 Check the brake pad friction material thickness (arrowed)

A leak in the cooling system will usually show up as white- or antifreeze-coloured deposits on the area adjoining the leak.

5 Underbonnet check for fluid leaks and hose condition

Caution: Renewal of air conditioning hoses must be left to a dealer service department or air conditioning specialist who has the equipment to depressurise the system safely. Never remove air conditioning components or hoses until the system has been depressurised.

General

1 High temperatures in the engine compartment can cause the deterioration of the rubber and plastic hoses used for engine, accessory and emission systems operation. Periodic inspection should be made for cracks, loose clamps, material hardening and leaks.

2 Carefully check the large top and bottom radiator hoses **(see Haynes Hint)**, along with the other smaller-diameter cooling system hoses and metal pipes; do not forget the heater hoses/pipes which run from the engine to the bulkhead. Inspect each hose along its entire length, renewing any that are cracked, swollen or shows signs of deterioration. Cracks may become more apparent if the hose is squeezed.

3 Make sure that all hose connections are tight. If the spring clamps that are used to secure some of the hoses appear to be slackening,

6.2 Check the condition of the steering rack gaiters

they should be updated with screw- type clips to prevent the possibility of leaks.

4 Some other hoses are secured to their fittings with screw-type clips. Where screw-type clips are used, check to be sure they haven't slackened, allowing the hose to leak. If clamps or screw-type clips aren't used, make sure the hose has not expanded and/or hardened where it slips over the fitting, allowing it to leak.

5 Check all fluid reservoirs, filler caps, drain plugs and fittings, etc, looking for any signs of leakage of oil, transmission and/or brake hydraulic fluid, coolant and power steering fluid. If the vehicle is regularly parked in the same place, close inspection of the ground underneath will soon show any leaks; ignore the puddle of water which will be left if the air conditioning system is in use. As soon as a leak is detected, its source must be traced and rectified. Where oil has been leaking for some time, it is usually necessary to use a steam cleaner, pressure washer or similar, to clean away the accumulated dirt, so that the exact source of the leak can be identified.

Vacuum hoses

6 It's quite common for vacuum hoses, especially those in the emissions system, to be numbered or colour-coded, or to be identified by coloured stripes moulded into them. Various systems require hoses with different wall thicknesses, collapse resistance and temperature resistance. When renewing hoses, be sure the new ones are made of the same material.

7 Often the only effective way to check a hose is to remove it completely from the vehicle. If more than one hose is removed, be sure to label the hoses and fittings to ensure correct installation.

8 When checking vacuum hoses, be sure to include any plastic T-fittings in the check. Inspect the fittings for cracks, and check the hose where it fits over the fitting for distortion, which could cause leakage.

9 A small piece of vacuum hose can be used as a stethoscope to detect vacuum leaks. Hold one end of the hose to your ear, and probe around vacuum hoses and fittings, listening for the hissing sound characteristic of a vacuum leak.

⚠ *Warning: When probing with the vacuum hose stethoscope, be very careful not to come into contact with moving engine components such as the auxiliary drivebelt, radiator electric cooling fan, etc.*

Fuel hoses

⚠ *Warning: Before carrying out the following operation, refer to the precautions given in Safety first! at the beginning of this manual, and follow them implicitly. Fuel is a highly dangerous and volatile liquid, and the precautions necessary when handling it cannot be overstressed.*

10 Check all fuel hoses for deterioration and chafing. Check especially for cracks in areas where the hose bends, and also just before fittings, such as where a hose attaches to the fuel filter.

11 High-quality fuel line, usually identified by the word Fluoroelastomer printed on the hose, should be used for fuel line renewal. Never, under any circumstances, use un-reinforced vacuum line, clear plastic tubing or water hose for fuel lines.

12 Spring-type clamps are commonly used on fuel lines. These clamps often lose their tension over a period of time, and can be 'sprung' during removal. Update all spring-type clamps with screw clips whenever a hose is renewed.

13 If a fuel leak is suspected, remember that any leak will be more obvious with the system at full pressure, such as when the engine is running, or shortly after switching off.

Metal lines

14 Sections of metal piping are often used for fuel line between the fuel filter and the engine. Check carefully to be sure the piping has not been bent or crimped, and that cracks have not started in the line.

15 If a section of metal fuel line must be renewed, only seamless steel piping should be used, since copper and aluminium piping don't have the strength necessary to withstand normal engine vibration.

16 Check the metal brake lines where they enter the master cylinder and ABS hydraulic unit for cracks in the lines or loose fittings. Any sign of brake fluid leakage calls for an immediate and thorough inspection of the brake system.

6 Steering and suspension check

Front suspension and steering

1 Apply the handbrake, then jack up the front of the vehicle and support it on axle stands (see *Jacking and vehicle support*).

2 Visually inspect the balljoint dust covers and the steering gear gaiters for splits, chafing or deterioration **(see illustration)**. Any wear of these components will cause loss of lubricant, together with dirt and water entry, resulting in rapid deterioration of the balljoints or steering gear.

3 Check the power steering fluid hoses for chafing or deterioration, and the pipe and hose unions for fluid leaks. Also check for signs of fluid leakage under pressure from the steering gear rubber gaiters, which would indicate failed fluid seals within the steering gear.

4 Check for signs of fluid leakage around the suspension strut body, or from the rubber boot around the piston rod (where fitted). Should any fluid be noticed, the shock absorber is defective internally, and renewal is necessary.

6.5 Grasp the wheel at the 12 o'clock and 6 o'clock positions, and try to rock it

5 Grasp the roadwheel at the 12 o'clock and 6 o'clock positions, and try to rock it **(see illustration)**. Very slight free play may be felt, but if the movement is appreciable, further investigation is necessary to determine the source. Continue rocking the wheel while an assistant depresses the footbrake. If the movement is now eliminated or significantly reduced, it is likely that the wheel bearings are at fault. If the free play is still evident with the footbrake depressed, then there is wear in the suspension joints or mountings.

6 Now grasp the wheel at the 9 o'clock and 3 o'clock positions, and try to rock it as before. Any movement felt now may again be caused by wear in the wheel bearings or the steering track rod end balljoints. If the outer track rod end is worn, the visual movement will be obvious. If the inner joint is suspect, it can be felt by placing a hand over the rack-and-pinion rubber gaiter, and gripping the track rod. If the wheel is now rocked, movement will be felt at the inner joint if wear has taken place.

7 Using a large screwdriver or flat bar, check for wear in the suspension mounting bushes by levering between the relevant suspension component and its attachment point. Some movement is to be expected as the mountings are made of rubber, but excessive wear should be obvious. Also check the condition of any visible rubber bushes, looking for splits, cracks or contamination of the rubber.

8 With the vehicle standing on its wheels, have an assistant turn the steering wheel back-and-forth, about an eighth of a turn each way. There should be very little, if any, lost movement between the steering wheel

and roadwheels. If this is not the case, closely observe the joints and mountings previously described, but in addition, check the steering column universal joints for wear, and also check the rack-and-pinion steering gear itself.
9 The efficiency of the shock absorber may be checked by bouncing the car at each front corner. Generally speaking, the body will return to its normal position and stop after being depressed. If it rises and returns on a rebound, the shock absorber is probably suspect. Examine also the shock absorber upper and lower mountings for any signs of wear or fluid leakage.

Rear suspension

10 Chock the front wheels, then raise the rear of the vehicle and support it on axle stands (see *Jacking and vehicle support*).
11 Check the rear hub bearings for wear, using the method described for the front hub bearings (paragraph 5).
12 Using a large screwdriver or flat bar, check for wear in the suspension mounting bushes by levering between the relevant suspension component and its attachment point. Some movement is to be expected as the mountings are made of rubber, but excessive wear should be obvious. Check the condition of the shock absorbers as described previously.

7 Driveshaft gaiter check

1 With the vehicle raised and securely supported on axle stands (see *Jacking and vehicle support*), turn the steering onto full lock, then slowly rotate the roadwheel. Inspect the condition of the outer constant velocity (CV) joint rubber gaiters, squeezing the gaiters to open out the folds **(see illustration)**. Check for signs of cracking, splits or deterioration of the rubber, which may allow the grease to escape, and lead to water and grit entry into the joint. Also check the security and condition of the retaining clips. Repeat these checks on the inner CV joints. If any damage or deterioration is found, the gaiters should be renewed as described in Chapter 8.
2 At the same time, check the general condition of the CV joints themselves by first holding the

7.1 Check the condition of the driveshaft gaiters (arrowed)

driveshaft and attempting to rotate the wheel. Repeat this check by holding the inner joint and attempting to rotate the driveshaft. Any appreciable movement indicates wear in the joints, wear in the driveshaft splines, or a loose driveshaft retaining nut.

8 Clutch hydraulic check

1 Check that the clutch pedal moves smoothly and easily through its full travel, and that the clutch itself functions correctly, with no trace of slip or drag.
2 Undo the two screws and remove the lower facia panel (above the pedals) for access to the clutch pedal, and apply a few drops of light oil to the pedal pivot. Refit the panel.
3 From within the engine compartment, check the condition of the fluid lines and hoses.

9 Pollen filter renewal

1 Undo the two screws and remove the lower facia panel from above the passenger's footwell **(see illustration)**.
2 Undo the four screws, remove the cover and pull the pollen filter downwards from the heater housing **(see illustrations)**.
3 Note there are two possible locations in the heater housing for the pollen filter. Standard filters slide up into the narrower of the two slots

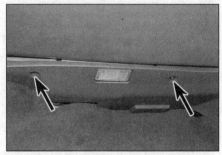

9.1 Undo the 2 screws (arrowed) and remove the lower facia panel on the passenger's side

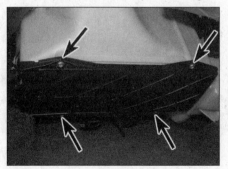

9.2a Undo the pollen filter cover screws (arrowed) . . .

9.2b . . . and slide the filter down

10.4 Unscrew the cell caps (arrowed)

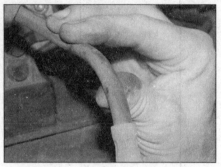

11.5 Check the condition of the brake hoses

in the housing, whilst multifilters (vehicles with an air quality sensor) slide up into the wider of the slots. **Note:** *Under no circumstances should both a standard and multifilter be fitted together.*
4 Slide the appropriate filter into place, then refit the cover and tighten the retaining screws securely.
5 Refit the lower facia panel.

10 Battery electrolyte level check

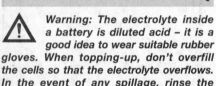

⚠ *Warning: The electrolyte inside a battery is diluted acid – it is a good idea to wear suitable rubber gloves. When topping-up, don't overfill the cells so that the electrolyte overflows. In the event of any spillage, rinse the electrolyte off without delay. Refit the cell covers and rinse the battery with copious quantities of clean water. Don't attempt to syphon out any excess electrolyte.*

1 The battery is located under the flooring in the luggage compartment. Lift up the flooring, and where applicable, unclip the cover from the battery.
2 Some models covered by this manual may be fitted with a maintenance-free battery as standard equipment, or may have had one fitted. If the battery in your vehicle is marked Freedom, Maintenance-Free or similar, no electrolyte level checking is required (the battery is often completely sealed, preventing any topping-up).
3 Batteries which do require their electrolyte level to be checked can be recognised by the presence of removable covers over the six battery cells – the battery casing can also be translucent, so that the electrolyte level can be more easily checked. One of the project vehicles seen in our workshop had a battery marked 'maintenance-free', which still had removable cell caps – in this case, check the electrolyte level as described, but consult a Volvo dealer if topping-up appears to be required.
4 Remove the cell caps or covers, and either look down inside the battery to see the level web, or check the level using any markings provided on the battery casing **(see illustration)**. The electrolyte should cover the battery plates by approximately 15 mm.

5 If necessary, top-up a little at a time with distilled (deionised) water until the level in all six cells is correct – don't fill the cells up to the brim. Wipe up any spillage, then refit the cell covers.
6 Further information on the battery, charging and jump starting can be found at the start of this manual and in Chapter 5A.

11 Underbody and fuel/brake line check

1 With the vehicle raised and supported on axle stands (see *Jacking and vehicle support*), or over an inspection pit, thoroughly inspect the underbody and wheel arches for signs of damage and corrosion. In particular, examine the bottom of the side sills, and any concealed areas where mud can collect.
2 Where corrosion and rust is evident, press and tap firmly on the panel with a screwdriver, and check for any serious corrosion which would necessitate repairs. If the panel is not seriously corroded, clean away the rust, and apply a new coating of underseal. Refer to Chapter 11 for more details of body repairs.
3 At the same time, inspect the treated lower body panels for stone damage and general condition.
4 Inspect all of the fuel and brake lines on the underbody for damage, rust, corrosion and leakage. Also make sure that they are correctly supported in their clips. Where applicable, check the PVC coating on the lines for damage.

12.2 Make sure all the exhaust rubber mountings are in good condition

5 Inspect the flexible brake hoses in the vicinity of the front calipers and rear axle, where they are subjected to most movement **(see illustration)**. Bend them between the fingers (but do not actually bend them double, or the casing may be damaged) and check that this does not reveal previously-hidden cracks, cuts or splits.

12 Exhaust system check

1 With the engine cold (at least three hours after the vehicle has been driven), check the complete exhaust system, from its starting point at the engine to the end of the tailpipe. Ideally, this should be done on a hoist, where unrestricted access is available; if a hoist is not available, raise and support the vehicle on axle stands (see *Jacking and vehicle support*).
2 Check the pipes and connections for evidence of leaks, severe corrosion, or damage. Make sure that all brackets and rubber mountings are in good condition, and tight; if any of the mountings are to be renewed, ensure that the new ones are of the correct type **(see illustration)**. Leakage at any of the joints or in other parts of the system will usually show up as a black sooty stain in the vicinity of the leak.
3 At the same time, inspect the underside of the body for holes, corrosion, open seams, etc, which may allow exhaust gases to enter the passenger compartment. Seal all body openings with silicone or body putty, with due consideration given to the heat generated by the exhaust system and gases.
4 Rattles and other noises can often be traced to the exhaust system, especially the rubber mountings. Try to move the system, silencer(s) and catalytic converter. If any components can touch the body or suspension parts, secure the exhaust system with new mountings.

13 Handbrake check and adjustment

In service, the handbrake should be fully applied within approximately 5 clicks of the handbrake lever ratchet. Adjustment will be necessary periodically to compensate for lining wear and cable stretch. Refer to Chapter 9 for the full adjustment procedure.

14 Seat belt check

1 Check the seat belts for satisfactory operation and condition. Inspect the webbing for fraying and cuts. Check that they retract smoothly and without binding into their reels.
2 Check the seat belt mountings, ensuring that all the bolts are securely tightened.

15 Door, boot and bonnet check and lubrication

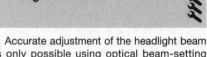

1 Check that the doors, bonnet and boot lid close securely. Check that the bonnet safety catch operates correctly. Check the operation of the door check straps.
2 Lubricate the hinges, door check straps, the striker plates and the bonnet catch sparingly with a little oil or grease.
3 If any of the doors or bonnet do not close effectively, or appear not to be flush with the surrounding panels, carry out the relevant adjustment procedures contained in Chapter 11.

16 Headlight beam alignment check

Accurate adjustment of the headlight beam is only possible using optical beam-setting equipment, and this work should therefore be carried out by a Volvo dealer or service station with the necessary facilities.

Basic adjustments can be carried out in an emergency, and further details are given in Chapter 12.

17 Coolant antifreeze concentration check

1 The cooling system should be filled with the recommended antifreeze and corrosion protection fluid. Over a period of time, the concentration of fluid may be reduced due to topping-up (this can be avoided by topping-up with the correct antifreeze mixture) or fluid loss. If loss of coolant has been evident, it is important to make the necessary repair before adding fresh fluid. The exact mixture of antifreeze-to-water which you should use depends on the relative weather conditions. The mixture should contain at least 40% antifreeze, but not more than 70%. Consult the mixture ratio chart on the antifreeze container before adding coolant. Hydrometers are available at most automotive accessory shops to test the coolant. Use antifreeze which meets the vehicle manufacturer's specifications.
2 With the engine cold, carefully remove the cap from the expansion tank. If the engine is not completely cold, place a cloth rag over the cap before removing it, and remove it slowly to allow any pressure to escape.
3 Antifreeze checkers are available from car accessory shops. Draw some coolant from the expansion tank and observe how many plastic balls are floating in the checker (see illustration). Usually, 2 or 3 balls must be floating for the correct concentration of antifreeze, but follow the manufacturer's instructions.

4 If the concentration is incorrect, it will be necessary to either withdraw some coolant and add antifreeze, or alternatively drain the old coolant and add fresh coolant of the correct concentration.

18 Service reminder indicator – resetting

2001 model year

1 Turn the ignition switch to position I.
2 Press and hold the mileage trip reset button, then turn the ignition switch to position II.
3 Service reminder indicator starts to flash after the button has been pressed for approx 10 seconds. Release the button within 5 seconds. An audible signal will be given when the reset is complete.

From 2002 model year

4 Turn the ignition switch to position I.
5 Press and hold the mileage trip reset button, then turn the ignition switch to position II within 2 seconds.
6 Hold the reset button in until the indicator has been reset. On models from 2003, a yellow light in the cluster will illuminate when the button is to be released. Release the reset button within 4 seconds. An audible signal will be given when the reset is complete.

19 Road test

Braking system

1 Make sure that the vehicle does not pull to one side when braking, and that the wheels do not lock when braking hard.
2 Check that there is no vibration through the steering when braking. Note that, under heavy braking, some vibration may be felt through the brake pedal – this is a normal feature of the Anti-lock Braking System (ABS) operation, and does not normally indicate a fault.
3 Check that the handbrake operates correctly, without excessive movement of the lever, and that it holds the vehicle stationary on a slope.

17.3 Use a hydrometer to check the strength of the antifreeze

4 With the engine switched off, test the operation of the brake servo unit as follows. Depress the footbrake four or five times to exhaust the vacuum, then start the engine. As the engine starts, there should be a noticeable give in the brake pedal as vacuum builds-up. Allow the engine to run for at least two minutes, and then switch it off. If the brake pedal is now depressed again, it should be possible to detect a hiss from the servo as the pedal is depressed. After about four or five applications, no further hissing should be heard, and the pedal should feel considerably harder.

Steering and suspension

5 Check for any abnormalities in the steering, suspension, handling or road feel.
6 Drive the vehicle, and check that there are no unusual vibrations or noises.
7 Check that the steering feels positive, with no excessive sloppiness or roughness, and check for any suspension noises when cornering and driving over bumps.

Drivetrain

8 Check the performance of the engine, transmission and driveline.
9 Check that the engine starts correctly, both when cold and hot.
10 Listen for any unusual noises from the engine and transmission.
11 Make sure that the engine runs smoothly when idling, and that there is no hesitation when accelerating.
12 On manual transmission models, check that all gears can be engaged smoothly without noise, and that the gear lever action is smooth and not abnormally vague or notchy.
13 On automatic transmission models, make sure that the drive seems smooth without jerks or engine speed flare-ups. Check that all the gear positions can be selected with the vehicle at rest.

Clutch

14 Check that the clutch pedal moves smoothly and easily through its full travel, and that the clutch itself functions correctly, with no trace of slip or drag. If the movement is uneven or stiff in places, check the system components with reference to Chapter 6.

Instruments and electrical equipment

15 Check the operation of all instruments and electrical equipment.
16 Make sure that all instruments read correctly, and switch on all electrical equipment in turn, to check that it functions properly.

20 Air conditioning system check

Warning: The air conditioning system is under high pressure. Do not loosen any fittings or remove

21.1a Drain screw (arrowed) – canister type fuel filter . . .

any components until after the system has been discharged. Air conditioning refrigerant must be properly discharged into an approved type of container, at a dealer service department or an automotive air conditioning repair facility capable of handling the refrigerant safely. Always wear eye protection when disconnecting air conditioning system fittings.

1 The following maintenance checks should be performed on a regular basis, to ensure that the system continues to operate at peak efficiency:

a) Check the auxiliary drivebelt. If it's worn or deteriorated, renew it (see Section 27).
b) Check the system hoses. Look for cracks, bubbles, hard spots and deterioration. Inspect the hoses and all fittings for oil bubbles and seepage. If there's any evidence of wear, damage or leaks, renew the hose(s).

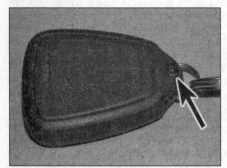

22.1 Undo the Torx bolt (arrowed) and lift up the cover

22.4 Prise up the rear edge of the cover

21.1b . . . and paper element type fuel filter (arrowed)

c) Inspect the condenser fins for leaves, insects and other debris. Use a 'fin comb' or compressed air to clean the condenser.

 Warning: Wear eye protection when using compressed air.

d) Check that the drain tube from the front of the evaporator is clear – note that it is normal to have clear fluid (water) dripping from this while the system is in operation, to the extent that quite a large puddle can be left under the vehicle when it is parked.

2 It's a good idea to operate the system for about 30 minutes at least once a month, particularly during the winter. Long term non-use can cause hardening, and subsequent failure, of the seals.

3 Because of the complexity of the air conditioning system and the special equipment necessary to service it, in-depth

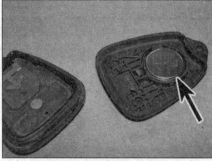

22.2 The battery (arrowed) fits positive side down in the cover

22.5 The battery is fitted positive side up

repairs are not included in this manual, apart from those procedures covered in Chapter 3.

4 The most common cause of poor cooling is simply a low system refrigerant charge. If a noticeable drop in cool air output occurs, the following quick check will help you determine if the refrigerant level is low.

5 Warm the engine up to normal operating temperature.

6 Place the air conditioning temperature selector at the coldest setting, and put the blower at the highest setting. Open the doors – to make sure the air conditioning system doesn't cycle off as soon as it cools the passenger compartment.

7 With the compressor engaged – the clutch will make an audible click, and the centre of the clutch will rotate – feel the inlet and outlet pipes at the compressor. One side should be cold, and one hot. If there's no perceptible difference between the two pipes, there's something wrong with the compressor or the system. It might be a low charge – it might be something else. Take the vehicle to a dealer service department or an automotive air conditioning specialist.

21 Fuel filter water draining

1 The fuel filter is located under the right-hand side of the vehicle, in front of the rear roadwheel. Position a container under the filter and slacken the drain screw on the underside of the filter **(see illustrations)**.
2 Drain off approximately 100 cc of fluid and tighten the drain screw.
3 Start the engine and check for leaks.

22 Remote control battery renewal

Up to 2003 model year

1 Undo the bolt and remove the cover from the remote control **(see illustration)**.
2 Remove the battery from the cover, noting its orientation – negative side up **(see illustration)**. Avoid touching the battery and contacts with bare fingers.
3 Fit the new battery into the cover (negative side up), then refit the cover and tighten the bolt.

From 2004 model year

4 Use a small, flat-bladed screwdriver to gently prise up the rear edge of the cover on the remote **(see illustration)**. Remove the cover.
5 Remove the battery from the control, noting its orientation – positive side up **(see illustration)**. Avoid touching the battery and contacts with bare fingers.
6 Fit the new battery into the control (positive side up), then refit the cover, ensuring the rubber seal is correctly fitted.

23.1 Disconnect the mass flow meter wiring plug

23.2 Slacken the air filter outlet hose clamp

23.3a Release the clips . . .

23.3b . . . lift up the air filter cover . . .

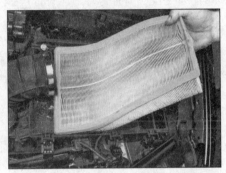

23.3c . . . and remove the filter element

23.8 Lift the ECM cover

Every 36 000 miles or 2 years

23 Air cleaner element renewal

D5244T/T2/T3 engines

1 Disconnect the mass airflow meter wiring plug – located in the air filter outlet **(see illustration)**.
2 Slacken the retaining clamp, and disconnect the outlet hose from the mass airflow meter **(see illustration)**.
3 Release the clips at the front edge, lift the cover upwards, and remove the air filter element **(see illustrations)**.
4 Wipe clean inside the housing and cover with a cloth. Be careful not to sweep debris into the air inlet.
5 Fit the new element, making sure it is the right way up. Press the seal on the rim of the element into the groove on the housing.
6 Refit the cover and secure it with the clips. Note that the rear of the cover can be difficult to refit. Take care to endure the three 'hinges' locate correctly in the air cleaner housing.
7 Reconnect the outlet hose, tighten the clamp, then reconnect the mass airflow meter wiring plug.

D5244T4/T5/T6/T7 engines

8 Lift off the cover from the ECM at the left-hand side of the engine compartment **(see illustration)**.

9 Undo the Torx bolts and lift the air cleaner housing cover **(see illustration)**.
10 Lift the air cleaner element from place, noting which way around it's fitted **(see illustration)**.
11 Fit the new element, refit the cover and tighten the Torx bolts.
12 Refit the cover over the ECM.

24 Automatic transmission fluid level check

Fluid level check

1 The level of the automatic transmission fluid should be carefully maintained. Low fluid level can lead to slipping or loss of drive, while overfilling can cause foaming, loss of fluid and transmission damage.
2 Ideally, the transmission fluid level should be checked when the transmission is hot – 80°C for 5-speed transmissions, and 50 to 60°C for 6-speed transmissions.

5-speed transmissions

3 Park the vehicle on level ground, firmly apply the handbrake, and start the engine. While the engine is idling, depress the brake pedal and move the selector lever through all gear positions (pausing in each position for at least 3 seconds), returning finally to the P position.
4 Wait two minutes then, with the engine still idling, remove the dipstick (yellow handle) from

23.9 Undo the Torx bolts (arrowed) and lift the air filter cover

23.10 Note which way around the filter element is fitted

24.4 The automatic transmission fluid level dipstick is located on the front face of the transmission casing (arrowed)

its tube which is located at the front of the engine **(see illustration)**. Note the condition and colour of the fluid on the dipstick.

5 Wipe the fluid from the dipstick with a clean rag, and re-insert it into the filler tube until the cap seats.

6 Pull the dipstick out again, and note the fluid level. The level should be between the MIN and MAX marks, on the side of the dipstick marked HOT **(see illustration)**. If the level is on the MIN mark, stop the engine, and add the specified automatic transmission fluid through the dipstick tube, using a clean funnel if necessary. It is important not to introduce dirt into the transmission when topping-up.

7 Add the fluid a little at a time, and keep checking the level as previously described until it is correct. The difference between the MIN and MAX marks on the dipstick is approximately 0.5 litre.

8 If the vehicle has not been driven and the engine and transmission are cold, carry out the procedures in paragraphs 3 to 7, but use the marks of the dipstick marked COLD. It is, however, preferable to check the level when the transmission is hot, as a more accurate reading will be obtained.

6-speed transmissions

9 Park the vehicle on level ground, firmly apply the handbrake, and remove the engine transmission undershield.

10 Remove the air cleaner housing as described in Chapter 4B.

11 Clean the area on the top of the trans-mission around the filler plug, then using a T55 Torx bit, unscrew the filler plug **(see illustration 24.34)**.

12 Position the end of a hose in the filler aperture, and attach a funnel to the other end. Temporarily refit the air cleaner housing.

13 Start the engine. While the engine is idling, depress the brake pedal and move the selector lever through all gear positions (pausing in each position for 2 seconds), returning finally to the P position.

14 With the engine still running, unscrew the level plug from the centre of the transmission drain plug using a T40 Torx bit **(see illus-tration 24.30)**. If no fluid emerges from the level aperture, add specified fluid through the funnel and hose until it does emerge. Refit the level plug and tighten it to the specified torque, using a new sealing washer.

15 Stop the engine, remove the air cleaner housing, and tighten the fluid filler plug to the specified torque, using a new sealing washer.

16 Refit the air cleaner housing as described in Chapter 4B, then refit the engine/transmission undershield.

All transmissions

17 The need for regular topping-up of the transmission fluid indicates a leak, which should be found and rectified without delay.

18 The condition of the fluid should also be checked along with the level. If the fluid at the end of the dipstick is black or a dark reddish-brown colour, or if it has a burned smell, the fluid should be changed. If you are in doubt about the condition of the fluid, purchase some new fluid, and compare the two for colour and smell.

19 If the car is used regularly for short trips, taxi work, or does a lot of towing, the transmission fluid should be renewed on a regular basis. Likewise, if a high mileage has been completed, or the history of the car is unknown, it might be worth renewing the fluid for peace of mind. Normally, however, renewal of the fluid is not a service requirement.

Fluid renewal

Note: *The automatic transmission fluid does not normally require changing. It's only necessary on vehicles which are used predominantly for towing or as taxis.*

20 Ideally, the transmission fluid level should be drained when the transmission is hot (at its normal operating temperature). If the vehicle has just been driven for about 30 minutes, and the transmission is hot. Note that on 6-speed transmissions, the fluid temperature must not be allowed to exceed 60°C, or an incorrect fluid level will result.

21 Jack up the front and rear of the vehicle and support it securely on axle stands (see *Jacking and vehicle support*). The vehicle should be level.

22 Release the screws and remove the engine undershield **(see illustration 3.2)**.

5-speed transmission

23 Position a container beneath the trans-mission and unscrew the drain plug **(see illustration)**. Discard the drain plug sealing washer, a new one must be fitted.

24 If required, detach the oil cooler hoses from the transmission and allow the fluid in the cooler and pipes to drain into the container.

25 Refit the drain plug with a new sealing washer, and tighten it to the specified torque. Refit the engine undershield, and lower the vehicle to the ground.

26 Ensure the handbrake is fully applied and the selector lever is in position P.

27 Pull out the fluid level dipstick, and with the aid of a funnel, pour approximately 2.0 litres of new fluid down through the dipstick guide tube **(see illustration 24.4)**.

28 Start the engine and allow it to idle for a few seconds, then turn it off, and add another 2.0 litre of fluid.

29 Start the engine, allow it to idle, then move the selector lever through all positions, pausing for at least 3 seconds in each position. Insert and remove the fluid level dipstick and check the level. With the transmission warm, the temperature of the fluid should be approaching 80°C. At this temperature the fluid level should be up to the mark adjacent to the 'Hot' marked on the dipstick. Add fluid as necessary. After adding fluid, move the selector lever through all positions, pausing for at least 3 seconds in each position as previously described.

6-speed transmission

30 Position a container beneath the trans-mission and unscrew the level plug from the centre of the drain plug using a T40 Torx bit **(see illustration)**.

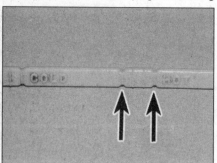

24.6 Maximum and minimum level marks (arrowed) when the fluid is hot

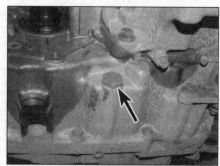

24.23 Automatic transmission drain plug (arrowed)

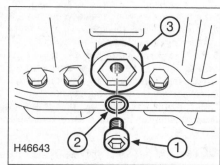

H46643

24.30 Transmission level plug (1), drain plug (2) and sealing washer (3)

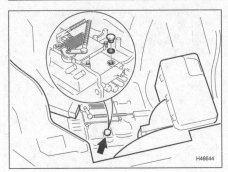

24.34 Transmission filler plug (arrowed)

25.3a Unscrew the filter from the housing – cartridge filter . . .

25.3b . . . and paper element type filter

31 Unscrew the drain plug from the transmission and allow the fluid to drain. Refit the drain plug with a new seal and tighten it to the specified torque.

32 Refit the level plug, but only finger-tighten it at this stage.

33 Remove the air cleaner housing as described in Chapter 4B.

34 Clean the area on the top of the transmission around the filler plug, then using a T55 Torx bit, unscrew the filler plug **(see illustration)**.

35 Disconnect the fluid return hose from the cooler adjacent to the radiator, and attach a length of clear hose to the cooler outlet. Volvo special tool No 999 7363 may be available for this purpose. Place the end of the hose into a container.

36 Using a funnel, add 4.0 litres of the specified fluid into the transmission casing through the filler hole.

37 Fully apply the handbrake, and check the selector lever is in position P.

38 Start the engine, and allow it to idle. Shift through all the selector positions, pausing for 2 seconds at each position. Switch the engine off when air bubbles are visible in the clear hose attached to the cooler.

39 Add 2.0 litres of the specified fluid, then start the engine again and allow it to idle. Switch the engine off when air bubbles are visible in the clear hose.

40 Add 2.0 litres of the specified fluid, then start the engine again and allow it to idle. Switch the engine off when air bubbles are visible in the clear hose.

41 Disconnect the clear hose from the cooler, and reconnect the fluid return hose.

42 Unscrew the level plug from the centre of the drain plug, and add fluid through the filler hole until it begins to run out of the level plug hole. Refit the level and filler plugs and tighten them to their specified torques.

43 Refit the air cleaner housing.

All transmissions

Note: *If the 'Gearbox oil change' indicator illuminates, this can only be reset using dedicated Volvo test equipment. Entrust this task to a Volvo dealer or suitably-equipped specialist.*

25 Fuel filter renewal

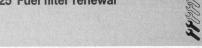

Note: *Ensure the fuel tank level is less than 3/4 full before removing the filter.*

1 The fuel filter is located under the right-hand side of the vehicle, in front of the rear roadwheel.

2 Place a container under the filter, then slacken the drain screw on the filter underside and allow the fluid to drain **(see illustration 21.1a and 21.1b)**.

3 Use a strap wench or filter removal tool to unscrew the filter from the housing **(see illustration)**. Be prepared for fluid spillage. Some models are fitted with a spin-on cartridge filter, whilst others are fitted with a

renewable paper element. Where applicable, pull the paper element from the filter housing **(see illustration)**.

4 On models with a spin-on cartridge, smear a layer of clean diesel around the filter seal **(see illustration)**, then fit the new filter to the housing. Tighten the filter by hand until the seal contacts the housing, then tighten it a further 1/2 to 3/4 of a turn.

5 On models with a paper element, ensure the small O-ring seal is fitted to the top of the element, then fit the large O-ring seal to the filter housing. Fit the new element into the filter housing, then fit the filter holder, ensuring the top of the holder locates in the housing **(see illustrations)**. Tighten the holder by hand until the seal contacts the holder, then tighten it a further 1/2 to 3/4 of a turn.

6 Start the engine and check for leaks.

25.4 Smear a little clean diesel around the filter

25.5a Renew the large O-ring seal (arrowed) . . .

25.5b . . . then push the new element into the housing . . .

25.5c . . . and refit the cover

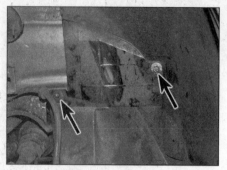

27.2a Undo the 2 nuts (arrowed), remove the metal plate . . .

27.2b . . . and fold the inner wheel arch panel forwards

27.5a Prise off the plastic cap from the centre of the tensioner pulley . . .

Every 90 000 miles or 5 years

26 Timing belt and tensioner renewal

Refer to Chapter 2B.

27 Auxiliary drivebelt renewal

1 The auxiliary drivebelt transmits power from the crankshaft pulley to the alternator, steering pump and air conditioning compressor (as applicable).

2 Although not strictly necessary, access to the lower belt run is easier through the right-hand wheel arch. Loosen the right-hand front wheel bolts, then jack up and support the front of the car on axle stands. Remove the roadwheel, then remove the two plastic nuts, remove the metal plate and fold forward the inner wheel arch panel to give access to the crankshaft pulley (see illustrations).

3 Before removing the old belt, note its fitted routing around all pulleys.

4 The correct drivebelt tension is continually maintained by an automatic adjuster and tensioner assembly. This device is bolted to the front of the engine, and incorporates a spring-loaded idler pulley.

D5244T/T2/T3 engines

5 Use a screwdriver to prise off the plastic cap (where fitted), then using a spanner on the tensioner nut, rotate the tensioner clockwise, thereby relieving the belt tension. Slip the belt off all the pulleys, then release the tensioner and remove the belt (see illustrations).

D5244T4/T5/T6/T7 engines

6 Unclip the power steering hose from the bracket, then undo the 2 Torx bolts and remove the auxiliary belt cover (see illustration).

7 Use Volvo tool No 999 7109, or a T60 Torx bit and spanner, to rotate the tensioner clockwise, thereby relieving the belt tension. Slip the belt off all the pulleys, then release the tensioner and remove the belt (see illustrations).

27.5b . . . then rotate the tensioner clockwise with a spanner

27.6 Undo the Torx bolts (arrowed) and remove the auxiliary belt cover

27.7a Use a spanner (arrowed) . . .

27.7b . . . on a T60 Torx bit to rotate the tensioner clockwise

All engines

8 Check the tensioner and idler pulleys for any roughness or damage. Renew as necessary.
9 Fit the new belt loosely over the pulleys and the tensioner wheel, ensuring that it is properly seated – leave the belt off the top (power steering pump) pulley, however **(see illustration)**.
10 Rotate the tensioner clockwise, then work the drivebelt over the top pulley. Release the tensioner, which will now automatically take up the adjustment.
11 If removed, refit the inner wheel arch panel, then refit the wheel and lower the car to the ground. Tighten the wheel bolts to the specified torque.

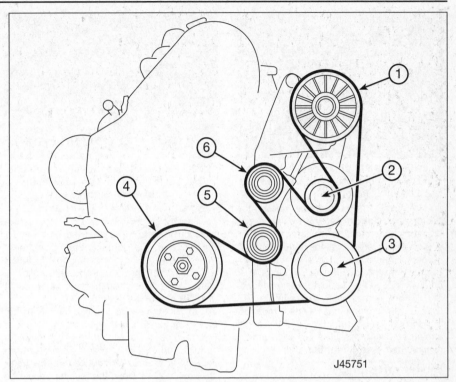

27.9 Auxiliary drivebelt routing

1 Power steering pump pulley
2 Alternator pulley
3 Air conditioning compressor pulley
4 Crankshaft pulley
5 Idler pulley
6 Tensioner pulley

Every 2 years, regardless of mileage

28 Brake fluid renewal

Warning: Brake hydraulic fluid can harm your eyes and damage painted surfaces, so use extreme caution when handling and pouring it. Do not use fluid that has been standing open for some time as it absorbs moisture from the air. Excess moisture can cause a dangerous loss of braking effectiveness.

The procedure is similar to that for the bleeding of the hydraulic system as described in Chapter 9, except that the brake fluid reservoir should be emptied by syphoning, and allowance should be made for the old fluid to be removed from the circuit when bleeding a section of the circuit.

Since the clutch hydraulic system uses the same fluid and reservoir as the braking system, it will probably be necessary to bleed the clutch system also (see Chapter 6).

HAYNES HINT *Old hydraulic fluid is invariably much darker in colour than the new, making it easy to distinguish between the two.*

Every 3 years, regardless of mileage

29 Coolant renewal

Warning: Wait until the engine is cold before starting this procedure. Do not allow antifreeze to come into contact with your skin, or with painted surfaces of the vehicle. Rinse off spills immediately with plenty of water. Never leave antifreeze lying around in an open container, or in a puddle in the driveway or on the garage floor. Children and pets are attracted by its sweet smell, but antifreeze can be fatal if ingested.
Note: *If genuine Volvo coolant has been continuously maintained in the system in the specified ratio then coolant renewal will not normally be necessary. However, to be absolutely sure about the integrity of the antifreeze and anti-corrosion properties of the coolant, periodic renewal is to be recommended.*

Coolant draining

1 To drain the system, first remove the expansion tank filler cap (see *Weekly checks*).
2 If the additional working clearance is required, raise the front of the vehicle and support it securely on axle stands (see *Jacking and vehicle support*).
3 Undo the screw at each end of the radiator undertray, then using a long screwdriver to depress the clip each side and pull the undertray to the rear and remove it **(see**

29.3a Viewed from underneath, undo the radiator undertray bolts at each end (arrowed) . . .

illustrations). Undo the screws and remove the engine undershield, then place a large drain tray underneath the radiator.

4 Slacken the drain tap at the bottom left-hand corner of the radiator and allow the coolant to drain into the tray. If no drain tap is fitted, carefully loosen the clamp and disconnect the radiator bottom hose (see illustration).

5 When the radiator has drained, move the tray to the rear right-hand side of the engine and unscrew the cylinder block drain tap (where fitted) (see illustration).

System flushing

6 With time, the cooling system may gradually lose its efficiency, as the radiator core becomes choked with rust, scale deposits from the water, and other sediment. This is especially likely if an inferior grade of antifreeze has been used. To minimise this, as well as using only the specified type of antifreeze and clean soft water, the system should be flushed as follows whenever any part of it is disturbed, and/or when the coolant is renewed.

7 With the coolant drained, close the drain taps and refill the system with fresh water. Refit the expansion tank filler cap, start the engine and warm it up to normal operating temperature, then stop it and (after allowing it to cool down completely) drain the system again. Repeat as necessary until only clean water can be seen to emerge, then refill finally with the specified coolant mixture.

8 If only clean, soft water and good-quality antifreeze has been used, and the coolant has been renewed at the specified intervals, the above procedure will be sufficient to keep the

29.3b . . . the release the clip at the front each side (arrowed – shown with the bumper removed)

system clean for a considerable length of time. If, however, the system has been neglected, a more thorough operation will be required, as follows.

9 First drain the coolant, then disconnect the radiator top and bottom hoses. Insert a garden hose into the top hose, and allow water to circulate through the radiator until it runs clean from the bottom outlet.

10 To flush the engine, remove the thermostat (see Chapter 3), insert the garden hose into the thermostat housing, and allow water to circulate until it runs clear from the bottom hose. If, after a reasonable period, the water still does not run clear, the radiator should be flushed with a good proprietary cleaning agent.

11 In severe cases of contamination, reverse-flushing of the radiator may be necessary. To do this, remove the radiator (see Chapter 3), invert it, and insert the garden hose into the bottom outlet. Continue flushing until clear water runs from the top hose outlet. A similar procedure can be used to flush the heater matrix.

12 The use of chemical cleaners should be necessary only as a last resort. Normally, use of the correct coolant will prevent excessive contamination of the system.

Coolant filling

13 With the cooling system drained and flushed, ensure that all disturbed components or hose unions are correctly fitted, and that the two drain taps are securely tightened. Refit the engine undershields removed for access. If it was raised, lower the vehicle to the ground.

14 Prepare a sufficient quantity of the specified coolant mixture; allow for a surplus, so as to have a reserve supply for topping-up.

15 Slowly fill the system through the expansion tank; since the tank is the highest point in the system, all the air in the system should be displaced into the tank by the rising liquid. Slow pouring reduces the possibility of air being trapped and forming airlocks. It helps also, if the large radiator hoses are gently squeezed during the filling procedure.

16 Continue filling until the coolant level reaches the expansion tank MAX level line, then wait for a few minutes. During this time, continue to squeeze the radiator hoses. When the level stops falling, top-up to the MAX level and refit the expansion tank cap.

17 Start the engine and run it at idle speed, until it has warmed-up to normal operating temperature. If the level in the expansion tank drops significantly, top-up to the MAX level line, to minimise the amount of air circulating in the system.

18 Stop the engine, allow it to cool down completely (overnight, if possible), then remove the expansion tank filler cap and top-up the tank to the MAX level line. Refit the filler cap, tightening it securely, and wash off any spilt coolant from the engine compartment and bodywork.

19 After refilling, always check carefully all components of the system (but especially any unions disturbed during draining and flushing) for signs of coolant leaks. Fresh antifreeze has a searching action, which will rapidly expose any weak points in the system.

Airlocks

20 If, after draining and refilling the system, symptoms of overheating are found which did not occur previously, then the fault is almost certainly due to trapped air at some point in the system, causing an airlock and restricting the flow of coolant; usually, the air is trapped because the system was refilled too quickly.

21 If an airlock is suspected, first try gently squeezing all visible coolant hoses. A coolant hose which is full of air feels quite different to one full of coolant, when squeezed. After refilling the system, most airlocks will clear once the system has cooled, and been topped-up.

22 While the engine is running at operating temperature, switch on the heater and heater fan, and check for heat output. Provided there is sufficient coolant in the system, lack of heat output could be due to an airlock in the system.

23 Airlocks can have more serious effects than simply reducing heater output – a severe airlock could reduce coolant flow around the engine. Check that the radiator top hose is hot when the engine is at operating temperature – a top hose which stays cold could be the result of an airlock (or a non-opening thermostat).

24 If the problem persists, stop the engine and allow it to cool down completely, before unscrewing the expansion tank filler cap or disconnecting hoses to bleed out the trapped air. In the worst case, the system will have to be at least partially drained (this time, the coolant can be saved for re-use) and flushed to clear the problem.

29.4 Radiator drain tap and bottom hose (arrowed)

29.5 Cylinder block drain tap (arrowed – engine removed for clarity)

Chapter 2 Part A:
Petrol engine in-car repair procedures

Contents

Degrees of difficulty

Easy, suitable for novice with little experience 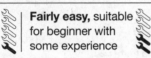	**Fairly easy,** suitable for beginner with some experience	**Fairly difficult,** suitable for competent DIY mechanic	**Difficult,** suitable for experienced DIY mechanic	**Very difficult,** suitable for expert DIY or professional

Specifications

General

Engine codes:
2.0 litre (1984 cc), turbocharged.	B5204 T
2.3 litre (2319 cc), turbocharged.	B5234 T
2.4 litre (2401 cc), turbocharged.	B5244 T4 and T5

2.4 litre (2435 cc):
Normally-aspirated (non-turbocharged)	B5244 S
Turbocharged	B5244 T3
2.5 litre (2521 cc), turbocharged.	B5254 T and T2

Bore:
1984 cc and 2319 cc litre engines	81.0 mm
2401 cc engines	81.3 mm
2435 cc and 2521 litre engines	83.0 mm

Stroke:
1984 cc engines	77.0 mm
2319 cc and 2435 cc engines	90.0 mm
2401 cc and 2521 cc engines	93.2 mm

Compression ratio:
B5204 T	9.5 : 1
B5234 T	8.5 : 1
B5244 T4	Not available
B5244 T5	8.5 : 1
B5244 S	10.3 : 1
B5244 T3	9.0 : 1
B5254 T	8.5 : 1
B5254 T2	9.0 : 1

Compression pressure:
Normally-aspirated engines	13 to 15 bars
Turbocharged engines	11 to 13 bars
Maximum difference between highest and lowest readings	2 bars
Firing order	1-2-4-5-3 (No 1 at timing belt end of engine)
Direction of crankshaft rotation	Clockwise (viewed from front of engine)

Camshaft

	Intake	Exhaust
Identification letter (stamped on end):		
Non-turbo engines	PGI	PGE
Turbo engines	PHI	PHE
Maximum lift (intake and exhaust):		
Non-turbo engines	8.45 mm	
Turbo engines	9.05 mm	
Camshaft endfloat	0.05 to 0.20 mm	
Valve clearances (engine cold):	Intake	Exhaust
Checking dimension	0.15 to 0.45 mm	0.35 to 0.60 mm
Setting dimension	0.20 ± 0.03 mm	0.40 ± 0.03 mm

Lubrication system

Oil pressure – engine warm:	
At idle speed	1.0 bar
At 4000 rpm	3.5 bars
Oil pump type	Gear, driven from crankshaft
Maximum pump gear to housing clearance	0.35 mm
Pressure relief valve spring free height:	
Non-turbo engines	82.13 mm
Turbo engines	76.22 mm

Torque wrench settings

	Nm	lbf ft
Camshaft position sensor housing	17	13
Camshaft position sensor signal wheel	17	13
Camshaft sprocket bolts (non-VVT)	20	15
Camshaft sprocket-to-VVT unit screws	10	7
Connecting rod cap bolt*:		
Waisted screw/machined face between cap and rod:		
Stage 1	20	15
Stage 2	Angle-tighten a further 90°	
Fully threaded screw/fractured cap/rod:		
Stage 1	30	22
Stage 2	Angle-tighten a further 90°	
Crankshaft pulley-to-sprocket bolts*:		
Stage 1	25	18
Stage 2:		
Up to 2002	Angle-tighten a further 30°	
From 2002	Angle-tighten a further 60°	
Crankshaft sprocket centre nut	180	133
Crankshaft stop tool hole plug in cylinder block	40	30
Cylinder head lower section to block*:		
Stage 1	20	15
Stage 2	60	44
Stage 3	Angle-tighten a further 130°	
Cylinder head upper section to lower section	17	13
Driveplate*:		
Stage 1	45	33
Stage 2	Angle-tighten a further 50°	
Engine compartment cross-stay	50	37
Engine oil drain plug	35	26
Flywheel*:		
Stage 1	45	33
Stage 2	Angle-tighten a further 65°	
Intermediate section-to-cylinder block (tighten in the following sequence):		
M10*	20	15
M10	45	33
M8	24	18
M7	17	13
M10	Angle-tighten a further 90°	
Oil filter	25	18
Oil pump to cylinder block	6	4
Oil pressure switch	25	18
Piston cooling jet	17	13
Piston cooling oil valve	36	27
Roadwheel bolts	140	103
Spark plugs	30	22

Torque wrench settings

	Nm	lbf ft
Subframe mounting bolts*:		
Up to 2004 model year:		
Stage 1	105	77
Stage 2	Angle-tighten a further 120°	
From 2005 model year	160	118
Subframe mounting brackets to body	50	37
Sump:		
Sump to engine	17	13
Sump to transmission:		
Stage 1	25	18
Stage 2	48	35
Timing belt front cover screws	12	9
Timing belt idler pulley	25	18
Timing belt tensioner bolt	20	15
Timing belt upper, inner cover screws	8	6
Torque converter	50	37
Valve clearance checking plug	20	15
Variable valve timing (VVT) central plug	35	26
Variable valve timing (VVT) unit central bolt	120	89

Engine/transmission mountings

	Nm	lbf ft
Engine lower steady bar bracket to subframe:		
Stage 1	65	48
Stage 2	Angle-tighten a further 60°	
Engine lower steady bar bracket to transmission*:	50	37
Engine lower steady bar bushes to brackets*:		
Stage 1	35	26
Stage 2	Angle-tighten a further 90°	
Engine right-hand mounting bracket to engine:		
10 mm bolts*:		
Stage 1	35	26
Stage 2	Angle-tighten a further 60°	
8 mm bolt*:		
Stage 1	20	15
Stage 2	Angle-tighten a further 60°	
Engine right-hand mounting to engine bracket*:		
Stage 1	35	26
Stage 2	Angle-tighten a further 90°	
Engine right-hand mounting to subframe*:		
Stage 1	65	48
Stage 2	Angle-tighten a further 60°	
Engine cross-stay:		
Mounting to engine	50	37
Mounting to cross-stay	80	59
Cross stay to suspension turrets	50	37
Transmission front mounting bracket to subframe	50	37
Transmission front mounting bracket to transmission	25	18
Transmission rear mounting nuts/bolts	50	37

* Do not re-use

1 General information

How to use this Chapter

This Part of Chapter 2 describes those repair procedures that can reasonably be carried out on the engine while it remains in the car. If the engine has been removed from the car and is being dismantled as described in Part C, any preliminary dismantling procedures can be ignored.

Note that, while it may be possible physically to overhaul items such as the piston/connecting rod assemblies while the engine is in the car, such tasks are not normally carried out as separate operations. Usually, several additional procedures (not to mention the cleaning of components and oilways) have to be carried out. For this reason, all such tasks are classed as major overhaul procedures, and are described in Part C of this Chapter.

Part C describes the removal of the engine/transmission from the vehicle, and the full overhaul procedures that can then be carried out.

Engine description

The five-cylinder engine is of the double overhead camshaft type, incorporating four valves per cylinder. The cylinders are in line and the engine is mounted transversely on a subframe in the engine bay. The engine codes (which appear only where necessary) are quite logical to follow – the first digit is the number of cylinders, the second and third together give the engine capacity in litres, and the final digit is the number of valves per cylinder. A T designation after the digits denotes a turbocharged engine. Thus, the B5234 T is a five-cylinder, 2.3 litre engine, with 4 valves per cylinder (total: 20 valves) and is turbocharged.

The entire engine is constructed of aluminium alloy, and consists of five sections. The cylinder head comprises an upper and lower section, with the cylinder block, intermediate section and sump forming the other three. The upper and lower sections of the cylinder head are mated along the centre-line of the camshafts, while the cylinder block and intermediate section are mated along the crankshaft centre-line. A conventional cylinder head gasket is used between the cylinder head and block, with liquid gaskets being used in the joints between the other main sections.

The cylinder block incorporates five cast-iron dry cylinder liners which are cast into the block and cannot be renewed. Cast-iron reinforcements are also used in the intermediate section as strengthening agents in the main bearing areas.

Drive to the camshaft is by a toothed timing belt and sprockets, incorporating an automatic tensioning mechanism. The timing belt also drives the coolant pump. All accessories are driven from the crankshaft pulley by a single multi-ribbed auxiliary drivebelt.

The cylinder head is of the crossflow type, the intake ports being at the front of the engine and the exhaust ports at the rear. The upper section of the cylinder head functions as a combined valve cover and camshaft cover, and the camshafts run in six plain bearings integral to the two cylinder head sections. Valve actuation is by solid tappets, acted upon directly by the camshaft lobes.

A variable valve timing system is fitted to the intake camshaft, exhaust camshaft, or both camshafts depending on model.

The crankshaft runs in six shell type main bearings; the connecting rod big-end bearings are also of the shell type. Crankshaft endfloat is taken by thrustwashers which are an integral part of the No 5 main bearing shells.

The lubrication system is of the full-flow, pressure-feed type. Oil is drawn from the sump by a gear type pump, driven from the front of the crankshaft. Oil under pressure passes through a filter before being fed to the various shaft bearings and to the valve gear. All models have an external oil cooler mounted on the rear of the sump. Turbo models also have an oil feed and return for the turbocharger bearings.

Operations with engine in car

The following work can be carried out with the engine in the car:

a) Compression pressure – testing.
b) Timing belt – removal and refitting.
c) Camshaft oil seals – renewal.

d) Camshafts and tappets – removal and refitting.
e) Cylinder head – removal and refitting.
f) Cylinder head and pistons – decarbonising.
g) Crankshaft oil seals – renewal.
h) Oil pump – removal and refitting.
i) Flywheel/driveplate – removal and refitting.
j) Engine mountings – removal and refitting.

2 Compression test – description and interpretation

1 When engine performance is down, or if misfiring occurs which cannot be attributed to the ignition or fuel systems, a compression test can provide diagnostic clues as to the engine's condition. If the test is performed regularly, it can give warning of trouble before any other symptoms become apparent.

2 The engine must be fully warmed-up to normal operating temperature, the battery must be fully-charged, and all the spark plugs must be removed (Chapter 1A). The aid of an assistant will also be required.

3 Disable the ignition system by disconnecting the wiring plugs from each coil. Also remove the injector fuse from the engine compartment fusebox to disable the fuel injectors, to prevent fuel from damaging the catalytic converter.

4 Fit a compression tester to the No 1 cylinder spark plug hole – the type of tester which screws into the plug thread is to be preferred.

5 Have the assistant hold the throttle wide open, and crank the engine on the starter motor; after one or two revolutions, the compression pressure should build up to a maximum figure, and then stabilise. Record the highest reading obtained.

6 Repeat the test on the remaining cylinders, recording the pressure in each.

7 All cylinders should produce very similar pressures; a difference of more than 2 bars between the highest and lowest reading indicates a fault.

8 Note that the compression should build-up quickly in a healthy engine; low compression on the first stroke, followed by gradually-increasing pressure on successive strokes, indicates worn piston rings.

9 A low compression reading on the first stroke, which does not build-up during successive strokes, indicates leaking valves or a blown head gasket (a cracked head could also be the cause). Deposits on the undersides of the valve heads can also cause low compression.

10 If the pressure in any cylinder is low, carry out the following test to isolate the cause. Introduce a teaspoonful of clean oil into that cylinder through its spark plug hole, and repeat the test.

11 If the addition of oil temporarily improves the compression pressure, this indicates that bore or piston wear is responsible for the pressure loss. No improvement suggests that leaking or burnt valves, or a blown head gasket, may be to blame.

12 A low reading from two adjacent cylinders is almost certainly due to the head gasket having blown between them; the presence of coolant in the engine oil will confirm this.

13 If one cylinder is about 20 percent lower than the others and the engine has a slightly rough idle, a worn camshaft lobe could be the cause.

14 If the compression reading is unusually high, the combustion chambers are probably coated with carbon deposits. If this is the case, the cylinder head should be removed and decarbonised.

15 On completion of the test, refit the spark plugs and reconnect the ignition system and fuel injectors.

3 Timing belt – removal and refitting

Removal

1 Disconnect the battery negative lead as described in Chapter 5A.

2 Undo the bolts/nuts and remove the engine compartment cross-stay between the brackets on the front suspension turrets (see illustrations).

3 Remove the auxiliary drivebelt as described in Chapter 1A.

4 Undo the two Torx bolts, release the two spring clips and remove the timing belt inner/upper cover (see illustration).

3.2a Undo the nut and bolt and each end of the engine cross-stay (arrowed) . . .

3.2b . . . then undo the centre mounting nut/bolt (arrowed) and remove the cross-stay

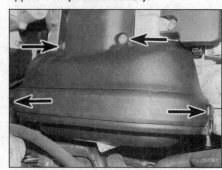

3.4 Release the two clips (arrowed) and undo the two Torx bolts (arrowed)

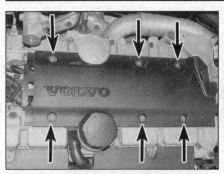

3.5 The spark plug cover is secured by 6 Torx bolts (arrowed)

3.6 Release the clip (arrowed) and lift the power steering fluid reservoir from its mountings

3.8a Undo the retaining bolt . . .

3.8b . . . then lift the cover to release the clips at the base (arrowed)

3.10a Undo the two plastic nuts (arrowed) and remove the wheel arch plate

3.10b Fold the wheel arch liner forwards

5 Where applicable, release the turbocharger intake ducting, then undo the six bolts and remove the spark plug cover from the centre of the cylinder head **(see illustration)**.

6 Release the power steering fluid reservoir from its mountings, and move it to one side without disconnecting the fluid hoses. Make sure the reservoir cap is secure, and that the reservoir is kept as upright as possible, to avoid fluid spillage **(see illustration)**.

7 Lift the cooling system expansion tank out of its mounting bracket, and place it to one side. Disconnect the wiring connector for the coolant level sensor, but there should be no need to disconnect the coolant hoses.

8 Undo the single bolt from the centre of the timing belt front cover, then pull the cover away from the engine, and lift it to release its retaining clips **(see illustrations)**.

9 Loosen the right-hand front wheel bolts, then jack up the front of the car and support it on axle stands (see *Jacking and vehicle support*). Remove the right-hand front roadwheel.

10 Release the two nuts securing the inner wheel arch liner plate, and fold forward the liner for access to the crankshaft pulley **(see illustrations)**.

11 Temporarily refit the timing belt inner-upper cover.

12 Using a socket on the crankshaft pulley centre nut, rotate the crankshaft clockwise (viewed from the right-hand side of the car) until the timing marks on the camshaft sprocket rims align with the notches on the timing belt upper cover **(see illustration)**.

13 In this position, the timing mark on the edge of the crankshaft sprocket flange should also be aligned with the cast projection on the oil pump housing **(see illustration)**.

14 The timing marks are not at all easy to see – the camshaft sprocket marks can be hardly more than faint scratches on the edges of the sprockets. Similarly, the mark on the crankshaft sprocket flange can only just be

3.12 Align the camshaft sprocket marks (A) with the marks (B) on the timing belt rear cover

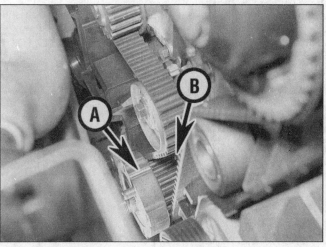

3.13 The crankshaft sprocket flange rib (A) should align with the oil pump housing mark (B)

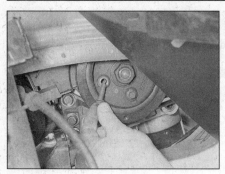

3.16a Slacken and remove two of the outer bolts . . .

3.16b . . . then fit the home-made pulley holding tool . . .

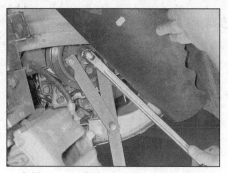

3.16c . . . and slacken the central nut

seen from above. It will probably take two or three attempts until you are sure that the marks are correctly aligned.

15 The crankshaft (auxiliary drivebelt) pulley must now be removed – this is secured to the crankshaft (timing belt) sprocket by four bolts, and to the crankshaft itself by a large central nut.

16 Loosen the four outer bolts, and remove two of them. Using a home-made sprocket holding tool bolted to the pulley using the two vacated bolt holes, hold the pulley as the central nut is loosened – this is tightened to a very high torque **(see illustrations)**.

17 Once the central nut is loose, check the alignment of the timing belt sprockets as described in paragraphs 13 and 14 before removing the pulley, and the upper timing belt cover.

18 The crankshaft pulley locates on a roll-pin, and a puller may be required to work the pulley off **(see illustration)**. Levering the pulley off is not advisable – the rim of the pulley itself is easily broken if care is not taken.

Up to 2006 model year

19 Insert a 6 mm Allen key into the hole in the tensioner arm, then loosen the timing belt tensioner retaining bolt, and rotate the tensioner assembly clockwise to approximately the 10 o'clock position to relieve the tension on the belt **(see illustration)**. If a new belt is being fitted, remove the tensioner completely, noting how the protruding lug on the tensioner engages with the engine. Volvo recommend that a new tensioner is fitted whenever a new timing belt is fitted.

From 2006 model year

Note: *Although Volvo state this type of spring-loaded tensioner is fitted to all petrol engines from 2006, we found vehicles later than this fitted with the earlier type of tensioner (as described in paragraph 19). Examine the tensioner fitted to your vehicle, and proceed according to tensioner type.*

20 Slacken the tensioner centre bolt slightly, then rotate the tensioner clockwise with a 6.0 mm Allen key. Insert a small diameter pin/drill bit to lock the tensioner in this position **(see illustration)**.

All vehicles

21 Mark the running direction of the belt if it is to be re-used, then slip it off the sprockets and idler pulleys and remove it. Clearance is very limited at the crankshaft sprocket, and a certain amount of manipulation is necessary. **Do not** rotate the crankshaft or camshafts with the belt removed.

22 Spin the idler pulley, to check for roughness or shake; renew if necessary.

23 Check the timing belt carefully for any signs of uneven wear or splitting. Pay particular attention to the roots of the teeth. Renew the belt if there is the slightest doubt about its condition.

24 If the engine is undergoing an overhaul, and has covered more than 36 000 miles with the existing belt fitted, renew the belt as a matter of course, regardless of its apparent condition. The cost of a new belt is nothing when compared to the cost of repairs, should the belt break in service.

25 If signs of oil or coolant contamination are found on the old belt, trace the source of the leak, and rectify it. Wash down the engine timing belt area and all related components, to remove all traces of oil.

26 Even if the old timing belt does not show signs of coolant contamination, examine the coolant pump carefully for any indication that it may be leaking. When a coolant pump fails, it often starts leaking from the 'weep hole' in the top of the unit, just behind the pump's timing belt sprocket (see Chapter 3, Section 7). A coolant leak normally shows up as a white, crusty stain. If the engine has covered a high mileage, and is known to be using the original pump, it would be worth considering renewing the coolant pump at the same time as the timing belt. If this is not done, and the pump subsequently starts leaking, the belt will have to be taken off again to fit a new pump.

27 Renew the tensioner assembly if there is any doubt about its condition – Volvo recommend that a new unit is fitted as a matter of course with a new belt.

Refitting and tensioning

28 Before refitting the timing belt, make sure that the sprockets are in the correct positions (paragraphs 13 and 14). It will be necessary to temporarily refit the timing belt upper cover to do this.

29 If removed, refit the belt tensioner in the same position as noted on removal, ensuring the tensioner 'fork' locates over the cylinder block rib. On vehicles up to 2006, with the tensioner arm at the 10 o'clock position,

3.18 The crankshaft pulley locates on a roll-pin (arrowed)

3.19 Slacken the tensioner retaining bolt (arrowed)

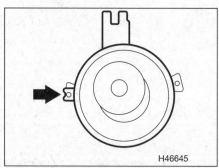

H46645

3.20 Rotate the tensioner clockwise until the locking pin (arrowed) can be inserted

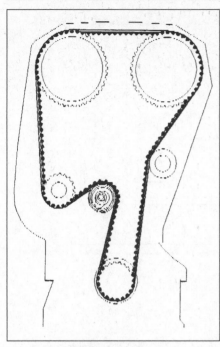

3.30 Timing belt run

lightly tighten the retaining bolt. On vehicles after this date, ensure the tensioner is in the locked position as described in paragraph 20.

30 Slip the belt over the crankshaft sprocket. Keeping it taut, and taking care not to rotate the camshaft sprockets in particular, feed the belt over the idler pulley, front camshaft sprocket, rear camshaft sprocket, coolant pump sprocket and finally over the tensioner pulley **(see illustration)**. Observe the correct running direction if the old belt is being re-used.

31 Recheck the alignment of the sprocket marks.

Up to 2006 model year

32 Using a 6 mm Allen key, turn the belt tensioner anti-clockwise until its pointer reaches the stop to the right of the central notch, then turn it back to align with the central notch **(see illustrations)**. The tensioner must always be set in this way, so that it is being set from the right of the central position.

33 With the tensioner aligned with the central notch, hold the tensioner using the Allen key, and tighten the retaining bolt to the specified torque **(see illustration)**.

34 Press on the belt at a point midway between the sprockets, and check that the tensioner pointer moves freely.

35 Turn the crankshaft clockwise through two complete revolutions, then check that all the timing marks can be realigned.

36 Also check that the tensioner pointer is aligned with the central notch. If not, loosen the tensioner retaining bolt, and reset the belt tension as described in paragraphs 32 to 36.

From 2006 model year

Caution: Refer the note at the beginning of paragraph 20.

37 Remove the locking pin/drill bit and allow the tensioner to tension the belt.
38 Press on the belt midway between the sprockets.
39 Turn the crankshaft through two complete revolutions, then check the timing marks can be realigned. Tighten the tensioner centre bolt to the specified torque.

All vehicles

40 Refit the crankshaft pulley over the roll-pin, then fit and tighten the central nut and the four outer bolts to the specified torques.
41 Fold back the wheel arch liner, and secure with the two nuts.
42 Refit the roadwheel and lower the car to the ground. Tighten the wheel bolts in a diagonal sequence to the specified torque.
43 Refit all the remaining components removed for access, using a reversal of the removal procedure.

---

4 Camshaft sprockets, VVT units and front oil seals – removal and refitting

Note: *For this procedure, the Volvo camshaft locking tool 999 5452 will be required to prevent the camshafts from rotating while the sprockets are removed. Details for fabricating a home-made alternative are given in the text. Do not attempt to carry out the work without locking the camshafts, or the valve timing will be lost.*

3.32b Timing belt tensioner aligned with the central notch (arrowed)

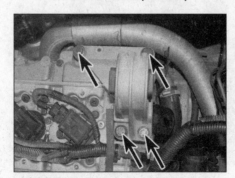

4.3 Undo the bolts (arrowed) and remove the mounting bracket from the top of the engine

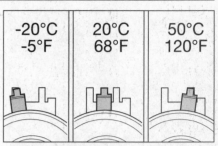

3.32a Timing belt tensioner settings at various ambient temperatures

Removal

1 Remove the timing belt as described in Section 3.
2 Referring to Chapter 4A, remove the air cleaner assembly and intake ducts as necessary for clear access to the rear end of both camshafts.
3 Undo the bolts and remove the cross-stay mounting bracket from the top of the engine **(see illustration)**.
4 On non-turbo models, undo the bolts remove the camshaft position sensor housing from the end of the intake camshaft **(see illustration)**.
5 On turbo models, undo the two screws and remove the sensor housing from the cylinder head at the rear of the exhaust camshaft. Undo the bolt and remove the sensor rotor plate from the end of the exhaust camshaft.
6 Undo the bolts and remove the bracket from the left-hand end of the cylinder head (where fitted) **(see illustration)**.

3.33 Hold the tensioner with an Allen key and tighten the nut

4.4 Undo the two Torx bolts (arrowed) and remove the camshaft position sensor housing

4.6 Undo the bolts and remove the bracket (arrowed) from the left-hand end of the cylinder head (non-turbo models only)

4.7 Use a screwdriver to prise out the blanking plug at the end of the intake or exhaust camshaft

7 Using a screwdriver and prise out the plastic blanking plug at the end of the intake camshaft (turbo models) or exhaust camshaft (non-turbo models) **(see illustration)**. Be prepared for oil spillage.

8 Observe the position of the slots in the rear of the camshafts. Before the sprockets are removed, the camshafts must be positioned so that these slots are parallel to the join between the upper and lower cylinder head sections, and then locked in that position. Note also that the slots are very slightly offset from the centre-line; one slightly above and one slightly below.

9 To lock the camshafts in the correct position

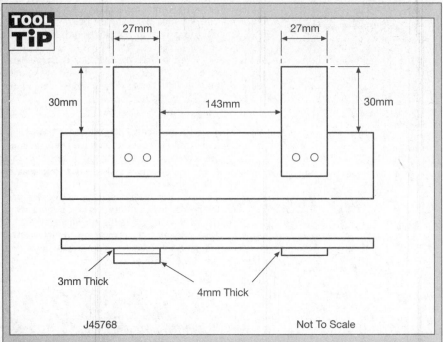

To make a camshaft locking tool, obtain a length of strip steel or angle-iron, and cut it so that it will fit across the left-hand end of the cylinder head. Obtain another length of strip steel of suitable thickness to fit snugly in the slots in the camshafts. Cut the strip into two lengths and drill accordingly so that both strips can be bolted to the angle-iron/strip. Using spacer washers, nut and bolts, position and secure the strips to the angle-iron/strip so that the camshafts can be locked with their slots horizontal. Pack out the strips with spacers to cater for the offset of the slots. Bear in mind that the tool must be strong enough to hold the camshafts whilst the VVT screws are tightened.

for refitting, obtain Volvo tool 999 5452 or fabricate a home-made alternative **(see Tool Tip above)**.

10 Check that the crankshaft sprocket timing marks are still aligned, then attach the Volvo tool or the home-made alternative to the rear of the cylinder head **(see illustration)**. It may be necessary to rotate the camshafts very slightly to bring their slots exactly to the horizontal position to allow the tool to fit.

11 If both camshaft sprockets are to be removed, suitably mark them, intake and exhaust for identification when refitting. The intake sprocket is nearest the front of the car.

12 If a sprocket with a variable valve timing unit is to be removed, use a Torx T55 key to undo and remove the plug at the front of the unit, then use the same key to undo the central retaining bolt. Pull the camshaft sprocket from the camshaft complete with the variable valve

4.10 Engage the locking tool with the slots in the end of the camshafts, to prevent the camshafts from rotating. The tool and the camshafts must be secure

4.12a Use a Torx T55 key to undo the VVT unit plug . . .

4.12b . . . followed by the VVT unit/ sprocket bolt . . .

4.12c . . . then remove the VVT unit

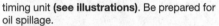

timing unit **(see illustrations)**. Be prepared for oil spillage.

13 If a sprocket without variable valve timing is to be removed, undo the three bolts and remove the sprocket for access to the failed seal. Restrain the sprockets with a suitable tool through the holes in their faces **(see Tool Tip right)**. Withdraw the sprocket from the camshaft.

14 Carefully extract the seal by prising it out with a small screwdriver or hooked tool. Do not damage the shaft sealing face.

Refitting

15 Clean the seal seat. Examine the shaft sealing face for wear or damage which could cause premature failure of the new seal.

16 Lubricate the new oil seal with clean engine oil. Fit the seal over the shaft, lips inwards, and tap it home with a large socket or piece of tube until its outer face is flush with the housing **(see illustration)**.

Non-variable valve timing sprocket

17 Refit the camshaft sprocket, with the timing marks aligned, and refit the retaining bolts but only tighten the bolts so that they just touch the sprockets and allow the sprockets to turn within the limits of their elongated bolt holes. Check that the crankshaft pulley marks still align as described in Section 3, paragraph 14.

Variable valve timing sprocket(s)

18 Check the crankshaft is still positioned as described in Section 3, then rotate it clockwise a few degrees.

19 Remove the starter motor as described in Chapter 5A.

20 Unscrew the blanking plug from the engine block, and insert Volvo tool 999 5451 **(see illustrations)**.

21 Rotate the crankshaft anti-clockwise until the crankweb stops against the Volvo tool.

22 Press the VVT unit/camshaft sprocket onto the camshaft, and refit the central retaining Torx bolt. Lightly tighten the bolt.

23 Slacken, but don't remove, the screws securing the camshaft sprocket to the VVT unit **(see illustration)**.

24 Position the sprocket screws so they are

TOOL TIP

To make a camshaft sprocket holding tool, obtain two lengths of steel strip about 6 mm thick by 30 mm wide or similar, on 600 mm long, the other 200 mm long (all dimensions are approximate). Bolt the two strips together to form a forked end, leaving the bolt slack so that the shorter strip can pivot freely. At the end of each 'prong' of the fork, bend the strips through 90° about 50 mm from their ends to act as fulcrums; these will engage with the holes in the sprockets. It may be necessary to grind or cut off the side slightly to allow them to fit in the sprocket holes.

4.16 Fit the oil seal over the end of the shaft, lips inwards

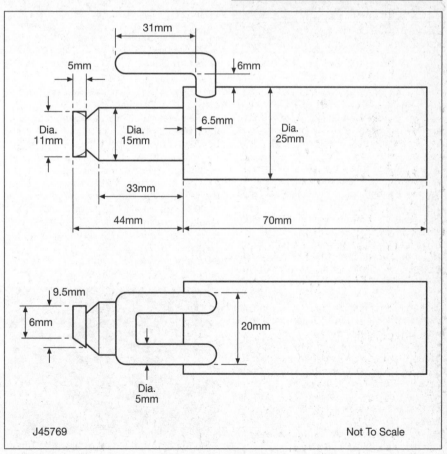

4.20a If you have access to a lathe, you may be able to produce a replica of the Volvo crankshaft stop tool

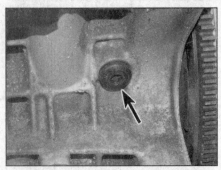

4.20b With the starter motor removed, undo the blanking plug (arrowed) . . .

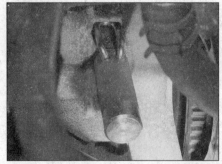

4.20c . . . and insert the crankshaft stop tool

4.20d Note the end of the crankshaft stop tool is chamfered

4.23 Slacken the sprocket-to-VVT unit screws (arrowed)

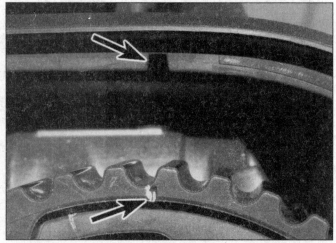

4.27 Rotate the VVT unit clockwise until the two marks (arrowed) align

in the centre of the slots on the VVT unit, and tighten them lightly.

25 Turn the VVT unit clockwise to the stop. Slacken the central retaining Torx bolt.

26 Temporarily refit the timing belt upper/inner cover.

27 Continue to rotate the VVT unit clockwise until the mark on the sprocket rim aligns with the mark on the upper/inner timing belt cover **(see illustration)**.

28 Tighten the VVT unit central retaining bolt to the specified torque. Do **not** allow the VVT unit to rotate whilst tightening the bolt.

29 Fit the new timing belt to the sprockets as described in paragraphs 28 to 39 of Section 3.

30 Slacken the screws securing the VVT unit(s) to the camshaft sprocket(s), and the bolts securing the non-VVT sprocket to the camshaft (where applicable).

31 Refit the centre plug to the VVT unit and tighten it to the specified torque.

32 Reset the torque wrench to 25 Nm (18 lbf ft), and apply this torque to the centre plug of the VVT unit whilst tightening the camshaft sprockets screws to their specified torque **(see illustration)**.

33 Tighten the non-VVT sprocket bolts to their specified torque.

34 On vehicles up to 2006 model year, check the position of the timing belt tensioner arm,

and adjust if necessary (see Section 3, paragraphs 32 to 36).

35 Remove the camshaft locking tools and the crankshaft stop tool.

36 Turn the crankshaft clockwise through two complete revolutions, then check that all the timing marks can be realigned.

37 Also check that the tensioner pointer is aligned with the central notch (vehicles up to 2006 model year only). If not, loosen the tensioner retaining bolt, and reset the belt tension as described in Section 3, paragraphs 32 to 36.

38 The remainder of refitting is a reversal of removal.

4.32 Apply 25 Nm (18 lbf ft) to the VVT unit centre plug, then tighten the camshaft sprocket-to-VVT unit screws

5 Camshaft rear oil seals – renewal

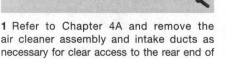

1 Refer to Chapter 4A and remove the air cleaner assembly and intake ducts as necessary for clear access to the rear end of both camshafts.

2 Disconnect the camshaft position sensor wiring at the connector on the transmission end of the cylinder head.

3 Undo the bolts and remove the sensor housing from the cylinder head at the rear of the camshaft **(see illustration 4.4)**. Undo the bolt and remove the sensor rotor plate from the end of the camshaft.

4 On camshafts without a position sensor, remove the two screws and take off the camshaft end cover.

5 Carefully extract the seal by prising it out with a small screwdriver or hooked tool. Do not damage the shaft sealing face.

6 Clean the seal seat. Examine the shaft sealing face for wear or damage which could cause premature failure of the new seal.

7 Lubricate the new oil seal with clean engine oil. Fit the seal over the shaft, lips inwards, and tap it home with a large socket or piece of tube until its outer face is flush with the housing **(see illustration)**. **Note:** *If the camshaft journal shows signs of wear, the seal can be pressed in up to 2.0 mm further so it bears upon an unworn part of the camshaft surface.*

8 Refit the components removed for access, using a reversal of removal.

9 Refit the air cleaner and ducts.

6 Camshafts and tappets – removal, inspection and refitting

Note : *For this procedure, Volvo tools 999 5452 and 999 5454 will be required to lock the camshafts in position in the cylinder head upper section during refitting, and to pull the upper section into place. Details for fabricating home-made alternatives are given in the text. Do not attempt to carry out the work without these tools. A tube of liquid gasket and a short-haired application roller (available from Volvo dealers) will also be required.*

Removal

1 Drain the cooling system as described in Chapter 1A.

2 Remove the timing belt as described in Section 3.

3 Referring to Chapter 4A, remove the air cleaner assembly and intake ducts as necessary for clear access to the rear end of both camshafts.

4 On turbocharged engines, release the clamps and remove the charge air pipe above the engine. Plug or seal the openings to prevent dirt ingress.

5 Undo the bolts/nuts and remove the cross-stay from between the suspension turrets **(see illustration 3.2a)**.

6 Undo the nut and remove the bolt securing the engine cross-stay to the bracket on the engine. Note that a new nut and bolt will be required for refitting **(see illustration 3.2b)**.

7 Undo the bolts and remove the engine

5.7 Fit the new oil seal with the lips facing inwards until its outer face is flush with the housing

cross-stay bracket from the cylinder head **(see illustration 4.3)**

8 Disconnect the camshaft position sensor wiring at the connector located at the transmission end of the engine.

9 On non-turbo models, undo the screws and remove the bracket from the left-hand end of the cylinder head, then prise out the exhaust camshaft blanking plug **(see illustrations 4.6 and 4.7)**.

10 On turbo models, prise out the rubber blanking plug at the left-hand end of the intake camshaft from the cylinder head **(see illustration 4.7)**

11 Undo the two screws and remove the sensor housing from the cylinder head at the rear of the exhaust or intake camshaft. Undo the bolt and remove the sensor rotor plate from the end of the camshaft **(see illustration 4.4)**.

12 Observe the position of the slots in the rear of the camshafts. Before the sprockets are removed, the camshafts must be positioned so that these slots are parallel to the join between the upper and lower cylinder head sections, and then locked in that position. Note also that the slots are very slightly offset from the centre-line; one slightly above and one slightly below.

13 To lock the camshafts in the correct

position for refitting, obtain Volvo tool 999 5452 or fabricate a home-made alternative **(see Tool Tip from Section 4, paragraph 9)**.

14 Check that the crankshaft sprocket timing marks are still aligned, then attach the Volvo tool or the home-made alternative to the rear of the cylinder head **(see illustration)**. It may be necessary to rotate the camshafts very slightly to bring their slots exactly to the horizontal position to allow the tool to fit.

15 Suitably mark both camshaft sprockets for identification when refitting. The intake sprocket is nearest the front of the car.

16 To remove a sprocket with a variable valve timing unit, use a Torx 55 key to undo and remove the plug at the front of the unit, then use the same key to undo the central retaining screw. Pull the camshaft sprocket from the camshaft complete with the variable valve timing unit **(see illustrations 4.12a, 4.12b and 4.12c)**. Be prepared for oil spillage.

17 To remove a sprocket without variable valve timing, undo the three bolts and remove the sprocket. Restrain the sprockets with a suitable tool through the holes in their faces **(see Tool Tip from Section 4, paragraph 13)**. Withdraw the sprocket from the camshaft.

18 Remove the ignition coils as described in Chapter 5A.

19 Disconnect the crankcase ventilation hose from the camshaft cover.

20 Disconnect the variable valve timing (VVT) solenoid(s) wiring plug, then remove the VVT solenoid(s) **(see illustration)**.

21 In a progressive diagonal sequence, working inwards, slacken then remove all the bolts securing the cylinder head upper section. Note the location of the earth leads on the rear bolts **(see illustration)**.

22 Using a soft-faced mallet, gently tap, or alternatively prise, the cylinder head upper section upwards off the lower section. Note that parting lugs are provided to allow the upper section to be struck or prised against without damage. Do not insert a screwdriver

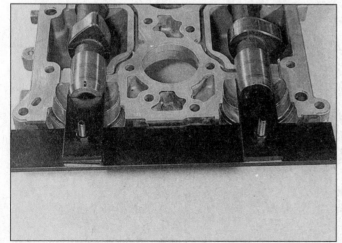

6.14 Home-made camshaft locking tool in position (cylinder head upper section removed for clarity)

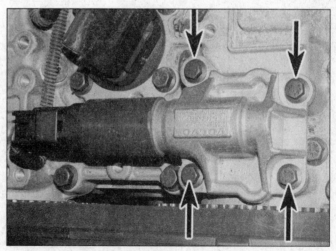

6.20 Undo the bolts (arrowed) and remove the VVT solenoid

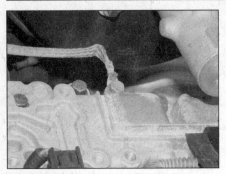

6.21 Note the earth lead(s) on the rear cylinder head cover bolts

6.29 Remove the tappets and place them in a segmented container

or similar tool into the joint between the two sections as a means of separation. In practice, the upper section will be quite tight as it is located on numerous dowels; patience is necessary.

23 Once the upper section is free, carefully lift it off. The camshafts will rise up under the pressure of the valve springs – be careful they don't tip and jam in the upper section.

24 Withdraw the sealing O-rings from the top of the spark plug recesses in the lower section. Obtain new O-rings for reassembly.

25 Suitably mark the camshafts, intake and exhaust, and lift them out complete with front and rear oil seals. Be careful of the lobes, which may have sharp edges.

26 Remove the oil seals from the camshafts, noting their fitted positions. Obtain new seals for reassembly.

27 Have ready a suitable box divided into twenty segments, or some containers and other means of storing and identifying the tappets after removal.

28 Mark the segments in the box or the containers with the cylinder number for each tappet, together with identification for intake and exhaust and front and rear or the particular cylinder.

29 Lift out the tappets, using a suction cup or magnet if necessary. Keep them identified for position, and place them upright in their

respective positions in the box or containers **(see illustration)**.

Inspection

30 Inspect the cam lobes and the camshaft bearing journals for scoring or other visible evidence of wear. Once the surface hardening of the lobes has been penetrated, wear will progress rapidly.

31 No specific bearing journal diameters or running clearances are specified by Volvo for the camshafts or journals. However, if there is a visual deterioration, then component renewal will be necessary.

32 Inspect the tappets for scuffing, cracking or other damage.

33 Note that if the camshafts, valves or cylinder head have been renewed, the valve clearances must be checked and, if necessary, the correct size tappet fitted as described below.

Preparation for refitting

34 Thoroughly clean the sealer from the mating surfaces of the upper and lower cylinder head sections. Use a suitable liquid gasket dissolving agent together with a soft putty knife; do not use a metal scraper, or the faces will be damaged. As there is no conventional gasket used, the condition of the faces is of the utmost importance.

35 Clean off any oil, dirt or grease from both components and dry with a clean lint free cloth. Ensure that all the oilways are completely clean.

Valve clearances checking and adjustment

36 If the camshaft(s), cylinder head or valves have been renewed, or the valve seats/faces ground, the valve clearances must be checked and if necessary adjusted.

37 Checking the valve clearances can be carried out before removing the timing belt, by attaching Volvo Tool No 999 5754 to the rear of the camshaft(s). If this tool is not available, the clearances must be set as described in paragraph 38 onwards. Remove the spark plugs (Chapter 1A) and the 20 inspection plugs for access to the valve clearances. Then rotate the engine clockwise until the marking on the Volvo tool aligns with the mark on the cylinder head cover, indicating which valve clearance to check. Insert the appropriate feeler gauge approximately 15 mm into the inspection plug hole and make a note of the clearance. Rotate the engine further and check the next set of clearances **(see illustrations)**. If any of these *Checking* clearances are outside those given in the *Specifications*, proceed as follows.

38 Install two tappets (intake or exhaust) for the first cylinder to be checked.

39 Lay the camshaft in position over the tappets with the relevant lobes pointing away from their tappets.

40 Use hand-pressure to clamp the camshaft onto the cylinder head, and measure the clearance between the underside of the camshaft and the tappet surface. If the measurement is different from that given in *Specifications*, make a note of the clearance, remove the camshaft and tappet. The tappet size is marked on its underside.

41 Once the size of the tappet is established, it must be changed for a thicker or thinner one to bring the previously recorded clearance within specification. For example, if the measured

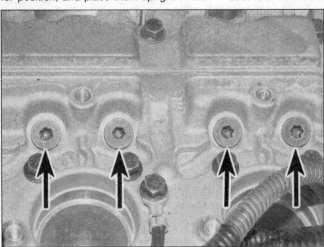

6.37a Remove the tappet clearance inspection plugs (4 arrowed)

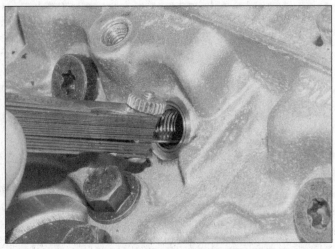

6.37b Insert the feeler gauge approximately 15 mm and make a note of the clearance

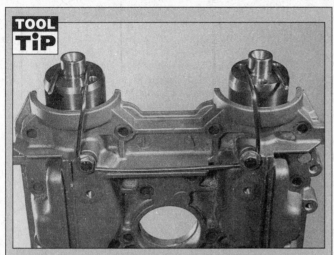

Tool Tip 1: To retain the camshafts in the cylinder head upper section at the front when refitting, make a retaining strap out of welding rod, bent to shape, which will located under the camshaft projections at the front and can be secured to the upper section with two bolts.

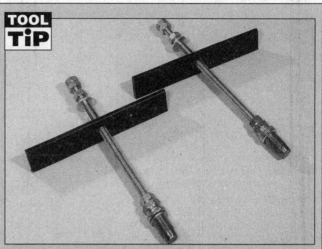

Tool Tip 2: To pull the cylinder head upper section down against valve spring pressure, obtain two old spark plugs and carefully break away all the porcelain so that only the lower threaded portion remains. Drill out the centre of the spark plugs as necessary, then fit a long bolt or threaded rod to each, and secure tightly with nuts. The bolts or rods must be long enough to project up from the spark plugs wells to above the level of the assembled cylinder head. Drill a hole in the centre of two 6 mm long strips or steel which are long enough to fit across the cylinder head upper section. Fit the strips then fit a nut and locknut to each bolt or rod.

valve clearance was 0.20 mm too great, a tappet *thicker* by this amount will be required. Conversely, if the clearance was 0.20 mm too small, a tappet thicker by this amount will be required. Note the different clearance specifications for *Checking* (with the camshaft cover, timing belt, etc, installed) and *Setting* (with the camshaft cover, etc, removed).

42 For reassembly, the camshafts are installed in the upper section, and retained in place in the correct position using special tools. This assembly is then fitted to the lower section, clamped in place against the pressure of the valve springs with more special tools, and finally bolted down. If possible, obtain the Volvo special tools mentioned in the note at the beginning of this section and use them in accordance with the instructions provided. Alternatively, fabricate a set of home-made tools as follows.

43 To position and secure the camshafts at the rear, make up the camshaft locking tool described in the Tool Tip in Section 4.

44 To secure the camshafts at the front, make up a strap as shown **(see Tool Tip 1)**.

45 Finally, it will be necessary to make up a tool which will allow the upper section to be clamped down against the pressure of the valve springs **(see Tool Tip 2)**.

Refitting

46 Commence refitting by liberally oiling the tappet bores and the camshaft bearings in the cylinder head lower section with clean engine oil.

47 Insert the tappets into their original bores (unless new tappets are being fitted).

48 Ensure that the mating faces of both cylinder head sections are clean and free of any oil or grease.

49 Check that the crankshaft timing marks are still aligned.

50 Using the short-haired roller, apply an even coating of Volvo liquid gasket solution (1161 059) to the mating face of the cylinder head upper section only **(see illustration)**. Ensure that the whole surface is covered, but take care to keep the solution out of the oilways; a thin coating is sufficient for a good seal.

51 Lubricate the camshaft journals in the upper section sparingly with oil, taking care not to allow the oil to spill over onto the liquid gasket.

52 Lay the camshafts in their correct

locations in the upper section, remembering that the intake camshaft must be at the front of the engine.

53 Turn the camshafts so that their slots are parallel to the upper section join, noting that the slots in each camshaft are offset with regards to the centre-line **(see illustration)**. When viewing the upper section the right way up, ie, as it would be when fitted, the slot on the intake camshaft is offset above the centre-line, and the exhaust camshaft slot is offset below the centre-line. Verify this by looking at the other end of the camshafts. Again, with the upper section the right way up, there should be two sprocket bolt holes above the centre-line on the intake camshaft, and two bolt holes below the centre-line on the exhaust camshaft.

54 With the camshafts correctly positioned,

6.50 Apply the liquid sealant using a short-haired roller

6.53 Position the camshafts so that their slots are parallel to the upper section join (see text)

6.55 Place new sealing O-rings around each spark plug well

lock them at the rear by fitting the rear locking and holding tool. It should not be possible to rotate the camshafts at all with the tool in place. Now secure the camshafts at the front using the holding tool or the home-made alternative.

55 Place new sealing O-rings into the recesses around each spark plug well in the lower section **(see illustration)**.

56 Lift up the assembled upper section, with camshafts, and lay it in place on the lower section.

57 Insert the pull-down tools into Nos 1 and 5 spark plug holes and tighten securely. If using the home-made tool, make sure that the bolt or threaded rod is a secure fit in the spark plug, or you will not be able to remove the tool later.

58 Lay the pull-down tool top plates, or the home-made steel strips, over the bolts or threaded rods, and secure with the nuts **(see illustration)**. Slowly and carefully tighten the nuts, a little at a time, so that the tools pull the upper section down onto the lower section. Remember there will be considerable resistance from the valve springs. Make sure that the upper section stays level, or the locating dowels will jam.

59 Refit the upper section retaining bolts and tighten them in a progressive diagonal sequence, working outwards, to the specified torque. Don't forget the earth lead on the rear bolt.

60 With the upper section secure, remove the pull-down tool and the camshaft front end

holding tool. Leave the rear locking tool in place.

61 Lubricate the lips of four new camshaft oil seals. Fit each seal the correct way round over the camshaft, and tap it home with a large socket or piece of tube until its outer face is flush with the housing (see Sections 4 and 5).

62 Refit the camshaft sprockets, timing belt, etc, as described in Section 4.

63 The remainder of refitting is a reversal of removal.

64 Refill the cooling system as described in Chapter 1A on completion.

7 Cylinder head – removal and refitting

Removal

1 Disconnect the battery negative lead (Chapter 5A).

2 Drain the engine coolant as described in Chapter 1A.

3 Remove the intake and exhaust manifolds as described in Chapter 4A.

4 Remove the camshafts and tappets as described in Section 6.

5 Where applicable, undo the bolt securing the timing belt rear cover to the cylinder head.

6 If not already done, undo the bolt and remove the earth lead(s) at the rear of the cylinder head.

7 Slacken the clips and remove the radiator top hose from the thermostat housing and radiator. Remove the expansion tank hose from the thermostat housing.

8 Undo the two bolts securing the coolant pipe flange to the rear of the cylinder head.

9 Slacken the cylinder head bolts, half a turn at a time to begin with, in the order shown **(see illustration)**. Remove the bolts. Note that new bolts will be required for refitting.

10 Lift off the cylinder head and set it down on wooden blocks to avoid damage to protruding valves. Recover the old head gasket.

11 If the cylinder head is to be dismantled for overhaul, refer to Part C of this Chapter.

Preparation for refitting

12 The mating faces of the cylinder head and cylinder block must be perfectly clean before refitting the head.

13 Use a plastic scraper to remove all traces of gasket and carbon; also clean the piston crowns. Take particular care during the cleaning operations, as aluminium alloy is easily damaged.

14 Make sure that the carbon is not allowed to enter the oil and water passages – this is particularly important for the lubrication system, as carbon could block the oil supply to the engine's components. Using adhesive tape and paper, seal the water, oil and bolt holes in the cylinder block. To prevent carbon entering the gap between the pistons and bores, smear a little grease in the gap. After cleaning each piston, use a small brush to remove all traces of grease and carbon from the gap, then wipe away the remainder with a clean rag. Clean all the pistons in the same way.

15 Check the mating surfaces of the cylinder block and the cylinder head for nicks, deep scratches and other damage. If slight, they may be removed carefully with a file, but if excessive, machining may be the only alternative to renewal.

16 If warpage of the cylinder head gasket surface is suspected, use a straight-edge to check it for distortion. Refer to Part C of this Chapter if necessary.

17 Check that the cylinder head bolt holes in the block are clean and dry. If available, run a correct-size tap down each threaded hole – failing this, an old head bolt with two slots cut along the length of the threads can be used. It is most important that no oil or coolant is present in the bolt holes, otherwise the block may be cracked by the hydraulic action as the head bolts are inserted and tightened.

Refitting

18 Commence refitting by placing a new head gasket on the cylinder block. Make sure it is the right way up; it should be marked TOP.

19 Lower the head into position, then lightly oil the threads of the new cylinder head bolts.

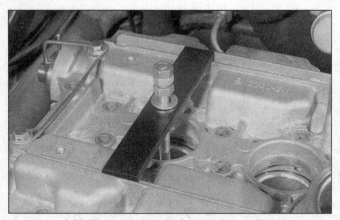

6.58 Home-made pull-down tool in position

7.9 Cylinder head bolt SLACKENING sequence

Fit the bolts and tighten them to the specified Stage 1 torque, in the reverse sequence to that shown (refer to illustration 7.9).

20 In the same sequence, tighten the bolts to the Stage 2 torque, then, again in the same sequence, tighten the bolts through the angle specified for Stage 3 using an angle-tightening gauge (see illustration).

21 Using a new gasket, refit the coolant pipe flange to the rear of the cylinder head and secure with the two bolts using thread sealant.

22 Refit the radiator top hose to the thermostat housing and radiator.

23 Refit the timing belt cover retaining bolt and the bolt securing the rear earth lead.

24 Refit the camshaft and tappets as described in Section 6, but do not reconnect the battery at this stage.

25 Refit the intake and exhaust manifolds as described in Chapter 4A.

26 Refill the engine cooling system as described in Chapter 1A.

8 Crankshaft oil seals – renewal

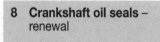

Front seal

1 Remove the timing belt as described in Section 3.

2 With the crankshaft pulley removed, insert two of the retaining bolts and draw the sprocket/flange off the crankshaft using a two-legged puller. Engage the puller legs with the protruding bolts at the rear (see illustration).

3 With the sprocket removed, carefully prise out the old oil seal. Do not damage the oil pump housing or the surface of the crankshaft. Alternatively, punch or drill two small holes opposite each other in the oil seal. Screw a self-tapping screw into each, and pull on the screws with pliers to extract the seal.

4 Clean the oil seal location and the crankshaft. Inspect the crankshaft for a wear groove or ridge left by the old seal.

5 Lubricate the housing, the crankshaft and the new seal using clean engine oil only. Fit the seal, lips inwards, and use a piece of tube (or the old seal, inverted) to tap it into place until flush.

6 Refit the crankshaft sprocket using the reverse of the removal procedure, aligning the master spline.

7 Refit the timing belt as described in Section 3.

Rear seal

8 Remove the flywheel or driveplate as described in Section 10.

9 Remove the old seal and fit the new one as described previously in paragraphs 3 to 5.

10 Refit the flywheel or driveplate as described in Section 10.

7.20 Tighten the bolts through the specified angle using an angle-tightening gauge

9 Oil pump – removal, inspection and refitting

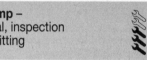

Removal

1 Carry out the operations described in Section 8, paragraphs 1 to 4.

2 Undo the four bolts securing the oil pump to the front of the cylinder block.

3 Carefully withdraw the pump assembly by levering behind the upper and lower parting lugs using a screwdriver (see illustration). Remove the pump and recover the gasket.

4 Thoroughly clean the pump and cylinder block mating faces and remove all traces of old gasket.

Inspection

5 Remove the two screws which hold the two halves of the pump together.

6 Remove the gear cover from the pump body. Be prepared for the ejection of the pressure relief valve spring.

7 Remove the relief valve spring and plunger and the pump gears.

8 Remove the crankshaft front oil seal by carefully levering it out of the cover. Obtain a new seal for refitting.

9 Clean all components thoroughly, then inspect the gears, body and gear cover for signs of wear or damage.

10 If any parts appear worn, or damaged, renew them. At the time of writing no information concerning valve spring length or rotor/gear clearance was available.

11 Refit the gears to the pump body, with the markings on the large gear uppermost.

12 Liberally lubricate the gears. Lubricate and fit the relief valve plunger and spring.

13 Fit a new O-ring seal to the pump body, then fit the cover and secure with the two screws.

Refitting

14 Using a new gasket, fit the pump to the block. Use the pump retaining bolts as guides, and draw the pump into place with the crankshaft pulley nut and spacers. With the pump seated, tighten the retaining bolts diagonally to the specified torque.

8.2 Us a puller to draw off the crankshaft pulley flange

15 Lubricate the cover, crankshaft and the new oil seal. Fit the seal, lips inwards, and use a piece of tube (or the old seal, inverted) to tap it into place until flush.

16 Refit the crankshaft sprocket and pulley using a reverse of the removal procedure.

17 Refit the timing belt as described in Section 3.

10 Flywheel/driveplate – removal, inspection and refitting

Note: New flywheel/driveplate retaining bolts will be required for refitting.

Removal

Flywheel

1 Remove the transmission as described in Chapter 7A.

2 Remove the clutch assembly as described in Chapter 6.

3 Make alignment marks so that the flywheel can be refitted in the same position relative to the crankshaft.

4 Loosen the flywheel bolts. Prevent crankshaft rotation by inserting a large screwdriver in the ring gear teeth and in contact with an adjacent dowel in the engine/transmission mating face.

5 With the flywheel supported, remove the bolts and lower it to the floor. Take care not to drop it, as it is heavy, and not easy to hold on to.

9.3 Parting lugs (arrowed) for oil pump removal

11.4a Engine cross-stay to engine mounting bracket

11.4b Engine lower steady bar

11.4c Engine right-hand mounting to subframe

Driveplate

6 Remove the automatic transmission as described in Chapter 7B.

7 Make alignment marks so that the driveplate can be refitted in the same position relative to the crankshaft.

8 Unbolt the driveplate and remove it as described in paragraphs 4 and 5.

Inspection

9 On manual transmission models, If the flywheel's clutch mating surface is deeply scored, cracked or otherwise damaged, the flywheel must be renewed. However, it may be possible to have it surface-ground; seek the advice of a Volvo dealer or engine reconditioning specialist. If the ring gear is badly worn or has missing teeth, flywheel renewal will also be necessary.

10 On models with a dual mass flywheel, check the radial play by turning the flywheel secondary mass one way until the spring begins to tension, then allow the flywheel to spring back – make an alignment mark between the primary and secondary masses. Now turn the flywheel in the opposite direction until the spring begins to tension – make another alignment mark between the two masses. The distance between the 2 marks must be less than 35 mm.

11 On models with automatic transmission, check the torque converter driveplate carefully for signs of distortion. Look for any hairline cracks around the bolt holes or radiating

outwards from the centre, and inspect the ring gear teeth for signs of wear or chipping. If any signs of wear or damage are found, the driveplate must be renewed.

Refitting

Flywheel

12 Clean the mating surfaces of the flywheel and crankshaft. Remove any remaining locking compound from the threads of the crankshaft holes, using the correct-size tap, if available.

> **HAYNES HiNT** *If a suitable tap is not available, cut two slots into the threads of one of the old flywheel bolts and use the bolt to remove the locking compound from the threads.*

13 Continue refitting by reversing the removal operations. Apply thread-locking compound to the new flywheel retaining bolts (if not already pre-coated) and tighten them to the specified torque.

14 Refit the clutch as described in Chapter 6, and the transmission as described in Chapter 7A.

Driveplate

15 Proceed as described above for manual transmission models, ignoring any references to the clutch. Refit the transmission as described in Chapter 7B.

11 Engine mountings – removal and refitting

Removal

1 The engine mountings can be renewed one at a time with the engine/transmission installed, providing suitable means of supporting the engine/transmission are available.

2 Ascertain which components are likely to impede removal and remove, or move aside as necessary, with reference to the relevant Chapters of this manual.

3 Attach suitable lifting equipment to the engine, or position a jack with protective wooden block under the sump or transmission as necessary.

4 With the engine supported, remove the nuts or bolts from the mounting to be removed **(see illustrations)**.

5 Take the weight off the mounting, raise the engine/transmission as necessary for clearance, and remove the mounting. Note any locating pegs or directional arrows as an aid to refitting. Take care not to raise the engine/transmission by more than 30 mm, otherwise the inner left-hand constant velocity joint will be damaged.

Refitting

6 Refit by reversing the removal operations, tightening all fastenings to the specified torque.

12 Sump – removal and refitting

Removal

1 Jack up the front of the vehicle and support it securely on axle stands (see *Jacking and vehicle support*).

2 Undo the screws and remove the engine undershield **(see illustration)**.

3 Drain the engine oil as described in Chapter 1A.

4 Undo the bolt/nut and pull the oil level dipstick guide tube from the sump.

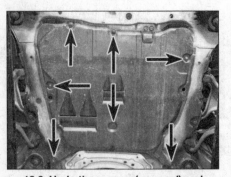

12.2 Undo the screws (arrowed) and remove the engine undershield

12.5 Oil cooler mounting bolts (arrowed)

5 The oil cooler (where fitted) is secured to the sump by four bolts. Undo the bolts and pull the cooler to the rear **(see illustration)**. Be prepared for oil spillage.

6 Undo the bolt securing the fuel pipe bracket to the sump.

7 Disconnect the oil level sensor wiring plug.

8 Remove all the screws securing the sump to the engine, with the exception of one screw in each corner, which should just be slackened a few turns.

9 Gently tap the sides and ends of the sump until the joint between the engine and sump releases. Undo the remaining screws and remove the sump. Discard the O-rings at the right-hand end of the sump, new ones must be fitted.

Refitting

10 Ensure the mating faces of the sump and engine are clean and free from any remaining gasket residue.

11 Using a short-haired roller, apply a thin layer of Volvo liquid sealant (1161 059-9) to the sump mating face.

12 Position the new O-rings, and refit the sump, securing it with a screw in each corner, finger-tightened only.

13 Insert the sump-to-transmission screws, and tighten them to the specified torque.

14 Refit the remaining sump-to-engine screws and tighten them to the specified torque starting from the transmission end.

15 The remainder of refitting is a reversal of removal, noting the following points:

a) *Refit the oil cooler to the sump using new O-ring seals.*

b) *Refit the oil level dipstick tube using a new O-ring seal.*

c) *Renew the oil filter and fill the engine with new oil as described in Chapter 1A.*

Notes

Chapter 2 Part B:
Diesel engine in-car repair procedures

Contents

Degrees of difficulty

Easy, suitable for novice with little experience	**Fairly easy,** suitable for beginner with some experience	**Fairly difficult,** suitable for competent DIY mechanic	**Difficult,** suitable for experienced DIY mechanic	**Very difficult,** suitable for expert DIY or professional

Specifications

General

Capacity	2401 cc	
Bore	81.3 mm	
Stroke	93.2 mm	
Engine code:	**Power output**	**Torque output**
D5244T	120 kW (163 bhp)	340 Nm at 1750 to 3000 rpm
D5244T2	96 kW (130 bhp)	280 Nm at 1750 to 3000 rpm
D5244T3	85 kW (110 bhp)	286 Nm at 1750 to 2750 rpm
D5244T4	136 kW (177 bhp)	400 Nm at 2000 to 2750 rpm
D5244T5	120 kW (163 bhp)	340 Nm at 1750 to 2750 rpm
D5244T6	90 kW (117 bhp)	300 Nm at 1750 to 2250 rpm
D5244T7	92 kW (125 bhp)	300 Nm at 1750 to 2250 rpm
Compression ratio	18.0 : 1	
Compression pressures:		
Nominal	24 to 31 bar	
Minimum	22 bar	
Maximum difference between cylinders	5.0 bar	
Firing order	1 – 2 – 4 – 5 – 3	
Cylinder No 1 location	Timing belt end	

Lubrication system

Oil pump type	Mounted on front of cylinder block and driven directly from crankshaft
Normal operating oil pressure:	
800 rpm	1.0 bar minimum (oil temperature 100°C)
4000 rpm	3.5 bar minimum (oil temperature 100°C)

Torque wrench settings

	Nm	lbf ft
Auxiliary drivebelt tensioner	35	26
Camshaft bearing cap	10	7
Camshaft cover	10	7
Camshaft end sealing/bearing caps (M7)	17	13
Camshaft position sensor	10	7
Camshaft sprocket bolt	30	22
Catalytic converter crossmember	25	18
Catalytic converter mounting screws	10	7
Connecting rod cap*:		
D5244T/T2/T3:		
Stage 1	20	15
Stage 2	Angle-tighten a further 100°	
D5244T4/T5/T6/T7:		
Stage 1	30	22
Stage 2	Angle-tighten a further 90°	
Coolant temperature sensor	22	16
Crankcase intermediate section (tighten in the following sequence):		
M10*	20	15
M10	40	30
M8	24	18
M7	17	13
M10	Angle-tighten a further 110°	
Crankshaft pulley/sprocket:		
Nut	300	221
Screws:		
Stage 1	35	26
Stage 2	Angle-tighten a further 50°	
Cylinder head bolts*:		
Stage 1	20	15
Stage 2	Slacken	
Stage 3	20	15
Stage 4	50	37
Stage 5	Angle-tighten a further 90°	
Stage 6	Angle-tighten a further 90°	
Driveplate*:		
Stage 1	45	33
Stage 2	Angle-tighten a further 50°	
Engine cross-stay brackets to suspension turrets	50	37
Engine cross-stay to brackets on the suspension turrets	80	59
Engine cross-stay to engine mounting bracket	80	59
Engine mounting (right-hand side)*:		
M8:		
Stage 1	20	15
Stage 2	Angle-tighten a further 60°	
M10:		
Stage 1	35	26
Stage 2	Angle-tighten a further 60°	
Engine mounting (rear or front, hydraulic)*	50	37
Engine mounting (on camshaft cover):		
7 mm bolt	17	13
8 mm bolt	50	37
Engine speed sensor	10	7
Exhaust pipe to turbocharger	30	22
Flywheel*:		
Stage 1	45	33
Stage 2	Angle-tighten a further 65°	
Fuel injection pump	20	15
Fuel rail/injector pipe unions*	28	21
Fuel rail mounting bolts	17	13
Glow plugs	8	6
Injector screws*:		
D5244T to D5244T3	28	21
D5244T4 to D5244T7	13	10
Lower torque rod-to-transmission bolts*:		
Stage 1	35	26
Stage 2	Angle-tighten a further 40°	

Torque wrench settings (continued)

	Nm	lbf ft
Lower torque rod to mounting bracket*:		
Stage 1	35	26
Stage 2	Angle-tighten a further 90°	
Lower torque rod mounting-to-subframe nut*:		
Stage 1	65	48
Stage 2	Angle-tighten a further 60°	
Oil filter	35	26
Oil pick-up pipe	17	13
Oil pressure switch	27	20
Oil pump screws	6	4
Piston cooling jets	17	13
Piston cooling valve	45	33
Roadwheel bolts	140	103
Subframe mounting bolts*:		
Up to 2004 model year:		
Stage 1	105	77
Stage 2	Angle-tighten a further 120°	
From 2005 model year	160	118
Subframe mounting brackets to body	50	37
Sump:		
Sump to transmission:		
Stage 1	25	18
Stage 2	48	35
Sump to engine	17	13
Sump drain plug (engine oil)	35	26
Timing belt idler pulley	25	18
Timing belt tensioner	27	20
Torque converter bolts*	60	44
Turbocharger oil drain pipe flange screws	12	9
Turbocharger-to-manifold nuts*	35	26

Do not re-use

1 General information

Using this Chapter

Chapter 2 is divided into three Parts: A, B and C. Repair operations that can be carried out with the engine in the vehicle are described in Part A (petrol engines) and Part B (diesel engines). Part C covers the removal of the engine/transmission as a unit, and describes the engine dismantling and overhaul procedures.

In Parts A and B the assumption is made that the engine is installed in the vehicle, with all ancillaries connected. If the engine has been removed for overhaul, the preliminary dismantling information which precedes each operation may be ignored.

Access to the engine bay can be improved by removing the bonnet as described in Chapter 11.

Engine description

The engines are water-cooled, double overhead camshaft, 20 valve, in-line five cylinder units with both the cylinder block and cylinder head made from aluminium-alloy, with cast iron cylinder sleeves. The engine is mounted transversely at the front of the vehicle, with the transmission bolted to the left-hand end of the engine.

The cylinder head carries the camshafts, which are driven by a toothed timing belt from the crankshaft to the intake camshaft. A toothed gear on the intake shaft drives a corresponding gear on the exhaust camshaft. An Oldham coupling on the left-hand end of the intake camshaft drives the low/high pressure fuel pump, whilst the vacuum pump is driven from the left-hand end of the exhaust camshaft. The cylinder head also incorporates the 20 intake and exhaust valves (4 per cylinder), which are closed by single coil springs, and which run in guides pressed into the cylinder head. The camshaft actuates the valves via roller type rocker arms acting upon hydraulic tappets, mounted in the cylinder head. The cylinder head contains internal oilways which supply and lubricate the hydraulic tappets.

All engines are of direct injection design where the swirl chambers are incorporated in the tops of the pistons. The cylinder head incorporates two separate intake ports per cylinder. These ports are of different length and geometry to ensure more efficient combustion and reduced emissions.

The forged steel crankshaft is of six-bearing type, and the No 5 (from the right) main bearing shells incorporate separate thrustwashers to control crankshaft endfloat. The intake camshaft is driven by a toothed belt from the crankshaft sprocket, and the belt also drives the water pump mounted on the rear of the block.

The pistons are manufactured from aluminium-silicon alloy, with graphite coated skirts to reduce friction. The pistons incorporate cooling channels, through which oil flows, supplied by fixed jets mounted at the base of the cylinders. As each piston reaches the lower end of its stroke, the oil jet aligns with a hole in the base of the piston, and oil is forced through the cooling channel.

The engine has a full-flow lubrication system. A duocentric internal gear type oil pump is mounted on the front of the crankshaft. The oil filter is of the paper element type, mounted on the front side of the cylinder block.

The specified power outputs are achieved using different turbochargers and ECM software.

Repairs with engine in vehicle

The following operations can be performed without removing the engine:

a) Auxiliary drivebelt – removal and refitting.
b) Camshafts – removal and refitting.
c) Camshaft oil seals – renewal.
d) Camshaft sprocket – removal and refitting.
e) Coolant pump – removal and refitting (refer to Chapter 3)
f) Crankshaft oil seals – renewal.
g) Crankshaft sprocket – removal and refitting.
h) Cylinder head – removal and refitting.
i) Engine mountings – inspection and renewal.
j) Oil pump and pickup assembly – removal and refitting.

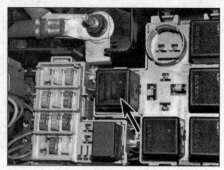

2.3 Pull the ECM relay (arrowed) from place

k) Sump – removal and refitting.

l) Timing belt, sprockets and cover – removal, inspection and refitting.

Note: *It is possible to remove the pistons and connecting rods (after removing the cylinder head and sump) without removing the engine from the vehicle. However, this procedure is not recommended. Work of this nature is more easily and thoroughly completed with the engine on the bench – refer to Chapter 2C.*

2 Cylinder compression test

Compression test

Note: *A compression tester specifically designed for diesel engines must be used for this test because of the higher pressures involved.*

1 When engine performance is down, or if misfiring occurs, a compression test can provide diagnostic clues as to the engine's condition. If the test is performed regularly, it can give warning of trouble before any other symptoms become apparent.

2 The tester is connected to an adapter which screws into the glow plug hole. It is unlikely to be worthwhile buying such a tester for occasional use, but it may be possible to borrow or hire one – if not, have the test performed by a garage.

3 Unless specific instructions to the contrary are supplied with the tester, observe the following points:

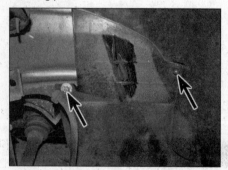

3.6a Undo the 2 nuts (arrowed), remove the metal plate . . .

a) *The battery must be in a good state of charge, the air filter must be clean, and the engine should be at normal operating temperature.*

b) *All the glow plugs should be removed before starting the test.*

c) *The engine management ECM relay must be removed from the fuse/relay box (see illustration).*

4 There is no need to hold the accelerator pedal down during the test, because the diesel engine air intake is not throttled.

5 The manufacturers specify a wear limit for compression pressure – refer to the *Specifications*. Seek the advice of a Volvo dealer or other diesel specialist if in doubt as to whether a particular pressure reading is acceptable.

6 The cause of poor compression is less easy to establish on a diesel engine than on a petrol one. The effect of introducing oil into the cylinders (wet testing) is not conclusive, because there is a risk that the oil will sit in the recess on the piston crown, instead of passing to the rings. However, the following can be used as a rough guide to diagnosis.

7 All cylinders should produce very similar pressures; a difference of more than 5.0 bars between any two cylinders indicates the existence of a fault. Note that the compression should build-up quickly in a healthy engine; low compression on the first stroke, followed by gradually-increasing pressure on successive strokes, indicates worn piston rings. A low compression reading on the first stroke, which does not build-up during successive strokes, indicates leaking valves or a blown head gasket (a cracked head could also be the cause).

8 A low reading from two adjacent cylinders is almost certainly due to the head gasket having blown between them.

Leakdown test

9 A leakdown test measures the rate at which compressed air fed into the cylinder is lost. It is an alternative to a compression test, and in many ways it is better, since the escaping air provides easy identification of where pressure loss is occurring (piston rings, valves or head gasket).

10 The equipment needed for leakdown

3.6b . . . then fold forward the wheel arch liner

testing is unlikely to be available to the home mechanic. If poor compression is suspected, have the test performed by a suitably-equipped garage.

3 Timing belt – removal, inspection and refitting

Note: *Whenever the timing belt is renewed, the tensioner and idler pulley should also be renewed as described in Section 4.*

Removal

1 The camshaft and coolant pump sprockets are driven by the timing belt from the crankshaft sprocket. The crankshaft and camshaft sprockets move in phase with each other to ensure correct valve timing. Should the timing belt slip or break in service, the valve timing will be disturbed and piston-to-valve contact will occur, resulting in serious engine damage.

2 The design of the engines covered in this Chapter is such that piston-to-valve contact will occur if the crankshaft is turned with the timing belt removed. For this reason, it is important that the correct phasing between the camshaft and crankshaft is preserved whilst the timing belt is off the engine. This is achieved by setting the engine in a reference condition (known as Top Dead Centre or TDC) before the timing belt is removed, and then not rotating the shafts until the belt is refitted. Similarly, if the engine has been dismantled for overhaul, the engine must be set to TDC during reassembly to ensure that the correct shaft phasing is restored.

3 TDC is the highest position a piston reaches within its respective cylinder – in a four-stroke engine, each piston reaches TDC twice per cycle, once on the compression stroke and once on the exhaust stroke. In general, TDC normally refers to No 1 cylinder on the compression stroke. The cylinders are numbered one to five, starting from the timing belt end of the engine. Note that on this particular engine, when the timing marks are aligned, the No 1 piston is positioned very slightly before TDC.

4 Before starting work, disconnect the battery (see Chapter 5A).

5 Slacken the right-hand front roadwheel bolts, then jack up the front of the vehicle and support it securely on axle stands (see *Jacking and vehicle support*). Remove the roadwheel.

6 Undo the two nuts, remove the metal protection plate, and fold the section of the right-hand wheel arch liner forwards for access to the crankshaft pulley, etc **(see illustrations)**.

7 Release the cable tie securing the servo hose to the engine cross-stay (where applicable).

8 Undo the nuts/bolts and remove the engine cross-stay from between the brackets on the front suspension turrets **(see illustrations)**.

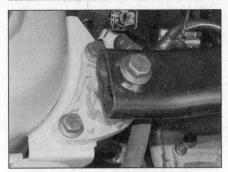

3.8a Undo the nut and bolt each side securing the engine cross-stay to the brackets on the suspension turrets . . .

3.8b . . . and the nut and bolt (arrowed) securing the cross-stay to the mounting on the cylinder head

3.9a Release the clips around the edge of the timing belt cover . . .

9 Release the four clips, undo the single bolt, and remove the timing belt outer cover **(see illustrations)**.

10 Release the return hose cable tie from the engine cross-stay mounting bracket, then release the top clip and lift the power steering fluid reservoir from place, and move it to one side over the top of the engine. Do not disconnect the hoses.

11 Remove the auxiliary drivebelt as described in Chapter 1B.

12 Undo the bolts and remove the timing belt lower guard **(see illustration)**.

13 Using a socket on the crankshaft pulley nut, rotate the crankshaft clockwise until the markings on the camshaft sprocket and timing belt rear cover align **(see illustration)**.

14 Undo the four bolts and one nut securing the crankshaft pulley to the crankshaft/sprocket and remove the crankshaft pulley, leaving the sprocket in place. Note that the centre nut is very tight. In order to prevent the crankshaft from rotating on manual models, engage top gear and have an assistant fully depress the brake pedal. On automatic models, remove the starter motor as described in Chapter 5A, and use a large flat-bladed screwdriver wedged between the driveplate ring gear teeth and the transmission housing.

3.9b . . . and undo the single bolt (arrowed)

15 Check that the marks on the camshaft sprocket and timing belt rear cover are still aligned, and the lug on the oil pump housing aligns with the mark cast into crankshaft pulley mounting boss. If the marks do not align, temporarily refit two of the crankshaft pulley retaining bolts and the centre nut loosely, and using a large screwdriver/lever, rotate the crankshaft clockwise until the marks are in alignment **(see illustration)**. In actual fact, in this position the No 1 piston is slightly before TDC.

16 Slacken the timing belt tensioner centre bolt slightly, and use a 6 mm Allen key to rotate

3.12 Undo the 2 bolts and remove the belt lower cover (pulley removed for clarity)

the tensioner arm clockwise to the 10 o'clock position, then lightly tighten the centre bolt.

17 Remove the timing belt from the sprockets, without turning the crankshaft or camshaft.

Inspection

18 Examine the belt for evidence of contamination by coolant or lubricant. If this is the case, find the source of the contamination before progressing any further. Check the belt for signs of wear or damage, particularly around the leading edges of the belt teeth. Renew the belt if its condition is in doubt; the cost of belt renewal is negligible compared

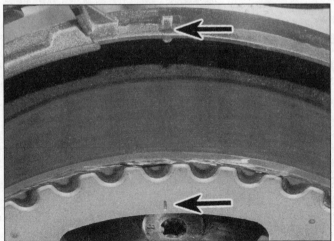

3.13 Align the mark on the camshaft sprocket with the mark on the timing belt cover (arrowed)

3.15 The mark on the crankshaft pulley

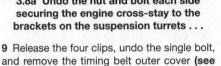

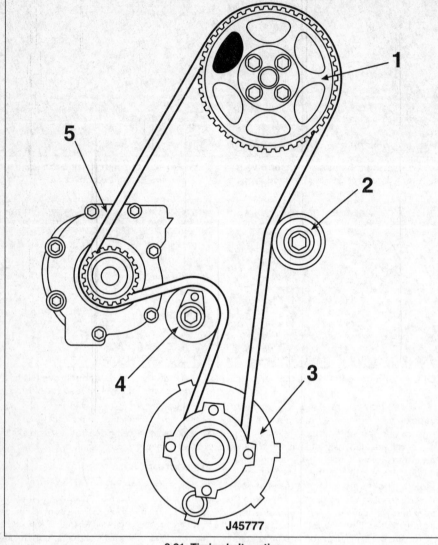

3.21 Timing belt routing

1	Camshaft sprocket	3	Crankshaft sprocket	5	Coolant pump
2	Idler pulley	4	Tensioner pulley		sprocket

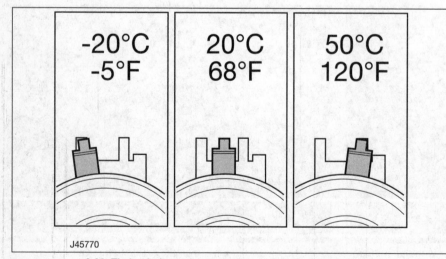

3.23 Timing belt tensioner settings at various temperatures

with potential cost of the engine repairs, should the belt fail in service. The belt must be renewed if it has covered the mileage stated by the manufacturer (see Chapter 1B), however if it has covered less it is prudent to renew it regardless of condition, as a precautionary measure. **Note:** *If the timing belt is not going to be refitted for some time, it is a wise precaution to hang a warning label on the steering wheel, to remind yourself (and others) not to attempt to start the engine.*

19 Spin the belt tensioner and idler pulleys and listen for noise which may indicate wear in the pulley bearings. If in any doubt, renew the pulleys as described in Section 4.

Refitting

20 Ensure that the crankshaft and camshaft are still aligned as described in paragraphs 13 and 15.

21 Fit the new belt around the crankshaft sprocket, idler pulley, camshaft sprocket, coolant pump sprocket, and finally, the tensioner pulley **(see illustration)**. Ensure the belt teeth seat correctly on the sprockets.

22 Ensure that the front run of the belt is taut – ie, all the slack should be in the section of the belt that passes over the tensioner roller.

23 Slacken the tensioner roller centre bolt slightly, then using a 6 mm Allen key, rotate the tensioner arm anti-clockwise until it passes the position shown, then rotate it clockwise until the indicator reaches the correct position **(see illustration)**.Tighten the centre bolt to the specified torque.

24 Gently press the belt between the camshaft sprocket and coolant pump sprocket, and check the tensioner arm moves freely as the belt is pressed.

25 Turn the crankshaft through two complete turns, then check that the timing marks on the crankshaft pulley boss and camshaft sprocket align correctly as described in paragraphs 13 and 15.

26 Check that the timing belt tensioner indicator is still position as described in paragraph 23. If not, repeat the operation described in paragraph 23.

27 The remainder of refitting is a reversal of removal, remembering to tighten all fasteners to their specified torque where given.

4 Timing belt tensioner and sprockets – removal and refitting

Note: *Whenever the timing belt is renewed, the tensioner and idler pulley should also be renewed as described in Section 4.*

Timing belt tensioner

Removal

1 Remove the timing belt as described in Section 3.

2 Undo the centre bolt and remove the tensioner.

3 Spin the tensioner roller, feeling and

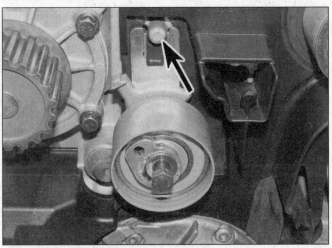

4.4 Endure the tensioner locates correctly over the rib (arrowed) on the cylinder block

4.7 Use a simple tool to counterhold the camshaft sprocket whilst slackening the bolts

4.10a Insert the camshaft aligning tool through the hole in the cylinder head and into the exhaust camshaft sprocket

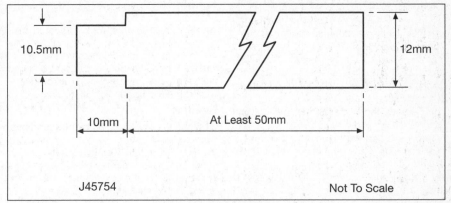

4.10b Camshaft aligning tool

listening for any roughness or noise, which would indicated wear in the tensioner roller bearing. If in any doubt as the condition of the tensioner, renew it.

Refitting

4 Refit the tensioner and insert the bolt – do not fully tighten the bolt at this stage. Ensure the tensioner 'fork' locates correctly over the rib on the cylinder block **(see illustration)**.

5 Refit and tension the timing belt as described in Section 3.

Camshaft sprocket

Removal

6 Remove the timing belt as described in Section 3.

7 Unscrew the camshaft sprocket bolts, while holding the sprocket stationary using a tool which engages the holes in the sprocket **(see illustration)**. Do not allow the camshaft to rotate.

8 Remove the sprocket from the camshaft.

Refitting

9 Remove the vacuum pump from the left-hand end of the exhaust camshaft as described in Chapter 9.

10 Insert a camshaft locking pin (Volvo No 999 7007) into the hole in the cylinder head and into the hole in the camshaft sprocket.

If necessary, rotate the camshaft slightly to enable the pin to be inserted. If the Volvo pin is not available, a home-made equivalent can be fabricated **(see illustrations)**.

11 Check the mark on the crankshaft sprocket still aligns with the mark on the oil pump housing as described in Section 3, then rotate the crankshaft clockwise (viewed from the timing belt end) approximately 15 degrees.

12 Refit the sprocket to the camshaft, but only tighten the retaining bolts sufficiently to allow the sprocket to just move independently

of the camshaft. Position the sprocket so the retaining bolts are not at the ends of the slots, and the mark on the sprocket edge aligns with the mark on the timing belt inner cover **(see illustration)**.

13 Unscrew the blanking plug from the front left-hand face of the cylinder block, and insert Volvo tool No 999 7005, then rotate the crankshaft anti-clockwise (viewed from the timing belt of the engine) until the crankshaft web of No 5 cylinder comes to a stop against the tool. Check the marks on the

4.12 Align the mark on the camshaft with the mark on the timing belt inner cover (arrowed)

4.13a Unscrew the blanking plug (arrowed) . . .

4.13b . . . and insert the crankshaft stop tool

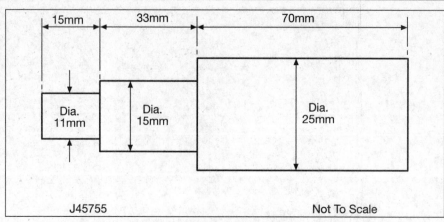

J45755   Not To Scale

4.13c Crankshaft stop tool

crankshaft pulley flange and oil pump housing align (see illustration 3.15). If the tool is not available, a home-made equivalent may be fabricated using the dimensions shown (see illustrations).

14 Refit the timing belt as described in Section 3

15 Ensure the marks of the crankshaft sprocket aligns with the mark on the oil pump housing, and the marks on the camshaft sprocket and timing belt inner cover align, then tighten the camshaft sprocket bolts to the specified torque, using the tool to counterhold the sprocket (see paragraph 7).

16 Remove the camshaft locking tool and crankshaft stop tool, and refit the vacuum pump as described in Chapter 9. Refit the blanking plug to the front face of the cylinder block.

17 Proceed as described from paragraph 24 of Section 3.

Crankshaft sprocket

Removal

18 Remove the timing belt as described in Section 3.

19 The crankshaft sprocket locates on a master spline on the crankshaft, and a puller may be required to work the sprocket off (see illustration). Levering the sprocket off is not advisable – the rim of the sprocket itself is easily broken if care is not taken.

Refitting

20 Wipe the sprocket and crankshaft mating surfaces clean.

21 Refit the sprocket to the crankshaft, and check the timing marks still align. Note the sprocket is located by means of a master spline on the crankshaft.

22 Install the timing belt around the crankshaft sprocket, idler pulley, camshaft sprocket, coolant pump, and finally the tensioner pulley.

23 Refit the pulley to the sprocket and refit the crankshaft nut – finger-tight only at this stage, then rotate the crankshaft anti-clockwise approximately 45°.

24 Stop the crankshaft from rotating and tighten the pulley nut to the specified torque, then tighten the pulley bolts to their specified torque.

25 Tension the timing belt and complete the refitting procedure as described in Section 3.

Idler pulley

Removal

26 Remove the timing belt as described in Section 3.

27 Undo the bolt and remove the idler pulley (see illustration).

Refitting

28 Refitting is a reversal of removal, remembering to tighten all fasteners to their specified torque where given.

| 5 | Camshaft cover – removal and refitting |

Removal

1 Release the cable tie securing the servo hose to the engine cross-stay (where applicable).

2 Undo the nuts/bolts and remove the engine cross-stay from between the brackets on the front suspension turrets (see illustrations 3.8a and 3.8b)

3 Pull the plastic engine cover straight up, and manoeuvre it from the engine compartment.

4 Remove the fuel injectors as described in Chapter 4B.

5 Release the clamp and disconnect the crankcase ventilation hose from the camshaft cover (see illustration).

6 Undo the screws and remove the hose bracket from the cylinder head/engine mounting (see illustration).

4.19 If necessary, use a puller to remove the crankshaft sprocket

4.27 Timing belt idler pulley

5.5 Disconnect the crankcase ventilation hose (arrowed)

5.6 Detach the hose bracket (arrowed)

7 Release the clamps and disconnect the intake hose from the intake manifold **(see illustration)**.

8 On D5244T4/T5/T6/T7 engines, slacken the clamp, disconnect the breather hose from the top of the oil separator at the front of the engine, then slacken the banjo bolt and rotate the fuel return pipe on the high-pressure pump to one side away from the camshaft cover **(see illustrations)**.

9 Undo the bolts and remove the upper/rear engine mounting bracket **(see illustration)**.

10 Disconnect the wiring plugs as necessary (camshaft position sensor, coolant temperature sensor, etc), then undo the cable duct screws (where fitted) and position the wiring harness to one side **(see illustration)**.

11 Undo the screws and remove the camshaft cover **(see illustration)**. Discard the gasket(s), new ones must be fitted.

12 Clean the mating surfaces of the cylinder head and camshaft cover thoroughly, removing all traces of oil and old gasket – take care to avoid damaging the surfaces as you do this.

5.7 Release the clamps and remove the intake hose

5.8a Release the clamp (arrowed) and detach the breather hose

Refitting

13 Refit the camshaft cover by following the removal procedure in reverse, noting the following points:

a) On D5244T/T2/T3 engines, ensure that the new gaskets are correctly seated on the cylinder head, and take care to avoid

displacing them as the camshaft cover is lowered into position **(see illustration)**. Note that the TOP on the centre gasket must be uppermost.

b) On D5244T4/T5/T6/T7 engines, the rubber sealing gasket is fitted to the underside of the camshaft cover **(see**

5.8b Slacken the bolt (arrowed) and rotate the fuel return union/ hose away from the camshaft cover

5.9 Remove the upper/rear engine mounting bracket

5.10 Undo the 2 screws (arrowed) and remove the cable duct

5.11 Undo the screws (arrowed) and remove the camshaft cover

5.13a Ensure the gaskets are not displaced when the cover is refitted (D5244T/T2/T3 engines)

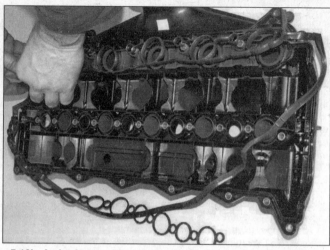

5.13b An intricate rubber gasket is fitted to the camshaft cover

6.3a Fit the new seal using a tubular spacer which bears only on the hard, outer surface of the seal

6.3b The outside edge of the seal should be flush with the outer edge of the sealing cap/cylinder head casting

illustration). Ensure the gasket remains in place whilst the cover is refitted.

c) *Tighten the camshaft cover retaining nuts to the specified torque, starting from the centre and working outwards.*

6 Camshaft oil seal – renewal

1 Remove the camshaft sprocket as described in Section 4.
2 Using a screwdriver or lever, carefully prise

out the oil seal taking care not to damage the camshaft surface.
3 Clean the seating in the bearing cap, then smear a little clean engine oil on the lips of the new oil seal. Fit the new oil seal and tap it into position carefully using a tubular spacer, socket or block of wood that bears only on the hard outer surface of the seal **(see illustrations)**. The outside edge of the seal should be flush with the outer edge of the sealing cap/cylinder head casting.
4 Refit the camshaft sprocket as described in Section 4.

7 Crankshaft oil seals – renewal

Right-hand oil seal

1 Remove the crankshaft sprocket, with reference to Section 4.
2 The seal may be renewed without removing the oil pump by drilling a small hole, inserting a self-tapping screw, and pulling on the head of the screw with pliers **(see illustrations)**. Take great care not to mark the crankshaft surface with the drill bit.
3 Wrap some adhesive tape around the end of the crankshaft to prevent damage to the new oil seal. Dip the new seal in clean engine oil and drive it into the oil pump housing with a block of wood or a socket until flush. Make sure that the closed end of the seal is facing outwards **(see illustrations)**.
4 Remove the adhesive tape.
5 Refit the crankshaft sprocket and timing belt, with reference to Section 4.

Left-hand oil seal

6 Remove the flywheel/driveplate with reference to Section 10.

7.2a Drill a small hole into the head, outer edge of the seal . . .

7.2b . . . then insert a self-tapping screw and pull the seal from place

7.3a Wrap tape around the shoulder on the crankshaft to protect the seal lips . . .

7.3b ... then use a tubular spacer or socket ...

7.3c ... to drive the seal home

7 Clean the surfaces of the block and crankshaft.

8 Remove the old oil seal and fit the new one as described in paragraphs 2 to 4 above.

9 Refit the flywheel/driveplate (Section 10).

8 Cylinder head – removal, inspection and refitting

Removal

1 Disconnect the battery negative (earth) lead (see Chapter 5A).

2 Jack up the front of the vehicle and support it securely on axle stands (see *Jacking and vehicle support*).

3 Drain the engine oil with reference to Chapter 1B.

4 Drain the cooling system with reference to Chapter 1B.

5 Loosen the clips and disconnect all coolant and vacuum hoses from the cylinder head noting their locations **(see illustrations)**.

6 Remove the air cleaner assembly as described in Chapter 4B.

7 Remove the timing belt as described in Section 3.

8 Remove the camshafts, rocker arm and hydraulic tappets as described in Section 9.

9 Disconnect the power steering pump support bracket from the cylinder head **(see illustration)**.

10 Undo the bolts securing the fuel rail and fuel pipes to the cylinder head **(see illustration)**.

11 Undo the retaining bolts and remove the heat shield above the exhaust manifold.

12 Slacken the EGR pipe clamp at the exhaust manifold, then undo the three bolts securing the EGR valve/cooler/pipe assembly to the cylinder head and move it to one side.

13 Remove the front section of the exhaust pipe, and undo the bolts securing the exhaust manifold to the cylinder head as described in Chapter 4B. Disconnect and remove the oil and coolant return and supply pipes (where applicable) from the turbocharger and engine block/cylinder head, then slacken the clamp and disconnect the turbocharger outlet pipe **(see illustration)**. Disconnect the vacuum hose (where applicable) from the turbocharger control valve, and the rubber intake hose from the turbocharger, then carefully lower the turbocharger and manifold assembly onto the driveshaft and steering rack. Discard the turbocharger oil/coolant supply and return pipe sealing washers – new ones must be fitted.

14 Undo the screws securing the coolant pipe to the cylinder head **(see illustration)**.

15 Make a final check to ensure all wiring plugs have been disconnected from the cylinder head.

16 Following the **reverse** of the tightening sequence **(see illustration 8.30)**, progressively slacken the cylinder head bolts, by half a turn at a time, until all bolts can be unscrewed by hand and removed. Discard the bolts – new ones must be fitted on reassembly.

17 Check that nothing remains connected to the cylinder head, then lift the head away from the cylinder block; seek assistance if possible, as it is heavy. Do not lay the cylinder head on the worktop face down – this may damage the sealing face.

18 Remove the gasket from the top of the block, noting the identification holes on its front edge. If the dowels are a loose fit,

8.5a Squeeze together the sides of the servo vacuum hose collar to disconnect it ...

8.5b ... then pull the vacuum hose from the port on the vacuum pump (arrowed)

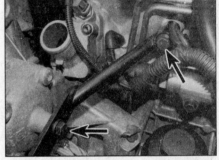

8.9 Undo the bolts (arrowed) and remove the power steering pump support bracket

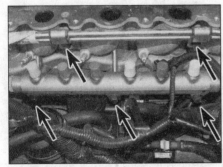

8.10 Undo the bolts (arrowed) securing the fuel rail and fuel pipes to the cylinder head

8.13 Slacken the clamp (arrowed) and disconnect the turbo outlet hose (viewed from underneath)

8.14 Undo the bolt (arrowed) securing the coolant pipe to the right-hand rear corner of the cylinder head

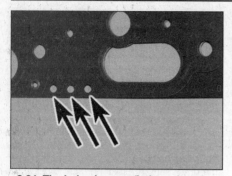

8.24 The holes (arrowed) along the edge of the cylinder head gasket indicate the thickness (see Chapter 2C for more information)

8.26 Ensure the cylinder head gasket locates over the dowels in the block surface

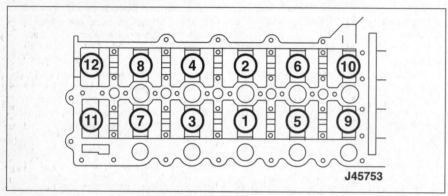

8.30 Cylinder head bolt tightening sequence

remove them and store them with the head for safe-keeping. Do not discard the gasket yet – it will be needed for identification purposes.

19 If the cylinder head is to be dismantled for overhaul, refer to Chapter 2C.

Inspection

20 The mating faces of the cylinder head and cylinder block/crankcase must be perfectly clean before refitting the head. Use a hard plastic or wood scraper to remove all traces of gasket and carbon; also clean the piston crowns. Take particular care during the cleaning operations, as aluminium alloy is easily damaged. Also, make sure that the carbon is not allowed to enter the oil and water passages – this is particularly important for

8.31 Use an angle-measuring gauge to accurately tighten the bolts

the lubrication system, as carbon could block the oil supply to the engine's components. Using adhesive tape and paper, seal the water, oil and bolt holes in the cylinder block/crankcase.

21 Check the mating surfaces of the cylinder block/crankcase and the cylinder head for nicks, deep scratches and other damage. If slight, they may be removed carefully with abrasive paper, but note that head machining will not be possible – refer to Chapter 2C.

22 If warpage of the cylinder head gasket surface is suspected, use a straight-edge to check it for distortion. Refer to Part C of this Chapter if necessary.

23 Clean out the cylinder head bolt drillings using a suitable tap. If a tap is not available, use an old head bolt with two slots cut along the length of the threads. It is most important that no oil or coolant is present in the bolts holes, otherwise the block may be cracked by the hydraulic action as the head bolts are inserted and tightened.

Refitting

24 Examine the old cylinder head gasket for manufacturer's identification markings. These are in the form of holes along the front edge of the gasket **(see illustration)**. Unless new pistons have been fitted, the new cylinder head gasket must be the same type as the old one.

25 If new piston assemblies have been fitted as part of an engine overhaul, before purchasing the new cylinder head gasket, refer to Chapter 2C and measure the piston projection. Purchase a new gasket according to the results of the measurement (see Chapter 2C Specifications).

26 Lay the new head gasket on the cylinder block, engaging it with the locating dowels. Ensure that the manufacturer's part number markings are facing upwards **(see illustration)**.

27 With the help of an assistant, place the cylinder head centrally on the cylinder block, ensuring that the locating dowels engage with the recesses in the cylinder head. Check that the head gasket is correctly seated before allowing the full weight of the cylinder head to rest on it.

28 Apply a smear of grease to the threads, and to the underside of the heads, of the new cylinder head bolts.

29 Carefully enter each bolt into its relevant hole (*do not drop them in*) and screw in, by hand only, until finger-tight.

30 Working progressively and in sequence, tighten the cylinder head bolts to their Stage 1 torque setting, using a torque wrench and socket. Then slacken the bolts in sequence (Stage 2) and tighten them to the Stage 3 Setting. Then working in sequence tighten them to the Stage 4 setting **(see illustration)**.

31 Once all the bolts have been tightened to their Stage 4 settings, working again in the given sequence, angle-tighten the bolts through the specified Stage 5 angle, using a socket and extension bar **(see illustration)**. It is recommended that an angle-measuring gauge is used during this stage of the tightening, to ensure accuracy. If a gauge is not available, use paint to make alignment marks between the bolt head and cylinder head prior to tightening; the marks can then be used to check the bolt has been rotated through the correct angle during tightening. Repeat the procedure, tightening the bolts to the Stage 6 angle.

32 The remainder of refitting is a reversal of removal, noting the following points:
 a) *No retightening of the cylinder head bolts is required.*
 b) *Tighten all fasteners to their specified torque where given.*
 c) *Refill the cooling system and replenish the engine oil as described in Chapter 1B.*

9 Camshafts, rocker arms and hydraulic tappets – removal, inspection and refitting

Removal

1 Remove the intake camshaft sprocket as described in Section 4.

2 Remove the camshaft cover as described in Section 5.

3 Undo the screw securing the timing inner

9.3 Inner timing cover screw (arrowed)

9.5a Undo the screws and remove the left-hand . . .

9.5b . . . and right-hand bearing caps

9.6 The bearing caps should be numbered, starting at the timing belt end

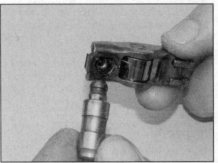

9.10 Unclip the tappets from the rocker arms

9.11 Spin the roller and listen for any noise

cover to the right-hand camshaft bearing cap **(see illustration)**.

4 Remove the vacuum pump (Chapter 9) and the fuel pump (Chapter 4B).

5 Undo the screws securing the right- and left-hand camshaft bearing/sealing caps **(see illustrations)**.

6 The camshaft bearing caps should be marked to indicate their position. If they are not, number them starting from the timing belt end **(see illustration)**. It is essential they are refitted to their original positions.

7 Starting on the intake camshaft, slacken each of the bearing cap screws one turn at a time until the camshaft is no longer under tension, then remove the screws and caps. The screws must be released gradually and evenly to prevent excess stress and possible damage to the camshaft. Repeat this procedure on the exhaust camshaft.

8 Lift out the camshafts, and discard the oil seal on the intake camshaft.

9 Carefully lift the rocker arms and hydraulic tappets from the cylinder head. Lay them out on a clean, dry surface, and using paint, mark their positions in the cylinder head. eg, E1, E2, (exhaust 1, exhaust 2, etc).

Inspection

10 Unclip the hydraulic tappets from the rocker arms, and check for any signs of damage **(see illustration)**. Renew as necessary.

11 Spin the roller on each of the rocker arms and listen for any noise from the bearing **(see illustration)**. Renew as necessary.

12 Inspect the cam lobes and the camshaft bearing journals for scoring or other visible

evidence of wear. Once the surface hardening of the lobes has been penetrated, wear will progress rapidly.

13 No specific bearing journal diameters or running clearances are given by Volvo for the camshafts. However, if there is a visual deterioration, then component renewal will be necessary.

Refitting

14 Clip each tappet onto the underside of their respective rocker arms.

15 Ensure the bores for the tappets in the cylinder head are clean and free of debris, then lubricate the tappets with clean engine oil, and lower them into their original positions. Check the ends of the rocker arms are correctly located over the valve stems **(see illustration)**.

16 Check to make sure the camshaft bearing positions in the cylinder head are clean, then

9.15 Ensure the end of the rocker arms are correctly located over the end of the valve stems

lubricate them, and the rocker arm rollers, with clean engine oil.

17 Position the camshafts together, so the marks on the drive gears align, then lower the camshafts into position on the cylinder head **(see illustration)**. Lubricate the camshaft journals with clean engine oil.

18 Refit the camshaft bearing caps and screws into their original positions, and hand-tighten the screws evenly until the caps lie flat against the camshaft journals. Do not install the right- and left-hand bearing/sealing caps yet.

19 Tighten the bearing cap screws one turn at a time on both camshafts until the bearing caps contact the cylinder head. It's essential the bearing caps are tightened down gradually and evenly, or damage to the camshaft may result. Finally, tighten the bearing cap screws to the specified torque.

20 Insert a camshaft locking pin (Volvo

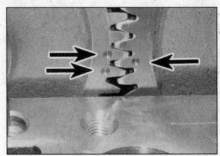

9.17 Position the camshafts together so the marks (arrowed) on the drive gears align

9.21 Apply sealant to the cylinder head/ bearing cap sealing surface

No 999 7007) though the hole in the cylinder head and into the hole in the camshaft sprocket. If necessary, rotate the camshaft slightly to enable the pin to be inserted using a large screwdriver in the camshaft end slots – do not turn the camshafts more than is absolutely necessary. If the Volvo pin is not available, a home-made equivalent can be fabricated **(see illustrations 4.10a and 4.10b)**.

21 Ensure the mating surfaces of the right- and left-hand camshaft bearing/sealing caps are clean and dry, then apply a light, even film of Volvo liquid sealant (Volvo No 11 61 059) to the mating surfaces **(see illustration)**. Ideally, use a short-haired roller.

22 Refit the right- and left-hand bearing/ sealing caps, and tighten the retaining screws to their specified torque.

23 Clean the oil seal seating in the bearing cap, then smear a little oil on the lips of the new camshaft oil seal. Wrap adhesive tape around the end of the camshaft, then fit the new oil seal and tap it into position carefully using a tubular bar or socket on the hard outer surface of the seal **(see illustrations 6.3a and 6.3b)**. Remove the tape on completion.

24 The remainder of refitting is a reversal of removal, noting the following points:

a) *Tighten all fasteners to the specified torque where given.*

b) *Wait a minimum of 30 minutes (or preferably, leave overnight) after fitting the hydraulic tappets before turning the engine over, to allow the tappets time to settle, otherwise the valve heads will strike the pistons.*

10.3 Undo the bolts and remove the engine speed sensor, complete with bracket

10 Flywheel/driveplate – removal, inspection and refitting

Removal

1 On manual gearbox models, remove the gearbox (see Chapter 7A) and clutch (see Chapter 6).

2 On automatic transmission models, remove the automatic transmission as described in Chapter 7B.

3 Undo the bolts and move the engine speed sensor, complete with bracket, to one side **(see illustration)**.

4 Temporarily insert a bolt in the cylinder block, and use a wide-bladed screwdriver to hold the flywheel/driveplate, or make up a holding tool **(see illustration)**.

5 Slacken and remove the multi-spline bolts securing the flywheel/driveplate to the crankshaft, and lift the flywheel/driveplate from place – the flywheel's heavy! Discard the flywheel bolts, new ones must be fitted.

Inspection

6 Check the flywheel/driveplate for wear and damage. Examine the starter ring gear for excessive wear to the teeth. If the driveplate or its ring gear are damaged, the complete driveplate must be renewed. The flywheel ring gear, however, may be renewed separately from the flywheel, but the work should be entrusted to an Volvo dealer. If the clutch friction face is discoloured or scored excessively, it may be possible to regrind it, but this work should also be entrusted to an Volvo dealer. Always renew the flywheel/ driveplate bolts.

7 On models with a dual mass flywheel, check the radial play by turning the flywheel secondary mass one way until the spring begins to tension, then allow the flywheel to spring back – make an alignment mark between the primary and secondary masses. Now turn the flywheel in the opposite direction until the spring begins to tension – make another alignment mark between the two masses. The distance between the 2 marks must be less than 35 mm.

10.4 Ideally, make up a tool to lock the flywheel in place

Refitting

8 Position the flywheel/driveplate against the crankshaft, aligning the locating dowel with the corresponding hole in the flywheel/ driveplate **(see illustration)**.

9 Insert the new bolts, and tighten them gradually and evenly, in a diagonal pattern to the Stage 1 torque setting, followed by the Stage 2 angle setting. Prevent the flywheel from rotating using the same method as during removal.

10 The remainder of refitting is a reversal of removal.

11 Engine mountings – inspection and renewal

Inspection

1 The front and rear engine mounting pads are hydraulic, with their hardness being vacuum-controlled by the engine management ECM. At approximately 1000 rpm, the pads change from soft to hard.

2 If improved access is required, raise the front of the car and support it securely on axle stands then remove the undershield.

3 Check the mounting rubbers to see if they are cracked, hardened or separated from the metal at any point; renew the mounting if any such damage or deterioration is evident.

4 Check that all the mounting's fasteners are securely tightened; use a torque wrench to check if possible.

5 Using a large screwdriver or a crowbar, check for wear in the mounting by carefully levering against it to check for free play. Where this is not possible, enlist the aid of an assistant to move the engine/transmission back-and-forth, or from side-to-side, while you watch the mounting. While some free play is to be expected even from new components (see paragraph 1), excessive wear should be obvious. If excessive free play is found, check first that the fasteners are correctly secured, then renew any worn components as described below.

10.8 Align the locating dowel in the crankshaft with the hole in the flywheel marked by the dimple (arrowed)

Renewal

Top, rear mounting

6 Pull the plastic cover on the engine straight upwards and remove it from the engine compartment.

7 Undo the bolts/nuts securing the engine cross-stay to the suspension turrets and top mounting **(see illustrations 3.8a and 3.8b)**.

8 Undo the retaining bolt and move the hose bracket to one side.

9 Undo the bolts and remove the rear mounting.

10 Position the mounting and tighten the screws to the correct torque as shown **(see illustration)**.

11 Refit the hose bracket, and engine cross-stay, tightening the fasteners to the specified torque.

12 Refit the plastic cover.

Lower torque rod

13 Jack up the front of the vehicle and support it securely on axle stands (see *Jacking and vehicle support*).

14 Undo the screws and remove the engine undershield.

15 Undo the bolts and manoeuvre the torque rod from place.

16 Position the torque rod and tighten the new fasteners to the correct torque as shown **(see illustration)**.

17 Refit the undershield and lower the vehicle to the ground.

Rear hydraulic mounting

18 Jack up the front of the vehicle and support it securely on axle stands (see *Jacking and vehicle support*). Undo the screws and remove the engine undershield.

19 Pull the plastic cover on the engine straight upwards and remove it from the engine compartment.

20 Undo the bolts/nuts securing the engine cross-stay to the suspension turrets and top mounting **(see illustrations 3.8a and 3.8b)**.

21 Disconnect the vacuum pipe from the rear mounting **(see illustration)**.

22 Remove the upper nut from the rear mounting.

23 Undo the 4 nuts/bolts securing the crossmember under the catalytic converter, unclip the brake pipe, undo the catalytic converter mounting screws, and remove the crossmember.

24 Undo the rear mounting lower screw. Discard the screw, a new one must be fitted **(see illustration)**.

25 Position a trolley jack under the transmission and lift the engine approximately 38 mm, and remove the rear hydraulic mounting.

26 Transfer the heat shield to the new mounting, and fit the mounting in place ensuing the guide pin at the top of the mounting locates correctly. Lower the engine and remove the jack.

27 Tighten the new mounting lower screw to the specified torque.

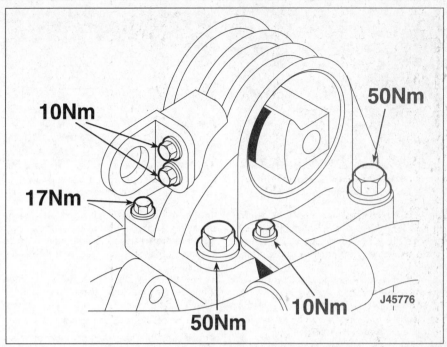

11.10 Top, rear engine mounting bolts tightening torques

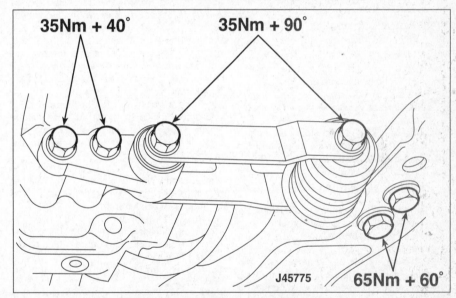

11.16 Lower torque rod bolts tightening torques

11.21 Disconnect the vacuum pipe (arrowed) from the rear mounting

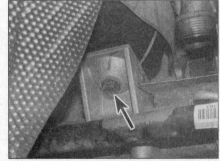

11.24 Undo the rear mounting lower screw (arrowed)

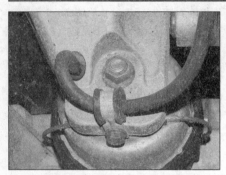

11.36 Disconnect the front mounting vacuum hose and undo the nut

11.37 Undo the front mounting lower screw (arrowed)

11.50 Right-hand engine mounting (shown with the engine removed for clarity)

28 Refit the crossmember under the catalytic converter, tighten the fasteners to the specified torque. Clip the brake pipe in place, and secure the catalytic converter mounting screws.

29 Refit the engine undershield and lower the vehicle to the ground.

30 Fit the new upper nut to the rear mounting, and tighten it to the specified torque, then reconnect the vacuum hose.

31 Refit the engine cross-stay and tighten the fasteners to the specified torque. Refit the plastic engine cover.

Front hydraulic mounting

32 Jack up the front of the vehicle and support it securely on axle stands (see *Jacking and vehicle support*). Undo the screws and remove the engine undershield.

33 Pull the plastic cover on the engine straight upwards and remove it from the engine compartment.

34 Undo the bolts/nuts securing the engine cross-stay to the suspension turrets and top mounting **(see illustrations 3.8a and 3.8b)**.

35 Release the clamps and remove the air hose from the intercooler to the intake manifold.

36 Disconnect the vacuum hose from the front mounting, and remove the mounting upper nut **(see illustration)**. Discard the nut, a new one must be fitted.

37 Remove the air intake cover, and the front mounting lower screw **(see illustration)**. Discard the screw, a new one must be fitted.

38 Remove the screw/nut securing the lower torque rod to the mounting on the transmission.

39 Place a trolley jack under the transmission, and lift the engine approximately 30 mm. Remove the front hydraulic engine mounting.

40 Fit the mounting in place and insert the new screw. Do not tighten the screw yet.

41 Lower the engine, ensuring the guide pin on the top of the mounting locates correctly. Tighten the lower screw to the specified torque, and remove the trolley jack.

42 Fit a new nut and screw to the lower torque rod and tighten them to the specified torque.

43 Refit the engine undershield, air intake cover, and lower the vehicle to the ground.

44 Fit a new upper nut to the engine mounting, and reconnect the vacuum hose.

45 Refit the air hose from the intercooler to the intake manifold, and secure the retaining clamps.

46 Refit the engine cross-stay and tighten the fasteners to the specified torque. Refit the plastic engine cover.

Right-hand engine mounting

47 Slacken the right-hand front roadwheel bolts, then jack up the front of the vehicle and support it securely on axle stands (see *Jacking and vehicle support*). Remove the roadwheel, undo the clips/screws and remove the engine undershield.

48 Undo the plastic nuts and remove the access panel from the right-hand front wheel arch liner to access the mounting **(see illustration 3.6)**.

49 Place a trolley jack under the right-hand end of the engine sump and take the weight. Position a block of wood between the jack head and sump to prevent damage to the casing.

50 Undo the four mounting bolts, raise the engine slightly with the jack, and remove the mounting. Discard the nuts, new ones must be fitted **(see illustration)**.

51 Position the mounting, and lower the engine as necessary for the bolt holes to align. Insert the new bolts and tighten them to the specified torque.

52 Remove the jack, and refit the engine undershield.

53 Refit the access panel in the wheel arch liner, refit the roadwheel and lower the vehicle to the ground. Tighten the roadwheel bolts to the specified torque.

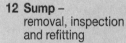

12 Sump –
removal, inspection and refitting

Removal

1 Jack up the front of the vehicle and support it securely on axle stands (see *Jacking and vehicle support*).

2 Undo the screws and remove the engine undershield.

3 Drain the engine oil as described in Chapter 1B.

4 Undo the bolt/nut and pull the oil level dipstick guide tube from the sump.

5 The oil cooler (where fitted) is secured to the sump by four bolts. Undo the bolts and pull the cooler to the rear **(see illustration 14.3)**. Be prepared for oil spillage.

6 Pull the plastic engine cover straight up from the top of the engine, and remove it.

7 Undo the fasteners and remove the engine cross-stay from between the suspension turrets.

8 Working underneath the vehicle, undo the front mounting screw for the charge air pipe.

9 Remove the upper nut from the rear hydraulic engine mounting, and disconnect the vacuum hose (see Section 11). Discard the nut, a new one must be fitted.

10 Release the clamp and disconnect the front hose from the charge air pipe. Plug the opening to prevent dirt ingress.

11 Remove the front hydraulic engine mounting lower screw. Discard the screw, a new one must be fitted.

12 Remove the screw/nut securing the lower torque rod to the transmission bracket.

13 Undo the two screws securing the charge air pipe to the transmission casing.

14 Position a trolley jack under the rear edge of the transmission casing, and lift the assembly slightly so the charge air pipe can be withdrawn.

15 Slacken the screws securing the sump, and remove them all apart from one screw in each corner.

16 Gently tap the sides and ends of the sump until the joint between the engine and sump releases. Undo the remaining screws and remove the sump. Discard the O-rings at the right-hand end/front edge of the sump, new ones must be fitted.

Refitting

17 Clean the contact faces of the sump and block.

18 Apply a thin and even layer of Volvo liquid sealant (No 11 61 059) to the sump mating face, and position the new O-ring seals on the engine block face **(see illustrations)**. Ideally, use a short-haired roller to apply the sealant.

19 Refit the sump casing and refit the

12.18a Apply a thin and even layer of Volvo sealant . . .

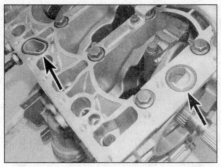

12.18b . . . and renew the O-ring seals (arrowed)

12.19 The 4 slightly shorter bolts are fitted at the transmission end

retaining screws, finger-finger tight only at this stage. Note that the three longest bolts are fitted to the oil pump end, and the four slightly shorter bolts are fitted at the transmission end **(see illustration)**.

20 Refit the transmission-to-sump bolts and tighten them to the Stage 1 torque setting, followed by the Stage 2 torque setting.

21 Starting from the transmission end, tighten the sump-to-engine bolts in pairs to the specified torque.

22 The remainder of refitting is a reversal of refitting, noting the following points:

 a) *Fit new engine mounting nuts and bolts.*
 b) *Renew the oil cooler-to-sump O-ring seals.*
 c) *Tighten all fasteners to their specified torque where given.*
 d) *Fit a new engine oil filter, and refill the engine with oil as described in Chapter 1B.*

13 Oil pump –
removal, inspection and refitting

Removal

1 Remove the crankshaft right-hand oil seal as described in Section 7.

2 Undo the four bolts securing the oil pump to the front of the cylinder block **(see illustration)**.

3 Carefully withdraw the pump assembly by levering behind the upper and lower parting lugs using a screwdriver. Remove the pump and recover the gasket.

4 Thoroughly clean the pump and cylinder block mating faces and remove all traces of old gasket. Discard the O-ring seal, a new one must be fitted.

Inspection

5 Undo the two pump cover retaining Allen screws whilst holding the two halves of the pump together, then remove the cover. Be prepared for the ejection of the pressure relief valve spring **(see illustration)**.

6 Note their fitted positions, then remove the pressure relief valve spring, plunger and pump rotors **(see illustrations)**.

7 In not already done so, lever out the crankshaft oil seal.

8 Clean all the components thoroughly, then inspect the rotors, body and cover for damage or signs of wear.

9 At the time of writing, no specifications concerning the overhaul or inspection of the pump were available, and it would appear that no pump internal parts are available separately.

10 Refit the inner rotor with the marks facing the pump body **(see illustration)**.

13.2 Undo the 4 oil pump bolts (arrowed)

13.5 Undo the 2 oil pump cover screws (arrowed)

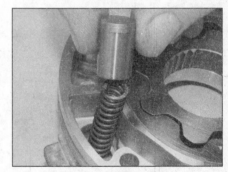

13.6a Remove the plunger . . .

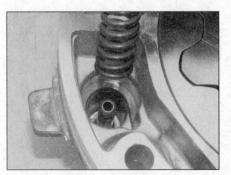

13.6b . . . spring . . .

13.6c . . . and rotors

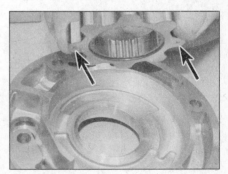

13.10 Fit the inner rotor with the marks (arrowed) facing the pump body . . .

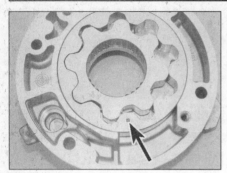

13.11 . . . and the outer rotor with the mark (arrowed) facing the cylinder block

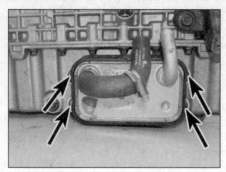

14.3 Undo the oil cooler bolts (arrowed)

14.4 Oil cooler O-ring seals

11 Refit the outer rotor to the body, ensuring the mark on the rotor faces the cylinder block **(see illustration)**.

12 Refit the pressure relief valve spring and plunger, and fit the cover, tightening the retaining screws securely.

Refitting

13 Using a new gasket and O-ring, fit the pump to the block. Use the pump retaining bolts as guides, and draw the pump into place with the crankshaft pulley nut and spacers. With the pump seated, tighten the retaining bolts diagonally to the specified torque.

14 Fit a new crankshaft right-hand oil seal as described in Section 7.

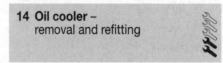

14 Oil cooler –
removal and refitting

Removal

1 Drain the engine oil and coolant as described in Chapter 1B.

2 Release the hose clamp and disconnect the coolant hoses from the cooler, located on the rear face of the sump.

3 Undo the bolts securing the cooler to the sump, and recover the O-ring seals as the cooler is withdrawn. Be prepared for fluid spillage **(see illustration)**.

Refitting

4 Check the mating faces of the sump and oil cooler are clean, then refit the cooler using new O-ring seals. Tighten the retaining bolts securely **(see illustration)**.

5 Reconnect the coolant hoses and secure them with new clips where necessary.

6 Refill the engine oil and cooling systems as described in Chapter 1B.

Chapter 2 Part C:
Engine removal and overhaul procedures

Contents

Degrees of difficulty

Easy, suitable for novice with little experience 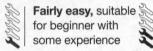	**Fairly easy,** suitable for beginner with some experience 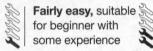	**Fairly difficult,** suitable for competent DIY mechanic 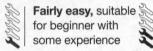	**Difficult,** suitable for experienced DIY mechanic	**Very difficult,** suitable for expert DIY or professional

Specifications

Cylinder head

Warp limit – maximum acceptable for use:
Lengthways	0.50 mm
Across	0.20 mm

Height:
Petrol engines	129.0 ± 0.05 mm
Diesel engines	149.4 ± 0.15 mm
Maximum height reduction after machining	0.30 mm

Cylinder head gasket selection – diesel engines only

Piston protrusion (see text)	Min	Max	Holes in gasket
	0.26 mm	0.47 mm	1
	0.47 mm	0.52 mm	2
	0.52 mm	0.57 mm	3
	0.57 mm	0.62 mm	4
	0.62 mm	0.74 mm	5

Intake valves

Head diameter:
Petrol engines	31.0 ± 0.15 mm
Diesel engines	28.0 ± 0.07 mm

Stem diameter:
Petrol engines:
Early models	6.955 to 6.970 mm
Late models	5.955 to 5.970 mm
Diesel engines	5.975 ± 0.015 mm

Length:
Petrol engines	102.00 ± 0.07 mm
Diesel engines	98.1 ± 0.07 mm

Valve seat angle:
Petrol engines	44° 30'
Diesel engines	45° ± 0.5°

Exhaust valves

Head diameter:
  Petrol engines . . . . 27.0 ± 0.15 mm
  Diesel engines . . . . 26.2 ± 0.1 mm
Stem diameter:
  Petrol engines:
    Early models . . . . 6.955 to 6.970 mm
    Late models . . . . 5.947 to 5.960 mm
  Diesel engines . . . . 5.975 ± 0.015 mm
Length:
  Petrol engines . . . . 101.05 ± 0.07 mm
  Diesel engines . . . . 97.7 ± 0.07 mm
Valve seat angle:
  Petrol engines . . . . 44° 30'
  Diesel engines . . . . 45.0° ± 0.5°

Valve guides

Valve stem-to-guide clearance:
  Petrol engines:
    New . . . . 0.03 to 0.06 mm
    Wear limit . . . . 0.15 mm
  Diesel engines . . . . Not available

Valve springs

Free length:
  Petrol engines . . . . 44.6 to 46.6 mm
  Diesel engines . . . . Not available

Piston rings

Clearance in groove:
  Petrol engines:
    Top compression . . . . 0.030 to 0.070 mm
    Second compression . . . . 0.030 to 0.070 mm
    Oil control . . . . 0.038 to 0.142 mm
  Diesel engines:
    Top compression . . . . 0.120 to 0.160 mm
    Second compression . . . . 0.070 to 0.110 mm
    Oil control . . . . 0.030 to 0.070 mm
End gap (measured in cylinder):
  Compression rings . . . . 0.20 to 0.40 mm
  Oil control . . . . 0.25 to 0.50 mm

Crankshaft

Endfloat:
  Petrol engines . . . . 0.19 mm max
  Diesel engines . . . . 0.08 to 0.19 mm

Torque wrench settings

Refer to Chapter 2A or 2B Specifications for torque wrench settings.

---

1 General information

Included in this part of Chapter 2 are details of removing the engine/transmission from the car and general overhaul procedures for the cylinder head, cylinder block and all other engine internal components.

The information ranges from advice concerning preparation for an overhaul and the purchase of parts, to detailed step-by-step procedures covering removal, inspection, renovation and refitting of engine internal components.

After Section 6, all instructions are based on the assumption that the engine has been removed from the car. For information concerning engine in-car repair, as well as removal and installation of those external components necessary for full overhaul, refer to Part A or B of this Chapter as applicable, and to Section 4. Ignore any preliminary dismantling operations described in Part A or Part B that are no longer relevant once the engine has been removed from the car.

2 Engine/transmission removal – preparation and precautions

If you have decided that an engine must be removed for overhaul or major repair work, several preliminary steps should be taken.

Locating a suitable place to work is extremely important. Adequate work space, along with storage space for the car, will be needed. If a workshop or garage is not available, at the very least, a flat, level, clean work surface is required.

If possible, clear some shelving close to the work area, and use it to store the engine components and ancillaries as they are removed and dismantled. In this manner, the components stand a better chance of staying clean and undamaged during the overhaul. Laying out components in groups together with their fixing bolts, screws, etc, will save time and avoid confusion when the engine is refitted.

Clean the engine compartment and engine/transmission before beginning the removal procedure; this will help visibility and help to keep tools clean.

The help of an assistant should be available; there are certain instances when one person cannot safely perform all of the operations required to remove the engine from the vehicle. Safety is of primary importance, considering the potential hazards involved in this kind of operation. A second person should always be in attendance to offer help in an emergency. If this is the first time you have removed an engine, advice and aid from someone more experienced would also be beneficial.

Plan the operation ahead of time. Before starting work, obtain (or arrange for the hire of) all of the tools and equipment you will need. Access to the following items will allow the task of removing and refitting the engine/ transmission to be completed safely and with relative ease: an engine hoist – rated in excess of the combined weight of the engine/ transmission, a heavy-duty trolley jack, complete sets of spanners and sockets as described at the rear this manual, wooden blocks, and plenty of rags and cleaning solvent for mopping-up spilled oil, coolant and fuel. A selection of different-sized plastic storage bins will also prove useful for keeping dismantled components grouped together. If any of the equipment must be hired, make sure that you arrange for it in advance, and perform all of the operations possible without it beforehand; this may save you time and money.

Plan on the vehicle being out of use for quite a while, especially if you intend to carry out an engine overhaul. Read through the whole of this Section and work out a strategy based on your own experience and the tools, time and workspace available to you. Some of the overhaul processes may have to be carried out by a Volvo dealer or an engineering works – these establishments often have busy schedules, so it would be prudent to consult them before removing or dismantling the engine, to get an idea of the amount of time required to carry out the work.

When removing the engine from the vehicle, be methodical about the disconnection of external components. Labelling cables and hoses as they removed will greatly assist the refitting process.

Always be extremely careful when lifting the engine/transmission assembly from the engine bay. Serious injury can result from careless actions. If help is required, it is better to wait until it is available rather than risk personal injury and/or damage to components by continuing alone. By planning ahead and taking your time, a job of this nature, although major, can be accomplished successfully and without incident.

On all models covered by this manual, the engine and transmission are removed as a complete assembly, upwards and out of the engine bay. The engine and transmission are then separated with the assembly on the bench.

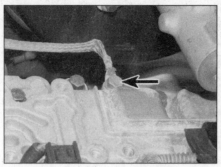

3.5 Disconnect the earth strap from the cylinder head (arrowed)

3 Engine and transmission – removal, separation and refitting

Removal

1 Open the bonnet. If there is any possibility of the engine hoist being obstructed, remove the bonnet as described in Chapter 11.

2 Disconnect the battery negative terminal as described in Chapter 5A.

3 Pull the plastic cover on top of the engine straight up (where fitted), then undo the fasteners and remove the engine cross-stay from between the brackets on the front suspension turrets.

4 Remove the air cleaner assembly, and all air ducting, including turbocharger inlet (where applicable) with reference to the relevant Part of Chapter 4.

5 Disconnect the earth straps from the top of the cylinder head (where fitted) **(see illustration)**.

6 Refer to the relevant Part of Chapter 1 and carry out the following:
  a) Drain the cooling system.
  b) If the engine is going to be dismantled, drain the engine oil.
  c) Remove the auxiliary drivebelt.

7 Unclip the plastic cover from the central electrical unit, and disconnect the engine wiring loom plug and the positive connection leading to the starter motor, then undo the two bolts and move the central electrical unit to one side **(see illustration)**.

3.11 Earth strap location (arrowed) – viewed from the front of the engine

3.7 Disconnect the engine wiring loom plug (arrowed) and the positive connection (arrowed)

8 Slacken the clamp and disconnect the fluid return pipe from the top of the power steering fluid reservoir, then release the clip and lift up the power steering fluid reservoir and lay it on top of the engine temporarily. Plug or seal the pipe and reservoir openings to prevent dirt ingress and fluid loss.

9 Disconnect bleed hose from the coolant expansion tank, slacken the clamp and disconnect the hose from the expansion tank to the coolant pipe on the rear of the cylinder head, and remove the expansion tank. Disconnect the tank level sensor wiring plug as it's withdrawn.

10 Note their fitted positions and disconnect all electrical wiring plugs from the engine/ transmission assembly. Note the routing of the wiring loom to aid refitting. Undo the bolts and release the loom from the retaining brackets on the engine/subframe and manoeuvre the loom clear of the engine/transmission.

11 Undo the bolts and detach the engine earth strap from the right-hand front corner of the transmission casing, then undo the bolt securing the strap-retaining bracket to the subframe **(see illustration)**.

12 Disconnect the brake servo vacuum hose from the intake manifold (petrol models) or the vacuum pump (diesel models).

13 Remove the radiator as described in Chapter 3.

14 Disconnect the selector/gearchange cables from the transmission as described in the relevant Part of Chapter 7.

15 Clamp the flexible rubber hose, then prise out the retaining clip and disconnect the metal pressure pipe from the clutch slave cylinder – refer to Chapter 6 where necessary.

16 Disconnect the fuel supply and return hoses at the connectors located above the right-hand driveshaft. The connectors maybe of the 'quick-release' type where a collar must be pressed into the connector, or a tool (a length of tube slit lengthways) must be inserted to spread the 'fingers' of the collar, or simply retained by a metal clamp **(see illustrations)**. On petrol models, disconnect the EVAP hose at the same point.

17 On all models, remove both driveshafts as described in Chapter 8.

18 Disconnect the air conditioning compressor wiring plug, the undo the four

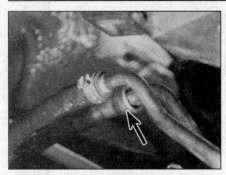

3.16a To disconnect the fuel supply pipe (arrowed) . . .

3.16b . . . the four clips inside the connection must be pushed outwards

3.20 Rotate the collars anti-clockwise to disconnect the heater hoses

3.23a Front engine mounting bolt (arrowed)

3.23b Rear engine mounting bolt (arrowed)

retaining bolts and detach the compressor from the engine, and tie it to the front panel. Take care not to damage the air conditioning pipes. There is no need to discharge the air conditioning refrigerant.

19 Remove the turbocharger as described in the relevant Part of Chapter 4.

20 Rotate the collars anti-clockwise and disconnect the heater hoses at the engine compartment bulkhead **(see illustration)**. Be prepared for coolant spillage.

21 Working through the holes in the pulley, undo the three bolts securing the power steering pump to the mounting bracket, then undo the bolts securing the bracket to the

rear of the pump and cylinder head. Lower the pump, along with the fluid reservoir, and secure it to the front of the subframe using cable ties.

22 Undo the remaining mounting bolt and remove the alternator.

23 Working underneath the vehicle, remove the bolt securing the front engine mounting to the subframe, and the bolt securing the rear engine/transmission mounting to the subframe **(see illustrations)**.

24 Undo the two bolts securing the roll restrictor to the underside of the transmission casing.

25 Attach a lifting chain/strap to the transport

brackets on the top of the engine, then manoeuvre an engine hoist/crane into position and take the weight of the engine **(see illustration)**.

26 Make a final check to ensure all hoses, pipes and electrical wiring between the engine/transmission and body have been disconnected.

27 Undo the bolts securing the right-hand engine mounting to the bracket on the cylinder block (adjacent to the crankshaft pulley), then lift and manoeuvre the engine/transmission assembly from the engine compartment **(see illustration)**. We found it necessary to undo the three bolts and detach the front engine mounting from the cylinder block. The aid of an assistant will be essential to support and manoeuvre the assembly without damaging the vehicle bodywork, etc.

Separation

28 Remove the starter motor.

Manual transmission models

29 Remove the bolts securing the trans-mission to the engine.

30 With the aid of an assistant, draw the transmission off the engine. Once it is clear of the dowels, do not allow it to hang on the input shaft.

3.25 Attach a lifting chain/strap to the transport brackets (arrowed)

3.27 Undo the two bolts securing the right-hand engine mounting bracket to the cylinder block (arrowed)

Automatic transmission models

31 Rotate the crankshaft, using a socket on the pulley nut, until one of the torque converter-to-driveplate retaining bolts becomes accessible through the opening on the rear facing side of the engine. Working through the opening, undo the bolt using a TX50 socket. Rotate the crankshaft as necessary and remove the remaining bolts in the same way. Note that new bolts will be required for refitting.

32 Remove the bolts securing the transmission to the engine.

33 With the aid of an assistant, draw the transmission squarely off the engine dowels making sure that the torque converter remains in position on the transmission. Use the access hole in the transmission housing to hold the converter in place.

Refitting

Manual transmission models

34 Make sure that the clutch is correctly centred and that the clutch release components are fitted to the bellhousing. Do not apply any grease to the transmission input shaft, the guide sleeve, or the release bearing itself, as these components have a friction-reducing coating which does not require lubrication.

35 Manoeuvre the transmission squarely into position, and engage it with the engine dowels. Refit the bolts securing the transmission to the engine, and tighten them to the specified torque. Refit the starter motor.

Automatic transmission models

36 Before refitting the transmission, flush out the fluid cooler with fresh transmission fluid. To do this, attach a hose to the upper union, pour ATF through the hose and collect it in a container positioned beneath the return hose.

37 Clean the contact surfaces on the torque converter and driveplate, and the transmission and engine mating faces. Lightly lubricate the torque converter guide projection and the engine/transmission locating dowels with grease.

38 Manoeuvre the transmission squarely into position, and engage it with the engine dowels. Refit the bolts securing the transmission to the engine and tighten lightly first in a diagonal sequence, then again to the specified torque.

39 Attach the torque converter to the driveplate using new bolts. Rotate the crankshaft for access to the bolts as was done for removal, then rotate the torque converter by means of the access hole in the transmission housing. Fit and tighten all the bolts hand-tight first, then tighten again to the specified torque.

All models

40 The remainder of refitting is essentially a reversal of removal, noting the following points:

 a) *Tighten all fastenings to the specified*

torque and, where applicable, torque angle. Refer to the relevant Chapters of this manual for torque wrench settings not directly related to the engine.

 b) *Ensure that the ABS sensor, and the sensor location in each hub carrier, are perfectly clean before refitting.*

 c) *When reconnecting the manual transmission selector cables, note that the outermost cable (marked with yellow paint) attaches to the vertical selector lever on the end of the transmission (also marked yellow).*

 d) *On automatic transmission models, reconnect and adjust the selector cable as described in Chapter 7B.*

 e) *Refit the air cleaner assembly as described in Chapter 4A or 4B.*

 f) *Refit the auxiliary drivebelt, then refill the engine with coolant and oil as described in the relevant Part of Chapter 1.*

 g) *Refill the transmission with lubricant if necessary as described in the relevant Part of Chapter 1, 7A or 7B as applicable.*

 h) *Refer to Section 16 before starting the engine.*

---

4 Engine overhaul – preliminary information

It is much easier to dismantle and work on the engine if it is mounted on a portable engine stand. These stands can often be hired from a tool hire shop. Before the engine is mounted on a stand, the flywheel/driveplate should be removed so that the stand bolts can be tightened into the end of the cylinder block/crankcase.

If a stand is not available, it is possible to dismantle the engine with it suitably supported on a sturdy, workbench or on the floor. Be careful not to tip or drop the engine when working without a stand.

If you intend to obtain a reconditioned engine, all ancillaries must be removed first, to be transferred to the new engine (just as they will if you are doing a complete engine overhaul yourself). These components include the following:

 a) *Engine mountings and brackets (Chapter 2A or 2B).*

 b) *Alternator including accessories mounting bracket (Chapter 5A).*

 c) *Starter motor (Chapter 5A).*

 d) *The ignition system and HT components including all sensors, ignition coils, spark plugs, as applicable (Chapters 1A and 5B).*

 e) *Exhaust manifold, with turbocharger if fitted (Chapter 4A or 4B).*

 f) *Intake manifold with fuel injection components (Chapter 4A or 4B).*

 g) *All electrical switches, actuators and sensors, and the engine wiring harness (Chapters 4A, 4B and 5B).*

 h) *Coolant pump, thermostat, hoses, and distribution pipe (Chapter 3).*

 i) *Clutch components – manual transmission models (Chapter 6).*

 j) *Flywheel/driveplate (Chapter 2A or 2B).*

 k) *Oil filter (the relevant Part of Chapter 1).*

 l) *Dipstick, tube and bracket.*

Note: *When removing the external components from the engine, pay close attention to details that may be helpful or important during refitting. Note the fitting positions of gaskets, seals, washers, bolts and other small items.*

If you are obtaining a 'short' engine (cylinder block/crankcase, crankshaft, pistons and connecting rods all assembled), then the cylinder head, timing belt (together with tensioner, tensioner and idler pulleys and covers) and auxiliary drivebelt tensioner will have to be removed also.

If a complete overhaul is planned, the engine can be dismantled in the order given below:

 a) *Intake and exhaust manifolds and turbocharger (where applicable).*

 b) *Timing belt, sprockets, tensioner, pulleys and covers.*

 c) *Cylinder head.*

 d) *Oil pump.*

 e) *Flywheel/driveplate.*

 f) *Sump.*

 g) *Oil pick-up pipe.*

 h) *Intermediate section.*

 i) *Pistons/connecting rods.*

 j) *Crankshaft.*

---

5 Cylinder head – dismantling, cleaning, inspection and reassembly

Note: *New and reconditioned cylinder heads are available from the manufacturer and from engine overhaul specialists. Specialist tools are required for the dismantling and inspection procedures, and new components may not be readily available. It may, therefore, be more practical and economical for the home mechanic to purchase a reconditioned head rather than dismantle, inspect and recondition the original head.*

Dismantling

1 Remove the cylinder head as described in Part A or B of this Chapter.

2 If still in place, remove the camshafts and tappets as described in Part A of this Chapter (petrol engines only).

3 According to components still fitted, remove the thermostat housing (Chapter 3), the spark plugs (Chapter 1A) and any other unions, pipes, sensors or brackets as necessary. On D5244T4/T5/T6/T7 engines, lift the swirl valve assembly from the top of the cylinder head.

4 Tap each valve stem smartly, using a light hammer and drift, to free the spring and associated items.

5 Fit a deep-reach type valve spring compressor to each valve in turn, and compress each spring until the collets are exposed

5.5 Compress the valve spring with a suitable valve spring compressor

(see illustration). Lift out the collets; a small screwdriver, a magnet or a pair of tweezers may be useful. Carefully release the spring compressor and remove it.

6 Remove the valve spring upper seat and the valve spring. Pull the valve out of its guide.

7 Pull off the valve stem oil seal with a pair of long-nosed pliers. It may be necessary to use a tool such as a pair of electrician's wire strippers, the 'legs' of which will engage under the seal, if the seal is tight.

8 Recover the valve spring lower seat. If there is much carbon build-up round the outside of the valve guide, this will have to be scraped off before the seat can be removed.

9 It is essential that each valve is stored together with its collets, spring and seats. The valves should also be kept in their correct sequence, unless they are so badly worn or burnt that they are to be renewed. If they are going to be kept and used again, place each valve assembly in a labelled polythene bag or similar container (see illustration).

10 Continue removing all the remaining valves in the same way.

Cleaning

11 Thoroughly clean all traces of old gasket material and sealing compound from the cylinder head upper and lower mating surfaces. Use a suitable liquid gasket dissolving agent together with a soft putty knife; do not use a metal scraper, or the faces will be damaged. Note that on diesel engines, the gasket surface cannot be refaced.

12 Remove the carbon from the combustion chambers and ports, then clean all traces of

5.9 Keep groups of components together in labelled bags or boxes

oil and other deposits from the cylinder head, paying particular attention to the bearing journals, tappet bores, valve guides and oilways.

13 Wash the head thoroughly with paraffin or a suitable solvent. Take plenty of time and do a thorough job. Be sure to clean all oil holes and galleries very thoroughly, dry the head completely and coat all machined surfaces with light oil.

14 Scrape off any heavy carbon deposits that may have formed on the valves, then use a power-operated wire brush to remove deposits from the valve heads and stems.

Inspection

Note: *Be sure to perform all the following inspection procedures before concluding that the services of an engineering works are required. Make a list of all items that require attention.*

Cylinder head

15 Inspect the head very carefully for cracks, evidence of coolant leakage, and other damage. If cracks are found, a new cylinder head should be obtained.

16 Use a straight-edge and feeler blade to check that the cylinder head gasket surface is not distorted (see illustration). If it is, it may be possible to resurface it (petrol models); consult your dealer or engine overhaul specialist.

17 Examine the valve seats in each of the combustion chambers. If they are severely pitted, cracked or burned, then they will need to be renewed or recut by an engine overhaul specialist. If they are only slightly pitted, this

can be removed by grinding-in the valve heads and seats with fine valve-grinding compound, as described below.

18 If the valve guides appear worn, indicated by a side-to-side motion of the valve, new guides must be fitted. Verify this by mounting a dial gauge on the cylinder head, and check the side-to-side rock with the valve lifted 2.0 to 3.0 mm clear of its seat (see illustration). If excessive, measure the diameter of the existing valve stems (see below) and the bore of the guides, renew the valves or guides as necessary. The renewal of valve guides should be carried out by an engine overhaul specialist.

19 If the valve seats are to be recut, this must be done *only after* the guides have been renewed.

20 The threaded holes in the cylinder head must be clean to ensure accurate torque readings when tightening fixings during reassembly. Carefully run the correct size tap (which can be determined from the size of the relevant bolt which fits in the hole) into each of the holes to remove rust, corrosion, thread sealant or other contamination, and to restore damaged threads. If possible, use compressed air to clear the holes of debris produced by this operation. Do not forget to clean the threads of all bolts and nuts as well.

21 Any threads which cannot be restored in this way can often be reclaimed by the use of thread inserts. If any threaded holes are damaged, consult your dealer or engine overhaul specialist and have them install any thread inserts where necessary.

Valves

22 Examine the head of each valve for pitting, burning, cracks and general wear, and check the valve stem for scoring and wear ridges. Rotate the valve, and check for any obvious indication that it is bent. Look for pits and excessive wear on the tip of each valve stem. Renew any valve that shows any such signs of wear or damage.

23 If the valve appears satisfactory at this stage, measure the valve stem diameter at several points, using a micrometer (see illustration). Any significant difference in the readings obtained indicates wear of the valve stem. Should any of these conditions be apparent, the valve(s) must be renewed.

5.16 Measure the distortion of the cylinder head surface with a straight-edge and feeler gauges

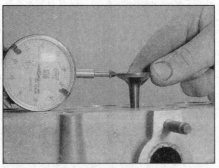

5.18 Measure the maximum deflection of the valve in its guide using a dial gauge

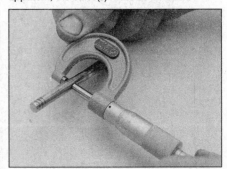

5.23 Measure the valve stem diameter with a micrometer

24 If the valves are in satisfactory condition, they should be ground (lapped) into their respective seats, to ensure a smooth gas-tight seal. If the seat is only lightly pitted, or if it has been recut, fine grinding compound *only* should be used to produce the required finish. Coarse valve-grinding compound should *not* be used unless a seat is badly burned or deeply pitted; if this is the case, the cylinder head and valves should be inspected by an expert, to decide whether seat recutting, or even the renewal of the valve or seat insert, is required.

25 Valve grinding is carried out as follows. Place the cylinder head upside-down on a bench, with a block of wood at each end to give clearance for the valve stems.

26 Smear a trace of (the appropriate grade) valve-grinding compound on the seat face, and press a suction grinding tool onto the valve head. With a semi-rotary action, grind the valve head to its seat, lifting the valve occasionally to redistribute the grinding compound. A light spring placed under the valve head will greatly ease this operation.

27 If coarse grinding compound is being used, work only until a dull, matt even surface is produced on both the valve seat and the valve, then wipe off the used compound, and repeat the process with fine compound. When a smooth unbroken ring of light grey matt finish is produced on both the valve and seat, the grinding operation is complete. *Do not* grind in the valves any further than absolutely necessary, or the seat will be prematurely sunk into the cylinder head.

28 When all the valves have been ground-in, carefully wash off *all* traces of grinding compound, using paraffin or a suitable solvent, before reassembly of the cylinder head.

Valve components

29 Examine the valve springs for signs of damage and discoloration, and also measure their free length by comparing each of the existing springs with a new component.

30 Stand each spring on a flat surface, and check it for squareness. If any of the springs are damaged, distorted, or have lost their tension, obtain a complete set of new springs. It is normal to fit new springs as a matter of course if a major overhaul is being carried out.

31 Renew the valve stem oil seals regardless of their apparent condition.

Reassembly

32 Oil the stem of one valve and insert it into its guide then fit the spring lower seat.

33 The new valve stem oil seals should be supplied with a plastic fitting sleeve to protect the seal when it is fitted over the valve. If not, wrap a thin piece of polythene around the valve stem allowing it to extend about 10 mm above the end of the valve stem.

34 With the fitting sleeve, or polythene in place around the valve, fit the valve stem oil seal, pushing it onto the valve guide as far as it

6.3 Oil cooler mounting bolts (arrowed)

will go with a suitable socket or piece of tube. Once the seal is seated, remove the protective sleeve or polythene.

35 Fit the valve spring and upper seat. Compress the spring and fit the two collets in the recesses in the valve stem. Carefully release the compressor.

 HAYNES HINT *Use a little dab of grease to hold the collets in position on the valve stem while the spring compressor is released.*

36 Cover the valve stem with a cloth and tap it smartly with a light hammer to verify that the collets are properly seated.

37 Repeat these procedures on all the other valves.

38 Refit the remainder of the disturbed components then refit the cylinder head as described in Part A or B of this Chapter.

6 Sump and intermediate section – removal

1 If not already done, drain the engine oil then remove the oil filter, referring to the relevant Part of Chapter 1 if necessary.

2 Remove the oil pump as described in Part A or B of this Chapter.

3 On models with an oil cooler mounted on the rear face of the sump, remove the four retaining bolts and take off the cooler, if

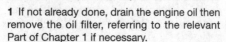

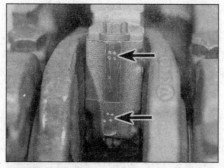

7.3 Mark the big-end caps and connecting rods with their cylinder numbers

6.6 Undo the oil pick up pipe bracket bolt (arrowed)

possible without disconnecting the coolant pipes (see illustration).

4 Undo the bolts securing the sump to the intermediate section, noting the different bolt lengths and their locations.

5 Carefully tap the sump free using a rubber or hide mallet. Recover the O-ring seals.

6 Undo the mounting bracket bolt and remove the oil pick-up pipe (see illustration). Recover the O-ring seal on the end of the pipe.

7 Remove the pistons and connecting rods as described in Section 7.

8 Undo all the M7 bolts securing the intermediate section to the cylinder block working from the outside in. With all the M7 bolts removed, undo the M8, then the M10 bolts in the same order.

9 Carefully tap the intermediate section free using a rubber or hide mallet. Lift off the intermediate section complete with crankshaft lower main bearing shells. If any of the shells have stayed on the crankshaft, transfer them to their correct locations in the intermediate section. Do not rotate the crankshaft with the intermediate section removed.

10 Remove the crankshaft oil seal.

7 Pistons and connecting rods – removal and inspection

Removal

1 Remove the cylinder head, oil pump and flywheel/driveplate as described in Part A or B of this Chapter. Remove the sump as described in Section 6.

2 Feel inside the tops of the bores for a pronounced wear ridge. Some experts recommend that such a ridge be removed (with a scraper or ridge reamer) before attempting to remove the pistons. However, a ridge big enough to damage the pistons and/or piston rings will almost certainly mean that a rebore and new pistons/rings are needed anyway.

3 Check that there are identification numbers or marks on each connecting rod and cap; paint or punch suitable marks if necessary, so that each rod can be refitted in the same position and the same way round (see illustration). Note their positions, eg, markings on the exhaust side, etc.

7.10 Remove the piston rings with the aid of feeler gauges

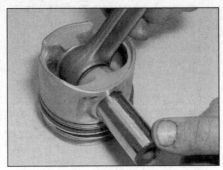

7.23 Push the gudgeon pin out of the piston and connecting rod

4 Remove the two connecting rod bolts. Tap the cap with a soft-faced hammer to free it. Remove the cap and lower bearing shell. Note that new bolts will be needed for reassembly. New shells should always be fitted.

5 Push the connecting rod and piston up and out of the bore. Recover the other half bearing shell if it is loose.

6 Refit the cap to the connecting rod, the correct way round, so that they do not get mixed up. Note that on some engines, the surface between the cap and rod is not machined, but fractured. Take great care not to damage or mark the fractured surfaces otherwise the cap will not fit properly with the shell, and new connecting rods will be required.

7 Check to see if there is an arrow on the top of the piston which should be pointing toward the timing belt end of the engine. If no arrow can be seen, make a suitable direction mark yourself.

8 Repeat the operations on the remaining connecting rods and pistons.

Inspection

9 Before the inspection process can be carried out, the piston/connecting rod assemblies must be cleaned, and the original piston rings removed from the pistons

10 Carefully expand the old rings and remove them from the top of the pistons. The use of two or three old feeler blades will be helpful in preventing the rings dropping into empty grooves **(see illustration)**. Be careful not to scratch the pistons with the ends of the ring. The rings are brittle and will snap if they are spread too far. They are also very sharp – protect your hands and fingers.

11 Scrape all traces of carbon from the top of the piston. A hand-held wire brush (or a piece of fine emery cloth) can be used, once the majority of the deposits have been scraped away.

12 Remove the carbon from the ring grooves in the piston, using an old ring. Break the ring in half to do this (be careful not to cut your fingers – piston rings are sharp). Be careful to remove only the carbon deposits – do not remove any metal, and do not nick or scratch the sides of the ring grooves.

13 Once the deposits have been removed, clean the piston/rod assemblies with paraffin or a suitable solvent, and dry thoroughly. Make sure the oil return holes in the ring grooves, are clear.

14 If the pistons and cylinder bores are not damaged or worn excessively, and if the cylinder block does not need to be rebored (where applicable), the original pistons can be refitted. Normal piston wear appears as even vertical wear on the piston thrust surfaces, and slight looseness of the top ring in its groove. New piston rings should always be used when the engine is reassembled.

15 Carefully inspect each piston for cracks around the skirt, around the gudgeon pin holes, and at the ring 'lands' (between the ring grooves).

16 Look for scoring and scuffing on the piston skirt, holes in the piston crown, and burned areas at the edge of the crown.

17 If the skirt is scored or scuffed, the engine may have been suffering from overheating and/or abnormal combustion, which caused excessively-high operating temperatures. The cooling and lubrication systems should be checked thoroughly. Scorch marks on the sides of the piston show that blow-by has occurred.

18 A hole in the piston crown or burned areas at the edge of the piston crown, indicates that abnormal combustion (pre-ignition, knocking, or detonation) has been occurring.

19 If any of the above piston problems

7.26 Measure the ring-to-groove clearance using feeler gauges

exist, the causes must be investigated and corrected, or the damage will occur again. The causes may include intake air leaks, incorrect fuel/air mixture or an emission control system fault.

20 Corrosion of the piston, in the form of pitting, indicates that coolant has been leaking into the combustion chamber and/or the crankcase. Again, the cause must be corrected, or the problem may persist in the rebuilt engine.

21 Examine each connecting rod carefully for signs of damage, such as cracks around the big-end and small-end bearings. Check that the rod is not bent or distorted. Damage is highly unlikely, unless the engine has been seized or badly overheated. Detailed checking of the connecting rod assembly can only be carried out by an engine overhaul specialist with the necessary equipment.

22 The gudgeon pins are of the floating type, secured in position by two circlips. Where necessary, the pistons and connecting rods can be separated as follows.

23 Remove one of the circlips which secure the gudgeon pin. Push the gudgeon pin out of the piston and connecting rod **(see illustration)**.

24 If any doubt exists concerning the condition of the pistons, have them measured by an automotive engine reconditioning specialist. If new pistons are required, the specialist will be able to supply new pistons and rebore the cylinder block to the appropriate size (where applicable).

25 If any one of the pistons is worn, then all five pistons must be renewed. Note that if the cylinder block was rebored during a previous overhaul, oversize pistons may have been fitted.

26 Hold a new piston ring in the appropriate groove, and measure the ring-to-groove clearance using a feeler blade **(see illustration)**. Note that the rings are of different sizes, so use the correct ring for the groove. Compare the measurements with those listed in the *Specifications*; if the clearances are outside the tolerance range, then the pistons must be renewed.

27 Check the fit of the gudgeon pin in the connecting rod bush and in the piston. If there is perceptible play, a new bush or an oversize gudgeon pin must be fitted. Consult a Volvo dealer or engine reconditioning specialist.

28 Examine all components and obtain any new parts required. If new pistons are purchased, they will be supplied complete with gudgeon pins and circlips. Circlips can also be purchased separately.

29 Oil the gudgeon pin. Reassemble the connecting rod and piston, making sure the rod is the right way round as noted during removal, and secure the gudgeon pin with the circlip. Position the circlip so that its opening is facing downward.

30 Repeat these operations for the remaining pistons.

8 Crankshaft – removal and inspection

Note: *If no work is to be done on the pistons and connecting rods, then removal of the cylinder head and pistons will not be necessary. Instead, the pistons need only be pushed far enough up the bores so that they are positioned clear of the crankpins.*

Removal

1 With reference to Part A or B of this Chapter, and earlier Sections of this part as applicable, carry out the following:
 a) *Remove the oil pump.*
 b) *Remove the sump and intermediate section.*
 c) *Remove the clutch components and flywheel/driveplate.*
 d) *Remove the pistons and connecting rods (refer to the Note above).*
2 Before the crankshaft is removed, it is advisable to check the endfloat. To do this, temporarily refit the intermediate section then mount a dial gauge with the stem in line with the crankshaft and just touching the crankshaft **(see illustration)**.
3 Push the crankshaft fully away from the gauge, and zero it. Next, lever the crankshaft towards the gauge as far as possible, and check the reading obtained. The distance that the crankshaft moved is its endfloat; if it is greater than specified, check the crankshaft thrust surfaces for wear. If no wear is evident, new thrustwashers (which are integral with the main bearing shells) should correct the endfloat.
4 Remove the intermediate section again, then lift out the crankshaft. Do not drop it, it is heavy.
5 Remove the upper half main bearing shells from their seats in the crankcase by pressing the end of the shell furthest from the locating tab. Keep all the shells in order.

Inspection

6 Clean the crankshaft using paraffin or a suitable solvent, and dry it, preferably with compressed air if available. Be sure to clean the oil holes with a pipe cleaner or similar probe to ensure that they are not obstructed.

 Warning: Wear eye protection when using compressed air.

7 Check the main and big-end bearing journals for uneven wear, scoring, pitting and cracking.
8 Big-end bearing wear is accompanied by distinct metallic knocking when the engine is running (particularly noticeable when the engine is pulling from low speed) and some loss of oil pressure.
9 Main bearing wear is accompanied by severe engine vibration and rumble – getting progressively worse as engine speed increases – and again by loss of oil pressure.
10 Check the bearing journal for roughness by

8.2 Check the crankshaft endfloat using a dial gauge

running a finger lightly over the bearing surface. Any roughness (which will be accompanied by obvious bearing wear) indicates that the crankshaft requires regrinding (where possible) or renewal.
11 Have the crankshaft measured and inspected by an engine reconditioning specialist. They will be able to advise concerning the availability of undersize bearings, and crankshaft reconditioning.

9 Cylinder block/crankcase – cleaning and inspection

Cleaning

1 Prior to cleaning, remove all external components and senders, and any gallery plugs or caps that may be fitted. Remove the piston cooling valve, and the cooling jets (where applicable) **(see illustrations)**.
2 If any of the castings are extremely dirty, all should be steam-cleaned.
3 After the castings are returned from steam-cleaning, clean all oil holes and oil galleries one more time. Flush all internal passages with warm water until the water runs clear. If you have access to compressed air, use it to speed the drying process, and to blow out all the oil holes and galleries.

 Warning: Wear eye protection when using compressed air.

4 If the castings are not very dirty, you can do an adequate cleaning job with hot soapy

water (as hot as you can stand) and a stiff brush. Take plenty of time, and do a thorough job. Regardless of the cleaning method used, be sure to clean all oil holes and galleries very thoroughly, and to dry all components completely. Apply clean engine oil to the cylinder bores to prevent rusting.
5 The threaded holes in the cylinder block must be clean to ensure accurate torque readings when tightening fixings during reassembly. Carefully run the correct size tap (which can be determined from the size of the relevant bolt which fits in the hole) into each of the holes to remove rust, corrosion, thread sealant or other contamination, and to restore damaged threads. If possible, use compressed air to clear the holes of debris produced by this operation. Do not forget to clean the threads of all bolts and nuts as well.
6 Any threads which cannot be restored in this way can often be reclaimed by the use of thread inserts. If any threaded holes are damaged, consult your dealer or engine overhaul specialist and have them install any thread inserts where necessary.
7 If the engine is not going to be reassembled right away, cover it with a large plastic bag to keep it clean; protect the machined surfaces as described above, to prevent rusting.

Inspection

8 Visually check the castings for cracks and corrosion. Look for stripped threads in the threaded holes. If there has been any history of internal coolant leakage, it may be worthwhile having an engine overhaul specialist check the cylinder block/crankcase for cracks with special equipment. If defects are found, have them repaired, if possible, or renew the assembly.
9 Check the condition of the cylinder head mating face and the intermediate section mating surfaces. Check the surfaces for any possible distortion using the straight-edge and feeler blade method described earlier for cylinder head inspection. If distortion is slight, consult an engine overhaul specialist as to the best course of action.
10 Check each cylinder bore for scuffing and scoring. Check for signs of a wear ridge at the top of the cylinder, indicating that the bore is excessively worn.

9.1a Unscrew the piston cooling valve . . .

9.1b . . . and the piston cooling jets

11 Have the bores inspected and measured by an automotive engine reconditioning specialist. They will be able to advise on possible cylinder reboring and supply appropriate replacement pistons to match.

12 If the bores are in reasonably good condition and not excessively-worn, then it may only be necessary to renew the piston rings.

13 If this is the case, the bores should be honed, to allow the new rings to bed in correctly and provide the best possible seal. Honing is an operation that will be carried out for you by an engine reconditioning specialist.

14 After all machining operations are completed, the entire block/crankcase must be washed very thoroughly with warm soapy water to remove all traces of abrasive grit produced during the machining operations. When the cylinder block/crankcase is completely clean, rinse it thoroughly and dry it, then lightly oil all exposed machined surfaces, to prevent rusting.

15 Refit the piston cooling jets to the base of the cylinder bores, and tighten the retaining bolts to the specified torque.

16 Fit a new sealing washer to the piston cooling oil valve, or apply thread sealing compound to valve threads (as applicable), then refit the valve and tighten it to the specified torque.

10 Main and big-end bearings – inspection and selection

Inspection

1 Even though the main and big-end bearing shells should be renewed during the engine overhaul, the old shells should be retained for close examination, as they may reveal valuable information about the condition of the engine.

2 Bearing failure occurs because of lack of lubrication, the presence of dirt or other foreign particles, overloading the engine, and corrosion **(see illustration)**. Regardless of the cause of bearing failure, the cause must be corrected (where applicable) before the engine is reassembled, to prevent it from happening again.

3 When examining the bearing shells, remove them from the cylinder block/crankcase and main bearing caps, and from the connecting rods and the big-end bearing caps, then lay them out on a clean surface in the same general position as their location in the engine. This will enable you to match any bearing problems with the corresponding crankshaft journal. *Do not* touch any of the shell's bearing surface with your fingers while checking it, or the delicate surface may be scratched.

4 Dirt or other foreign matter gets into the engine in a variety of ways. It may be left in the engine during assembly, or it may pass through filters or the crankcase ventilation system. It may get into the oil, and from there

into the bearings. Metal chips from machining operations and normal engine wear are often present. Abrasives are sometimes left in engine components after reconditioning, especially when parts are not thoroughly cleaned using the proper cleaning methods.

5 Whatever the source, any foreign objects often end up embedded in the soft bearing material, and are easily recognised. Large particles will not embed in the material, and will score or gouge the shell and journal. The best prevention for this cause of bearing failure is to clean all parts thoroughly, and to keep everything spotlessly-clean during engine assembly. Frequent and regular engine oil and filter changes are also recommended.

6 Lack of lubrication (or lubrication breakdown) has a number of inter-related causes. Excessive heat (which thins the oil), overloading (which squeezes the oil from the bearing face) and oil leakage (from excessive bearing clearances, worn oil pump or high engine speeds) all contribute to lubrication breakdown. Blocked oil passages, which usually are the result of misaligned oil holes in a bearing shell, will also starve a bearing of oil, and destroy it.

7 When lack of lubrication is the cause of bearing failure, the bearing material is wiped or extruded from the shell's steel backing. Temperatures may increase to the point where the steel backing turns blue from overheating.

8 Driving habits can have a definite effect on bearing life. Full-throttle, low-speed operation (labouring the engine) puts very high loads on bearings, which tends to squeeze out the oil film. These loads cause the shells to flex, which produces fine cracks in the bearing face (fatigue failure). Eventually, the bearing material will loosen in pieces, and tear away from the steel backing.

9 Short-distance driving leads to corrosion of bearings, because insufficient engine heat is

produced to drive off condensed water and corrosive gases. These products collect in the engine oil, forming acid and sludge. As the oil is carried to the engine bearings, the acid attacks and corrodes the bearing material.

10 Incorrect shell refitting during engine assembly will lead to bearing failure as well. Tight-fitting shells leave insufficient bearing running clearance, and will result in oil starvation. Dirt or foreign particles trapped behind a bearing shell result in high spots on the bearing, which lead to failure.

11 *Do not* touch any shell's bearing surface with your fingers during reassembly; there is a risk of scratching the delicate surface, or of depositing particles of dirt on it.

Bearing selection

12 Have the crankshaft measured and examined by an automotive engine reconditioning specialist, who will be able to supply the appropriate bearing shells.

11 Engine overhaul – reassembly sequence

1 Before reassembly begins, ensure that all new parts have been obtained and that all necessary tools are available. Read through the entire procedure to familiarise yourself with the work involved, and to ensure that all items necessary for reassembly of the engine are at hand. In addition to all normal tools and materials, thread-locking compound will be needed in most areas during engine reassembly. A tube of Volvo liquid gasket solution together with a short-haired application roller will also be needed to assemble the main engine sections.

2 In order to save time and avoid problems, engine reassembly can be carried out in the following order:
   a) Crankshaft.
   b) Intermediate section.
   c) Pistons/connecting rods.
   d) Sump.
   e) Oil pump.
   f) Flywheel/driveplate.
   g) Cylinder head.
   h) Camshaft and tappets.
   i) Timing belt, tensioner, sprockets and idler pulleys.
   j) Engine external components.

3 At this stage, all engine components should be absolutely clean and dry, with all faults repaired. The components should be laid out (or in individual containers) on a completely clean work surface.

12 Crankshaft – refitting

1 Crankshaft refitting is the first stage of engine reassembly following overhaul. It

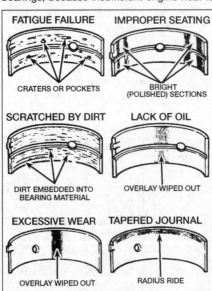

10.2 Typical bearing failures

FATIGUE FAILURE — CRATERS OR POCKETS

IMPROPER SEATING — BRIGHT (POLISHED) SECTIONS

SCRATCHED BY DIRT — DIRT EMBEDDED INTO BEARING MATERIAL

LACK OF OIL — OVERLAY WIPED OUT

EXCESSIVE WEAR — OVERLAY WIPED OUT

TAPERED JOURNAL — RADIUS RIDE

H 28395

is assumed at this point that the cylinder block/crankcase and crankshaft have been cleaned, inspected and repaired or reconditioned as necessary, and the piston cooling jets and valve have been refitted. Position the cylinder block on a clean level work surface, with the crankcase facing upwards.

2 If they're still in place, remove the old bearing shells from the block and the intermediate section.

3 Wipe clean the main bearing shell seats in the crankcase and clean the backs of the new bearing shells. Insert the previously-selected upper shells into their correct position in the crankcase. Note the shells incorporating the thrustwashers must be fitted to the No 5 bearing position. Press the shells home so that the tangs engage in the recesses provided. Note the thicker of the two shells must be fitted to the intermediate section.

4 Liberally lubricate the bearing shells in the crankcase with clean engine oil.

5 Wipe clean the crankshaft journals, then lower the crankshaft into position. Make sure that the shells are not displaced.

6 Inject oil into the crankshaft oilways, then wipe any traces of excess oil from the crankshaft and intermediate section mating faces.

7 Using the short-haired application roller, apply an even coating of Volvo liquid gasket solution (No 11 61 059) to the cylinder block mating face of the intermediate section. Ensure that the whole surface is covered, but note that a thin coating is sufficient for a good seal.

8 Wipe clean the main bearing shell seats in the intermediate section and clean the backs of the bearing shells. Insert the previously-selected lower shells into their correct position in the intermediate section. Press the shells home so that the tangs engage in the recesses provided.

9 Lightly lubricate the bearing shells in the intermediate section, but take care to keep the oil away from the liquid gasket solution.

10 Lay the intermediate section on the crankshaft and cylinder block, and insert the retaining bolts. Tighten the bolts in the five stages listed in the *Specifications*, to the specified torque and torque angle, starting from the outside in **(see illustration)**.

11 Rotate the crankshaft. Slight resistance is to be expected with new components, but there must be no tight spots or binding.

12 It is a good idea at this stage to once again check the crankshaft endfloat as described in Section 8. If the thrust surfaces of the crankshaft have been checked and new bearing shells have been fitted, then the endfloat should be within specification.

13 Lubricate the oil seal location, the crankshaft, and a new oil seal. Fit the seal, lips inwards, and use a piece of tube (or the old seal, inverted) to tap it into place until flush.

13 Pistons and piston rings – assembly

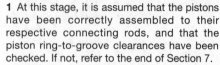

1 At this stage, it is assumed that the pistons have been correctly assembled to their respective connecting rods, and that the piston ring-to-groove clearances have been checked. If not, refer to the end of Section 7.

2 Before the rings can be fitted to the pistons, the end gaps must be checked with the rings inserted into the cylinder bores.

3 Lay out the piston assemblies and the new ring sets so the components are kept together in their groups, during and after end gap checking. Position the cylinder block on the work surface, on its side, allowing access to the top and bottom of the bores.

4 Take the No 1 piston top ring and insert it into the top of the first cylinder. Push it down the bore using the top of the piston; this will ensure that the ring remains square with the cylinder walls. Position the ring near the bottom of the cylinder bore, at the lower limit of ring travel. Note that the top and second compression rings are different. The second ring is easily identified by the step on its lower surface.

5 Measure the ring gap using feeler blades.

6 Repeat the procedure with the ring at the top of the cylinder bore, at the upper limit of its travel, and compare the measurements with the figures given in the *Specifications*.

7 If new rings are being fitted, it is unlikely that the end gaps will be too small. If a measurement is found to be undersize, it must be corrected, or there is the risk that

the ring ends may contact each other during engine operation, possibly resulting in engine damage. Ideally, new piston rings providing the correct end gap should be fitted; however, as a last resort the end gaps can be increased by filing the ring ends very carefully with a fine file. Mount the ring in a vice equipped with soft jaws, slip the ring over the file with the ends contacting the file face, and slowly move the ring to remove material from the ends. Take care, as piston rings are sharp and are easily broken.

8 It is equally unlikely that the end gap will be too large. If the gaps are too large, check that you have the correct rings for your engine and for the cylinder bore size.

9 Repeat the checking procedure for each ring in the first cylinder, and then for the rings in the remaining cylinders. Remember to keep rings, pistons and cylinders matched up.

10 Once the ring end gaps have been checked and if necessary corrected, the rings can be fitted to the pistons.

11 Fit the piston rings using the same technique as for removal. Fit the bottom scraper ring first, and work up. On petrol engines, the lower oil scraper ring is a 3-part ring – install the spring-like expander ring first, followed by the two plain rings either side. Observe the text markings on one side of the top and bottom rings; this must face upwards when the rings are fitted. The middle ring is bevelled, and the bevel must face downwards when installed **(see illustrations)**. Do not expand the compression rings too far, or they will break. **Note:** *Always follow any instructions supplied with the new piston ring sets – different manufacturers may specify*

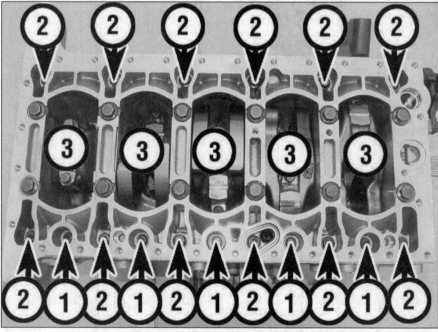

12.10 Intermediate section bolts

1 M7   2 M8   3 M10

different procedures. Do not mix up the top and second compression rings, as they have different cross-sections.

12 When all the rings are in position, arrange the ring gaps 120° apart, with the exception of the 3-part oil scraper ring where the two plain rings should be 90° apart from each other.

14 Pistons and connecting rod assemblies – refitting

1 Before refitting the piston/connecting rod assemblies, the cylinder bores must be perfectly clean, and the crankshaft and intermediate section must be in place.

2 Remove the big-end bearing cap from No 1 cylinder connecting rod (refer to the marks noted or made on removal). Remove the original bearing shells, and wipe the bearing recesses of the connecting rod and cap with a clean, lint-free cloth. They must be kept spotlessly-clean. Ensure that new big-end bearing cap retaining bolts are available.

3 Clean the back of the new upper bearing shell, fit it to No 1 connecting rod, then fit the other shell of the bearing to the big-end bearing cap. Note that shell with the black-coloured size marker on its edge must be fitted to the connecting rod. On 'fractured' type rods and caps, no locating notch for the bearing shell tab is provided. On these rods/caps, simply position the shells as centrally as possible. Where tabs and notches are provided, make sure the tab on each shell fits into the notch in the rod or cap recess.

4 Position the piston ring gaps in their correct positions around the piston, lubricate the piston and rings with clean engine oil, and attach a piston ring compressor to the piston. Leave the skirt protruding slightly, to guide the piston into the cylinder bore. The rings must be compressed until they're flush with the piston.

5 Rotate the crankshaft until No 1 big-end journal is at BDC (Bottom Dead Centre), and apply a coat of engine oil to the cylinder walls.

6 Arrange the No 1 piston/connecting rod assembly so that the arrow on the piston crown points to the timing belt end of the engine (petrol engines), or the channel in the base of the piston aligns with the piston cooling jet at the base of the cylinder bore. Gently insert the assembly into the No 1 cylinder bore, and rest the bottom edge of the ring compressor on the engine block.

7 Tap the top edge of the ring compressor to make sure it's contacting the block around its entire circumference.

8 Gently tap on the top of the piston with the end of a wooden hammer handle while guiding the connecting rod big-end onto the crankpin. The piston rings may try to pop out of the ring compressor just before entering the cylinder bore, so keep some pressure on the ring compressor. Work slowly, and if any resistance is felt as the piston enters the cylinder, stop immediately. Find out what is binding, and fix it before proceeding. *Do not*, for any reason, force the piston into the cylinder – you might break a ring and/or the piston. Take great care not to damage the piston cooling jets.

9 Make sure the bearing surfaces are perfectly clean, then apply a uniform layer of clean engine oil, to both of them. You may have to push the piston back up the cylinder bore slightly to expose the bearing surface of the shell in the connecting rod.

10 Slide the connecting rod back into place on the big-end journal, refit the big-end bearing cap. Lubricate the bolt threads, fit the bolts and tighten them in two stages to the specified torque.

11 Repeat the entire procedure for the remaining piston/connecting rod assemblies.

12 The important points to remember are:

a) *Keep the backs of the bearing shells and the recesses of the connecting rods and caps perfectly clean when assembling them.*

b) *Make sure you have the correct piston/rod assembly for each cylinder.*

c) *The arrow on the piston crown must face the camshaft drivebelt end of the engine (petrol engines), or the channel in the base of the piston must align with the piston cooling jet.*

d) *Lubricate the cylinder bores with clean engine oil.*

e) *Lubricate the bearing surfaces before fitting the big-end bearing caps.*

13 After all the piston/connecting rod assemblies have been properly installed, rotate the crankshaft a number of times by hand, to check for any obvious binding.

Diesel engines

14 If new pistons, connecting rods, or crankshaft are fitted, or if a new short engine is installed, the projection of the piston crowns above the cylinder head surface at TDC must be measured, to determine the correct head gasket required.

15 Fit the sump as described in Section 15.

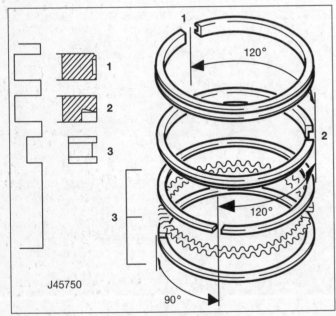

J45750

13.11a Piston ring details – petrol models

1 *Top compression ring*
2 *2nd compression ring*
3 *Oil scraper ring assembly*

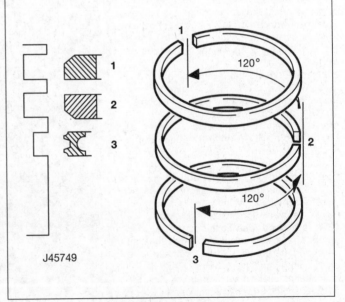

J45749

13.11b Piston ring details – diesel models

1 *Top compression ring*
2 *2nd compression ring*
3 *Oil scraper ring*

14.16 Measure the piston protrusion using a dial gauge

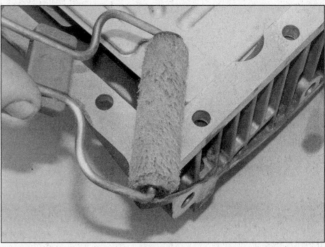

15.3 Apply sealant to the sump mating face using a short-haired roller

16 Anchor a DTI gauge to the cylinder block, and zero it on the head gasket mating surface. Rest the gauge probe on No 1 piston crown and turn the crankshaft slowly by hand so that the piston reaches TDC (Top Dead Centre). Measure and record the maximum projection at TDC **(see illustration)**.

17 Repeat the measurement for the remaining pistons and record.

18 If the measurements differ from piston to piston, take the highest figure and use this to determine the head gasket type required – refer to the *Specifications* for details.

15 Sump – refitting

1 Place a new O-ring on the oil pick-up pipe, and insert the pipe into its location. Secure with the bracket retaining bolt tightened to the specified torque where given.

2 Wipe off any oil smears from the sump and intermediate section joint faces, then locate new O-rings in the recesses in the intermediate section.

3 Using the short-haired application roller, apply an even coating of Volvo liquid gasket solution to the sump mating face **(see illustration)**. Ensure that the whole surface is covered, but note that a thin coating is sufficient for a good seal.

4 Place the sump in position, and insert four of the retaining bolts, tightened finger-tight only.

5 Using a straight edge, ensure that the rear edges of the sump and cylinder block are flush, then tighten the four bolts to just hold the sump in position.

6 Refit the remaining bolts and tighten them in pairs, starting from the transmission end, to the specified torque.

7 On completion, where applicable, refit the oil cooler to the rear face of the sump, tightening the retaining bolts securely. Also check that the coolant hoses are undamaged, and the hose clamps secure.

16 Engine – initial start-up after overhaul and reassembly

1 Refit the remainder of the engine components in the order listed in Section 11, with reference to the relevant Sections of this part of Chapter 2, and Part A or B. Refit the engine and transmission to the vehicle as described in Section 3 of this Part. Double-check the engine oil and coolant levels and make a final check that everything has been reconnected. Make sure that there are no tools or rags left in the engine compartment.

2 Remove the spark plugs and disable the ignition system by disconnecting the camshaft position sensor wiring at the connector. Disconnect the fuel injector wiring connectors to prevent fuel being injected into the cylinders.

3 Turn the engine over on the starter motor until the oil pressure warning light goes out.

If the light fails to extinguish after several seconds of cranking, check the engine oil level and that the oil filter is fitted securely. Assuming these are correct, check the security of the oil pressure sensor wiring – do not progress any further until you are sure that oil is being pumped around the engine at sufficient pressure.

4 Refit the spark plugs and ignition wiring (ignition coils and wiring), and reconnect the camshaft position sensor and fuel injector wiring connectors.

5 Start the engine, noting that this also may take a little longer than usual, due to the fuel system components being empty.

6 While the engine is idling, check for fuel, coolant and oil leaks. Don't be alarmed if there are some odd smells and smoke from parts getting hot and burning off oil deposits. Note also that it may initially be a little noisy until the hydraulic tappets fill with oil.

7 Keep the engine idling until hot water is felt circulating through the top hose, check that it idles reasonably smoothly and at the usual speed, then switch it off.

8 After a few minutes, recheck the oil and coolant levels, and top-up as necessary (see the relevant Part of Chapter 1).

9 If new components such as pistons, rings or crankshaft bearings have been fitted, the engine must be run-in for the first 500 miles. Do not operate the engine at full-throttle, or allow it to labour in any gear during this period. It is recommended that the oil and filter be changed at the end of this period.

Notes

Chapter 3
Cooling, heating and air conditioning systems

Contents

Degrees of difficulty

Easy, suitable for novice with little experience	**Fairly easy,** suitable for beginner with some experience	**Fairly difficult,** suitable for competent DIY mechanic	**Difficult,** suitable for experienced DIY mechanic	**Very difficult,** suitable for expert DIY or professional

Specifications

General
System type	Water-based coolant, pump-assisted circulation, thermostatically controlled

Thermostat
Opening commences	90°C
Fully open at	105°C

Coolant temperature sensor
Resistance at (all values are approximate):

-20°C	15 040 ohms
0°C	5740 ohms
10°C	3700 ohms
20°C	2450 ohms
30°C	1660 ohms
40°C	1150 ohms
50°C	811 ohms
60°C	584 ohms
70°C	428 ohms
80°C	318 ohms

Torque wrench settings

	Nm	lbf ft
Auxiliary heater glow plugs	15	11
Compressor mounting bolts	24	18
Coolant pump bolts	17	13
Coolant temperature sensor*	22	16
Expansion valve screws	10	7
Front subframe mounting bolt*:		
Stage 1	105	77
Stage 2	Angle-tighten a further 120°	
Thermostat housing:		
Petrol models	Not available	
Diesel models	17	13

* Do not re-use

1 General information and precautions

General information

The cooling system is of pressurised semi-sealed type with the inclusion of an expansion tank to accept coolant displaced from the system when hot and to return it when the system cools.

Water-based coolant is circulated around the cylinder block and head by the coolant pump which is driven by the engine timing belt. As the coolant circulates around the engine it absorbs heat as it flows then, when hot, it travels out into the radiator to pass across the matrix. As the coolant flows across the radiator matrix, airflow created by the forward motion of the vehicle cools it, and it returns to the cylinder block. Airflow through the radiator matrix is assisted by a two-speed electric fan, which is controlled by the engine management system ECM.

A thermostat is fitted to control coolant flow through the radiator. When the engine is cold, the thermostat valve remains closed so that the coolant flow which occurs at normal operating temperatures through the radiator matrix is interrupted.

As the coolant warms-up, the thermostat valve starts to open and allows the coolant flow through the radiator to resume.

The engine temperature will always be maintained at a constant level (according to the thermostat rating) whatever the ambient air temperature.

Most models have an oil cooler mounted on the rear of the sump – this is basically a heat exchanger with a coolant supply, to take heat away from the oil in the sump.

The vehicle interior heater operates by means of coolant from the engine cooling system. Coolant flow through the heater matrix is constant; temperature control being achieved by blending cool air from outside the vehicle with the warm air from the heater matrix in the desired ratio.

Air entering the passenger compartment is filtered by a pleated paper filter element, sometimes known as a pollen filter. Also available instead of a pollen filer is a multi-filter, which is a carbon impregnated filter which absorbs incoming smells, etc. With this system a pollution sensor monitors the quality of the incoming air, and opens and closes the recirculation flaps accordingly.

The standard climate control (air conditioning) systems are described in detail in Section 9.

Available as options are additional electric and fuel-fired cabin and engine block heaters. These can be remotely operated, or programmed to operate for a suitable period before the vehicle is required.

Precautions

 Warning: Do not attempt to remove the expansion tank filler cap, or to disturb any part of the cooling system, while it or the engine is hot, as there is a very great risk of scalding. If the expansion tank filler cap must be removed before the engine and radiator have fully cooled down (even though this is not recommended) the pressure in the cooling system must first be released. Cover the cap with a thick layer of cloth, to avoid scalding, and slowly unscrew the filler cap until a hissing sound can be heard. When the hissing has stopped, showing that pressure is released, slowly unscrew the filler cap further until it can be removed; if more hissing sounds are heard, wait until they have stopped before unscrewing the cap completely. At all times, keep well away from the filler opening.

 Warning: Do not allow antifreeze to come in contact with your skin, or with the painted surfaces of the vehicle. Rinse off spills immediately with plenty of water. Never leave antifreeze lying around in an open container, or in a puddle in the driveway or on the garage floor. Children and pets are attracted by its sweet smell, but antifreeze is fatal if ingested.

Warning: Refer to Section 9 for precautions to be observed when working on vehicles equipped with air conditioning.

2 Cooling system hoses – disconnection and renewal

Note: *Refer to the warnings given in Section 1 of this Chapter before proceeding. Hoses should only be disconnected once the engine has cooled sufficiently to avoid scalding.*

1 If the checks described in Chapter 1A or 1B reveal a faulty hose, it must be renewed as follows.

2 First drain the cooling system (see Chapter 1A or 1B); if the antifreeze is not due for renewal, the drained coolant may be re-used, if it is collected in a clean container.

2.3 Use a screwdriver to slacken screw-type clamps

3 To disconnect any hose, use a pair of pliers to release the spring clamps (or a screwdriver to slacken screw-type clamps), then move them along the hose clear of the union **(see illustration)**. Carefully work the hose off its stubs. The hoses can be removed with relative ease when new – on an older vehicle they may have stuck.

4 If a hose proves to be difficult to remove, try to release it by rotating it on its unions before attempting to work it off. Gently prise the end of the hose with a blunt instrument (such as a flat-bladed screwdriver), but do not apply too much force, and take care not to damage the pipe stubs or hoses. Note in particular that the radiator hose unions are fragile; do not use excessive force when attempting to remove the hoses.

> **HAYNES HiNT** *If all else fails, cut the hose with a sharp knife, then slit it so that it can be peeled off in two pieces. Although this may prove expensive if the hose is otherwise undamaged, it is preferable to buying a new radiator.*

5 When refitting a hose, first slide the clamps onto the hose, then engage the hose with its unions. Work the hose into position, then check that the hose is settled correctly and is properly routed. Slide each clip along the hose until it is behind the union flared end before tightening it securely.

> **HAYNES HiNT** *If the hose is stiff, use a little soapy water as a lubricant, or soften the hose by soaking it in hot water. Do not use oil or grease, which may attack the rubber.*

6 Refill the system with coolant (Chapter 1A or 1B).

7 Check carefully for leaks as soon as possible after disturbing any part of the cooling system.

3 Antifreeze – general information

Note: *Refer to the warnings given in Section 1 of this Chapter before proceeding.*

1 The cooling system should be filled with Volvo antifreeze in a ratio of 50/50 with pure water. At this strength, the coolant will protect against freezing down to -35°C. Antifreeze also provides protection against corrosion, and increases the coolant boiling point. As the engine is of all-aluminium construction, the corrosion protection properties of the antifreeze are critical. Only Volvo antifreeze should be used in the system, and should never be mixed with different antifreeze types.

2 The cooling system should be maintained according to the schedule described in

4.1a Twist up and remove the air intake pipe – early models

4.1b Push-in the centre pin, prise out the plastic rivet (arrowed) and pull the intake flap assembly – late models

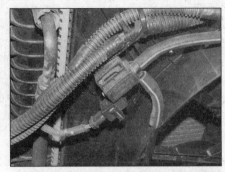

4.2 Detach the carbon canister purge valve from the fan shroud – petrol models only

Chapter 1A or 1B. If antifreeze is used that is not to Volvo's specification, old or contaminated coolant mixtures are likely to cause damage, and encourage the formation of corrosion and scale in the system.

3 Before adding antifreeze, check all hoses and hose connections, because antifreeze tends to leak through very small openings. Engines don't normally consume coolant, so if the level goes down, find the cause and correct it.

4 The specified mixture is 50% antifreeze and 50% clean soft water (by volume). Mix the required quantity in a clean container and then fill the system as described in Chapter 1A or 1B and *Weekly checks*. Save any surplus mixture for topping-up.

4.7a Disconnect the cooling fan wiring plug (arrowed) – early models . . .

4.7b . . . and late models (arrowed)

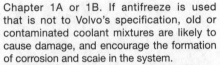

4 Radiator cooling fan – removal and refitting

Removal

1 Disconnect the air intake pipe from the connection above the radiator, by twisting the pipe up (see illustrations).

2 On petrol models, detach the carbon canister purge valve from the radiator shroud (see illustration).

3 On turbocharged engines, release the clamps and remove the charge air pipe/hose on the right-hand side. In cold weather use a hot air gun to soften the pipe/hose prior to removal.

4 Detach the boost pressure sensor from the front plate (petrol turbocharged models only).

5 On all models, release the wiring looms

from the upper part, and the right-hand side of the fan shroud.

6 Lift the coolant expansion hose from the clips at the top of the fan shroud.

7 Disconnect the fan motor wiring plugs (see illustrations).

4.8a Undo the cooling fan shroud bolt (arrowed) each side . . .

8 Undo the fan shroud retaining screws, and lift the shroud and fan assembly up from position (see illustrations).

9 Release the cable and connector from the shroud, then undo the screws, and remove the fan motor and control unit (see illustrations).

4.8b . . . and lift the cooling fan shroud from place

4.9a Fan motor . . .

4.9b . . . and control unit – early models

4.9c Fan motor and control unit – later models

5.3 Disconnect the charge air pipes from the intercooler (turbocharged models only)

5.4a Disconnect the upper hose . . .

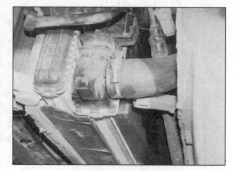
5.4b . . . and lower hose

5.5 Radiator screws (arrowed)

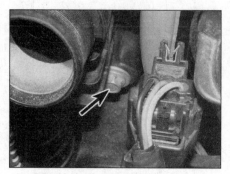
5.6a Undo the upper bolts on the right-hand side (arrowed) . . .

5.6b . . . and on the left-hand side (arrowed)

Refitting

10 Refitting is the reversal of removal. Align the shroud with the holes at the side of the radiator.

5 Radiator – removal and refitting

HAYNES HiNT *If leakage is the reason for wanting to remove the radiator, bear in mind that minor leaks can often be cured using a radiator sealant with the radiator in situ.*

Removal

1 Drain the cooling system (see Chapter 1A or 1B).
2 Remove the radiator cooling fan as described in Section 4.
3 On turbocharged engines, release the clamps and disconnect the charge air pipes from the intercooler **(see illustration)**.
4 On all models, release the clamps and disconnect the radiator upper and lower hoses **(see illustrations)**.
5 Undo the screws securing the radiator to the bonnet slam panel **(see illustration)**.
6 Undo the two upper radiator retaining screws **(see illustrations)**.
7 Working underneath the vehicle, undo the bolts, release the clips and remove the

air baffle assembly under the radiator **(see illustrations)**.
8 On automatic transmission models, disconnect the fluid cooler lines from the radiator left-hand side tank. Be prepared for fluid spillage **(see illustration)**. Plug or cap the lines to keep dirt out.
9 Reach up from underneath and disconnect the wiring plug from the pressure switch on the top of the air conditioning receiver, and the wiring harness from the holder on the right-hand side of the radiator.
10 Secure the condenser to the vehicle body using cable ties (or similar).
11 Undo the two retaining screws at the lower edge of the radiator **(see illustrations)**.
12 Undo the screw each side securing the

5.7a Working through the wheel arch, undo the bolt (arrowed) each side securing the air baffle (shown with the bumper removed) . . .

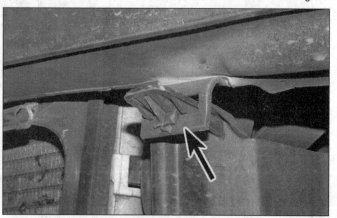
5.7b . . . then reach up and release the clip (arrowed) each side at the front of the air baffle

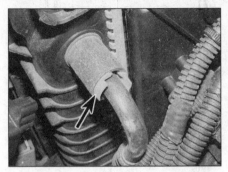

5.8 Prise out the collar (arrowed) and disconnect the cooler pipe

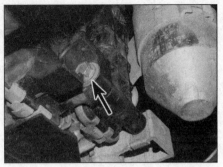

5.11a Undo the bolt (arrowed) on the lower right-hand side . . .

5.11b . . . and the left-hand side (arrowed)

5.12a Undo the mounting bolt (arrowed) on the right-hand side (viewed from underneath) . . .

5.12b . . . and the left-hand side (arrowed)

radiator and intercooler (where fitted), and manoeuvre the radiator (and intercooler where applicable) downwards. Release the clamp and disconnect the expansion tank hose as the radiator is withdrawn **(see illustrations)**. **Note:** *Where metal crimp type hose clamps are fitted, update them with traditional worm-drive type clamps.*

Refitting

13 Refit by reversing the removal operations. With reference to Chapter 1A or 1B, refill the cooling system on completion, and where applicable top-up the automatic transmission fluid and engine oil.

---

6 Coolant temperature sensor – testing, removal and refitting

Testing

1 The coolant temperature sensor is located in the thermostat housing, and is used by both the engine management system and the instrument panel temperature gauge to supply an engine temperature source signal.
2 In the event of a fault in the sensor, or a loss of signal due to poor electrical connections, a fault code will be logged in the engine management system ECM, which can be read out via the diagnostic connector in the centre console (using a suitable fault code reader).
3 Should a fault code be logged, a careful check should be made of the sensor wiring

and the wiring connector. Apart from testing by substitution with a new unit, further checks require the use of Volvo test equipment and should be entrusted to a dealer or suitably-equipped specialist.

Removal

4 Partially drain the cooling system (see Chapter 1A or 1B) to below the level of the sensor unit (approximately 2.0 litres).

Petrol models up to and including 2001 model year

5 Remove the two Torx bolts, and lift off the thermostat housing cover.
6 Disconnect the wiring at the adjacent connector, then unscrew the sensor from its location in the thermostat housing **(see illustrations)**. Where fitted, discard the sensor seal – a new one must be fitted.

Petrol models from 2002 model year

7 Undo the clips/screws and remove the upper timing belt cover, and disconnect the sensor wiring plug.
8 Remove the sensor from the thermostat housing. Where fitted, discard the sensor seal – a new one must be fitted.

Diesel models

9 Pull the plastic cover on the top of the engine straight up and remove it from the engine compartment.
10 Disconnect the wiring plug, then unscrew the sensor from the housing **(see illustration)**. Where fitted, discard the seal – a new one must be fitted.

Refitting

11 Screw in the new sensor unit, using a

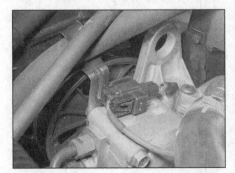

6.6a Disconnect the temperature sensor wiring plug above the power steering pump

6.6b Coolant temperature sensor (arrowed)

6.10 Unscrew the coolant temperature sensor from the housing (arrowed)

7.3a Undo the coolant pump bolts

7.3b Note the locating dowels (arrowed)

smear of sealant on the threads or new seal as applicable. Reconnect the wiring connector. Refit the thermostat housing, tightening the screws securely, and reconnect the radiator hose or refit the timing belt cover/engine cover as applicable..

12 Top-up the coolant level as described in *Weekly checks*.

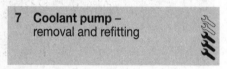

7 Coolant pump – removal and refitting

Note: *Refer to the warnings given in Section 1 of this Chapter before proceeding.*

Removal

1 Drain the cooling system as described in Chapter 1A or 1B.

2 Refer to the relevant Part of Chapter 2 and remove the timing belt. To improve access, it may also be necessary to loosen some of the timing belt rear cover fasteners.

3 Undo the bolts, and remove the coolant pump from its locating dowels **(see illustration)**. Access is very limited, and patience is needed. Recover the gasket after removing the pump.

4 Thoroughly clean all traces of old gasket from the pump and cylinder block mating faces.

Refitting

5 Using a new gasket, locate the pump in position.

6 Apply a little thread-locking compound,

then tighten the bolts progressively and in a diagonal sequence to the specified torque.

7 Refit the timing belt as described in Chapter 2, and top-up the coolant as described in Chapter 1A or 1B.

8 Thermostat – removal, testing and refitting

1 As the thermostat ages, it will become slower to react to changes in water temperature. Ultimately, the unit may stick in the open or closed position, and this causes problems. A thermostat which is stuck open will result in a very slow warm-up; a thermostat which is stuck shut will lead to rapid overheating.

2 Before assuming the thermostat is to blame for a cooling system problem, check the coolant level. If the system is draining due to a leak, or has not been properly filled, there may be an airlock in the system (see Chapter 1A or 1B).

3 If the engine seems to be taking a long time to warm up (based on heater output or temperature gauge operation), the thermostat is probably stuck open.

4 Equally, a lengthy warm-up period might suggest that the thermostat is missing – it may have been removed or inadvertently omitted by a previous owner or mechanic. Don't drive the vehicle without a thermostat – the engine management system's ECM will then stay in warm-up mode for longer than necessary, causing emissions and fuel economy to suffer.

5 If the engine runs hot, use your hand to check the temperature of the radiator top

hose. If the hose isn't hot, but the engine is, the thermostat is probably stuck closed, preventing the coolant inside the engine from escaping to the radiator – renew the thermostat. Again, this problem may also be due to an airlock (see Chapter 1A or 1B).

6 If the radiator top hose is hot, it means that the coolant is flowing and the thermostat is open. Consult the *Fault diagnosis* section at the end of this manual to assist in tracing possible cooling system faults.

7 To gain a rough idea of whether the thermostat is working properly when the engine is warming-up, without dismantling the system, proceed as follows.

8 With the engine completely cold, start the engine and let it idle, while checking the temperature of the radiator top hose. Periodically check the temperature indicated on the coolant temperature gauge – if overheating is indicated, switch the engine off immediately.

9 The top hose should feel cold for some time as the engine warms up, and should then get warm quite quickly as the thermostat opens.

10 The above is not a precise or definitive test of thermostat operation, but if the system does not perform as described, remove and test the thermostat as described below.

Removal

Note: *Refer to the warnings given in Section 1 of this Chapter before proceeding.*

11 The engine must be completely cold before starting this procedure – the engine should have been switched off for several hours, and ideally left to cool overnight.

12 Partially drain the cooling system (see Chapter 1A or 1B) to below the level of the thermostat housing (approximately 2.0 litres).

13 On diesel models, pull the plastic engine cover straight up and remove it from the engine compartment.

Models with 'horizontal' thermostat

14 Release the radiator top hose and expansion tank hose from the thermostat housing.

15 Release the clips/undo the screws and remove the timing belt upper cover.

16 Undo the two cover retaining bolts **(see illustration)**.

17 Lift off the cover, and remove the thermostat and sealing ring **(see illustrations)**.

8.16 Thermostat cover bolts (arrowed – horizontal thermostat)

8.17a Lift off the thermostat cover . . .

8.17b . . . and remove the thermostat

Models with 'vertical' thermostat

18 Remove the timing belt upper cover, and disconnect the engine coolant sensor wiring plug.

19 Remove the auxiliary drivebelt as described in Chapter 1A or 1B.

20 Use a hose clamp on the power steering fluid supply hose, then disconnect the hose from the pump.

21 Undo the bolts and move the power steering pump to one side, see Chapter 10.

22 Undo the bolts and remove the thermostat housing (see illustration).

23 Undo the bolts and remove the thermostat cover, followed by the thermostat. Note the fitted position of the thermostat (see illustrations). Discard the gasket.

Testing

Note: *Frankly, if there is any question about the operation of the thermostat, it's best to renew it – they are not usually expensive items. Testing involves heating in, or over, an open pan of boiling water, which carries with it the risk of scalding. A thermostat which has seen more than five years' service may well be past its best already.*

24 Check the temperature marking stamped on the thermostat, which will typically be 90°C.

25 Using a thermometer and container of water, heat the water until the temperature corresponds with the temperature marking stamped on the thermostat.

26 Suspend the (closed) thermostat on a length of string in the water, and check that maximum opening occurs within two minutes.

27 Remove the thermostat and allow it to cool down; check that it closes fully.

28 If the thermostat does not open and close as described, or if it sticks in either position, it must be renewed.

Refitting

29 Fit a new sealing ring/gasket to the thermostat/cover, and refit the thermostat and cover, tightening the bolts securely.

8.22 The lower thermostat housing bolt is accessible through a hole in the power steering pump bracket

30 Refit the thermostat housing (where applicable) and secure with the two bolts.

31 The remainder of refitting is a reversal of removal. Top-up the cooling system as described in Chapter 1A or 1B.

9 Heating, ventilation and air conditioning systems – general information and precautions

Manual climate control system

1 On models equipped with a manual climate control system, the heater system may be fitted in conjunction with a manually-controlled air conditioning unit.

2 The heater is of the fresh air type. Air enters through a grille in front of the windscreen, and passes to the various vents, a variable proportion of the air passes through the heater matrix, where it is warmed by engine coolant flowing through the matrix.

3 Distribution of air to the vents, and through or around the matrix, is controlled by flaps. These are operated by an electric motor. Separate temperature controls are provided for the driver and front passenger, and these are cable-operated.

4 A variable speed electric fan is fitted to boost the airflow through the heater with a pollen/pollution filter fitted after the fan.

5 The air conditioning system works in conjunction with the heater to enable any reasonable air temperature to be achieved inside the car. It also reduces the humidity of the incoming air, aiding demisting even when cooling is not required.

6 The refrigeration side of the air conditioning system functions in a similar way to a domestic refrigerator. A compressor, belt-driven from the crankshaft pulley, draws refrigerant in its gaseous phase from an evaporator. The compound refrigerant passes through a condenser where it loses heat and enters its liquid phase. After dehydration the refrigerant returns to the evaporator where it absorbs heat from air passing over the evaporator fins. The refrigerant becomes a gas again and the cycle is repeated.

7 Various subsidiary controls and sensors protect the system against excessive temperature and pressures. Additionally, engine idle speed is increased when the system is in use, to compensate for the additional load imposed by the compressor.

Automatic climate control system

8 On models with automatic climate control, the temperature inside the car can be automatically maintained at the level selected by the operator, irrespective of outside temperature. The computer-controlled system operates the heater, air conditioner and fan functions as necessary to achieve this. The refrigeration side of the system is the same as for models with manual climate control; the fully automatic electronic control operates as follows.

9 An electronic control module (ECM) receives signal inputs from sensors that detect the air duct temperatures on the driver's and passenger's side, interior temperature on the driver's and passenger's side. A solar sensor is used to detect the presence of sunlight.

8.23a The thermostat locates on the 'bridge' (arrowed) in the housing

8.23b The 'bleed valve' (arrowed) must be at the top

9.13a The air conditioning refrigerant circuit high- and low-pressure service ports are located on the right-hand side of the bonnet slam panel (arrowed) . . .

9.13b . . . and adjacent to the timing cover (arrowed)

Many car accessory shops sell one-shot air conditioning recharge aerosols. These generally contain refrigerant, compressor oil, leak sealer and system conditioner. Some also have a dye to help pinpoint leaks.

⚠️ *Warning: These products must only be used as directed by the manufacturer, and do not remove the need for regular maintenance.*

Signals are also received from the dampers (air flaps) on their position at any given time. Information on engine temperature, outside temperature, whether or not the engine is running, and if so, the vehicle roadspeed, are also sent to the ECM from the engine management system.

10 When the automatic function is engaged, the ECM can establish the optimum settings needed, based on the sensor signals, for the selected temperature and air distribution. These settings can then be maintained irrespective of driving conditions and weather.

11 Distribution of air to the various vents, and the blending of hot or cold air to achieve the selected temperature, are controlled by dampers (flaps). These are operated by electric motors, which are in turn controlled by

the ECM. A variable speed fan which can be manually or automatically controlled is used to boost airflow through the system.

12 Should a fault occur, the ECM stores a series of fault codes for subsequent read-out via the diagnostic connector located in the lower facia panel above the driver's pedals.

Precautions

13 When an air conditioning system is fitted, it is necessary to observe special precautions whenever dealing with any part of the system, or its associated components. If for any reason the system must be discharged, entrust this task to your Volvo dealer or a refrigeration engineer. The air conditioning system high- and low-pressure service ports are located in the engine compartment, on the right-hand side of the bonnet slam panel, and

the right-hand chassis leg, adjacent to the timing belt cover **(see illustrations)**.

⚠️ *Warning: The refrigeration circuit contains R134a liquid refrigerant, and it is therefore dangerous to disconnect any part of the system without specialised knowledge and equipment.*

14 The refrigerant is potentially dangerous, and should only be handled by qualified persons **(see Tool tip)**. If it is splashed onto the skin, it can cause frostbite. It is not itself poisonous, but in the presence of a naked flame (including a cigarette) it forms a poisonous gas. Uncontrolled discharging of the refrigerant is dangerous, and potentially damaging to the environment.

10 Climate control system components – removal and refitting

Control panel

Note: *The control panel contains the ECM and the temperature sensor for the system. If the control panel assembly is renewed, it will need to be programmed prior to use. This can only be carried out by a Volvo dealer or suitably-equipped specialist.*

1 Remove the ignition key, then wait at least 3 minutes before proceeding.

2 Move the gear/selector lever to the rearmost position, then prise up the rear edge and lift the gear selector panel from place **(see illustrations)**.

Up to and including 2004 model year

3 Undo the 2 bolts at the lower edge of the control panel, then pull out the lower edge of the panel and detach if from the audio panel above **(see illustrations)**.

10.2a Prise the penholder from position . . .

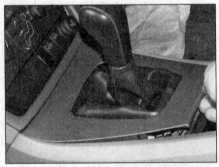

10.2b . . . or prise up the rear edge of the gear/selector lever panel

10.3a Undo the 2 Torx bolts (arrowed) . . .

10.3b . . . then pull out the lower edge, and pull the upper edge of the control panel rearwards . . .

10.3c . . . to release it from the 2 clips (arrowed)

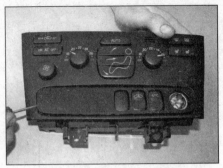

10.5 Unclip the switch panel

10.6a Unscrew the bulbholder from the rear of the control panel . . .

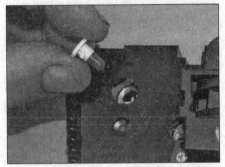

10.6b . . . and pull out the bulb and holder

10.8a Undo the 2 Torx bolts (arrowed) . . .

10.8b . . . and pull the complete infotainment and dashboard environment panel from place

4 Disconnect the wiring plugs as the panel is withdrawn.

5 If required, the front face of the control panel can be removed by releasing the clips and pulling it from place **(see illustration)**.

6 If required, the panel illumination bulbs can be removed by unscrewing the bulbholder. The bulb is integral with the holder **(see illustrations)**.

7 Refit by reversing the removal operations.

From 2005 model year

8 Working underneath the panel, depress the 4 catches and remove the panel from the gaiter. Undo the two screws at the lower edge of the control panel, then pull out the lower edge of the complete infotainment and dashboard environment panel **(see illustrations)**.

9 Disconnect the wiring plugs as the panel is withdrawn. Take great care not to damage the fibre optic cables. The bend radius must not be less the 25 mm.

10 Undo the 3 bolts and the top of the panel,

the release the 6 catches and remove the panel surround **(see illustrations)**.

11 Undo the 4 bolts and remove the climate control panel **(see illustrations)**.

12 If required, the front panel can be removed by releasing the catches and pulling the panel

from place. Note that the panel is secured by double-sided adhesive tape.

13 Refit by reversing the removal operations.

14 If the front panel has been removed, clean all traces of the old double-sided adhesive tape before applying the new tape.

10.10a Undo the 3 Torx bolts (arrowed) . . .

10.10b . . . release the 6 clips around the edge of the surround . . .

10.10c . . . and detach it from the panel

10.11a Undo the 4 Torx bolts (arrowed) . . .

10.11b . . . and withdraw the control panel

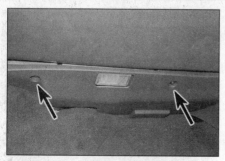

10.16 Undo the 2 screws (arrowed) and remove the passenger's side lower facia panel

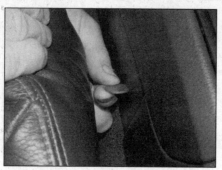

10.17a Undo the fastener . . .

10.17b . . . then pull the side panel rearwards

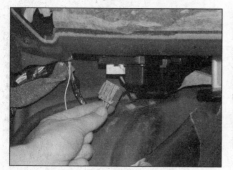

10.20 Disconnect the heater blower motor wiring plug

10.21 Undo the 2 screws and remove the heater blower motor (2 rearmost screws arrowed)

19 Release the floor carpet at the front edge, and fold the carpet rearwards.

20 Working through the glovebox aperture, disconnect the blower motor wiring connector **(see illustration)**.

21 Undo the five screws and remove the blower motor from the heater unit **(see illustration)**.

22 If required, squeeze together the sides of the cover to remove it, then undo the two bolts and separate the fan and motor from the cover **(see illustrations)**.

23 Refit by reversing the removal operations.

Heater blower motor

15 Pull the passenger's door sill trim straight up and remove it from the vehicle.

16 Undo the two screws and pull the passenger's side lower facia panel downwards and to the rear **(see illustration)**.

17 Slide the passenger's seat as far as possible to the rear, then rotate the fastener 90° anti-clockwise and pull the centre console side panel rearwards **(see illustrations)**.

18 Remove the passenger's side glovebox as described in Chapter 11.

Blower motor resistor

24 Remove the blower motor, and separate it from the cover as described previously.

25 Undo the two bolts and remove the resistor **(see illustration)**.

26 Refitting is a reversal of removal.

Heater matrix

Note: *Refer to the warnings given in Section 1 of this Chapter before proceeding.*

27 Remove the heater housing as described in this Section.

28 Pull out the evaporator temperature sensor (where applicable), then undo the three screws securing the fan/evaporator housing to the heater housing **(see illustrations)**.

29 Undo the two screws and remove the distribution flap motor from the left-hand side of the heater housing **(see illustration)**.

30 Release the matrix pipes from the bracket on the fan/evaporator housing, and separate

10.22a Squeeze together the sides of the cover and remove it

10.22b Undo the 2 Torx bolts, and separate the cover from the motor

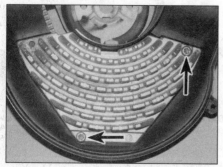

10.25 Undo the 2 Torx bolts (arrowed) and remove the resistor

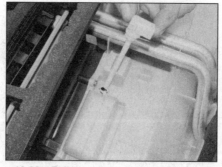

10.28a Pull the evaporator temperature sensor from place . . .

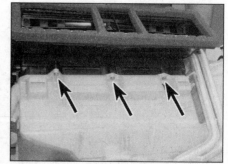

10.28b . . . and undo the 3 screws (arrowed)

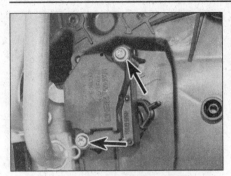

10.29 Undo the screws (arrowed) and remove the distribution flap motor

10.30 Note how the evaporator housing engages with the heater housing

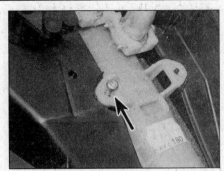

10.31a Undo the matrix retaining screw (arrowed) . . .

the fan/evaporator housing from the heater housing **(see illustration)**.

31 Remove the matrix retaining screw, and pull the matrix from the housing, prise out the clips and detach the pipes as the matrix is withdrawn **(see illustrations)**.

32 Refit by reversing the removal operations. Use new O-rings on the heater pipes and top-up the cooling system as described in *Weekly checks* on completion.

Air recirculation flap motor

33 The air distribution flap motor is located on the left-hand side of the main heater housing (ie, to the left of the central facia section).

34 Remove the glovebox compartment as described in Chapter 11.

35 Undo the screw securing the motor bracket to the heater housing **(see illustration)**.

36 Use a screwdriver to detach the operating lever from the motor, the detach the motor bracket from the housing.

37 Undo the three screws and detach the motor from the bracket. Disconnect the motor wiring plug as the motor is withdrawn.

38 Refitting is a reversal of removal.

Distribution flap motor

39 Remove the glovebox compartment as described in Chapter 11.

40 Working through the glovebox aperture, disconnect the damper motor wiring connector from the side of the heater blower housing.

41 Undo the two screws and remove the flap motor from the side of the heater blower motor housing **(see illustration 10.29)**.

42 Refit by reversing the removal operations.

Facia panel vents

Centre vents

43 Insert a blunt lever between the vent and the facia, release the 4 catches and pull the vent out of the facia panel. Use a piece of card beneath it to protect the facia. Disconnect the wiring plugs from the vents as they are withdrawn (where applicable).

44 Refitting is a reversal of removal.

Side vents

45 Open the front door(s), and starting at the rear edge using a plastic or wooden tool, carefully prise the facia end trim(s) from place.

10.31b . . . then unclip the matrix pipes . . .

46 If removing the driver's side vent, reach behind and press the headlight switch from the facia panel. Release the two clips on the lower edge of the vent, then push the lower edge rearwards from the facia. Remove the vent(s).

47 Refitting is a reversal of removal.

Windscreen defrost side vents – driver's side

48 Remove the driver's side vent as described previously. Reach through the end of the facia and release the clips and press the defrost vent upwards from the facia.

49 Refitting is a reversal of removal.

Windscreen defrost side vent – passenger's side

50 Remove the glovebox as described in Chapter 11. Reach through the glovebox aperture, release the clips and push the defrost vent upwards from the facia.

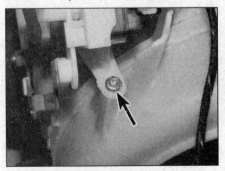

10.35 Undo the motor bracket screw (arrowed)

10.31c . . . and lift the matrix from the housing

51 Refitting is a reversal of removal.

Heater housing

52 Have the air conditioning refrigerant discharged by a suitably-equipped specialist (where applicable).

53 Use hose clamps on the heater hoses at the engine compartment bulkhead, or drain the cooling system as described in Chapter 1A or 1B, then press in the collars, and rotate them anti-clockwise to disconnect the heater hose couplings from the pipes at the bulkhead **(see illustration)**.

54 Plug the heater pipes to prevent dirt ingress.

55 Undo the two screws and remove the cover plate and seal from the heater pipes at the bulkhead **(see illustration)**.

56 Undo the two nuts and remove the heat shield, plate and rubber insulation from the air conditioning expansion valve on the bulkhead **(see illustration)**.

10.53 Rotate the collars anti-clockwise and disconnect the heater hoses

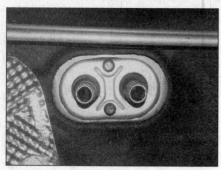

10.55 Undo the 2 screws and remove the cover plate

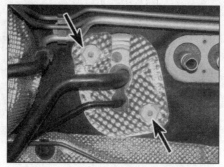

10.56 Undo the 2 nuts (arrowed) and remove the heat shield

10.57 Undo the bolt (arrowed) and disconnect the air conditioning pipes

10.60 Heater housing drain tube (arrowed)

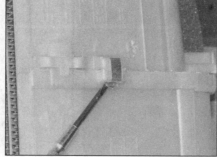

10.68a Use a small screwdriver to release the various clips . . .

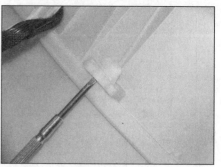

10.68b . . . holding the evaporator housing together

57 Undo the bolt and disconnect the air conditioning pipes from the bulkhead. Discard the O-ring seals, new ones must be fitted **(see illustration).**
58 Remove the windscreen wiper assembly as described in Chapter 12.
59 Remove the complete facia assembly and facia crossmember as described in Chapter 11.
60 Disconnect the air ducts and drain tubes from the heater housing **(see illustration).**
61 Note their fitted positions, then make a final check to ensure all wiring plugs have been disconnected from the heater housing, and manoeuvre it from the passenger cabin. Have an assistant lift and support the facia crossmember whilst the housing is manoeuvred from position. Mop-up any spilled coolant immediately.

Evaporator

Note: *Whenever disconnecting air*

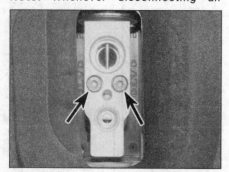

10.69 Undo the 2 screws (arrowed) and detach the expansion valve

conditioning pipes or components, always plug the openings to prevent dirt ingress, and to prevent the receiver/drier from becoming saturated.
62 Remove the heater housing as described in this Section.
63 Pull out the evaporator temperature sensor, then undo the three screws securing the fan/evaporator housing to the heater housing **(see illustrations 10.28a and 10.28b).**
64 Undo the two screws and remove the distribution flap motor from the left-hand side of the heater housing **(see illustration 10.29).**
65 Release the matrix pipes from the bracket on the fan/evaporator housing, and separate the fan/evaporator housing from the heater housing **(see illustration 10.30).**
66 Undo the screws and slide the heater blower motor down from the housing **(see illustration 10.21).**
67 Undo the screw securing the recirculation motor bracket to the fan housing.
68 Use a screwdriver to release the retaining clips where the upper section of the housing joins the lower section, then lift the upper section away **(see illustrations).**
69 Lift the evaporator from place, and if required undo the two screws and detach the expansion valve from the air conditioning pipes **(see illustration).** Discard the O-ring seals, new ones must be fitted.
70 Refitting is a reversal of removal, noting the following points:
   a) *Fit new O-ring seals to the expansion valve and air conditioning pipe connections at the engine compartment bulkhead.*

   b) *Upon completion have the air conditioning system recharged, and checked for leaks.*

Condenser

Note: *Whenever disconnecting air conditioning pipes or components, always plug the openings to prevent dirt ingress, and to prevent the receiver/drier from becoming saturated.*
71 Have the air conditioning refrigerant discharged by a suitably-equipped specialist.
72 Detach the cooling pipe from the control module box (where fitted).
73 Undo the bolt each side securing the radiator/intercooler/condenser (where applicable) together **(see illustrations 5.6a and 5.6b).**
74 Remove the two screws from the bonnet slam panel securing the radiator **(see illustration 5.5).**
75 Jack up the front of the vehicle, and support it securely on axle stands (see *Jacking and vehicle support*).
76 Working under the front of the vehicle, undo the screw each side, release the clips and remove the air baffle assembly **(see illustrations 5.7a and 5.7b).**
77 Undo the bolt and disconnect the air conditioning pipe from the receiver/drier **(see illustration).** Discard the O-ring seal, a new one must be fitted. Note that the receiver/drier is removed with the condenser – disconnect the wiring plug at the top of the unit.
78 The condenser/radiator assembly is held in place by one bolt each side, accessed from under the vehicle. Slacken the right-hand bolt,

10.77 Undo the bolt (arrowed) and disconnect the pipe from the receiver/drier

10.79 Undo the bolt (arrowed) and disconnect the pipe from the condenser

10.84 Remove the engine cross-stay (arrowed)

and completely remove the left-hand bolt **(see illustrations 5.11a and 5.11b)**.

79 Lower the left-hand side of the condenser to access and remove the air conditioning pipe connection bolt on the condenser **(see illustration)**. Detach the pipe and discard the O-ring seal, a new one must be fitted.

80 Remove the two lower screws securing the condenser to the radiator, then pull the radiator/intercooler backwards, and lower the condenser from position **(see illustrations 5.12a and 5.12b)**.

81 If required, undo the screw securing the pipes to the receiver/drier, then slacken the clamp screws and detach the receiver/drier from the condenser **(see illustration 10.91)**.

82 Refitting is a reversal of removal, noting the following points:

a) Fit new O-ring seals to the air conditioning pipe connections.

b) Upon completion, have the air conditioning system recharged, and checked for leaks.

Expansion valve

Note: Whenever disconnecting air conditioning pipes or components, always plug the openings to prevent dirt ingress, and to prevent the receiver/drier from becoming saturated.

83 Have the air conditioning refrigerant discharged by a suitably-equipped specialist.

84 Undo the fasteners and remove the engine cross-stay from between the brackets on the front suspension turrets **(see illustration)**.

85 Release the clamp securing the air conditioning pipes to the inner wing.

86 Undo the two nuts and remove the heat shield from the air conditioning pipe connection at the engine compartment bulkhead **(see illustration 10.56)**.

87 Undo the screw securing the air conditioning pipes to the expansion valve, and pull the pipes forwards to detach them **(see illustration 10.57)**. Discard the O-ring seals, new ones must be fitted.

88 Undo the two screws securing the expansion valve to the passenger's compartment air conditioning pipes, and remove the valve **(see illustration 10.69)**. Discard the O-ring seals, new ones must be fitted.

89 Refitting is a reversal of removal, noting the following points:

a) Tighten the expansion valve screws to the specified torque.

b) Renew all O-ring seals where disturbed.

c) Upon completion, have the air conditioning system recharged and checked for leaks.

Receiver/drier

Note: Whenever disconnecting air conditioning pipes or components, always plug the openings to prevent dirt ingress, and to prevent the receiver/drier from becoming saturated.

90 Remove the condenser as described previously in this Section.

91 Undo the screws and detach the air conditioning pipes from the receiver/drier **(see illustration)**. Discard the O-ring seal, a new one must be fitted.

92 Slacken the clamp screws and slide the receiver/drier from the bracket.

93 Refitting is a reversal of removal.

Compressor

Note: Whenever disconnecting air conditioning pipes or components, always plug the openings to prevent dirt ingress, and to prevent the receiver/drier from becoming saturated.

94 Have the air conditioning refrigerant discharged by a suitably-equipped specialist.

95 Remove the auxiliary drivebelt as described in Chapter 1A or 1B.

96 Jack up the front of the vehicle and support it securely on axle stands (see Jacking and vehicle support). Undo the clips/screws and remove the engine undershield.

97 Remove the two screws holding the front splash shield, then release the clips at the front edge, and pull the shield rearwards to remove it **(see illustrations 5.7a and 5.7b)**.

98 Undo the screw securing the cable ducting to the subframe.

99 Undo the screws and detach the air conditioning pipes from the compressor. Discard the O-ring seals, new ones must be fitted.

100 Disconnect the wiring plug, then remove the 4 bolts securing the compressor to the engine, and manoeuvre it downwards and out from the vehicle **(see illustration)**.

101 Refitting is a reversal of removal, noting the following points:

a) Renew all O-ring seals where disturbed.

b) Upon completion, have the air conditioning system recharged and checked for leaks.

Solar sensor

102 The solar sensor is combined with the anti-theft alarm system diode, and is located on top of the facia cover.

103 Carefully prise up the sensor using a screwdriver inserted under its base at the side **(see illustration)**.

104 Disconnect the wiring connector and remove the sensor.

105 Refitting is a reversal of removal.

10.91 Undo the bolts and disconnect the pipes from the receiver/drier

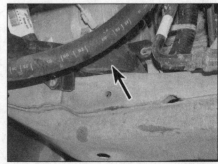

10.100 Undo the bolts securing the cable ducting (arrowed) at the front of the subframe

10.103 Carefully prise the solar sensor upwards from the facia

11.5 Undo the screws and bolts (arrowed) and remove the bumper slide mounting

Evaporator temperature sensor

106 Remove the heater housing as described in this Section.
107 Pull the sensor from the housing, and disconnect the wiring plug **(see illustration 10.28a)**.
108 Refitting is a reversal of removal.

11 Auxiliary/parking heater – general information, removal and refitting

General information

1 Available as an option on most models is a fuel-powered auxiliary heater, which can be operated directly by the driver, operated remotely, or programmed to come on at a preset time. The heater raises the temperature of the coolant in the system, thus raising the temperature of the engine and passenger cabin. The system consists of a fuel pump, a heat exchanger with fuel injection nozzle, a coolant pump, glow plugs, control module and the associated pipes, wiring and thermostatic controls.

Heater assembly

2 Disconnect the battery negative lead as described in Chapter 5A.

3 Remove the front bumper as described in Chapter 11.
4 Undo the screws, release the clips and remove the air baffle **(see illustrations 5.7a and 5.7b)**.
5 Undo the screws and remove the left-hand side bumper slide mounting **(see illustration)**.
6 Clamp the coolant hoses to and from the heater assembly, then release the clips and disconnect the hoses. Be prepared for coolant spillage.

Models up to September 2001

7 Disconnect the fuel pipe from the heater at the quick-release coupling, and disconnect the wiring plug from the heater. Plug the end of the fuel pipe to prevent fuel spillage.
8 The heater assembly may be secured to the subframe by three screws, or have a bracket which is retained by the subframe mounting bolt. Undo the screws/bolt and remove the heater assembly **(see illustration)**.Note the subframe bolt may not be re-used.
9 Refit by reversing the removal operations, remembering to top-up the cooling system as described in Chapter 1A or 1B. Tighten the new subframe bolt to the specified torque (where applicable).

Models from October 2001

10 Release the clamp and disconnect the fuel pipe from the heater. Plug the open end of the fuel pipe to prevent spillage and dirt ingress. Undo the upper mounting nut, and the two screws securing the bracket to the vehicle body, then unhook the heater from the upper mounting and remove it from position. Any further dismantling of the heater should be entrusted to a Volvo dealer or suitably-equipped specialist.
11 Refit by reversing the removal operations, remembering to top-up the cooling system as described in Chapter 1A or 1B.

Control module

Removal

12 Disconnect the battery negative lead as described in Chapter 5A.

Models up to September 2001

13 Undo the 4 screws, release the clips and remove the air baffle from the front underside of the vehicle **(see illustrations 5.7a and 5.7b)**.
14 Slide out the locking catch and disconnect the control module wiring plug.
15 Slacken the two mounting screws and remove the module from position.
16 Refit by reversing the removal operations.

Models from October 2001

17 Remove the front bumper as described in Chapter 11. Undo the two screws, release the clips and remove the air baffle **(see illustrations 5.7a and 5.7b)**.
18 Undo the four screws and remove the left-hand side bumper slide mounting **(see illustration 11.5)**.
19 Cut the cable tie securing the module wiring loom.

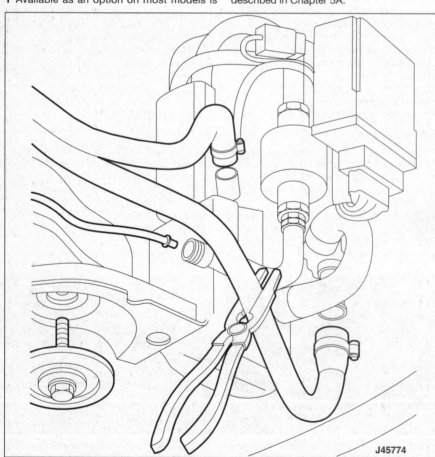

J45774

11.8 Early auxiliary heaters may be retaining by the subframe bolt

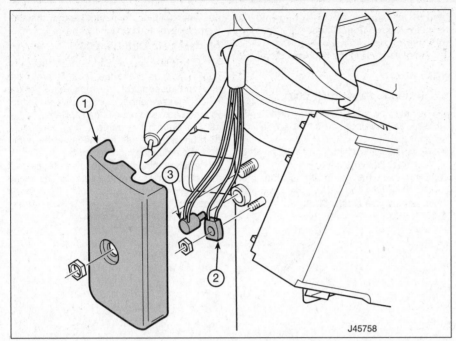

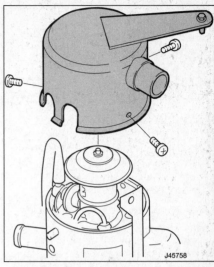

11.40 Undo the 3 screws and remove the shroud

11.39 Auxiliary heater overheat protection thermostat (2), coolant temperature sensor (3) and cover (1)

20 Slacken the upper mounting nut, and remove the lower mounting nut, then pull the module from its mounting.

21 Slide out the locking catch, and disconnect the module wiring plug as it's withdrawn.

22 Refit by reversing the removal operations.

Glow plugs

23 Disconnect the battery negative lead as described in Chapter 5A.

Models up to September 2001

24 Undo the 4 screws, release the clips and remove the air baffle from the front underside of the vehicle **(see illustrations 5.7a and 5.7b)**.

25 Peel back the protective cap, then undo the nut and disconnect the glow plug wiring connector. Unscrew the glow plug from position.

26 Refit the glow plug, tighten it to the specified torque, then reconnect the wiring plug.

27 The remainder of refitting is a reversal of removal, but allow the engine to idle for a few seconds prior to operating the heater.

Models from October 2001

28 Remove the front bumper as described in Chapter 11. Undo the screws, release the clips and remove the left-hand air baffle **(see illustrations 5.7a and 5.7b)**.

29 Undo the screws and remove the left-hand side bumper slide mounting **(see illustration 11.5)**.

30 Pull the wiring plug from the glow plug, then unscrew it from position.

31 Refit the glow plug, tighten it to the specified torque, then reconnect the wiring plug.

32 The remainder of refitting is a reversal of

removal, but allow the engine to idle for a few seconds prior to operating the heater.

Coolant pump

33 Remove the control module as previously described in this Section, but do not disconnect the module wiring plug. Position the module to one side.

34 Clamp the coolant hoses to and from the pump, then release the clips and disconnect the hoses. Be prepared for coolant spillage.

35 Cut the cable tie and remove the protective cap over the pump, then disconnect the pump wiring plug.

36 Note the pump's fitted position, then remove the mounting screw/nut and manoeuvre the pump from the mounting and withdrawn it from the vehicle.

37 Refitting is a reversal of removal, but allow the engine to idle for a few seconds prior to operating the heater.

Overheat protection thermostat, flame sensor and coolant temperature sensor

38 Remove the heater assembly as described previously in this Section.

39 Undo the nut and remove the cover over the coolant temperature sensor and thermostat. Pull the temperature sensor from place, then undo the nut and remove the thermostat **(see illustration)**.

40 Detach the control module from the heater as previously described in this Section, then detach the intake hose, release the three screws and remove the fan shroud from the top of the heater **(see illustration)**.

41 Disconnect the fan motor wiring plug, and pull the flame sensor from place **(see illustration)**. On models up to September 2001, it will be necessary to cut the wiring, and splice

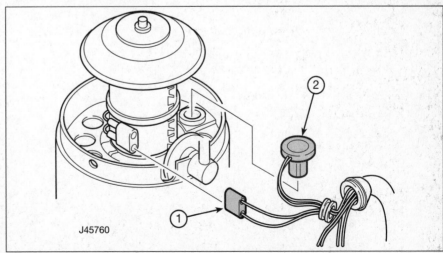

11.41 Fan motor wiring plug (1) and flame sensor (2)

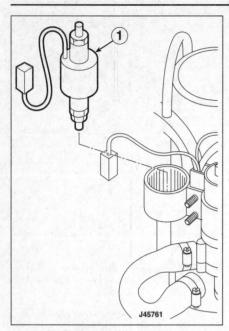

11.45 Fuel pump (1) – models up to September 2001

the new sensor/thermostat wiring into the loom. On models from October 2001, remove the wiring harness from the vehicle.

42 Refit by reversing the removal operations.

Fuel pump

Models up to September 2001

43 Remove the heater assembly and control module as previously described in this Section.

44 Cut off the metal clamps and disconnection the fuel pipes from the pump.

45 Disconnect the pump wiring plug, then undo the two nuts and remove the pump from the assembly **(see illustration)**.

46 When refitting the pump use new metal or worm drive clamps on the fuel hoses.

Models from October 2001

47 The fuel pump is located at the front right-hand side of the fuel tank. Depress the clip and disconnect the fuel hoses at the quick-release connectors on the fuel pump. Plug the hoses to prevent fuel spillage.

48 Disconnect the pump wiring connector, then undo the nut and manoeuvre the pump from the mounting, noting its fitted position.

49 When refitting the pump, it's essential that it's refitted in its original position. The pump was originally fitted at an angle of 15° to the horizontal.

Chapter 4 Part A:
Fuel and exhaust systems – petrol models

Contents

Degrees of difficulty

Easy, suitable for novice with little experience	Fairly easy, suitable for beginner with some experience	Fairly difficult, suitable for competent DIY mechanic	Difficult, suitable for experienced DIY mechanic	Very difficult, suitable for expert DIY or professional

Specifications

System type

Turbocharged engines . . . .   Bosch ME7.01 engine management system
Non-turbocharged engines . . . .   Denso engine management system

Fuel system data

Idle speed* . . . .   850 rpm
Regulated fuel pressure:
  Bosch ME7.01 . . . .   3.8 bar
  Denso . . . .   3.0 bar
Non-adjustable – controlled by ECM

Torque wrench settings

	Nm	lbf ft
Camshaft position solenoid bolts.	10	7
Crankshaft position/speed sensor nut*	10	7
Engine cross-stay to engine stabiliser	80	59
Engine cross-stay to suspension turrets	50	37
Exhaust manifold nuts*.	25	18
Exhaust pipe to turbocharger.	30	22
Exhaust pipe-to-manifold nuts*	25	18
Fuel gauge sender unit plastic retaining nut	30	22
Fuel pump plastic retaining nut	40	30
Fuel rail to intake manifold.	10	7
Intake manifold bolts	20	15
Throttle control unit	10	7
Turbocharger to manifold	25	18

Do not re-use

1.5 The fuel pressure relief valve (arrowed) is located at the left-hand end of the fuel rail

1 General information

General information

The fuel system consists of a centrally-mounted fuel tank, an electric fuel pump, a fuel filter and a fully-electronic fuel injection system. Further details of the fuel injection systems will be found in Sections 6 and 8.

Depending on engine type, models for some market territories are also equipped with an exhaust gas recirculation (EGR) system, as part of an emissions control package. Further details of these systems will be found in Part C of this Chapter.

Depressurising the fuel system

Before working on any part of the fuel system, it is recommended that the residual fuel pressure is relieved. Even if the engine has been switched off for some time, there is a risk that, when fuel lines are disconnected, the residual fuel pressure will cause fuel to spray out uncontrollably. This is at best unpleasant (if it sprays in your face, for instance), and at worst, presents a fire risk.

Whenever a fuel line is to be disconnected, particularly if the system pressure has not been relieved, wrap plenty of absorbent rag around the connection to be disturbed. Loosen the fittings or clips slowly, and remove any pipes carefully, so that the pressure is

relieved in a controlled fashion, and/or so that any fuel spillage can be contained.

Place rags around the fuel pressure relief valve on the fuel rail, then unscrew the cap and use a screwdriver to depress the valve core **(see illustration)**. Be prepared for fuel spillage.

Note that a pressure relief valve is also fitted in the fuel supply line to the fuel filter under the car. This valve is similar in design to a normal tyre valve, and may be used as described in Chapter 1A, Section 25, to relieve system pressure.

Remember that relieving the system pressure does not remove the risk of fuel spillage – fuel will still be present in the lines, and it is wise to place absorbent rags around any connection which is to be disturbed.

Precautions

⚠️ *Warning: Petrol is extremely flammable – great care must be taken when working on any part of the fuel system. Do not smoke or allow any naked flames or uncovered light bulbs near the work area. Note that gas powered domestic appliances with pilot flames, such as heaters, boilers and tumble dryers, also present a fire hazard – bear this in mind if you are working in an area where such appliances are present. Always keep a suitable fire extinguisher close to the work area and familiarise yourself with its operation before starting work. Wear eye protection when working on fuel systems and wash off any fuel spilt on bare skin immediately with soap and water. Note that fuel vapour is just as dangerous as liquid fuel; a vessel that has just been emptied of liquid fuel will still contain vapour and can be potentially explosive. Petrol is a highly dangerous and volatile liquid, and the precautions necessary when handling it cannot be overstressed.*

• Many of the operations described in this Chapter involve the disconnection of fuel lines, which may cause an amount of fuel spillage. Before commencing work, refer to the above Warning and the information in Safety first! at the beginning of this manual; also see the information on depressurising

the fuel system, given previously in this Section.

• It is strongly advised that, wherever possible, the battery negative lead is disconnected whenever there is a danger of fuel spillage. This reduces the risk of a spark causing a fire, and also prevents the fuel pump running, which could be dangerous if the fuel lines have been disconnected.

• When working with fuel system components, pay particular attention to cleanliness – dirt entering the fuel system may cause blockages which will lead to poor running.

2 Air cleaner assembly and air ducts – removal and refitting

Removal

Air cleaner assembly

1 Slacken the clamp and disconnect the air outlet hose from the mass airflow meter on the air cleaner housing, then disconnect the meter wiring plug **(see illustration)**.

2 Detach the wiring loom from the front of the air cleaner housing.

3 Note their fitted positions, then disconnect the vacuum hoses from the rear of the housing.

4 Pull the hot air hose and intake hose from the side of the air cleaner housing **(see illustration)**.

5 Pull the housing upwards and release it from the mountings **(see illustration)**.

Air ducts

6 All ducting is retained either by simple snap-fit connectors or by hose clips. The routing of the ducts varies between normally-aspirated and turbo models, but in all cases removal is straightforward and self-explanatory. To gain access to the lower ducts, it will be necessary to remove the air cleaner assembly as previously described.

Refitting

7 In all cases, refit by reversing the removal operations.

2.1 Slacken the air outlet hose clamp (arrowed)

2.4 Pull the air intake hose (arrowed) from the side of the air cleaner housing

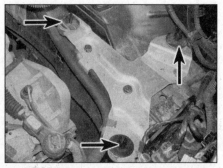

2.5 Pull the housing from the 3 mountings (arrowed)

3 Accelerator pedal – removal and refitting

Removal

1 Undo the two screws and remove the trim panel above the pedals in the driver's footwell **(see illustration)**.
2 Undo the three nuts securing the assembly to the bulkhead **(see illustration)**.
3 Release the cable tie, and disconnect the position sensor wiring plug as the pedal assembly is removed. No further dismantling of the assembly is recommended.

Refitting

4 Refit by reversing the removal operations.

4 Fuel gauge sender/ pump units – removal and refitting

Note: *Observe the precautions in Section 1 before working on any component in the fuel system.*

Removal

1 Disconnect the battery negative lead (see Chapter 5A).
2 Remove the rear seat cushion and backrest as described in Chapter 11.
3 Fold the floor carpet forwards to expose the fuel tank access covers.
4 Undo the nuts and remove the access

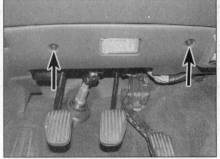

3.1 Undo the 2 screws (arrowed) securing the trim panel

covers over the fuel pump and sender unit (right-hand side) and the left-hand sender unit **(see illustration)**.
5 Trace the wiring for the sender unit/pump or sender unit, and disconnect the relevant connector, release any cable-ties, then feed the wiring back and through the sender unit aperture in the floor.
6 Press in the buttons and disconnect the hoses from the right-hand pump/sender unit **(see illustration)**.
7 Unscrew the left-hand sender unit plastic retaining collar using a pair of large, crossed screwdrivers, or improvise a tool such as an old two-legged puller and an adjustable spanner **(see illustration)**.
8 Withdraw the left-hand sender from the fuel tank, then depress the clip and slide the fuel transfer ejector from the sender, and disconnect the wiring plug from the underside of the sender cover **(see illustration)**. Recover

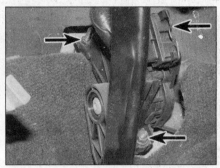

3.2 The accelerator pedal assembly is secured by 3 nuts (arrowed)

the O-ring seal from between the sender cover and the tank opening.
9 Attach a length of wire (or similar) to the transfer ejector hose to aid refitting. The wire must be long enough to reach across the full width of the fuel tank **(see illustration)**.
10 Unscrew the right-hand sender/pump unit retaining collar from the tank.
11 Carefully lift the sender/pump unit, pushing the float arm down and squeezing the sender and pump holder so the float arm is held in its lowest position **(see illustration)**. Manoeuvre the sender/pump assembly from the tank, pulling the hose/wiring assembly across from the left-hand side of the tank. Ensure the wire attached to the plugs (paragraph 9) is long enough to allow the assembly to be removed without disappearing into the tank. Free the routing wire from the plugs and leave it in place ready for refitting. Recover the O-ring seal from between the sender cover and the tank opening.

4.4 Undo the nuts and remove the left- and right-hand access covers (arrowed)

4.6 Press in the buttons (arrowed) and disconnect the hoses

4.7 We used an old two-legged puller to unscrew the plastic retaining collar

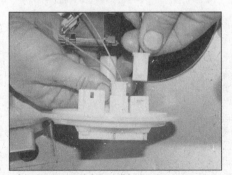

4.8 Disconnect the wiring plug from the underside of the sender cover

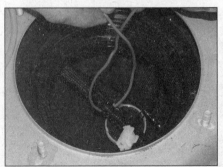

4.9 Attach a length of wire to the transfer hose to aid refitting

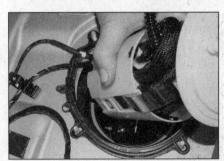

4.11 With the float arm held in its lowest position, manoeuvre the sender/pump assembly from the tank

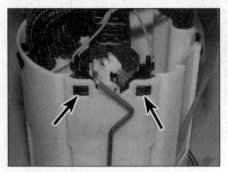

4.12 Release the clips (arrowed) and detach the sender from the pump

4.13 Attach the routing wire to the transfer hose and pull the hose/wiring across to the left-hand side of the tank

4.15 Both sender unit covers must be positioned with the mark (arrowed) pointing towards the rear of the vehicle

12 If required, the right-hand sender unit can be unclipped from the fuel pump assembly **(see illustration)**.

Refitting

13 Attach the routing wire to the plugs/hose assembly (see paragraph 9), and insert the sender/pump unit, pulling the hose/wiring assembly across to the left-hand side of the tank, and ensuring the float arm and float are inserted into place without any damage **(see illustration)**.

14 Reconnect the wiring plugs to the underside of the left-hand sender unit, and detach the routing wire.

15 The remainder of refitting is a reversal of removal, bearing in mind the following points:

a) Use a new seal smeared with petroleum jelly.

b) Position the sender/pump units, so the arrows on the covers point towards the rear of the vehicle, and aligns between the marks on the tank **(see illustration)**.

c) Route the wiring over the top of the fuel tank and out through the fuel pump aperture. Reconnect and secure with cable-ties, where applicable.

5 Fuel tank –
removal and refitting

Note: *Observe the precautions in Section 1 before working on any component in the fuel system.*

Removal

1 Before the tank can be removed, it must be drained of as much fuel as possible. To avoid the dangers and complications of fuel handling and storage, it is advisable to carry out this operation with the tank almost empty.

2 Disconnect the battery negative lead (see Chapter 5A).

3 Slacken the left-rear roadwheel bolts, then chock the front wheels then jack up the rear of the vehicle and support it on axle stands (see *Jacking and vehicle support*). Remove the roadwheel.

4 Carry out the operations described in Section 4, paragraphs 2 to 6.

5 Remove the rear section of the exhaust system as described in Section 13. Support the front section of the system to avoid placing any strain on the flexible section.

6 Unclip ABS wiring from both sides of the fuel tank.

7 Undo the two Torx bolts at the front of the heat shield under the tank, and unclip the brake pipes from the clips at the front of the tank retaining straps **(see illustrations)**.

8 Disconnect the left-hand handbrake cable from the brake assembly as described in Chapter 9, release the retaining brackets and position both cables in front of the tank.

9 Disconnect hose from the fuel filter at the quick-release coupling (press in the buttons on the coupling) **(see illustration)**.

10 Release the hose clamps and disconnect the fuel filler hose and shut-off pipe from the tank.

11 Position a trolley jack under the centre of the

tank. Insert a protective wooden pad between the jack head and tank base, then raise the jack to just take the weight of the tank.

12 Undo the tank retaining straps, and carefully lower the jack and tank slightly.

13 Lower the jack and tank, and remove the tank from under the car.

14 If the tank is contaminated with sediment or water, remove the gauge sender unit and the fuel pump as described previously. Swill the tank out with clean fuel.

15 The tank is moulded from a synthetic material and if damaged, it should be renewed. However, in certain cases it may be possible to have small leaks or minor damage repaired. Seek the advice of a dealer or suitable specialist concerning tank repair.

16 If a new tank is to be fitted, transfer all the components from the old tank to the new. Always renew the seals and plastic nuts securing the fuel pump and gauge sender unit. Once used, they may not seat and seal properly on a new tank.

Refitting

17 Refitting is a reversal of removal, bearing in mind the following points:

a) Locate the tank in position, and tighten the rear strap mountings. Push the tank forwards, and centre the fuel gauge sender unit and fuel pump plastic nuts with respect to their access holes in the floor. Now tighten the front strap mountings.

b) On completion, refill the tank with fuel and check exhaustively for signs of leakage before driving the car on the road.

5.7a Undo the heat shield Torx bolts (arrowed) . . .

5.7b . . . and release the brake pipes from the clips on the tank straps

5.9 Depress the button (arrowed), and pull the coupling from the filter connection

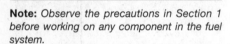

6 Fuel injection systems – general information

Bosch ME7.01 system

ME7.01 is a microprocessor-controlled engine management system, designed to meet stringent emission control legislation whilst still providing excellent engine performance and fuel economy. This is achieved by continuously monitoring the engine using various sensors, whose data is input to the system's electronic control module (ECM). Based on this information, the ECM program and memory then determine the exact amount of fuel necessary, which is injected directly sequentially into the intake manifold, for all actual and anticipated driving conditions. The ECM also controls the engine ignition functions (see Chapter 5B), and the engine emission control systems (see Chapter 4C).

The main components of the fuel side of the system are as follows.

Electronic control module (ECM)

• The ECM is a microprocessor, which controls the entire operation of the fuel, ignition, engine cooling fan, camshaft positions, turbocharger and emission systems. Contained in the module memory are programnes which control the fuel supply to the injectors, and their opening duration. The program enters sub-routines to alter these parameters, according to inputs from the other components of the system. In addition to this, the engine idle speed is also controlled by the ECM, which uses a motorised throttle unit. The ECM also incorporates a self-diagnostic facility, in which the entire fuel/ignition system is continuously monitored for correct operation. Any detected faults are logged as fault codes which can be downloaded using a piece of equipment called a fault code reader. In the event of a fault in the system due to loss of a signal from one of the sensors, the ECM reverts to an emergency (limp-home) program. This will allow the car to be driven, although engine operation and performance will be limited.

The ECM has several adaptive (self-learning) function, enabling it to continually adapt to changing circumstances through the life of the vehicle (wear, fuel differences, etc). The ECM has an integral atmospheric pressure sensor, and on some models, an integral air temperature sensor to monitor the temperature inside the plastic box in which the module sits, and if necessary, activate the box cooling fan.

Fuel injectors

• Each fuel injector consists of a solenoid-operated needle valve, which opens under commands from the ECM. Fuel from the fuel rail is then delivered sequentially through the injector nozzle into the intake manifold.

Coolant temperature sensor

• This resistive device is screwed into the thermostat housing, where its element is in direct contact with the engine coolant. Changes in coolant temperature are detected by the ECM as a change in sensor resistance. Signals from the coolant temperature sensor are also used by the temperature gauge in the instrument panel.

Mass airflow sensor

• The MAF sensor measures the mass of air drawn into the engine. The sensor is of the hot-film type, containing four different resistive elements and related circuitry. The unit is located in the air cleaner intake, and uses the intake air to alter the resistance of the elements. By comparing the changing resistance values with a calibration resistance, the ECM can establish the intake air temperature, and from its cooling effect, the intake air volume.

Accelerator pedal position sensor

• The accelerator pedal position sensor contains two potentiometers and an analogue-to-digital converter. The pedal shaft is connected to the potentiometers, whose resistance changes relative to pedal position. The sensor transmits both an analogue and digital signal to the ECM, informing it of the pedal position and rate of change. This information is used be the ECM to control the motorised throttle control unit. No throttle cable is fitted.

Motorised throttle control unit

• The throttle control unit regulates the amount of air entering the intake manifold. It consists of a throttle valve (disc), a DC motor and gears, and two potentiometers which report the position of the throttle valve to the ECM. There is no throttle cable fitted – the position of the throttle valve is controlled by the ECM via the electric motor.

Fuel pump

• The electric fuel pump is located in the fuel tank, and totally submerged in the fuel. The unit is a two-stage device consisting of an electric motor which drives an impeller pump to draw in fuel, and a gear pump to discharge it under pressure. The fuel is then supplied to the fuel rail on the intake manifold via an in-line fuel filter.

Fuel pressure regulator

• The function of the fuel pressure regulator is incorporated into the fuel tank-mounted pump module.

Stop-light switch

• Informs the ECM of the brake pedal position, for cruise control functions.

Clutch pedal switch

• Informs the ECM of the clutch pedal position, for cruise control functions.

Air conditioning pressure sensor

• Located in the high-pressure side of the

air conditioning system, this sensor informs the ECM of the system pressure to enable control of the engine cooling fan (to cool the condenser) and the compressor, and adjust the idle speed relative to compressor load.

Turbocharger boost pressure sensor

• Fitted to the outlet pipe from the intercooler, this sensor informs the ECM of the pressure of the air entering the intake manifold. Not fitted to all turbocharged engines.

Intake air temperature sensor

• This sensor informs the ECM of the air temperature as it exits the intercooler. The resistance of the sensor changes according to the temperature of the air passing over it.

Ambient air temperature sensor

• Positioned at the base of the left-hand door mirror, the sensor informs the ECM of the temperature of the air outside the vehicle. The resistance of the sensor changes according to the air temperature around it.

Crankshaft position/speed sensor

• As the engine flywheel rotates, a series of drilled/punch holes (6° apart) on its circumference pass the tip of the sensor, fitted at the rear of the engine above the flywheel. As the sensor is inductive with a permanent magnet, the passing flywheel/holes generate an AC voltage in the sensor. The frequency of this voltage is directly proportional to the speed of the engine. In order to monitor the position of the crankshaft, one hole (at 72° BTDC) is missing. This missing hole creates an anomaly in the signal, from which the ECM can determine the exact position of the crankshaft. Although the rotational position of the crankshaft can be monitored, the sensor cannot determine which 'stroke' (compression or exhaust) the engine is one. For this information, the ECM must rely on the camshaft position sensor.

Camshaft position sensor

• In order to determine the position of the camshaft, this sensor is located adjacent the camshaft flanges. On each flange are four 'flanks' which have one tooth each. These teeth are not equally spaced (the flanks are not symmetrical), so as they pass by the sensor tip, the permanent magnetic in the sensor generates an AC voltage – the pattern of which informs the ECM of the position, and the frequency represents the speed.

Fuel pressure/temperature sensor

• This Piezo resistor sensor is fitted to the fuel rail on some models. As pressure acts upon the sensor, the output voltage varies proportionally to the pressure. The temperature detection element of the sensor is a resistor sensitive to temperature – as the temperature increases, the voltage output drops – and vice versa.

Camshaft position solenoid

• This solenoid, fitted to the cylinder head, controls the flow of oil to the continuously

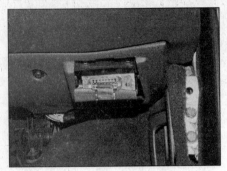

7.2 Pull down the flap to access the diagnostic plug, located under the driver's side of the facia

variable valve timing (CVVT) units on the camshafts. The flow of oil to these units determines the camshaft's radial position. The voltage to the solenoid(s) is controlled by the engine management ECM.

Turbocharger boost control valve

• Fitted to a hose between the intake manifold and the turbocharger pressure servo, the valve controls the pressure output of the turbocharger. The valve is controlled by the engine management ECM and controls the vacuum applied to the pressure servo.

Denso system

The Denso system components and their operation are very similar to the Bosch ME7.01, with the main difference being the lack of components to monitor or control the turbocharger operation.

8.3 Undo the 2 screws (arrowed) and remove the mass airflow sensor

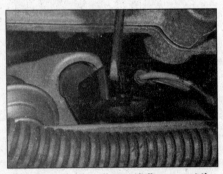

8.11 Depress the clips and disconnect the fuel injector's wiring plugs

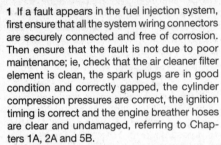

7 Fuel injection system – testing and adjustment

1 If a fault appears in the fuel injection system, first ensure that all the system wiring connectors are securely connected and free of corrosion. Then ensure that the fault is not due to poor maintenance; ie, check that the air cleaner filter element is clean, the spark plugs are in good condition and correctly gapped, the cylinder compression pressures are correct, the ignition timing is correct and the engine breather hoses are clear and undamaged, referring to Chapters 1A, 2A and 5B.

2 If these checks fail to reveal the cause of the problem, a diagnostic connector is under the driver's side facia above the pedals, into which a fault code reader can be plugged (see illustration). The test equipment is capable of interrogating the engine management system electronically and accessing its internal fault log.

3 Fault codes can only be extracted from the ECM using a dedicated fault code reader. A Volvo dealer will obviously have such a reader, but they are also available from other suppliers. It is unlikely to be cost-effective for the private owner to purchase a fault code reader, but a well-equipped local garage or auto-electrical specialist will have one.

4 Using this equipment, faults can be pin-pointed quickly and simply, even if their occurrence is intermittent. Testing all the system components individually in an attempt to locate the fault by elimination is

8.5 Intake air temperature sensor (arrowed)

8.12 Remove the injector rail mounting bolts (arrowed)

a time-consuming operation that is unlikely to be fruitful (particularly if the fault occurs dynamically), and carries high risk of damage to the ECM's internal components.

5 Experienced home mechanics equipped with an accurate tachometer and a carefully-calibrated exhaust gas analyser may be able to check the exhaust gas CO content and the engine idle speed; if these are found to be out of specification, then the vehicle must be taken to a suitably-equipped Volvo dealer or specialist for assessment. Neither the air/fuel mixture (exhaust gas CO content) nor the engine idle speed are manually adjustable; incorrect test results indicate the need for maintenance (possibly, injector cleaning) or a fault within the fuel injection system.

8 Fuel injection system components – removal and refitting

Note: *Refer to the precautions in Section 1 before working on any component in the fuel system. The following procedures are applicable to all fuel injection systems unless otherwise stated.*

Mass airflow sensor

1 Release the clip and disconnect the hose from the mass airflow sensor (see illustration 2.1).

2 Disconnect the wiring connector from the sensor.

3 Undo the two screws and remove the sensor from the air cleaner cover (see illustration).

4 Refit by reversing the removal operations.

Intake air temperature sensor

Turbo models up to 2002 model year

Note: *On non-turbocharged models, the intake air temperature sensor is incorporated into the mass airflow sensor, and on 2003-on turbocharged models, the sensor is incorporated into the boost pressure sensor.*

5 Disconnect the wiring plug from the sensor located on the pipe from the intercooler to the manifold (see illustration).

6 Release the clips and pull the sensor from place.

7 Refit by reversing the removal operations.

Fuel rail and injectors

Note: *If an injector problem is suspected, it might be worth trying the effect of a proprietary injector cleaner petrol treatment before removing the injectors.*

8 Depressurise the fuel system as described in Section 1.

9 On turbocharged engines, release the clips and remove the charge air pipe from over the top of the engine.

10 Undo the two Torx bolts and remove the cover over the fuel rail.

11 Release the clips and disconnect the wiring plug from each of the injectors (see illustration).

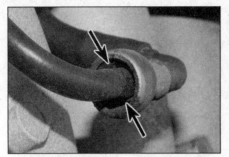

8.13 Push back the sleeves inside the coupling (arrowed), then pull the coupling apart

8.14 Withdraw the fuel rail and injectors from the manifold

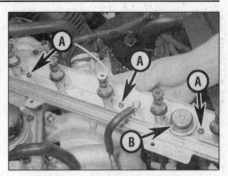

8.15 Injector retaining plate screws (A) and fuel pressure damper (B)

12 Clean the area around the injectors, then remove the fuel rail mounting bolts **(see illustration)**.

13 Disconnect the quick-release fuel line coupling from the fuel rail by pushing back the coupling sleeves **(see illustration)**. Be prepared for fuel spillage as the coupling is released. Plug the coupling after disconnection to prevent further loss of fuel.

14 Gently work the injectors loose, and pull the rail upwards to release the injectors from the manifold, and remove the rail complete with injectors and fuel pressure damper **(see illustration)**.

15 Remove the screws securing the injector retaining plate to the fuel rail **(see illustration)**. The injectors can now be unclipped from the retaining plate, and removed.

16 Refit by reversing the removal operations, and noting the following points:

a) *Check that the injector O-rings and manifold seals are in good condition, and renew them if necessary **(see illustration)**.*

b) *Smear the O-rings with petroleum jelly or silicone grease as an assembly lubricant.*

c) *Ensure that all wiring and fuel line connections are correctly and securely made.*

d) *Tighten the fuel rail retaining bolts to the specified torque setting.*

Fuel pressure damper

17 Remove the fuel rail and injectors as described previously. The fuel pressure damper can be unclipped from the fuel rail retaining plate in the same way as the injectors.

18 Refitting is a reversal of removal.

Motorised throttle control unit

Note: *If a new throttle control unit is fitted, it must be programmed and matched to the engine management ECM using dedicated Volvo test equipment. Entrust this task to a Volvo dealer or suitably-equipped specialist.*

Turbocharged models

19 Release the clamps and remove the intake ducting from the front panel and the air cleaner housing.

20 Release the clamps and remove the intake ducting from the intercooler to the throttle control unit.

8.16 Check the condition of the injector O-rings (A) and manifold seals (B)

21 Disconnect the wiring plug, undo the four bolts and remove the throttle control unit **(see illustration)**. Discard the gasket, a new one must be fitted.

22 Refitting is a reversal of removal, using a new gasket, and tighten the throttle control unit retaining bolts to the specified torque.

Non-turbocharged models

23 Release the clamp and disconnect the intake hose from the throttle control unit **(see illustration)**.

24 Disconnect the wiring plug, undo the four screws and remove the throttle control unit **(see illustration)**. Discard the gasket, a new one must be fitted.

25 Refit by reversing the removal operations, using a new gasket. Fit new hose clips if necessary, and tighten the throttle control unit retaining screws to the specified torque.

8.21 Throttle control unit retaining bolts (arrowed)

Coolant temperature sensor

26 Refer to Chapter 3.

Electronic control module

Note: *If a new control module is fitted, it must be programmed using dedicated Volvo test equipment. Entrust this task to a Volvo dealer or suitably-equipped specialist.*

Note: *The engine management ECM and, where applicable, the automatic transmission ECM, are all located in the ECM box, which is situated at the front right-hand side of the engine compartment.*

27 Ensure that the ignition is switched off. *Caution: Wait at least two minutes after the ignition has been switched off for any residual energy to drain from the main system relay.*

28 Clean off the top of the ECM box lid, to

8.23 Slacken the clamp (arrowed) securing the intake hose to the throttle control unit

8.24 Undo the 4 screws (arrowed) and remove the throttle control unit

8.28 Release the clips (arrowed) and remove the ECM box lid

8.29a Insert the tool alongside the ECM, and slide the connector locking catches forwards alternately, a little at a time

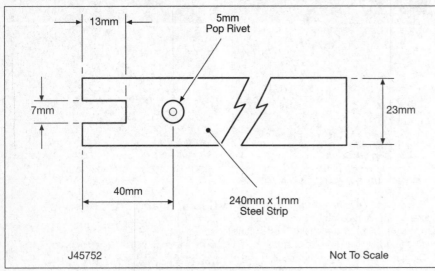

13mm

5mm
Pop Rivet

7mm

23mm

40mm

240mm x 1mm
Steel Strip

J45752

Not To Scale

8.29b Home-made ECM connector releasing tool

In order for the tool to slide down alongside the ECM, it will be necessary to file or grind the rivet to about half its original height

make sure no debris falls inside when it is removed. Release the catch on the side of the ECM module box lid. Lift off the lid and place it to one side **(see illustration)**.

29 To remove the ECM, insert Volvo tool No 999 5722 around the ECM and push the top of the tool rearwards as far as it will go, releasing the connector and the module. If the tool is not available, we managed to release the connectors using a strip of steel with a slot cut in the end and a 5 mm rivet as a

pivot, shaped as shown. Insert the homemade tool alongside the ECM and slide the catches forwards alternately, a little at a time as shown **(see illustrations)**. As the catches are slid forward the ECM will rise and detach from the connectors. **Note:** *Do not touch the control module terminal pins with bare hands – there is a danger of damage due to static electricity.*

30 Locate the ECM in the box, engaging it with the connector in the base.

31 Position the Volvo tool around the ECM

and pull the top of the tool as far forward as possible. If using the homemade tool, gently press the ECM downwards at the same time as levering the catches rearwards alternately a little at a time.

32 Refit the ECM box lid.

Outside temperature sensor

33 Remove the driver's door mirror as described in Chapter 11.

34 Carefully prise the sensor from the base of the mirror housing **(see illustration 6.23** in Chapter 12).

35 Disconnect the terminal pin from the connector.

36 Refitting is a reversal of removal.

Crankshaft position/speed sensor

Non-turbocharged engines

37 Remove the throttle control unit as previously described in this Section.

38 The sensor is located on the top of the transmission housing, adjacent to the cylinder block. Disconnect the sensor wiring plug, undo the bolt/nut and remove the sensor **(see illustration)**.

39 Refitting is a reversal of removal, tightening the new sensor retaining nut to the specified torque.

Turbocharged engines

40 Release the clamps and disconnect the hoses from the air cleaner to the turbocharger.

41 Disconnect the sensor wiring plug, then undo the nut/bolt and remove the sensor, located on the top of the transmission housing, adjacent to the engine block.

42 Refitting is a reversal of removal, tightening the new retaining nut/bolt to the specified torque.

Camshaft position sensor

Non-turbocharged engines

43 Remove the throttle control unit, as described previously in this Section.

44 Disconnect the sensor wiring plug, undo the bolt and remove the sensor **(see illustration)**.

45 Refitting is a reversal of removal,

Turbocharged engines

46 At the left-hand end of the cylinder head, disconnect the sensor wiring plug.

47 Undo the retaining bolt and remove the sensor **(see illustration)**.

48 Refitting is a reversal of removal.

Camshaft position solenoid

49 Undo the clips/screws, and remove the timing belt upper, inner cover **(see illustration)**.

50 Clean the area around the solenoid to prevent any dirt ingress, then disconnect the solenoid wiring plug.

51 Undo the retaining bolts, and remove the solenoid **(see illustration)**. Discard the gasket.

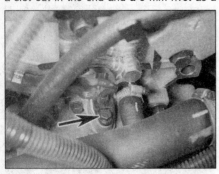

8.38 Undo the bolt (arrowed) and remove the crankshaft position/speed sensor

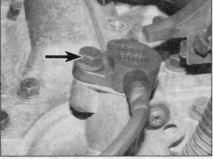

8.44 Undo the bolt (arrowed) and withdraw the camshaft position sensor

52 Ensure the mating faces are clean, then refit the solenoid using a new gasket, and tighten the retaining bolts to the specified torque.
53 Refit the timing cover.

Turbo boost pressure sensor

54 The boost pressure sensor is fitted into the pipe from the intercooler to the manifold. Disconnect the sensor wiring plug.
55 Undo the retaining screw, or release the clips, and remove the sensor **(see illustration)**.
56 Refitting is a reversal of removal.

Turbocharger control valve

57 Release the clip and detach the valve from the air cleaner housing cover.
58 Disconnect the valve wiring plug.
59 Note their fitted positions, then disconnect the hoses from the valve.
60 Refitting is a reversal of removal.

Clutch pedal position switch

61 Refer to Chapter 6.

Stop-light switch

62 Refer to Chapter 9.

9 Cruise control – general information

When fitted, the cruise control allows the vehicle to maintain a steady speed selected by the driver, regardless of gradients or prevailing winds.

The main components of the system is the control software (part of the steering wheel module), and a control switch. Brake and (when applicable) clutch pedal switches protect the engine against excessive speeds or loads should a pedal be depressed whilst the system is in use.

In operation, the driver accelerates to the desired speed, and then brings the system into use by means of the switch. The control software then monitors vehicle speed (from the wheel speed sensors) and opens or closes the throttle by means of the motorised throttle control unit. If the switch is moved to OFF, or the brake or clutch pedal is depressed, the control software immediately closes the throttle. The set speed is stored in the control module memory and the system can be reactivated by moving the switch to RESUME, provided that vehicle speed has not dropped below 25 mph.

The driver can override the cruise control for overtaking simply by depressing the throttle pedal. When the pedal is released, the set speed will be resumed.

The cruise control cannot be engaged at speeds below 25 mph, and should not be used in slippery or congested conditions.

For removal and refitting procedures:
a) *Steering wheel module – Chapter 10, Section 16.*

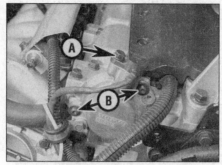

8.47 Camshaft position sensor retaining bolt (A) and end cover screws (B)

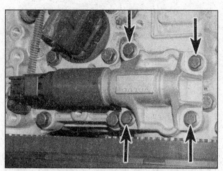

8.51 Undo the camshaft position sensor solenoid bolts (arrowed)

b) *Cruise control switch – Chapter 12.*
c) *Motorised throttle control unit – Section 8 of this Chapter.*

10 Intake manifold – removal and refitting

Note: *Observe the precautions in Section 1 before working on any component in the fuel system.*

Removal

1 Disconnect the battery negative lead (see Chapter 5A).
2 Remove the fuel rail and injectors as described in Section 8.
3 Remove the motorised throttle control unit as described in Section 8.

10.5 Undo the bolts and remove the cover (arrowed) over the ignition coils

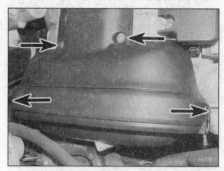

8.49 Release the clips and screws (arrowed), then remove the timing belt inner, upper cover

8.55 Turbocharger boost pressure sensor (arrowed – models up to 2002 shown)

4 Note their fitted positions, and disconnect the various vacuum hoses from the manifold.
5 Unscrew the oil filler cap, then undo the Torx bolts and remove the cover over the ignition coils **(see illustration)**.
6 Disconnect the engine breather hose from the camshaft cover **(see illustration)**.
7 Undo the screw/nut and detach the oil level dipstick guide tube bracket from the manifold **(see illustration)**.
8 Slacken the lower row of manifold retaining bolts, then remove the upper and outer bolts and lift the manifold from the engine. Discard the gasket. Note that on some models, a support bracket is fitted to the underside of the manifold – undo the screw and detach the bracket from the manifold.

Refitting

9 Refit by reversing the removal operations,

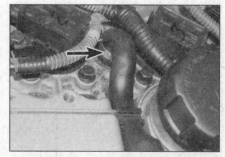

10.6 Release the clamp and disconnect the breather hose (arrowed) from the camshaft cover

10.7 Undo the bolt (arrowed) securing the oil level dipstick guide tube to the intake manifold

using a new manifold gasket, and new seals and O-rings for the injectors if necessary.

10 Locate the manifold gasket on the cylinder head, and place the manifold in position **(see illustration)**. Where applicable, remember to feed the crankcase ventilation hose up between the second and third ducts. Tighten the bolts to the specified torque setting.

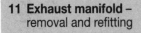

11 Exhaust manifold –
removal and refitting

Removal

1 Disconnect the battery negative lead (see Chapter 5A).

Turbocharged models

2 Remove the turbocharger as described in Section 12.

3 Undo the bolts and remove the heat shield from the exhaust manifold.

4 Undo the screws securing the support bracket to the cylinder block.

5 Undo the nuts, recover the washers, and remove the exhaust manifold. Discard the nuts and the gaskets, new ones must be fitted.

Non-turbocharged models

6 Undo the fasteners, and remove the engine cross-stay between the brackets on the front suspension turrets.

7 Detach the preheating pipe from the heat shield over the manifold, then undo the screws and remove the heat shield.

12.7 Turbocharger upper coolant retaining pipe and oil inlet pipe unions (arrowed)

10.10 Use the lower bolts to retain the gasket when refitting the manifold

8 Slacken the front left-hand roadwheel nuts/bolts, then jack up the front of the vehicle and support it securely on axle stands (see *Jacking and vehicle support*). Remove the roadwheel.

9 Undo the screws and remove the engine undershield.

10 Release the oxygen sensor wiring from the steering rack and the rear engine mounting.

11 Undo the nuts securing the front exhaust section to the manifold.

12 Undo the screws securing the cross-member under the front section of the exhaust pipe (just behind the steering rack), and release the brake pipe from the clips on the crossmember.

13 Carefully push the front section of the exhaust pipe rearwards and off the manifold studs. **Note:** *Take great care not to damage the oxygen sensor wiring or the flexible section of the exhaust pipe.*

14 Undo the nuts, and remove the manifold upwards and out of the engine compartment. Discard the gaskets, new ones must be fitted.

Refitting

15 Ensure the mating faces of the cylinder head and exhaust manifold are clean, then install the new gaskets over the studs in the cylinder head. Apply anti-seize grease (Copper slip) to the manifold studs.

16 Position the manifold, and fit the washers (where applicable) and new nuts. Tighten the nuts to the specified torque.

17 The remainder of refitting is a reversal of removal, noting the following points:

a) *Use new nuts to secure the front section*

12.9 Turbocharger pipe clamp bolt, oil return pipe flange, support bracket and manifold flange (arrowed)

of the exhaust pipe to the manifold/turbocharger.

b) *Tighten all fasteners to their specified torque where given.*

c) *Reconnect the battery negative lead as described in Chapter 5A.*

12 Turbocharger –
removal and refitting

Removal

1 Undo the fasteners and remove the engine cross-stay between the brackets on the suspension turrets.

2 Undo the screws/nuts and remove the heat shield over the turbocharger.

3 Release the clamps and remove the charge air pipe over the top of the engine.

4 Release the clamps and remove the intake hose between the air cleaner housing and the turbocharger.

5 Drain the cooling system as described in Chapter 1A.

6 Remove the right-hand driveshaft as described in Chapter 8.

7 Undo the upper coolant return pipe and oil intake pipe unions, and recover the seals **(see illustration)**.

8 Undo the upper nuts securing the front exhaust pipe to the turbocharger, and the upper nuts securing the turbocharger to the manifold.

9 Undo the bolt and remove the clamp bracket securing the oil feed and return pipes **(see illustration)**.

10 Undo the union and detach the oil feed pipe from the cylinder block.

11 Undo the union and detach the oil return pipe from the cylinder block. Recover the seals.

12 Undo the nuts securing the turbocharger to the manifold, and the front section of the exhaust pipe to the turbocharger.

13 Working in the engine compartment, pull the exhaust pipe rearwards and tie it to one side.

14 Note their fitted positions, then detach the vacuum hoses from the turbocharger assembly.

15 Remove the turbocharger from the manifold studs, and lay it on top of the steering rack.

16 Working underneath the vehicle, manoeuvre the turbocharger downwards, and away from the vehicle.

Refitting

17 Refitting is a reversal of removal, noting the following points:

a) *Return any studs that were removed with their nuts back to their original locations, with suitable thread-locking compound. If any of the studs are badly corroded, it may be advisable to renew all studs and nuts as a set.*

13.6 Undo the nuts securing the front section to the rear section

13.7a Undo the bolts and remove the front . . .

13.7b . . . and rear stiffener plates/ crossmembers

b) *Thoroughly clean the turbocharger and manifold mating faces prior to refitting.*
c) *Use a new manifold gasket, and use new seals on all disturbed unions.*
d) *Tighten all fasteners to their specified torque where given.*
e) *Refill the cooling system as described in Chapter 1A on completion.*

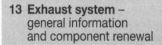

13 Exhaust system –
general information
and component renewal

General information

1 The exhaust system consists of a front section which comprises a front pipe and catalytic converter, and a rear section comprising an intermediate pipe, silencer and tailpipe. The system is suspended from the underbody on rubber mountings, and bolted to the exhaust manifold/turbocharger at the front. The front pipe-to-manifold/turbocharger connection is by a flange joint incorporating a flexible lattice type coupling.

2 The exhaust system should be examined for leaks, damage and security at regular intervals (see Chapter 1A). To do this, apply the handbrake, and allow the engine to idle in a well-ventilated area. Lie down on each side of the car in turn, and check the full length of the system for leaks, while an assistant temporarily places a wad of cloth over the end of the tailpipe. If a leak is evident, stop the engine and use a proprietary repair kit to seal it. If the leak is excessive, or damage is

evident, renew the section. Check the rubber mountings for deterioration, and renew them if necessary.

Removal

Front section

3 With the handbrake applied, jack up the front (and preferably the rear) of the car, and support it securely on axle stands (see *Jacking and vehicle support*). Undo the screws and remove the engine undershield.
4 Disconnect the two heated oxygen sensor wiring connectors, and release the wiring from any cable-ties.
5 Undo the nuts securing the front pipe flange to the manifold/turbocharger. On some models, access may be improved from above after removing the heat shield over the manifold.
6 Undo the nuts and bolts connecting the front and rear sections **(see illustration)**.
7 Unclip the metal brake pipe from the front stiffener plate/crossmember, then undo the bolts and remove the front and central stiffener plates/crossmembers from the underbody **(see illustrations)**.
8 Separate the front pipe-to-manifold/turbocharger joint, and remove the front section from under the car.

Rear section

9 Chock the front wheels, then jack up the rear (and preferably the front) of the car, and support it on axle stands (see *Jacking and vehicle support*).
10 Undo the nuts and bolts connecting the

front to the rear section, then undo the bolts and remove the stiffener plate/crossmember under the rear section **(see illustration 13.6)**.
11 Release the tailpipe and silencer from their rubber mountings **(see illustrations)**, and slide the rear section forward until the tailpipe is clear of the rear suspension. Remove the system from under the car.

Refitting

12 Refitting is a reversal of removal, bearing in mind the following points:
a) *Use a new sealing ring or flange gasket, as applicable, on the front pipe-to-manifold joint.*
b) *When refitting the front section, loosely attach the front pipe to the manifold, and the catalytic converter to the intermediate pipe. Align the system, then tighten the front pipe-to-manifold nuts first, followed by the intermediate pipe clamp nuts.*
c) *Ensure that there is a minimum clearance of 20 mm between the exhaust system and underbody/suspension components.*

Rear silencer

13 If the rear silencer is the only part of the system requiring renewal, cut the old silencer from the rear section of the system using pipe cutters, 27 mm from the welded joint in front of the silencer **(see illustration)**. Free the silencer from its mountings, and remove it from the vehicle.
14 Clean up and de-burr the end of the existing exhaust pipe with a file/emery tape, etc.

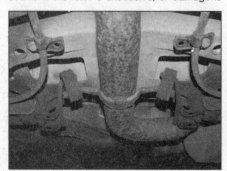

13.11a Exhaust rear section rubber mountings . . .

13.11b . . . and beside the tailbox

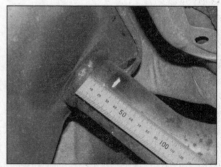

13.13 Cut the old silencer from the pipe, 27 mm from the welded joint

15 Rear silencers are available which slip over the end of the existing exhaust pipe, and are clamped in place. Slip the new silencer over the pipe, engage the rubber silencer mountings, then tighten the pipe clamp securely.

14 Intercooler – removal and refitting

1 The intercooler is attached to the engine cooling system radiator at the front of the vehicle. To remove the intercooler, remove the radiator as described in Chapter 3.

2 Release the clips and detach the intercooler from the radiator.

3 Refitting is a reversal of removal.

Chapter 4 Part B:
Fuel and exhaust systems – diesel engines

Contents

Degrees of difficulty

Easy, suitable for novice with little experience	**Fairly easy,** suitable for beginner with some experience	**Fairly difficult,** suitable for competent DIY mechanic	**Difficult,** suitable for experienced DIY mechanic	**Very difficult,** suitable for expert DIY or professional

Specifications

General

System type:

D5244T/T2/T3 engines	Direct injection common rail with Bosch high pressure delivery pump and Electronic Diesel Control EDC15C11
D5244T4/T5/T6/T7 engines	Direct injection common rail with Bosch high pressure delivery pump with Electronic Diesel Control EDC16C31
Fuel tank pump pressure	2.0 bar maximum
Fuel injection pump	Tandem pump (high pressure and low pressure) driven by the intake camshaft
Injection pressure.	300 to 1600 bar
Turbocharger type:	Variable nozzle
Turbocharger boost pressure	2.09 bar (maximum)
Idle speed*	700 rpm

* Not adjustable – controlled by engine control module (ECM)

Torque wrench settings

	Nm	lbf ft
Camshaft position sensor	10	7
Catalytic converter to turbocharger*	24	18
Engine cross-stay brackets to suspension turrets	50	37
Engine cross-stay to brackets on the suspension turrets	80	59
Engine cross-stay to engine mounting bracket	80	59
Exhaust front pipe to intermediate pipe	24	18
Exhaust front pipe-to-flange nuts/bolts*	30	22
Exhaust gas temperature sensor	45	33
Exhaust manifold to cylinder head	30	22
Fuel high-pressure pipe union nuts*	28	21
Fuel injection pump mounting screws	20	15
Fuel injector clamp screws*	13	10
Fuel pressure safety valve	95	70
Fuel pressure sensor:		
D5244T/T2/T3 engines	20	15
D5244T4/T5/T6/T7 engines	70	52
Fuel pressure sensor adapter to common rail	60	44
Fuel rail-to-cylinder head bolts:		
D5244T/T2/T3 engines	17	13
D5244T4/T5/T6/T7 engines	26	19
Fuel temperature sensor	20	15
Heated oxygen sensor	45	33
Manifold absolute pressure sensor (MAP)	10	7
Turbocharger coolant pipe screws	26	19
Turbocharger oil feed to cylinder block	38	28
Turbocharger oil feed to turbocharger	18	13
Turbocharger oil return flange bolts	12	9
Turbocharger to exhaust manifold*:		
D5244T/T2/T3 engines	30	22
D5244T4/T5/T6/T7 engines	37	27

Do not re-use

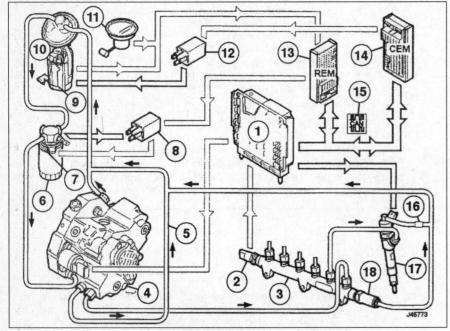

1.4 Common rail fuel injection system

1 Engine management ECM
    EDC15C11
2 Fuel pressure sensor
3 Common fuel rail
4 Tandem (high and low
    pressure) pump
5 Return line
6 Fuel filter with
    temperature sensor
7 Fuel heater element
8 Fuel heater element relay
9 Fuel level sensor
10 Fuel pressure sensor
11 Fuel level sensor
12 Fuel pump relay
13 Rear electronic module
14 Central electronic module
15 CAN databus
16 Check valve
17 Fuel injector
18 Relief valve

1 General information and precautions

General information

The operation of the fuel injection system is described in more detail in Section 5.

Fuel is drawn from a tank under the rear of the vehicle by a tank-immersed electric pump, and then forced through a filter to the injection pump. The intake camshaft driven injection pump is a tandem pump on D5244T/T2/T3 engines – a low pressure gear-type pump which supplies the high-pressure pump with fuel at a constant pressure, and a high-pressure piston-type pump which supplies fuel to the common fuel rail at variable pressure. Fuel is supplied from the common fuel rail to the injectors. Also inside the injection pump assembly is a pressure control valve which regulates the quantity of fuel to the high-pressure pump, and a bypass valve which returns excess fuel back to the low pressure pump. The injectors are operated by solenoids controlled by the ECM, based on information supplied by various sensors. The engine ECM also controls the preheating side of the system – refer to Chapter 5A for more details.

The EDC (electronic diesel control) system fitted, incorporates a 'drive-by-wire' system, where the traditional accelerator cable is

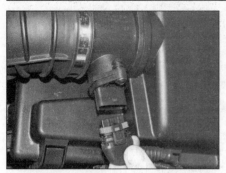

2.1a Unplug the mass airflow meter wiring plug . . .

2.1b . . . then slacken the clamp (arrowed) and disconnect the outlet hose

2.2 Unclip the vacuum valve and wiring loom

2.7 Slacken the clamp (arrowed) and disconnect the outlet hose

2.9a Press in the centre pin, prise out the plastic rivet (arrowed) . . .

2.9b . . . and manoeuvre the intake flap assembly from place

replaced by an accelerator pedal position sensor. The position and rate-of-change of the accelerator pedal is reported by the position sensor to the ECM, which then adjusts the fuel injectors and fuel pressure to deliver the required amount of fuel, and optimum combustion efficiency

The exhaust system incorporates a turbocharger, catalytic converter, particle filter, and an EGR system (depending on model/market). Further detail of the emission control systems can be found in Chapter 4C **(see illustration)**.

Precautions

• When working on diesel fuel system components, scrupulous cleanliness must be observed, and care must be taken not to introduce any foreign matter into fuel lines or components.
• After carrying out any work involving disconnection of fuel lines, it is advisable to check the connections for leaks; pressurise the system by cranking the engine several times.
• Electronic control units are very sensitive components, and certain precautions must be taken to avoid damage to these units as follows.
• When carrying out welding operations on the vehicle using electric welding equipment, the battery and alternator should be disconnected.
• Although the underbonnet-mounted modules will tolerate normal underbonnet conditions, they can be adversely affected by excess heat or moisture. If using welding equipment or pressure-washing equipment in

the vicinity of an electronic module, take care not to direct heat, or jets of water or steam, at the module. If this cannot be avoided, remove the module from the vehicle, and protect its wiring plug with a plastic bag.
• Before disconnecting any wiring, or removing components, always ensure that the ignition is switched off.
• Do not attempt to improvise ECM fault diagnosis procedures using a test lamp or multimeter, as irreparable damage could be caused to the module.
• After working on fuel injection/engine management system components, ensure that all wiring is correctly reconnected before reconnecting the battery or switching on the ignition.

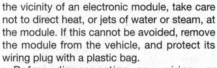

2 Air cleaner assembly – removal and refitting

Removal

D5244T/T2/T3 engines

1 Disconnect the mass airflow meter wiring plug, slacken the clamp and disconnect the outlet hose from the air cleaner cover **(see illustrations)**.
2 Unclip the engine mounting vacuum valve (where fitted) and wiring from the front of the air cleaner housing **(see illustration)**.
3 Pull the housing upwards sharply to release it from the three mounting grommets. Remove the air intake duct as the housing is withdrawn.

D5244T4/T5/T6/T7 engines

4 Remove the ECM as described in Section 11.
5 Pull up the plastic cover from the top of the engine.
6 Disconnect the mass airflow meter wiring plug.
7 Slacken the clamp and disconnect the outlet hose from the mass airflow meter **(see illustration)**.
8 Unclip the engine mounting vacuum valve from the front of the air cleaner housing, and unclip the wiring loom on the right-hand side of the housing.
9 Push-in the centre pin, prise out the plastic expansion rivet, and manoeuvre the air intake ducting from the bonnet cross panel **(see illustrations)**.
10 Pull the housing upwards sharply to release it from the three mounting grommets.

Refitting

11 Refitting is a reversal of removal. Make sure the outlet and intake ducts are clipped securely into position (where applicable).

3 Fuel tank – removal and refitting

Note: *Observe the precautions in Section 1 before working on any component in the fuel system.*

Removal

1 Before the tank can be removed, it must be drained of as much fuel as possible. To

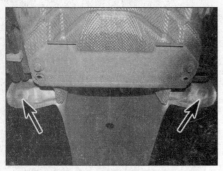

3.7a Undo the heat shield Torx bolts
(arrowed) . . .

3.7b . . . and release the brake pipes from
the clips on the tank straps

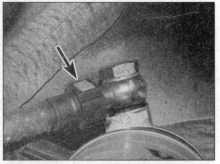

3.9a Depress the button (arrowed), and
pull the coupling from the filter connection

3.9b Disconnect the wiring plugs from the
filter

avoid the dangers and complications of fuel handling and storage, it is advisable to carry out this operation with the tank almost empty.
2 Disconnect the battery negative lead (see Chapter 5A).
3 Slacken the left-rear roadwheel bolts, then chock the front wheels then jack up the rear of the vehicle and support it on axle stands (see *Jacking and vehicle support*). Remove the roadwheel.
4 Carry out the operations described in Section 7, paragraphs 2 to 6.
5 Remove the rear section of the exhaust system as described in Section 17. Support the front section of the system to avoid placing any strain on the flexible section.
6 Unclip ABS wiring from both sides of the fuel tank.
7 Undo the two Torx bolts at the front of the heat shield under the tank, and unclip the

brake pipes from the clips at the front of the tank retaining straps **(see illustrations)**.
8 Disconnect the left-hand handbrake cable from the brake assembly as described in Chapter 9, release the retaining brackets and position both cables in front of the tank.
9 Disconnect hose from the fuel filter at the quick-release coupling (press in the buttons on the coupling), and disconnect the wiring plugs from the filter **(see illustrations)**.
10 Release the hose clamps and disconnect the fuel filler hose and shut-off pipe from the tank.
11 Position a trolley jack under the centre of the tank. Insert a protective wooden pad between the jack head and tank base, then raise the jack to just take the weight of the tank.
12 Undo the tank retaining straps, and carefully lower the jack and tank slightly.
13 Lower the jack and tank, and remove the tank from under the car.

14 If the tank is contaminated with sediment or water, remove the gauge sender unit and the fuel pump as described in Section 7. Swill the tank out with clean fuel.
15 The tank is moulded from a synthetic material and if damaged, it should be renewed. However, in certain cases it may be possible to have small leaks or minor damage repaired. Seek the advice of a dealer or suitable specialist concerning tank repair.
16 If a new tank is to be fitted, transfer all the components from the old tank to the new. Always renew the seals and plastic nuts securing the fuel pump and gauge sender unit. Once used, they may not seat and seal properly on a new tank.

Refitting

17 Refitting is a reversal of removal, bearing in mind the following points:
  a) *Locate the tank in position, and tighten the rear strap mountings. Push the tank forwards, and centre the fuel gauge sender unit and fuel pump plastic nuts with respect to their access holes in the floor. Now tighten the front strap mountings.*
  b) *On completion, refill the tank with fuel and check exhaustively for signs of leakage before driving the car on the road.*

4 Accelerator pedal – removal and refitting
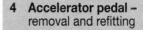

Removal

1 Undo the two screws and remove the trim panel above the pedals in the driver's footwell.
2 Undo the three nuts securing the assembly to the bulkhead **(see illustration)**.
3 Release the cable tie, and disconnect the position sensor wiring plug as the pedal assembly is removed. No further dismantling of the assembly is recommended **(see illustration)**.

Refitting

4 Refit by reversing the removal operations.

5 Fuel injection system – general information

The system is under the overall control of the Electronic Diesel Control (EDC) system, which also controls the preheating system (see Chapter 5A).
Fuel is supplied from the rear-mounted fuel tank, via an electrically-powered lift pump (controlled by the central electronic module), and fuel filter, to the fuel injection pump. The fuel injection pump supplies fuel under high pressure to the common fuel rail. The fuel rail provides a reservoir of fuel under pressure ready for the injectors to deliver direct to

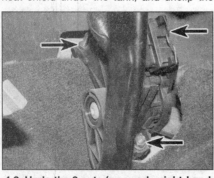

4.2 Undo the 3 nuts (arrowed – right-hand
upper one hidden)

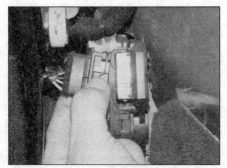

4.3 Depress the clip and disconnect the
wiring plug

the combustion chamber. The individual fuel injectors incorporate solenoids, which when operated, allow the high-pressure fuel to be injected. The solenoids are controlled by the EDC electric control module (ECM). The fuel injection pump purely provides high-pressure fuel. The timing and duration of the injection is controlled by the ECM based on the information received from the various sensors. In order to increase combustion efficiency and reduce combustion noise (diesel 'knock'), a small amount of fuel is injected before the main injection takes place – this is known as Pre- or Pilot-injection. The fuel filter incorporates a heater element and a temperature sensor – the rear electronic module activates the heater at temperatures below -3° C and deactivates it at 5° C.

Additionally, the engine management ECM activates the preheating system (Chapter 5A), and the exhaust gas recirculation (EGR) system (see Chapter 4C).

The system uses the following sensors.

a) *Crankshaft sensor – informs the ECM of the crankshaft speed and position.*

b) *Coolant temperature sensor – informs the ECM of engine temperature.*

c) *Mass airflow/intake air temperature sensor – informs the ECM of the mass and temperature of air entering the intake tract.*

d) *Wheel speed sensor – informs the ECM of the vehicle speed.*

e) *Accelerator pedal position sensor – informs the ECM of throttle position, and the rate of throttle opening/closing.*

f) *Fuel high-pressure sensor – informs the ECM of the pressure of the fuel in the common rail.*

g) *Camshaft position sensor – informs the ECM of the camshaft position so that the engine firing sequence can be established.*

h) *Stop-light switch – informs the ECM when the brakes are being applied.*

i) *Manifold absolute pressure sensor – informs the ECM of the boost pressure generated by the turbocharger.*

j) *Air conditioning pressure sensor – informs the ECM of the high-pressure side of the air conditioning circuit, in case a raised idle speed is required to compensate for compressor load.*

On all models, a 'drive-by-wire' throttle control system is used. The accelerator pedal is not physically connected to the fuel injection pump with a traditional cable, but instead is monitored by a dual potentiometer mounted on the pedal assembly, which provides the engine control module (ECM) with a signal relating to accelerator pedal movement.

The signals from the various sensors are processed by the ECM, and the optimum fuel quantity and injection timing settings are selected for the prevailing engine operating conditions.

Catalytic converter(s), a particle filter (depending on model and market) and an exhaust gas recirculation (EGR) system are fitted, to reduce harmful exhaust gas emissions. Details of this and other emissions control system equipment are given in Chapter 4C.

If there is an abnormality in any of the readings obtained from any sensor, the ECM enters its back-up mode. In this event, the ECM ignores the abnormal sensor signal, and assumes a pre-programmed value which will allow the engine to continue running (albeit at reduced efficiency). If the ECM enters this back-up mode, the warning light on the instrument panel will come on, and the relevant fault code will be stored in the ECM memory.

If the warning light comes on, the vehicle should be taken to a Volvo dealer or specialist at the earliest opportunity. A complete test of the Electronic Diesel Control (EDC) system can then be carried out, using a special electronic test unit which is simply plugged into the system's diagnostic connector. The connector is located below the driver's side of the facia above the pedals **(see illustration)**.

6 Fuel system – priming and bleeding

1 Volvo state that the no priming or bleeding is required, as the system is self-bleeding. However, If the vehicle has run out of diesel, or major parts of the fuel system have been changed, replenish the tank or check there is sufficient fuel in the tank (as applicable) then operate the fuel tank-mounted pump for 1 to 2 minutes by turning the ignition key to position 2 prior to attempting to the start

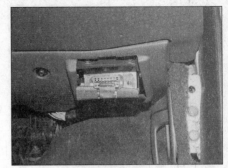

5.8 Unclip the cover to access the diagnostic plug

the engine. This should ensure sufficient fuel reaches the engine mounted pump prior to starting.

7 Fuel gauge sender/ pump units – removal and refitting

Note: *Observe the precautions in Section 1 before working on any component in the fuel system.*

Removal

1 Disconnect the battery negative lead (see Chapter 5A).

2 Remove the rear seat as described in Chapter 11.

3 Fold the floor carpet forwards to expose the fuel tank access covers.

4 Undo the nuts and remove the access covers over the fuel pump and sender unit (right-hand side) or the left-hand sender unit **(see illustration)**.

5 Trace the wiring for the sender unit/pump or sender unit, and disconnect the relevant connector, release any cable-ties, then feed the wiring back and through the sender unit aperture in the floor.

6 Press in the buttons and disconnect the hoses from the right-hand pump/sender unit **(see illustration)**.

7 Unscrew the left-hand sender unit plastic retaining collar using a pair of large, crossed-screwdrivers, or improvise a tool such as an old two-legged puller and an adjustable spanner **(see illustration)**.

7.4 Undo the nuts and remove the left- or right-hand access covers (arrowed)

7.6 Press in the buttons (arrowed) and disconnect the hoses

7.7 We used and old two-legged puller to unscrew the plastic retaining collar

7.8 Disconnect the wiring plug from the underside of the sender cover

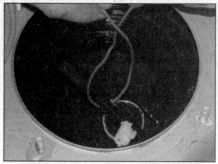

7.9 Attach a length of wire to the transfer hose to aid refitting

7.11 With the float arm held in its lowest position, manoeuvre the sender/pump assembly from the tank

8 Withdraw the left-hand sender from the fuel tank, then depress the clip and slide the fuel transfer ejector from the sender, and disconnect the wiring plug from the underside of the sender cover **(see illustration)**. Recover the O-ring seal from between the sender cover and the tank opening.

9 Attached a length of wire (or similar) to the transfer ejector hose to aid refitting. The wire must be long enough to reach across the full width of the fuel tank **(see illustration)**.

10 Unscrew the right-hand sender/pump unit retaining collar from the tank.

11 Carefully lift the sender/pump unit, pushing the float arm down and squeezing the sender and pump holder so the float arm is held in its lowest position **(see illustration)**. Manoeuvre the sender/pump assembly from the tank, pulling the hose/wiring assembly across from the left-hand side of the tank. Ensure the wire attached to the plugs (paragraph 9) is long enough to allow the assembly to be removed without disappearing into the tank. Free the routing wire from the plugs and leave it in place ready for refitting. Recover the O-ring seal from between the sender cover and the tank opening.

12 If required, the right-hand sender unit can be unclipped from the fuel pump assembly **(see illustration)**.

Refitting

13 Attach the routing wire to the plugs/hose assembly (see paragraph 9), and insert the sender/pump unit, pulling the hose/wiring assembly across to the left-hand side of the tank, and ensuring the float arm and float are

inserted into place without any damage **(see illustration)**.

14 Reconnect the wiring plugs to the underside of the left-hand sender unit, and detach the routing wire.

15 The remainder of refitting is a reversal of removal, bearing in mind the following points:

a) *Use a new seal smeared with petroleum jelly.*

b) *Position the sender/pump units, so the arrows on the covers point towards the rear of the vehicle **(see illustration)**.*

c) *Route the wiring over the top of the fuel tank and out through the fuel pump aperture. Reconnect and secure with cable-ties, where applicable.*

8 Fuel injection system – testing and adjustment

Testing

1 If a fault appears in the fuel injection system, first ensure that all the system wiring connectors are securely connected and free from corrosion. Ensure that the fault is not due to poor maintenance; ie, check that the air cleaner filter element is clean, that the cylinder compression pressures are correct (see Chapter 2B), and that the engine breather hoses are clear and undamaged (see Chapter 4C).

2 If the engine will not start, check the condition of the glow plugs (see Chapter 5A).

3 If these checks fail to reveal the cause of the problem, the vehicle should be taken to a

Volvo dealer or specialist for testing using special electronic equipment which is plugged into the diagnostic connector (see Section 5). The tester should locate the fault quickly and simply, avoiding the need to test all the system components individually, which is time-consuming, and also carries a risk of damaging the ECM.

Adjustment

4 The engine idle speed, maximum speed and fuel injection pump timing are all controlled by the ECM. Whilst in theory it is possible to check the settings, if they are found to be in need of adjustment, the car will have to be taken to a suitably-equipped Volvo dealer or specialist. They will have access to the necessary diagnostic equipment required to test and (where possible) adjust the settings.

9 Fuel injection pump – removal and refitting

Caution: Be careful not to allow dirt into the injection pump or injector pipes during this procedure.
Note: *Any rigid high-pressure fuel pipes disturbed must be renewed.*

Removal

1 Disconnect the battery negative lead (see Chapter 5A).

2 Remove the plastic cover from the top of the engine, by pulling it straight up from its mountings.

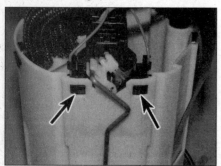

7.12 Release the clips (arrowed) and detach the sender from the pump

7.13 Attach the routing wire to the transfer hoses and pull the hose/wiring across to the left-hand side of the tank

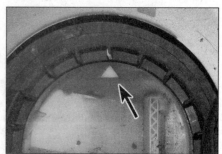

7.15 Both sender unit covers must be positioned with the mark (arrowed) pointing towards the rear of the vehicle

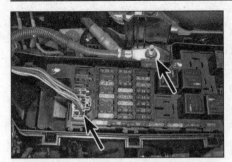

9.5a Undo the positive power supply cable nut (arrowed) and disconnect the engine loom wiring plug (arrowed)

9.5b Undo the 2 bolts (arrowed) and move the electrical box to one side

9.6 Undo the screws and remove the breather hose bracket (arrowed)

9.8a Release the clamps (arrowed) and disconnect the fuel supply and return hoses from the pump – D5244T/T2/T3 engines

9.8b Fuel supply hose (arrowed) . . .

9.8c . . . and return hose (arrowed) – D5244T4/T5/T6/T7 engines

3 Remove the air cleaner assembly as described in Section 2

4 Release the clamp and disconnect the turbocharger intake hose, then undo the mounting bracket bolt and remove the hose.

D5244T/T2 and T3 engines

5 Undo the nut and disconnect the positive power supply cable and engine wiring loom plug from the central electrical unit adjacent to the left-hand suspension turret, then undo the 2 mounting bolts and move the electrical unit to one side **(see illustrations)**.

6 Undo the 2 retaining screws securing the crankcase breather pipe bracket **(see illustration)**.

All engines

7 Slacken the unions, then remove high-pressure fuel pipe between the pump and the common (fuel) rail. Discard the pipe, a new one must be fitted. Plug or cover the fuel rail and pump ports to prevent dirt ingress.

8 Release the clamps/undo the bolts and disconnect the supply and return hoses from the pump **(see illustrations)**. If the metal hose clamps are damaged during removal, update them with traditional worm-drive clamps. Plug or seal the pump ports to prevent dirt ingress.

9 Disconnect the pump control valve and fuel temperature sensor wiring plugs **(see illustrations)**.

10 Remove the three retaining screws, and remove the fuel pump. Recover the connecting piece between the end of the camshaft and the pump drive – this is easily lost as the pump is

removed **(see illustrations)**. Discard the seal, a new one must be fitted. With the exception of the control valve and temperature sensor (see Section 11), no internal components of the pump are available. If the pump is faulty,

9.9a Control valve wiring plug . . .

the complete unit may have to be replaced – consult a Volvo dealer or specialist.

Caution: Do not rotate the pump once removed – it's important that it retains its original position if refitted.

9.9b . . . and temperature sensor wiring plug (arrowed)

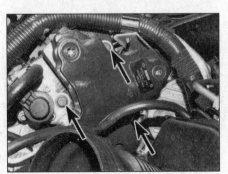

9.10a Pump retaining screws (arrowed)

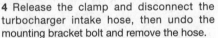
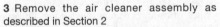

9.10b The connecting piece is easily lost as the pump is removed

9.12 The pump connection piece must align with the slots in the end of the intake camshaft

Refitting

11 Ensure that the mating surfaces of the pump and engine are clean and dry, and fit the new O-ring seal to the pump. Lubricate the seal with clean engine oil.

12 Position the fuel pump, ensuring the connecting piece is in place, then tighten the mounting screws to the specified torque **(see illustration)**.

13 Reconnect the fuel supply and return hoses to the pump, and secure them with new clamps.

14 Fit the new high-pressure fuel pipe between the pump and common rail, then tighten to the specified torque, using a crows-foot adapter **(see illustration)**.

15 The remainder of refitting is a reversal of removal, bearing in mind the following points:

10.2 Slacken the clamps and remove the hose

10.6b ... use a second spanner to prevent the port on the injector from turning whilst slackening the union

9.14 Use a crows-foot adapter to tighten the pump union, and a second spanner to counterhold the pump port. Do not allow the pump port to rotate

a) *Prior to starting the engine, turn the ignition key to position 2 for at least 80 seconds. This activates the tank-mounted pump, and ensures sufficient fuel reaches the injection pump for lubrication purposes prior to starting.*

b) *Depress the accelerator pedal to the floor then start the engine as normal (this may take longer than usual – operate the starter in ten second bursts with 5 seconds rest in between each operation). Run the engine at a fast idle speed for a minute or so to purge any remaining trapped air from the fuel lines. After this time the engine should idle smoothly at a constant speed.*

c) *Once the engine has started, thoroughly check for fuel leaks from the disturbed pipes/hoses.*

10.6a Undo the pipe union on the common rail ...

10.7a Prise out the clip ...

Caution: Be careful not to allow dirt into the injection pump or injector pipes during this procedure.

Removal

1 Remove the plastic cover from the top of the engine by pulling it straight up from its mountings.

D5244T/T2/T3 engines

2 Release the clamps and remove the charge air hose connected to the intake manifold **(see illustration)**.

3 Disconnect the crankcase breather hose from the cylinder head cover.

4 Pull the connectors from the glow plugs.

5 Make sure the areas around the high-pressure fuel pipe unions from the fuel rail to the injectors are scrupulously clean and free from debris, etc. If possible, use a vacuum cleaner and a degreaser to clean the area.

6 Undo the unions, then remove the high-pressure fuel pipes from the fuel rail to the injectors. Discard the fuel pipes, new ones must be fitted. Use a second open-ended spanner on the injector port to counterhold when slackening the pipe union **(see illustrations)**. Be prepared for fuel spillage and plug/cover the ports in the injectors and fuel rail to prevent dirt ingress.

7 Prise out the clips, then disconnect the fuel return hoses from the top of each injector **(see illustrations)**.

8 Note their fitted positions, then disconnect the injector wiring plugs.

9 Unscrew the two Torx bolts securing each injector clamp, and remove the injectors. Slide the copper sealing washer from the end of each injector, then prise off the circlip, remove the washer followed by the clamp ring. Discard the sealing washers, clamp rings, circlips and mounting screws – new ones must be fitted **(see illustrations)**. If the injectors are to be refitted, mark them for identification, so they can refitted to their original locations.

D5244T4/T5/T6/T7 engines

10 Undo the bolts/nuts and remove the

10.7b ... and disconnect the return hose from the top of the injector (note the Class number – arrowed)

cross-stay between the suspension turrets in the engine compartment.

11 Undo the 4 nuts and remove the rubber shield over the fuel injectors **(see illustration)**. Unclip the wiring connectors from the rear of the shield as it's withdrawn.

12 Make sure the areas around the high-pressure fuel pipe unions from the fuel rail to the injectors are scrupulously clean and free from debris, etc. If possible, use a vacuum cleaner and a degreaser to clean the area.

13 Undo the unions, then remove the high-pressure fuel pipes from the fuel rail to the injectors. Discard the fuel pipes, new ones must be fitted. Use a second spanner on the injector port to counterhold when slackening the pipe union **(see illustrations 10.6a and 10.6b)**. Be prepared for fluid spillage, and plug/cover the ports in the injectors and fuel rail to prevent contamination.

14 Prise out the clips, then disconnect the fuel return hoses from the top of each injector **(see illustrations 10.7a and 10.7b)**.

15 Note their fitted positions, then disconnect the injector wiring plugs, and unclip the wiring loom from No.1 injector.

16 Unscrew the two screws (complete with spacers where fitted) securing each injector clamp, and remove the injectors. Recover the metal washers beneath each clamp **(see illustrations)**.

17 Slide the copper sealing washer from the end of each injector, followed by the clamp ring. Discard the sealing washers, clamp rings and mounting screws – new ones must be fitted **(see illustrations)**. If the injectors are

10.9a Undo the injector clamp screws (arrowed) . . .

10.9c Slide off the copper washer . . .

to be refitted, mark them for identification, so they can refitted to their original locations.

All engines

18 If the injectors are to be refitted, plug all openings, and store them upright in their

10.9b . . . and carefully remove the injector (don't lever against the solenoid at the top)

10.9d . . . then prise off the circlip

original order. They must be refitted to their original positions **(see illustration)**.

Refitting

19 Ensure that the injectors and seats in

10.11 Undo the 4 nuts (arrowed) and remove the rubber shield

10.16a Injector retaining screws (arrowed)

10.16b Recover the metal washers beneath the clamps (arrowed)

10.17a Renew the copper sealing washers . . .

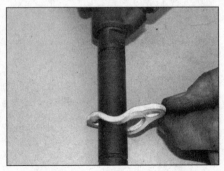

10.17b . . . and the clamp rings

10.18 The injectors should be stored upright

11.2 Pull the plastic cover on top of the engine straight up from its mountings

11.8 Undo the bolt (arrowed) and remove the crankshaft position/speed sensor

11.10 Disconnect the mass airflow sensor wiring plug

cylinder head are clean, dry and free from soot. It's essential the sealing surfaces are dirt-free, otherwise leakage will occur.

20 Fit new clamp rings, washers, circlips (where applicable) and sealing washers to the injectors, and refit them to the cylinder head. Where applicable, fit the metal washers between the injector clamp ring and the camshaft cover. Only finger-tighten the new retaining screws at this point. Ensure the screws are tightened evenly. **Note:** *On D5244T4/T5/T6/T7 engines, the clamp rings are supplied with new screws. The new screws are shorter than the original ones, and must be fitted without the original spacers between the screw head and clamp ring.*

21 Fit the new rigid high-pressure pipes between the common rail and the injectors. Starting at the common rail, tighten the pipe unions to the specified torque. Repeat this procedure on the pipe unions at the injectors. Use a second open-ended spanner to counter-hold the injector ports whilst tightening the pipe unions **(see illustrations 10.6a and 10.6b)**.

22 Now tighten the injector retaining screws to the specified torque. It's essential that the screws are tightened evenly – half a turn at a time.

23 The remainder of refitting is a reversal of removal, bearing in mind the following points:
 a) *Check the condition of the fuel return hoses, and replace if any appear damaged or perished.*
 b) *On D5244T/T2/T3 engines, make a note of the 'Class' identification number on the top of each injector* **(see illustration 10.7b)**.

11.15 Mass airflow sensor Torx bolts (arrowed)

Only 2 Classes are available as spare parts. Class 1 is replaced with Class 1, whereas Class 2 replaces Class 2 and Class 3. If 3 or more injectors of Class 3 are replaced, new software must be downloaded to the engine management ECM. Entrust this task to a Volvo dealer or suitably-equipped specialist.
 c) *On D5244T4/T5/T6/T7 engines, if new injectors are fitted, new software must be downloaded to the engine management ECM from Volvo. Entrust this task to a Volvo dealer or specialist.*
 d) *Depress the accelerator pedal to the floor then start the engine as normal (this may take longer than usual – operate the starter in ten second bursts with 5 seconds rest in between each operation). Run the engine at a fast idle speed for a minute or so to purge any remaining trapped air from the fuel lines. After this time the engine should idle smoothly at a constant speed.*
 e) *Once the engine has started, thoroughly check for fuel leaks from the disturbed pipes/hoses.*

11 Electronic Diesel Control (EDC) system components – removal and refitting

Crankshaft position/speed sensor

1 Remove the air cleaner assembly as described in Section 2.
2 Remove the plastic cover over the top of the engine by pulling it straight up from its mountings **(see illustration)**.
3 Disconnect the EGR solenoid valve wiring plug, located at the left-hand end of the cylinder head.
4 Undo the retaining screw, then remove the charge air pipe from the left-hand end of the cylinder head.
5 On models with automatic transmission, undo the bolts/nuts and remove the vacuum pump from the end of the exhaust camshaft (see Chapter 9).
6 Remove the EGR cooler, and valve assembly, as described in Chapter 4C.

7 Trace the wiring back from the sensor, and disconnect the wiring plug.
8 Slacken and remove the retaining bolt and carefully remove the sensor from the bracket **(see illustration)**.
9 Refitting is the reverse of removal, tightening the retaining bolt securely.

Mass airflow/ intake air temperature sensor

D5244T/T2/T3 engines

10 Ensure the ignition is switched off then release the retaining clip and disconnect the wiring connector from the airflow sensor **(see illustration)**.
11 Slacken the retaining clip and detach the intake duct from the airflow sensor.
12 Undo the screws then remove the airflow sensor from the air cleaner housing, along with its sealing ring.
13 Refitting is the reverse of removal, lubricating the new sealing ring.

D5244/T4/T5/T6/T7 engines

14 Remove the air cleaner assembly as described in Section 2.
15 Undo the 2 bolts and remove the mass airflow sensor **(see illustration)**.
16 Refitting is the reversal of removal, lubricating the new sealing ring.

Coolant temperature sensor

17 Refer to Chapter 3 for removal and refitting details.

Accelerator pedal position sensor

18 The sensor is secured to the accelerator pedal. Refer to Section 4 of this Chapter on pedal removal. Note that at the time of writing, the sensor was not available separately from the pedal assembly.

Turbo boost pressure sensor

19 On vehicles up to 2003 model year, then sensor is mounted on the right-hand end of the intake manifold. On vehicles after this date, the sensor is mounted on the intercooler outer pipe **(see illustration)**.
20 Ensure the ignition is switched off then disconnect the wiring connector from the sensor.

11.19 Turbo boost pressure sensor

11.25 Release the clips (arrowed) and remove the ECM box lid

11.26a Insert the tool alongside the ECM, and slide the connector locking catches forwards alternately, a little at a time

21 Slacken and remove the retaining bolt and remove the sensor from the vehicle.

22 Refitting is the reverse of removal, tightening the sensor retaining bolt securely.

Stop-light switch

23 The engine control module receives a signal from the stop-light switch which indicates when the brakes are being applied. Stop-light switch removal and refitting details can be found in Chapter 9.

Electronic control module (ECM)

Note: *If a new control module is fitted, it must be programmed using dedicated Volvo test equipment. Entrust this task to a Volvo dealer or suitably-equipped specialist.*

24 Disconnect the battery negative lead (see Chapter 5A), then wait at least 2 minutes before commencing work, to allow any stored electrical energy to dissipate.

D5244T/T2/T3 engines

25 The ECM box is located on the right-hand side inner wing. Clean off the top of the ECM box lid, to make sure no debris falls inside when it is removed. Release the catch on the side of the ECM module box lid. Lift off the lid and place it to one side **(see illustration)**.

26 To remove the ECM, insert Volvo tool No 999 5722 around the ECM and push the top of the tool rearwards as far as it will go, releasing the connector and the module. If the tool is not available, we managed to release the connectors using a strip of steel with a slot cut in the end and a 5 mm rivet as a pivot, shaped as shown. Insert the homemade

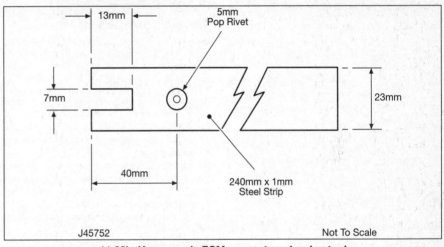

11.26b Home-made ECM connector releasing tool

In order for the tool to slide down alongside the ECM, it will be necessary to file or grind the rivet to about half its original height

tool alongside the ECM and slide the catches forwards alternately, a little at a time as shown **(see illustrations)**. As the catches are slid forward the ECM will rise and detach from the connectors. **Note:** *Do not touch the control module terminal pins with the bare hands – there is a danger of damage due to static electricity.*

27 To refit, locate the ECM in the box, engaging it with the connector in the base.

28 Position the Volvo tool around the ECM and pull the top of the tool as far forward as possible. If using the homemade tool, gently press the ECM downwards at the same time

as levering the catches rearwards alternately a little at a time.

29 Refit the ECM box lid.

D5244T4/T5/T6/T7 engines

30 The ECM is located on the left-hand side of the engine compartment. Pull the cover straight upwards **(see illustration)**.

31 Lever over the catches and disconnect the ECM wiring plugs **(see illustration)**.

32 Undo the 6 screws and remove the ECM **(see illustration)**. Recover the rubber seal beneath the ECM.

33 Refitting is a reversal of removal.

11.30 Lift off the ECM cover

11.31 Lever over the catches (arrowed) to disconnect the ECM wiring plugs

11.32 ECM screws (arrowed)

11.36 Release the clip (arrowed) and disconnect the hose from the fuel pressure safety valve

11.43 Turbo boost pressure control solenoid valve (arrowed)

11.48 Fuel pressure sensor – D5244T/T2/T3 engines

Fuel pressure safety valve

D5244T/T2/T3 engines only

34 Remove the plastic cover from over the top of the engine by pulling it straight up from its mountings.

35 Release the clamps and remove the hose from the intake manifold **(see illustration 10.2)**.

36 Undo the union and disconnect the return pipe from the safety valve **(see illustration)**.

37 Unscrew the valve from the common rail. Discard the seal, a new one must be fitted.

38 Refit the valve to the common rail with a new seal. Tighten the valve to the specified torque.

39 Refit the return pipe, using a new clip where necessary.

40 The remainder of refitting is a reversal of removal.

Turbocharger boost pressure control solenoid valve

D5244T/T2/T3 engines only

41 Remove the plastic cover from over the top of the engine by pulling it straight up from its mountings.

42 Release the clamps and remove the hose from the intake manifold **(see illustration 10.2)**.

43 Ensure that the ignition is switched off, and disconnect the wiring plug from the solenoid valve **(see illustration)**.

44 Slacken the lower retaining screw, then undo the upper retaining screw and lift the valve upwards.

45 Note their fitted locations, and disconnect the vacuum hoses from the solenoid valve.

46 Refitting is a reversal of removal.

Fuel pressure sensor

47 Remove the plastic cover from the top of the engine, by pulling it straight up from its mountings.

D5244T/T2/T3 engines

48 The fuel high-pressure sensor is located in the left-hand end of the common fuel rail. Ensure that the ignition is switched off, and disconnect the wiring plug from the sensor **(see illustration)**.

49 Using a suitable deep socket, unscrew the sensor from the adapter on the rail. Plug the port of the common rail to prevent contamination.

50 If required, unscrew the adapter from the common rail.

51 Refitting is a reversal of removal, tightening the adapter and sensor to their specified torque.

D5244T4/T5/T6/T7 engines

52 Remove the swirl control valve/motor as described in this Section.

53 Disconnect the wiring plug from the sensor, located at the right-hand end of the fuel rail **(see illustration)**.

54 Unscrew the pressure sensor. Plug the openings to prevent contamination.

55 Refitting is a reversal of removal, tightening the sensor to the specified torque.

Fuel pressure control valve – D5244T/T2/T3 engines

56 Remove the air cleaner assembly as described in Section 2.

57 Disconnect the control valve wiring plug, then undo the screws and detach the valve from the fuel pump **(see illustration)**.

58 Refitting is a reversal of removal, tightening the retaining screws securely.

Fuel pressure control valve – D5244T4/T5/T6/T7 engines

Fuel rail mounted valve

59 Pull the plastic cover on the top of the engine upwards to remove it.

60 Remove the air intake hose between the bonnet slam panel and the air cleaner.

61 Remove the hose from the EGR valve-to-the intake manifold, and the intake manifold hose.

62 Release the clamps/clips and move aside the crankcase breather pipes assembly.

63 Undo the unions and remove the high-pressure fuel pipes from the fuel rail to the injectors and the pump. Discard the pipes, new ones must be fitted.

64 Disconnect the wiring plugs from the control valve and pressure sensor on the fuel rail.

65 Release the clamp and disconnect the fuel return hose from the fuel rail. Be prepared for fluid spillage, and plug the openings to prevent contamination.

66 Undo the 2 bolts and remove the fuel rail.

67 Unscrew the control valve from the fuel rail **(see illustration)**.

68 Refitting is a reversal of removal.

Pump mounted valve

69 Remove the air cleaner assembly as described in Section 2.

11.53 Fuel pressure sensor (arrowed) – D5244T4/T5/T6/T7 engines

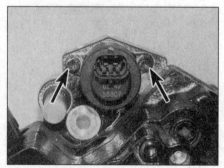

11.57 The fuel pressure control valve is secured to the pump by 2 screws (arrowed)

11.67 Fuel rail-mounted control valve (arrowed)

11.70 Fuel pump-mounted control valve (arrowed)

11.75a Camshaft position sensor (arrowed) – D5244T/T2/T3 engines . . .

11.75b . . . and D5244T4/T5/T6/T7 engines (arrowed)

70 Clean the area around the valve on the pump, then disconnect the valve wiring plug **(see illustration)**.

71 Undo the 3 Torx bolts and remove the valve by slowing rotating it and pulling it from the pump. Be prepared for fluid spillage. Plug or cover the openings to prevent contamination.

72 Refitting is a reversal of removal, lubricating the valve O-ring before fitting.

Camshaft position sensor

73 Remove the plastic cover from over the top of the engine, by pulling it straight up from its mountings.

74 On D5244T4/T5/T6/T7 engines, undo the 4 nuts and remove the shield at the rear of the cylinder head **(see illustration 10.11)**.

75 Ensure that the ignition is switched off, and disconnect the wiring plug from the sensor, located on the left-hand side of the camshaft cover **(see illustrations)**.

76 Undo the screw and remove the sensor. Discard the seal, a new one must be fitted.

77 To refit the sensor, ensure the mating face of the camshaft cover and sensor are clean, and fit the new seal.

78 Fit the sensor into the cover, and tighten the screw to the specified torque.

Swirl control valve/motor

D5244T4/T5/T6/T7 engines only

79 Remove the plastic cover from over the top of the engine, by pulling it straight up from its mountings.

80 Pull the control arm from the valve/motor **(see illustration)**.

81 Undo the 2 bolts and remove the control valve/motor **(see illustration)**. Disconnect the wiring plug and No 1 glow plug as the assembly is withdrawn.

82 Refitting is a reversal of removal. Note that if a new valve/motor has been fitted, the values stored in the ECM must be reset using dedicated diagnostic equipment. Entrust this task to a Volvo dealer or suitably-equipped specialist.

Turbocharger boost control motor

D5244T4/T5/T6/T7 engines only

83 On these engines, the position of the variable vane within the turbocharger (and

therefore the boost output) is controlled by an electric motor attached to the vane control arm **(see illustration)**. The motor is controlled by the engine management ECM. At the time of writing it would appear that the motor is not available separately from the turbocharger, and if faulty, the complete turbocharger assembly must be renewed as described in Section 13.

Fuel temperature sensor

D5244T4/T5/T6/T7 engines only

84 Remove the plastic cover from over the top of the engine, by pulling it straight up from its mountings.

85 The sensor is located on the top/front edge of the high-pressure pump at the left-hand end of the cylinder head. Disconnect the sensor wiring plug **(see illustration 9.9b)**.

86 Clean the area around the sensor, then unscrew it from the pump. Be prepared for

fluid spillage. Plug the opening to prevent contamination.

87 Refitting is a reversal of removal, tightening the sensor to the specified torque.

Throttle body

D5244T4/T5/T6/T7 engines only

88 Remove the air cleaner assembly as described in Section 2.

89 Slacken the clamp and disconnect the air hose from the throttle body. Move the hose to one side.

90 Disconnect the wiring plug, then undo the 4 retaining bolts and remove the throttle body **(see illustration)**. Discard the gasket, a new one must be fitted.

91 Refitting is a reversal of removal. If a new throttle body has been fitted, the stored values in the engine management ECM must be reset. Entrust this task to a Volvo dealer or suitably-equipped specialist.

11.80 Pull the arm from the swirl control motor

11.81 Swirl control motor retaining bolts (arrowed)

11.83 Turbocharger and boost control motor assembly

11.90 Throttle body retaining bolts (arrowed)

13.2a Undo the nut/bolt (arrowed) securing the cross-stay to the engine mounting on the cylinder head cover . . .

12 Turbocharger –
description and precautions

Description

A turbocharger increases engine efficiency by raising the pressure in the intake manifold above atmospheric pressure. Instead of the air simply being sucked into the cylinders, it is forced in. Additional fuel is supplied by the injection pump in proportion to the increased air intake.

Energy for the operation of the turbocharger comes from the exhaust gas. The gas flows through a specially-shaped housing (the turbine housing) and in so doing, spins the turbine wheel. The turbine wheel is attached to a shaft, at the end of which is another vaned wheel known as the compressor wheel. The compressor wheel spins in its own housing and compresses the inducted air on the way to the intake manifold.

The compressed air passes through an intercooler. This is an air-to-air heat exchanger, mounted with the radiator at the front of the vehicle. The purpose of the intercooler is to remove from the inducted air some of the heat gained in being compressed. Because cooler air is denser, removal of this heat further increases engine efficiency.

The turbocharger has adjustable guide vanes controlling the flow of exhaust gas into the turbine. The vanes are swivelled by

13.2b . . . and the ones securing the cross-stay to the brackets on the suspension turrets

the boost pressure control solenoid valve (D5244T/T2/T3 engines) or electric control valve/motor (D5244T4/T5/T6/T7 engines), controlled by the engine management ECM. At lower engine speeds, the vanes close together, giving a smaller exhaust gas entry port, and therefore higher gas speed, which increases boost pressure at low engine speed. At high engine speed, the vanes are turned to give a larger exhaust gas entry port, and therefore lower gas speed, effectively maintaining a reasonably constant boost pressure over the engine rev range. This is known as a Variable Nozzle Turbocharger (VNT).

The turbo shaft is pressure-lubricated by an oil feed pipe from the main oil gallery. The shaft 'floats' on a cushion of oil. A drain pipe returns the oil to the sump.

Precautions

• The turbocharger operates at extremely high speeds and temperatures. Certain precautions must be observed to avoid premature failure of the turbo or injury to the operator.
• **Do not** operate the turbo with any parts exposed. Foreign objects falling onto the rotating vanes could cause excessive damage and (if ejected) personal injury.
• **Do not** race the engine immediately after start-up, especially if it is cold. Give the oil a few seconds to circulate.
• **Always** allow the engine to return to idle speed before switching it off – do not blip the throttle and switch off, as this will leave the turbo spinning without lubrication.

• Allow the engine to idle for several minutes before switching off after a high-speed run.
• Observe the recommended intervals for oil and filter changing, and use a reputable oil of the specified quality (see *Lubricants and fluids*). Neglect of oil changing, or use of inferior oil, can cause carbon formation on the turbo shaft and subsequent failure.

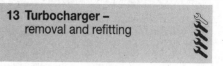

13 Turbocharger –
removal and refitting

Removal

1 Remove the plastic cover from over the top of the engine by pulling it straight up from its mountings.
2 Undo the fasteners, and remove the engine cross-stay from between the brackets on the front suspension turrets **(see illustrations)**.

D5244T/T2/T3 engines

3 Undo the 5 bolts and remove the heat shield from above the exhaust manifold. Note that it may be necessary to soak the bolts in releasing fluid prior to attempting their removal.
4 Undo the two screws, and detach the oil supply pipe from the turbocharger and engine block **(see illustration)**.
5 Remove the two upper nuts securing the turbocharger to the exhaust manifold.
6 Remove the front section of the exhaust pipe as described in Section 17.
7 Undo the screw securing the bracket to the vacuum pump at the left-hand end of the cylinder head, release the clamp, and remove the turbocharger intake pipe.
8 Release the clamp securing the oil pressure pipe to the coolant pipe.
9 Release the clamp and disconnect the charge air pipe from the turbocharger **(see illustration)**. Move the pipe to one side.
10 Undo the two Torx bolts securing the oil return pipe for the underside of the turbocharger, then pull the pipe from the cylinder block. Discard the seals, new ones must be fitted **(see illustrations)**.
11 Disconnect the vacuum hose from the nozzle control valve **(see illustration)**.

13.4 Turbocharger oil supply pipe – turbocharger end

13.9 Slacken the clamps and remove the charge air pipe (arrowed) from the turbocharger

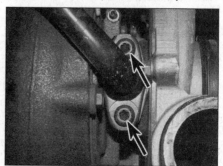

13.10a Undo the 2 Torx bolts (arrowed) securing the oil return pipe to the turbocharger . . .

13.10b . . . then pull the pipe from the engine block – recover the seal (arrowed)

13.11 Disconnect the vacuum hose from the turbocharger nozzle control valve (arrowed)

13.16 Unscrew the oxygen sensor and temperature sensor (arrowed) from the top of the catalytic converter

13.17 Heat shield bolts (arrowed)

13.18 Undo the Torx bolts and detach the oil pressure and coolant pipes from the top of the turbocharger

12 Undo the lower nut securing the turbocharger to the exhaust manifold, then lower the assembly down through the transmission tunnel and out from under the vehicle.

D5244T4/T5/T6/T7 engines

13 Drain the cooling system as described in Chapter 1B.
14 Remove the air cleaner as described in Section 2.
15 Undo the 4 nuts and remove the rubber shield from the rear of the cylinder head **(see illustration 10.11)**.
16 Unscrew the heated oxygen sensor

and temperature sensor from the top of the catalytic converter **(see illustration)**.
17 Undo the 5 bolts securing the heat shield to the exhaust manifold **(see illustration)**. Note the springs fitted to the 2 upper, right-hand bolts.
18 Disconnect oil pressure pipe and coolant pipe from the top of the turbocharger **(see illustration)**. Recover the sealing washers and remove the heat shield.
19 Remove the right-hand driveshaft as described in Chapter 8, then undo the nuts and remove the plastic cover over the driveshaft, where it enters the wheel arch area **(see illustration)**.

20 Working through the right-hand wheel arch, undo the banjo bolt securing the turbocharger oil supply pipe to the cylinder block. Recover the sealing washers.
21 Disconnect the turbocharger boost control motor wiring plug.
22 Undo the bolt securing it to the base of the vacuum pump, then slacken the clamp and remove the turbocharger intake hose.
23 Undo the 3 bolts securing the catalytic converter to the turbocharger, and the 2 bolts securing it to the support bracket **(see illustrations)**.
24 Working underneath the vehicle, release

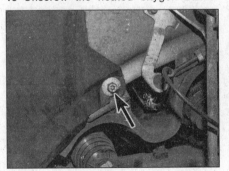

13.19 Undo the nut (arrowed) and remove the driveshaft cover

13.23a Catalytic converter-to-turbocharger upper bolts

13.23b Catalytic converter support bracket bolts (arrowed – viewed from underneath)

13.24a Slacken the clamp (arrowed) securing the charge air pipe to the turbocharger . . .

13.24b . . . then undo the bolts (arrowed) and remove the pipe

13.25 Undo the Torx bolts (arrowed) and detach the oil return and coolant pipes from the turbocharger

13.28a Turbocharger-to-manifold upper nuts (arrowed)

13.28b Renew the turbocharger-to-manifold metal gasket

the clamps, undo the bolts and remove the charge air pipe from the turbocharger (see illustrations).

25 Disconnect the coolant pipe and oil return pipe from the underside/rear of the turbocharger (see illustration). Recover the sealing washers and gasket.

26 Slacken the bolt and release the clamp securing the turbocharger oil supply pipe to the underside of the coolant pipe at the rear of the cylinder head. Manoeuvre the oil pipe from position.

27 Undo the Torx bolt securing the differential pressure sensor pipes support bracket to the rear of the turbocharger.

28 Undo the nuts securing the turbocharger to the exhaust manifold and lower it from place. Discard the metal gasket – a new one must be fitted. Volvo insist that no further dismantling of the turbocharger/wastegate actuator motor is carried out (see illustrations).

Refitting

29 Refitting is a reversal of removal, noting the following points:
a) Ensure all mating surfaces are clean and dry.
b) Renew all O-rings, seals and gasket.
c) Tighten all fasteners to the specified torque where available.
d) Fit new exhaust front section/catalytic converter-to-turbocharger nuts/bolts.

14 Turbocharger – examination and overhaul

With the turbocharger removed, inspect the housing for cracks or other visible damage.

Spin the turbine or the compressor wheel to verify that the shaft is intact and to feel for excessive shake or roughness. Some play is normal since in use the shaft is 'floating' on a film of oil. Check that the wheel vanes are undamaged.

The wastegate and actuator are integral with the turbocharger, and cannot be checked or renewed separately. Consult a Volvo dealer or other specialist if it is thought that the wastegate may be faulty.

If the exhaust or induction passages are oil-contaminated, the turbo shaft oil seals have probably failed. (On the induction side, this will also have contaminated the intercooler, where applicable, which if necessary should be flushed with a suitable solvent.)

No DIY repair of the turbo is possible. A new unit may be available on an exchange basis.

15 Intercooler – removal and refitting

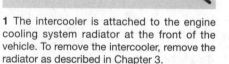

1 The intercooler is attached to the engine cooling system radiator at the front of the vehicle. To remove the intercooler, remove the radiator as described in Chapter 3.

2 Release the clips and detach the intercooler from the radiator.

3 Refitting is a reversal of removal.

16 Manifolds – removal and refitting

Intake manifold

1 The intake manifold is integral with the cylinder head cover – refer to Chapter 2B.

Exhaust manifold

Removal

2 Remove the turbocharger as described in Section 13.

3 Release the clamp and disconnect the EGR pipe from the exhaust manifold (see illustration).

4 Slacken and remove the nuts retaining the exhaust manifold, and remove it from the engine (see illustration). Discard the gasket, a new one must be fitted.

16.3 Release the EGR pipe clamp (arrowed)

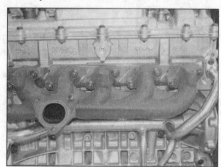

16.4 Undo the exhaust manifold nuts

Refitting

5 Examine all the manifold studs for signs of damage and corrosion; remove all traces of corrosion, and repair or renew any damaged studs.

6 Ensure the mating surfaces of the exhaust manifold and cylinder head are clean and dry. Position new gasket, and refit the exhaust manifold to the cylinder head. Tighten the nuts to the specified torque.

7 The remainder of refitting is a reversal of removal, noting the following points:

a) *Tighten all fasteners to their specified torque where available.*

b) *Check and, if necessary, top-up the oil level as described in 'Weekly checks'.*

17 Exhaust system –
general information and component renewal

General information

1 The exhaust system consists of two sections: the front pipe with the catalytic converters/particle filters (where applicable), and the rear section with the intermediate and rear silencers.

2 If required, the rear silencer can be renewed independently of the remainder of the system, by cutting the old silencer from the pipe, and slipping the new one over the cut end – details are given in this Section.

Removal

Front section

3 Jack up the front of the car and support it securely on axle stands (see *Jacking and vehicle support*). Alternatively, position the car over an inspection pit or on car ramps.

4 Undo the screws and remove the engine undershield.

5 On D5244T4/T5/T6/T7 engines, unscrew the exhaust gas temperature sensor and heated oxygen sensor from the catalytic converter **(see illustration 13.16)**.

6 Undo the 5 bolts and remove the heat shield from above the exhaust manifold. It may be necessary to soak the bolts in releasing fluid prior to attempting their removal.

7 Undo the nuts securing the catalytic converter to the turbocharger, then undo the nuts securing the catalytic converter to the particle filter/rear section of the exhaust pipe **(see illustration)**. For ease of access, undo the bolts securing the front exhaust pipe/catalytic converter mounting bracket to the rear of the cylinder block, and manoeuvre the bracket from place.

8 Undo the bolts securing the front and middle cross-plates under the exhaust pipe, and release the clips securing the heat shields and brake pipes to the cross-plates, then undo the bolts securing the front exhaust pipe to the subframe. Manoeuvre the exhaust pipe from under the vehicle. Note the catalytic

17.7 The 2 upper front exhaust pipe/catalytic converter-to-turbocharger nuts/bolts can be accessed from above

17.11 Release the rear exhaust pipe from the various rubber mountings

converters are integral with the front pipe and cannot be renewed independently.

Rear section

9 Jack up the rear of the car and support it securely on axle stands (see *Jacking and vehicle support*). Alternatively, position the car over an inspection pit or on car ramps.

10 Slacken and remove the nuts securing the exhaust rear section to the front section **(see illustration)**.

11 Release the exhaust rear section from the various mountings, and remove it from under the vehicle **(see illustration)**.

Rear silencer

12 If the rear silencer is the only part of the system requiring renewal, cut the old silencer from the rear section of the system using pipe cutters 27 mm from the welded joint in front of the silencer **(see illustration)**. Free the silencer from its mountings, and remove it from the vehicle.

13 Clean up and deburr the end of the existing exhaust pipe with a file/emery tape, etc.

14 Rear silencers are available which slip over the end of the existing exhaust pipe, and are clamped in place. Slip the new silencer over the pipe, engage the rubber silencer mountings, then tighten the pipe clamp securely.

Refitting

15 Each section is refitted by reversing the removal sequence, noting the following points:

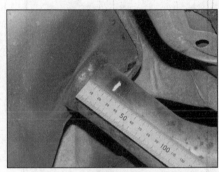

17.10 Remove the nuts securing the rear exhaust section to the front

17.12 Cut the old silencer from the pipe, 27 mm from the welded joint

a) *Ensure that all traces of corrosion have been removed from the flanges and renew all gaskets.*

b) *Inspect the rubber mountings for signs of damage or deterioration, and renew as necessary.*

c) *Prior to tightening the exhaust system fasteners to the specified torque, ensure that all rubber mountings are correctly located, and that there is adequate clearance between the exhaust system and vehicle underbody.*

18 Swirl duct –
removal and refitting

Note: *D5244T4/T5/T6/T7 engines only.*

Removal

1 The swirl duct is fitted to the cylinder head to control the flow of air into the intake tracts. The duct contains valves which alter the flow of air into the intake ducts depending on engine speed and load, generating a swirl motion for increased combustion efficiency and lower exhaust emissions. To remove the duct, begin by removing the cylinder head cover/intake manifold as described in Chapter 2B.

2 Disconnect the actuating arm from the swirl control motor.

3 Undo the bolts and remove the swirl duct.

Refitting

4 Refitting is a reversal of removal, tightening all fasteners securely.

Notes

Chapter 4 Part C:
Emission control systems

Contents

Degrees of difficulty

Easy, suitable for novice with little experience	Fairly easy, suitable for beginner with some experience	Fairly difficult, suitable for competent DIY mechanic	Difficult, suitable for experienced DIY mechanic	Very difficult, suitable for expert DIY or professional

Specifications

Torque wrench settings	Nm	lbf ft
EGR valve/cooler:		
M6	10	7
M8	27	20
Exhaust gas temperature sensor	45	33
Heated oxygen sensor	45	33
Oil separator bolts	20	15

1 General information

All models covered by this manual have various features built into the fuel and exhaust systems to help minimise harmful emissions. These features fall broadly into three categories; crankcase emission control, evaporative emission control, and exhaust emission control. Additionally, diesel models may be equipped with a particulate emission filter which uses porous silicon carbide substrate to trap particulates of carbon as the exhaust gases pass through.

The main features of these systems are as follows.

Crankcase emission control

Petrol models

To reduce the emissions of unburned hydrocarbons from the crankcase into the atmosphere, a Positive Crankcase Ventilation (PCV) system is used. The engine is sealed, and the blow-by gases and oil vapour are drawn from inside the crankcase, through an oil separator, into the intake tract, to be burned by the engine during normal combustion.

Under conditions of high manifold depression (idling, deceleration) the gases will be sucked positively out of the crankcase. Under conditions of low manifold depression (acceleration, full-throttle running) the gases are forced out of the crankcase by the (relatively) higher crankcase pressure; if the engine is worn, the raised crankcase pressure (due to increased blow-by) will cause some of the flow to return under all manifold conditions.

Diesel models

Crankcase gases are taken via hoses from the cylinder head and the cylinder block, into a cyclone type oil separator. Here, the gases are forced to twist past two cones. As the gases pass the cones, oil is thrown out and condenses on the walls of the separator, where it then returns to the sump. The gases are admitted into the intake system, via a pressure limiting valve.

Evaporative emission control

Petrol models

The evaporative emission control (EVAP) system is used to minimise the escape of unburned hydrocarbons into the atmosphere. To do this, the fuel tank filler cap is sealed, and a carbon canister is used to collect and store petrol vapours generated in the tank. When the engine is running, the vapours are cleared from the canister by an ECM controlled electrically operated EVAP purge valve, into the intake tract, to be burned by the engine during normal combustion.

To ensure that the engine runs correctly when idling, the valve only opens when the engine is running under load; the valve then opens to allow the stored vapour to pass into the intake tract.

Exhaust emission control

Petrol models

To minimise the amount of pollutants which escape into the atmosphere, all models are fitted with a catalytic converter in the exhaust system. The system is of the closed-loop type, in which two heated oxygen sensors in the exhaust system provide the engine management ECM with constant feedback on the oxygen content of the exhaust gases. This enables the ECM to adjust the mixture by altering injector opening time, thus providing the best possible conditions for the converter to operate. The system functions in the following way.

The oxygen sensors (also known as a lambda sensors) have built-in heating elements, activated by the ECM to quickly bring the sensor's tip to an efficient operating temperature. The sensor's tip is sensitive to oxygen, and sends the control module a varying voltage depending on the amount of oxygen in the exhaust gases; if the intake air/fuel mixture is too rich, the exhaust gases are low in oxygen, so the sensor sends a voltage signal proportional to the oxygen detected, the voltage altering as the mixture weakens and the amount of oxygen in the exhaust gases rises. Peak conversion efficiency of all major pollutants occurs if the intake air/fuel mixture is maintained at the chemically-correct ratio for complete combustion of petrol – 14.7 parts (by weight) of air to 1 part of fuel (the stoichiometric ratio). The sensor output voltage alters in a large step at this point, the ECM using the signal change as a reference point, and correcting the intake air/fuel mixture accordingly, by altering the fuel injector opening time.

Diesel models

The exhaust gas recirculation (EGR) system is designed to recirculate small quantities of exhaust gas into the intake tract, and therefore into the combustion process. This reduces the level of oxides of nitrogen present in the final exhaust gas which is released into the atmosphere.

The volume of exhaust gas recirculated is controlled by an electrically-operated solenoid valve. The solenoid, valve, and cooler is an assembly mounted at the left-hand end of the cylinder head between the intake and exhaust manifold.

The EGR system is controlled by the engine management ECM, which receives information on engine operating parameters from its various sensors.

Particulate filter system

Diesel models

The particulate filter is combined with the catalytic converter in the exhaust system, and its purpose it to trap particulates of carbon (soot) as the exhaust gases pass through, in order to comply with latest emission regulations.

The filter can be automatically regenerated (cleaned) by the system's ECM on-board the vehicle. The engine's high pressure injection system is utilised to inject fuel into the exhaust gases during the post-injection period; this causes the filter temperature to increase sufficient to oxidise the particulates, leaving an ash residue.

2 Catalytic converter – general information and precautions

On petrol models, a three-way catalytic converter is incorporated into the front section of the exhaust pipe, whilst on diesel models, an oxidation catalytic converter is fitted, again incorporated into the front section of the exhaust pipe. Refer to Part A or B of this Chapter for removal procedures.

The catalytic converter is a reliable and simple device, which needs no maintenance in itself, but there are some facts of which an owner should be aware if the converter is to function properly for its full service life.

Petrol models

a) *DO NOT use leaded petrol – the lead will coat the precious metals, reducing their converting efficiency, and will eventually destroy the converter.*

b) *Always keep the ignition and fuel systems well-maintained in accordance with the manufacturer's schedule (see Chapter 1A).*

c) *If the engine develops a misfire, do not drive the vehicle at all (or at least as little as possible) until the fault is cured.*

d) *DO NOT push – or tow-start the vehicle – this will soak the catalytic converter*

in unburned fuel, causing it to overheat when the engine does start.

e) *DO NOT switch off the ignition at high engine speeds, ie, do not blip the throttle immediately before switching off.*

f) *DO NOT use fuel or engine oil additives – these may contain substances harmful to the catalytic converter.*

g) *DO NOT continue to use the vehicle if the engine burns oil to the extent of leaving a visible trail of blue smoke.*

h) *Remember that the catalytic converter operates at very high temperatures. DO NOT, therefore, park the vehicle in dry undergrowth, over long grass or piles of dead leaves, after a long run.*

i) *Remember that the catalytic converter is FRAGILE. Do not strike it with tools during servicing work.*

j) *In some cases, a sulphurous smell (like that of rotten eggs) may be noticed from the exhaust. This is common to many catalytic converter-equipped vehicles. Once the vehicle has covered a few thousand miles, the problem should disappear – in the meantime, try changing the brand of petrol used.*

k) *The catalytic converter used on a well-maintained and well-driven vehicle should last for between 50 000 and 100 000 miles. If the converter is no longer effective, it must be renewed.*

Diesel models

Refer to the information given in parts f, g, h, i, and k of the petrol engine information given above.

3 Crankcase emission control system – checking and component renewal

Checking

1 The components of this system require no attention other than to check that the hoses are clear and undamaged.

Oil separator renewal

2 The oil separator is located on the front facing side of the cylinder block, below the intake manifold **(see illustration)**.

3.2 The oil separator is located on the front of the cylinder block (arrowed)

3 Remove the intake manifold as described in Part A of this Chapter (petrol models) or the oil level dipstick guide tube (diesel models).

4 Remove the clips securing the connecting hoses to the cylinder block connecting sleeves. If the clips are in less than perfect condition, obtain new clips for reassembly.

5 Undo the two bolts and remove the unit from the engine.

6 Refit the oil separator using a reversal of removal. Refit the intake manifold as described in Part A of this Chapter, or the oil level dipstick guide tube.

4 Evaporative emission control system – checking and component renewal

Checking

1 Poor idle, stalling and poor driveability can be caused by an inoperative canister vacuum valve, a damaged canister, split or cracked hoses, or hoses connected to the wrong fittings. Check the fuel filler cap for a damaged or deformed gasket.

2 Fuel loss or fuel odour can be caused by liquid fuel leaking from fuel lines, a cracked or damaged canister, an inoperative canister vacuum valve, and disconnected, misrouted, kinked or damaged vapour or control hoses.

3 Inspect each hose attached to the canister for kinks, leaks and cracks along its entire length. Repair or renew as necessary.

4 Inspect the canister. If it is cracked or damaged, renew it. Look for fuel leaking from the bottom of the canister. If fuel is leaking, renew the canister, and check the hoses and hose routing.

Component renewal

Carbon canister

5 The canister is located behind the left-hand rear wheel arch underneath the vehicle.

6 Slacken the left-hand rear roadwheel bolts/nuts, the jack up the rear of the vehicle and support it securely on axle stands (see *Jacking and vehicle support*). Remove the roadwheel.

7 Remove the rear section of the exhaust system as described in Chapter 4A.

8 Undo the plastic nut securing the plastic wheel arch liner.

9 Drill out the two rivets securing the heat shield to the rear subframe mounting and the 3rd rivet on the rear bracket of the exhaust system. Remove the heat shield.

10 Press the large diameter pipe towards the canister, squeeze together the clips and disconnect it from the canister.

11 Depress the clips and disconnect the small diameter pipe from the canister.

12 Detach the rubber hose and cable tie from the canister.

13 Undo the two bracket retaining screws and lower the canister from place.

14 Refitting is a reversal of removal.

Canister purge valve (EVAP)

15 The canister purge valve is mounted in the engine compartment, on the radiator coolant fan shroud.

16 Note their fitted positions, then disconnect the vacuum pipes and wiring plug from the valve (see illustrations).

17 Unclip the valve from the shroud.

18 Refitting is a reversal of removal.

5 Exhaust emission control systems – checking and component renewal

1 Checking of the system as a whole entails a close visual inspection of all hoses, pipes and connections for condition and security. Apart from this, any known or suspected faults should be attended to by a Volvo dealer or suitably-equipped specialist.

Heated oxygen (lambda) sensor

Note: *The sensor is delicate, and will not work if it is dropped or knocked, if its power supply is disrupted, or if any cleaning materials are used on it.*

2 Apply the handbrake, then jack up the front of the car and support it on axle stands (see *Jacking and vehicle support*). Release the screws and remove the engine undershield.

Front sensor

3 Disconnect the heated oxygen sensor wiring connector, and release the wiring from any cable-ties.

4 Unscrew the sensor from the exhaust, and collect the sealing washer (where fitted) (see illustrations).

5 On refitting, clean the sealing washer (where fitted) and renew it if it is damaged or worn. Apply a smear of anti-seize compound to the sensor's threads, then refit the sensor, tightening it to the specified torque. Reconnect the wiring and secure with cable-ties where applicable.

Rear sensor – petrol models

6 On some models, it may be necessary to remove the catalytic converter as described in Chapter 4A.

7 Unscrew the sensor from the exhaust system, and collect the sealing washer (where fitted) (see illustration).

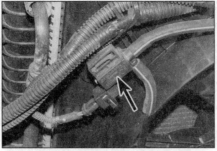

4.16a The canister purge valve is located on the radiator cooling fan shroud (arrowed) . . .

8 On refitting, clean the sealing washer (where fitted) and renew it if it is damaged or worn. Apply a smear of anti-seize compound to the sensor's threads, then refit the sensor, tightening it to the specified torque. Reconnect the wiring and secure with cable-ties where applicable.

Catalytic converter(s)

9 The catalytic converter(s) is part of the exhaust system front section. Refer to Part A or B of this Chapter for renewal procedures and additional information.

EGR actuator – diesel models

D5244T/T2/T3 engines

10 The EGR actuator is located at the left-hand end of the cylinder head. In order to access it, pull the plastic cover on the top of the engine straight up from its mountings.

11 Remove the air cleaner assembly as described in Chapter 4B.

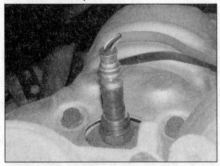

5.4a The front oxygen sensor is located in the exhaust manifold – petrol models . . .

5.17 Viewed down the rear of the cylinder head, slacken the clamp (arrowed) and disconnect the EGR intake hose

4.16b . . . or under the intake manifold (arrowed)

12 Drain the cooling system as described in Chapter 1B.

13 Disconnect the wiring plug from the EGR actuator.

14 Release the clamp and disconnect the air intake hose, then remove the hose complete with mass airflow sensor. Disconnect the sensor wiring plug as it is withdrawn.

15 Undo the screw securing the charge air pipe to the vacuum pump at the left-hand end of the exhaust camshaft, then release the clamp and remove the pipe.

16 On models with automatic transmission, remove the vacuum pump as described in Chapter 9.

17 Disconnect the intake hose from the EGR cooler (see illustration).

18 Undo the screw securing the cooler assembly beneath the fuel injection pump (see illustration).

19 Undo the two screws securing the bracket at the rear edge of the cooler.

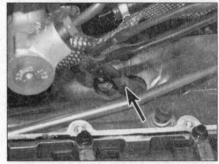

5.4b . . . and diesel models (arrowed)

5.18 EGR cooler mounting bolt (arrowed)

5.7 Rear oxygen sensor

5.20 EGR coolant hoses (arrowed)

5.22 Undo the screws and withdraw the EGR solenoid

5.31 EGR cooler upper coolant hose (arrowed)

20 Release the clamps and disconnect the coolant hoses from the cooler **(see illustration)**.
21 Remove the EGR cooler complete with actuator.
22 Undo the 4 screws and detach the actuator **(see illustration)**.
23 Refitting is a reversal of removal, renewing the gasket where applicable.

D5244T4/T5/T6/T7 engines

24 Remove the throttle body as described in Chapter 4B.
25 Disconnect the actuator wiring plug.
26 Undo the 4 bolts and remove the actuator.
27 Refitting is a reversal of removal.

EGR cooler – diesel models

D5244T/T2/T3 engines

28 EGR cooler removal is described within the EGR actuator removal procedure.

D5244T4/T5/T6/T7 engines

29 Remove the air cleaner and throttle body as described in Chapter 4B.
30 Drain the cooling system as described in Chapter 1B.
31 Undo the clamps and detach the coolant pipes from the EGR cooler located at the left-hand end of the cylinder head **(see illustration)**.
32 Release the clamps securing the EGR pipe to the cooler.
33 Undo the 3 mounting bolts and remove the cooler assembly.
34 Refitting is a reversal of removal.

Particulate filter – diesel models

35 Raise the front of the vehicle and support it securely on axle stands (see *Jacking and vehicle support*).
36 Unscrew the rear temperature sensor **(see illustration)**.
37 Note their fitted positions, then release the

clips and detach the hoses from the filter **(see illustration)**.
38 Undo the 4 retaining bolts, and remove the crossmember plate under the rear of the filter **(see illustration)**.
39 Undo the flange nuts at the front and rear of the particulate filter, then release the rubber mountings and lower it from place.
40 Refitting is a reversal of removal, using new nuts to secure the filter in place. **Note:** *After renewing a particulate filter, the 'counter' within the ECM must be reset. This requires access to dedicated Volvo diagnostic equipment, and should be entrusted to a Volvo dealer or suitably-equipped specialist.*

Particulate filter differential pressure sensor

41 Pull the plastic cover on the top of the engine straight up from its mountings.
42 Undo the bolts and remove the cross-stay between the suspension turrets in the engine compartment.
43 Undo the 4 nuts and remove the rubber shield at the rear of the cylinder head **(see illustration)**.
44 Disconnect the sensor wiring plug.
45 Undo the 2 mounting Torx bolts, then note their fitted locations, and disconnect the hoses to the sensor as it's withdrawn **(see illustration)**. **Note:** *After renewing the pressure differential sensor, the values for the sensor stored in the ECM must be adapted. This requires access to dedicated Volvo diagnostic equipment, and should be entrusted to a Volvo dealer or suitably-equipped specialist.*

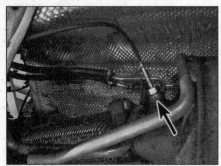

5.36 Particulate filter rear temperature sensor (arrowed)

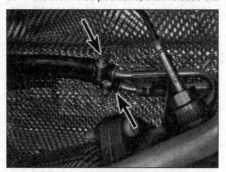

5.37 Particulate filter pressure hoses (arrowed)

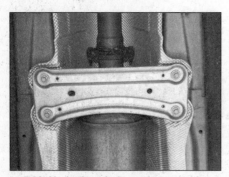

5.38 Undo the 4 bolts and remove the crossmember plate

5.43 Undo the 4 nuts (arrowed) and remove the rubber shield at the rear of the cylinder head

5.45 The particle filter pressure differential sensor is located at the left-hand rear of the cylinder head – access is limited

Chapter 5 Part A:
Starting and charging systems

Contents

Degrees of difficulty

Easy, suitable for novice with little experience 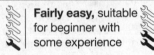	Fairly easy, suitable for beginner with some experience	Fairly difficult, suitable for competent DIY mechanic	Difficult, suitable for experienced DIY mechanic	Very difficult, suitable for expert DIY or professional

Specifications

System type . . . . 12 volt, negative earth

Battery
Type . . . . Low-maintenance or maintenance-free sealed for life
Capacity . . . . 45 to 90 Ah (depending on model)
Charge condition:
   Poor . . . . 12.5 volts
   Normal . . . . 12.6 volts
   Good . . . . 12.7 volts

Alternator
Type . . . . Bosch
Output . . . . 120, 140 or 160 A
Brush minimum length . . . . 5.0 mm

Starter motor
Type . . . . Bosch 1.4, 2.0 or 2.2 kW

Glow plugs
Resistance:
   D5244T/T2/T3 engines . . . . 0.685 ± 0.08 Ω at 20°C
   D5244T4/T5/T6/T7 engines . . . . Not available

Torque wrench setting	Nm	lbf ft
Alternator mounting bolts	24	18
Alternator pulley:		
Fixed pulley	65	48
Freewheel pulley	80	59
Compressor mounting bolts	24	18
Glow plugs	8	6
Starter motor mounting bolts	40	30

1 General information and precautions

General information

The engine electrical system consists mainly of the charging, starting and diesel preheating systems. Because of their engine-related functions, these components are covered separately from the body electrical devices such as the lights, instruments, etc (which are covered in Chapter 12). Information on the ignition system is covered in Part B of this Chapter.

The electrical system is of the 12 volt negative earth type.

The battery is of the low-maintenance or maintenance-free (sealed for life) type, and is charged by the alternator, which is belt-driven from the crankshaft pulley.

The starter motor is of the pre-engaged type, incorporating an integral solenoid. On starting, the solenoid moves the drive pinion into engagement with the flywheel ring gear before the starter motor is energized. Once the engine has started, a one-way clutch prevents the motor armature being driven by the engine until the pinion disengages from the flywheel.

Further details of the various systems are given in the relevant Sections of this Chapter. While some repair procedures are given, the usual course of action is to renew the component concerned.

Precautions

⚠️ *Warning: It is necessary to take extra care when working on the electrical system to avoid damage to semiconductor devices (diodes and transistors), and to avoid the risk of personal injury. In addition to the precautions given in Safety first!, observe the following when working on the system:*

• *Always remove rings, watches, etc, before working on the electrical system.* Even with the battery disconnected, capacitive discharge could occur if a component's live terminal is earthed through a metal object. This could cause a shock or nasty burn.

• *Do not reverse the battery connections.* Components such as the alternator, electronic control units, or any other components having semiconductor circuitry could be irreparably damaged.

• Never disconnect the battery terminals, the alternator, any electrical wiring or any test instruments when the engine is running.

• Do not allow the engine to turn the alternator when the alternator is not connected.

• Never test for alternator output by 'flashing' the output lead to earth.

• Always ensure that the battery negative lead is disconnected when working on the electrical system.

• If the engine is being started using jump leads and a slave battery, connect the batteries *positive-to-positive* and *negative-to-negative* (see *Jump starting*). This also applies when connecting a battery charger.

• *Never use an ohmmeter of the type incorporating a hand-cranked generator for circuit or continuity testing.*

• Before using electric-arc welding equipment on the car, *disconnect the battery, alternator and components such as the electronic control units* (where applicable) to protect them from the risk of damage.

2 Battery – testing and charging

Testing

Standard and low-maintenance battery

1 If the vehicle covers a small annual mileage, it is worthwhile checking the specific gravity of the electrolyte every three months to determine the state of charge of the battery. Use a hydrometer to make the check, and compare the results with the following table. Note that the specific gravity readings assume an electrolyte temperature of 15°C ; for every 10°C below 15°C subtract 0.007. For every 10°C above 15°C add 0.007.

	Ambient temperature	
	Above 25°C	Below 25°C
Fully-charged	1.210 to 1.230	1.270 to 1.290
70% charged	1.170 to 1.190	1.230 to 1.250
Discharged	1.050 to 1.070	1.110 to 1.130

2 If the battery condition is suspect, first check the specific gravity of electrolyte in each cell. A variation of 0.040 or more between any cells indicates loss of electrolyte or deterioration of the internal plates.

3 If the specific gravity variation is 0.040 or more, the battery should be renewed. If the cell variation is satisfactory but the battery is discharged, it should be charged as described later in this Section.

Maintenance-free battery

4 In cases where a sealed for life maintenance-free battery is fitted, topping-up and testing of the electrolyte in each cell may not be possible. The condition of the battery can therefore only be tested using a battery condition indicator or a voltmeter.

5 Certain models my be fitted with a maintenance-free battery, with a built-in charge condition indicator. The indicator is located in the top of the battery casing, and indicates the condition of the battery from its colour. The charge conditions denoted by the colour of the indicator should be printed on a label attached to the battery – if not, consult a Volvo dealer or automotive electrician for advice.

All battery types

6 If testing the battery using a voltmeter, connect the voltmeter across the battery and note the voltage. The test is only accurate if the battery has not been subjected to any kind of charge for the previous six hours. If this is not the case, switch on the headlights for 30 seconds, then wait four to five minutes before testing the battery after switching off the headlights. All other electrical circuits must be switched off, so check that the doors and tailgate are fully shut when making the test.

7 If the voltage reading is less than 12.2 volts, then the battery is discharged, whilst a reading of 12.2 to 12.4 volts indicates a partially-discharged condition.

8 If the battery is to be charged, remove it from the vehicle and charge it as described later in this Section.

Charging

Note: *The following is intended as a guide only. Always refer to the manufacturer's recommendations (often printed on a label attached to the battery) before charging a battery.*

Standard and low-maintenance battery

9 Charge the battery at a rate equivalent to 10% of the battery capacity (eg, for a 45 Ah battery charge at 4.5 A) and continue to charge the battery at this rate until no further rise in specific gravity is noted over a four-hour period.

10 Alternatively, a trickle charger charging at the rate of 1.5 amps can safely be used overnight.

11 Specially rapid boost charges which are claimed to restore the power of the battery in 1 to 2 hours are not recommended, as they can cause serious damage to the battery plates through overheating. If the battery is completely flat, recharging should take at least 24 hours.

12 While charging the battery, note that the temperature of the electrolyte should never exceed 38°C.

Maintenance-free battery

13 This battery type takes considerably longer to fully recharge than the standard type, the time taken being dependent on the extent of discharge, but it can take anything up to three days.

14 A constant voltage type charger is required, to be set, when connected, to 13.9 to 14.9 volts with a charger current below 25 amps. Using this method, the battery should be useable within three hours, giving a voltage reading of 12.5 volts, but this is for a partially-discharged battery and, as mentioned, full charging can take far longer.

15 If the battery is to be charged from a fully-discharged state (condition reading less than 12.2 volts), have it recharged by your Volvo dealer or local automotive electrician, as the charge rate is higher, and constant supervision during charging is necessary.

3.3 Slacken the bolt and disconnect the clamp from the negative terminal

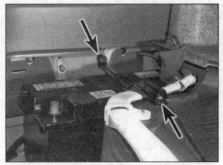

3.4 Undo the nut and bolt (arrowed) and remove the retaining bracket

3.6 Lift the up the plastic cover and disconnect the positive terminal clamp

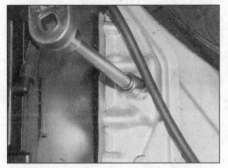

3.7 Undo the battery retaining clamp bolt

3.8a Pull the vent tube from the battery . . .

3.8b . . . and lift the battery from place

3 Battery – removal and refitting

Note: *On models with auxiliary heating with remote starting, once the battery has been disconnected the personal code is reset to the factory default (1234).*

Caution: Wait at least 5 minutes after turning off the ignition switch before disconnecting the battery. This is to allow sufficient time for the various control modules to store information.

Removal

1 The battery is located under the floor in the luggage compartment.
2 Lift the luggage compartment floor, and remove the storage tray.
3 Slacken the clamp bolt and disconnect the clamp from the battery negative (earth) terminal **(see illustration)**.
4 Undo the retaining nuts/bolt and remove the battery retaining bracket **(see illustration)**.
5 Lift the large plastic cover from the battery, or fold up the cover from the positive terminal as applicable.
6 Disconnect the positive terminal lead in the same way **(see illustration)**.
7 Unscrew the bolt and remove the battery retaining clamp **(see illustration)**.
8 Disconnect the vent tube, and lift the battery out of the engine compartment **(see illustrations)**.

Refitting

9 Position the battery in the luggage compartment floor.
10 Refit the retaining clamp and tighten the retaining bolt securely.
11 Reconnect the vent tube.
12 Reconnect the battery positive lead, followed by the negative lead. Smear a little petroleum jelly on the terminals.
13 Where applicable, refit the battery cover, then position the retaining bracket and tighten the retaining nuts securely.
14 After reconnecting the battery, the engine may run erratically until it's been driven for a few minutes to allow the ECM to relearn. Initialise the upper electronic module by unlocking the vehicle using the remote control. It will also be necessary to recalibrate the blower fan (manual or standard climate control), and the sunroof as follows:

4.1 Check the security of the alternator connections (arrowed)

Blower fan calibration

15 With the ignition turned on, set the blower speed switch to the maximum position, then to the minimum position. Calibration is now complete.

Sunroof calibration

16 Turn the ignition switch to position I.
17 Operate the sunroof switch to position the sunroof in the tilt position, then release the switch.
18 Press the switch again for at least 5 seconds, so the sunroof closes. The calibration is complete. **Note:** *If the sunroof hasn't moved to the correct position, press the switch and completely open the sunroof, then release the switch – press the switch again for at least 5 seconds to fully close the sunroof. The calibration should now be complete.*

4 Charging system – testing

Note: *Refer to the warnings given in Safety first! and in Section 1 of this Chapter before starting work.*

1 If the ignition/no-charge warning light fails to illuminate when the ignition is switched on, first check the alternator wiring connections for security **(see illustration)**. If all is satisfactory, the alternator maybe at fault and should be renewed or taken to an auto-electrician for testing and repair.
2 If the ignition warning light illuminates when the engine is running, stop the engine

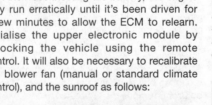
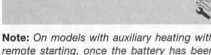

5.5 Disconnect the alternator lead and plug(s)

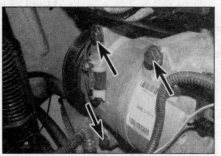

5.6 Slacken the lower air conditioning compressor bolt, but completely remove the upper ones (arrowed)

5.14 Alternator upper mounting bolt (arrowed)

and check that the drivebelt is correctly tensioned (see Chapter 1A or 1B) and that the alternator connections are secure. If all is so far satisfactory, have the alternator checked by an auto-electrician for testing and repair.

3 If the alternator output is suspect even though the warning light functions correctly, the regulated voltage may be checked as follows.

4 Connect a voltmeter across the battery terminals and start the engine.

5 Increase the engine speed until the voltmeter reading remains steady; the reading should be between 13.5 and 14.8 volts.

6 Switch on as many electrical accessories (eg, the headlights, heated rear window and heater blower) as possible, and check that the alternator maintains the regulated voltage between 13.5 and 14.8 volts.

7 If the regulated voltage is not as stated, the fault may be due to worn brushes, weak brush springs, a faulty voltage regulator, a faulty diode, a severed phase winding, or worn or damaged slip-rings. The brushes and slip-ring may be checked (see Section 6), but if the fault persists the alternator should be renewed or taken to an auto-electrician for testing and repair.

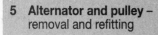

5 Alternator and pulley – removal and refitting

Alternator removal

1 Disconnect the battery negative lead (see Section 3).

2 Remove the auxiliary drivebelt as described in Chapter 1A or 1B.

Petrol engines up to 2005

3 On turbocharged models, release the clamps and remove the air intake hose from the front panel to the air cleaner housing, and the charge air pipe over the top of the engine to the intercooler.

4 On all engines, remove the radiator cooling fan and shroud as described in Chapter 3.

5 Disconnect the wiring plug(s) and the leads from the terminal studs at the rear of the alternator **(see illustration)**.

6 Slacken the air conditioning compressor mounting bolts/nut, then remove the retaining bolts and remove the alternator towards the air cleaner housing, and manoeuvre it from the engine compartment **(see illustration)**.

Petrol engines from 2005

7 Remove the power steering pump and position it to one side, as described in Chapter 10.

8 Release the clamp and disconnect the hose from the turbocharger to the intercooler and move it to one side (turbocharged models only).

9 Drain the cooling system to below the level of the radiator top hose (see Chapter 1A), then disconnect the hose from the radiator, and move it to one side.

10 Disconnect the wiring multiplugs and the leads from the terminal studs at the rear of the alternator.

11 Slacken the air conditioning compressor mounting bolts/nut, then remove the retaining bolts and remove the alternator.

Diesel engines up to 2005

12 Use a hose clamp on the supply hose to the power steering pump, then disconnect the hose from the pump. Undo the union and disconnect the pressure hose from the pump. Be prepared for fluid spillage, and protect the alternator with rags, etc.

13 Disconnect the wiring plug(s) and the leads from the terminal studs at the rear of the alternator.

14 Slacken the air conditioning compressor lower mounting bolts/nut, unscrew the upper ones, then remove the retaining bolts and remove the alternator **(see illustration)**.

Diesel engines from 2005

15 Remove the plastic cover from the top of the engine by pulling it straight up from its mountings.

16 Undo the 3 bolts and remove the mounting strut from between the rear of the power steering pump and the engine **(see illustration)**.

17 Release the clamps and remove the hose from the charge air pipe to the intercooler.

18 Working through the holes in the drive pulley, undo the 3 bolts securing the power steering pump **(see illustration)**. There's no need to remove the pump, merely tilt it forward as the alternator is removed.

19 Disconnect the wiring multiplugs and the leads from the terminal studs at the rear of the alternator.

20 Slacken the 2 lower air conditioning compressor mounting bolts, then remove the upper 2.

21 Undo the remaining retaining bolt and remove the alternator **(see illustration)**.

5.16 Remove the strut (arrowed) at the rear of the power steering pump

5.18 Undo the power steering pump mounting bolts

5.21 Remove the remaining alternator mounting bolt (arrowed)

Alternator refitting

22 Refitting is a reversal of removal. Remembering to tighten the various fasteners to their specified torque where given.

Drive pulley removal

23 On diesel models, the alternator drive pulley is fitted with a one-way clutch to reduced wear and stress on the auxiliary drivebelt. In order to remove the pulley, a special tool (Volvo No 999 5760) will be required to hold the alternator shaft whilst unscrewing the pulley. An equivalent to this tool should be available from auto electrical specialists/automotive tool specialists.

24 Prise the plastic cap from the pulley.

25 Insert the special tool into the splines of the pulley, engaging the central Torx bit with the alternator shaft **(see illustrations)**. Unscrew the pulley anti-clockwise whilst holding the shaft with the Torx bit, and remove the pulley.

26 Fit the pulley to the alternator shaft, and tighten it securely using the special tool.

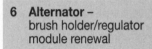

6 Alternator – brush holder/regulator module renewal

1 Remove the alternator, as described in Section 5.

2 Place the alternator on a clean work surface, with the pulley facing down.

3 Undo the cover nuts and screw(s), then lift the plastic cover from the rear of the alternator **(see illustration)**.

4 Undo the three screws and carefully remove the voltage regulator/brush holder from the alternator **(see illustrations)**.

5 Measure the free length of the brushes **(see illustration)**. Check the measurement with the Specifications; renew the module if the brushes are worn below the minimum limit.

6 Clean and inspect the surfaces of the slip-rings at the end of the alternator shaft. If they are excessively worn, or damaged, the alternator must be renewed.

7 Reassemble the alternator by following the dismantling procedure in reverse. On completion, refer to Section 5 and refit the alternator.

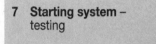

7 Starting system – testing

Note: *Refer to the precautions given in Safety first! and in Section 1 of this Chapter before starting work.*

1 If the starter motor fails to operate when the ignition key is turned to the appropriate position, the following possible causes may be to blame:

a) The battery is faulty.
b) The electrical connections between the switch, solenoid, battery and starter

5.25a Use a special tool that engages with the splines in the shaft and the pulley centre

motor are somewhere failing to pass the necessary current from the battery through the starter to earth.
c) The solenoid is faulty.
d) The starter motor is mechanically or electrically defective.

2 To check the battery, switch on the headlights. If they dim after a few seconds, this indicates that the battery is discharged – recharge (see Section 2) or renew the battery. If the headlights glow brightly, operate the ignition switch and observe the lights. If they dim, then this indicates that current is reaching the starter motor, therefore the fault must lie in the starter motor. If the lights continue to glow brightly (and no clicking sound can be heard from the starter motor solenoid), this indicates that there is a fault in the circuit or solenoid – see following paragraphs. If the starter motor turns slowly when operated, but the battery

6.3 Prise off the plastic cap, undo the 2 nuts and 1 screw, then lift off the plastic cover (arrowed)

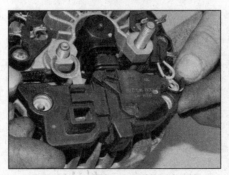

6.4b . . . and lift away the voltage regulator/brush holder

5.25b Counterhold the shaft whilst unscrewing the pulley centre

is in good condition, then this indicates that either the starter motor is faulty, or there is considerable resistance somewhere in the circuit.

3 If a fault in the circuit is suspected, disconnect the battery leads (including the earth connection to the body), the starter/solenoid wiring and the engine/transmission earth strap. Thoroughly clean the connections, and reconnect the leads and wiring, then use a voltmeter or test light to check that full battery voltage is available at the battery positive lead connection to the solenoid, and that the earth is sound. Smear petroleum jelly around the battery terminals to prevent corrosion – corroded connections are amongst the most frequent causes of electrical system faults.

4 If the battery and all connections are in good condition, check the circuit by disconnecting the wire from the solenoid blade terminal.

6.4a Undo the 3 screws (arrowed) . . .

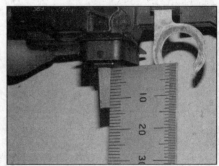

6.5 Measure the free length of the brushes

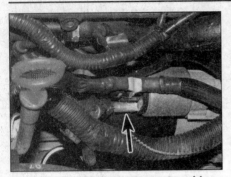

8.6 Disconnect the starter motor wiring plug (arrowed)

Connect a voltmeter or test light between the wire end and a good earth (such as the battery negative terminal), and check that the wire is live when the ignition switch is turned to the start position. If it is, then the circuit is sound – if not, the circuit wiring can be checked as described in Chapter 12.

5 The solenoid contacts can be checked by connecting a voltmeter or test light between the battery positive feed connection on the starter side of the solenoid, and earth. When the ignition switch is turned to the start position, there should be a reading or lighted bulb, as applicable. If there is no reading or lighted bulb, the solenoid is faulty and should be renewed.

6 If the circuit and solenoid are proved sound, the fault must lie in the starter motor. In this event, it may be possible to have the starter motor overhauled by a specialist, but check on the cost of spares before proceeding, as it may prove more economical to obtain a new or exchange motor.

8 Starter motor – removal and refitting

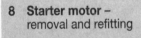

Removal

1 Disconnect the battery negative lead (see Section 3).

2 On petrol engines, release the clamps and remove the air intake hose between the front panel and the air cleaner assembly.

3 On turbocharged petrol engines, release

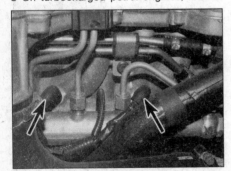

10.2 Pull the wiring plugs from the glow plug terminals (arrowed)

8.7 Note the position of the locating dowel (arrowed)

the clamps and remove the hose between the intercooler and the throttle control unit.

4 On all models, remove the air cleaner assembly as described in Chapter 4A or 4B.

5 Unbolt the starter motor rear support bracket from the cylinder block – where fitted.

6 Disconnect the wiring from the starter motor solenoid **(see illustration)**.

7 Undo the bolts securing the starter motor to the transmission bellhousing, and manoeuvre the unit from its location. Note the position of the locating dowel, and ensure it is in place when refitting **(see illustration)**.

Refitting

8 Refitting is a reversal of removal. Tighten all fasteners to their specified torque where given.

9 Starter motor – testing and overhaul

If the starter motor is thought to be suspect, it should be removed from the vehicle and taken to an auto-electrician for testing. Most auto-electricians will be able to supply and fit brushes at a reasonable cost. However, check on the cost of repairs before proceeding, as it may prove more economical to obtain a new or exchange motor.

10 Preheating system – general information and component renewal

General information

To assist cold starting, diesel engine models are fitted with a preheating system, which comprises a relay, and five glow plugs. The system is controlled by the Electronic Diesel Control (EDC) system, using information provided by the coolant temperature sensor (see Chapter 4B).

The glow plugs are miniature electric heating elements, encapsulated in a metal case with a probe at one end, and an electrical connection at the other. The combustion chambers have a glow plug threaded into it. When the glow plug is energised, it heats up rapidly causing

the temperature of the air charge drawn into each of the combustion chambers to rise. Each glow plug probe is positioned directly in line with the incoming spray of fuel from the injector. Hence the fuel passing over the glow plug probe is also heated, allowing its optimum combustion temperature to be achieved more readily.

The duration of the preheating period is governed by the Electronic Diesel Control (EDC) system control module (ECM), using information provided by the coolant temperature sensor. The ECM alters the preheating time (the length for which the glow plugs are supplied with current) to suit the prevailing conditions.

A warning light informs the driver that preheating is taking place. The lamp extinguishes when sufficient preheating has taken place to allow the engine to be started, but power will still be supplied to the glow plugs for a further period, known as post-heating, to reduce exhaust emissions. If no attempt is made to start the engine, the power supply to the glow plugs is switched off to prevent battery drain and glow plug burn-out.

Component renewal

Glow plugs

1 Remove the plastic cover from the top of the engine by pulling it straight up from its mountings.

2 The glow plugs are fitted into the front face of the cylinder head. Pull the wiring plugs from each of the glow plugs **(see illustration)**.

3 Using a deep socket, unscrew and remove the glow plugs **(see illustration)**.

4 Inspect the glow plugs for signs of damage. Burt or eroded glow plug tips can be caused by a bad injector spray pattern. Have the injectors checked if this sort of damage is found.

5 The glow plugs can be energised by applying 12 volts (D5244T/T2/T3 engines), or 7 volts (D5244T4/T5/T6/T7 engines) to them to verify that they heat up evenly and in the required time. Observe the following precautions:

a) Support the glow plug by clamping it carefully in a vice or self-locking pliers. Remember it will be red hot.

10.3 Unscrew the glow plug from the cylinder head

b) *Make sure that the power supply or test lead incorporates a fuse or overload trip to protect against damage from a short-circuit.*

c) *After testing, allow the glow plug to cool for several minutes before attempting to handle it.*

6 A glow plug in good condition will start to glow red at the tip after drawing current for 5 seconds or so. Any plug which takes much longer to start glowing, or which starts glowing in the middle instead of at the tip, is probably defective.

7 Thoroughly clean the glow plugs, and the glow plug seating areas in the cylinder head.

8 Apply a smear of anti-seize compound to the glow plug threads, then refit the glow plug and tighten it to the specified torque.

9 Reconnect the wiring to the glow plug. The connectors are a push-fit.

Glow plug relay

10 Remove the air cleaner as described in Chapter 4B.

11 Depress the clip and detach the relay bracket by sliding it upwards **(see illustration)**.

12 Depress the catch and pull the relay upwards from the bracket.

13 Disconnect the wiring plug as the relay is withdrawn.

14 Refitting is a reversal of removal.

10.11 The glow plug relay is located in front of the air cleaner housing (arrowed)

Notes

Notes

Chapter 5 Part B:
Ignition system

Contents

Degrees of difficulty

Easy, suitable for novice with little experience	Fairly easy, suitable for beginner with some experience	Fairly difficult, suitable for competent DIY mechanic	Difficult, suitable for experienced DIY mechanic	Very difficult, suitable for expert DIY or professional

Specifications

General
System type:

All engines .... Distributorless engine management system

Firing order .... 1-2-4-5-3 (No 1 cylinder at timing belt end of engine)

Spark plugs
Type .... See Chapter 1A Specifications

Ignition timing
The ignition timing is constantly altered by the engine management ECM, and connect be checked without specialist equipment.

Ignition coil
Primary resistance .... Not available

Secondary resistance .... Not available

Knock sensor
Resistance .... 200 kohms

Torque wrench settings

	Nm	lbf ft
Ignition coil	10	7
Knock sensors	20	15

1 General information

The ignition system is responsible for igniting the compressed fuel/air charge in each cylinder in turn at precisely the right moment for the prevailing engine speed and load. This is achieved by using a sophisticated engine management system, which utilises computer technology and electromagnetic circuitry to achieve the required ignition characteristics.

The main components of the ignition side of the system are the ignition coils (with integral power stage and HT caps), the spark plugs and knock sensor(s). The ignition system is under the overall control of the engine management ECM, therefore many of the sensors used by the ECM have an influence on the ignition system. The operation of the system is as follows.

The ECM computes engine speed and crankshaft position from a series of holes drilled in the periphery of the engine flywheel, with an RPM sensor whose inductive head runs just above the drilled flywheel periphery. As the crankshaft rotates, the land (or 'teeth') between the drilled holes in the flywheel, passes the crankshaft position/speed sensor, which transmits a pulse to the ECM every time a tooth passes it. There is one missing hole in the flywheel periphery, which allows the land (or tooth) at that point to be twice as wide as the others. The ECM recognises the absence of a pulse from the position/speed sensor at this point, and uses it to establish the TDC position for No 1 piston. The time interval between pulses, and the location of the missing pulse, allow the ECM to accurately determine the position of the crankshaft

and its speed. The camshaft position sensor enhances this information by detecting whether a particular piston is on an intake or an exhaust cycle.

Information on engine load is supplied to the ECM via the mass airflow sensor and the manifold absolute pressure sensor on certain models. The engine load is determined by computation based on the quantity of air being drawn into the engine. Further information is sent to the ECM from one (non-turbo engines) or two knock sensors (turbo engines). These sensors are sensitive to vibration, and detect the knocking which occurs when the engine starts to pink (pre-ignite). Sensors monitoring coolant temperature, accelerator pedal position, roadspeed, automatic transmission gear position (where applicable) and air conditioning system operation provide additional input signals to the ECM on vehicle operating conditions.

From this constantly-changing data, the ECM selects, and if necessary modifies, a particular ignition advance setting from a map of ignition characteristics stored in its memory.

With the firing point established, the ECM sends a signal to the ignition power stage, which is an electronic switch controlling the current to the ignition coil primary windings. On receipt of the signal from the ECM, the power stage interrupts the primary current to the ignition coil, which induces a high-tension voltage in the coil secondary windings. This HT voltage is passed through the integral HT caps to the spark plugs. Each cylinder has its own small ignition coil, attached directly to each spark plug, and wired back to the ECM.

In the event of a fault in the system due to loss of a signal from one of the sensors, the ECM reverts to an emergency (limp-home) program. This will allow the car to be driven, although engine operation and performance will be limited. A warning light on the instrument panel will illuminate if the fault is likely to cause an increase in harmful exhaust emissions.

To facilitate fault diagnosis, the ignition system is provided with an on-board diagnostic facility, which can be interrogated using suitable diagnostic equipment (fault code reader). The diagnostic connector is located under the driver's side of the facia, above the pedals **(see illustration)**.

2 Ignition system – testing

⚠ Warning: Voltages produced by an electronic ignition system are considerably higher than those produced by conventional ignition systems. Extreme care must be taken when working on the system if the ignition is switched on. Persons with surgically-implanted cardiac pacemaker devices should keep well clear of the ignition circuits, components and test equipment.

General

1 The components of the ignition system are normally very reliable; most faults are far more

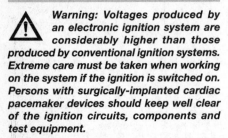

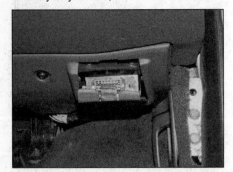

1.8 Pull down the plastic cover to expose the diagnostic connector

likely to be due to loose or dirty connections, or to tracking of HT voltage due to dirt, dampness or damaged insulation, than to the failure of any of the system's components. **Always** check all wiring thoroughly before condemning an electrical component, and work methodically to eliminate all other possibilities before deciding that a particular component is faulty.

2 The old practice of checking for a spark by holding the live end of an HT cap a short distance away from the engine is **not** recommended; not only is there a high risk of a powerful electric shock, but the ECM or HT coil may be damaged. Similarly, **never** try to diagnose misfires by pulling off one HT coil at a time.

3 The following tests should be carried out when an obvious fault such as non-starting or a clearly detectable misfire exists. Some faults, however, are more obscure and are often disguised by the fact that the ECM will adopt an emergency program (limp-home) mode to maintain as much driveability as possible. Faults of this nature usually appear in the form of excessive fuel consumption, poor idling characteristics, lack of performance, knocking or pinking noises from the engine under certain conditions, or a combination of these conditions. Where problems such as this are experienced, the best course is to refer the car to a suitably-equipped garage for diagnostic testing using dedicated test equipment.

Engine will not start

Note: *Remember that a fault with the anti-theft alarm or immobiliser will give rise to apparent starting problems. Make sure that the alarm or immobiliser has been deactivated, referring to the vehicle handbook for details.*

4 If the engine either will not turn over at all, or only turns very slowly, check the battery and starter motor. Connect a voltmeter across the battery terminals (meter positive probe to battery positive terminal) then note the voltage reading obtained while turning the engine over on the starter for (no more than) ten seconds. If the reading obtained is less than approximately 9.5 volts, first check the battery, starter motor and charging system as described in Part A of this Chapter.

Engine misfires

5 An irregular misfire is probably due to a loose connection to one of the ignition coils or system sensors.

6 With the ignition switched off, check carefully through the system, ensuring that all connections are clean and securely fastened.

7 Regular misfiring indicates a problem with one of the ignition coils or spark plugs. As no resistance values are available, testing the coils is best left to a Volvo dealer or suitably-equipped specialist.

8 Any further checking of the system components should be carried out after first checking the ECM for fault codes.

3 Fault finding – general information and preliminary checks

Note: *Both the ignition and fuel systems must ideally be treated as one inter-related engine management system. Although the contents of this section is mainly concerned with the ignition side of the system, many of the components perform dual functions, and some of the following procedures of necessity relate to the fuel system.*

General information

1 The fuel and ignition systems on all engines covered by this manual incorporate an on-board diagnostic system to facilitate fault finding and system testing. Should a fault occur, the ECM stores a series of fault codes for subsequent read-out via the 16-pin diagnostic connector located under the driver's side of the facia above the pedals.

2 If driveability problems have been experienced and engine performance is suspect, the on-board diagnostic system can be used to pinpoint any problem areas, but this requires special test equipment. Once this has been done, further tests may often be necessary to determine the exact nature of the fault; ie, whether a component itself has failed, or whether it is a wiring or other inter-related problem.

3 Apart from visually checking the wiring and connections, any testing will require the use of a fault code reader at least. A Volvo dealer will obviously have such a reader, but they are also available from other suppliers. It is unlikely to be cost-effective for the private owner to purchase a fault code reader, but a well-equipped local garage or auto-electrical specialist will have one.

Preliminary checks

Note: *When carrying out these checks to trace a fault, remember that if the fault has appeared only a short time after any part of the vehicle has been serviced or overhauled, the first place to check is where that work was carried out, however unrelated it may appear, to ensure that no carelessly-refitted components are causing the problem.*

If you are tracing the cause of a partial engine fault, such as lack of performance, in addition to the checks outlined below, check the compression pressures. Check also that the fuel filter and air cleaner element have been renewed at the recommended intervals.

Remember that any fault codes which have been logged will have to be cleared from the ECM memory using a dedicated fault code reader (see paragraph 3) before you can be certain the cause of the fault has been fixed.

4 Open the luggage compartment, lift the floor and check the condition of the battery connections (see Chapter 5A) – remake the connections or renew the leads if a fault is found. Use the same techniques to ensure that all earth points in the engine compartment provide good electrical contact through clean, metal-to-metal joints, and that all are securely fastened.

5 Next work methodically around the engine compartment, checking all visible wiring, and the connections between sections of the wiring loom. What you are looking for at this stage is wiring that is obviously damaged by chafing against sharp edges, or against moving suspension/transmission components and/or the auxiliary drivebelt, by being trapped or crushed between carelessly-refitted components, or melted by being forced into contact with hot engine castings, coolant pipes, etc. In almost all cases, damage of this sort is caused in the first instance by incorrect routing on reassembly after previous work has been carried out (see the note at the beginning of this sub-Section).

6 Obviously wires can break or short together inside the insulation so that no visible evidence betrays the fault, but this usually only occurs where the wiring loom has been incorrectly routed so that it is stretched taut or kinked sharply; either of these conditions should be obvious on even a casual inspection. If this is thought to have happened and the fault proves elusive, the suspect section of wiring should be checked very carefully during the more detailed checks which follow.

7 Depending on the extent of the problem, damaged wiring may be repaired by rejoining the break or splicing-in a new length of wire, using solder to ensure a good connection, and remaking the insulation with adhesive insulating tape or heat-shrink tubing, as desired. If the damage is extensive, given the implications for the vehicle's future reliability, the best long-term answer may well be to renew that entire section of the loom, however expensive this may appear.

8 When the actual damage has been repaired, ensure that the wiring loom is re-routed correctly, so that it is clear of other components, is not stretched or kinked, and is secured out of harm's way using the plastic clips, guides and ties provided.

9 Check all electrical connectors, ensuring that they are clean, securely fastened, and that each is locked by its plastic tabs or wire clip, as appropriate. If any connector shows external signs of corrosion (accumulations of white or green deposits, or streaks of 'rust'), or if any is thought to be dirty, it must be unplugged and cleaned using electrical contact cleaner. If the connector pins are severely corroded, the connector must be renewed; note that this may mean the renewal of that entire section of the loom.

10 If the cleaner completely removes the corrosion to leave the connector in a satisfactory condition, it would be wise to pack the connector with a suitable material which will exclude dirt and moisture, and

prevent the corrosion from occurring again; a Volvo dealer may be able to recommend a suitable product.

11 Working methodically around the engine compartment, check carefully that all vacuum hoses and pipes are securely fastened and correctly routed, with no signs of cracks, splits or deterioration to cause air leaks, or of hoses that are trapped, kinked, or bent sharply enough to restrict airflow. Check with particular care at all connections and sharp bends, and renew any damaged or deformed lengths of hose.

12 Working from the fuel tank, via the filter, to the fuel rail (and including the feed and return), check the fuel lines, and renew any that are found to be leaking, trapped or kinked. Check particularly the ends of the hoses – these can crack and perish sufficiently to allow leakage.

13 Unclip the air cleaner cover, and check that the air filter is not clogged or soaked. A clogged air filter will obstruct the intake airflow, causing a noticeable effect on engine performance. Renew the filter if necessary; refer to the relevant Section of Chapter 1A for further information, if required.

14 Start the engine and allow it to idle.

Caution: Working in the engine compartment while the engine is running requires great care if the risk of personal injury is to be avoided; among the dangers are burns from contact with hot components, or contact with moving components such as the radiator cooling fan or the auxiliary drivebelt. Refer to Safety first! at the front of this manual before starting, and ensure that your hands, and any long hair or loose clothing, are kept well clear of hot or moving components at all times.

15 Working from the air intake, via the air cleaner assembly and the mass airflow sensor to the throttle control unit and intake manifold (and including the various vacuum hoses and pipes connected to these), check for air leaks. Usually, these will be revealed by sucking or hissing noises, but minor leaks may be traced by spraying a solution of soapy water on to the suspect joint; if a leak exists, it will be shown by the change in engine note and the accompanying air bubbles (or sucking-in of the liquid, depending on the pressure difference at that point). If a leak is found at any point, tighten the fastening clamp and/or renew the faulty components, as applicable.

16 Similarly, work from the cylinder head, via the manifold to the tailpipe, to check that the exhaust system is free from leaks. The simplest way of doing this, if the vehicle can be raised and supported safely and with complete security while the check is made, is to temporarily block the tailpipe while listening for the sound of escaping exhaust gases; any leak should be evident. If a leak is found at any point, tighten the fastening clamp bolts and/or nuts, renew the gasket, and/or renew the faulty section of the system, as necessary, to seal the leak.

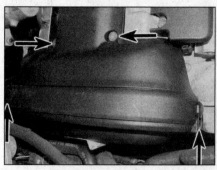

4.2 Undo the two screws and release the two clips (arrowed)

17 It is possible to make a further check of the electrical connections by wiggling each electrical connector of the system in turn as the engine is idling; a faulty connector will be immediately evident from the engine's response as contact is broken and remade. A faulty connector should be renewed to ensure that the future reliability of the system; note that this may mean the renewal of that entire section of the loom.

18 If the preliminary checks have failed to reveal the fault, the car must be taken to a Volvo dealer or suitably-equipped garage for diagnostic testing using electronic test equipment.

4 Ignition HT coils – removal and refitting

Removal

1 On turbocharged engines, release the clamps and remove the charge air hose from the turbocharger to the intercooler (over the top of the engine).

2 Remove the two screws, and release the two spring clips securing the timing belt upper cover, and unclip the cover from the spark plug cover in the centre of the cylinder head **(see illustration)**.

3 Remove the six retaining screws, and lift the cover away for access to the ignition coils **(see illustration)**.

4 Starting at the coil nearest the timing belt, disconnect the wiring plug from the coil **(see**

4.3 Undo the 6 screws and remove the cover over the coils

4.4 Press down on the clip and disconnect the wiring plug from the coil (arrowed)

4.5 Undo the single retaining bolt, and pull the ignition coil from the top of the spark plug

5.4 Rear knock sensor retaining bolt (arrowed)

illustration). It is safest to work on one coil at a time. However, if the coils and their wiring plugs are marked for position, all five could be removed at once.

5 Unscrew the coil retaining bolt, then pull the coil and HT cap out of the recess in the cylinder head **(see illustration)**.

Refitting

6 Align the coil with the mounting bolt hole, then push it down firmly onto the spark plug. Tighten the retaining bolt to the specified torque.

7 Press the wiring plug until it can be heard to 'click' into place.

8 The remainder of refitting is a reversal of removal.

5 Knock sensor(s) –
   removal and refitting

Removal

1 The two knock sensors are located on the front facing side of the cylinder block under the intake manifold.

2 Refer to Chapter 4A and remove the intake manifold.

3 Disconnect the wiring connector from the front or rear knock sensor as applicable.

4 Undo the retaining bolt and remove the sensor **(see illustration)**.

Refitting

5 On non-turbocharged engines, located the sensor on the cylinder block, and refit and tighten the retaining bolt to the specified torque. Whilst tightening the bolt, hold the sensor with its connector at the 4 o'clock position.

6 On turbocharged engines, locate the sensor on the cylinder block, and refit and tighten the retaining bolt to the specified torque. When tightening the bolt, hold the front sensor (nearest the timing belt) with its connector at the 3 o'clock position, and the rear sensor with its connector at the 5 o'clock position.

7 Refit the intake manifold as described in Chapter 4A.

Chapter 6
Clutch

Contents

Degrees of difficulty

Easy, suitable for novice with little experience	Fairly easy, suitable for beginner with some experience	Fairly difficult, suitable for competent DIY mechanic	Difficult, suitable for experienced DIY mechanic	Very difficult, suitable for expert DIY or professional

Specifications

General
Clutch type . . . . Single dry plate, diaphragm spring, self-adjusting, hydraulic actuation

Pressure plate
Warp limit . . . . 0.2 mm

Torque wrench settings

	Nm	lbf ft
Master cylinder retaining nuts	25	18
Pedal retaining screws	25	18
Pressure plate retaining screws	25	18
Release bearing and slave cylinder mounting bolts	10	7

---

1 General information

A single dry plate diaphragm spring clutch is fitted to all manual transmission models. The clutch is hydraulically operated via a master and slave cylinder. All models have an internally-mounted slave cylinder and release bearing combined into one unit.

The main components of the clutch are the pressure plate (or clutch cover), the driven plate (sometimes called the friction plate or disc) and the release bearing. The pressure plate is bolted to the flywheel, with the driven plate sandwiched between them. The centre of the driven plate carries female splines which mate with the splines on the transmission input shaft. The release bearing acts on the diaphragm spring fingers of the pressure plate.

When the engine is running and the clutch pedal is released, the diaphragm spring clamps the pressure plate, driven plate and flywheel firmly together. Drive is transmitted through the friction surfaces of the flywheel and pressure plate to the linings of the driven plate, and thus to the transmission input shaft.

The slave cylinder is incorporated into the release bearing – when the slave cylinder operates, the release bearing moves against the diaphragm spring fingers. As the spring pressure on the pressure plate is relieved, the flywheel and pressure plate spin without moving the driven plate. As the pedal is released, spring pressure is restored and the drive is gradually taken up.

The clutch hydraulic system consists of a master cylinder, a slave cylinder and the associated pipes and hoses. The fluid reservoir is shared with the brake master cylinder.

All models are fitted with a self-adjusting clutch, which compensates for driven plate wear by altering the attitude of the diaphragm spring fingers by means of a sprung mechanism within the pressure plate cover. This ensures a consistent clutch pedal 'feel' over the life of the clutch.

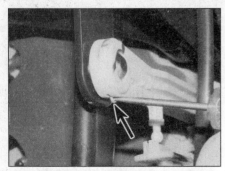

2.2 Prise out the clip (arrowed) and pull the pushrod from the pedal – shown with the facia removed for clarity

2.3a Use a 24 mm spanner (arrowed) to counterhold the pedal shaft bolt

2.3b Recover the pedal return spring

2 Clutch pedal –
removal and refitting

Removal

1 Undo the two screws and pull downwards/rearwards the trim panel above the pedals.

2 Prise out the retaining clip, and pull the master cylinder pushrod from the pedal **(see illustration)**. If necessary, pull the clutch pedal position sensor pushrod from the master cylinder pushrod.

3 Undo the screws, and lower the pedal assembly from position. Recover the return spring as the pedal is withdrawn **(see illustrations)**. Use a 24 mm spanner to counterhold the pedal shaft.

4 If required, pull the pedal shaft out and recover the bushes.

Refitting

5 Refit by reversing the removal operations. Apply grease to the pedal bushes.

3 Clutch master cylinder –
removal and refitting

⚠ *Warning: Hydraulic fluid is poisonous; wash off immediately and thoroughly in the case of skin contact, and seek immediate medical advice if any fluid is swallowed or gets into*

the eyes. Certain types of hydraulic fluid are inflammable, and may ignite when allowed into contact with hot components; when servicing any hydraulic system, it is safest to assume that the fluid IS inflammable, and to take precautions against the risk of fire as though it is petrol that is being handled. Hydraulic fluid is also an effective paint stripper, and will attack plastics; if any is spilt, it should be washed off immediately, using copious quantities of clean water. Finally, it is hygroscopic (it absorbs moisture from the air) – old fluid may be contaminated and unfit for further use. When topping-up or renewing the fluid, always use the recommended type, and ensure that it comes from a freshly-opened sealed container.

Note: *At the time of writing, it would appear that master cylinder internal components are not available separately, and therefore no repair or overhaul of the cylinder is possible. In the event of a hydraulic system fault, or any sign of visible fluid leakage on or around the master cylinder or clutch pedal, the unit should be renewed – consult a Volvo dealer or specialist.*

Removal

1 Undo the fasteners, and remove the engine cross-stay from between the brackets on the front suspension turrets.

2 Disconnect the brake fluid reservoir and servo wiring plugs, then move the loom to one side.

3 Undo the two screws, and pull rearwards the trim panel above the pedals.

4 Prise off the retaining clip, and pull the master cylinder pushrod from the pedal **(see illustration 2.2)**.

5 Pull the clutch pedal position sensor from place.

6 Working under the facia, undo the two nuts securing the master cylinder to the bulkhead **(see illustration)**.

7 Prise out the clip and disconnect the pressure pipe union from the master cylinder **(see illustration)**. Be prepared for further fluid spillage. Cover the open pipe union with a piece of polythene and a rubber band to keep dirt out.

8 Pull the master cylinder slightly away from the bulkhead, rotate it half a turn and release the fluid supply hose from the retaining clip, then use a clamp on the hose before disconnecting it from the master cylinder. Be prepared for further fluid spillage. Cover the open pipe union with a piece of polythene and a rubber band to keep dirt out.

9 Remove the master cylinder from the engine compartment.

Refitting

10 Refit by reversing the removal operations, noting the following points:

a) If a new master cylinder is being fitted, transfer the fluid supply hose from the old cylinder to the new one prior to installation.

b) Tighten the master cylinder retaining nuts to the specified torque.

c) Bleed the clutch hydraulic system on completion (Section 5).

4 Clutch slave cylinder –
removal and refitting

Note 1: *Slave cylinder internal components are not available separately, and no repair or overhaul of the cylinder is possible. In the event of a hydraulic system fault, or any sign of fluid leakage, the unit should be renewed.*

Note 2: *Refer to the warning at the beginning of Section 3 before proceeding.*

Removal

1 Remove the transmission as described in

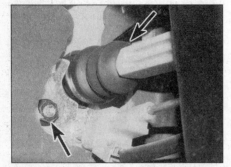

3.6 Clutch master cylinder nuts (arrowed – upper one hidden)

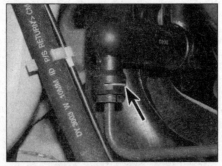

3.7 Prise out the clip (arrowed) and disconnect the pipe from the master cylinder

Chapter 7A. The internal slave cylinder cannot be removed with the transmission in place.

2 Release the rubber seal from the transmission, and move it inwards down the pipe.

3 Prise out the clip and disconnect the fluid pipe junction from the pipe **(see illustration)**.

4 Remove the two mounting bolts securing the cylinder and release bearing assembly to the transmission, and remove the assembly, feeding the fluid pipe in through the transmission aperture **(see illustration)**.

Refitting

5 Refit by reversing the removal operations, noting the following points:

  a) *Tighten the release bearing assembly mounting bolts to the specified torque.*

  b) *Volvo recommend renewing the seals when refitting the quick-release pipe connections.*

  c) *Refit the transmission as described in Chapter 7A.*

  d) *Bleed the clutch hydraulic system on completion (Section 5).*

5 Clutch hydraulic system – bleeding

Note: *Refer to the warning at the beginning of Section 3 before proceeding.*

1 Top-up the hydraulic fluid reservoir on the brake master cylinder with fresh clean fluid of the specified type (see *Weekly checks*).

2 Remove the dust cover, and fit a length of clear hose over the bleed screw on the slave cylinder **(see illustration)**. Place the other end of the hose in a jar containing a small amount of hydraulic fluid.

3 Slacken the bleed screw, then have an assistant depress the clutch pedal. Tighten the bleed screw when the pedal is depressed. Have the assistant release the pedal, then slacken the bleed screw again.

4 Repeat the process until clean fluid, free of air bubbles, emerges from the bleed screw. Tighten the screw at the end of a pedal downstroke, and remove the hose and jar. Refit the dust cover.

5 Top-up the hydraulic fluid reservoir.

6 One-way valve or pressure bleeding equipment may be used if preferred – refer to the information in Chapter 9, Section 2.

6 Clutch assembly – removal, inspection and refitting

Warning: Dust created by clutch wear and deposited on the clutch components may contain asbestos, which is a health hazard. DO NOT blow it out with compressed air or inhale any of it. DO NOT use petrol or petroleum-based solvents to clean off the dust. Brake system cleaner or methylated spirit should be used to flush the dust into a suitable

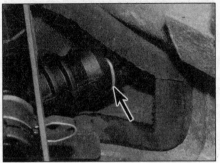

4.3 Prise out the clip (arrowed) and disconnect the junction from the pipe

receptacle. After the clutch components are wiped clean with rags, dispose of the contaminated rags and the used cleaner in a sealed, marked container.

Note: *Volvo tools 999 5677 (M56 transmission), 999 7068 (M58 transmission) and 999 5662 may be required to reset the self-adjusting mechanism and compress the diaphragm spring prior to clutch removal, although it is possible to successfully carry out the procedure using improvised home-made tools. Volvo insist that if the clutch assembly is removed without using the special tools, the pressure and driven plate must not be re-used.*

Removal

1 Access to the clutch may be gained in one of two ways. Either the engine/transmission assembly can be removed as described in Chapter 2C, and the transmission then separated from the engine, or the engine may be left in the car and the transmission removed independently as described in Chapter 7A. If the clutch is to be refitted, use paint or marker pen to mark the position of the pressure plate relative to the flywheel.

With Volvo special tools

2 Fit Volvo 'counterhold' tool 999 5677 (M56 transmission) or 999 7068 (M58 transmission) to the pressure plate to reset the self-adjusting mechanism. The pins of the tool must engage in the groove in front of the adjuster springs, then hold the tool against the plate. Engage the hooks at the end of the counter tool springs in the centre of the three holes, located at 120° intervals along the circumference of the pressure plate.

5.2 Prise off the cap (arrowed) to access the bleed screw

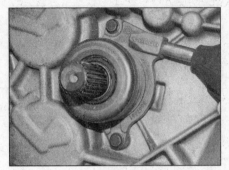

4.4 Undo the two bolts and remove the slave cylinder

3 Fit the Volvo compression tool 999 5662 to the pressure plate, and compress the diaphragm spring so that the self-adjusting spring is not under tension. Ensure that hooks on the underside of the compressor engage correctly without clamping the adjuster mechanism springs. Continue to screw in the compression tool spindle until the diaphragm spring has pressed the pressure plate to a 'free' position. A distinct 'click' will be heard when the pressure plate is in the 'free' position.

With or without Volvo special tools

4 Undo the screws and remove the pressure plate, followed by the driven plate **(see illustration)**. Note the orientation of the driven plate.

5 It is important that no oil or grease is allowed to come into contact with the friction material or the pressure plate and flywheel faces during inspection and refitting. **Note:** *If the pressure plate is to be refitted, do not allow the diaphragm spring to remain in the compressed state for a long period of time, as the spring may be permanently weakened.*

Inspection

6 With the clutch assembly removed, clean off all traces of clutch dust using a dry cloth. This is best done outside or in a well-ventilated area.

7 Examine the linings of the driven plate for wear and loose rivets, and the rim for distortion, cracks, broken torsion springs and worn splines. The surface of the friction linings

6.4 Undo the clutch pressure plate screws

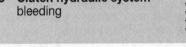

6.15a The driven plate should be marked (arrowed) to indicate which side faces the flywheel

6.15b Fit the driven plate with the longer side of the centre boss towards the flywheel

may be highly glazed, but, as long as the friction material pattern can be clearly seen, this is satisfactory.

8 If there is any sign of oil contamination, indicated by a continuous or patchy, shiny black discolouration, the plate must be renewed and the source of the contamination traced and rectified. This will be either a leaking crankshaft oil seal or transmission input shaft oil seal – or both.

9 The driven friction must also be renewed if the lining thickness has worn down to, or just above, the level of the rivet heads. Given the amount of dismantling work necessary to gain access to the driven plate, it may be wise to fit a new plate regardless of the old one's condition.

10 Check the machined faces of the flywheel and pressure plate. If either is grooved, or heavily scored, renewal is necessary. Providing the damage is not too serious, the flywheel can be removed as described in Chapter 2A or 2B, and taken to an engineering works, who may be able to clean up the surface by machining.

11 The pressure plate must be renewed if any cracks are apparent, if the diaphragm spring is damaged or its pressure suspect, or if there is excessive warpage of the pressure plate face.

12 With the transmission removed, check the condition of the release bearing, as described in Section 7.

Refitting

13 It is advisable to refit the clutch assembly with clean hands, and to wipe down the

pressure plate and flywheel faces with a clean dry rag before assembly begins.

14 Fit an appropriate centring tool into the hole at the end of the crankshaft. The tool must be a sliding fit in the crankshaft hole and the driven plate centre. Volvo centring tool 999 5663 may be available, or a suitable equivalent may be fabricated.

15 Place the driven plate in position with the longer side of the centre boss towards the flywheel, or as noted on removal. Note that the new driven plate will be marked to indicate which side faces the flywheel **(see illustrations)**.

With Volvo special tools

16 Fit the counterhold tool 999 5677 or 999 7068 (as applicable) to the pressure plate, ensuring the three pins engage in the grooves in front of the adjuster springs, then hold the tool against the plate. Engage the hooks at the end of the counter tool springs in the centre of the three holes, located at 120° intervals along the circumference of the pressure plate.

17 Fit the Volvo compression tool 999 5662 to the pressure plate, and compress the diaphragm spring so that the self-adjusting springs are not under tension. Ensure that hooks on the underside of the compressor engage correctly without clamping the adjuster mechanism springs. From the initial 'loose' state, the compressor spindle should be turned no more the 5.0 turns or a distinct 'click' will be heard when the pressure plate is in the 'free' position.

Without Volvo special tools

18 Using a length of threaded rod, some circular spacers and two nuts, compress the diaphragm spring fingers and the pressure plate together as shown. Once the fingers are compressed, use a screwdriver to move and hold the adjusting ring anti-clockwise until the pointers align with the marks by the adjustment springs **(see illustrations)**.

19 Slowly undo the nuts to uncompress the pressure plate assembly. The self-adjusting ring/spring marks should remain in the same place (see paragraph 18). Remove the threaded rod, etc.

With or without Volvo special tools

20 Position the pressure plate assembly over the dowels on the flywheel, aligning the previously-made marks (where applicable).

21 Working in a diagonal pattern, fit and evenly tighten the pressure plate retaining screws to the specified torque.

22 Slowly release the compressor, then remove the counterhold too from the clutch – where applicable.

23 Pull the centring tool from the plate/crankshaft, and check visually that the driven plate appears centrally located.

24 The engine and/or transmission can now be refitted by referring to the appropriate Chapters of this manual.

7 Clutch release bearing – removal, inspection and refitting

Removal

1 Access to the clutch release bearing may be gained in one of two ways. Either the engine/transmission assembly can be removed as described in Chapter 2C, and the transmission then separated from the engine, or the engine may be left in the car and the transmission removed independently as described in Chapter 7A.

2 The release bearing and slave cylinder are combined into one unit, and cannot be separated. Refer to the slave cylinder removal procedure in Section 4.

6.18a Compress the diaphragm spring fingers and the pressure plate together . . .

6.18b . . . then rotate the adjuster ring anti-clockwise . . .

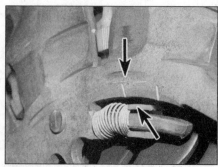

6.18c . . . until the pointers align with the marks by the adjustment springs (arrowed)

Inspection

3 Check the bearing for smoothness of operation, and renew it if there is any roughness or harshness as the bearing is spun. It is a good idea to renew the bearing as a matter of course during clutch overhaul, regardless of its apparent condition, considering the amount of dismantling work necessary to gain access to it.

Refitting

4 Refer to Section 4.

8 Clutch pedal position sensor – renewal

1 Undo the two screws and remove the trim panel above the driver's pedals.
2 Using a flat-bladed screwdriver, carefully prise the sensor from the balljoints on the master cylinder and the pushrod **(see illustration)**. Disconnect the wiring plug as the sensor is withdrawn.
3 Refitting is a reversal of removal.

8.2 Carefully prise the position sensor from the balljoints on the arm and master cylinder

Notes

Chapter 7 Part A:
Manual transmission

Contents

Degrees of difficulty

Easy, suitable for novice with little experience	**Fairly easy,** suitable for beginner with some experience	**Fairly difficult,** suitable for competent DIY mechanic	**Difficult,** suitable for experienced DIY mechanic	**Very difficult,** suitable for expert DIY or professional

Specifications

General

Designation	M56, M58 or M66

Transmission type:

M56 or M58	Five forward gears and one reverse. Synchromesh on all gears
M66.	Six forward gears and one reverse. Synchromesh on all gears

Lubrication

Lubricant type	See end of *Weekly checks*

Capacity:

M56 or M58	2.1 litres
M66.	2.0 litres

Torque wrench settings

	Nm	lbf ft
Anti-roll bar link to anti-roll bar.	60	44
Auxiliary heater mounting nuts.	25	18
Engine cross-stay:		
To suspension turrets.	50	37
To engine mounting bracket.	80	59
Engine lower stabiliser*:		
Stage 1	50	37
Stage 2	Angle-tighten a further 40°	
Engine mounting nuts/bolts.	See Chapter 2 Specifications	
Engine rear mounting bracket to transmission.	50	37
Engine undershield screws.	25	18
Gear lever housing bolts	25	18
Lower torque rod-to-subframe nut:		
Stage 1	65	48
Stage 2	Angle-tighten a further 60°	
Lower torque rod to transmission:		
Stage 1	35	26
Stage 2	Angle-tighten a further 40°	
Oil filler/drain plugs.	35	26
Reversing light switch	25	18
Roadwheel bolts.	140	103
Starter motor mounting bolts.	40	30
Steering gear crash guard bolts.	80	59
Steering gear-to-subframe nuts*	50	37
Subframe mounting bolts:*		
Up to 2004 model year:		
Stage 1	105	77
Stage 2	Angle-tighten a further 120°	
From 2005 model year	160	118
Subframe mounting brackets to body	50	37
Transmission-to-engine bolts.	48	35

* Do not re-use

2.2a Squeeze together the clips (arrowed) and pull the locking collar downwards . . .

2.2b . . . then pull the knob straight upwards . . .

2.2c . . . followed by the support ring . . .

2.2d . . . and gaiter

1 General information

The manual transmission and final drive are housed in an aluminium casing, bolted directly to the left-hand side of the engine. Gear selection is by a remotely-sited lever assembly, operating the transmission selector mechanism via cables.

On M56 and M58 transmissions, the internal components comprise the input shaft, the upper and lower layshafts, the final drive differential and the selector mechanism. The input shaft contains the fixed 1st, 2nd and 5th gears, the freewheeling 3rd and 4th gearwheels and the 3rd/4th synchro unit. The upper layshaft contains the freewheeling 5th and reverse gearwheels, the 5th/reverse

synchro unit and a final drive pinion. The lower layshaft contains the fixed 3rd and 4th gears, the freewheeling 1st, 2nd and reverse intermediate gearwheels, the 1st/2nd synchro unit and a final drive pinion. On M66 transmissions, the input shaft contains the 6th, 5th gear idler wheels, and the 4th, 1st, and 3rd gearwheels. The two intermediate shafts contain the 5th and 6th gearwheels, 1st, 2nd, 3rd and 4th gear idler wheels, and the final drive gearwheels.

Drive from the engine is transmitted to the input shaft by the clutch. The gears on the input shaft are permanently meshed with the gears on the two layshafts, but when drive is transmitted, only one gear at a time is actually locked to its shaft, with the others freewheeling. The selection of gears is by sliding synchro units; movement of the gear lever is transmitted to selector forks which

slide the appropriate synchro unit towards the gear to be engaged, and lock it to the relevant shaft. In neutral, none of the gears are locked; all are freewheeling.

Reverse gear is obtained by locking the reverse gearwheel to the upper layshaft. Drive is transmitted through the input shaft to the reverse intermediate gearwheel on the lower layshaft, then to the reverse gearwheel and final drive pinion on the upper layshaft. Reverse is therefore obtained by transmitting power through all three shafts, instead of only two as in the case of the forward gears. By eliminating the need for a separate reverse idler gear, synchromesh can also be provided on reverse gear.

2 Gear lever housing – removal and refitting

Removal

1 Remove the centre console as described in Chapter 11.
2 On models with a gear lever gaiter, pull the gaiter and panel upwards around the knob, then squeeze together the two catches and pull the gaiter locking collar downwards, followed by the gaiter. Pull the knob straight upwards and remove it followed by the support ring and the gaiter from the lever **(see illustrations)**.
3 Undo the four bolts securing the housing assembly to the floor **(see illustration)**.
4 Lift up the housing, and prise off the selector inner cable socket joints from the base of the gear lever. Note that on some models, the cable ends may be secured by clips **(see illustration)**.
5 Release the retaining clips securing the selector outer cables to the housing **(see illustration)**, and remove the assembly from the car.

Refitting

6 Refit by reversing the removal operations. Tighten the four securing bolts to the specified torque. Refit the centre console as described in Chapter 11.

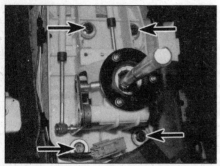

2.3 Undo the four bolts (arrowed) securing the housing to the floor

2.4 Prise the inner cable socket joints from the lever

2.5 Release the clips and slide the outer cables up from the housing

3.4a Prise the inner cables from the balljoints . . .

3.4b . . . then pull back the collars, and slide the outer cables up from the brackets on the transmission

3.4c On some models, prise out the clip securing the cable end to the balljoint . . .

3 Selector cables – removal and refitting

Removal

1 Refer to the relevant Part of Chapter 4 and remove the air cleaner assembly.

2 Slacken the front left-hand roadwheel nuts, then jack up the front of the vehicle and support it securely on axle stands (see *Jacking and vehicle support*). Remove the roadwheel.

3 Undo the two plastic nuts securing the wheel arch liner, and remove the splash guard over the driveshaft.

4 Note their fitted positions, prise inner cable ends from the transmission selector levers, then pull back the collars and pull the outer cables from the brackets on the transmission **(see illustrations)**. Note that on some models, the cable ends may be retained by clips, and the blue plastic spacers must slide up from place before the outer cable collars can be pulled back.

5 Remove the centre console as described in Chapter 11.

6 Undo the four screws securing the gear lever housing to the floor, and disconnect the cables from the housing and levers, as described in Section 2, paragraphs 3, 4 and 5.

7 Fold back the carpet on the left-hand side under the facia to access the cable grommet/cable entry plate.

8 Undo the nuts securing the grommet/cable entry plate to the bulkhead **(see illustration)**.

9 Note the routing of the cables under the facia, and in the engine compartment, as an aid to refitting, then attach welding rod (or similar) to the ends of the cables in the engine compartment. Release any adjacent components as necessary, then pull the cables one at a time into the passenger compartment, then unhook the welding rods leaving them in place to assist refitting. Remove the cables from the car.

Refitting

10 From inside the car, hook the cables end onto the welding rod, then carefully feed/pull the cables through into the engine compartment, ensuring that they are routed

3.4d . . . and slide up the blue plastic spacer before pulling back the outer cable collar

correctly. Note that the cable which is attached to the gear lever housing left-hand link plate, and the link plate itself, are marked with white paint.

11 Reconnect the cables to the gear lever housing, and refit the housing as described in Section 2.

12 Refit the grommet/cable entry plate, and the carpet.

13 Refit the centre console (see Chapter 11).

14 Attach the outer cables to the transmission brackets, refitting the blue clips where applicable.

15 To set the cable with the adjuster, pull forward the spring-loaded collar, and push up the locking button to hold the collar in place. Ensure the gear lever is in the neutral position, then press the inner cable ends onto the selector levers. Press the locking button down to release the spring-loaded collar **(see illustrations)**.

3.15a Pull forward the spring-loaded collar (arrowed) . . .

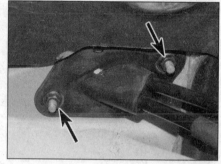

3.8 Undo the two nuts (arrowed) securing the cable grommet

16 Refit the air cleaner assembly as described in the relevant Part of Chapter 4.

4 Oil seals – renewal

Driveshaft seals

1 Remove the left- or right-hand driveshaft (as appropriate) with reference to Chapter 8.

2 Using a large screwdriver or suitable lever, carefully prise the oil seal out of the transmission casing, taking care not to damage the casing **(see illustration)**.

3 Wipe clean the oil seal seating in the transmission casing.

4 Apply a small amount of general purpose grease to the new seal lips, then press it a little way into the casing by hand, making sure that it is square to its seating.

3.15b . . . and press down the locking button (arrowed)

4.2 Use a piece of wood to protect the casing when levering out the driveshaft oil seal(s)

4.5 Use a socket or tubular spacer to drive in the oil seal

4.9a Drill a small hole in the hard outer edge of the oil seal, then insert a self-tapping screw . . .

4.9b . . . and use pliers to pull the screw and seal from place

5 Using suitable tubing or a large socket, carefully drive the oil seal fully into position until it is flush with the casing edge **(see illustration)**.

6 Refit the driveshaft(s) as described in Chapter 8.

Input shaft oil seal

7 Remove the transmission as described in Section 7.

8 Remove the clutch release bearing/slave cylinder as described in Chapter 6.

9 Note its fitted depth, then drill a small hole in the hard outer surface of the seal, insert a self-tapping screw, and use pliers to extract the seal **(see illustrations)**.

10 Lubricate the new seal with grease and fit it to the bellhousing, lips pointing to the gearbox side. Use a deep socket or suitable tubing to seat it **(see illustration)**.

11 Refit the release bearing/slave cylinder using a reversal of removal.

4.10 Use a suitable tube to drive in the seal

12 Refit the transmission as described in Section 7.

5 Reversing light switch – removal and refitting

Removal

1 The reversing light switch is located on the upper face of the transmission, between the two gear selector levers. Remove the air cleaner assembly as described in the relevant Part of Chapter 4.

M66 transmissions

2 Disconnect the ends of the selector cables from the levers on the transmission, then release the outer cables from the bracket as described in Section 3.

3 Disconnect the switch wiring plug, unclip

the loom, then undo the 3 bolts and remove the selector cable support bracket from the transmission **(see illustration)**.

4 Slide a deep socket over the switch and unscrew it from the transmission **(see illustration)**.

M56/58 transmissions

5 Clean around the switch, disconnect the wiring connector **(see illustration)** and unscrew the switch.

Refitting

6 Refit by reversing the removal operations.

6 Manual transmission oil – draining and refilling

Note: *Renewal of the transmission oil is not a service requirement and will normally only be necessary if the unit is to be removed for overhaul or replacement. However, if the car has completed a high mileage, or is used under arduous conditions (eg, extensive towing or taxi work), it would be advisable to change the oil as a precaution, especially if the gearchange quality has deteriorated.*

Draining

1 Slacken the left-hand front roadwheel bolts, then jack up the front of the vehicle and support it securely on axle stands (see *Jacking and vehicle support*). Remove the roadwheel.

2 Release the screws and remove the engine

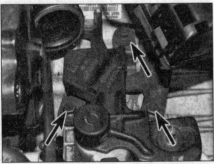

5.3 Undo the 3 bolts (arrowed) and remove the cable support bracket

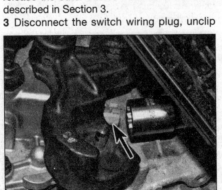

5.4 Use a deep socket to unscrew the reversing light switch (arrowed)

5.5 Disconnect the reversing light switch wiring plug (arrowed)

undershield, then position a suitable container beneath the transmission.

3 On the left-hand side of the transmission casing, you will see the filler/level plug and the drain plug. Unscrew and remove the drain plug (the lower of the two) and allow the oil to drain into the container **(see illustration)**. Check the condition of the drain plug sealing washer, and renew if necessary.

4 When all the oil has drained, refit the drain plug and tighten it to the specified torque.

Refilling

Note: *For the level check to be accurate, the car must be completely level. If the front of the car has been jacked up, the rear should be jacked up also.*

5 Wipe clean the area around the filler/level plug, and unscrew the plug from the casing **(see illustration)**.

6 Fill the transmission through the filler plug orifice with the correct type of oil until the oil begins to run out of the orifice.

7 Refit the filler/level plug with a new seal, and tighten it to the specified torque.

8 Dispose of the old oil safely in accordance with environmental regulations.

7 Manual transmission – removal and refitting

Note: *Arrangements must be made to support the engine from above, to allow the subframe to be detached on the left-hand side. The best way to support the engine is with a bar resting in the bonnet channels with an adjustable hook appropriately placed. Trolley jacks and the help of an assistant will also be required throughout the procedure.*

Removal

1 Set the steering wheel and roadwheels in the straight-ahead position. Release the steering column adjuster, and push the steering wheel in and upwards as far as it will go. Lock it in this position.

2 Put the gear lever in neutral.

3 Refer to Section 6 and drain the transmission oil. This is not absolutely essential, but will remove the potential problem of oil spillage when the driveshafts are removed, or when the transmission is moved out of the car.

4 Disconnect the battery negative lead as described in Chapter 5A.

5 Refer to the relevant Part of Chapter 4 and remove the air cleaner assembly, and all relevant intake ducting around the left-hand side of the engine. On 6-speed transmissions, remove the air cleaner bracket from the transmission.

6 Disconnect the gearchange cables from the transmission as described in Section 3.

7 On diesel models, remove the plastic cover over the top of the engine by pulling it straight up from its mountings.

8 Undo the fasteners and remove the engine

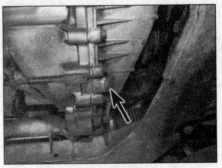

6.3 Oil drain plug (arrowed)

cross-stay between the brackets on the front suspension turrets.

9 On turbo models, release the clamps/undo the bolts and remove the charge air pipe from the intercooler to the turbo, and the intercooler to the intake manifold/throttle housing.

10 Undo the nut securing the rear engine mounting pad to the bracket **(see illustration)**. Where applicable, disconnect the vacuum hose from the mounting pad.

11 Clamp the hoses, rotate the collars anti-clockwise and disconnect the heater hoses from the unions at the engine compartment bulkhead **(see illustration)**.

12 Clamp the fluid supply hose from the brake fluid reservoir to the clutch master cylinder, then extract the circlip and withdraw the slave cylinder supply pipe from the transmission. Have ready a container and rags to catch the fluid which will spill. Cover the open pipe union with a piece of polythene and a rubber band to keep dirt out.

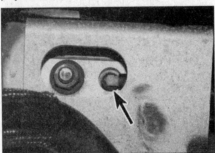

7.10 Looking down the back of the engine, unscrew the mounting pad nut and disconnect the vacuum hose (arrowed)

7.13 Disconnect the earth strap from the front of the transmission casing

6.5 Transmission oil filler/level plug (arrowed)

13 Disconnect the earth cable from the subframe and transmission **(see illustration)**.

14 Undo the screw securing the power steering hose clamp to the subframe.

15 Tap out the retaining pin and remove the vertical selector lever on the end of the transmission.

16 Disconnect the wiring connector at the reversing light switch, then undo the bolts and remove the cable guide from the top of the transmission.

17 Undo all the transmission-to-engine retaining bolts that are accessible from above.

18 Referring to Chapter 8, remove both driveshafts completely.

19 Undo the screws/clips and remove the engine undershield, if not already done so.

20 Undo the screws, release the clips and remove the air baffle from the front underside of the vehicle **(see illustration)**.

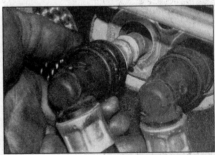

7.11 Rotate the collars anti-clockwise and pull the heater hoses from the bulkhead pipes

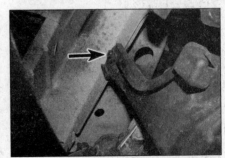

7.20 Viewed from under the wheel arch, undo the bolt (arrowed) each end securing the air baffle from under the radiator

7.25 Undo the two bolts (arrowed) securing the engine lower steady bar bracket to the transmission casing

7.29 Undo the steering universal joint pinch-bolt (arrowed)

7.32 Undo the bolts each side securing the subframe rear mounting to the vehicle body

21 Remove the clips and release the pipe(s) running under the front of the subframe.

22 On models with a fuel-powered auxiliary heater, undo the two mounting screws, and leave the heater hanging from its upper mounting. Detach the fuel hose from its retaining bracket on the subframe.

23 Working underneath the vehicle, undo the screws and remove the reinforcement plates under the exhaust system. Release the brake pipe from the clips on the front reinforcement plate.

24 On right-hand drive models, undo the two steering rack crash guard bolts at the rear of the subframe, and the nut securing the crash guard base to the subframe.

25 Undo the two bolts securing the engine lower steady bar bracket to the transmission **(see illustration)**.

26 With reference to the note at the beginning of this Section, suitably support the engine from above, and adjust the support so that the load is just taken off the engine mountings.

27 Undo the bolt securing the engine front mounting to the subframe.

28 Disconnect the left-hand steering track rod end from the hub carrier as described in Chapter 10.

29 Make alignment marks between the steering rack pinion and the steering column lower universal joint, then undo the pinch-bolt and push the joints upwards from the pinion **(see illustration)**.

30 Position a sturdy trolley jack beneath, and in contact with, the left-hand side of the subframe. Ensure that the engine is securely supported from above.

31 Undo the nut securing the left-hand link to the anti-roll bar (see Chapter 10).

32 Undo the bolts each side securing the subframe rear mounting brackets to the body **(see illustration)**.

33 Slacken the two subframe mounting bolts on the right-hand side by at least 5 turns. Note that new bolts will be required for refitting.

34 Undo the two subframe mounting bolts on the left-hand side. Collect the mounting bracket when the rear bolt is removed. Note that new bolts will be required for refitting.

35 Slacken the bolt securing the engine rear mounting to the steering gear, then undo the

five nuts securing the steering gear to the subframe. Note that new nuts will be required for refitting.

36 Undo the bolts and remove the rear engine mounting bracket from the transmission and mounting pad.

37 Carefully lower the jack, and allow the subframe to drop on the left-hand side by approximately 100 mm.

38 Refer to Chapter 5A and remove the starter motor.

39 Release the oxygen sensor wiring from the rear engine mounting bracket cover. Remove the cover, then remove the mounting bracket from the transmission.

40 Lower the jack completely, and allow the subframe to hang free from the right-hand side mountings.

41 Lower the engine/transmission by means of the overhead support, until sufficient clearance exists to enable the transmission to be withdrawn. Take care not to lower the unit too far, or the exhaust downpipe will foul the steering gear. Also, make sure that the engine oil dipstick tube clears the radiator fan, and that no hoses or leads are trapped.

42 Securely and safely support the transmission from below on a trolley jack.

43 Undo the remaining bolts securing the transmission to the engine. Withdraw the transmission squarely off the engine dowels, taking care not to allow the weight of the transmission to hang on the input shaft.

44 Lower the jack and remove the unit from under the car.

Refitting

45 Do not apply any grease to the transmission input shaft, the guide sleeve, or the release bearing itself, as these components have a friction-reducing coating which does not require lubrication.

46 Manoeuvre the transmission squarely into position, and engage it with the engine dowels. Refit the lower bolts securing the transmission to the engine, and tighten them to the specified torque.

47 Raise the engine to its approximate fitted position. Refit the rear engine mounting bracket and cover, and secure with the three bolts tightened to the specified torque.

48 Refit the engine rear mounting to the transmission bracket and steering gear, but do not fully tighten the nut and bolt at this stage.

49 Secure the oxygen sensor wiring to the mounting bracket cover.

50 On right-hand drive models, raise the subframe to within 100 mm of the body, align the steering gear and crash guard with their subframe locations. Tighten all the clamp bolts to the specified torque.

51 On all models, raise the subframe to its fitted position, ensuring that the steering gear bolts engage in their locations.

52 Fit the new subframe mounting bolts and rear mounting bracket and bolts on the left-hand side. Tighten the subframe bolts to the specified torque using a torque wrench, then further, through the specified angle, using an angle-tightening gauge. Tighten the mounting bracket bolts to the specified torque.

53 Support the right-hand side of the subframe on the jack, and remove the two previously-slackened subframe bolts. Fit the new bolts and the two mounting bracket bolts, and tighten them as described in the previous paragraph.

54 Secure the steering gear to the subframe using five new nuts tightened to the specified torque.

55 Refit the engine front mounting bolt, then tighten the engine front and rear mountings to the specified torque.

56 On right-hand-drive models, refit the two steering gear crash guard bolts at the rear of the subframe, and the nut securing the crash guard base to the subframe. Tighten to the specified torque.

57 The remainder of refitting is a reversal of removal, noting the following points:

a) *Tighten all fasteners to the their specified torque where given.*

b) *Top-up the gearbox oil as described in Section 6 of this Chapter.*

c) *Top-up the cooling system as described in the relevant Part of Chapter 1.*

d) *Bleed the clutch hydraulic system (if necessary) as described in Chapter 6.*

e) *Reconnect the battery negative lead as described in Chapter 5A.*

8 Manual transmission overhaul – general information

Overhauling a manual transmission is a difficult job for the do-it-yourselfer. It involves the dismantling and reassembly of many small parts. Numerous clearances must be precisely measured and, if necessary, changed with selected spacers and circlips. As a result, if transmission problems arise, while the unit can be removed and refitted by a competent do-it-yourselfer, overhaul should be left to a transmission specialist. Rebuilt transmissions may be available – check with your dealer parts department, motor factors, or transmission specialists. At any rate, the time and money involved in an overhaul is almost sure to exceed the cost of a rebuilt unit.

Nevertheless, it's not impossible for an experienced mechanic to rebuild a transmission, providing the special tools are available, and the job is done in a deliberate step-by-step manner, so nothing is overlooked.

The tools necessary for an overhaul include: internal and external circlip pliers, a bearing puller, a slide hammer, a set of pin punches, a dial test indicator, and possibly a hydraulic press. In addition, a large, sturdy workbench and a vice or transmission stand will be required.

During dismantling of the transmission, make careful notes of how each part comes off, where it fits in relation to other parts, and what holds it in place.

Before taking the transmission apart for repair, it will help if you have some idea what area of the transmission is malfunctioning. Certain problems can be closely tied to specific areas in the transmission, which can make component examination and renewal easier. Refer to the *Fault finding* section at the rear of this manual for information regarding possible sources of trouble.

Notes

Chapter 7 Part B:
Automatic transmission

Contents

Degrees of difficulty

Easy, suitable for novice with little experience	**Fairly easy,** suitable for beginner with some experience	**Fairly difficult,** suitable for competent DIY mechanic	**Difficult,** suitable for experienced DIY mechanic	**Very difficult,** suitable for expert DIY or professional

Specifications

General

Type	Computer-controlled five or six-speed, one reverse, with torque converter lock-up on three highest gears (five-speed box) or 5 highest gears (six-speed box)
Designation:	
Five-speed	AW50-50/51
Six-speed	TF-80SC

Lubrication

Lubricant type	See end of *Weekly checks*
Capacity (drain and refill):	
AW50-50/51	7.1 litres (approximately)
TF-80SC	8.0 litres (approximately)

Torque wrench settings

	Nm	lbf ft
Anti-roll bar link to anti-roll bar	60	44
Auxiliary heater mounting nuts	25	18
Engine cross-stay:		
To suspension turrets	50	37
To engine mounting bracket	80	59
Engine lower stabiliser*:		
Stage 1	50	37
Stage 2	Angle-tighten a further 40°	
Engine mounting nuts/bolts	See Chapter 2 Specifications	
Engine rear mounting bracket to transmission	50	37
Engine undershield screws	25	18
Fluid drain plug	40	30
Gear lever housing bolts	25	18
Gearshift position sensor screws	25	18
Lower torque rod-to-subframe nut:		
Stage 1	65	48
Stage 2	Angle-tighten a further 60°	
Lower torque rod to transmission:		
Stage 1	35	26
Stage 2	Angle-tighten a further 40°	
Reversing light switch	25	18
Roadwheel bolts	140	103
Starter motor mounting bolts	40	30
Steering rack crash guard bolts	80	59
Steering rack-to-subframe nuts*	50	37
Subframe mounting bolts*:		
Up to 2004 model year:		
Stage 1	105	77
Stage 2	Angle-tighten a further 120°	
From 2005 model year	160	118
Subframe mounting brackets to body	50	37
Torque converter-to-driveplate bolts*	60	44
Transmission-to-engine bolts	48	35

* Do not re-use

1 General information

The AW 50-50/51 is a computer-controlled fully automatic five-speed transmission, with torque converter lock-up on the highest three gears. The TF-80SC is also a computer-controlled automatic transmission, but has 6 forward speeds, with torque converter lock-up on the 5 highest speeds. It is also equipped with a Geartronic function that allows the driver to manually shift between transmission speeds in a sequential fashion – lever forward to change up, and backward to change down.

The units are controlled by a transmission control module (TCM) which receives signal inputs from various sensors relating to transmission operating conditions. Information on engine parameters are also sent to the TCM from the engine management system. From this data, the TCM can establish the optimum gear shifting speeds and lock-up engagement points according to the driving mode selected.

Drive is taken from the engine to the transmission by a torque converter. This is a type of fluid coupling, which under certain conditions has a torque multiplying effect. The torque converter is mechanically locked to the engine, under the control of the TCM, when the transmission is operating in the three, or five highest gears (depending on model). This eliminates losses due to slip, and improves fuel economy.

The engine can only be started in position P, thanks to a safety/security feature called Shiftlock. With this system, the ignition key can only be removed from the ignition/steering lock if the selector lever is placed in position P. On restarting the car, the selector lever can only be moved from the P position once the ignition switch is turned to position II.

Most models with automatic transmission feature a Winter mode selector, with the switch located alongside the selector lever. In this mode, the transmission will allow starting from rest in a higher than normal gear to avoid wheelspin in poor road conditions. This mode can also be used to restrict gearchanging when road conditions dictate the need for more direct control of gear selection.

A kickdown facility causes the transmission to shift down a gear (subject to engine speed) when the throttle is fully depressed. This is useful when extra acceleration is required. Kickdown, like the other transmission functions, is controlled by the TCM.

A shiftlock facility is also incorporated into the gear selector mechanism on certain models. This security device prevents movement of the selector lever when the engine has been stopped, or when the ignition is switched off with the selector lever in the P position.

In addition to control of the transmission, the TCM incorporates a built-in fault diagnosis facility. If a transmission fault occurs, the transmission warning light on the instrument panel will flash; the TCM will revert to an emergency (limp-home) program which ensures that some forward gears and reverse will always be available, but gearchanging may need to be performed manually. If a fault of this nature does occur, the TCM stores a series of signals (or fault codes) which can be read and interpreted using suitable diagnostic equipment, for quick and accurate fault diagnosis (see Section 8). The TCM also has a facility for recording the amount of time the gearbox fluid spends above a 150°C – normally this temperature is only achieved by continuous taxi-use, or continuous use as a tow vehicle. Once a predetermined amount of time at or above this temperature is exceeded, the TCM will store a fault code, and illuminate a warning light on the instrument cluster, indicating that the fluid must be changed. However, changing the fluid will not extinguish the warning light – this must be carried out using dedicated Volvo test equipment.

The automatic transmission is a complex unit, but if it is not abused, it is reliable and long-lasting. Repair or overhaul operations are beyond the scope of many dealers, let alone the home mechanic; specialist advice should be sought if problems arise which cannot be solved by the procedures given in this Chapter.

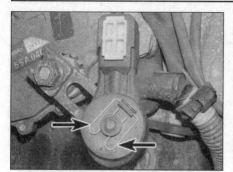

2.2a Spread the two sides (arrowed) of the clip and pivot it upwards

2.2b On models without a retaining clip, prise the cable end from the lever

2.3 Slide the outer cable up from the bracket

2 Selector cable – removal, refitting and adjustment

Removal

1 Park the car on a level surface (with the transmission selector lever in position P), then refer to the relevant Part of Chapter 4 and remove the air cleaner assembly.

2 Working in the engine compartment, extract the locking clip and washer securing the selector inner cable to the transmission selector lever. Note that on some models, no locking clip is fitted – the cable end fitting must be prised up from place **(see illustrations)**.

3 Use a screwdriver to prise the outer cable up from the bracket on the transmission **(see illustration)**.

4 Remove the centre console as described in Chapter 11.

5 Extract the retaining clip securing the selector inner cable to the gear selector lever, and slide the selector outer cable from the gear selector housing **(see illustrations)**.

6 Pull back the carpet under the passenger's side of the facia to access the cable entry cover plate.

7 Undo the bolts securing the cable entry cover plate to the bulkhead **(see illustration)**. Where applicable, release the shiftlock cable from the selector cable.

8 Note the routing of the cable under the facia, and in the engine compartment, as an aid to refitting. Release any adjacent components as necessary, then pull the cable into the passenger compartment and remove it from the car.

Refitting and adjustment

9 From inside the car, carefully feed the cable through into the engine compartment, ensuring that it is correctly routed.

10 Reconnect the cable to the selector lever and housing, and secure with the retaining clips.

11 Refit the cable entry cover plate.

12 Refit the centre console as described in Chapter 11.

13 Move the gear selector lever to position P (Park). Ensure that the gear lever and cable position do not move during subsequent operations.

14 Move the selector lever on the trans-mission as far forward as it will go to the P (Park) position. Ensure that P is selected by releasing the handbrake and trying to roll the car; the transmission should be locked. Re-apply the handbrake.

15 On some transmissions, lever up the locking tab on the end of the cable, and fit the cable outer to the support bracket on the transmission, and the cable end to the selector lever. Check the selector lever in the passenger cabin is still in the P position, then press down

2.5a Expand the selector cable clip . . .

2.5b . . . and detach the end of the cable from the lever . . .

2.5c . . . then slide the outer cable from the housing

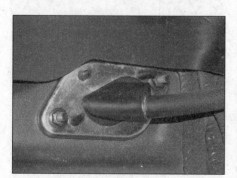

2.7 Pull back the carpet to expose the cable grommet

2.15a Lever up the locking tab on the end of the cable . . .

2.15b . . . or pull back the spring-loaded collar, and push up the lock button

3.4a Pull the yellow locking sleeve outwards to release the cable

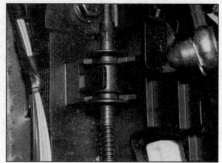

3.4b Unclip the cable from the bracket

3.8 Insert a 5 mm drill bit through the hole in the side of the housing, and into the hole in the interlock lever

the locking tab on the end of the cable. On other transmissions, pull the spring-loaded locking collar forwards, push up the lock button, then fit the outer cable to the support bracket, and the cable end to the selector lever. Check the selector lever in the passenger cabin is still in the P position, then press down the lock button **(see illustrations)**.

16 Refit the locking clip and washer securing the cable to the transmission selector lever (where applicable).

17 On completion, refit the air cleaner assembly (the relevant Part of Chapter 4).

3 Selector housing – removal and refitting

Removal

1 Remove the centre console as described in Chapter 11.

2 Extract the retaining clip securing the selector inner cable to the gear selector lever **(see illustrations 2.5a and 2.5b)**.

3 Extract the retaining clip securing the selector outer cable to the gear selector housing **(see illustration 2.5c)**.

4 Slightly pull out the yellow locking sleeve, and unclip the interlock cable from the bracket and disconnect it from the lever **(see illustrations)**. Note that the locking sleeve must not be reused.

5 Where applicable, disconnect the shiftlock solenoid wiring connector.

6 Undo the bolts securing the housing to the floor and remove it from the car.

4.2 Unclip the ECM box lid

Refitting

7 Refitting is a reversal of removal, setting the interlock cable as follows.

8 Turn the ignition switch to position 0, and move the selector lever to position P. Insert a 5 mm drill bit into the housing above the new yellow locking sleeve, to position the lever in the 'secured' position **(see illustration)**. Fit the outer cable to the housing, and the threaded end in the groove on the yellow locking sleeve. Press the locking sleeve so that it locks the cable. Remove the drill and check the operation of the interlock.

4 Transmission control module – removal and refitting

Note: *If a new control module is fitted, it must be programmed using dedicated Volvo test equipment. Entrust this task to a Volvo dealer or suitably-equipped specialist.*

Removal

1 Disconnect the battery negative terminal as described in Chapter 5A.

Caution: Wait at least two minutes after the battery negative lead has been disconnected for any residual energy to dissipate from the main system relay.

Five-speed transmissions (AW50-50/51)

2 The transmission control module (TCM) is located alongside the engine management ECM in the right-hand corner of the engine compartment. Clean off the top of the ECM box lid, to make sure no debris falls inside when it is removed. Release the catch on the side of the ECM module box lid. Lift off the lid and place it to one side **(see illustration)**.

3 To remove the TCM, insert Volvo tool No 999 5722 around the TCM and push the top of the tool rearwards as far as it will go, then pull the module upwards. If the tool is not available, fabricate a homemade equivalent as shown **(see illustrations)**. **Note:** *Do not touch the control module terminal pins with bare hands – there is a danger of damage due to static electricity.*

Six-speed transmissions (TF-80SC)

4 The transmission control module (TCM) is

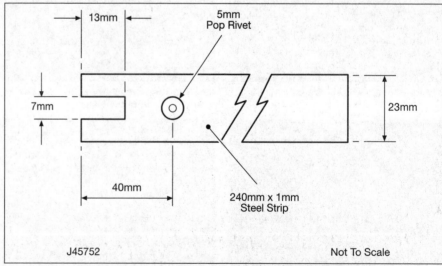

4.3a Home-made ECM connector releasing tool

In order for the tool to slide down beside the ECM, it will be necessary to file or grind the rivet to about half its original height

located on the top of the transmission casing. Remove the air cleaner assembly as described in the relevant Part of Chapter 4.

5 Disconnect the wiring plug from the TCM.

6 Undo the nut securing the selector lever to the shaft and pull the lever upwards from position (**see illustration**).

7 Undo the 3 bolts and remove the TCM.

Refitting

Five-speed transmissions (AW50-50/51)

8 Locate the TCM in the box, engaging it with the connector in the base.

9 Position the Volvo tool (or homemade equivalent) on the ECM and pull the top of the tool as far forward as possible to slide the connector rearwards.

10 Refit the ECM box lid, and reconnect the battery negative lead (see Chapter 5A).

Six-speed transmissions (TF-80SC)

11 Ensure the selector lever is in the N (neutral) position. Refit the TCM to the transmission casing ensuring the arrow on the shaft aligns with the arrow on the TCM (**see illustration**). Tighten the retaining screws securely.

12 Refit the lever to the shaft, and tighten the retaining nut securely.

13 Reconnect the wiring plug.

14 Refit the air cleaner assembly.

15 Reconnect the battery negative lead as described in Chapter 5A.

5 Gear shift position sensor – removal and refitting

Note: *This procedure applies only to 5-speed AW50-50/51 transmissions. On 6-speed transmissions (TF-80SC) the function of the position sensor is incorporated into the transmission control module (TCM).*

Removal

1 Disconnect the selector cable from the lever on the transmission as described in Section 2, then undo the two screws securing the support bracket, and move the cable and bracket to one side.

4.11 Ensure the arrows on the TCM cover and shaft align (arrowed)

4.3b Insert the tool alongside the ECM, and slide the connector locking catches forwards alternately, a little at a time

4.3c Automatic transmission control module (arrowed – nearest the engine)

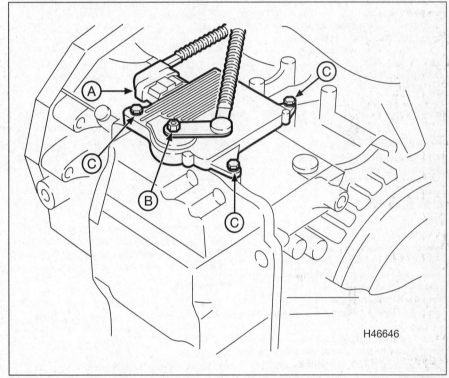

H46646

4.6 Disconnect the wiring plug (A), undo the nut (B) securing the lever to the shaft, then unscrew the 3 retaining bolts (C)

2 Undo the nut and remove the lever from the shift lever rod. Recover the nut, lockwasher and rubber washer.

3 Undo the nut securing the cable duct and move it to one side.

4 Undo the two screws and carefully lift the position sensor off the linkage rod. Disconnect the sensor wiring plug as it is withdrawn.

Refitting

5 Reconnect the wiring plug, then refit the sensor over the linkage rod, but only finger-tighten the retaining screws at this stage.

6 Refit the rubber washer, lockwasher and nut to the linkage rod. Tighten the nut securely, and lock it in place with the lockwasher.

7 Rotate the sensor housing as necessary to align the mark on the housing with a centre line parallel with the flats on the shift linkage

rod (**see illustration**). Tighten the sensor retaining screws to the specified torque.

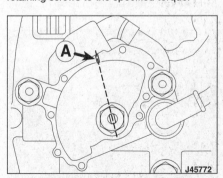

5.7 Align the mark on the sensor housing (A) with a centre line parallel with the flats on the shift linkage rod

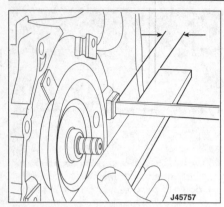

6.7 When correctly fitted, the distance between the end of the transmission casing and the mounting tabs on the converter should be 14 mm (5-speed) or 13 mm (6-speed)

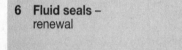

6 Fluid seals – renewal

Driveshaft seals

1 The procedure is the same as that described for the manual transmission in Chapter 7A.

Input shaft/ torque converter seal

2 Remove the transmission (see Section 7).
3 Pull the torque converter squarely out of the transmission. Be careful, as it is full of fluid.
4 Pull or lever out the old seal. Clean the seat and inspect the seal rubbing surface on the torque converter.
5 Lubricate the new seal with transmission fluid and fit it, lips inwards. Seat it with a piece of tube.
6 Lubricate the torque converter sleeve with transmission fluid, and slide the converter into place, pushing it in as far as it will go.
7 Check that the torque converter is fully seated by measuring the distance from the edge of the transmission housing face to the retaining bolt tabs on the converter. The dimension should be approximately 14 mm (5-speed transmissions) or 13 mm (6-speed transmissions) **(see illustration)**.

7.12 Rotate the collars anti-clockwise and disconnect the heater hoses

8 Refit the transmission as described in Section 7.

Gear shift linkage rod seal

9 Remove the gear shift position sensor as described in Section 5 (5-speed transmissions) or the TCM as described in Section 4 (6-speed transmissions).
10 Carefully prise the old oil seal from position using a small screwdriver. Take care not to damage the linkage rod.
11 Smear the lips of the new oil seal with clean automatic transmission fluid, the guide the seal over the rod (lips towards the transmission), and seat it in place using a suitable tubular spacer.
12 Refit the gear shift position sensor as described in Section 5, or the TCM as described in Section 4 (as applicable).

All seals

13 Check the transmission fluid level as described in the relevant Part of Chapter 1 on completion.

7 Automatic transmission – removal and refitting

Note: *Arrangements must be made to support the engine from above, to allow the subframe to be detached on the left-hand side. The best way to support the engine is with a bar resting in the bonnet channels with an adjustable hook appropriately placed. Trolley jacks and the help of an assistant will also be required throughout the procedure.*

Removal

1 Set the steering wheel and roadwheels in the straight-ahead position. Release the steering column adjuster, and push the steering wheel in and upwards as far as it will go. Lock it in this position.
2 Move the gear selector lever to P (Park).
3 Slacken the front roadwheel bolts/nuts, then jack up the front of the vehicle, and support it securely on axle stands (see *Jacking and vehicle support*). Remove both front roadwheels.
4 Undo the screws and remove the engine undershield.

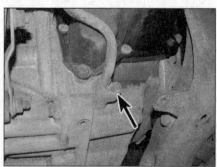

7.15 Disconnect the oil pipe (arrowed) from the front of the transmission casing

5 Refer to the relevant Part of Chapter 1 and drain the transmission fluid. This is not absolutely essential, but will remove the potential problem of fluid spillage when the driveshafts are removed, or when the transmission is moved out of the car.
6 Refer to Chapter 5A disconnect the battery negative lead.
7 Drain the coolant as described in Chapter 1A or 1B.
8 On diesel models, remove the plastic cover over the top of the engine by pulling it straight up from its mountings.
9 Undo the fasteners, and remove the engine cross-stay from between the brackets on the front suspension turrets.
10 Refer to the relevant Part of Chapter 4 and remove the air cleaner assembly and all relevant inlet ducting around the left-hand side of the engine.
11 On turbocharged models, release the clamps and remove the charge air ducts to and from the intercooler.
12 Rotate the collars anti-clockwise and disconnect the two heater hoses from the unions on the engine compartment bulkhead **(see illustration)**.
13 Slacken the rear engine mounting pad upper nut by a few threads.
14 Disconnect the selector cable from the lever on the transmission as described in Section 2, then undo the two screws securing the cable support bracket to the transmission casing, and move the cable to one side.
15 Disconnect the oil pipe/hose from the front of the transmission casing **(see illustration)**.
16 Unhook the transmission wring connector bracket from the air cleaner bracket, then disconnect all the connectors. Note the routing of the harness. On 6-speed transmissions, disconnect the TCM wiring plug.
17 On diesel models, remove the vacuum pump as described in Chapter 9, and the EGR cooler as described in Chapter 4C.
18 Disconnect the transmission earth lead from the subframe.
19 Disconnect the coolant pipe at the rear of the engine.
20 Disconnect the vacuum hoses from the engine mounting pads (where applicable).
21 Undo the retaining screw, and release the power steering pipe from the clamp on the subframe.
22 Remove the starter motor as described in Chapter 5A.
23 Undo the upper bolts securing the transmission bellhousing to the engine cylinder block.
24 Referring to Chapter 8, remove both driveshafts completely.
25 Undo the screws, release the clips and remove the air baffle from the front underside of the vehicle **(see illustration)**.
26 Remove the clips and release the pipe(s) running under the front of the subframe.
27 On models with a fuel-powered auxiliary heater, undo the two mounting screws, and leave the heater hanging from its upper

mounting. Detach the fuel hose from its retaining bracket on the subframe.

28 Working underneath the vehicle, undo the screws and remove the reinforcement plates under exhaust system. Release the brake pipe from the clips on the front reinforcement plate.

29 On right-hand drive models, undo the two steering rack crash guard bolts at the rear of the subframe, and the nut securing the crash guard base to the subframe.

30 Undo the bolts securing the engine lower steady bar bracket to the transmission (see illustration).

31 With reference to the note at the beginning of this Section, suitably support the engine from above, and adjust the support so that the load is just taken off the engine mountings.

32 Undo the bolt securing the engine front mounting to the subframe.

33 Disconnect the left-hand steering track rod end from the hub carrier as described in Chapter 10.

34 Make alignment marks between the steering rack pinion and the steering column lower universal joint, then undo the pinch-bolt and push the joints upwards from the pinion (see illustration).

35 Position a sturdy trolley jack beneath, and in contact with, the left-hand side of the subframe. Ensure that the engine is securely supported from above.

36 Undo the nut securing the left-hand link to the anti-roll bar (see Chapter 10).

37 Undo the two bolts each side securing the subframe rear mounting brackets to the body (see illustration).

38 Slacken the two subframe mounting bolts on the right-hand side by at least 5 turns. Note that new bolts will be required for refitting.

39 Undo the two subframe mounting bolts on the left-hand side. Collect the mounting bracket when the rear bolt is removed. Note that new bolts will be required for refitting.

40 Slacken the bolt securing the engine rear mounting to the steering rack, then undo the nuts securing the steering rack to the subframe. Note that new nuts will be required for refitting.

41 Undo the bolts and remove the rear engine mounting bracket from the transmission and mounting pad.

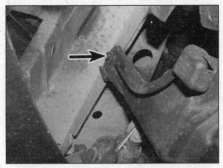

7.25 Looking through the wheel arch, undo the bolt each side (arrowed) securing the air baffle to the underside of the radiator

42 Carefully lower the jack, and allow the subframe to drop on the left-hand side by approximately 100 mm.

43 Release the oxygen sensor wiring from the rear engine mounting bracket cover (where applicable). Remove the cover, then remove the mounting bracket from the transmission.

44 Lower the jack completely, and allow the subframe to hang free from the right-hand side mountings.

45 Lower the engine/transmission by means of the overhead support, until sufficient clearance exists to enable the transmission to be withdrawn. Take care not to lower the unit too far, or the exhaust downpipe will foul the steering rack. Also, make sure that the engine oil dipstick tube clears the radiator fan, and that no hoses or leads are trapped or stretched.

46 Securely and safely support the transmission from below on a trolley jack.

47 Rotate the crankshaft, using a socket on the pulley nut, until one of the torque converter-to-driveplate retaining bolts becomes accessible through the opening on the rear facing side of the engine. Working through the opening, undo the bolt using a TX50 socket. Rotate the crankshaft as necessary and remove the remaining bolts in the same way. Note that new bolts will be required for refitting.

48 Remove the remaining bolts securing the transmission to the engine.

49 With the aid of an assistant, draw the transmission squarely off the engine dowels making sure that the torque converter remains

in position on the transmission. Use the access hole in the transmission housing to hold the converter in place.

50 Lower the jack and remove the unit from under the car.

Refitting

51 Clean the contact surfaces on the torque converter and driveplate, and the transmission and engine mating faces. Lightly lubricate the torque converter guide projection and the engine/transmission locating dowels with grease.

52 Check that the torque converter is fully-seated by measuring the distance from the edge of the transmission housing face to the retaining bolt tabs on the converter. The dimension should be approximately 14 mm (five-speed transmission) or 13 mm (six-speed transmission) (see illustration 6.7).

53 Manoeuvre the transmission squarely into position, and engage it with the engine dowels. Refit the bolts securing the transmission to the engine and tighten lightly first in a diagonal sequence, then again to the specified torque.

54 Attach the torque converter to the driveplate using new bolts. Rotate the crank shaft for access to the bolts as was done for removal, then rotate the torque converter by means of the access hole in the transmission housing. Fit and tighten all the bolts hand-tight first, then tighten again to the specified torque.

55 Raise the engine to its approximate fitted position. Refit the rear engine mounting bracket and cover, and secure with the three bolts tightened to the specified torque.

56 Refit the engine rear mounting to the transmission bracket and steering rack, but do not fully tighten the nut and bolt at this stage.

57 Secure the oxygen sensor wiring (where applicable) to the mounting bracket cover.

58 On right-hand drive models, raise the subframe to within 100 mm of the body, align the steering rack and crash guard with their subframe locations. Tighten all the clamp bolts to the specified torque.

59 On all models, raise the subframe to its fitted position, ensuring that the steering rack bolts engage in their locations.

60 Fit the new subframe mounting bolts

7.30 Undo the bolts securing the engine steady to the front of the transmission

7.34 Undo the lower steering column universal pinch-bolt

7.37 Undo the 2 bolts each side (arrowed) securing the rear of the subframe

and rear mounting bracket and bolts on the left-hand side. Tighten the subframe bolts to the specified torque using a torque wrench, then further, through the specified angle, using an angle-tightening gauge. Tighten the mounting bracket bolts to the specified torque.

61 Support the right-hand side of the subframe on the jack, and remove the two previously-slackened subframe bolts. Fit the new bolts and the two mounting bracket bolts, and tighten them as described in the previous paragraph.

62 Secure the steering rack to the subframe using five new nuts tightened to the specified torque.

63 Refit the engine front mounting bolt, then tighten the engine front and rear mountings to the specified torque.

64 On right-hand-drive models, refit the two steering rack crash guard bolts at the rear of the subframe, and the nut securing the crash guard base to the subframe. Tighten to the specified torque.

65 The remainder of refitting is a reversal of removal, noting the following points:

a) *Tighten all fasteners to their specified torque where given.*

b) *Top-up the transmission fluid as described in the relevant Part of Chapter 1.*

c) *Top-up the cooling system as described in the relevant Part of Chapter 1.*

d) *Reconnect the battery negative lead as described in Chapter 5A.*

8 Automatic transmission – fault diagnosis

The automatic transmission electronic control system incorporates an on-board diagnostic facility as an aid to fault finding and system testing. The diagnostic system is a feature of the transmission control module (TCM) which continually monitors the system components and their operation. Should a fault occur, the TCM stores a series of signals (or fault codes) for subsequent read-out.

If a fault occurs, indicated by the flashing of the warning light on the instrument panel, the on-board diagnostics can be accessed using a fault code reader, for quick and accurate diagnosis. A Volvo dealer will obviously have such a reader, but they are also available from other suppliers. It is unlikely to be cost-effective for the private owner to purchase a fault code reader, but a well-equipped local garage or auto electrical specialist will have one.

In many instances, the fault may be nothing more serious than a corroded, trapped or loose wiring connection, or a loose, dirty, or badly-fitted component. Remember that if the fault has appeared only a short time after any part of the vehicle has been serviced or overhauled, the first place to check is where that work was carried out, however unrelated it may appear, to ensure that no carelessly-refitted components are causing the problem.

Even if the source of the problem is found and fixed, diagnostic equipment may still be required, to erase the fault code from the TCM memory, and stop the warning light flashing.

If the fault cannot be easily cured, the only alternatives possible at this time are the substitution of a suspect component with a known good unit (where possible), or entrusting further work to a Volvo dealer or suitably-equipped specialist.

Chapter 8
Driveshafts

Contents

Degrees of difficulty

Easy, suitable for novice with little experience 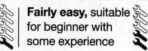	Fairly easy, suitable for beginner with some experience	Fairly difficult, suitable for competent DIY mechanic	Difficult, suitable for experienced DIY mechanic	Very difficult, suitable for expert DIY or professional

Specifications

General

Driveshaft type . . . .   Equal-length solid-steel shafts, splined to inner and outer constant velocity joints. Intermediate shaft incorporated in right-hand driveshaft assembly

Outer constant velocity joint type. . . . .   Ball-and-cage

Inner constant velocity joint type:

   Manual transmission models . . . .   Ball-and-cage

   Automatic transmission models . . . .   Tripod

Lubrication

Lubricant type . . . .   Special grease supplied in repair kit, or suitable molybdenum disulphide grease – consult a Volvo dealer

Torque wrench settings

	Nm	lbf ft
ABS wheel speed sensor.	10	7
Brake caliper mounting bolts*	100	74
Driveshaft screw*:		
Stage 1.	35	26
Stage 2.	Angle-tighten a further 90°	
Hub carrier to suspension strut:		
Stage 1.	105	77
Stage 2.	Angle-tighten a further 90°	
Lower arm balljoint to hub carrier*	80	59
Right-hand driveshaft support bearing cap bolts	25	18
Roadwheel bolts.	140	103

* Do not re-use

1 General information

Drive is transmitted from the differential to the front wheels by means of two solid-steel, equal-length driveshafts equipped with constant velocity (CV) joints at their inner and outer ends. Due to the position of the transmission, an intermediate shaft and support bearing are incorporated into the right-hand driveshaft assembly.

A ball-and-cage type CV joint is fitted to the outer end of each driveshaft. The joint has an outer member, which is splined at its outer end to accept the wheel hub, and is threaded so that it can be fastened to the hub by a large screw. The joint contains six balls within a cage, which engage with the inner member. The complete assembly is protected by a flexible gaiter secured to the driveshaft and joint outer member.

At the inner end, the driveshaft is splined to engage with a ball-and-cage type CV joint on manual transmission models, or a tripod type CV joint, containing needle roller bearings and cups, on automatic transmission versions. On the left-hand side, the driveshaft inner CV joint engages directly with the differential sun wheel. On the right-hand side, the inner joint is integral with the intermediate shaft, the inner end of which engages with the differential sun wheel. As on the outer joints, a flexible gaiter secured to the driveshaft and CV joint outer member protects the complete assembly.

2 Driveshafts – removal and refitting

Removal

1 Firmly apply the handbrake and chock the rear wheels. When the driveshaft screw is to be loosened (or tightened), it is preferable to do so with the car resting on its wheels. If the car is jacked up, this places a high load on the jack, and the car could slip off.

2 If the car has steel wheels, remove the wheel trim on the side being worked on – the driveshaft screw can then be loosened with the wheel on the ground. On models with alloy wheels, the safest option is to remove the wheel on the side being worked on, and to fit the temporary spare (see *Wheel changing* at the front of this Manual) – this wheel allows access to the driveshaft screw.

3 With an assistant firmly depressing the brake pedal, slacken the driveshaft retaining screw using a socket and a long extension bar **(see illustration)**. Note that this screw is extremely tight – ensure that the tools used to loosen it are of good quality, and a good fit.

4 Loosen the front wheel bolts, then jack up the front of the car and support it on axle stands (see *Jacking and vehicle support*). Remove the appropriate front roadwheel, then undo the screws and remove the engine undershield.

5 Remove the previously-slackened driveshaft retaining screw. Discard the screw – a new one must be fitted.

6 Remove the ABS wheel sensor from the hub carrier, and release the sensor wiring from the suspension strut bracket **(see illustration)**.

7 Undo the mounting bolts, remove the lock restrictor, and slide the brake caliper and mounting bracket from the disc, then use a length of wire (or similar) to suspend the caliper from the suspension or vehicle bodywork. Do not place any strain on the brake hose.

8 Free the driveshaft CV joint from the hub flange by tapping it inwards approximately 10 to 15 mm with a plastic or copper mallet.

9 Undo the nut securing the hub carrier lower balljoint to the suspension control arm, using a Torx bit to counterhold the balljoint shank. Push down on the suspension arm using a stout bar to release the balljoint shank from the control arm **(see illustrations)**. Take care not to damage the balljoint dust cover during and after disconnection.

10 Swivel the suspension strut and hub carrier assembly outwards, and withdraw the driveshaft CV joint from the hub flange. **Note:** *Later models have a rubber seal on the CV joint adjacent to the ABS signal ring – take care not to damage the seal (see illustration).*

11 If removing the left-hand driveshaft, free the inner CV joint from the transmission by levering between the edge of the joint and the transmission casing with a large screwdriver or similar tool. Take care not to damage the transmission oil seal or the inner CV joint gaiter. Withdraw the driveshaft from under the wheel arch.

12 If removing the right-hand driveshaft, undo the two bolts and remove the cap from the intermediate shaft support bearing **(see illustration)**. Pull the intermediate shaft out of

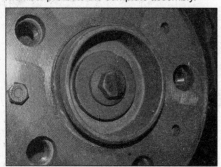

2.3 Slacken the driveshaft screw

2.6 Undo the bolt (arrowed) and pull the ABS sensor from the hub carrier

2.9a Unscrew the balljoint-to-lower arm nut . . .

2.9b . . . then use a bar to pull the lower arm down and release the balljoint shank

2.10 Later models have a rubber seal between the driveshaft and the hub carrier

2.12 Undo the two bolts (arrowed) and remove the intermediate shaft support bearing cap

the transmission, and remove the driveshaft assembly from under the wheel arch. **Note:** *Do not pull the outer shaft from the intermediate shaft – the coupling will separate.*

Refitting

13 Refitting is a reversal of removal, but observe the following points.

a) *Prior to refitting, remove all traces of rust, oil and dirt from the splines of the outer CV joint, and lubricate the splines of the inner joint with wheel bearing grease.*

b) *Renew the rubber seal on the CV joint adjacent to the ABS signal ring (where applicable) if it shows any signs of wear or damage. Note that the seal will only fit properly on the driveshaft one way around.*

c) *If working on the left-hand driveshaft, ensure that the inner CV joint is pushed fully into the transmission, so that the retaining circlip locks into place in the differential gear.*

d) *Always use a new driveshaft-to-hub retaining screw (see illustration).*

e) *Fit the same wheel as was used for loosening the driveshaft screw, and lower the car to the ground.*

f) *Tighten all nuts and bolts to the specified torque (see Chapters 9 and 10 for brake and suspension component torque settings). When tightening the driveshaft screw, tighten first using a torque wrench, then further, through the specified angle, using an angle-tightening gauge.*

g) *Ensure that the ABS sensor, and sensor location in the hub carrier, are perfectly clean before refitting.*

2.13 Always renew the driveshaft screw

h) *Where applicable, refit the alloy wheel on completion. Tighten the roadwheel bolts to the specified torque.*

3 Outer constant velocity joint gaiter – renewal

1 Remove the driveshaft (Section 2).
2 Cut off the gaiter retaining clips, then slide the gaiter down the shaft to expose the outer constant velocity joint **(see illustration)**.
3 Scoop out as much grease as possible from the joint, then measure and note the distance from the inner groove on the shaft to the inner face of the outer CV joint **(see illustration)**.
4 Tap the exposed face of the inner ball hub with a hammer and brass drift to separate the joint from the driveshaft **(see illustration)**. Slide the gaiter off the driveshaft.

5 With the constant velocity joint removed from the driveshaft, clean the joint using paraffin, or a suitable solvent, and dry it thoroughly. This is especially important if the old gaiter was badly split, as dust and grit may be embedded in the lubricating grease, which will otherwise cause rapid wear of the joint. Remove the retaining circlip from the shaft, and obtain a new one for reassembly (normally supplied in the gaiter kit).
6 Move the inner splined driving member from side-to-side, and remove each ball in turn, then rotate the ball cage 90° to the upright position and lift it from the outer part of the joint **(see illustrations)**. Examine the balls for cracks, flat spots or signs of surface pitting.
7 Inspect the ball tracks on the inner and outer members. If the tracks have widened, the balls will no longer be a tight fit. At the same time, check the ball cage windows for wear or cracking between the windows. At the time of writing, it would appear that only complete exchange driveshafts are available – if the joints appear worn, complete renewal may be the only option – check with a Volvo dealer or specialist.
8 If the joint is in satisfactory condition, obtain a repair kit from your Volvo dealer, consisting of a new gaiter, retaining clips, driveshaft screw, circlip and grease.
9 Refit the inner driving member and cage into the outer part of the joint, and insert the balls one at a time.
10 Pack the joint with the half of the grease supplied, working it well into the ball tracks, and into the driveshaft opening in the inner member **(see illustration)**.

3.2 Cut the old clips from the gaiter

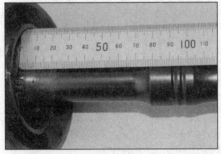

3.3 Measure the distance from the inner groove on the shaft to the inner face of the CV joint

3.4 Use a brass drift and hammer to drive the inner joint hub from the driveshaft

3.6a Remove the balls one at a time . . .

3.6b . . . then rotate the cage 90° and lift out the cage

3.10 Pack the joint with half the grease supplied in the gaiter kit

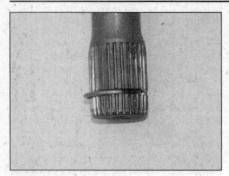

3.11 Fit the new circlip to the end of the shaft

3.13 Apply the remaining grease to the inside of the gaiter

3.14a Use pincers to compress the raised section of the outer clip . . .

3.14b . . . and the inner clip

11 Slide the rubber gaiter onto the shaft, fit the new circlip to the end of the shaft **(see illustration)**.
12 Engage the constant velocity joint with the driveshaft splines, and tap it onto the shaft until the internal circlip locates in the driveshaft groove. This can by verified by measuring the distance from the outer groove to the inner groove on the shaft and comparing the dimension with that obtained in paragraph 3.
13 Check that the circlip holds the joint securely on the driveshaft, then apply the remaining grease to the joint and the inside of the gaiter **(see illustration)**.
14 Locate the outer lip of the gaiter in the groove on the joint outer member, then fit the two retaining clips. Remove any slack in the clips by carefully compressing the raised section using a pair of pincers **(see illustrations)**.

15 Check that the constant velocity joint moves freely in all directions, then refit the driveshaft as described in Section 2.

4 Inner constant velocity joint gaiter – renewal

1 Remove the outer CV joint gaiter as described in Section 3.
2 Cut through the metal clips, and slide the gaiter from the inner CV joint.
Caution: Do not attempt to pull the inner joint from the shaft. The joint will easily slide from the shaft displacing the cage and balls, which are very difficult to reassemble.
3 Clean the joint as described in the previous

4.4 Ensure the smaller diameter of the new gaiter locates over the grooves in the shaft (arrowed)

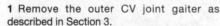

4.5 Fit the new clips and crimp them using a pair of pincers

Section, taking care not to pull the joint from the shaft.
4 Repack the joint with the grease supplied in the kit, and slide the new gaiter into place ensuring the smaller diameter of the gaiter locates over the grooves in the shaft **(see illustration)**.
5 Fit the new retaining clips and outer CV joint gaiter as described in the previous Section **(see illustration)**.

Automatic models with a vibration damper fitted

6 On these vehicles, after removing the outer CV joint, measure and note the distance from the end of the shaft to the edge of the damper. The damper must then be pressed from the shaft, the inner joint boot fitted as described above, then the damper pressed back into its original position using the dimensions previously noted. If access to a hydraulic press in not available, most engineering workshops (automotive or otherwise) would be prepared to carry out this task for a modest fee.

5 Right-hand driveshaft support bearing – removal and refitting

Note: *At the time of writing, it would appear the support bearing was not available as a separate part. If the bearing is worn of damaged, the complete driveshaft must be renewed. Exchange driveshafts may be available – check with a Volvo dealer or specialist.*

6 Driveshaft overhaul – general information

Road test the car, and listen for a metallic clicking from the front as the car is driven slowly in a circle with the steering on full-lock. Repeat the check on full-left and full-right lock. This noise may also be apparent when pulling away from a standstill with lock applied. If a clicking noise is heard, this indicates wear in the outer constant velocity joints.

If vibration, consistent with roadspeed, is felt through the car when accelerating, there is a possibility of wear in the inner constant velocity joints.

If the joints are worn or damaged, it would appear at the time of writing that no parts are available, other than boot replacement kits, and the complete driveshaft must be renewed. *Exchange driveshafts may be available – check with a Volvo dealer or specialist.*

Chapter 9
Braking system

Contents

Degrees of difficulty

Easy, suitable for novice with little experience | **Fairly easy,** suitable for beginner with some experience | **Fairly difficult,** suitable for competent DIY mechanic | **Difficult,** suitable for experienced DIY mechanic | **Very difficult,** suitable for expert DIY or professional

Specifications

General
System type:
Footbrake . . . . Dual-circuit hydraulic with servo assistance. Disc brakes front and rear. Anti-lock braking (ABS) on all models
Handbrake . . . . Mechanical to drums incorporated in rear brake discs

Front brakes
Type . . . . Ventilated disc, with single-piston sliding calipers
Brake pad friction material minimum thickness . . . . 2.0 mm
Disc diameter . . . . 286 or 305 mm
Disc thickness:
  286 mm diameter discs:
    New . . . . 26.0 mm
    Wear limit . . . . 23.0 mm
  305 mm diameter discs:
    New . . . . 28.0 mm
    Wear limit . . . . 25.0 mm
Maximum disc run-out . . . . 0.04 mm
Maximum disc thickness variation . . . . . . 0.008 mm

Rear brakes
Type . . . . Solid disc, with twin-piston fixed calipers
Brake pad minimum lining thickness . . . . . 2.0 mm
Disc diameter . . . . 295 mm
Disc thickness:
  New . . . . 13.0 mm
  Wear limit . . . . 10.0 mm
Maximum disc run-out . . . . 0.08 mm
Maximum disc thickness variation . . . . . . 0.008 mm

Handbrake
Drum diameter . . . . 178 mm
Maximum drum run-out . . . . 0.15 mm
Maximum drum out-of-round . . . . . . 0.15 mm

Torque wrench settings

	Nm	lbf ft
ABS ECM mounting bolts	5	4
ABS wheel sensor mounting bolts	10	7
Auxiliary heater mountings	30	22
Brake pedal bolts	40	30
Engine cross-stay:		
To suspension turrets	50	37
To engine bracket	80	59
Flexible hose unions	18	13
Front caliper bracket bolts*	100	74
Front caliper guide bolts	30	22
Handbrake lever bolts	25	18
Master cylinder mounting nuts	25	18
Rear caliper bracket bolts*	60	44
Rear caliper guide bolts	30	22
Rigid pipe unions	14	10
Roadwheel bolts	140	103
Steering column joint pinch-bolt	25	18
Subframe front and rear mounting bolts*:		
Up to 2004 model year:		
Stage 1	105	77
Stage 2	Angle-tighten a further 120°	
From 2005 model year	160	118
Subframe rear mounting brackets to body	50	37
Vacuum pump bolts	17	13
Vacuum servo unit mounting nuts	25	18

* Do not re-use

1 General information

The brake pedal operates disc brakes on all four wheels by means of a dual circuit hydraulic system with servo assistance. The handbrake operates separate drum brakes on the rear wheels by means of cables. An anti-lock braking system (ABS) is fitted to all models, and is described in further detail in Section 18.

The hydraulic system is split into two circuits, so that in the event of failure of one circuit, the other will still provide adequate braking power (although pedal travel and effort may increase). An axle-split system is employed, in which one circuit serves the front brakes and the other circuit the rear brakes.

The brake servo is of the direct-acting type, being interposed between the brake pedal and the master cylinder. The servo magnifies the effort applied by the driver. It is vacuum-operated, the vacuum being derived from the inlet manifold on petrol models, and a camshaft-driven vacuum pump on diesel models.

Instrument panel warning lights alert the driver to low fluid level by means of a level sensor in the master cylinder reservoir. Other warning lights remind when the handbrake is applied, and indicate the presence of a fault in the ABS system.

Note: *When servicing any part of the system, work carefully and methodically; also observe scrupulous cleanliness when overhauling any part of the hydraulic system. Always renew components (in axle sets, where applicable) if in doubt about their condition, and use only genuine Volvo parts, or at least those of known good quality. Note the warnings given in Safety first! and at relevant points in this Chapter concerning the dangers of asbestos dust and hydraulic fluid.*

2 Hydraulic system – bleeding

⚠️ *Warning: Hydraulic fluid is poisonous; wash off immediately and thoroughly in the case of skin contact, and seek immediate medical advice if any fluid is swallowed or gets into the eyes. Certain types of hydraulic fluid are inflammable, and may ignite when allowed into contact with hot components; when servicing any hydraulic system, it is safest to assume that the fluid IS inflammable, and to take precautions against the risk of fire as though it is petrol that is being handled. Hydraulic fluid is also an effective paint stripper, and will attack plastics; if any is spilt, it should be washed off immediately, using copious quantities of clean water. Finally, it is hygroscopic (it absorbs moisture from the air). The more moisture is absorbed by the fluid, the lower its boiling point becomes, leading to a dangerous loss of braking under hard use. Old fluid may be contaminated and unfit for further use. When topping-up or renewing the fluid, always use the recommended type, and ensure that it comes from a freshly-opened sealed container.*

General

1 The correct functioning of the brake hydraulic system is only possible after removing all air from the components and circuit; this is achieved by bleeding the system.

2 During the bleeding procedure, add only clean, fresh hydraulic fluid of the specified type; never re-use fluid that has already been bled from the system. Ensure that sufficient fluid is available before starting work.

3 If there is any possibility of incorrect fluid being used in the system, the brake lines and components must be completely flushed with uncontaminated fluid and new seals fitted to the components.

4 If brake fluid has been lost from the master cylinder due to a leak in the system, ensure that the cause is traced and rectified before proceeding further.

5 Park the car on level ground, apply the handbrake, and switch off the ignition.

6 Check that all pipes and hoses are secure, unions tight, and bleed screws closed. Remove the dust caps and clean any dirt from around the bleed screws.

7 Unscrew the master cylinder reservoir cap, and top-up the reservoir to the MAX level line. Refit the cap loosely, and remember to maintain the fluid level at least above the MIN level line throughout the procedure, otherwise there is a risk of further air entering the system.

8 There are a number of one-man, do-it-yourself, brake bleeding kits currently available from motor accessory shops. It is recommended that one of these kits is used wherever possible, as they greatly simplify the

bleeding operation, and also reduce the risk of expelled air and fluid being drawn back into the system. If such a kit is not available, the basic (two-man) method must be used, which is described in detail below.

9 If a kit is to be used, prepare the car as described previously, and follow the kit manufacturer's instructions, as the procedure may vary slightly according to the type being used; generally, they are as outlined below in the relevant sub-section.

10 Whichever method is used, the same sequence must be followed (paragraphs 11 and 12) to ensure the removal of all air from the system.

Bleeding sequence

11 If the hydraulic system has only been partially disconnected and suitable precautions were taken to minimise fluid loss, it should only be necessary to bleed that part of the system (ie, the primary or secondary circuit).

12 If the complete system is to be bled, then it should be done in the following sequence:
a) Front left-hand brake
b) Front right-hand brake.
c) Rear brakes (in any order).

Bleeding

Basic (two-man) method

13 Collect a clean glass jar of reasonable size and a suitable length of plastic or rubber tubing, which is a tight fit over the bleed screw, and a ring spanner to fit the screws. The help of an assistant will also be required.

14 If not already done, remove the dust cap from the bleed screw of the first wheel to be bled **(see illustration)**, and fit the spanner and bleed tube to the screw. Place the other end of the tube in the jar, and pour in sufficient fluid to cover the end of the tube.

15 Ensure that the master cylinder reservoir fluid level is maintained at least above the MIN level line throughout the procedure.

16 Have the assistant fully depress the brake pedal several times to build-up pressure, then maintain it on the final downstroke.

17 While pedal pressure is maintained, unscrew the bleed screw (approximately one turn) and allow the compressed fluid and air to flow into the jar. The assistant should maintain pedal pressure, following it down to the floor if necessary, and should not release it until instructed to do so. When the flow stops, tighten the bleed screw again have the assistant release the pedal slowly, and recheck the reservoir fluid level.

18 Repeat the steps given in paragraphs 16 and 17 until the fluid emerging from the bleed screw is free from air bubbles. If the master cylinder has been drained and refilled, and air is being bled from the first screw in the sequence, allow approximately five seconds between cycles for the master cylinder passages to refill.

19 When no more air bubbles appear, tighten

the bleed screw securely, remove the tube and spanner, and refit the dust cap. Do not overtighten the bleed screw.

20 Repeat these procedures on the remaining calipers in sequence until all air is removed from the system and the brake pedal feels firm again.

Using a one-way valve kit

21 As their name implies, these kits consist of a length of tubing with a one-way valve fitted, to prevent expelled air and fluid being drawn back into the system; some kits include a translucent container, which can be positioned so that the air bubbles can be more easily seen flowing from the end of the tube.

22 The kit is connected to the bleed screw, which is then opened **(see illustration)**. The user returns to the driver's seat, depresses the brake pedal with a smooth steady stroke, and slowly releases it; this is repeated until the expelled fluid is clear of air bubbles.

23 Note that these kits simplify work so much that it is easy to forget the master cylinder fluid level; ensure that this is maintained at least above the MIN level line at all times.

Using a pressure-bleeding kit

24 These kits are usually operated by the reserve of pressurised air contained in the spare tyre. However, note that it will probably be necessary to reduce the pressure to a lower level than normal; refer to the instructions supplied with the kit.

25 By connecting a pressurised, fluid-filled container to the master cylinder reservoir, bleeding is then carried out by simply opening each bleed screw in turn (in the specified sequence) and allowing the fluid to run out, until no more air bubbles can be seen in the expelled fluid.

26 This method has the advantage that the large reservoir of fluid provides an additional safeguard against air being drawn into the system during bleeding.

27 Pressure-bleeding is particularly effective when bleeding difficult systems, or when bleeding the complete system at the time of routine fluid renewal. It is also the method recommended by Volvo if the hydraulic system has been drained either wholly or partially.

All methods

28 When bleeding is complete, and firm pedal feel is restored, wash off any spilt fluid, tighten the bleed screws securely, and refit their dust caps.

29 Check the hydraulic fluid level in the master cylinder reservoir, and top-up if necessary.

30 Discard any hydraulic fluid that has been bled from the system; it will not be fit for re-use.

31 Check the feel of the brake pedal. If it feels at all spongy, air must still be present in the system, and further bleeding is required. Failure to bleed satisfactorily after a reasonable

2.14 Pull the dust cap (arrowed) from the bleed screw

repetition of the bleeding operations may be due to worn master cylinder seals.

32 Check the operation of the clutch. Any problems noted would indicate a need to bleed the clutch system also – see Chapter 6.

3 Hydraulic pipes and hoses – renewal

Note: *Before starting work, refer to the warning at the beginning of Section 2 concerning the dangers of hydraulic fluid.*

1 If any pipe or hose is to be renewed, minimise hydraulic fluid loss by removing the master cylinder reservoir cap, placing a piece of plastic film over the reservoir and sealing it with an elastic band. Alternatively, flexible hoses can be sealed, if required, using a proprietary brake hose clamp; metal brake pipe unions can be plugged (if care is taken not to allow dirt into the system) or capped immediately they are disconnected. Place a wad of rag under any union that is to be disconnected, to catch any spilt fluid.

2 If a flexible hose is to be disconnected, unscrew the brake pipe union nut before removing the spring clip which secures the hose to its mounting, where applicable. Some of the flexible hose unions are protected by a rubber cover – in this case, the pipe will have to be removed from its mounting bracket first, and the cover slid down the pipe, before the nut can be unscrewed.

3 To unscrew the union nuts, it is preferable to obtain a brake pipe spanner of the correct

2.22 Connect the kit and open the bleed screw

size; these are available from most large motor accessory shops. Failing this, a close-fitting open-ended spanner will be required, though if the nuts are tight or corroded, their flats may be rounded-off if the spanner slips. In such a case, a self-locking wrench is often the only way to unscrew a stubborn union, but it follows that the pipe and the damaged nuts must be renewed on reassembly.

4 Always clean a union and surrounding area before disconnecting it. If disconnecting a component with more than one union, make a careful note of the connections before disturbing any of them.

5 If a brake pipe is to be renewed, it can be obtained, cut to length and with the union nuts and end flares in place, from Volvo dealers. All that is then necessary is to bend it to shape, following the line of the original, before fitting it to the car. Alternatively, most motor accessory

shops can make up brake pipes from kits, but this requires very careful measurement of the original, to ensure that the new one is of the correct length. The safest answer is usually to take the original to the shop as a pattern.

6 Before refitting, blow through the new pipe or hose with dry compressed air. Do not overtighten the union nuts. It is not necessary to exercise brute force to obtain a sound joint.

7 If flexible rubber hoses are renewed, ensure that the pipes and hoses are correctly routed, with no kinks or twists, and that they are secured in the clips or brackets provided. Original equipment flexible hoses have white lines along their length which clearly show if the hose is twisted.

8 After fitting, bleed the hydraulic system as described in Section 2, wash off any spilt fluid, and check carefully for fluid leaks.

4 Front brake pads – renewal

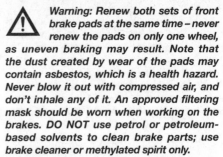

Warning: Renew both sets of front brake pads at the same time – never renew the pads on only one wheel, as uneven braking may result. Note that the dust created by wear of the pads may contain asbestos, which is a health hazard. Never blow it out with compressed air, and don't inhale any of it. An approved filtering mask should be worn when working on the brakes. DO NOT use petrol or petroleum-based solvents to clean brake parts; use brake cleaner or methylated spirit only.

1 Apply the handbrake, then slacken the front roadwheel bolts. Jack up the front of the vehicle and support it on axle stands (see *Jacking and vehicle support*). Remove both front roadwheels.

2 Follow the accompanying photos **(see illustrations 4.2a to 4.2t)** for the actual pad renewal procedure. Be sure to stay in order and read the caption under each illustration, and note the following points:

a) New pads may have an adhesive foil on the backplates. Remove this foil prior to installation.

b) Thoroughly clean the caliper guide surfaces, and apply a little brake assembly (Molykote P37 or Copper slip) grease.

c) When pushing the caliper piston back to accommodate new pads, keep a close eye on the fluid level in the reservoir.

4.2a Prise out the ends . . .

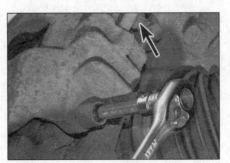

4.2b . . . and remove the retaining spring

4.2c Prise out the rubber cap . . .

4.2d . . . then use a 7 mm hexagon key to undo the lower and upper guide pins (arrowed)

4.2e Slide the caliper from place. Note the inner pad is clipped to the caliper piston

4.2f Remove the outer brake pad . . .

4.2g . . . and unclip the inner

4.2h If new pads are fitted, push the piston back into the caliper. Check the fluid reservoir doesn't overflow!

4.2i Use a wire brush to clean the pad mounting surfaces on the caliper bracket

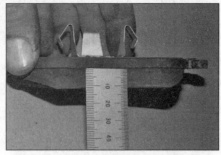

4.2j Measure the thickness of the pad's friction material. If it's 2.0 mm or less, renew all the front pads

4.2k Apply a thin smear of anti-seize compound to the rear of the brake pads . . .

4.2l . . . and where the pads contact the caliper bracket (arrowed)

4.2m Clip the inner pad into the caliper piston . . .

4.2n . . . and fit the outer pad to the caliper bracket

4.2o Slide the caliper with the inner pad fitted over the disc and outer pad

4.2p Refit the caliper guide pins . . .

4.2q . . . and tighten them to the specified torque

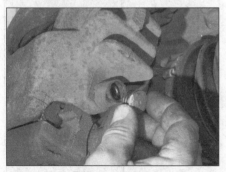

4.2r Refit the rubber caps

4.2s Hook one end of the retaining spring into place . . .

4.2t . . . and use pliers to insert the other end

3 Depress the brake pedal repeatedly, until the pads are pressed into firm contact with the brake disc, and normal (non-assisted) pedal pressure is restored.
4 Repeat the above procedure on the remaining front brake caliper.

5 Refit the roadwheels, then lower the vehicle to the ground and tighten the roadwheel bolts to the specified torque.
6 Check the hydraulic fluid level as described in *Weekly checks*.

Caution: New pads will not give full braking efficiency until they have bedded-in. Be prepared for this, and avoid hard braking as far as possible for the first hundred miles or so after pad renewal.

5 Rear brake pads – renewal

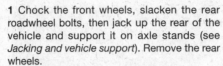

Warning: Renew both sets of rear brake pads at the same time – never renew the pads on only one wheel, as uneven braking may result. Note that the dust created by wear of the pads may contain asbestos, which is a health hazard. Never blow it out with compressed air, and don't inhale any of it. An approved filtering mask should be worn when working on the brakes. DO NOT use petrol or petroleum-based solvents to clean brake parts; use brake cleaner or methylated spirit only.

1 Chock the front wheels, slacken the rear roadwheel bolts, then jack up the rear of the vehicle and support it on axle stands (see *Jacking and vehicle support*). Remove the rear wheels.

2 With the handbrake lever fully released, follow the accompanying photos **(see illustrations 5.2a to 5.2r)** for the actual pad renewal procedure. Be sure to stay in order and read the caption under each illustration, and note the following points:

a) *If re-installing the original pads, ensure they are fitted to their original positions.*
b) *Thoroughly clean the caliper guide surfaces and guide pins, and apply a little brake assembly (Molykote P37 or Copper slip) grease.*
c) *If new pads are to be fitted, use a piston retraction tool or G-clamp to push the piston back – keep an eye on the fluid level in the reservoir whilst retracting the piston.*

3 Depress the brake pedal repeatedly, until the pads are pressed into firm contact with the brake disc, and normal (non-assisted) pedal pressure is restored.

4 Repeat the above procedure on the remaining brake caliper.

5 Refit the roadwheels, then lower the vehicle to the ground and tighten the roadwheel bolts to the specified torque.

6 Check the hydraulic fluid level as described in *Weekly checks*.

Caution: New pads will not give full braking efficiency until they have bedded-in. Be prepared for this, and avoid hard braking as far as possible for the first hundred miles or so after pad renewal.

5.2a Prise out the ends . . .

5.2b . . . and remove the caliper retaining springs

5.2c Prise out the rubber caps . . .

5.2d . . . and use a 7.0 mm hexagon bit to unscrew the upper and lower guide pins

5.2e Slide the caliper and pads from place

5.2f The outer pad may be stuck to the caliper . . .

5.2g . . . and the inner pad is clipped into the caliper piston

5.2h Use a wire brush to clean the pad mounting surfaces on the caliper bracket

5.2i If new pads are to be fitted, push the piston back into the caliper. Check the fluid level in the master cylinder reservoir!

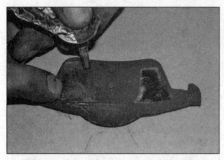

5.2j Apply a thin smear of anti-seize compound to the rear of the pads where they contact the piston . . .

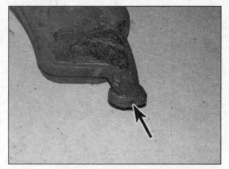

5.2k . . . and the caliper bracket (arrowed)

5.2l Fit the outer pad to the caliper bracket . . .

5.2m . . . and clip the inner pad to the caliper piston

5.2n Slide the caliper, with the inner pad in place, over the disc and outer pad

5.2o Refit the guide pins, tighten them to the specified torque . . .

5.2p . . . and refit the rubber caps

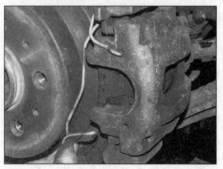

5.2q Insert one end of the retaining spring into place . . .

5.2r . . . then use pliers to insert the other end

---

6 Front brake disc –
inspection, removal
and refitting

Note: *Before starting work, refer to the warning at the beginning of Section 4 concerning the dangers of asbestos dust.*

Inspection

Note: *If either disc requires renewal, BOTH should be renewed at the same time, to ensure even and consistent braking. New brake pads should also be fitted.*

1 Remove the front brake pads as described in Section 4.
2 Inspect the disc friction surfaces for cracks or deep scoring (light grooving is normal and may be ignored). A cracked disc must be renewed; a scored disc can be reclaimed by

machining, provided that the thickness is not reduced below the specified minimum.
3 Check the disc run-out using a dial test indicator with its probe positioned near the outer edge of the disc. If the run-out exceeds the figures given in the *Specifications*, machining may be possible, otherwise disc renewal will be necessary.

> **HAYNES HiNT**
> *If a dial test indicator is not available, check the run-out by positioning a fixed pointer near the outer edge, in contact with the disc face. Rotate the disc and measure the maximum displacement of the pointer with feeler blades.*

4 Excessive disc thickness variation can also cause judder. Check this using a micrometer **(see illustration).**

Removal

5 With the brake pads and caliper removed (Section 4), undo the two mounting bolts and

6.4 Measure the disc thickness using a micrometer

6.5 Undo the two bolts (arrowed) and remove the caliper mounting bracket

remove the brake caliper bracket and limiter bracket **(see illustration)**. Note that new bolts will be required for refitting.

6 Check whether the position of the disc in relation to the hub is marked, and if not, make your own mark as an aid to refitting. Remove the bolt which holds the disc to the hub, and lift off the disc **(see illustration)**.

Refitting

7 Ensure that the hub and disc mating faces are spotlessly clean. Clean any rustproofing compound off a new disc with degreaser and a rag.

8 Locate the disc on the hub with the orientation marks aligned, then refit and tighten then retaining spigot pin.

9 Refit the brake caliper bracket and limiter bracket, then tighten the new bolts to the specified torque.

10 Refit the brake pads as described in Section 4.

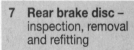

<table>
<tr><td>7</td><td>**Rear brake disc –**
inspection, removal
and refitting</td></tr>
</table>

Note: *Before starting work, refer to the warning at the beginning of Section 5 concerning the dangers of asbestos dust.*

Inspection

Note: *If either disc requires renewal, BOTH should be renewed at the same time, to ensure even and consistent braking. New brake pads should also be fitted.*

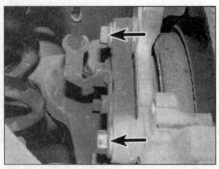

7.3 Undo the caliper mounting bracket bolts (arrowed)

6.6 Disc retaining bolt

1 With the rear brake pads removed (Section 5), the inspection procedures are the same as for the front brake disc, and reference should be made to Section 6, paragraphs 2 to 4 inclusive. Additionally, after removal, check the condition of the handbrake drums. Refinishing, run-out and out-of-round limits are given in the *Specifications*. The drums are unlikely to wear, unless the handbrake is habitually used to stop the car.

Removal

2 If not already done, remove the rear brake pads as described in Section 5. Suitably support the caliper, or suspend it using string or wire tied to a convenient suspension component.

3 Undo the two caliper mounting bracket bolts, and withdraw the bracket **(see illustration)**. Note that new bolts will be required for refitting.

4 Unscrew the disc retaining screw **(see illustration)**.

5 Mark the position of the disc in relation to the hub, then pull off the disc. Tap it with a soft-faced mallet if necessary to free it. If it is not possible to remove the disc due to it binding on the handbrake shoes, proceed as follows.

6 From inside the car, prise out the centre console trim panel adjacent to the handbrake lever **(see illustration 13.3)**.

7 Working through the panel aperture, slacken the adjuster nut at the rear of the handbrake lever until there is slack in the handbrake cables **(see illustration 13.4)**.

7.4 Rear disc retaining bolt

Refitting

8 Ensure that the hub and disc mating faces are spotlessly clean. Clean any rustproofing compound off a new disc with degreaser and a rag.

9 Locate the disc on the hub with the orientation marks aligned, and refit the retaining screw.

10 Refit the brake caliper mounting bracket and tighten the new bolts to the specified torque.

11 Refit the brake pads as described in Section 5.

12 Adjust the handbrake as described in Section 13.

<table>
<tr><td>8</td><td>**Front brake caliper –**
removal, overhaul and refitting</td></tr>
</table>

Note: *Before starting work, refer to the warning at the beginning of Section 2 concerning the dangers of hydraulic fluid, and to the warning at the beginning of Section 4 concerning the dangers of asbestos dust.*

Removal

1 Apply the handbrake and chock the rear wheels. Loosen the front wheel bolts, then jack up the front of the car and support it on axle stands (see *Jacking and vehicle support*). Remove the roadwheel.

2 To minimise fluid loss, unscrew the master cylinder reservoir filler cap and place a piece of polythene over the filler neck. Secure the polythene with an elastic band ensuring that an airtight seal is obtained. Preferably, use a brake hose clamp, a G-clamp, or a similar tool with protected jaws, to clamp the front flexible hydraulic hose **(see illustration)**.

3 Clean the area around the hydraulic hose-to-caliper union, then slacken the hose union half a turn. Be prepared for fluid spillage.

4 Remove the brake pads as described in Section 4.

5 Unscrew the caliper from the hydraulic hose, and wipe up any spilled brake fluid immediately. Plug or cap the open unions.

6 If it is wished to remove the caliper bracket, undo the two bolts which secure it to the steering knuckle. Note that new bolts will be required for refitting.

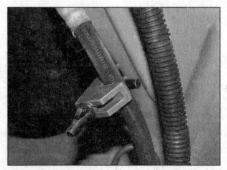

8.2 Use a hose clamp on the flexible brake hose

Overhaul

Note: *At the time of writing it was unclear whether overhaul kits were available for the calipers. Check with a Volvo dealer or specialist prior to dismantling the caliper.*

7 With the brake caliper removed, clean it externally with degreaser and a soft brush.

8 Remove the bleed screw and empty any remaining hydraulic fluid out of the caliper.

9 Remove the piston dust boot and pull the piston out of the caliper bore. If the caliper piston is reluctant to move, refit the bleed screw and apply low air pressure (eg, from a foot pump) to the fluid inlet, but note that the piston may be ejected with some force.

10 Hook out the piston seal from the bore using a blunt instrument.

11 Withdraw the two guide pin rubber bushes from their locations.

12 Clean the piston and caliper bore with a lint-free rag and some clean brake fluid or brake cleaner. Slight imperfections may be polished out with steel wool. If any pitting, scoring or wear ridges are evident, the caliper must be renewed.

13 Renew all rubber components (seal, dust boot and guide pin bushes) as a matter of course. Blow through the fluid inlet and bleed screw hole with compressed air.

14 Lubricate the new piston seal with clean brake fluid. Insert the seal into the groove in the bore, using your fingers only.

15 Fit a new dust boot to the piston, ensuring that it is properly seated in the piston groove. Extend the dust boot ready for fitting.

16 Lubricate the piston and bore with clean brake fluid.

17 Offer the piston and dust boot to the caliper. Engage the dust boot with the groove in the caliper, then push the piston through the dust boot into the caliper bore.

18 Fit the new guide pin rubber bushes, then refit the caliper bleed screw.

Refitting

19 If removed, refit the caliper bracket using new bolts tightened to the specified torque.

20 Refit the brake pads as described in Section 4, but screw the caliper onto the flexible hose before refitting it to the caliper bracket.

21 Tighten the flexible hose union ensuring that the hose is not kinked.

22 Remove the brake hose clamp or polythene, where fitted, and bleed the hydraulic system as described in Section 2.

23 Apply the footbrake two or three times to settle the pads, then refit the roadwheel and lower the car. Tighten the wheel bolts in a diagonal sequence to the specified torque.

9 Rear brake caliper – removal, overhaul and refitting

Note: *Before starting work, refer to the warning at the beginning of Section 2 concerning the dangers of hydraulic fluid, and to the warning at the beginning of Section 5 concerning the dangers of asbestos dust.*

Removal

1 To minimise fluid loss, unscrew the master cylinder reservoir filler cap, and place a piece of polythene over the filler neck. Secure the polythene with an elastic band, ensuring that an airtight seal is obtained. Preferably, use a brake hose clamp, a G-clamp, or a similar tool with protected jaws, to clamp the rear flexible hydraulic hose.

2 Clean around the hydraulic union on the caliper, then slacken the pipe union half a turn.

3 Remove the rear brake pads as described in Section 5.

4 Undo the caliper from the flexible pipe union. Be prepared for fluid spillage, and plug or cap the open unions.

Overhaul

Note: *At the time of writing it was unclear whether overhaul kits were available for the calipers. Check with a Volvo dealer or specialist prior to dismantling the caliper.*

5 This is essentially the same procedure as that described for the front caliper (see Section 8).

Refitting

6 Refit the brake pipe to the caliper, and tighten the union securely.

7 Refit the brake pads as described in Section 5.

8 Remove the brake hose clamp or polythene, where fitted, and bleed the hydraulic system as described in Section 2.

9 Apply the footbrake two or three times to settle the pads, then refit the roadwheel and lower the car. Tighten the wheel bolts in a diagonal sequence to the specified torque.

10 Brake master cylinder – removal and refitting

Note: *Before starting work, refer to the warning at the beginning of Section 2 concerning the dangers of hydraulic fluid.*

Note: *Overhaul of the master cylinder is not possible, and internal components are not available separately. In the event of a fault in the master cylinder, the unit must be renewed.*

Removal

1 Disconnect the battery negative lead (see Chapter 5A).

2 Depress the brake pedal repeatedly to collapse any residual vacuum in the servo, then syphon as much fluid as possible from the master cylinder reservoir, using a hydrometer or old poultry baster.

Caution: *Do not syphon the fluid by mouth – it is poisonous.*

3 Undo the fasteners and remove the engine cross-stay from between the brackets on the front suspension turrets.

4 Disconnect any wiring connectors from the reservoir/master cylinder.

5 On manual transmission models, release the spring clip and disconnect the clutch master cylinder fluid hose from the side of the reservoir **(see illustration)**. Be prepared for fluid spillage. Plug the open end of the hose and the reservoir orifice.

6 Disconnect the hydraulic pipe unions from the master cylinder **(see illustration)**. Be prepared for further fluid spillage. Cap the open unions to keep dirt out. Do not bend the pipes – if necessary slacken the unions securing the pipes to the ABS modulator to allow the pipes to clear the master cylinder.

7 Undo the retaining nut and pull the heat shield from the master cylinder mounting studs.

8 Remove the nuts which secure the master cylinder to the servo **(see illustration)**. Pull the master cylinder off the servo studs and remove it. Discard the O-ring seal, a new one

10.5 Disconnect the clutch master cylinder fluid hose (arrowed) from the reservoir

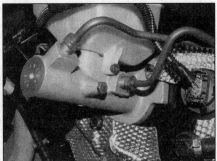

10.6 Undo the unions and disconnect the brake pipes

10.8 Undo the master cylinder retaining nuts (arrowed)

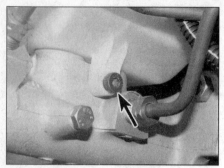

10.9 Undo the screw (arrowed) and lift the reservoir from the cylinder

must be fitted. Be careful not to spill hydraulic fluid on the paintwork.

9 If required, undo the screw and lift the reservoir from the master cylinder body **(see illustration)**. Discard the two seals, new ones must be fitted.

Refitting

10 If removed, refit the reservoir to the master cylinder, using new seals, and tighten the retaining screw securely.
11 Place the master cylinder (with a new seal) in position on the servo unit, and secure with the nuts tightened to the specified torque.
12 Refit the heat shield and retaining nut.
13 Refit the brake pipes, but do not tighten the union nuts fully at this stage.
14 Refit the fluid hose to the reservoir. Lubricate the hose end with brake hydraulic fluid to ease fitting.

11.2 Spread the bracket apart, and move the relay box rearwards and downwards

11.4a Brake pedal shaft bolt (arrowed)

15 Reconnect the reservoir/master cylinder electrical connectors.
16 Place absorbent rags under the brake pipe unions on the master cylinder, then fill the reservoir with clean hydraulic fluid of the specified type.
17 When hydraulic fluid can be seen seeping out, tighten the brake pipe unions securely.
18 Bleed the hydraulic system as described in Section 2 on completion. On manual transmission models, bleed the clutch hydraulic system as described in Chapter 6.
19 After the system has been bled, pressure test the master cylinder by depressing the brake pedal hard and holding it down for 30 seconds. Release the pedal and check for leaks around the master cylinder pipe unions.

11 Brake pedal – removal and refitting

Removal

1 Undo the two screws, and pull the panel above the pedals rearwards to remove.
2 Spread the bracket apart, pull the relay box rearwards/downwards, and position it to one side **(see illustration)**.
3 Release the retaining clip and disconnect the servo pushrod from the pedal **(see illustration)**.
4 Undo the two retaining bolts and lower the pedal assembly. Disconnect the return spring as the pedal is withdrawn **(see illustrations)**.

11.3 Prise the clip (arrowed) securing the pushrod to the pedal

11.4b Use a 24 mm spanner to counterhold the pedal bolt

Use a 24 mm open-ended spanner to counterhold the pedal shaft.
5 If required, pull the pivot shaft from the pedal, and extract the two bushes.

Refitting

6 If removed, refit the bushes and pivot shaft to the pedal assembly.
7 Manoeuvre the pedal into position, and reconnect the return spring. Tighten the retaining bolts to the specified torque.
8 Reconnect the servo pushrod to the pedal, and secure it with the retaining clip.
9 Refit the relay box and facia trim panel.
10 Check the operation of the brake lights.

12 Vacuum servo unit – removal and refitting

Removal

1 Disconnect the battery negative lead (see Chapter 5A), then depress the brake pedal several times to dissipate any vacuum in the servo unit.
2 Undo the fasteners and remove the engine cross-stay from between the suspension turrets.
3 Note their fitted positions, then disconnect any wiring connectors from the reservoir/master cylinder/servo.
4 Remove the nuts which secure the master cylinder to the servo. Pull the master cylinder off the servo studs and position it to one side, taking care not to damage any of the rigid brake pipes. Discard the O-ring seal between the servo and the master cylinder, a new one must be fitted. Keep the master cylinder horizontal to prevent air from entering the system.
5 Disconnect the servo vacuum feed by levering out the non-return valve on the front of the servo unit.
6 Release the wiring loom and ducting around the servo as necessary for improved access.
7 Undo the two screws, and pull the trim panel under the facia on the driver's side rearwards to remove it.
8 Disconnect the servo pushrod and linkage from the brake pedal by removing the retaining clip **(see illustration 11.3)**.
9 Undo the four nuts securing the servo unit to the bulkhead **(see illustrations)**.
10 In order to remove the servo, it's necessary to lower the front subframe and engine/transmission a little. Jack up the front of the vehicle, and support it securely on axle stands (see *Jacking and vehicle support*).
11 Undo the screw securing the cable ducting to the front underside of the subframe, adjacent to the radiator **(see illustration)**.
12 Undo the 10 screws securing the three crossmembers under the exhaust system.
13 With the steering in the straight-ahead position, and the steering lock engaged, undo the pinch-bolt and pull the lower steering

12.9a Servo nuts (arrowed) on the left- . . .

12.9b . . . and right-hand side (arrowed)

12.11 Undo the two bolts (arrowed) securing the cable ducting to the front subframe

column universal joint from the steering rack pinion.

14 On models with an auxiliary fuel-fired heater, undo the heater mounting nuts, release the heater fuel lines from the retaining brackets on the subframe. Suspend the heater from the bodywork.

15 On turbocharged engines, release the clamps and remove the charge air pipes to and from the intercooler.

16 Position a mobile jack under the front subframe then, with the subframe supported, remove the subframe mounting bolts one at a time, and substitute each of them with a length of studded rod with washers and locknuts fitted.

17 Undo the four bolts securing the brackets at the rear of the subframe.

18 Starting at the front, gradually lower the subframe, until sufficient clearance exists to manoeuvre the servo from the engine compartment. Recover the seal between the servo unit and the bulkhead.

Refitting

19 Refitting is a reversal of removal bearing in mind the following points:
  a) Ensure that the seal is in position before fitting the servo.
  b) Tighten all nuts and bolts to the specified torque.
  c) Refit the master cylinder as described in Section 10.
  d) Check and if necessary, bleed the hydraulic system as described in Section 2 on completion.

13 Handbrake – adjustment

1 Before carrying out the adjustment, drive the car slowly on a quiet road for about 400 metres with the handbrake applied by a few notches. This will clean any rust and deposits from the handbrake shoes and drum.

2 From inside the car, pull up the handbrake lever and check that full braking effect is achieved on the rear wheels between 2 and 5 clicks of the handbrake lever ratchet. If this is not the case, proceed as follows.

3 Prise up the gaiter panel around the lever on the console, and lift up the plastic cover over the lever **(see illustration)**.

4 Working through the cover panel aperture, turn the adjuster nut until the handbrake performs as described in paragraph 2 **(see illustration)**. Release the handbrake lever, and check that the rear wheels are both free to turn without binding.

5 Refit the centre console cover panel and handbrake lever gaiter.

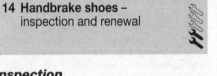

14 Handbrake shoes – inspection and renewal

Inspection

1 Remove the rear brake disc (Section 7).

2 Inspect the shoes for wear, damage or oil/

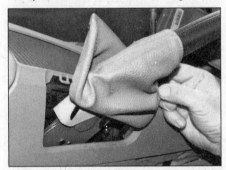

13.3 Prise up the gaiter panel around the handbrake lever

14.4a Press in the retaining spring . . .

fluid contamination. Renew them if necessary as described below. As with the brake pads, the shoes must be renewed in axle sets.

3 If the shoes are contaminated, identify and rectify the source of any contamination before the new shoes are fitted; one possible problem area could be the hub bearing grease seal. Unfortunately, if this has failed, the hub assembly must be renewed complete (See Chapter 10).

Renewal

4 Depress the brake retaining springs, and slide them sideways to disengage the hook on the end of the spring from the slotted bracket on the backplate **(see illustrations)**.

5 Pull the brake shoes from the expander bracket, then disconnect the two return springs **(see illustrations)**.

6 Clean the backplate, the inside of the brake disc and the actuator mechanism.

13.4 Lift the plastic flap and turn the nut (arrowed) to adjust the handbrake

14.4b . . . and slide it sideways to disengage it (shown here with the shoes removed for clarity)

14.5a Pull the shoes from the expander bracket . . .

7 Apply a smear of high melting-point grease to the shoe contact areas on the brake backplate, and to the actuator mechanism **(see illustration)**.

8 Refitting is a reversal of removal. Take care not to get grease or oil onto the brake linings or the disc friction surface.

9 Refit the brake disc as described in Section 7, then adjust the handbrake as described in Section 13.

15 Handbrake cable – removal and refitting

Removal

1 Loosen the rear wheel bolts and chock the front wheels. Jack up the rear of the car and support it on axle stands (see *Jacking and vehicle support*). Remove the rear roadwheels.

15.3 Disconnect the equaliser plate from the end of the cables

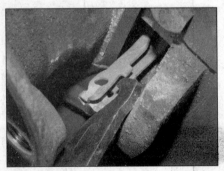

15.8 Unhook the expander from the sleeve

14.5b . . . and disconnect the return springs

2 Refer to Chapter 11 and remove the centre console. Also remove the rear seat and carpets as necessary to gain access to the cable entry in the floorpan.

3 Ensure that the handbrake is released, then with reference to Section 13, slacken the handbrake adjuster nut at the lever until there is enough slack in the cables to disconnect the equaliser bracket from the end of the cables **(see illustration)**.

4 Remove the rear discs as described in Section 7.

5 Remove the rear seat cushion as described in Chapter 11, then fold the rear floor carpet forwards to expose the outer brake cables.

6 Working inside the rear of the passenger cabin, press the cable rubber grommet rearwards into the bodywork.

7 Attach a length of strong wire to the front end of the cables, to assist refitting **(see illustration)**.

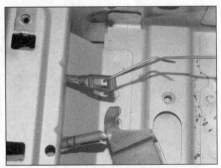

15.7 Attach a length of wire to the cable to aid refitting

15.9 Depress the clip (arrowed) and slide the inner cable end from the actuator sleeve

14.7 Apply high-melting point grease (Copper slip) to the shoe contact areas on the backplate

8 Unhook the brake shoe return spring, then unhook the expander from the actuator sleeve **(see illustration)**.

9 Detach the handbrake inner cable from the actuator sleeve **(see illustration)**.

10 Carefully prise the cable guide sleeve from the hub carrier assembly.

11 Note their fitted locations, then release the cable from any clips or brackets along its route.

12 Pull the front of the cable out from the passenger cabin, until the length of wire appears (see paragraph 7), then detach the wire, leaving it in place ready to attach to the new cable.

Refitting

13 Attach the end of the inner cable to the handbrake shoe actuator, and pull the actuator into position on the brake backplate. Reconnect the shoe return spring.

14 Push the guide sleeve back into position on the hub carrier. Ensure the lug on the sleeve locates correctly in the hub carrier **(see illustration)**.

15 Attach the front end of the cable to the guide wire and pull it, and the rubber grommet, into position through to the inside of the car, and reconnect the inner cable end to the handbrake lever equaliser plate. Detach the guide wire.

16 Refit the cable to the retaining/support brackets along its route.

17 The remainder is a reversal of refitting.

18 Operate the handbrake two or three times to settle the cable, then adjust the handbrake as described in Section 13.

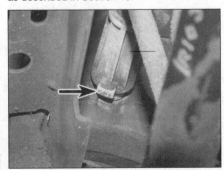

15.14 Ensure the lug (arrowed) engages correctly with the hub carrier

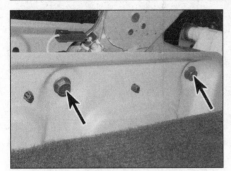

16.5 Undo the 2 bolts (arrowed) securing the handbrake lever

17.4 Pull the locking sleeve (arrowed) towards the switch plunger

17.5 Squeeze together the retaining catches (arrowed)

16 Handbrake lever – removal and refitting

Removal

1 Remove the centre console as described in Chapter 11.
2 Undo the cable adjuster nut from the handbrake cable **(see illustration 13.4)**.
3 Disconnect the wiring connector from the handbrake warning light switch.
4 Undo the warning light switch mounting bolt and remove the switch.
5 Undo the bolts securing the lever assembly to the floor **(see illustration)**.

Refitting

6 Refitting is a reversal of removal. Adjust the handbrake as described in Section 13 on completion.

17 Stop-light switch – removal and refitting

Removal

1 Ensure the ignition is switched off.
2 Undo the two screws, and remove the trim panel under the facia on the driver's side.
3 Depress the brake pedal slightly, then push the stop-light switch towards the pedal to release the locking sleeve.
4 Pull the white locking sleeve towards the switch plunger as far as it will go **(see illustration)**.
5 Compress the switch side retaining catches and withdraw the switch from the pedal bracket. Disconnect the wiring connector(s) and remove the switch **(see illustration)**.

Refitting

6 Make sure that the switch locking sleeve is fully extended towards the switch plunger.
7 Reconnect the wiring then, with the brake pedal depressed, locate the switch in the pedal bracket. Push the switch into the bracket until a click is heard as the retaining catches clip into the bracket.

8 Pull the brake pedal up as far as it will go; this will automatically adjust the switch.
9 Gently rock the switch to ensure that it is securely in place, and check the operation of the stop-lights.
10 Refit the panels removed for access.

18 Anti-lock braking system (ABS) – general information

The anti-lock braking system fitted as standard equipment on all models monitors the rotational speed of the wheels under braking. Sudden deceleration of one wheel, indicating that lock-up is occurring, causes the hydraulic pressure to that wheels brake to be reduced or interrupted momentarily.

The main components of the system are the wheel sensors, the electronic control module (ECM) and the hydraulic modulator assembly.

One sensor is fitted to each wheel, together with a pulse wheel carried on the wheel/ driveshaft hub. The sensors monitor the rotational speeds of the wheels, and are able to detect when there is a risk of wheel locking (low rotational speed). The wheel sensors also provide vehicle speed information to the speedometer.

Information from the sensors is fed to the ECM, which operates solenoid valves in the hydraulic modulator. The solenoid valves restrict the hydraulic fluid supply to any caliper detected to be on the verge of locking.

Should a fault develop in the system, the ECM illuminates a warning light on the instrument panel and disables the system. Normal braking will still be available, but without the anti-lock function. In the event of a fault, the ECM stores a series of signals (or fault codes) for subsequent read-out using diagnostic equipment (see Section 20).

Electronic Brake Force (EBD) distribution is incorporated into the ABS system, and regulates the proportion of braking force applied to the front and rear wheels.

On cars equipped with a traction control system (TRACS), the ABS system performs a dual role. In addition to detecting when a wheel is locking under braking, the system also detects a wheel that is spinning under acceleration.

When this condition is detected, the brake on that wheel is momentarily applied to reduce, or eliminate, the wheel spin. When the rotational speed of the spinning wheel is detected to be equal to the other wheels, the brake is released. On vehicles equipped with stability control (STC or DSTC) The same sensors, solenoids and pipes are used by models equipped with Stability and Traction Control (STC) or Dynamic Stability Control (DSTC). However, vehicles with DSTC are also equipped with a combined yaw rate and lateral acceleration sensor, and a steering wheel angle sensor.

19 Anti-lock braking system (ABS) components – removal and refitting

Removal

Front wheel sensor

1 Loosen the appropriate front wheel bolts and chock the rear wheels. Jack up the front of the car and support it on axle stands (see *Jacking and vehicle support*). Remove the roadwheel.
2 Disconnect the wiring plug for the wheel sensor – the plugs are located in each rear corner of the engine compartment. Once the plug is disconnected, feed the wiring down into the wheel arch.
3 Undo the bolt which secures the sensor to the hub carrier. Withdraw the sensor, and unclip the wiring from the brackets on the suspension strut and inner wing **(see illustration)**.

19.3 Undo the bolt (arrowed) and remove the front wheel speed sensor

19.6 Undo the bolt (arrowed) and remove the rear wheel speed sensor (viewed from above)

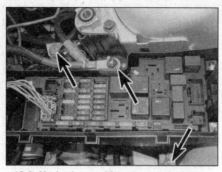

19.9 Undo the positive connection, then undo the two screws and move the engine compartment relay/fusebox to one side (arrowed)

Front pulse wheel

4 The front pulse wheel is a press fit on the driveshaft constant velocity joint, and special tools are required for removal. This work should be entrusted to a Volvo dealer.

Rear wheel sensor

5 Loosen the appropriate rear wheel bolts and chock the front wheels. Jack up the rear of the car and support it on axle stands (see *Jacking and vehicle support*). Remove the roadwheel.
6 Undo the bolt which secures the sensor to the stub axle (see illustration). Withdraw the sensor and disconnect the wiring connector. On certain models, it will be necessary to trace the wiring back until the connector is located and can then be disconnected. This may entail removal of the rear seats or luggage compartment trim panels (see Chapter 11).

Brake control module (BCM)

7 Disconnect the battery negative lead as described in Chapter 5A.
8 Remove the air cleaner housing as described in Chapter 4A or 4B.
9 Undo the positive wiring connections, then undo the two screws and move the engine compartment relay/fusebox to one side (see illustration).
10 Disconnect the hydraulic pump motor wiring plug from the BCM, then undo the four Torx bolts and detach the BCM from the modulator assembly.

Hydraulic modulator

Note: *Before starting work, refer to the warning*

at the beginning of Section 2 concerning the dangers of hydraulic fluid.
11 Disconnect the battery negative lead (see Chapter 5A).
12 Drain the hydraulic fluid from the braking system. This is essentially the same operation as bleeding the system (see Section 2), but no fluid is added to the master cylinder reservoir during the procedure. Note, however, that when the system is bled on completion, pressure-bleeding equipment will be necessary.
13 Remove the complete air cleaner assembly as described in Chapter 4A or 4B. Additionally, on turbo models, remove the inlet duct between the air cleaner assembly and the turbocharger.
14 Undo the positive wiring connections, then undo the two screws and move the engine compartment relay/fusebox to one side (see illustration 19.9).
15 Wipe clean all the brake pipe unions at the hydraulic modulator. Place absorbent rags beneath the pipe unions to catch any spilt fluid.
16 Before disconnecting the fluid pipes from the hydraulic modulator, mark them for position (eg, by wrapping labels around the pipes). Undo the union nuts on the brake pipes on the side of the hydraulic modulator. Carefully withdraw the pipes, and cover the open unions and pipe ends.
17 Unclip the cover from the large wiring connector at the side of the modulator. Release the connector locking clip and disconnect the wiring plug.

18 Disconnect the ABS pump motor wiring connector.
19 Undo the bolts securing the hydraulic modulator mounting bracket to the inner wing. Move the wiring aside, and lift out the modulator assembly and bracket.
20 If required (such as for renewal of the BCM), the modulator can be separated from the mounting bracket by removing the mounting bolts.
21 Note that the modulator is a sealed precision assembly, and must not under any circumstances be dismantled.

Brake pedal position sensor

22 Depress the brake pedal two or three times to dissipate any vacuum remaining in the servo unit.
23 Disconnect the wiring connector from the pedal sensor located on the front face of the vacuum servo unit (see illustration).
24 Open the circlip and withdraw the sensor from the servo. Recover the O-ring and spacer sleeve from the sensor.

Refitting

25 In all cases, refitting is a reversal of the removal operations but note the following points:
  a) *Clean off all dirt from the wheel sensors and mounting locations before refitting, and also clean the pulse wheels with a stiff brush.*
  b) *Bleed the hydraulic system as described in Section 2 after refitting the hydraulic modulator.*
  c) *Use a new O-ring on the brake pedal position sensor, and ensure that the colour-coded spacer sleeve matches the colour code of the servo unit.*

20 Anti-lock braking system (ABS) – fault diagnosis

General information

1 The anti-lock braking system incorporates an on-board diagnostic system to facilitate fault finding and system testing. Should a fault occur, the BCM stores a series of signals (or fault codes) for subsequent read-out via the diagnostic plug located under the facia, above the driver's pedals (see illustration).
2 If problems have been experienced, the on-board diagnostic system can be used to pinpoint any problem areas, but this requires special test equipment. Once this has been done, further tests may often be necessary to determine the exact nature of the fault; ie, whether a component itself has failed, or whether it is a wiring or other inter-related problem. Apart from visually checking the wiring and connections, any testing will require the use of a fault code reader at least. A Volvo dealer will obviously have such a reader, but they are also available from other suppliers. It is unlikely to be cost-effective for the private

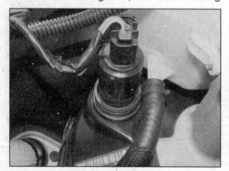

19.23 Brake pedal position sensor

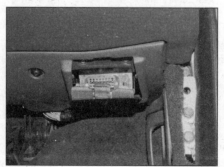

20.1 The diagnostic plug is located under the facia, above the driver's pedals

owner to purchase a fault code reader, but a well-equipped local garage or auto-electrical specialist will have one.

Preliminary checks

Note: *When carrying out these checks to trace a fault, remember that if the fault has appeared only a short time after any part of the vehicle has been serviced or overhauled, the first place to check is where that work was carried out, however unrelated it may appear, to ensure that no carelessly-refitted components are causing the problem.*

Remember that any fault codes which have been logged will have to be cleared from the ECM memory using a dedicated fault code reader (see paragraph 2) before you can be certain the cause of the fault has been fixed.

3 Lift the luggage compartment floor and check the condition of the battery connections – remake the connections or renew the leads if a fault is found. Use the same techniques to ensure that all earth points in the engine compartment provide good electrical contact through clean, metal-to-metal joints, and that all are securely fastened.

4 Next work methodically around the engine compartment, checking all visible wiring, and the connections between sections of the wiring loom. What you are looking for at this stage is wiring that is obviously damaged by chafing against sharp edges, or against moving suspension/transmission components and/or the auxiliary drivebelt, by being trapped or crushed between carelessly-refitted components, or melted by being forced into contact with hot engine castings, coolant pipes, etc. In almost all cases, damage of this sort is caused in the first instance by incorrect routing on reassembly after previous work has been carried out (see the note at the beginning of this sub-Section).

5 Obviously wires can break or short together inside the insulation so that no visible evidence betrays the fault, but this usually only occurs where the wiring loom has been incorrectly routed so that it is stretched taut or kinked sharply; either of these conditions should be obvious on even a casual inspection. If this is thought to have happened and the fault proves elusive, the suspect section of wiring should be checked very carefully during the more detailed checks which follow.

6 Depending on the extent of the problem, damaged wiring may be repaired by rejoining the break or splicing-in a new length of wire, using solder to ensure a good connection, and remaking the insulation with adhesive insulating tape or heat-shrink tubing, as desired. If the damage is extensive, given the implications for the vehicle's future reliability, the best long-term answer may well be to renew that entire section of the loom, however expensive this may appear.

7 When the actual damage has been repaired, ensure that the wiring loom is re-routed correctly, so that it is clear of other components, is not stretched or kinked, and

21.5a Disconnect the small vacuum hose from the pump (arrowed) . . .

is secured out of harm's way using the plastic clips, guides and ties provided.

8 Check all electrical connectors, ensuring that they are clean, securely fastened, and that each is locked by its plastic tabs or wire clip, as appropriate. If any connector shows external signs of corrosion (accumulations of white or green deposits, or streaks of 'rust'), or if any is thought to be dirty, it must be unplugged and cleaned using electrical contact cleaner. If the connector pins are severely corroded, the connector must be renewed; note that this may mean the renewal of that entire section of the loom.

9 If the cleaner completely removes the corrosion to leave the connector in a satisfactory condition, it would be wise to pack the connector with a suitable material which will exclude dirt and moisture, and prevent the corrosion from occurring again; a Volvo dealer may be able to recommend a suitable product.

10 Working methodically around the engine compartment, check carefully that all vacuum hoses and pipes are securely fastened and correctly routed, with no signs of cracks, splits or deterioration to cause air leaks, or of hoses that are trapped, kinked, or bent sharply enough to restrict airflow. Check with particular care at all connections and sharp bends, and renew any damaged or deformed lengths of hose.

11 Check the brake lines, and renew any that are found to be leaking, corroded or crushed. Check particularly the flexible hoses at the brake calipers.

12 It is possible to make a further check of the electrical connections by wiggling each electrical connector of the system in turn as the engine is idling; a faulty connector will be immediately evident from the engine's response (or that of the warning light) as contact is broken and remade. A faulty connector should be renewed to ensure that the future reliability of the system; note that this may mean the renewal of that entire section of the loom.

13 Ensure that the wiring and connections to the wheel sensors are thoroughly checked – the wheel sensors are subjected to water, road salt and general dirt, and are often responsible for the ABS warning light coming on.

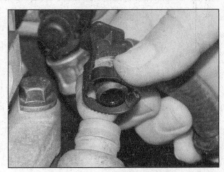

21.5b . . . then squeeze together the sides of the collar and disconnect the brake servo hose from the pump

14 If the preliminary checks have failed to reveal the fault, the car must be taken to a Volvo dealer or suitably-equipped garage for diagnostic testing using electronic test equipment.

21 Vacuum pump – removal and refitting

Note: *The camshaft driven vacuum pump is only fitted to diesel models.*

Removal

1 Remove the air cleaner assembly, complete with mass airflow sensor, as described in Chapter 4B.

2 Pull the plastic cover from over the engine straight up from its mountings.

D5244T/T2/T3 engines

3 Undo the positive wiring connections, then undo the two screws and move the engine compartment relay/fusebox to one side (see illustration 19.9).

4 Release the clamps, undo the mounting bracket bolt and remove the air pipe from the turbocharger to the air filter.

5 Note their fitted positions, and disconnect the vacuum hoses from the pump (see illustrations).

6 Undo the two screws securing the ventilation pipe, and move it aside to access the pump (see illustration).

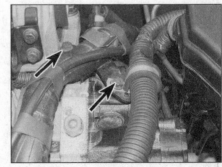

21.6 Undo the two screws (arrowed) and move the hose to one side

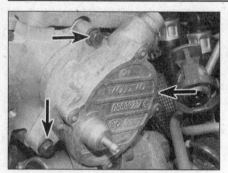

21.7 Undo the bolts (arrowed – 3rd bolt hidden) and remove the vacuum pump

21.9a Renew the vacuum pump O-rings (arrowed)

21.9b Ensure the drive lugs align with the slots in the end of the exhaust camshaft (arrowed)

D5244T4/T5/T6/T7 engines

7 Note their fitted positions and disconnect the vacuum hoses from the pump (see illustration).

All engines

8 Undo the three bolts and remove the pump from the cylinder head. Be prepared for fluid spillage. Discard the O-ring seals, new ones must be fitted. No dismantling of the pump is recommended.

Refitting

9 Fit new O-ring seals to the pump mating face, then align the pump drive lugs with the slots in the end of the exhaust camshaft, and fit the pump to the cylinder head – tighten the bolts to the specified torque (see illustrations).

10 The remainder of refitting is a reversal of removal.

Chapter 10
Suspension and steering

Contents

Degrees of difficulty

Easy, suitable for novice with little experience | **Fairly easy,** suitable for beginner with some experience | **Fairly difficult,** suitable for competent DIY mechanic | **Difficult,** suitable for experienced DIY mechanic | **Very difficult,** suitable for expert DIY or professional

Specifications

Front suspension
Type . . . . Independent, with MacPherson struts incorporating coil springs and telescopic shock absorbers. Anti-roll bar fitted to all models

Rear suspension
Type . . . . Fully-independent, multi-link with coil springs fitted over hydraulic telescopic shock absorbers. Anti-roll bar fitted to all models

Steering
Type . . . . Power-assisted rack-and-pinion
Steering fluid type . . . . See end of *Weekly checks*

Wheel alignment and steering angles
Front wheel:
 Camber angle. . . . . -0.3° ± 0.9°
 Castor angle. . . . . 4.0° ± 1.0°
 Toe setting . . . . 0.10° ± 0.10°' toe-in
Rear wheel:
 Camber angle. . . . . 0.0° ± 1.0°
 Toe setting . . . . 0.20° ± 0.20°' toe -in

Tyres
Tyre pressures . . . . See sticker on the inside of the fuel filler flap

Torque wrench settings

	Nm	lbf ft
Front suspension		
ABS sensor	10	7
Anti-roll bar clamp bolts	50	37
Anti-roll bar connecting link nuts*	50	37
Balljoint-to-hub carrier bolts*	40	30
Bearing housing to hub carrier*:		
Stage 1	20	15
Stage 2	65	48
Stage 3	Angle-tighten a further 60°	
Brake caliper mounting bracket bolts*	100	74
Control arm to subframe*:		
Front bolt:		
Stage 1	65	48
Stage 2	Angle-tighten a further 90°	
Rear bolt:		
Stage 1	105	77
Stage 2	Angle-tighten a further 90°	
Driveshaft screw*:		
Stage 1	35	26
Stage 2	Angle-tighten a further 90°	
Hub carrier balljoint-to-control arm nut:		
Stage 1	50	37
Stage 2	Angle-tighten a further 35°	
Position sensor	10	7
Subframe mounting bolts*:		
Up to 2004 model year:		
Stage 1	105	77
Stage 2	Angle-tighten a further 120°	
From 2005 model year	160	118
Subframe mounting brackets to body	50	37
Suspension strut to hub carrier*:		
Stage 1	105	77
Stage 2	Angle-tighten a further 90°	
Suspension strut piston nut	70	52
Suspension strut 'star' nut	70	52
Suspension strut upper mounting to body	25	18
Rear suspension		
Anti-roll bar-to-subframe bolts	80	59
Anti-roll bar to lower control arms	80	59
Lower control arm to hub carrier and subframe	80	59
Rear hub bearing assembly*:		
Stage 1	20	15
Stage 2	65	48
Stage 3	Angle-tighten a further 60°	
Shock absorber lower mounting bolt	80	59
Shock absorber upper mounting nut	60	44
Subframe mounting bolts*	80	59
Tie-rod bolts	80	59
Trailing arm bolts*	80	59
Upper control arm to hub carrier and subframe	80	59
Steering		
Power steering pipes to steering rack	25	18
Power steering pump mounting bolts	25	18
Steering column mounting bolts	25	18
Steering rack crash guard bolts	80	59
Steering rack to engine mounting	50	37
Steering rack to subframe nuts/bolt*	50	37
Steering shaft universal joint pinch-bolts*	30	22
Steering wheel bolt*:		
Stage 1	30	22
Stage 2	Angle-tighten a further 30°	
Track rod end balljoint nuts*:		
Aluminium hub carrier:		
Stage 1	50	37
Stage 2	Angle-tighten a further 40°	
Steel hub carrier	70	52
Track rod locknuts	70	52
Roadwheels		
Wheel bolts	140	103

* Do not re-use

1 General information

The independent front suspension is of the MacPherson strut type, incorporating coil springs and integral telescopic shock absorbers. The struts are located by transverse control arms, which are attached to the front subframe via rubber bushes at their inner ends, and incorporate a balljoint at their outer ends. The hub carriers, which carry the hub bearings, brake calipers and the hub/disc assemblies, are bolted to the MacPherson struts, and connected to the control arms through the balljoints. A front anti-roll bar is fitted to all models, and is attached to the subframe and to the MacPherson struts via link arms.

The rear suspension is of the fully independent, multi-link type, consisting of an upper and lower control arm mounted via rubber bushes to the hub carrier and rear subframe. The hub carrier is located by a trailing arm and an upper stay each side. Coil springs are fitted over telescopic shock absorbers between the lower control arm and the vehicle body.

Models equipped with the dynamic stability control system (DSTC) may also have the option of having the 'Four-C' active chassis system (Continuously Controlled Chassis Concept). Here, each shock absorber has its damping effect controlled by an electronic suspension module (SUM). The SUM receives vehicle movement data from various sensors on the suspension and vehicle body, from which it determines the optimal comfort or grip level, and adjusts the damping of the shock absorbers up to 500 times a second.

Power-assisted rack and pinion steering is fitted as standard equipment. Power assistance is derived from a hydraulic pump, belt-driven from the crankshaft pulley.

Note: *Many of the components described in this Chapter are secured by nuts and bolts tightened by the angle-tightening method. These particular nuts and bolts are indicated in the torque wrench settings section of the specifications. When these fastenings are disturbed, it is often required that **new** nuts and/or bolts are always used when refitting, as indicated in the Specifications. Self-locking nuts are also used in many areas, and these should also be renewed, particularly if resistance cannot be felt when the locking portion passes over the bolt or stud thread.*

2 Front hub carrier and bearing – removal and refitting

Note: *The hub bearing is a sealed, pre-adjusted and pre-lubricated, double-row ball type, and is intended to last the car's entire service life without maintenance or attention.*

2.2 Undo the driveshaft screw

2.3 Use a Torx bit to counterhold the anti-roll bar link balljoint shank

The bearing housing, hub flange and bearing are serviced as a complete assembly, and these components cannot be dismantled or renewed individually.

Removal

1 Loosen the appropriate front wheel bolts, then jack up the front of the car and support it on axle stands (see *Jacking and vehicle support*). Remove the appropriate front roadwheel.
2 Slacken and remove the screw securing the driveshaft to the hub **(see illustration)**. Have an assistant depress the brake pedal to prevent the hub from rotating. Discard the screw, a new one must be used.
3 Undo the nut securing the anti-roll bar link to the shock absorber. Use a Torx bit in the end of the balljoint shank to counterhold the nut **(see illustration)**.
4 Remove the ABS wheel sensor from the hub carrier, and release the sensor wiring from the suspension strut bracket.
5 Undo the two bolts securing the brake caliper bracket and lock-limiter bracket to the hub carrier. Note that new bolts will be required for refitting. Slide the caliper assembly, complete with brake pads off the disc and suspend it from the coil spring using string or wire.
6 Check whether the position of the brake disc in relation to the hub is marked, and if not, make your own mark as an aid to refitting. Remove the spigot pin which holds the disc to the hub and lift off the disc.

7 Free the driveshaft CV joint from the hub flange by tapping it inwards approximately 10 to 15 mm with a plastic or copper mallet.
8 Undo the retaining nut, then disconnect the steering track rod end balljoint from the hub carrier. If necessary, use a balljoint separator tool **(see illustration 22.3)**.
9 Using vernier calipers (or similar) measure the distance from the outer edge of the hub carrier mounting lug to the back of the shock absorber body **(see illustration)**. This will enable the camber setting of the front wheels to be preserved when reassembled.
10 Remove the bolts securing the hub carrier to the shock absorber, and pull the hub carrier outwards from the shock absorber. Note which way the bolts are inserted – from the front **(see illustration)**.
11 Undo the nut and detach the suspension control arm balljoint from the hub carrier. Use a stout bar to lever the control arm downwards and over the end of the balljoint shank **(see illustrations)**. Take care not to damage the balljoint dust cover during and after disconnection.
12 Swivel the hub carrier assembly outwards, and withdraw the driveshaft CV joint from the hub flange.
13 Undo the four bolts and withdraw the bearing housing assembly from the hub carrier **(see illustration)**. Note that new bolts will be required for reassembly.

Refitting

14 Prior to refitting, remove all traces of metal

2.9 Measure the distance from the back of the shock absorber to the outer edge of the hub carrier mounting lug

2.10 The shock absorber-to-hub carrier bolts are inserted from the front

2.11a Undo the control arm balljoint nut . . .

2.11b . . . then lever down the control arm and pull out the hub carrier

2.13 Undo the four bolts and detach the bearing housing from the hub carrier

adhesive, rust, oil and dirt from the splines and threads of the driveshaft outer CV joint and the bearing housing mating surface on the hub carrier.

15 Locate the bearing housing on the hub carrier. Refit the new bolts and tighten them progressively, in a diagonal sequence, first to the specified torque settings using a torque wrench, then through the specified angle using an angle-tightening gauge.

16 The remainder of refitting is a reversal of removal, but observe the following points:

a) *Ensure that the hub and brake disc mating faces are spotlessly clean, and refit the disc with the orientation marks aligned.*

b) *When refitting the hub carrier to the shock absorber, ensure the distance from the outer edge of the carrier lug to the back of the shock absorber is as measured earlier. If not, the vehicle must be taken to a dealer or specialist to have the front suspension geometry checked and adjusted.*

c) *Lubricate the threads of the CV joint with engine oil before refitting the screw. A new driveshaft screw should be used.*

d) *Ensure that the ABS sensor, and the sensor location in the hub carrier, are perfectly clean before refitting.*

e) *Tighten all nuts and bolts to the specified torque (see Chapter 9 for brake component torque settings). When tightening the driveshaft screw, tighten first using a torque wrench, then further, through the specified angle, using an angle-tightening gauge.*

3 Front suspension strut – removal and refitting

Removal

1 Loosen the appropriate front wheel bolts. Chock the rear wheels and apply the handbrake, then jack up the front of the car and support it on axle stands (see *Jacking and vehicle support*). Remove the appropriate front roadwheel.

2 Remove the ABS wheel sensor from the hub carrier, and release the sensor wiring from the suspension strut or hub carrier bracket **(see illustration)**.

3 Undo the retaining nut, and separate the anti-roll bar connecting link from the bracket on the suspension strut. Use a Torx key to counterhold the nut **(see illustration 2.3)**. Discard the nut, a new one must be fitted.

4 On models with Four-C (Active suspension), undo the screw remove the position sensor from the shock absorber. Position the sensor to one side.

5 Using vernier calipers (or similar) measure the distance from the outer edge of the hub carrier mounting lug to the back of the shock absorber body **(see illustration 2.9)**. This will enable the camber setting of the front wheels to be preserved when reassembled.

6 Position a jack beneath the suspension control arm, and raise the jack to just take the weight of the suspension assembly.

7 On models with Four-C, working in the engine compartment, trace the wires from the

suspension strut back to the connector and unplug the connector.

8 Undo the two nuts and remove the bolts securing the suspension strut to the hub carrier. Note that new nuts will be required for refitting **(see illustration 2.10)**.

9 From within the engine compartment, undo the three nuts securing the strut upper mounting to the body – **do not** attempt to loosen the centre nut **(see illustration)**. Note that new nuts will be required for refitting.

10 Free the suspension strut from the hub carrier, and manoeuvre the strut out from underneath the wheel arch.

Refitting

11 Refitting is a reversal of removal, but observe the following points:

a) *Tighten all nuts and bolts to the specified torque, using new nuts/bolts where necessary.*

b) *When refitting the hub carrier to the shock absorber, ensure the distance from the outer edge of the carrier lug to the back of the shock absorber is as measured earlier. If not, the vehicle must be taken to a dealer or specialist to have the front suspension geometry checked and adjusted.*

c) *Ensure that the ABS sensor, and the sensor location in the hub carrier, are perfectly clean before refitting.*

4 Front suspension strut – dismantling, inspection and reassembly

⚠ *Warning: Before attempting to dismantle the suspension strut, a suitable tool to hold the coil spring in compression must be obtained. Adjustable coil spring compressors which can be positively secured to the spring coils are readily available, and are recommended for this operation. Any attempt to dismantle the strut without such a tool is likely to result in damage or personal injury.*

Dismantling

1 Remove the strut from the car as described in Section 3.

2 Prise off the plastic cap, then slacken the strut mounting nut 1/2 a turn, while holding

3.2 Undo the bolt and pull the ABS sensor from the hub carrier

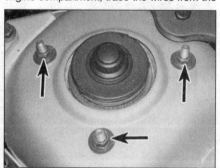

3.9 Undo the three nuts (arrowed) securing the shock absorber to the vehicle body

4.2 Prise off the plastic cap

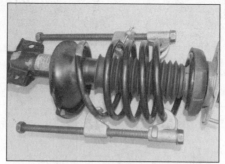

4.3 Fit spring compressors to the coil spring

4.4a Unscrew the piston nut . . .

4.4b . . . followed by the rubber washer . . .

4.4c . . . and 'star' nut

4.5a Remove the upper mounting . . .

the protruding portion of the piston rod with a Torx bit **(see illustration)**. Do not remove the nut at this stage.

3 Fit the spring compressors to the coil spring, and tighten the compressors until the load is taken off the spring seats **(see illustration)**.

4 Remove the piston nut, rubber washer and special 'star' nut **(see illustrations)**.

5 Remove the upper mounting and spring seat, followed by the spring, bump stop and gaiter **(see illustrations)**.

Inspection

6 With the strut assembly now completely dismantled, examine all the components for wear, damage or deformation. Renew any of the components as necessary.

7 Examine the shock absorber for signs of fluid leakage, and check the strut piston for signs of pitting along its entire length. Test the operation of the shock absorber, while holding it in an upright position, by moving the piston through a full stroke and then through short strokes of 50 to 100 mm. In both cases, the resistance felt should be smooth and continuous. If the resistance is jerky, or uneven, or if there is any visible sign of wear or damage, renewal is necessary.

8 If any doubt exists about the condition of the coil spring, gradually release the spring compressor, and check the spring for distortion and signs of cracking. Since no minimum free length is specified by Volvo, the only way to check the tension of the spring is to compare it to a new component. Renew the spring if it is damaged or distorted, or if there is any doubt as to its condition.

9 Inspect all other components for signs of damage or deterioration, and renew any that are suspect.

10 If a new shock absorber is being fitted, hold it vertically and pump the piston a few times to prime it.

4.5b . . . followed by the spring seat . . .

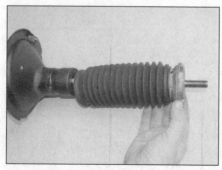

4.5d . . . gaiter and bump stop

Reassembly

11 Reassembly is a reversal of dismantling, but ensure that the spring is fully compressed before fitting. Make sure that the spring ends are correctly located in the upper

4.5c . . . spring . . .

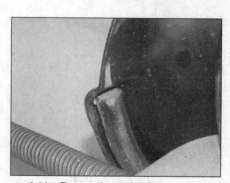

4.11a Ensure the spring is correctly located in its seats

4.11b Modify an old socket to fit the 'star' nut

and lower seats, then tighten the 'star' nut, shock absorber piston retaining nut and strut mounting nuts to the specified torque. Note that in order to tighten the 'start' nut correctly, Volvo tool No 999 5469 will be required, or modify an old socket to fit (see illustrations).

5 Front suspension control arm/balljoint – removal, overhaul and refitting

Removal

1 Loosen the appropriate front wheel bolts. Chock the rear wheels and apply the handbrake, then jack up the front of the vehicle and support it on axle stands (see *Jacking and vehicle support*). Remove the appropriate front roadwheel, then release the screws and remove the engine undershield.

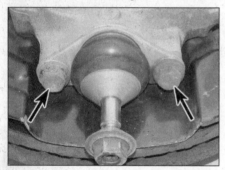

5.3 Undo the balljoint bolts (arrowed)

5.4b . . . control arm rear mounting bolt

2 Undo the nut securing the balljoint shank to the control arm. Use a Torx bit to counterhold the nut, then use a bar to lever the arm downwards over the end of the balljoint shank (see illustrations 2.11a and 2.11b).

3 If required, undo the two bolts and remove the balljoint from the base of the hub carrier (see illustration). If the balljoint is difficult to remove, use a slide hammer attached to the balljoint shank and pull it from the hub carrier.

Left-hand control arm

4 Undo the two inner mounting bolts, withdraw the bolts and remove the arm from the car (see illustrations). Note that new bolts will be required for refitting.

Right-hand control arm

5 In order to remove the control arm-to-subframe bolts, it's necessary to raise the engine approximately 25 mm. Pull the plastic cover on top of the engine straight up from its mountings.

6 Undo the bolts securing the engine cross-stay to the brackets on the suspension turrets.

7 Position a workshop jack under the engine sump, with a block of wood on the jack head to protect the sump casing.

8 Undo the bolts securing the right-hand engine mounting to the cylinder block.

9 Undo the bolts/nuts securing the front engine tie rod and rear mounting pad to the subframe.

10 Use the jack to raise the engine approximately 25 mm to access the control arm inner bolts. Undo the bolts and manoeuvre

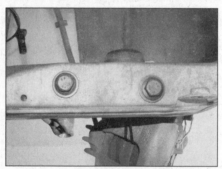

5.4a The two bolts for the left-hand control arm pass through the subframe . . .

5.10 In order to remove these right-hand control arm front mounting bolts, the engine must be lowered approximately 25 mm

the arm from the car (see illustration). Note that new bolts will be required.

Overhaul

11 Thoroughly clean the control arm and the area around the control arm mountings. Inspect the arm for any signs of cracks, damage or distortion, and carefully check the inner pivot bushes for signs of swelling, cracks or deterioration of the rubber.

12 If either bush requires renewal, the work should be entrusted to a Volvo dealer or specialist. A hydraulic press and suitable spacers are required to remove and refit the bushes and a setting gauge is needed for accurate positioning of the bushes in the arm.

Refitting

13 Locate the arm in its mountings, and fit the new mounting bolts and nuts. Tighten the nuts to their specified torque.

14 If removed, refit the balljoint to the hub carrier and tighten the new retaining bolts to the specified torque.

15 Engage the balljoint shank in the control arm, then tighten the new nut to the specified torque, followed by the specified angle.

16 The remainder of refitting is a reversal of removal.

6 Front anti-roll bar – removal and refitting

Removal

1 Loosen the front wheel bolts. Chock the rear wheels, then jack up the front of the vehicle and support it on axle stands (see *Jacking and vehicle support*). Remove both front roadwheels.

2 Undo the retaining nut, and separate the anti-roll bar connecting links on each side from the ends of the anti-roll bar. If necessary, use a Torx bit in the end of the balljoint shank to counterhold the nut (see illustration).

3 Release the screws and remove the engine undershield.

4 On right-hand-drive models, undo the two steering rack crash guard bolts at the rear of the front subframe (see illustration).

5 Undo the nuts/bolts securing the steering

6.2 Undo the nut (arrowed) and separate the connecting link from the anti-roll bar

rack to the subframe and, on right-hand-drive models, the nut at the base of the steering rack crash guard.

6 Undo the steering rack fluid pipe retaining clip bolts at the front and rear of the subframe.

7 Position a sturdy trolley jack beneath, and in contact with, the rear of the subframe. *Caution: Make sure that the subframe is well-supported, and that the jack being used is capable of taking the combined weight of the engine/transmission and subframe.*

8 Undo the bolt each side securing the subframe rear mounting brackets to the body.

9 Undo the bolts each side securing the rear mounting brackets to the subframe, and recover the washers. Note that new bolts will be required for refitting.

10 Slacken the two subframe front mounting bolts by no more than 10 to 15 mm, then carefully lower the jack and allow the subframe to drop slightly at the rear (approximately 90 mm). Ensure that the steering rack mounting bolts are clear of the subframe. On right-hand-drive models, check that the crash guard does not trap the steering rack fluid pipes as the subframe is lowered. Note that new subframe front mounting bolts will be required for refitting.

11 Undo the bolts securing the anti-roll bar clamps on each side of the subframe, and manipulate the anti-roll bar out from under the car **(see illustration)**. On right-hand-drive models, withdraw the steering rack crash guard from its location as the anti-roll bar is removed.

12 Examine the anti-roll bar for signs of damage or distortion, and the connecting links and mounting bushes for signs of deterioration of the rubber. The bushes are vulcanised to the anti-roll bar, and are not available separately.

Refitting

13 Manipulate the anti-roll bar into position on the subframe, together with the steering rack crash guard on right-hand-drive models. Refit the clamp bolts and tighten to the specified torque.

14 Raise the subframe at the rear, then engage the steering rack bolts and, where applicable, the crash guard bolt.

15 Refit the rear mounting brackets to the body, and tighten the bolts hand-tight only at this stage.

16 Secure the rear mounting brackets to the subframe using the washers and new bolts, also tightened hand-tight only.

17 Move the jack to the front of the subframe, and raise it to just take the subframe weight. Unscrew the subframe front mounting bolts, fit two new bolts and tighten them hand-tight only.

18 Tighten the two subframe mounting bolts on the left-hand side of the car to the specified torque using a torque wrench, then further, where necessary, through the specified angle, using an angle-tightening gauge. Now tighten

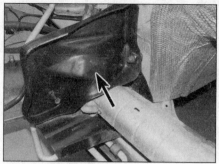

6.4 Steering rack crash guard (arrowed – engine removed for clarity)

the two mounting bolts on the right-hand side in the same way. Finally tighten the four mounting bracket-to-body bolts to the specified torque.

19 Secure the steering rack using new nuts tightened to the specified torque.

20 On right-hand-drive models, refit the steering rack crash guard nut and the two bolts.

21 Refit the steering rack fluid pipe retaining clip bolts.

22 Refit the engine undershield.

23 Refit the anti-roll bar connecting links on each side to the brackets on the suspension struts.

24 Refit the roadwheels, lower the car and tighten the wheel bolts in a diagonal sequence to the specified torque.

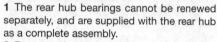

7 Rear hub bearings – renewal

1 The rear hub bearings cannot be renewed separately, and are supplied with the rear hub as a complete assembly.

2 Remove the brake disc as described in Chapter 9.

3 Undo the bolt and remove the ABS wheel speed sensor from the hub carrier **(see illustration)**.

4 Undo the four bolts and withdrawn the bearing assembly from the hub carrier. Note in order to remove the lower rear fixing bolt (once the hub has been removed) on some

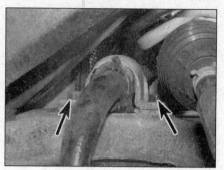

6.11 Front anti-roll bar clamp bolts (arrowed)

models, the bolt's integral flange must be partially ground down.

5 Fit the new assembly to the hub carrier then insert and tighten the new bolts (supplied in the bearing/hub kit) to the specified torque. Note that the bolt without an integral flange has a washer included in the kit, and must be screwed into the lower rear bolt hole in the bearing housing.

6 Refit the ABS wheel speed sensor and brake disc as described in Chapter 9.

8 Rear hub carrier – removal and refitting

Removal

1 Remove the rear brake disc and handbrake shoes on the relevant side, as described in Chapter 9.

2 Undo the retaining bolt and withdraw the ABS wheel sensor from hub carrier. Do not disconnect the wheel sensor connector.

3 Undo the four bolts, and remove the brake backplate **(see illustration)**. Remove the backplate gasket; obtain a new one for refitting if the original is in any way damaged.

4 Prise up the handbrake lever surround trim from the console **(see illustration)**.

5 Working through the cover panel aperture and turn the adjuster nut until there is sufficient slack in the cables to enable the handbrake shoe actuator to be pulled from the hub carrier, and then use a screwdriver to release

7.3 Undo the bolt (arrowed) and pull out the ABS speed sensor (viewed from above)

8.3 The brake backplate is secured by four bolts (arrowed)

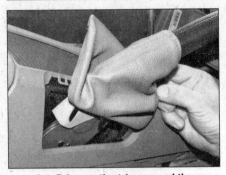

8.4 Prise up the trim around the handbrake lever

8.5 Release the clip and detach the cable

8.6 To set the suspension in the 'normal' position, the distance from the wheel arch to the hub centre is 373 mm

the clip and detach the handbrake inner cable **(see illustration)**.

6 Position a trolley jack under the shock absorber mounting of the lower control arm and raise the hub carrier assembly to the 'normal' position. Measure the distance from the lower edge of the top of the wheel arch to the centre of the wheel hub **(see illustration)**. This distance is 373 mm.

7 Note their fitted positions, then undo the bolts securing the trailing arm, upper and lower control arms, and the tie-rod to the hub carrier. Discard the bolts – new ones must be fitted. Withdrawn the hub carrier from the vehicle.

8 If any of the various metal-elastic bushes on the hub carrier appear damaged or worn, have them renewed by a Volvo dealer or specialist, as access to special tools and a hydraulic press is required.

Refitting

9 Position the hub carrier, connect the various link arms, and fit the new bolts. Only finger-tighten the bolts at this stage.

10 Check the hub carrier is in the 'normal' position as described in paragraph 6.

11 Now tighten the various link arms mounting bolts to the specified torque.

12 The remainder of refitting is a reversal of removal, remembering to adjust the handbrake as described in Chapter 9.

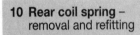

9 Rear shock absorber – removal and refitting

Removal

1 Fold down the rear seat backrest and release the front edge of the luggage compartment side trim panel for access to the shock absorber upper mounting.

2 Chock the front wheels then jack up the rear of the vehicle and support it on axle stands (see *Jacking and vehicle support*). Although not essential, access will be improved if the rear wheel is removed.

3 On models equipped with the Four-C Active chassis, trace the wiring back from the shock absorbers to the connectors above the rear subframe, and disconnect the wiring plugs.

4 Position a jack under the outer end of the lower control arm, and raise the jack sufficiently to take the load off the shock absorber.

5 From inside the luggage compartment, undo the nut securing the shock absorber upper mounting to the body **(see illustration)**. Use a Torx key to counterhold the nut.

6 Undo the shock absorber lower mounting bolt, and slide the unit down through the lower control arm **(see illustrations)**.

7 Check the condition of the shock absorber and renew as necessary.

Refitting

8 Refitting is a reversal of removal, tightening all nuts and bolts to the specified torques and, where applicable, through the specified angle.

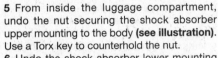

10 Rear coil spring – removal and refitting

Note: *Despite our best efforts in the workshop, we were unable to come up with a safe method of removing the coil springs without using Volvo springs compressors. Consequently, if access to these tools is not available, entrust this task to a Volvo dealer or suitably-equipped specialist.*

Removal

1 Remove the rear shock absorber from the appropriate side as described in Section 9.

2 Undo the bolts and remove the brake caliper mounting bracket from the hub carrier. Discard the bolts, new ones must be fitted. Do not disconnect the fluid pipe – suspend the caliper from the vehicle bodywork to prevent any strain on the flexible brake hose.

3 Undo the bolt and remove the ABS wheel speed sensor from the hub carrier. Position the sensor to on side.

4 Attach the Volvo spring compressors (Nos 951 2911, 9512913 and 951 2937) and compress the spring.

5 Lift out the spring from its location.

6 Examine all the components for wear or damage, and renew as necessary.

Refitting

7 Refit the compressed spring onto the seat in the lower control arm. Rotate the spring until a gap of 15 mm exists between the end of the spring coil and the raised section of the spring seat **(see illustration)**.

9.5 Undo the shock absorber upper mounting nut (arrowed)

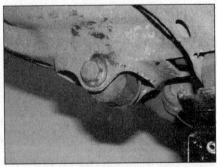

9.6a Undo the shock absorber lower mounting bolt . . .

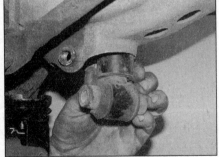

9.6b . . . and slide it down through the lower control arm

8 Raise the control arm by means of the jack, and engage the upper end of the spring in its recess in the body.

9 Refit the shock absorber, securing it in place before removing the jack. Tighten all nuts and bolts to the specified torque.

10 Release and remove the spring compressor.

11 Remainder of refitting is a reversal of removal.

11 Rear suspension link arms – removal and refitting

Removal

1 Loosen the rear wheel bolts. Chock the front wheels, then jack up the rear of the vehicle and support it on axle stands (see *Jacking and vehicle support*). Remove the appropriate rear roadwheel(s).

Trailing arm

2 Position a trolley jack under the shock absorber mounting of the lower control arm and raise the hub carrier assembly to the 'normal' position. Measure the distance from the lower edge of the top of the wheel arch to the centre of the wheel hub **(see illustration 8.6)**. This distance is 373 mm. If necessary, place some ballast in the luggage compartment to increase the weight of the vehicle, so that the suspension can be compressed enough by the jack without lifting the vehicle from the axle stands.

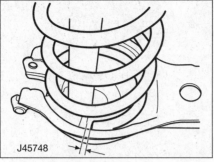

10.7 Leave a gap of 15 mm between the end of the spring and the edge of the seat

3 Undo the bolt and remove the brake pipe support bracket adjacent to the front of the arm **(see illustration)**.

4 Undo the bolt at each end of the arm and remove it from the vehicle **(see illustrations)**. Discard the bolts – new ones must be fitted.

Tie-rod

5 Release the handbrake cable from the clip on the tie-rod.

6 Make alignment marks between the tie-rod and the eccentric washer integral with the bolt at its inner end, then undo the bolt **(see illustration)**.

7 Undo the outer bolt and remove the tie-rod **(see illustration)**.

Upper control arm

8 To remove the upper control arm the complete rear subframe must be lowered. The metal-elastic bushes must then be pulled from their mountings in the subframe before

the arm can be removed. Although subframe removal is described in this Chapter, specialist tools are required to extract and press in the bushes – this should be entrusted to a Volvo dealer or specialist. If you are attempting to renew the bushes, note their exact fitted position, and fitted depth before extracting them, and ensure the new ones are fitted in exactly the same positions.

Lower control arm

9 Remove the coil spring as described in Section 10.

10 Undo the nut and disconnect the suspension ride height sensor link arm from the bracket on the control arm – where applicable **(see illustration)**.

11 Undo the bolt securing the rear of the trailing arm to the hub carrier, then pull the end of the arm downwards from the hub carrier.

12 Undo the bolts securing the inner end of the lower control arm to the subframe, and the outer end to the hub carrier. Detach the lower control arm.

Refitting

13 Refitting any of the link arms is essentially a reversal of removal, noting the following points:
a) *Always renew the trailing arms mounting bolts.*
b) *Tighten all fasteners to their specified torque where given.*
c) *Before tightening any links arm mounting bolts, ensure the suspension is in the 'normal' position as described in paragraph 2 of this Section.*

11.3 Remove the brake pipe support bracket (arrowed)

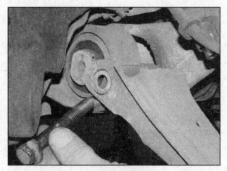

11.4a Remove the trailing arm front bolt . . .

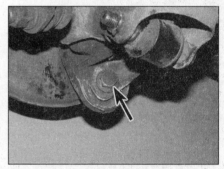

11.4b . . . and rear bolt (arrowed)

11.6 To aid refitting, make alignment marks between the eccentric washer and the tie-rod

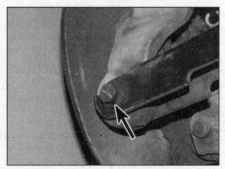

11.7 Tie-rod outer bolt (arrowed)

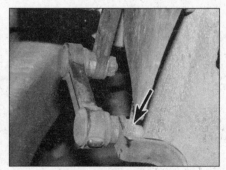

11.10 Undo the nut (arrowed) and disconnect the ride height sensor link arm

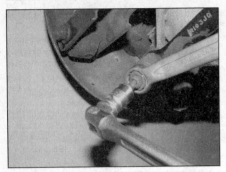

12.6 Use a Torx bit in the end of the balljoint shank to counterhold the nut

12.7 Undo the rear anti-roll bar clamps (right-hand clamp arrowed)

12 Rear anti-roll bar – removal and refitting

Removal

1 Chock the front wheels, then jack up the rear of the vehicle and support it on axle stands (see *Jacking and vehicle support*).

2 Remove the exhaust system as described in Chapter 4A or 4B.

3 Unclip the handbrake cables from the clips on the subframe and tie-rod.

4 Position a jack under the outer end of the left-hand lower control arm, and raise the jack sufficiently to take the load off the shock absorber.

5 Undo the right-hand shock absorber lower mounting bolt (see illustration 9.6a), and push the unit up into the coil spring.

6 Undo the nuts securing the outer ends of the anti-roll bar, using a Torx bit to counterhold the nuts (see illustration). Take care not to damage the rubber boots.

7 Undo the screws securing the anti-roll bar clamps to the subframe, manoeuvre the anti-roll bar to the right-hand side, past the disconnected shock absorber and withdraw it from the vehicle (see illustration).

Refitting

8 Insert the anti-roll bar from the right-hand side, manoeuvring the left-hand of the bar past the disconnected shock absorber. Ensure the handbrake cable lies above the anti-roll bar.

13.10a Rear subframe front mounting (left-hand side shown) . . .

Fit and tighten the bolts securing the anti-roll bar clamps to the subframe.

9 Use the jack to position the lower control arm so the bolts securing the outer ends of the anti-roll bar, and the lower end of the shock absorber can be refitted and tightened to the specified torque.

10 The remainder of refitting is a reversal of removal.

13 Rear subframe assembly – removal and refitting

Removal

1 Remove both rear brake discs as described in Chapter 9.

2 Undo the retaining bolt and withdraw the ABS wheel speed sensor from the rear of hub carrier, and release the sensor wiring from the various clips, then position the sensor to one side. Do not disconnect the wheel sensor connector.

3 Remove both handbrake cables as described in Chapter 9.

4 Remove the exhaust system as described in Chapter 4A or 4B.

5 Remove the rear coil springs as described in Section 10.

6 On petrol models, undo the screw securing the carbon canister to the subframe.

7 Undo the bolt securing the brake pipe support bracket to the subframe.

8 Undo the wheel arch liner plastic nut, and

13.10b . . . and rear mounting (right-hand shown)

drill out the rivet securing the heat shield at the subframe rear-left mounting.

9 Position two trolley jacks under the subframe, make alignment marks between the subframe mountings and the vehicle body to aid refitment.

10 Undo the bolts securing the subframe mountings and brackets to the vehicle body (see illustrations). Gradually lower the subframe, releasing the brake pipes from the retaining clips, and the fuel filter bracket (petrol models) as the subframe is lowered. When the assembly is clear of the underbody, withdraw it rearwards and out from under the car.

Refitting

11 Refitting is a reversal of removal bearing in mind the following points:

a) Manoeuvre the subframe assembly into position using the jacks and secure with the four new mounting bolts each side, align the previously-made marks and tighten the bolts to the specified torque.

b) Adjust the handbrake as described in Chapter 9.

14 Suspension control module – general information, removal and refitting

General information

1 On models equipped with the Four-C (Continuously Controlled Chassis Concept) active suspension system, an electronic control module, known as the SUM (suspension module) is fitted, which correlates the information from the suspension sensors, calculates the desired damper setting, and signals the valves at each damper to operate accordingly – at up to 500 times a second.

Removal

2 Ensure the ignition is switched off, and move the passenger's seat to the rearmost position.

3 Rotate the clip anti-clockwise, remove the left-hand panel from the side of the centre console, and fold back the carpet a little (see illustration).

14.3 Slide the centre console side panel rearwards and remove it

4 Undo the SUM retaining screws, and disconnect the wiring plugs as it is withdrawn **(see illustration)**.

Refitting

5 Reconnect the wiring plugs, position the SUM and tighten the retaining screws securely.
6 Push the carpet back into place and secure the centre console side panel.
7 If a new SUM has been fitted, it must be programmed prior to use using software downloaded via Volvo test equipment. Entrust this task to a Volvo dealer or suitably-equipped specialist.

15 Steering wheel – removal and refitting

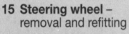

⚠ **Warning: Handle the airbag unit with extreme care as a precaution against personal injury, and always hold it with the cover facing away from the body. If in doubt concerning any proposed work involving the airbag unit or its control circuitry, consult a Volvo dealer.**

Removal

1 Drive the car forwards, and park it with the front wheels in the straight-ahead position.
2 Disconnect the battery negative lead (Chapter 5A), and wait for 10 minutes before proceeding.
3 Place a piece of masking tape on the top of the steering wheel hub, and another piece on the top of the steering column upper shroud. Draw a pencil line across both pieces of tape to act as an alignment mark to centralise the steering wheel when refitting.
4 Remove the airbag unit from the steering wheel as described in Chapter 12.
5 Ensure the steering wheel is in the 'straight-ahead' position, then remove the lower screw from its storage position and insert it into the hole to lock the rotary contact reel **(see illustrations)**.
6 Undo the steering wheel centre retaining bolt. Discard the bolt – a new one must be fitted.
7 Lift the steering wheel off the column shaft, and feed the wiring and plastic strip through the hole in the wheel.

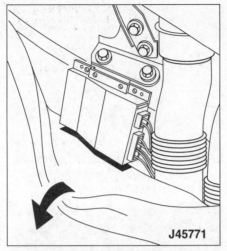

14.4 Pull back the carpet a little, undo the screws and remove the SUM

Refitting

8 Ensure that the front wheels are still in the straight-ahead position.
9 Feed the wiring through the hole in the steering wheel, then engage the wheel with the steering column shaft. Ensure that the marks made on removal are aligned, and that the pegs on the contact reel engage with the recesses on the steering wheel hub **(see illustration)**. Note that the upper shroud is attached to the instrument panel surround. Do not attempt to turn the steering wheel with the contact reel locked, otherwise the reel will be damaged.

15.5a Remove the airbag contact unit locking screw from the storage position (arrowed) . . .

15.9 Ensure the peg (arrowed) on the contact reel engages with the recess (arrowed) on the steering wheel

10 Fit the new steering wheel retaining bolt, and tighten it finger-tight only.
11 Referring to the information in Chapter 12, remove the airbag contact reel locking screw, and refit the screw and plastic strip to the location provided in the steering wheel.
12 Tighten the steering wheel retaining bolt to the specified torque.
13 Refit the airbag unit to the steering wheel as described in Chapter 12.

16 Steering column – removal and refitting

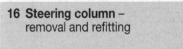

Removal

1 Disconnect the battery negative lead – see Chapter 5A.
2 Fully extend the steering column, then remove the steering wheel (see Section 15).
3 Undo the three screws from under the steering column lower shroud, and prise the upper and lower shrouds apart to release the retaining pegs. Remove the lower shroud, and lift the upper shroud out of the way **(see illustrations)**.
4 Remove the trim panel under the facia on the driver's side, which is secured by two screws, and is then pulled out of its locating slots at the top. Disconnect the wiring plug from the footwell light.
5 Disconnect the wiring plug, then depress the clip and pull the transponder unit from the end of the ignition switch **(see illustration)**.

15.5b . . . and insert it into the hole (arrowed) to lock the contact unit

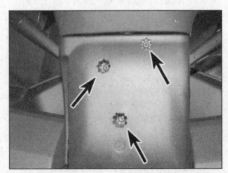

16.3a Undo the 3 Torx bolts (arrowed) securing the lower shroud . . .

16.3b . . . and lift the upper shroud from place

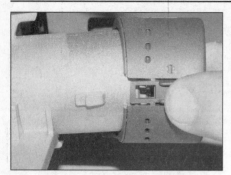

16.5 Depress the clip and pull the transponder from the ignition switch barrel

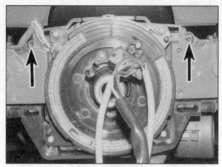

16.7 Steering wheel module retaining screws (arrowed)

16.9 Undo the intermediate shaft universal joint pinch-bolt (arrowed)

16.10 Pull the steering column rearwards . . .

16.11 . . . then turn it upside-down and manoeuvre it through the facia

16.12 Drill out the security screws (arrowed) and detach the steering lock from the column

6 On automatic transmission models, turn the ignition switch to position I, then press-in the catch and pull the interlock cable from the side of the switch.

7 Disconnect the two wiring plugs, undo the 2 screws, release the two clips on the underside and pull the steering wheel module from steering column (see illustration).

8 Detach the wiring loom guide from the underside of the column, and allow it to hang down.

9 Undo the pinch-bolt/nut at the universal joint on the intermediate steering column shaft, and pull the joint up from the lower shaft (see illustration). Discard the bolt and nut – new ones must be fitted.

10 Undo the four bolts securing the column to the facia, and pull the assembly rearwards (see illustration).

11 Rotate the column assembly to the upside

17.1 Remove the lower steering column pinch-bolt (arrowed)

down position and manoeuvre it from the vehicle (see illustration).

12 If required, drill out the security screws, and remove the steering lock from the column (see illustration). No further dismantling of the assembly is recommended.

Refitting

13 Refitting is a reversal of removal, bearing in mind the following points:

a) *Lubricate the intermediate shaft splines with grease before engaging the steering column.*

b) *When refitting the column retaining bolts, tighten the rearmost bolts first.*

c) *Use a new universal joint pinch-bolt.*

d) *If refitting the steering lock, tighten the new security screws until their heads snap off.*

e) *On automatic models, when refitting the interlock cable, ensure the selector lever is in position P and the ignition switch in position I. Insert the cable into the switch housing, checking its properly connected, then remove the ignition key and check the selector lever is locked in position.*

f) *On models equipped with DSTC (Dynamic stability and traction control) system, after refitting the column the system must be recalibrated. This can be achieved in the workshop if Volvo's dedicated test equipment is available. Alternatively, the car must be driven for at least 30 km (18.6 miles) on roads that are smooth (no potholes etc), and with low lateral acceleration (no high corner speeds or sharp turns).*

17 Steering shaft, gaiter and bearing – removal and refitting

Removal

1 Working in the engine compartment, using a ratchet, socket and several extension pieces, slacken and remove the pinch-bolt securing the lower shaft to the steering rack pinion (see illustration). Discard the bolt, a new one must be fitted.

2 Undo the screws and remove the trim panel over the driver's pedals.

3 Undo the pinch-bolt at the universal joint between the intermediate shaft and lower shaft (see illustration 16.9). Discard the pinch-bolt nut, a new one must be fitted. Push the intermediate shaft upwards into the upper column.

4 Fold back the floor carpet, fold up the top portion of the rubber boot at the base of the steering shaft.

5 Prise out the locking ring from the rubber boot lower portion, and remove the rubber boot and bearing assembly, followed by the shaft (see illustrations).

Refitting

6 Engage the universal joint with the steering rack pinion shaft, and push it fully home. The universal joint slot must be aligned with the groove on the pinion shaft.

7 Refit the new pinch-bolt and tighten it to the specified torque.

8 Lubricate the needle bearing in the rubber boot with grease, and the boot lower portion with soapy water (eg, washing-up liquid).

9 With the top portion of the boot folded up, fit the lower portion to the collar on the bulkhead ensuring a good seal.

10 Press the locking ring into position around the boot lower portion and the bulkhead.

11 Fold down the top portion of the boot so that it seals around the locking ring flange, and refit the carpet.

12 Refit the intermediate shaft universal joint to the lower shaft and tighten the new pinch-bolt nut to the specified torque.

13 Refit the trim panel over the driver's pedals.

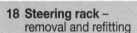

18 Steering rack – removal and refitting

Removal

1 Drive the car forwards and park it with the steering wheels in the straight-ahead position. Remove the ignition key to lock the steering in this position.

2 Ensure the ignition is turned off and remove the ignition key to engage the steering lock. On diesel models, pull the plastic cover over the engine straight up from its mountings.

3 Loosen the front wheel bolts. Chock the rear wheels then jack up the front of the vehicle and support it on axle stands (see *Jacking and vehicle support*). Remove both front roadwheels.

4 Unscrew the left-hand track rod end balljoint nut to the end of its threads. Separate the balljoint from the steering arm with a proprietary balljoint separator, then remove the nut and disengage the balljoint from the arm. Separate the right-hand track rod end from the steering arm in the same way.

5 Measure the length of the track rod on one side, relative to the steering rack housing, and make a note of the dimension measured.

6 Release the screws and remove the engine undershield.

7 Undo the bolts securing the exhaust pipe front crossmember to the vehicle body, then release the brake pipes from the retaining clips and remove the crossmember.

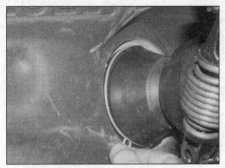

17.5a Release the locking clip . . .

8 From under the car, undo the steering rack fluid pipe retaining clip bolts at the front and rear of the subframe.

9 On right-hand-drive models, undo the two steering rack crash guard bolts at the rear of the front subframe, and remove the crash guard (**see illustration 6.4**).

10 On models with speed-sensitive power steering, trace the wiring back from the rack to the wiring plugs and disconnect them.

11 Wipe clean the area around the fluid pipe unions on the steering rack pinion housing. Place a suitable container under the steering rack, unscrew the union nuts and carefully pull the pipes clear (**see illustration**).

12 Undo the four nuts and one screw securing the steering rack to the subframe (**see illustrations**).

13 Position a sturdy trolley jack beneath, and in contact with, the rear of the subframe.

Caution: Make sure that the subframe is well-supported, and that the jack being used is capable of taking the combined weight of the engine/transmission and subframe.

14 Undo the two bolts each side securing the subframe rear mounting brackets to the body.

15 Undo the single bolt each side securing the rear mounting brackets to the subframe, and recover the washers. Note that new bolts will be required for refitting.

16 Slacken the two subframe front mounting bolts by no more than 10 to 15 mm, then carefully lower the jack and allow the subframe to drop approximately 90 mm at the rear. Ensure that the steering rack mounting bolts are clear of the subframe. Note that new

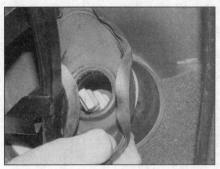

17.5b . . . and remove the boot and bearing assembly

subframe front mounting bolts will be required for refitting.

17 Undo the nut and remove the clamp bolt from the steering shaft universal joint. Push the universal joint upwards off the steering rack pinion shaft.

18 Undo the bolt securing the steering rack to the rear engine mounting.

19 Manipulate the steering rack out from the right-hand (RHD models) or left-hand (LHD models) side of the car.

20 If a new steering rack assembly is to be fitted, transfer the heat shield from the old rack.

Refitting

21 Set the length of the track rod to the previously-recorded dimension by turning the pinion shaft as necessary.

22 Manipulate the steering rack into position on the subframe.

23 Support the steering rack on the rear engine mounting, position it so that it is straight relative to the subframe, and tighten the engine mounting bolt to the specified torque.

24 Engage the steering shaft universal joint with the pinion shaft, and push it fully home. The universal joint slot must be aligned with the groove below the pinion shaft splines.

25 Fit the new universal joint pinch-bolt and tighten it to the specified torque.

26 Raise the subframe at the rear, and engage the steering rack bolts.

27 Refit the rear mounting brackets to the body, and tighten the bolts hand-tight only at this stage.

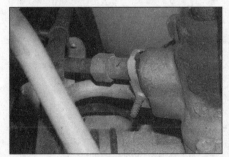

18.11 Undo the union nuts and disconnect the pipes from the steering rack pinion housing

18.12a Steering rack mounting nuts on the right-hand side (arrowed) . . .

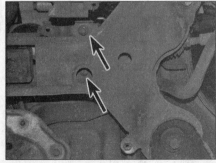

18.12b . . . and the left-hand side (arrowed)

19.3a Steering rack boot inner gaiter clip (arrowed) . . .

19.3b . . . and outer clip

28 Secure the rear mounting brackets to the subframe, using the washers and new bolts also tightened hand-tight only.

29 Move the jack to the front of the subframe, and raise it to just take the subframe weight. Unscrew the subframe front mounting bolts, fit two new bolts and tighten them hand-tight only.

30 Tighten the two subframe mounting bolts on the left-hand side of the car to the specified torque. Now tighten the two mounting bolts on the right-hand side. Finally tighten the four mounting bracket-to-body bolts to the specified torque.

31 Secure the steering rack using new nuts/bolt tightened to the specified torque.

32 Reconnect the oil pipes to the steering rack using new O-ring seals. Tighten the unions to the specified torque.

33 On right-hand-drive models, refit the steering rack guard.

34 Refit the exhaust pipe front crossmember, clip the brake pipes in position, then securely tighten the retaining bolts.

35 Refit the track rod ends to the hub carriers, and secure with new nuts tightened to the specified torque.

36 On models with speed-sensitive power steering, reconnect the wiring plugs.

37 On diesel models, refit the plastic cover over the engine.

38 Refit the engine undershield.

39 Refit the roadwheels then bleed the steering rack as described in Section 20.

40 With the car lowered, tighten the wheel bolts in a diagonal sequence to the specified torque.

21.4 Remove the pipe union lock bracket (arrowed)

41 Have the front wheel toe-in checked and adjusted by a Volvo dealer or suitably-equipped repairer.

19 Steering rack gaiters – renewal

1 Count and record the number of exposed threads on the track rod, from the end of the rod to the track rod end locknut.

2 Remove the track rod end on the side concerned as described in Section 22. Unscrew the locknut from the track rod.

3 Release the two clips and peel off the gaiter **(see illustrations)**.

4 Clean out any dirt and grit from the inner end of the track rod and (when accessible) the rack.

5 Wrap insulating tape around the track rod threads to protect the new gaiter whilst installing.

6 Refit the track rod end locknut, and position it so that the same number of threads counted on removal are visible.

7 Refit the track rod end as described in Section 22.

20 Steering rack – bleeding

1 The power steering fluid reservoir is located on the right-hand side of the engine compartment, just in front of the coolant

21.7 Working through the pulley holes, undo the pump mounting bolts

expansion tank. Wipe clean the area around the reservoir filler neck, and unscrew the filler cap/dipstick from the reservoir.

2 The fluid level in the reservoir is checked by means of a dipstick in the filler cap. The dipstick has two sides so that the fluid level can be checked with the engine cold, or hot after the car has been driven. Fluid level should not exceed the COLD or HOT mark as applicable, nor drop below the ADD mark.

3 If topping-up is necessary, use clean fluid of the specified type (see *Weekly checks*). Check for leaks if frequent topping-up is required. Do not run the engine without fluid in the reservoir.

4 After component renewal, or if the fluid level has been allowed to fall so low that air has entered the hydraulic system, bleeding must be carried out as follows.

5 Fill the reservoir to the correct level as described above.

6 Chock the rear wheels, then jack up the front of the vehicle and support it on axle stands (see *Jacking and vehicle support*).

7 Turn the steering wheel repeatedly from full lock one way, to full lock the other way, and top-up the fluid level as necessary.

8 Lower the car to the ground then start the engine and allow it to idle.

9 Turn the steering wheel slowly to the full right lock position, and hold it there for 2 seconds.

10 Now turn the steering wheel slowly to the full left lock position, and hold it there for 2 seconds.

11 Top-up the fluid level again if necessary.

12 Repeat paragraphs 9 and 10 ten times. Repeatedly check and if necessary top-up the fluid level during this operation.

13 On completion, stop the engine, recheck the fluid level then refit the reservoir filler cap.

21 Steering pump – removal and refitting

Removal

1 Remove the auxiliary drivebelt as described in Chapter 1A or 1B.

2 Release the fluid supply hose from the clip above the pump pulley.

3 Clamp the fluid supply hose as close as possible to the pump to reduce fluid loss.

4 Undo the pressure pipe union lock bracket bolt a few turns and remove the bracket (where fitted) **(see illustration)**.

5 Place absorbent rags below the pump. Unscrew the pressure pipe union, and recover the O-ring.

6 Separate the fluid supply hose from the pipe stub on the pump – do not use excessive force, or the hose may be damaged.

7 Working through the access holes in the pulley, undo the three pump mounting bolts **(see illustration)**.

21.8 On diesel models, remove the support bracket (arrowed) from the rear of the pump

22.2 Slacken the track rod end locknut (arrowed)

22.3 Hold the track rod end balljoint with a second spanner whilst slackening the retaining nut

8 On diesel models, remove the bracket at the rear of the pump **(see illustration).**

9 If it is suspected that the power steering fluid is contaminated, raise and support the front of the car so that the wheels are just clear of the ground.

10 Position a suitable container beneath the front of the car, and collect the fluid from the hoses as the steering is turned from lock-to-lock.

11 If a new pump is to be fitted, have the pulley and (where applicable) the reservoir transferred to it by a dealer or suitably-equipped repairer, as special tools are required.

Refitting

12 Refitting is a reversal of removal, bearing in mind the following points:

a) Use a new O-ring on pressure pipe union.
b) Tighten the mounting bolts to the specified torque.
c) Refit the auxiliary drivebelt as described in Chapter 1A or 1B.
d) Ensure the pressure pipe union locking bracket fits around the hexagon section of the union.
e) Refill/top-up the fluid reservoir, and bleed the system as described in Section 20.

22 Track rod end – removal and refitting

Removal

1 Loosen the appropriate front wheel bolts. Chock the rear wheels, then jack up the front of the vehicle and support it on axle stands (see *Jacking and vehicle support*). Remove the appropriate front roadwheel.

2 Counterhold the track rod, and slacken the track rod end locknut by half a turn **(see illustration).** If the locknut is now left in this position, it will act as a further guide for refitting.

3 Unscrew the track rod end balljoint nut. Separate the balljoint from the steering arm with a proprietary balljoint separator, then remove the nut and disengage the balljoint from the arm **(see illustration).**

4 Unscrew the track rod end from the track rod, counting the number of turns needed to remove it. Make a note of the number of turns, so that the tracking can be reset (or at least approximated) on refitting.

Refitting

5 Screw the track rod end onto the track rod by the same number of turns noted during removal.

6 Engage the balljoint in the steering arm. Fit a new nut and tighten it to the specified torque.

7 Counterhold the track rod and tighten the locknut.

8 Refit the front wheel, lower the car and tighten the wheel bolts in a diagonal sequence to the specified torque.

9 Have the front wheel toe-in (tracking) checked and adjusted by a Volvo dealer or suitably-equipped repairer.

23 Steering rack solenoid – renewal

Renewal

1 On models with speed-sensitive power steering, an electrical solenoid is fitted to the

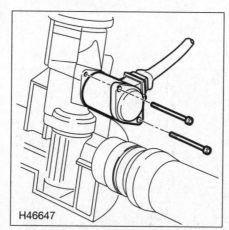

H46647

23.3 Steering rack solenoid mounting screws

steering rack. To remove the solenoid, remove the rack as described in Section 18.

2 Clean the area around the solenoid.

3 Undo the 2 screws securing the solenoid and withdrawn it from the rack **(see illustration).** Be prepared for fluid spillage.

4 Remove the filter in the mounting hole in the steering rack, and press a new one into place (a new filter is normally supplied with a new solenoid).

5 Lubricate the new O-rings with clean power steering fluid, then install the new solenoid and tighten the retaining screws securely.

6 Refit the steering rack as described in Section 20.

24 Wheel alignment and steering angles – general information

1 A car's steering and suspension geometry is defined in four basic settings – all angles are expressed in degrees (toe settings are also expressed as a measurement); the relevant settings are camber, castor, steering axis inclination, and toe setting **(see illustration).** On the models covered by this manual, only the front camber and the front and rear wheel toe settings are adjustable.

2 Camber is the angle at which the front wheels are set from the vertical when viewed from the front or rear of the car. Negative camber is the amount (in degrees) that the wheels are tilted inward at the top from the vertical.

3 The front camber angle is adjusted by slackening the steering knuckle-to-suspension strut mounting bolts and repositioning the hub carrier assemblies as necessary.

4 Castor is the angle between the steering axis and a vertical line when viewed from each side of the car. Positive castor is when the steering axis is inclined rearward at the top.

5 Steering axis inclination is the angle (when viewed from the front of the vehicle) between the vertical and an imaginary line drawn through the front suspension strut upper mounting and the control arm balljoint.

6 Toe setting is the amount by which the distance between the front inside edges of the roadwheels (measured at hub height) differs

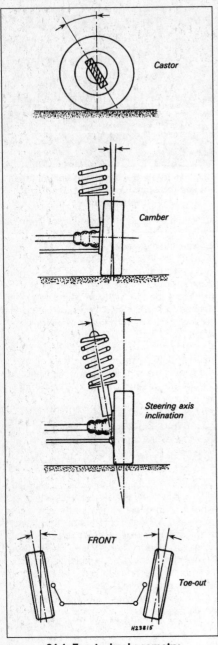

25.2 Undo the nut (arrowed) and disconnect the sensor link arm from the bracket on the control arm

25.3 Release the clip and remove the sensor

from the diametrically opposite distance measured between the rear inside edges of the roadwheels. Toe-in is when the roadwheels point inwards, towards each other at the front, while toe-out is when they splay outwards from each other at the front.

7 The front wheel toe setting is adjusted by altering the length of the steering track rods on both sides. This adjustment is normally referred to as the tracking.

8 The rear wheel toe setting is adjusted by altering the position of the rear suspension transverse arm-to-trailing arm mountings.

9 With the exception of the front and rear toe settings, and the front camber angles, all other suspension and steering angles are set during manufacture, and no adjustment is possible. It can be assumed, therefore, that unless the vehicle has suffered accident damage, all the preset angles will be correct.

10 Special optical measuring equipment is necessary to accurately check and adjust the front and rear toe settings and front camber angles, and this work should be carried out by a Volvo dealer or similar expert. Most tyre-fitting centres have the expertise and equipment to carry out at least a front wheel toe setting (tracking) check for a nominal charge.

25 Suspension ride height sensor – removal and refitting

1 Jack up the rear of the vehicle and support it securely on axle stands (see *Jacking and vehicle support*).

2 Undo the nut and disconnect the link arm from the bracket on the lower control arm **(see illustration)**.

3 Disconnect the sensor wiring plug, then release the clip and remove the sensor **(see illustration)**.

4 Refitting is a reversal of removal.

24.1 Front wheel geometry

Chapter 11
Bodywork and fittings

Contents

Degrees of difficulty

Easy, suitable for novice with little experience	Fairly easy, suitable for beginner with some experience	Fairly difficult, suitable for competent DIY mechanic	Difficult, suitable for experienced DIY mechanic	Very difficult, suitable for expert DIY or professional

Specifications

Torque wrench settings	Nm	lbf ft
Facia crossmember:		
To A-post	48	35
To centre console brackets	25	18
Front seat belt anchorage to seat	48	35
Front seat belt tensioner/inertia reels.	48	35
Rear seat belt inertia reel nut	48	35
Rear seat belt lower anchorages	48	35

1 General information

The bodyshell is made of pressed-steel sections, and is available only as a four-door Saloon. Most components are welded together, but some use is made of structural adhesives. The doors and door pillars are reinforced against side impacts as part of the side impact protection system (SIPS).

A number of structural components and body panels are made of galvanised steel to provide a high level of protection against corrosion. Extensive use is also made of plastic materials, mainly in the interior, but also in exterior components. The front and rear bumpers are moulded from a synthetic material that is very strong and yet light. Plastic components such as wheel arch liners are fitted to the underside of the vehicle to further improve corrosion resistance.

2 Maintenance – bodywork and underframe

The general condition of a vehicle's bodywork is the one thing that significantly affects its value. Maintenance is easy but needs to be regular. Neglect, particularly after minor damage, can lead quickly to further deterioration and costly repair bills. It is important also to keep watch on those parts of the vehicle not immediately visible, for instance the underside, inside all the wheel arches and the lower part of the engine compartment.

The basic maintenance routine for the bodywork is washing preferably with a lot of water, from a hose. This will remove all the loose solids which may have stuck to the vehicle. It is important to flush these off in such a way as to prevent grit from scratching the finish. The wheel arches and underframe need washing in the same way to remove any accumulated mud which will retain moisture and tend to encourage rust. Oddly enough, the best time to clean the underframe and wheel arches is in wet weather when the mud is thoroughly wet and soft. In very wet weather the underframe is usually cleaned of large accumulations automatically and this is a good time for inspection.

Periodically, except on vehicles with a wax-based underbody protective coating, it is a good idea to have the whole of the underframe of the vehicle steam-cleaned, engine compartment included, so that a thorough inspection can be carried out to see what minor repairs and renovations are necessary. Steam-cleaning is available at many garages, and is necessary for removal of the accumulation of oily grime which sometimes is allowed to become thick in certain areas. If steam-cleaning facilities are not available, there are one or two excellent grease solvents available which can be brush applied; the dirt

can then be simply hosed off. Note that these methods should not be used on vehicles with wax-based underbody protective coating, or the coating will be removed. Such vehicles should be inspected annually, preferably just prior to winter, when the underbody should be washed down and any damage to the wax coating repaired using underseal. Ideally, a completely fresh coat should be applied. It would also be worth considering the use of such wax-based protection for injection into door panels, sills, box sections, etc, as an additional safeguard against rust damage where such protection is not provided by the vehicle manufacturer.

After washing paintwork, wipe off with a chamois leather to give an unspotted clear finish. A coat of clear protective wax polish will give added protection against chemical pollutants in the air. If the paintwork sheen has dulled or oxidised, use a cleaner/polisher combination to restore the brilliance of the shine. This requires a little effort, but such dulling is usually caused because regular washing has been neglected. Care needs to be taken with metallic paintwork, as special non-abrasive cleaner/polisher is required to avoid damage to the finish.

Always check that the door and ventilator opening drain holes and pipes are completely clear, so that water can be drained out. Brightwork should be treated in the same way as paintwork. Windscreens and windows can be kept clear of the smeary film which often appears by the use of a proprietary glass cleaner. Never use any form of wax or other body or chromium polish on glass, especially not on the windscreen or tailgate.

3 Maintenance – upholstery and carpets

Mats and carpets should be brushed or vacuum cleaned regularly to keep them free of grit. If they are badly stained, remove them from the vehicle for scrubbing or sponging, and make quite sure they are dry before refitting. Seats and interior trim panels can be kept clean by wiping with a damp cloth and a proprietary upholstery cleaner. If they do become stained (which can be more apparent on light-coloured upholstery) use a little liquid detergent and a soft nail brush to scour the grime out of the grain of the material. Do not forget to keep the headlining clean in the same way as the upholstery. When using liquid cleaners inside the vehicle, do not over-wet the surfaces being cleaned. Excessive damp could get into the seams and padded interior causing stains, offensive odours or even rot.

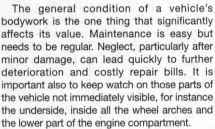 **HAYNES HINT** *If the inside of the vehicle gets wet accidentally, it is worthwhile taking some trouble to dry it out properly, particularly where carpets are involved. Do not leave oil or electric heaters inside the vehicle for this purpose.*

4 Minor body damage – repair

Minor scratches

If the scratch is very superficial, and does not penetrate to the metal of the bodywork, repair is very simple. Lightly rub the area of the scratch with a paintwork renovator, or a very fine cutting paste, to remove loose paint from the scratch, and to clear the surrounding bodywork of wax polish. Rinse the area with clean water.

In the case of metallic paint, the most commonly-found 'scratches' are not in the paint, but in the lacquer top coat, and appear white. If care is taken , these can sometimes be rendered less obvious by very careful use of paintwork renovator (which would otherwise not be used on metallic paintwork); otherwise, repair of these scratches can be achieved by applying lacquer with a fine brush.

Apply touch-up paint to the scratch using a fine paint brush; continue to apply fine layers of paint until the surface of the paint in the scratch is level with the surrounding paintwork. Allow the new paint at least two weeks to harden: then blend it into the surrounding paintwork by rubbing the scratch area with a paintwork renovator or a very fine cutting paste. Finally, apply wax polish.

Where the scratch has penetrated right through to the metal of the bodywork, causing the metal to rust, a different repair technique is required. Remove any loose rust from the bottom of the scratch with a penknife, then apply rust-inhibiting paint, to prevent the formation of rust in the future. Using a rubber or nylon applicator fill the scratch with bodystopper paste. If required, this paste can be mixed with cellulose thinners, to provide a very thin paste which is ideal for filling narrow scratches. Before the stopper-paste in the scratch hardens, wrap a piece of smooth cotton rag around the top of a finger. Dip the finger in cellulose thinners, and then quickly sweep it across the surface of the stopper-paste in the scratch; this will ensure that the surface of the stopper-paste is slightly hollowed. The scratch can now be painted over as described earlier in this Section.

Dents

When deep denting of the vehicle's bodywork has taken place, the first task is to pull the dent out, until the affected bodywork almost attains its original shape. There is little point in trying to restore the original shape completely, as the metal in the damaged area will have stretched on impact, and cannot be reshaped fully to its original contour. It is better to bring the level of the dent up to a point which is about 3 mm below the level of the surrounding bodywork. In cases where the dent is very shallow anyway, it is not worth trying to pull it out at all. If the underside of the dent is accessible, it can be hammered out gently from behind, using a mallet with a wooden or plastic head. Whilst doing this, hold a suitable block of wood firmly against the outside of the panel to absorb the impact from the hammer blows and thus prevent a large area of the bodywork from being 'belled-out'.

Should the dent be in a section of the bodywork which has a double skin or some other factor making it inaccessible from behind, a different technique is called for. Drill several small holes through the metal inside the area – particularly in the deeper section. Then screw long self-tapping screws into the holes just sufficiently for them to gain a good purchase in the metal. Now the dent can be pulled out by pulling on the protruding heads of the screws with a pair of pliers.

The next stage of the repair is the removal of the paint from the damaged area, and from an inch or so of the surrounding 'sound' bodywork. This is accomplished most easily by using a wire brush or abrasive pad on a power drill, although it can be done just as effectively by hand using sheets of abrasive paper. To complete the preparation for filling, score the surface of the bare metal with a screwdriver or the tang of a file, or alternatively, drill small holes in the affected area. This will provide a really good 'key' for the filler paste.

To complete the repair, see the Section on filling and re-spraying.

Rust holes or gashes

Remove all paint from the affected area, and from an inch or so of the surrounding 'sound' bodywork, using an abrasive pad or a wire brush on a power drill. If these are not available, a few sheets of abrasive paper will do the job just as effectively. With the paint removed, you will be able to gauge the severity of the corrosion, and therefore decide whether to renew the whole panel (if this is possible) or to repair the affected area. New body panels are not as expensive as most people think, and it is often quicker and more satisfactory to fit a new panel than to attempt to repair large areas of corrosion.

Remove all fittings from the affected area, except those which will act as a guide to the original shape of the damaged bodywork. Then, using tin snips or a hacksaw blade, remove all loose metal and any other metal badly affected by corrosion. Hammer the edges of the hole inwards in order to create a slight depression for the filler paste.

Wire-brush the affected area to remove the powdery rust from the surface of the remaining metal. Paint the affected area with rust-inhibiting paint; if the back of the rusted area is accessible treat this also.

Before filling can take place, it will be necessary to block the hole in some way. This can be achieved by the use of aluminium or plastic mesh, or aluminium tape.

Aluminium or plastic mesh or glass fibre matting is probably the best material to use for a large hole. Cut a piece to the approximate size and shape of the hole to be filled, then position it in the hole so that its edges are below the level of the surrounding bodywork. It can be retained in position by several blobs of filler paste around its periphery.

Aluminium tape should be used for small or very narrow holes. Pull a piece off the roll and trim it to the approximate size and shape required, then pull off the backing paper (if used) and stick the tape over the hole; it can be overlapped if the thickness of one piece is insufficient. Burnish down the edges of the tape with the handle of a screwdriver or similar, to ensure that the tape is securely attached to the metal underneath.

Filling and re-spraying

Before using this Section, see the Sections on dent, deep scratch, rust holes and gash repairs.

Many types of bodyfiller are available, but generally speaking those proprietary kits which contain a tin of filler paste and a tube of resin hardener are best for this type of repair; some can be used directly from the tube. A wide, flexible plastic or nylon applicator will be found invaluable for imparting a smooth and well contoured finish to the surface of the filler.

Mix up a little filler on a clean piece of card or board – measure the hardener carefully (follow the maker's instructions on the pack) otherwise the filler will set too rapidly or too slowly. Using the applicator, apply the filler paste to the prepared area; draw the applicator across the surface of the filler to achieve the correct contour and to level the filler surface. As soon as a contour that approximates to the correct one is achieved, stop working the paste – if you carry on too long the paste will become sticky and begin to 'pick up' on the applicator. Continue to add thin layers of filler paste at twenty-minute intervals until the level of the filler is just proud of the surrounding bodywork.

Once the filler has hardened, excess can be removed using a metal plane or file. From then on, progressively finer grades of abrasive paper should be used, starting with a 40-grade production paper and finishing with 400-grade wet-and-dry paper. Always wrap the abrasive paper around a flat rubber, cork, or wooden block – otherwise the surface of the filler will not be completely flat. During the smoothing of the filler surface the wet-and-dry paper should be periodically rinsed in water. This will ensure that a very smooth finish is imparted to the filler at the final stage.

At this stage the 'dent' should be surrounded by a ring of bare metal, which in turn should be encircled by the finely 'feathered' edge of the good paintwork. Rinse the repair area with clean water, until all of the dust produced by the rubbing-down operation has gone.

Spray the whole repair area with a light coat of primer – this will show up any imperfections in the surface of the filler. Repair these imperfections with fresh filler paste or bodystopper, and once more smooth the surface with abrasive paper. If bodystopper is used, it can be mixed with cellulose thinners to form a really thin paste which is ideal for filling small holes. Repeat this spray and repair procedure until you are satisfied that the surface of the filler, and the feathered edge of the paintwork are perfect. Clean the repair area with clean water and allow to dry fully.

The repair area is now ready for final spraying. Paint spraying must be carried out in a warm, dry, windless and dust free atmosphere. This condition can be created artificially if you have access to a large indoor working area, but if you are forced to work in the open, you will have to pick your day very carefully. If you are working indoors, dousing the floor in the work area with water will help to settle the dust which would otherwise be in the atmosphere. If the repair area is confined to one body panel, mask off the surrounding panels; this will help to minimise the effects of a slight mis-match in paint colours. Bodywork fittings (eg chrome strips, door handles etc) will also need to be masked off. Use genuine masking tape and several thicknesses of newspaper for the masking operations.

Before commencing to spray, agitate the aerosol can thoroughly, then spray a test area (an old tin, or similar) until the technique is mastered. Cover the repair area with a thick coat of primer; the thickness should be built up using several thin layers of paint rather than one thick one. Using 400 grade wet-and-dry paper, rub down the surface of the primer until it is really smooth. While doing this, the work area should be thoroughly doused with water, and the wet-and-dry paper periodically rinsed in water. Allow to dry before spraying on more paint.

Spray on the top coat, again building up the thickness by using several thin layers of paint. Start spraying in the centre of the repair area and then, with a single side-to-side motion, work outwards until the whole repair area and about 50 mm of the surrounding original paintwork is covered. Remove all masking material 10 to 15 minutes after spraying on the final coat of paint.

Allow the new paint at least two weeks to harden, then, using a paintwork renovator or a very fine cutting paste, blend the edges of the paint into the existing paintwork. Finally, apply wax polish.

Plastic components

With the use of more and more plastic body components by the vehicle manufacturers (eg bumpers, spoilers, and in some cases major body panels), rectification of more serious damage to such items has become a matter of either entrusting repair work to a specialist in this field, or renewing complete components. Repair of such damage by the DIY owner is not really feasible owing to the cost of the equipment and materials required for effecting such repairs. The basic technique involves making a groove along the line of the crack in the plastic using a rotary burr in a

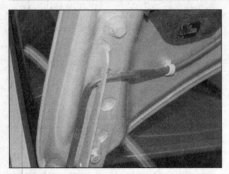

6.4 Make alignment marks between the hinge and bonnet, then undo the bolts

power drill. The damaged part is then welded back together by using a hot-air gun to heat up and fuse a plastic filler rod into the groove. Any excess plastic is then removed and the area rubbed down to a smooth finish. It is important that a filler rod of the correct plastic is used, as body components can be made of a variety of different types (eg polycarbonate, ABS, polypropylene).

Damage of a less serious nature (abrasions, minor cracks etc) can be repaired by the DIY owner using a two-part epoxy filler repair material. Once mixed in equal proportions, this is used in similar fashion to the bodywork filler used on metal panels. The filler is usually cured in twenty to thirty minutes, ready for sanding and painting.

If the owner is renewing a complete component himself, or if he has repaired it with epoxy filler, he will be left with the problem of finding a suitable paint for finishing which is compatible with the type of plastic used. At one time the use of a universal paint was not possible owing to the complex range of plastics encountered in body component applications. Standard paints, generally speaking, will not bond to plastic or rubber satisfactorily. However, it is now possible to obtain a plastic body parts finishing kit which consists of a pre-primer treatment, a primer and coloured top coat. Full instructions are normally supplied with a kit, but basically the method of use is to first apply the pre-primer to the component concerned and allow it to dry for up to 30 minutes. Then the primer is applied and left to dry for about an hour before finally applying the special coloured top coat.

The result is a correctly-coloured component where the paint will flex with the plastic or rubber, a property that standard paint does not normally possess.

5 Major body damage – repair

Where serious damage has occurred or large areas need renewal due to neglect, completely new sections or panels will need welding in – this is best left to professionals. If the damage is due to impact, it will also be necessary to check completely the alignment of the body shell structure. Due to the principle of construction, the strength and shape of the whole can be affected by damage to a part. In such instances, the services of a Volvo agent with specialist checking jigs are essential. If a body is left misaligned, it is first of all dangerous as the car will not handle properly and secondly uneven stresses will be imposed on the steering, engine and transmission, causing abnormal wear or complete failure. Tyre wear may also be excessive.

6 Bonnet – removal, refitting and adjustment

Removal

1 Open the bonnet, prise out the two plastic caps and disconnect the tubes from the base of the washer jets. Pull the tubing back through the bonnet, release it from the retaining clip and lay it to one side.
2 Where applicable, disconnect the washer jets wiring plugs and pull the loom from the bonnet.
3 Mark around the hinge bracket on the underside of the bonnet with a felt tip pen for reference when refitting.
4 With the aid of an assistant, support the bonnet and remove the hinge bolts **(see illustration)**. Lift off the bonnet and store it in a safe place.

Refitting and adjustment

5 Before refitting, place pads of rags under

the corners of the bonnet near the hinges to protect the paintwork from damage.
6 Fit the bonnet and insert the hinge bolts. Just nip the bolts up in their previously-marked positions.
7 Reconnect the washer tube and wiring plugs.
8 Shut the bonnet and check its fit. If necessary slacken the bolts and reposition the bonnet.
9 Tighten the hinge bolts securely when adjustment is correct.

7 Bonnet release cable – removal, refitting and adjustment

Removal

1 Remove the front indicator lights and headlights as described in Chapter 12.
2 Undo the 12 bolts securing the bonnet slam panel to the vehicle body **(see illustration)**.
3 On LHD models, remove the air cleaner assembly as described in the relevant Part of Chapter 4.
4 Undo the two screws, and remove the trim panel above the driver's pedals.
5 Prise of the cover, undo the screw and detach the bonnet release handle from the footwell **(see illustration)**.
6 Disconnect the cable ends from the lock levers and release catch, release the cable-ties and remove the cable by pulling it forwards from the white sleeving **(see illustration)**.

Refitting

7 Refit by reversing the removal operations. Insert the new cable into the white sleeving, into the passenger's compartment.

8 Bonnet lock – removal and refitting

Removal

1 Remove the front headlights as described in Chapter 12.
2 Undo the 12 bolts securing the bonnet slam panel to the vehicle body **(see illustration 7.2)**.

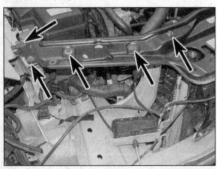

7.2 Five of the bonnet slam panel bolts (arrowed)

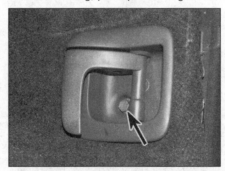

7.5 Undo the bolt (arrowed) and detach the handle assembly from the footwell

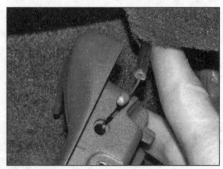

7.6 Detach the end of the release cable from the lever

3 Undo the two catch retaining screws and detach the cable end **(see illustration)**.

Refitting

4 Refitting is a reversal of removal. Only finger-tighten the catch retaining screws, then shut the bonnet to centralise the catch. Tighten the retaining screws securely.

9 Doors –
removal, refitting and adjustment

Removal

1 Disconnect the battery negative lead (see Chapter 5A).
2 Open the door and support it with a jack or axle stand, using rags to protect the paintwork.
3 Disconnect the front door electrical wiring. Pull back the rubber boot, then use a small screwdriver to release the clip at the top and unplug the connector **(see illustration)**. If removing a rear door, release the convoluted sleeve from the door pillar, pull the connector from the pillar, depress the clip and separate the two halves of the connector **(see illustration)**.
4 Release the door check strap by undoing the bolt securing it to the pillar bracket.
5 Undo the bolt securing the hinge brackets **(see illustration)**.
6 With the help of an assistant, lift the door upwards to disengage the hinge pins, then remove the door.

Refitting and adjustment

7 Refit the door by reversing the removal operations then adjust as follows.
8 Close the door and check the alignment with the surrounding body panels. The gap should be equal all round, and the door must be flush with the outside of the car. The rear edge of the front door should be 0 to 1.5 mm outside the front edge of the rear door.
9 Fore-and-aft adjustment of the door at the top and bottom is by shims inserted between the hinges and the door. Shims are available in thicknesses of 0.3 and 0.5 mm, and can be slid into place after slackening the hinge retaining bolts.

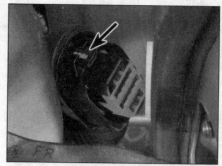

8.3 The bonnet catch bolts (arrowed) are accessed from the front of the bonnet slam panel

9.3b Depress the clip and disconnect the two halves of the rear door connector

10 Vertical and lateral adjustment is made by slackening the hinge retaining bolts slightly and moving the door as necessary.
11 Once the correct door fit is obtained, adjust the striker plate so that the door opens and closes easily but firmly. With the door handle pulled out, shut the door and check that the lock slides over the striker plate without scraping.

10 Door interior trim panel –
removal and refitting

Removal

1 Ensure the ignition is switched off, and remove the key from the lock. This is to ensure the ignition is not accidentally switched on, and the airbag systems energised. Wait at

9.3a Lift the clip (arrowed) to unplug the front door connector

9.5 Undo the bolt (arrowed) and lift the door from the hinge

least one minute for any stored electrical energy to dissipate before commencing work.

Front doors

2 Carefully prise the mirror triangular trim panel from the door mirror mounting **(see illustration)**.
3 Use a flat-bladed tool to prise out the bottom edge of the door pull handle cover, pull it from the panel, then undo the 2 Torx bolts exposed **(see illustrations)**.
4 The door trim panel is further secured by 8 plastic expansion rivets around the base and front/rear edges of the panel. Push in the centre pins, then prise out the complete rivet using a wide-bladed tool. On later models, prise the plastic inserts from the panel **(see illustrations)**.
5 Lift the panel upwards, then pull the panel away from the door sufficiently to gain access to the various wiring plugs/cables behind it.

10.2 Prise off the mirror trim panel

10.3a Carefully pull the handle cover from place – early models . . .

10.3b . . . and later models . . .

10.3c ... and undo the 2 Torx bolts (arrowed)

10.4a Push in the centre pins and prise out the plastic rivets

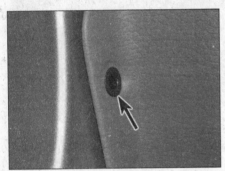

10.4b On later models, prise out the plastic inserts (arrowed) from the panel

10.6 Prise apart the upper and lower clip (arrowed) and pull the cable end fitting from the handle

Noting their locations, disconnect the wiring from the window, door mirror and door locking switches.

6 Release the clips and disconnect the cable end from the interior handle (where applicable) **(see illustration)**.

Rear doors

7 Prise out the cap and undo the screw in the pull-handle recess **(see illustrations)**.

8 Push in the centre pins and prise out the plastic expansion rivets at the outer edges of the panel **(see illustration 10.4a and 10.4b)**.

9 Lift the panel from the door frame, spread the two retaining clips and disconnect the interior handle operating cable **(see illustration)**. Disconnect the wiring plugs as the panel is withdrawn.

Refitting

10 Refitting is a reversal of removal. Obtain and fit new fasteners for the base/edges of the panel if any were broken during removal. Check the operation of all switches before finally fitting the trim panel into place.

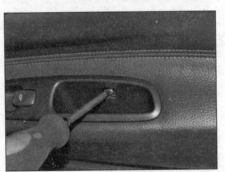

10.7a Prise out the plastic cap ...

10.7b ... and undo the screw in the recess

| 11 Door handle and lock components – removal and refitting | |

Outer handle

Removal – non-deadlocking models

1 Remove the door inner trim panel as described in Section 10, then carefully pull away the door sealing panel. Use a sharp knife or scalpel to cut through the sealant **(see illustrations)**. **Note:** *Where removal of the sealing panel is prevented by a riveted bracket, drill out one of the rivets, and lift the panel over the bracket.*

2 Press the link rod between the exterior handle and the lock unit forwards to disconnect it from the lock unit **(see illustration)**.

3 Undo the two retaining nuts, then twist the retaining plate to remove it **(see illustration)**.

10.9 Spread apart the clips and pull the cable end fitting from the handle

11.1a Use a sharp knife to cut through the door sealing panel sealant

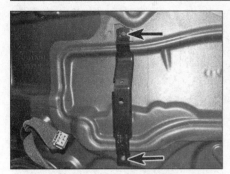

11.1b Drill out the rivets and remove the bracket (arrowed)

11.2 Reach up inside the door and pull the link rod (arrowed) forwards from the retaining clip

11.3 Peel away the tape and undo the two nuts (arrowed)

Peel away the tape (where fitted) to access the rearmost nut. Take care not to damage the vehicle paintwork.

4 From inside the door, lift up the 2 rubber clips at the lower edge of the handle surround, then manoeuvre the handle assembly from the door (see illustrations).

Removal – deadlocking models (applies to the driver's door only)

5 Remove the door window as described in Section 12.

6 Using a 3.5 mm drill bit, remove the lower rivet, and remove the window rear guide from the door (see illustrations). Note how the top of the guide engages with the lower section of the window frame guide (see illustration 11.15).

7 Undo the single screw, then note its fitted position and manoeuvre the lock cover from the door frame (see illustration).

8 Undo the two retaining nuts, then manoeuvre the retaining plate from place (see illustration).

9 Working inside the door, lift up the 2 clips at the lower edge of the handle rubber surround, pull the lower edge of the handle from the door, and manoeuvre it from place (see illustrations 11.4a and 11.4b). Take care not to damage the vehicle paintwork. Disconnect the lock cylinder operating rod from the lock motor.

Refitting

10 Refitting is a reversal of removal. When refitting the cylinder link rod back into the

11.4a Push up the clips (arrowed) . . .

spring clip on the lock lever, position the lever so that the hole in the lever aligns with the hole in the lock body, then press the rod into the clip (see illustration). Check for correct operation before refitting the door trim.

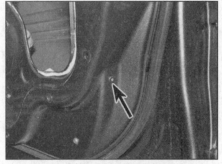

11.6a Drill out the rivet (arrowed) . . .

11.4b . . . and manoeuvre the handle from the door

Front door lock cylinder

Removal

11 Remove the outer handle as described previously.

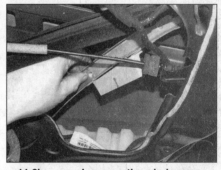

11.6b . . . and remove the window rear guide

11.7 Undo the lock cover retaining screw (arrowed)

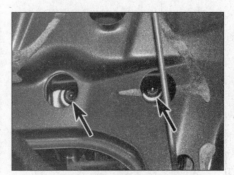

11.8 Undo the retaining plate nuts (arrowed)

11.10 Align the hole in the lock body with the hole in the lever (arrowed) then press the rod into the clip

11.12a Prise out the lock cylinder retaining clips . . .

11.12b . . . and pull the cylinder from the handle

11.15 Note how the top of the guide engages with the frame guide

12 Prise out the ends tabs of the cylinder retaining clip a little, and slide the cylinder from the handle assembly **(see illustrations)**.

Refitting

13 Refitting is a reversal of removal, noting the following points:

a) *Make sure the lock cylinder is inserted the correct way round.*

b) *Do not insert the key in the lock cylinder when it is being refitted, or the cylinder may be installed in the wrong position.*

c) *Check for correct operation before refitting the door trim.*

Front door lock assembly

Removal

14 Remove the window glass as described in Section 12.

15 Using a 3.5 mm drill bit, remove the lower

rivet, and lower the window rear guide from the door **(see illustration 11.6a and 11.6b)**. Note how the top of the guide engages with the lower section of the window frame guide **(see illustration)**.

16 On models with deadlocking, undo the screw and remove the cover over the lock assembly **(see illustration 11.7)**.

17 Using a screwdriver, disconnect the link rods to the lock from the exterior handle, lock button and lock cylinder (where applicable) **(see illustration)**.

18 Undo the three Torx bolts securing the lock to the end of the door, and manoeuvre the lock assembly from position, disconnecting the wiring plug as the lock is withdrawn. If required, the interior handle operating cable can be disconnected by releasing the retaining tabs, sliding the outer cable from the support bracket, and disengaging the inner cable from the lever **(see illustrations)**.

Refitting

19 Refitting is a reversal of the removal procedure. Check for correct operation before refitting the door trim. **Note:** *If a new lock assembly has been fitted, the clip which determines the position on the link for the lock cylinder must be removed once the lock and link rods have been fitted. Rotate the clip 90° anti-clockwise and pull it from the lock.*

Rear door lock assembly

Removal

20 Remove the door exterior handle as described in this Section. This is necessary as a rubber water deflector is located on the top of the lock, which cannot be removed or refitted with the handle is place.

21 Undo the 3 Torx bolts securing the lock assembly to the door frame, pull out the plastic bung securing the water deflector,

11.17 Prise the link rods forwards from the retaining clips

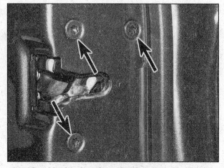

11.18a Undo the door lock retaining bolts (arrowed)

11.18b Slide the operating cable from the support bracket . . .

11.18c . . . and disengage the cable from the lever

11.21a Undo the 3 bolts (arrowed) . . .

11.21b . . . prise out the rubber bung . . .

then manoeuvre the lock from position, disconnecting the interior handle cable, lock button rod and wiring plugs as the lock is withdrawn (see illustrations).

Refitting

22 Refitting is a reversal of the removal procedure. Ensure the rubber fitting is correctly located on the lock prior to refitting (see illustration). Check for correct operation before refitting the door trim.

Front and rear interior handles

23 The interior handle is integral with the door trim. If faulty, the handle must be renewed as described in Section 10.

---

12 Window regulator and glass – removal and refitting

Front window regulator/motor

Removal

1 Lower the window to approximately the halfway position.
2 Remove the door inner trim panel as described in Section 10, then carefully pull away the door sealing panel. Use a sharp knife or scalpel to cut through the sealant

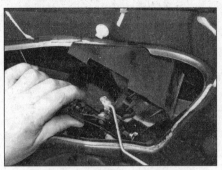

11.21c . . . and manoeuvre the lock assembly from the door

(see illustration 11.1a). Note: *Where removal of the sealing panel is prevented by a riveted bracket, drill out one of the rivets, and lift the panel over the bracket.*
3 Prise away the plastic wiring loom panel at the front of the door frame, then prise out the two retaining clips and use a screwdriver or pliers to separate the regulator arm balljoints from the window lift channels (see illustrations).
4 Raise the window, and secure it in the raised position with adhesive tape over the top of the door frame.
5 Drill out the four rivets, and manoeuvre the regulator assembly from the door frame (see

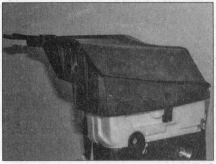

11.22 Ensure the rubber fitting is correctly located before refitting the lock

illustration). Disconnect the motor wiring connector as the assembly is withdrawn.
6 If required, undo the screws and separate the motor from the regulator assembly.

Refitting

7 Refitting is a reversal of the removal procedure, but the new rivets must be installed in the sequence shown (see illustration). Before use, the window position must be initialised as follows: Use the manual control to fully lower, and then raise the window to its limit positions. Note that on all models from model year 2003, the window will automatically lower approximately 10 mm and then fully close during the initialisation procedure.

12.3a Prise away the plastic wiring loom cover

12.3b Slide out the regulator balljoint retaining clips . . .

12.3c . . . and lever the balljoints from the window lift channels

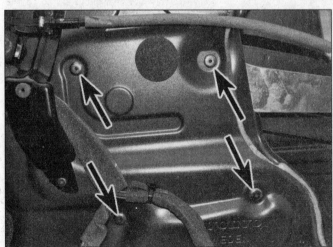

12.5 Drill out the window regulator rivets (arrowed)

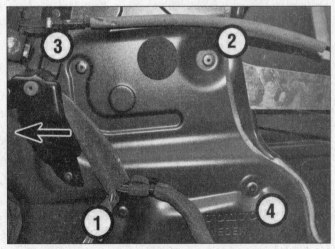

12.7 Rivet the window regulator to the door in the sequence shown. The arrow indicates the front of the door

12.10 Drill out the 2 rivets securing the regulator to the window lift channel

12.11 The window regulator is secured by 2 rivets and 1 nut (arrowed)

12.16 Prise up the inner sealing strip from the door

Rear window regulator/motor

Removal

8 Lower the window to approximately the halfway position.

9 Remove the door inner trim panel as described in Section 10, then carefully pull away the door sealing panel. Use a sharp knife or scalpel to cut through the sealant **(see illustration 11.1a)**. **Note:** *Where removal of the sealing panel is prevented by a riveted bracket, drill out the rivets and remove the bracket.*

10 Carefully drill out the two rivets or undo the two bolts (as applicable) securing the regulator to the window lift channel, then raise the window and secure it in the fully-closed position using adhesive tape **(see illustration)**.

11 The regulator is secured to the door frame by two rivets at its lower end and one nut at

12.18 Lift the rear edge first, and manoeuvre the glass from the door

the top **(see illustration)**. Drill out the rivets, undo the nut, and manoeuvre the regulator assembly from the door. Disconnect the wiring plug as the unit is withdrawn.

12 At the time of writing, it was unclear as to whether the motor was available separately from the regulator. Check with a Volvo dealer or specialist.

Refitting

13 Refitting is a reversal of the relevant removal procedure. Check for correct operation before refitting the door trim.

Front window glass

Removal

14 Lower the window to approximately the halfway position.

15 Remove the door inner trim panel as described in Section 10, then carefully pull away the door sealing panel. Use a sharp

knife or scalpel to cut through the sealant **(see illustration 11.1a)**. **Note:** *Where removal of the sealing panel is prevented by a riveted bracket, drill out one of the rivets, and lift the panel over the bracket.*

16 Carefully prise up and remove the window inner sealing strip from the door **(see illustration)**.

17 Prise away the plastic wiring loom panel at the front of the door frame, then prise out the two retaining clips and use a screwdriver or pliers to separate the regulator arm balljoints from the window lift channels **(see illustrations 12.3a, 12.3b and 12.3c)**.

18 Lift the rear edge of the glass first, and manoeuvre it upwards and out of the door frame. Recover the plastic inserts from the window lift channels **(see illustration)**.

Refitting

19 Refitting is a reversal of removal.

Rear window glass

Removal

20 Lower the window to the halfway position.

21 Remove the door inner trim panel as described in Section 10, then carefully pull away the door sealing panel. Use a sharp knife or scalpel to cut through the sealant **(see illustration 11.1a)**. **Note:** *Where removal of the sealing panel is prevented by a riveted bracket, drill out the rivets, and remove the bracket.*

22 Use a flat-bladed tool to prise out and remove the rubber strip from the window guide channel, and the inner rubber weatherstrip from the door **(see illustrations)**.

23 Drill out the two rivets securing the glass to the regulator **(see illustration 12.10)**, and manoeuvre the glass up and through the outside of the window frame **(see illustration)**.

Refitting

24 Refitting is a reversal of removal, however, lower the window into the door, then refit the rubber strip to the window guide channel before re-rivetting the glass clamp to the regulator.

Rear side quarter-light glass

25 Remove the rear door window glass as described previously in this Section, then remove the exterior window rubber weatherstrip.

12.22a Pull up the inner weather strip . . .

12.22b . . . then prise out the window channel rubber from the door frame

12.23 Rotate the glass 90° and manoeuvre it from the door

12.26a The quarter-light glass frame is secured by a bolt down through the door frame (arrowed) . . .

12.26b . . . and a lower bolt (arrowed)

12.26c Pull the quarter-light frame forwards from place

26 Undo the 2 bolts securing the guide channel, slide the glass unit forwards and manoeuvre it from the door **(see illustrations)**.
27 Refitting is a reversal of removal, but use a soap solution around the edge of the glass unit to aid refitting.

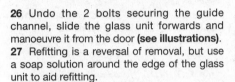

13 Boot lid –
removal and refitting

Removal

1 Rotate the fasteners anti-clockwise and remove the warning triangle from the trim panel (where fitted).
2 Release the clips and remove the boot inner trim panel **(see illustration)**.
3 Note their fitted positions, then disconnect

the boot wiring plugs, and release the loom grommet from the boot lid.
4 Mark around the hinges to aid alignment on refitting, then undo the two bolts each side securing the hinges to the boot lid **(see illustration)**. Have an assistant support the boot lid, pull the wiring loom out from the boot lid as it's withdrawn.

Refitting

5 Refit by reversing the removal operations. Check the fit and closure of the boot lid, and adjust as necessary.

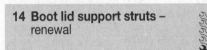

14 Boot lid support struts –
renewal

1 Support the boot lid, prise out the retaining

clips, and pull the top and bottom of the struts from the balljoint mountings **(see illustration)**. Remove the struts from the car.
2 Refitting is a reversal of removal. Note that the struts contain gas under pressure – if new ones have been fitted, the old ones should be disposed of safely, and should on no account be incinerated.

15 Boot lid lock components –
removal and refitting

Removal

Lock assembly

1 Rotate the fasteners anti-clockwise and remove the warning triangle from the trim panel.
2 Release the clips and remove the boot inner trim panel **(see illustration 13.2)**.
3 Undo the three bolts and remove lock assembly, disconnecting the wiring plug as it withdrawn **(see illustration)**.
4 Undo the 2 nuts securing the lock cylinder assembly, and pull it from the boot lid.
5 Pull the outer cable from the lock cylinder assembly then disconnect the inner cable fitting.

Lock cylinder

6 Open the boot and remove the inner trim panel as described in paragraphs 1 and 2.
7 Undo the two retaining nuts and pull the cylinder assembly from the boot lid **(see illustration)**.

13.2 Prise out the clips and remove the boot inner trim panel

13.4 Mark around the hinges, then remove the 2 bolts each side

14.1 Prise out the boot lid strut retaining clips

15.3 Undo the boot lock bolts (arrowed)

15.7 Lock cylinder nuts (arrowed)

15.8 Disengage the cable from the lever

15.11 Handle retaining screws (arrowed)

Door mirror glass removal

Up to and including 2006 model year

1 Pivot the mirror glass into the mirror housing as far as possible on the inside edge.
2 Insert a blunt, flat-bladed tool between the inner edge of the mirror glass and the housing, then twist the tool whilst pulling the outer edge of the glass rearwards to release the clips (see illustration). Take care – excessive force will cause the glass to break. Disconnect the wiring plugs as the glass is withdrawn.

2007 and 2008 model years

3 Push the lower edge of the glass into the mirror housing.
4 Insert a blunt, flat-bladed tool between the top edge of the glass and the housing, and release the clip (see illustration). Disconnect the wiring plugs as the glass is withdrawn.

Door mirror glass refitting

5 Reconnect the glass heating element wiring plugs.

Up to and including 2003 model year

6 Fold out the glass mounting on the motor, hook the glass into the mounting, and press the glass into the motor to engage the clips.

From 2004 to 2006 model year

7 Align the mirror guides with the slots in the housing, hook the inside edge of the glass over the motor, and press it into position to engage the clips.

2007 and 2008 model years

8 Align the mirror guide with the slots in the housing, position the glass against the motor and press it into place.

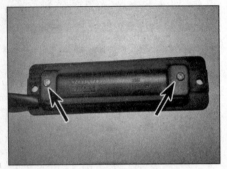

15.12a Undo the 2 bolts (arrowed) . . .

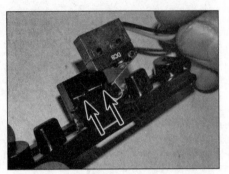

15.12b . . . and slide the microswitch up from the locating pegs (arrowed)

16 Windscreen and other fixed glass – removal and refitting

Special equipment and techniques are needed for successful removal and refitting of the windscreen and rear window. Have the work carried out by a Volvo dealer or a windscreen specialist.

17 Mirrors and associated components – removal and refitting

⚠ **Warning: If the mirror glass is broken, wear gloves to protect your hands. This is good advice, in fact, even if the glass is not broken, due to the risk of glass breakage.**

8 Slide the outer cable from the cylinder housing, and disengage the inner cable fitting from the operating lever (see illustration).

Handle

9 Open the boot and remove the inner trim panel as described in paragraphs 1 and 2.
10 Disconnect the handle wiring plug.
11 Undo the 2 Torx bolts and pull the handle from the boot lid (see illustration).
12 If required, undo the 2 screws and remove the button cover. The microswitch can then be withdrawn (see illustrations). Note that the switch wiring loom is integral with the loom for the number plate lights.

Refitting

13 Refitting is a reversal of the relevant removal procedure.

Door mirror motor

9 Remove the mirror cover as described previously
10 On vehicles up to and including 2006 model year, the motor is retained by 3 screws or clips, whilst on vehicles after this date, the motor is retained by a single central screw and 3 clips. Undo the retaining screw(s) and release the clips as applicable, and remove the motor (see illustration), disconnecting the wiring connector as it becomes accessible.
11 Refitting is a reversal of removal.

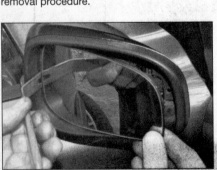

17.2 Twist the tool to force the mirror outwards, then pull the outer edge rearwards

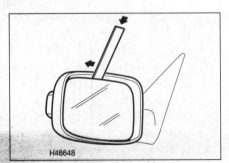

17.4 Insert a tool between the mirror and housing, then move it sideways to release the clip

17.10 Mirror motor retaining clips (arrowed)

17.13a Release the clip . . .

17.13b . . . and remove the mirror cover

17.17 Mirror retaining nut (arrowed)

17.19a Carefully prise the lenses from place . . .

17.19b . . . pull down the cover in the middle . . .

17.19c . . . and release the clips (arrowed)

Door mirror cover

12 Remove the mirror glass as described previously.

13 Insert a screwdriver through the access hole, release the clip and carefully prise the cover from the mirror **(see illustrations)**.

14 Refitting is a reversal of removal.

Door mirror (complete unit)

15 Remove the door interior trim panel as described in Section 10.

16 Disconnect the motor wiring at the connector inside the door.

17 Support the mirror, then undo the retaining nut and withdraw the mirror from the door **(see illustration)**. Release the rubber grommet from the door as the mirror is withdrawn.

18 Refitting is a reversal of removal.

Interior mirror

19 Prise the lenses from place, then pull down

the small cover at the front of the interior light assembly, release the 4 catches, and remove the cover **(see illustrations)**.

20 Undo the two screws at the front, release the clips and lower the light/mirror assembly from the headlining **(see illustration)**.

21 Prise out the plastic cover on the front

17.20 Light/mirror assembly retaining screws (arrowed)

side of the mirror, and the cable retaining spring, then insert a small screwdriver into the hole at the lower edge of the mirror and release the clip securing the mirror wiring plug **(see illustrations)**.

22 Undo the Torx bolt and remove the mirror **(see illustration)**.

17.21a Prise open the plastic cover . . .

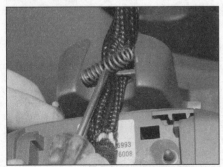

17.21b . . . prise out the cable retaining spring . . .

17.21c . . . then release the clip and pull out the wiring plug

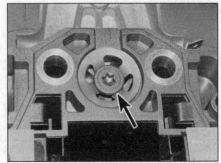

17.22 Undo the Torx bolt (arrowed) and remove the mirror

18.2 Lift up the cover and under the wiper retaining nut (arrowed)

18.3a Prise out the trim starting at the inner end . . .

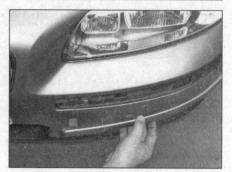

18.3b . . . and pull the trim from below each headlight

18.4 Undo the bolt beneath each headlight (arrowed)

18.5a Push in the centre pins . . .

18.5b . . . and prise out the plastic rivets at the top edge of the bumper

18 Bumpers – removal and refitting

Note: *The bumpers consist of several sections,*

and once the bumper assembly has been removed as described below, the outer cover can be unclipped and the bumper dismantled. It is unclear at the time of writing whether the individual sections that make up the bumper are available separately.

Front bumper removal

1 Open the bonnet.

2 On models with headlight wipers, lift up the cover and remove the wiper arm securing nut on each side. Pull off the washer supply hose, and remove the wiper arms (**see illustration**).

3 Using a wooden or plastic tool, carefully prise the plastic trim strips from the bumper below each headlamp (**see illustrations**).

Up to and including 2003 model year

4 Using a deep socket and extension, undo the retaining bolt each side below the headlamps (**see illustration**).

5 Press in the centre pins, and remove the 6 plastic expansion rivets at the top edge of the bumper, and the 2 screws on the bumper underside (**see illustrations**).

6 Working in the wheel arch, slacken the bumper side mounting retaining screw each side until only 3 threads remain engaged, then push the screws forwards to release the mounting (**see illustration**).

From 2004 model year

7 Undo the Torx bolt each side securing the bumper to the wing (**see illustration**).

8 Undo the screw each side in the trim recess under the headlights (**see illustration**).

9 Press in the centre pins, and remove the 6 plastic expansion rivets (**see illustration**) at the top edge of the bumper (**see illustration 18.5a and 18.5b**).

10 Press in the centre pins and remove the 2 clips on the rear lower outside edges of the bumper (**see illustration**).

18.6 Slacken the screw (arrowed) in the wheel arch each side until only 3 threads remain engaged, then push the screws forwards

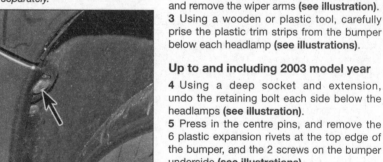

18.7 Undo the Torx bolt (arrowed) securing the bumper to the wing

18.8 Remove the screw each side under the headlights (arrowed)

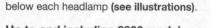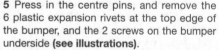

18.9 Remove the plastic rivets at the top edge of the bumper (arrowed)

18.10 Push in the centre pins and remove the plastic clip on the rear, lower edges of the bumper

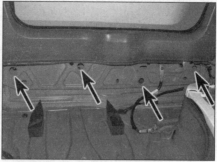

18.16 Undo the 4 nuts (arrowed) securing the bumper to the rear panel

18.17 Drill out the rivet each side at the front, lower edge of the bumper

All models

11 With the help of an assistant, pull the bumper sides outwards slightly, then pull it forward and remove it from the vehicle. Note their fitted positions and disconnect the various wiring plugs as the bumper is withdrawn. On models with headlight washers, separate the hose at the quick-release connector.

Front bumper refitting

12 Refitting is a reversal of removal. Take care when offering the bumper into position that the side mounting slides engage correctly.

Rear bumper removal

Up to and including 2004 model year

13 Remove the luggage compartment floor panel and tool tray/subwoofer (where fitted).
14 Unclip and remove the right-hand side access cover behind the rear light cluster, and disconnect the bumper aerial wiring plug.
15 Remove the battery as described in Chapter 5A.
16 Fold down the soundproofing on the rear panel, and undo the four nuts **(see illustration)**. Take care not to drop the nuts – they will be difficult to retrieve. If a nut is dropped, it can be retrieved once the bumper is removed, using a magnetic tool.
17 Drill out the rivet each side securing the front-underside edge of the bumper to the wheelarch liner **(see illustration)**.
18 Working in the wheelarch, slacken the bumper slide mounting retaining screw each side until only 3 threads remain engaged,

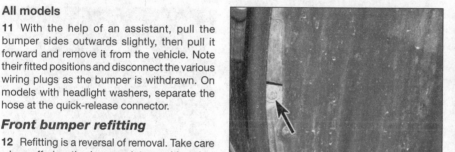

18.18a Undo the screw (arrowed) in the wheel arch until only 3 threads remain engaged . . .

18.18b . . . then push the screws and the mounting rearwards (arrowed)

then push the screws rearwards to release the mountings **(see illustrations)**.

From 2005 model year

19 Remove the Torx bolt each side securing the front-top edge of the bumper to the wheel arch, and the Torx bolt at the lower edge **(see illustrations)**.
20 Remove the luggage compartment floor panel and tool tray (where fitted).
21 Prise out the covers, and undo the four nuts **(see illustration 18.16)**. Take care not to drop the nuts – they will be difficult to retrieve.
22 Unclip and remove the right-hand side access cover behind the rear light cluster, and disconnect the bumper wiring plug(s).

All models

23 With the help of an assistant, pull the bumper front sides outwards slightly, then pull it rearwards and remove it from the vehicle.

Rear bumper refitting

24 Refitting is a reversal of removal. Take care when offering the bumper into position that the side mounting slides engage correctly (where applicable). If riveting equipment is not available, it may be possible to secure the bumper ends using suitable self-tapping screws (where applicable).

---

19 Front grille panel – removal and refitting

Removal

1 Remove the front bumper as described in Section 18.
2 Release the retaining clips and remove the grille **(see illustration)**.

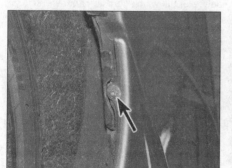

18.19a Undo the Torx bolt in the wheel arch (arrowed) . . .

18.19b . . . and the bolt under each side of the bumper (arrowed)

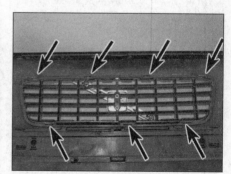

19.2 Release the clips (arrowed) and remove the front grille

20.3a Prise up the covers . . .

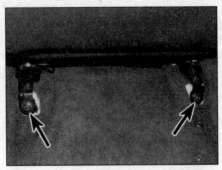

20.3b . . . then undo the bolts (arrowed) at the rear . . .

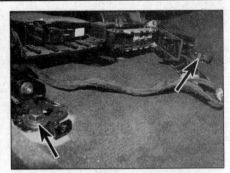

20.3c . . . and the front (arrowed)

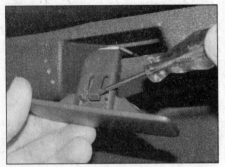

20.5 Release the clip and pull the knob from the seat lever

20.6 Pull up the front edge of the switch panel, followed by the rear edge

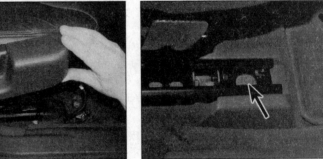

20.7 Depress the clip (arrowed) and slide the cover forwards

Refitting

3 Refit by reversing the removal operations.

20 Front seat – removal and refitting

Note: *All models are equipped with a SIPS airbag, fitted into the side of the front seat backrest, as part of the Side Impact Protection System. Various labels around the car will confirm whether the vehicle is so equipped; refer to Chapter 12 for further information on the SRS and SIPS systems.*

Removal

1 Raise the seat base to its maximum height. Ensure that the ignition is switched off, then disconnect the battery negative lead as described in Chapter 5A. Wait at least 5 min-

20.9 Undo the screw (arrowed) and disconnect the wiring plug

utes for any residual electrical energy to dissipate before proceeding.

2 It's advisable to 'earth' the seat frame before removal to protect against static electricity discharge. Strip the insulation from both ends of a long length of electrical cable, and secure one end to the metal parts of the seat frame and the other end to a bare metal part of the vehicle body or similar.

Up to and including 2004 model year

3 Prise up the plastic covers (the front covers pull straight up, whilst the rear ones pull up at an angle of 45 degrees) and undo the four seat retaining bolts **(see illustrations)**. *Note: Due to the design of the covers, it is quite likely they will be damaged during the removal process.*

4 At the front underside of the seat, pull forward the locking lever, and disconnect the wiring plugs. Take great care not to damage the connectors.

20.10 Slide a small screwdriver down the side of the rail to release the cover clip

5 On models with manual seats, release the clips and pull the knobs from the control levers **(see illustration)**. Pull up the front edge, then pull the panel rearwards to release the retaining clips and remove the panel.

6 On models with electrically-powered seats, pull up the front edge of the panel followed by the rear edge, then release the cable ties, and disconnect the wiring plugs under the seat cushion **(see illustration)**. If required, undo the three screws and remove switch console from the panel.

From 2005 model year

7 Depress the clip and slide forwards the plastic cover over the front mountings of the seat rail each side of the seat **(see illustration)**.

8 Undo the bolts securing the seat mounting rails at the front.

9 Undo the screw and separate the two halves of the wiring connector under the front of the seat **(see illustration)**.

10 Prise the plastic covers over the rear mounting bolts rearwards to release them **(see illustration)**. *Note: It is quite likely that the plastic covers will be damaged during removal.*

11 Undo the bolts securing the seat mounting rails at the rear.

12 On models with manual seats, undo the bolt at the front edge of the seat side panel, lift up the front edge of the panel, undo the retaining Torx bolt and remove the side handle. Pull the panel upwards to remove it **(see illustrations)**.

13 On models with electrically-powered

20.12a Undo the Torx bolt at the front edge of the panel (arrowed) . . .

20.12b . . . then undo the bolt securing the side handle (arrowed) . . .

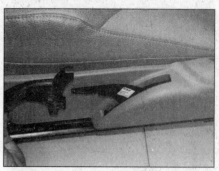

20.12c . . . and slid the handle forwards

seats, undo the bolt at the front edge of the seat side panel **(see illustration 20.12a)**, then pull up the front edge, then pull the panel rearwards to release the retaining clips and remove the panel.

All models

14 Depress the quick-release catch at the side **(see illustration)**, and pull the seat belt lower anchorage from the outside of the seat.
15 Lift the seat and manoeuvre it from the vehicle. As the seats are very heavy, the help of an assistant would be a good idea.
16 On models with electric motorised seats, the motors can be removed once the 2 retaining Torx bolts are moved, and the flexible drives disconnected.

Refitting

17 Locate the seat over the guide pins, reconnect the wiring, and insert the retaining bolts. Tighten the bolts securely and refit the bolt covers.
18 Refit the seat belt anchorage plate to the side of the seat (if removed) and tighten the Torx bolt to the specified torque.
19 Reconnect the seat belt lower anchorage, ensuring that the catch is fully engaged.
20 On models with manual seats, refit the side panel and height adjustment handle, tightening the retaining screws securely.
21 On models with electrically-powered seats, refit the switch console to the side panel (if removed), reconnect the wiring plug under the seat cushion, secure the cable with ties, and refit the side panel. Tighten the side panel screw securely.
22 Make sure that no-one is inside the car, then reconnect the battery negative lead (see Chapter 5A).

21 Rear seat –
removal and refitting

Removal

1 Free the seat cushion from its retaining clips by lifting the front edge, then remove the cushion **(see illustration)**. **Note:** *It is quite likely that one or more of the retaining clips will break during removal.*

20.12d Pull the side panel upwards to remove it

2 Fold down the backrest, reach behind the side cushion and release the clips at the top of the side cushion **(see illustrations)**. Pull the top of the cushion forwards.
3 Reach behind the lower section of the

21.1 Pull the front edge of the seat cushion upwards to release the clips

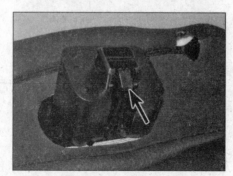

21.2b Side cushion upper clip (arrowed)

20.14 Depress the clip and pull the seat belt lower anchorage from the mounting

cushion, release the clip and lift the cushion upwards from position **(see illustration)**.
4 Undo the bolt securing the outside of each backrest to the vehicle body. Remove the backrest, disconnecting the wiring

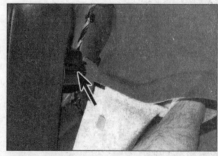

21.2a Reach behind the panel and release the clip (arrowed) at the top of the side cushion

21.3 Side cushion lower clip (arrowed)

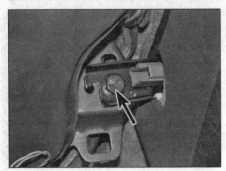

21.4 Undo the bolt (arrowed) at the lower, outer edge of the backrest

connectors as the backrest is withdrawn **(see illustration)**.

Refitting

5 Refit by reversing the removal operations.

22 Interior trim – removal and refitting

Note: *Refer to earlier Sections of this Chapter for specific procedures covering door and tailgate interior trim panels.*

Interior trim panels – general

1 The interior trim panels are secured using either screws or various types of trim fasteners, usually studs or clips.
2 Check that there are no other panels overlapping the one to be removed, or other components hindering removal; usually there

is a sequence that has to be followed, and this will only become obvious on close inspection.
3 Some of the interior panels will additionally be retained by the screws which are used to secure other items, such as the grab handles.
4 Remove all visible retainers such as screws, noting that these may be hidden under small plastic caps. If the panel will not come free, it is held by internal clips or fasteners. These are usually situated around the edges of the panel, and can be prised up to release them; note, however, that they can break quite easily, so new ones should be available. The best way of releasing such clips is to use a large flat-bladed screwdriver or other wide-bladed tool. Note that in many cases, the adjacent sealing strip must be prised back to release a panel.
5 When removing a panel, **never** use excessive force or the panel may be damaged; always check carefully that all fasteners or other relevant components have been removed or released before attempting to withdraw a panel.
6 Refitting is a reversal of removal; secure the fasteners by pressing them firmly into place and ensure that all disturbed components are correctly secured to prevent rattles.

Rear parcel shelf

7 Fold down the rear seat backrest, and remove the side cushion as described in Section 21.
8 Remove the C-pillar trim panel as described in this Section.
9 Lift the parcel shelf at the front edge

22.9 Pull up the front edge of the parcel shelf to release the clips (arrowed)

22.20a Note how the door sill trim fits under the B-pillar trim

22.18 Pull the top of the A-pillar trim inwards, and release the safety clip (arrowed) by turning it through 90°

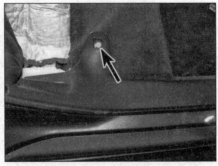

22.20b Prise out the clip (arrowed) and pull the rear door sill trim upwards

to release the three retaining clips **(see illustration)**.
10 Undo the bolts securing the lower ends of the rear seatbelts.
11 Lift the parcel shelf and pull it forwards. As the shelf is being removed, lift it slightly in the centre to ease it over the rear speakers. Prise out the seat belt guide trims and thread the belts through the shelf as it's withdrawn.
12 Refitting is a reversal of removal.

Carpets

13 The passenger compartment floor carpet is in three sections; front left, front right and rear, and is secured at the sides by the front and rear sill trim panels.
14 Carpet removal and refitting is reasonably straightforward, but is very time-consuming because all adjoining trim panels must be removed first, as must components such as the seats, centre console and seat belt lower anchorages.

Headlining

15 The headlining is clipped to the roof, and can be withdrawn only once all fittings such as grab handles, sunvisors, sunroof (if fitted), fixed window glass, and related trim panels have been removed and the relevant sealing strips have been prised clear.
16 Note that headlining removal and refitting requires considerable skill and experience if it is to be carried out without damage, and is therefore best entrusted to a dealer or automotive upholstery specialist.

A-pillar trims

17 Pull the rubber weatherstrip from the door aperture adjacent to the A-pillar.
18 Pull the top of the A-pillar trim inwards towards the centre of the passenger cabin to release the clips/hooks, then lift the trim from the lugs at the lower edge. On models equipped with safety clips, twist the clip through 90 degrees and detach it from the trim **(see illustration)**.
19 Refitting is a reversal of removal. On all versions, if any clips are damaged, new ones should be used when refitting, so as not to impair the inflatable safety curtain performance.

B-pillar trims

20 Pull the front door sill trim panel straight up to release it from the retaining clips. Remove the rear seat cushion as described in Section 21, then pull the rear door sill trim panel upwards to release the clips **(see illustrations)**.
21 Remove the seat side panel as described in Section 20, then depress the quick-release catch at the side **(see illustration 20.14)**, and remove the seat belt lower anchorage from the outside of the seat.
22 Move the front seat as far forward as possible, then pull the rubber weatherstrips from the door apertures adjacent to the B-pillar.

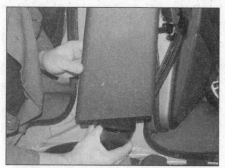

22.23a Pull the lower edge of the B-pillar trim inwards and disconnect the air ducting

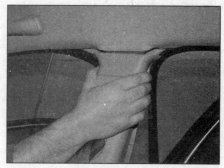

22.23b Squeeze together the sides at the top of the trim and pull it downwards

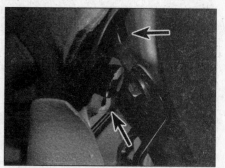

22.23c Note how the clip (arrowed) engages with the hole in the pillar (arrowed)

22.27a Prise out the plastic cover . . .

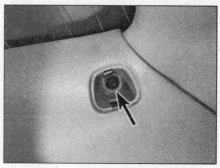

22.27b . . . and undo the Torx bolt (arrowed)

22.28 Pull the trim inwards and forwards from the C-pillar to release the clips (arrowed)

23 Pull the lower edge of the B-pillar trim in towards the centre of the cabin to release the clips and disengage the air ducting (where applicable), then pull it downwards at the same time as squeezing together the sides at the top of the trim to release the retaining clips (see illustrations).

24 Feed the seat belt through the panel and remove it from the cabin.

25 Refitting is a reversal of removal.

C-pillar trims

26 Pull the rubber weatherstrip from the door aperture adjacent to the pillar trim.

27 Prise out the cover and undo the trim retaining Torx bolt (see illustrations).

28 Pull the trim inwards and then forwards to release the clips (see illustration).

Caution: Do not touch the inflatable safety curtain with bare hands, as this may cause a deformity in the cover.

29 Refitting is a reversal of removal.

Luggage compartment side panel

30 Lift out the floor panel from the boot, then fold down the rear seat backrest.

31 Open the side panel access flaps, then release the 2 clips/1 nut (passenger's side) or 3 clips (driver's side) and remove the panel (see illustrations).

32 Refitting is a reversal of removal.

Glovebox

33 Undo the two screws, and pull the lower facia panel downwards to remove it.

34 Open the glovebox, slide the two hooks

past the tabs, and release the strut or return mechanism from the lid (see illustration).

35 Undo the 8 screws, and pull the glovebox from the facia, disconnect the light unit as it's withdrawn (see illustration).

22.31a Prise out the side panel clip, undo the nut in the luggage compartment (arrowed) . . .

22.34 Release the return mechanism from the glovebox lid

36 Refitting is a reversal of removal.

Sunvisor

37 Carefully prise off the outer mounting cover, and undo the two screws (see illustration).

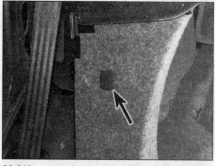

22.31b . . . and prise out the side panel clip behind the rear seat backrest (arrowed)

22.35 Remove the 8 glovebox retaining screws (arrowed)

22.37 Prise off the cover and undo the screws

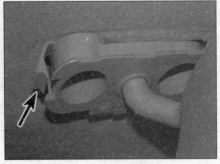

22.38 Depress the clip (arrowed) and pull the mounting out

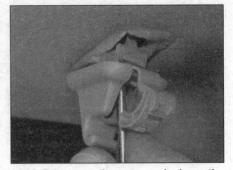

22.39 Prise open the cover and release the rear clip

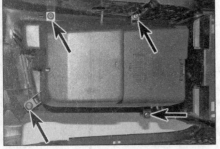

22.42a Undo the Torx bolts (arrowed) and remove the central drinks holder – early models . . .

22.42b . . . and later models

3 When the system is triggered, the explosive gas in the tensioner mechanism retracts and locks the seat belt through a cable which acts on the inertia reel. This prevents the seat belt moving, and keeps the occupant firmly in position in the seat. Once the tensioner has been triggered, the seat belt will be permanently locked and the assembly must be renewed. If any abnormal rattling noises are heard when pulling out or retracting the belt, this also indicates that the tensioner has been triggered.

4 There is a risk of injury if the system is triggered inadvertently when working on the vehicle, and it is therefore strongly recommended that any work involving the seat belt tensioner system is entrusted to a Volvo dealer. Note the following warnings before contemplating any work on the front seat belts.

> ⚠ *Warning: Switch off the ignition, disconnect the battery negative lead, and wait for at least 5 minutes for any residual electrical energy to dissipate before starting work involving the front seat belts.*
> • *Do not expose the tensioner mechanism to temperatures in excess of 100°C.*
> • *If the tensioner mechanism is dropped, it must be renewed, even it has suffered no apparent damage.*
> • *Do not allow any solvents to come into contact with the tensioner mechanism.*
> • *Do not attempt to open the tensioner mechanism, as it contains explosive gas.*
> • *Tensioners from other vehicles, even from the same model and year, must not be fitted as replacement parts.*
> • *Tensioners must be discharged before they are disposed of, but this task should be entrusted to a Volvo dealer or specialist.*

38 Depress the clip, swing the sunvisor outwards and remove it. Disconnect the wiring plug as the sunvisor is withdrawn **(see illustration)**.

39 To remove the inboard mounting, prise open the cover, insert a screwdriver and release the rear clip, then pull the rear of the mounting downwards, and pull it backwards from the headlining **(see illustration)**.

40 Refitting is a reversal of removal.

Central drinks holder

41 Remove the centre console as described in Section 24.

42 Invert the console, then undo the 4 Torx bolts securing the holder **(see illustrations)**, and lift it from position.

43 If required, release the clip and remove the holder insert **(see illustrations)**.

44 Refitting is a reversal of removal.

22.43a Release the clip . . .

22.43b . . . and remove the holder insert

23 Seat belts – general information, removal and refitting

1 All models are equipped with pyrotechnical front seat belt tensioners as part of the Supplemental Restraint System (SRS). The system is designed to instantaneously take up any slack in the seat belt in the case of a sudden frontal impact, therefore reducing the possibility of injury to the front seat occupants. Each front seat is fitted with the system, the tensioner being situated behind the upper B-pillar trim panel.

2 The seat belt tensioner is triggered, along with the driver's and passenger's airbag, by a frontal impact above a predetermined force. Lesser impacts, including impacts from behind, will not trigger the system.

Removal

Front seat belts

5 Switch off the ignition, then disconnect the battery negative lead as described in Chapter 5A. Wait for at least 5 minutes before proceeding.

6 Remove the B-pillar trim as described in Section 22.

7 Confirm that the battery is disconnected,

23.7a Squeeze together the side of the plugs clips (arrowed) . . .

23.7b . . . and pull it from the tensioner

23.8 Undo the 2 bolts (arrowed) and remove the reel/tensioner

then unplug the wiring connector from the seat belt tensioner by squeezing together the two plug retaining clips **(see illustrations)**. This wiring plug should never be disconnected (or reconnected) while the battery negative lead is connected.

8 Unscrew and remove the two reel/tensioner retaining bolts and remove the seat belt reel and tensioner from the car **(see illustration)**.

9 To detach the lower anchorage from the seat, remove the seat side panel as described in Section 20.

10 To remove the belt buckle, remove the seat first, as described in Section 20. The buckles are secured with a large Torx bolt.

Rear seat belts

11 Remove the rear seat cushion as described in Section 21.

12 Remove the rear parcel shelf as described in Section 22.

13 Confirm that the battery is disconnected, then unplug the wiring connector from the seat belt tensioner by squeezing together the two plug retaining clips **(see illustration)**. This wiring plug should never be disconnected (or reconnected) while the battery negative lead is connected.

14 Unbolt the seat belt anchorages **(see illustration)**. Note the fitted position of the anchorages – the lug on the bracket must locate in the hole in the vehicle body.

15 Undo the seat belt inertia reel retaining nut, and remove the rear belts from the car.

16 If required, the rear belt buckles can be unbolted and removed from the floor mountings.

Refitting

17 In all cases, refit by reversing the removal operations. Tighten the seat belt mountings to the specified torque. When refitting the seat belts, note the following points:

a) *Reconnect the front seat belt lower anchorage, ensuring that the catch is fully engaged.*

b) *Make sure that no-one is inside the car. Switch on the ignition, then reconnect the battery negative lead. Switch the ignition off, then on again, and check that the SRS warning light comes on, then goes out within 15 seconds.*

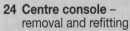

23.13 Disconnect the rear seat belt tensioner wiring plug (arrowed)

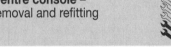

24 Centre console – removal and refitting

Removal

1 Fully apply the handbrake, then move the gear or selector lever to neutral – note that it may be necessary to move the gear or selector lever as the console is removed.

2 Ensure the front seats are in the fully lowered, rearmost position.

Models with a pen holder

3 Using a flat-bladed plastic or wooden tool, carefully prise out the pen holder panel in front of the gear/selector lever **(see illustration)**.

4 Rotate the fastener 90° anti-clockwise and slide the console side panel rearwards to

23.14 Rear seat belt anchorage bolt (arrowed)

remove it. Repeat this procedure on the other side of the console **(see illustrations)**.

5 Pull the coin holder straight up from the storage compartment, then release the catch

24.3 Carefully prise the pen holder from place

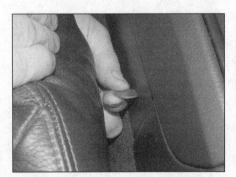

24.4a Use a coin to undo the fastener . . .

24.4b . . . then slide the console side panel to the rear and remove it

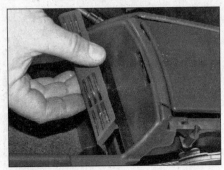

24.5a Pull the coin holder straight up . . .

24.5b . . . then release the catch and lift out the CD holder

24.6 Fold out the rear drinks holder and unclip the rear panel

24.7a Undo the 2 Torx bolts at the front of the console (arrowed) . . .

24.7b . . . and the 2 at the rear (arrowed)

24.8 Depress the clips at the front of the lever surround trim

24.9 Release the 2 clips at the front edge and lift out the lever surround trim

24.10a Undo the Torx bolt (arrowed) . . .

24.10b . . . and lift out the panel mounting bracket

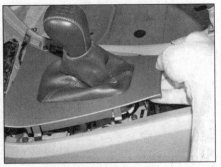

24.11 Starting at the rear edge, prise up the lever panel

at the front edge and lift out the CD holder (see illustration). On models without a coin holder/CD holder, lift out the rubber mat from the storage compartment (see illustration).

6 Open the rear ashtray past the hooks, then release the catch each side and pull the ashtray from the rear of the console. Disconnect the wiring plug as the ashtray is withdrawn. On models without a rear ashtray, fold out the rear drinks holder (where fitted), unclip the rear panel and disconnect the wiring plug (see illustration).

7 Undo the Torx bolts at the front and rear of the console (see illustrations).

8 On manual transmission models, release the two clips, and lift the front edge of the gear lever surround trim, and pull the gaiter/trim up around the gear lever knob (see illustration).

9 On automatic transmission models, release the 2 clips at the front edge and remove the selector lever surround panel (see illustration).

10 On automatic transmission models, undo the Torx bolt at the rear of the selector lever aperture/panel mounting bracket, then lift the rear edge and remove it (see illustrations).

Models without a pen holder

11 Carefully prise up the rear edge of the gear/selector lever panel (see illustration).

12 On manual transmission models, proceed as described in paragraphs 4 to 7. Pull up the gaiter around the gear lever knob. There is no need to pull the gaiter over the knob, as the lever panel will fit through the aperture as the console is lifted away.

13 On automatic transmission models, proceed as described in paragraphs 4 to 7, then paragraphs 9 and 10.

All models

14 Apply the handbrake fully, then carefully prise free the trim panel below the handbrake lever. The panel must be moved upwards to disengage the main retaining clip. Unclip the panel, then carefully work the gaiter over the lever and remove the trim panel (see illustrations).

15 Lifting the rear edge first, manoeuvre the centre console over the handbrake and

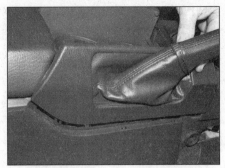

24.14a Prise up the handbrake lever surround trim – early models . . .

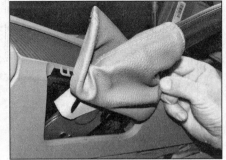

24.14b . . . and later models

24.15 Lift the rear edge first, and remove the centre console

gearchange/selector levers, and out from the vehicle **(see illustration)**. Feed the lever panel through the aperture as the console is removed.

16 The various sections of the console are held together by various nuts and screws, visible from beneath.

Refitting

17 Refitting is a reversal of removal.

25 Facia – removal and refitting

Removal

1 Ensure the front seats are in the rearmost positions, then disconnect the battery negative lead (see Chapter 5A), and wait at

least 5 minutes before proceeding to allow any residual electrical energy to dissipate.

2 Remove the A-pillar trim panels as described in Section 22.

3 Remove the lower facia panels in the driver's and passenger's footwell. Each panel is retained by two screws **(see illustrations)**.

4 Carefully prise the footwell illumination lights from place and disconnect the wiring plugs.

5 Detach the diagnostic plug from its mounting under the driver's side of the lower facia, above the pedals. On some models, simply release the retaining clip, and on other models the plug is fitted to a bracket retained by two Torx bolts **(see illustration)**.

6 Remove the steering wheel as described in Chapter 10.

7 Undo the three screws from under the steering column lower shroud, and prise the upper and lower shrouds apart to release the

retaining pegs. Remove the lower shroud, and lift the upper shroud out of the way **(see illustrations)**.

8 Disconnect the two wiring plugs, undo the 2 screws, pull the contact unit wiring plug from the back of the switch module, then release the two clips and pull the steering wheel switch module from steering column **(see illustration)**.

9 Remove the instrument panel as described in Chapter 12.

10 Remove the centre console as described in Section 24.

11 Remove the facia mounted audio unit as described in Chapter 12.

12 On automatic transmission models, disconnect the interlock cable from the selector lever housing, with reference to Chapter 7B, Section 3.

13 Carefully prise off the end trim panels from the facia **(see illustration)**. Reach through the

25.3a Undo the 2 screws (arrowed) and remove the passenger's lower facia panel . . .

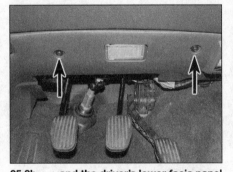

25.3b . . . and the driver's lower facia panel

25.5 Undo the 2 bolts (arrowed) and detach the diagnostic plug

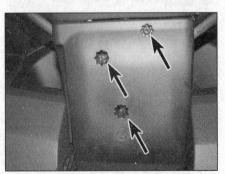

25.7a The lower steering column shroud is secured by 3 screws (arrowed)

25.7b Lift the upper shroud from place

25.8 Undo the 2 screws (arrowed) retaining the switch module

25.13 Prise the end trim panels from the facia

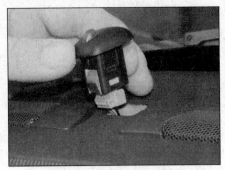

25.14 Prise the sunlight sensor from the centre of the facia

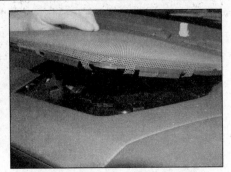

25.15a Prise up the centre speaker grille . . .

25.15b . . . and undo the 4 screws (arrowed) . . .

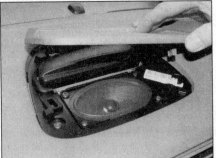

25.15c . . . or prise up the speaker/display grille/surround . . .

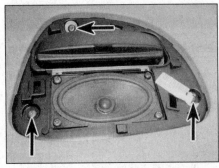

25.15d . . . and undo the 3 screws (arrowed)

right-hand end of the facia and disconnect the lighting switch wiring plug.

14 Prise up the sunlight sensor from the middle of the facia and disconnect the wiring plug (where fitted) **(see illustration)**.

15 Use a plastic or wooden flat-bladed tool to prise up the grille, then undo the screws securing the display screen/loudspeaker assembly from the centre of the facia **(see illustrations)**. Note their fitted positions and disconnect the wiring plugs as the assembly is withdrawn.

16 Reach down and press the hazard warning switch from the facia.

17 Open the glovebox, slide the two hooks past the opening limit stops, and release the return mechanism/strut from the lid **(see illustration 22.34)**.

18 Undo the 8 screws, and manoeuvre the passenger glovebox from the facia **(see illustration 22.35)**. Note their fitted positions and disconnect the wiring plugs as the glovebox is withdrawn.

19 Working through the glovebox aperture, release the clips and disconnect the passenger's airbag module wiring plug **(see illustration)**.

20 The facia panel is secured by two bolts at each end, one bolt in the instrument panel aperture, one bolt accessible through the central display screen/loudspeaker aperture, two under the passenger's side of the facia, and two in the audio unit aperture **(see illustrations)**. Undo the bolts, and pull the facia rearwards slightly. The help of an assistant will be invaluable.

21 Check to ensure all necessary wiring plugs, cable loom clips, etc, have been disconnected/released, and manoeuvre the facia from the vehicle.

⚠️ *Warning: Position the facia and airbag module in a safe place, with the mechanism facing downwards as a precaution against accidental operation. Do not attempt to open or repair the airbag module, or apply any electrical current to it. Do not re-use any airbag which is visibly damaged, or which has been tampered with.*

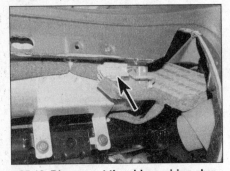

25.19 Disconnect the airbag wiring plug

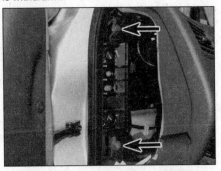

25.20a The facia is secured by 2 bolts at each end (arrowed) . . .

25.20b . . . one bolt in the instrument panel aperture (arrowed) . . .

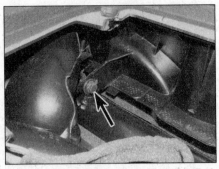

25.20c . . . one bolt in the central display/ speaker aperture (arrowed) . . .

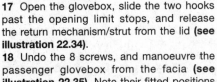

22 If required, undo the various bolts (including the steering column mounting bolts), and remove the facia crossmember. Note the routing of the various cable looms to aid refitting, then release the cable-ties. **Note:** *In order to access one of the right-hand crossmember mounting bolts, it will be necessary to remove the wiper motor and linkage as described in Chapter 12, then release the clips, open the cover and disconnect the electrical connector on the right-hand side. If the crossmember is being removed as part of the heater housing removal procedure, it is not necessary to completely remove it. Have an assistant help move the crossmember upwards and rearwards, whilst the heater housing is manoeuvred from place.*

Refitting

23 Refitting is a reversal of removal.
24 On cars equipped with a passenger's airbag, make sure that no-one is inside the car. Switch on the ignition, then reconnect the battery negative lead. Switch the ignition off, then on again, and check that the SRS warning light comes on, then goes out within 15 seconds.

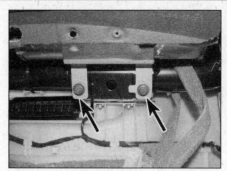

25.20d ... 2 bolts under the passenger's side (arrowed) ...

26 Sunroof – general information

An electrically-operated sunroof is available as standard or optional equipment, according to model.

The sunroof is maintenance-free, but any adjustment or removal and refitting of the component parts should be entrusted to a dealer or specialist, due to the complexity of

25.20e ... and 2 in the audio unit aperture (arrowed)

the unit and the need to remove much of the interior trim and headlining to gain access. The latter operation is involved, and requires care and specialist knowledge to avoid damage.

If the sunroof action becomes sluggish, the slides and/or cables may need lubricating – consult a Volvo dealer or specialist for advice on a suitable product to use. Further checks in the event of non-operation are limited to checking the fuse and wiring, with reference to the wiring diagrams at the end of Chapter 12.

Chapter 12
Body electrical system

Contents

Degrees of difficulty

Easy, suitable for novice with little experience	**Fairly easy,** suitable for beginner with some experience	**Fairly difficult,** suitable for competent DIY mechanic	**Difficult,** suitable for experienced DIY mechanic	**Very difficult,** suitable for expert DIY or professional

Specifications

General

System type.	12 volt, negative earth
Fuses	See wiring diagrams at end of Chapter and sticker on control box lid for specific vehicle details

Bulbs

	Wattage
Direction indicator side repeater lights.	5 wedge
Direction indicators (front and rear)	21 bayonet PY (yellow)
Door mirror ground light.	6 wedge
Door warning lights	5 wedge
Foglight:	
Front.	55 H1
Rear	21
Footwell illumination.	5 festoon
Headlight:	
Bi-Xenon.	35 D2R
Halogen dipped beam	55 H7
Halogen main beam:	
Up to and including 2004 model year.	55 HB3
From 2005 model year	65 H9
High-level brake light	LED type (non-renewable)
Luggage compartment illumination	5 wedge
Number plate light	5 wedge
Reversing light	21 bayonet
Side marker lights:	
Front.	3 wedge
Rear	5 wedge
Sidelights	5 wedge
Stop-light	21 bayonet
Tail light.	5 bayonet
Vanity mirror illumination	1.2 festoon

Torque wrench settings

	Nm	lbf ft
Airbag fasteners	10	7
Brake fluid pressure sensor	25	18
Headlight securing bolts	10	7
Headlight wiper arm nuts	4	3
Oil pressure sensor	27	20
SRS control module	10	7
SRS side crash sensors	6	4
Windscreen wiper arm nuts	16	12
Windscreen wiper motor crank arm nut	20	15

1 General information and precautions

The electrical system is of 12 volt negative earth type. Power for the lights and all electrical accessories is supplied by a lead-acid type battery, which is charged by the belt-driven alternator.

This Chapter covers repair and service procedures for the various electrical components not associated with the engine. Information on the battery, alternator, preheating system and starter motor can be found in Chapter 5A.

⚠ **Warning: Before carrying out any work on the electrical system, read through the precautions given in Safety first! at the beginning of this manual and in Chapter 5A.**

2 Electrical fault finding – general information

Note: *Refer to the precautions given in Safety first! and in Section 1 of this Chapter before starting work. The following tests relate to testing of the main electrical circuits, and should not be used to test delicate electronic circuits, particularly where an electronic control module is used.*

General

1 A typical electrical circuit consists of an electrical component, any switches, relays, motors, fuses, fusible links or circuit breakers related to that component, and the wiring and connectors which link the component to both the battery and the chassis. To help to pinpoint a problem in an electrical circuit, wiring diagrams are included at the end of this Chapter.

2 Before attempting to diagnose an electrical fault, first study the appropriate wiring diagram, to obtain a complete understanding of the components included in the particular circuit concerned. The possible sources of a fault can be narrowed down by noting if other components related to the circuit are operating properly. If several components or circuits fail at one time, the problem is likely to be related to a shared fuse or earth connection.

3 Electrical problems usually stem from simple causes, such as loose or corroded connections, a faulty earth connection, a blown fuse, a melted fusible link, or a faulty relay. Visually inspect the condition of all fuses, wires and connections in a problem circuit before testing the components. Use the wiring diagrams to determine which terminal connections will need to be checked in order to pinpoint the trouble-spot.

4 The basic tools required for electrical fault finding include a circuit tester or voltmeter (a 12 volt bulb with a set of test leads can also be used for certain tests); an ohmmeter (to measure resistance and check for continuity); a battery and set of test leads; and a jumper wire, preferably with a circuit breaker or fuse incorporated, which can be used to bypass suspect wires or electrical components. Before attempting to locate a problem with test instruments, use the wiring diagram to determine where to make the connections.

⚠ **Warning: Under no circumstances may live measuring instruments such as ohmmeters, voltmeters or a bulb and test leads be used to test any of the SRS airbag, SIPS bag, or pyrotechnical seat belt circuitry. Any testing of these components must be left to a Volvo dealer, as there is a danger of activating the system if the correct procedures are not followed.**

Caution: *The Volvo S60 electrical system is extremely complex. Many of the ECMs are connected via a 'Databus' system, where they are able to share information from the various sensors, and communicate with each other. For instance, as the automatic gearbox approaches a gear ratio shift point, it signals the engine management ECM via the Databus. As the gearchange is made by the transmission ECM, the engine management ECM retards the ignition timing, momentarily reducing engine output to ensure a smoother transition from one gear ratio to the next. Due to the design of the Databus system, it is not advisable to backprobe the ECMs with a multimeter in the traditional manner. Instead, the electrical systems are equipped with a sophisticated self-diagnosis system, which can interrogate the various ECMs to reveal the stored fault codes, and help pinpoint faults. In order to access the self-diagnosis system, specialist test equipment (fault code reader/scanner) is required. Refer to your Volvo dealer or suitably-equipped specialist.*

5 To find the source of an intermittent wiring fault (usually due to a poor or dirty connection, or damaged wiring insulation), a wiggle test can be performed on the wiring. This involves wiggling the wiring by hand to see if the fault occurs as the wiring is moved. It should be possible to narrow down the source of the fault to a particular section of wiring. This method of testing can be used in conjunction with any of the tests described in the following sub-Sections.

6 Apart from problems due to poor connections, two basic types of fault can occur in an electrical circuit – open-circuit, or short-circuit.

7 Open-circuit faults are caused by a break somewhere in the circuit, which prevents current from flowing. An open-circuit fault will prevent a component from working.

8 Short-circuit faults are caused by a short somewhere in the circuit, which allows the current flowing in the circuit to escape along an alternative route, usually to earth. Short-circuit faults are normally caused by a breakdown in wiring insulation, which allows a feed wire to touch either another wire, or an earthed component such as the bodyshell. A short-circuit fault will normally cause the relevant circuit fuse to blow.

Finding an open-circuit

9 To check for an open-circuit, connect one lead of a circuit tester or the negative lead of a voltmeter either to the battery negative terminal or to a known good earth.

10 Connect the other lead to a connector in the circuit being tested, preferably nearest to the battery or fuse. At this point, battery voltage should be present, unless the lead from the battery or the fuse itself is faulty (bearing in mind that some circuits are live only when the ignition switch is moved to a particular position).

11 Switch on the circuit, then connect the tester lead to the connector nearest the circuit switch on the component side.

12 If voltage is present (indicated either by the tester bulb lighting or a voltmeter reading, as applicable), this means that the section of the circuit between the relevant connector and the switch is problem-free.

13 Continue to check the remainder of the circuit in the same fashion.

14 When a point is reached at which no voltage is present, the problem must lie between that point and the previous test point with voltage. Most problems can be traced to a broken, corroded or loose connection.

Finding a short-circuit

15 To check for a short-circuit, first disconnect the load(s) from the circuit (loads are the components which draw current from a circuit, such as bulbs, motors, heating elements, etc).

16 Remove the relevant fuse from the circuit, and connect a circuit tester or voltmeter to the fuse connections.

17 Switch on the circuit, bearing in mind that some circuits are live only when the ignition switch is in a particular position.

18 If voltage is present (indicated either by the tester bulb lighting or a voltmeter reading, as applicable), this means that there is a short-circuit.

19 If no voltage is present during this test, but the fuse still blows with the load(s) reconnected, this indicates an internal fault in the load(s).

Finding an earth fault

20 The battery negative terminal is connected to earth – the metal of the engine/transmission and the vehicle body – and many systems are wired so that they only receive a positive feed, the current returning via the metal of the car body **(see illustrations)**. This means that the component mounting and the body form part of that circuit. Loose or corroded mountings can therefore cause a range of electrical faults, ranging from total failure of a circuit, to a puzzling partial failure. In particular, lights may shine dimly (especially when another circuit sharing the same earth point is in operation), motors (eg, wiper motors or the radiator cooling fan motor) may run slowly, and the operation of one circuit may have an apparently-unrelated effect on another.

21 Note that on many vehicles, earth straps are used between certain components, such as the engine/transmission and the body, usually where there is no metal-to-metal contact between components, due to flexible rubber mountings, etc.

22 To check whether a component is properly earthed, disconnect the battery and connect one lead of an ohmmeter to a known good earth point. Connect the other lead to the wire or earth connection being tested. The resistance reading should be zero; if not, check the connection as follows.

23 If an earth connection is thought to be faulty, dismantle the connection, and clean both the bodyshell and the wire terminal (or the component earth connection mating surface) back to bare metal. Be careful to remove all traces of dirt and corrosion, then use a knife to trim away any paint, so that a clean metal-to-metal joint is made. On reassembly, tighten the joint fasteners securely; if a wire terminal is being refitted, use serrated washers between the terminal and the bodyshell, to ensure a clean and secure connection.

24 When the connection is remade, prevent the onset of corrosion in the future by applying a coat of petroleum jelly or silicone-based grease, or by spraying on (at regular intervals)

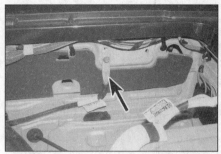

2.20a The battery negative (earth) terminal is connect to the vehicle body (rear panel) via an earth strap (arrowed)

2.20c . . . under the rear seats . . .

a proprietary ignition sealer, or a water-dispersant lubricant.

3 Fuses and relays – general information

Fuses

1 The fuses are located in the central fusebox situated in the engine compartment on the passenger's side, just in front of the suspension turret, in the passenger cabin fusebox under a panel on the right-hand end of the facia (RHD models), under the driver's side of the facia (on the CEM), and on the left-hand side of the luggage compartment.

2 If a fuse blows, the electrical circuit(s) protected by that fuse will cease to operate. The fuse positions and the circuits protected depends on vehicle specification, model year

3.3a Engine compartment fuse/relay box

2.20b Earth connections on the inner front wings (both sides) . . .

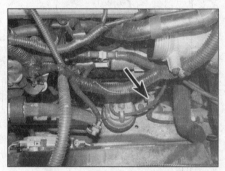

2.20d . . . and at the front of the transmission casing (arrowed)

and country. Refer to the wiring diagrams at the end of this Chapter, and the sticker on the fusebox lid which gives details for the particular vehicle.

3 To remove a fuse, first switch off the ignition, then lift up the cover on the central fusebox. Using the plastic removal tool provided, pull the fuse out of its terminals **(see illustrations)**. The wire within the fuse should be visible; if the fuse is blown, the wire will be broken or melted.

4 Always renew a fuse with one of an identical rating; never use a fuse with a different rating from the original, or substitute anything else, as it may lead to a fire. Never renew a fuse more than once without tracing the source of the trouble. The fuse rating is stamped on top of the fuse; note that fuses are also colour-coded for easy recognition. Spare fuses are provided in the fusebox.

5 Persistent blowing of a particular fuse indicates a fault in the circuit(s) protected.

3.3b The passenger compartment fusebox is located behind a panel at the right-hand end of the facia

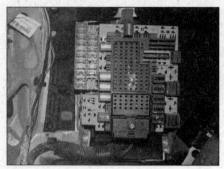

3.3c The luggage compartment fuse/relay box is located behind the left-hand access panel

3.3d Using the plastic tool provided, pull the fuse from place

Where more than one circuit is involved, switch on one item at a time until the fuse blows, so showing in which circuit the fault lies.

6 Besides a fault in the electrical component concerned, a blown fuse can also be caused by a short-circuit in the wiring to the component. Look for trapped or frayed wires allowing a live wire to touch vehicle metal, and for loose or damaged connectors.

7 Note that **only** the blade-type fuses should ever be renewed by the DIY mechanic. If one of the large fusible links in the main fusebox blows, this indicates a serious electrical fault, which should be diagnosed by a Volvo dealer or automotive electrical specialist.

Relays

8 A relay is an electrically-operated switch, which is used for the following reasons:
  a) A relay can switch a heavy current

remotely from the circuit in which the current is flowing, allowing the use of lighter-gauge wiring and switch contacts.
  b) *A relay can receive more than one control input, unlike a mechanical switch.*
  c) *A relay can have a timer function – for example an intermittent wiper delay.*

9 If a circuit which includes a relay develops a fault, remember that the relay itself could be faulty. A basic test of relay operation is to have an assistant switch on the item concerned, while you listen for a click from the relay. This would at least determine whether the relay is switching or not, but is not conclusive proof that a relay is working.

10 Most relays have four or five terminals – two terminals supplying current to its solenoid winding to provide the switching, a main current input and either one or two outputs to either supply or isolate the

component concerned (depending on its configuration). Using the wiring diagrams at the end of this Chapter, test to ensure that all connections deliver the expected voltage or good earth.

11 Ultimately, testing is by substitution of a known good relay, but be careful – relays which look similar are not necessarily identical for purposes of substitution.

12 The relays are found in the central and main fuseboxes, on the passenger's side rear of the engine compartment, and in the luggage compartment fusebox (see illustrations 3.3a and 3.3c).

13 To remove a relay, make sure that the ignition is switched off, then pull the relay from its socket. Push the new relay firmly in to refit.

4 Switches – removal and refitting

Steering column switches

1 Disconnect the battery negative lead (see Chapter 5A). Set the steering wheel to the straight-ahead position.

2 Release the steering wheel/column adjuster, and pull the steering wheel away from the facia as far as possible.

3 Remove the steering wheel as described in Chapter 10.

4 Undo the three bolts from under the steering column lower shroud, and prise the upper and lower shrouds apart to release the retaining pegs. Remove the lower shroud, and lift the upper shroud out of the way (see illustrations).

5 Remove the switch in question. Each switch is secured by two screws (see illustration). Remove the screws, pull the switch out to the side carefully.

6 Refit the relevant switch using a reversal of removal.

Ignition/starter switch

7 Undo the three bolts from under the steering column lower shroud, and prise the upper and lower shrouds apart to release the retaining pegs. Remove the lower shroud, and lift the upper shroud out of the way (see illustrations 4.4a and 4.4b).

8 Disconnect the wiring plug, then depress the clip and pull the transponder unit from the end of the ignition switch (see illustration).

9 On automatic transmission models, turn the ignition switch to position I, then press in the catch and pull the interlock cable from the side of the switch.

10 On all models, disconnect the ignition switch wiring connector.

11 Undo the two screws and remove the switch (see illustration).

12 Refitting is a reversal of removal. Insert the ignition key into the new switch when refitting.

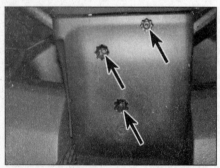

4.4a The lower steering column shroud is secured by 3 Torx bolts (arrowed)

4.4b Unclip the upper shroud and lift it out of the way, noting that it is attached to the instrument cluster surround

4.5 Undo the 2 screws (arrowed) and pull the switch to the side

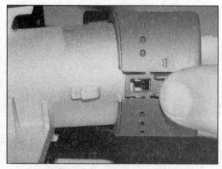

4.8 Depress the catch and pull the transponder from the ignition switch

4.11 Undo the 2 ignition switch screws

4.14 Reach through the end of the facia and push the headlight switch from place

4.19 Withdraw the hazard switch and disconnect the wiring plug

Headlight switch

13 Open the driver's door, and prise open the panel at the end face of the facia **(see illustration 3.3b)**.
14 Reach behind the facia and push the light switch from position **(see illustration)**.
15 Withdraw the switch, and disconnect the wiring connector at the rear.
16 Refitting is a reversal of removal.

Hazard warning light switch

17 Use a plastic or wooden flat-bladed tool to prise up the grille, then undo the screws securing the display screen/loudspeaker assembly from the centre of the facia **(see illustrations 19.1a and 19.1b)**. Note their fitted positions and disconnect the wiring plugs as the assembly is withdrawn.
18 Reach down behind, squeeze together the retaining clips and press the switch from the facia.

19 Withdraw the switch, and disconnect the wiring connector at the rear **(see illustration)**.
20 Refitting is a reversal of removal.

Centre console switches

21 Ensure the ignition is turned off, and wait at least 3 minutes for any residual electrical energy to dissipate before commencing work.
22 Remove the heater/air conditioning control panel as described in Chapter 3.
23 Release the three retaining clips on the lower edge of the switch panel, and remove the panel **(see illustrations)**.
24 The switches pull straight out from place **(see illustration)**.
25 Refitting is a reversal of removal.

Door panel switches/module

Front doors

26 The switch panel fitted to the front doors are integral with electronic modules which controls

the operation of the electric windows, door locks, door mirror and door open warning lights.
27 Remove the door trim panel as described in Chapter 11.
28 Undo the screw/nut securing the module, press in the retaining clips and push the assembly upwards and out of the door panel **(see illustrations)**.
29 Refitting is a reversal of removal, but test the operation of the switch before refitting the door trim panel. **Note:** *If a new switch/module has been fitted, it may need to be programmed using dedicated Volvo test equipment – entrust this task to Volvo dealer or suitably-equipped specialist.*

Rear doors

30 Remove the door trim panel as described in Chapter 11.
31 Release the four catches and pull the switch from the panel **(see illustration)**.
32 Refitting is a reversal of removal.

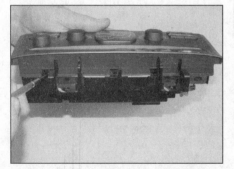

4.23a Release the 3 clips at the lower edge . . .

4.23b . . . and remove the panel . . .

4.24 . . . then pull the switch from place

4.28a Undo the switch/module screw (arrowed) . . .

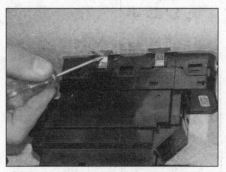

4.28b . . . and depress the retaining clips

4.31 Release the 4 catches and remove the switch

4.36 Drill out the rivet (arrowed) securing the handbrake warning switch to the bracket

Courtesy light switches

33 The courtesy light microswitches are incorporated in the door/boot lock assembly, together with the central locking motor.

Stop-light switch

34 Refer to Chapter 9.

Handbrake warning light switch

35 Remove the centre console as described in Chapter 11.
36 Drill out the rivet securing the switch to the bracket at the base of the handbrake lever **(see illustration)**.
37 Lift out the switch, disconnect the spade connector and remove it.
38 Refitting is a reversal of removal. Check for correct operation of the switch before refitting the console.

Steering wheel switches

39 Remove the driver's airbag as described in Section 23.
40 Undo the screw, and release the clip securing the relevant switch **(see illustration)**. Disconnect the wiring plugs as the switch is withdrawn.
41 Refitting is a reversal of removal.

Sunroof switch

42 Remove the overhead interior light unit as described in Section 9.
43 Lever out the retaining clips slightly, then pull the switch outwards and upwards. Disconnect the wiring plug as the unit is withdrawn.
44 Refitting is a reversal of removal.

4.40 Undo the screw, release the clip (arrowed) and remove the steering wheel switch

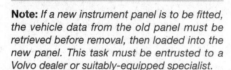

5 Instrument panel – removal and refitting

Note: *If a new instrument panel is to be fitted, the vehicle data from the old panel must be retrieved before removal, then loaded into the new panel. This task must be entrusted to a Volvo dealer or suitably-equipped specialist.*

Removal

1 The instrument panel is linked into the Volvo on-board diagnosis system (OBD), which means that any faults occurring in the instrument panel will be logged, and can be read out using diagnostic equipment (typically, a fault code reader). It is advisable, therefore, to have any less-than-obvious faults investigated by a dealer or suitably-equipped garage in the first instance. The diagnostic test equipment will be able to locate the fault, and the dealer can advise on the best course of action. In this case, take the car to the dealer – do not remove the instrument panel for diagnosis.
2 Turn the ignition off, and remove the key to prevent the ignition from being turned on.
3 Undo the three bolts and remove the steering column lower shroud, then fold back the upper shroud **(see illustrations 4.4a and 4.4b)**
4 Pull the instrument panel surround from place **(see illustration)**. Note that the upper column shroud is attached to the surround.
5 Undo the four screws and pull the instrument panel rearwards **(see illustration)**.
6 Disconnect the wiring connectors at the

rear of the instrument panel, noting their fitted positions.
7 Remove the instrument panel completely, and recover the soundproofing material above the panel. No further dismantling is recommended, apart from on models up to and including 2003 model year, where the illumination bulbs can be renewed – see Section 9. Vehicles from model year 2004 onwards are equipped with LEDs which cannot be renewed independently of the instrument panel.

Refitting

8 Refitting is a reversal of removal.

6 Electrical system sensors – removal and refitting

Note: *Not all sensors are fitted to all models.*

Vehicle speed sensor

1 Vehicle speed information for the speedometer is provided by the anti-lock braking system (ABS) wheel sensors, and this replaces the vehicle speed sensor which is often found on modern cars. If the speedometer does not work, therefore, this indicates a possible problem with the signal from the ABS wheel sensors. Check the wiring connections to the wheel sensors, and to the ABS control unit – if no fault is revealed, refer to a Volvo dealer or suitably-equipped garage for diagnostic testing.

Brake fluid level sensor

2 The brake fluid level sensor is a float incorporated in the master cylinder reservoir **(see illustration)**. The sensor and reservoir are an assembly; renew the reservoir if the unit is faulty – see Chapter 9.

Coolant level sensor

3 Wait until the engine is cold before starting this procedure. The cooling system need not be drained.
4 Lift the power steering fluid reservoir from its mounting, and place it to one side.
5 Slowly unscrew the cooling system expansion tank filler cap to release any pressure remaining in the system. Refit the cap securely.
6 Lift the expansion tank out of its mounting,

5.4 Pull the instrument panel surround from place

5.5 Undo the 4 screws (arrowed) and remove the instrument panel

6.2 Brake/clutch fluid level sensor wiring plug

6.7 Coolant lever sensor (expansion tank inverted)

and as far as possible turn it upside-down without disconnecting any of the hoses.

7 Disconnect the wiring connector at the sensor located in the base of the tank **(see illustration)**.

8 Taking care to avoid spilling any coolant, pull the sensor out of its sealing grommet.

9 Refitting is a reversal of removal. Top-up the expansion tank as described in *Weekly checks* if any coolant was lost.

Oil pressure sensor

10 The oil pressure sensor is located on the front facing side of the cylinder block, between the dipstick and the starter motor.

11 Wait until the engine is cold. Chock the rear wheels, then jack up the front of the car and support it on axle stands (see *Jacking and vehicle support*).

12 Release the screws and remove the engine undershield.

13 On diesel models, release the clamps and disconnect the hose from the charge air pipe to the intercooler.

14 On all models, disconnect the wiring connector from the sensor **(see illustration)**.

15 Unscrew the sensor and remove it from the engine.

16 Refitting is a reversal of removal, tightening the sensor to the specified torque.

Washer fluid level sensor

17 Remove the washer fluid reservoir as described in Section 14.

18 Prise the sensor's rubber grommet from the reservoir, and pull the sensor out. Disconnect the wiring connector **(see illustration)**.

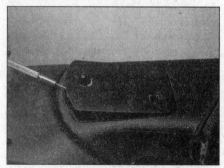

6.23 Prise the temperature sensor from the mirror housing

6.14 The oil pressure sensor (arrowed) is located on the front face of the cylinder block

19 Refitting is a reversal of removal.

Fuel level sender unit

20 Refer to Chapter 4A or 4B.

Coolant temperature sensor

21 Refer to Chapter 3.

Outside temperature sensor

Up to and including 2006 model year

22 The temperature sensor is mounted underneath the driver's door mirror. Remove the mirror assembly as described in Chapter 11.

23 Carefully prise the sensor from the mirror housing, using a flat-bladed screwdriver **(see illustration)**.

24 Extract the terminal pin from the wiring plug, and remove the sensor and wiring from the mirror housing.

From 2007 model year

25 Remove the driver's door mirror motor and cover as described in Chapter 11.

26 Release the clips and push the sensor from the mirror housing. Disconnect the wiring plug as the sensor is withdrawn.

27 Refit by reversing the removal operations.

Air quality sensor

28 Remove the windscreen wiper arms as described in Section 15.

29 Prise up the centre pins, and lever out the plastic expansion rivets, then remove the scuttle trim panel from in front of the windscreen **(see illustration 16.3 and 16.4)**.

30 The sensor is located in the air intake vent on the left-hand side of the scuttle.

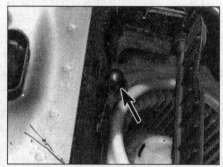

6.32 Air quality sensor (arrowed)

6.18 The level sensor (arrowed) is located on the underside of the washer fluid reservoir

31 On 2001 model year vehicles, release the retaining clip and remove the sensor. Disconnect the wiring plug as the sensor is withdrawn.

32 On 2002 model year-on vehicles, rotate the sensor 60° anti-clockwise and remove it **(see illustration)**. Disconnect the wiring plug as the sensor is withdrawn.

33 Refitting is a reversal of removal.

Evaporator temperature sensor

34 Refer to Chapter 3.

Clutch pedal position sensor

35 Refer to Chapter 6.

Brake fluid pressure sensor

36 The sensor is located on the underside of the master cylinder. Place rags or paper towels under the sensor to collect the spilt brake fluid.

37 Disconnect the sensor wiring plug, then using a deep 24 mm socket, unscrew the sensor. Immediately plug the port in the master cylinder to limit fluid loss.

38 Refitting is a reversal of removal, remembering to tighten the sensor to the specified torque, and bleed the brakes (if necessary) as described in Chapter 9.

Yaw rate/ lateral acceleration sensor

39 Remove the driver's seat as described in Chapter 11.

40 Pull the driver's side sill trim panel upwards from position.

41 Fold the carpet under the seat forwards a little, then undo the screws securing the sensor to the floor **(see illustration)**. If Note

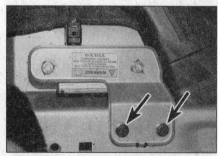

6.41 Undo the 2 screws (arrowed) and remove the yaw rate/lateral acceleration sensor

6.43 Prise the plastic cover from the sensor on the windscreen

the sensor fitted position, and disconnect the wiring plug as the sensor is withdrawn.

42 Refitting is a reversal of removal. **Note:** *If a new sensor has been fitted, it must be calibrated using Volvo dedicated test equipment. Entrust this task to a Volvo dealer or suitably-equipped specialist.*

Rain sensor

43 Carefully prise the plastic cover from the sensor **(see illustration)**.
44 Disconnect the wiring plug, then prise open the clips and remove the sensor **(see illustration)**. **Note:** *Do not touch the front face of the sensor with bare skin or the surface maybe contaminated.*
45 Refitting is a reversal of removal.

7 Control modules – general information, removal and refitting

General information

1 There are three main control modules for the vehicle body electrical system:
a) *The central electronic module (CEM) manages the functions of the headlights, foglights, windscreen washers, brake lights, headlamp washers (where applicable), central locking, immobiliser, headlamp range adjustment, indicators, blindspot information system, courtesy lighting, rear electric windows, fuel pump, starter motor, speed-sensitive power steering, heated seats, and*

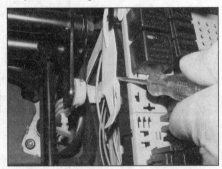

7.4 Spread the retaining bracket and swivel the base of the CEM rearwards

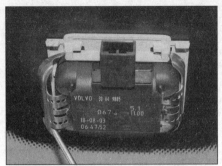

6.44 Prise open the rain sensor retaining clips

the horn, but also acts as a bridge between the high-speed and low-speed communication networks (databuses). Consequently, it monitors the signals between most of the vehicles sensors, actuators and control modules. As the CEM communicates with all other modules, it contains the vehicle's self-diagnosis system and stores any fault codes generated. The CEM also contains information specific to the vehicle: VIN, build details, and vehicle equipment options. Consequently, if the CEM needs renewing, the stored information must be retrieved prior to removal, and then programmed into the new unit once fitted.
b) *The upper electronic control module (UEM) manages the functions of the alarm siren, sunroof, movement sensor, rain sensor, interior ceiling lights, sunvisor lighting, auto-dipping rear view mirror, tyre pressure warning system, compass and the seat belt reminder system. The UEM communicates directly with the CEM via the CAN databus information network.*
c) *The rear electronic control module (REM) manages the certain functions of the alarm system, central locking, headlamp range control (Xenon headlights only), fuel level, diesel filter preheating, rear foglights, reversing lights, high-level brake lights, rear screen demisting, electric head restraints, luggage compartment lighting, rear electric windows and parking assistance system (where applicable). The REM communicates directly with the CEM via the CAN databus information network.*

7.9a Release the catches and remove the cover . . .

Central electronic control module

Note: *If the CEM is to be renewed, stored information must be retrieved and then programmed into the new CEM. As this task requires the use of dedicated Volvo test equipment, entrust it to a Volvo dealer or suitably-equipped specialist.*
2 Disconnect the battery negative lead as described in Chapter 5A.

Up to and including 2004 model year

3 Undo the two screws, and remove the lower facia trim panel above the driver's pedals.
4 Prise open the retaining bracket, swivel the base of the CEM rearwards, then pull it downwards from the facia **(see illustration)**.
5 Undo the screw and disconnect the CEM wiring plug. Take care not to damage any of the terminal pins.
6 Note their fitted locations, then pull out the relays mounted on the CEM.
7 Release the catch on the rear of the box, and slide out the CEM.

From 2005 model year

8 Remove the windscreen wiper linkage/motor as described in Section 16.
9 Working in the right-hand side of the wiper motor recess, release the 5 catches, remove the cover/foam insert, then note their fitted positions, undo the screws/release the catches, and disconnect the wiring plugs from the CEM **(see illustrations)**.
10 Undo the two screws, and remove the facia trim panel above the driver's pedals.
11 Note their fitted locations, and disconnect the wiring plugs from the CEM. Use a screwdriver to spread the brackets and manoeuvre the CEM from under the bracket **(see illustration 7.4)**.
12 Note their fitted positions, and remove the fuses from the CEM.

All models

13 Refitting is a reversal of removal, taking great care not to damage the fragile pins in the control module connectors.

Upper electronic control module

14 The UEM is integral with the interior mirror, and must be renewed as a complete assembly. Refer to Chapter 11.

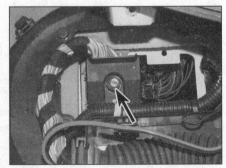

7.9b . . . then undo the screw (arrowed) and disconnect the wiring plugs

Rear electronic control module

15 Ensure the ignition is turned off, then remove the left-hand side panel from the luggage compartment (see Chapter 11).

16 Prise up the retaining clip and manoeuvre the integrated relay/fusebox from position **(see illustration)**.

17 Undo the screw and disconnect the REM wiring plug **(see illustration)**. Take care not to damage any of the terminal pins.

18 Note their fitted locations, then pull out the relays mounted on the REM.

19 Release the catch on the rear of the box, and slide out the REM.

20 Refitting is a reversal of removal, taking great care not to damage the fragile pins in the control module connectors.

8 Bulbs (exterior lights) – renewal

General

1 Whenever a bulb is renewed, note the following points:

a) Remember that if the light has just been in use, the bulb may be extremely hot.

b) Always check the bulb contacts and holder, ensuring that there is clean metal-to-metal contact between the bulb and its live(s) and earth. Clean off any corrosion or dirt before fitting a new bulb.

c) Wherever bayonet-type bulbs are fitted,

7.16 Prise up the retaining clip (arrowed)

ensure that the live contact(s) bear firmly against the bulb contact.

d) Always ensure that the new bulb is of the correct rating and that it is completely clean before fitting it; this applies particularly to headlight/foglight bulbs (see below).

e) With quartz halogen bulbs (headlights and similar applications), use a tissue or clean cloth when handling the bulb; do not touch the bulb glass with the fingers. Even small quantities of grease from the fingers will cause blackening and premature failure. If a bulb is accidentally touched, clean it with methylated spirit and a clean rag.

Halogen headlight main beam

H9 bulbs

2 Open the bonnet. Peel away the inner rubber cap **(see illustration)**.

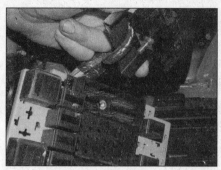

7.17 Undo the screw and disconnect the wiring plug

3 Press the bulb in, rotate it anti-clockwise and pull it from place **(see illustrations)**. Note how the bulb fits in the reflector.

4 Lift the clip and pull the wiring plug from the bulbholder **(see illustration)**.

5 When fitting the new bulb, do not touch the glass (paragraph 1). Make sure that the lugs on the bulb flange engage with the slots in the holder.

6 Refitting is a reversal of removal.

HB3 bulbs

7 Open the bonnet. Rotate the inner plastic cover on the rear of the light unit anti-clockwise and lift off **(see illustration)**.

8 Disconnect the wiring plug, then twist the bulbholder anti-clockwise and remove it from the headlight **(see illustration)**.

9 The bulb is integral with the holder.

10 When fitting the new bulb, do not touch the glass (paragraph 1).

8.2 Peel away the inner rubber cap

8.3a Press in the bulb (arrowed), rotate it anti-clockwise . . .

8.3b . . . and pull it from place

8.4 Lift the clip and disconnect the wiring plug

8.7 Rotate the inner cover anti-clockwise (arrowed)

8.8 Twist the bulbholder anti-clockwise and remove it

8.11 Peel away the outer rubber cap

8.12a Pull the wiring plug from the bulb . . .

8.12b . . . release the wiring clip . . .

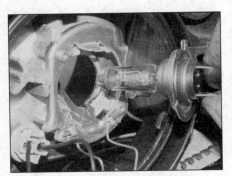

8.12c . . . and remove the bulb

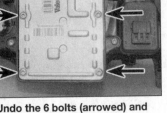

8.15a Undo the 6 bolts (arrowed) and remove the igniter/ballast unit . . .

8.15b . . . then disconnect the bulbholder wiring plug (arrowed)

Halogen headlight dipped beam

11 Open the bonnet. Rotate the outer plastic cover on the rear of the light unit-anticlockwise and lift it off, or on later models, peel away the rubber cap **(see illustration)**. **Note:** *If renewing*

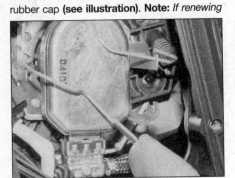

8.16 Release the bulbholder retaining clip

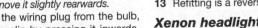
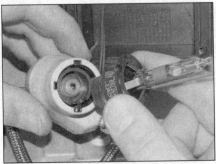

8.17 Rotate the bulb anti-clockwise and remove it from the holder

the left-hand bulb and more access is required, pull the air filter housing upwards from its rubber mountings and move it slightly rearwards.

12 Disconnect the wiring plug from the bulb, then release the clip by pressing it inwards, and remove the bulb **(see illustrations)**. Note

how the bulb fits in the reflector – it will only fit in one position.

13 Refitting is a reversal of removal.

Xenon headlight

Bulbs

Caution: Xenon bulbs are pressurised to approximately 10 bar. The bulbs must be handled delicately or there is a risk of explosion. Always wear gloves and safety goggles when handling Xenon bulbs.

14 Due to the high voltages (approximately 22 000 volts) required by Xenon gas discharge bulbs, disconnect the battery negative lead (see Chapter 5A) then turn on the main and dipped beams alternately to dissipate any residual electrical energy – allow the bulb(s) to cool before commencing.

15 Open the bonnet. Rotate the outer plastic cover anti-clockwise and remove it. If improved access is required, remove the headlight as described in Section 10. Slide the connector down from the bulbholder **(see illustrations)**.

16 Release the spring clip, then twist the bulbholder anti-clockwise and remove it from the headlight **(see illustration)**.

17 Note the fitted position of the bulb in the holder, then carefully press in the bulb, rotate it anti-clockwise and remove it from the holder **(see illustration)**. Do not touch the glass envelope of the bulb.

18 Press the new bulb into the holder and rotate it clockwise to the position shown **(see illustration)**.

19 Insert the bulb and holder into the rear of the reflector, ensuring the slots on the bulb

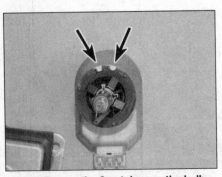

8.18 Ensure the 2 notches on the bulb flange are positioned as shown

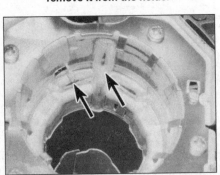

8.19 Ensure the notches on the bulb flange align with the lugs (arrowed) in the reflector

8.27 Pull the sidelight bulbholder from the reflector

flange align with the lugs in the reflector **(see illustration)**.

20 Rotate the bulbholder clockwise to the locked position, and secure it in place with the retaining clips.

21 Refit the cover.

Ballast/igniter

22 Due to the high voltages (approximately 22 000 volts) required by Xenon gas discharge bulbs, disconnect the battery negative lead (see Chapter 5A) then turn on the main and dipped beams alternately to dissipate any residual electrical energy – allow the bulb(s) to cool before commencing.

23 Remove the relevant headlight as described in Section 10.

24 Undo the Torx bolts securing the ballast/igniter, then disconnect the wiring plug and remove it **(see illustration 8.15a)**.

25 Refitting is a reversal of removal.

Sidelight

Halogen headlights

26 Open the bonnet. Rotate the dipped beam plastic cover on the rear of the light unit anti-clockwise and remove it, or on later models, peel away the rubber cap. **Note:** *If renewing the left-hand bulb and more access is required, pull the air filter housing upwards from its rubber mountings and move it slightly rearwards.*

27 Pull the bulbholder (located adjacent to the dipped beam bulb) from the rear of the headlight – there is no need to disconnect the wiring plug **(see illustration)**.

Xenon headlights

28 Prise off the plastic cover on the rear of the headlight **(see illustration)**. **Note:** *If renewing the left-hand bulb, undo the clips and remove the air filter cover to improve access (see Chapter 4A or 4B).*

29 Using a pair of thin-nosed pliers, depress the retaining catches and pull the bulbholder from position.

All headlights

30 Pull the wedge-base bulb out of the holder **(see illustration)**.

31 Refitting is a reversal of removal.

Front foglight

32 The foglight bulb is accessed from behind

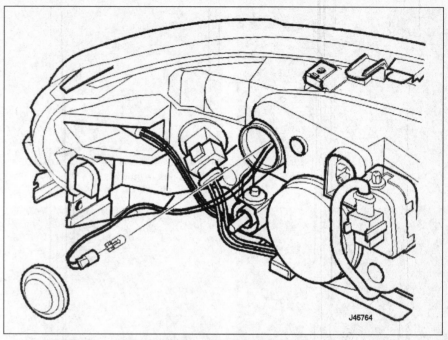

8.28 Remove the plastic cover and pull the bulbholder from the reflector (Xenon headlight)

the light unit – if preferred, jack up the front of the car for better access.

33 The bulbholder has two tabs to make it easier to turn – twist the bulbholder anti-clockwise to release it from the back of the light unit **(see illustration)**.

34 Remove the bulb from the bulbholder **(see illustration)**.

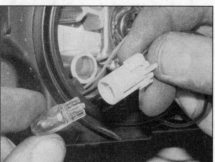

8.30 Pull the sidelight wedge bulb from the holder

8.34 Pull the foglight bulb from the holder

35 Refitting is a reversal of removal.

Front direction indicator

36 If renewing the right-hand side indicator bulb, undo the screw and pull the washer fluid reservoir filler neck from the reservoir **(see illustration)**. **Note:** *If renewing the left-hand bulb and more access is required, pull the*

8.33 Twist the foglight bulbholder anti-clockwise and remove it

8.36 Undo the screw (arrowed) and pull the reservoir filler neck from position

8.37 Rotate the bulbholder anti-clockwise

8.38 Push and twist the bulb anti-clockwise to remove it

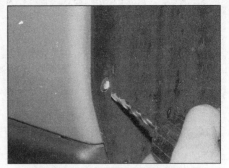

8.40a Drill out the 4 rivets securing the wheel arch liner to the wing . . .

8.40b . . . then reach behind and squeeze together the retaining clips (arrowed) to remove the side repeater

8.42 Pull the side repeater wedge bulb from the holder

8.44 Remove the access panel behind the rear lights

air filter housing upwards from its rubber mountings and move it slightly rearwards.
37 Regardless of which side, rotate the bulbholder clockwise and remove it from the rear of the headlight assembly **(see illustration)**.
38 Push in and twist the bulb anti-clockwise to remove it from the bulbholder **(see illustration)**.
39 Refitting is a reversal of removal.

Direction indicator side repeater

40 Volvo suggest that it's possible to open the relevant front door halfway, then reach behind the wing and press the repeater light from the wing. However, we found this impossible with adult-sized hands (as well as dangerous – do not attempt this in windy conditions). Consequently we found in necessary to drill out the 4 rivets securing the lower part of the wheel arch liner, then reach behind the liner/

wing to squeeze together the clips and push the repeater from the wing **(see illustrations)**.
41 Twist the bulbholder through a quarter-turn anti-clockwise to release it from the light unit, and withdraw the holder.
42 Pull the bulb from its holder, and press the new one into position **(see illustration)**.
43 Refitting is a reversal of removal.

Rear light cluster

44 From within the boot, rotate the retaining catch anti-clockwise to the vertical position, then fold down the access panel behind the rear light cluster **(see illustration)**.
45 Squeeze together the retaining clips and remove the bulbholder assembly from the rear of the light unit **(see illustration)**.
46 Push in and twist the bulb anti-clockwise to remove it from the bulbholder.
47 Refitting is a reversal of removal.

High-level brake light

48 The high-level brake light does not contain conventional light bulbs, but rather a row of LEDs (light-emitting diodes). As a result, if the high-level brake light stops working, it may ultimately be necessary to renew the light unit complete – see Section 10. Before deciding that this is necessary, however, check the fuse and all wiring, using the information in Section 2 and the wiring diagrams at the end of this Chapter.

Number plate light

49 Undo the Torx bolt securing the relevant light unit to the boot lid **(see illustration)**.
50 Carefully prise out the light unit **(see illustration)**.
51 Rotate the bulbholder anti-clockwise and pull it from the light unit.
52 Pull the wedge-type bulb out of the holder.
53 Refitting is a reversal of removal.

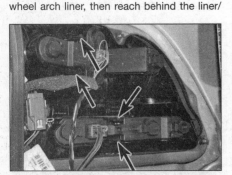

8.45 Squeeze together the clips (arrowed) and pull the bulbholder from the rear light cluster

8.49 Undo the number plate light retaining bolt . . .

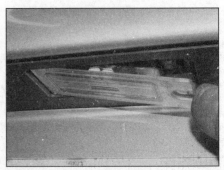

8.50 . . . and prise the light unit from the boot lid

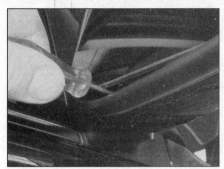

8.54a Insert a small screwdriver to release the clip . . .

8.54b . . . and pull the light unit from the underside of the door mirror

8.58 Rotate the bulbholder anti-clockwise (left-hand side light) or clockwise (right-hand side light)

Door mirror ground light bulb

54 Angle the mirror glass upwards and outwards, then using a screwdriver, release the retaining clip and pull the light unit from the mirror **(see illustrations)**.
55 Twist the bulbholder from the light unit, and pull out the bulb.
56 Refitting is a reversal of removal.

Side marker bulb

57 Remove the front indicator bulbholder, as described in this Section, to access the side marker bulbholder.
58 Rotate the bulbholder anti-clockwise (left-hand side) or clockwise (right-hand side) and pull it from the headlight **(see illustration)**.
59 Pull the wedge type bulb from the holder.
60 Refitting is a reversal of removal.

9	Bulbs (interior lights) – renewal

General

1 Whenever a bulb is renewed, note the following points:
a) Remember that if the light has just been in use, the bulb may be extremely hot.
b) Always check the bulb contacts and holder, ensuring that there is clean metal-to-metal contact between the bulb and its live(s) and earth. Clean off any corrosion or dirt before fitting a new bulb.

c) Wherever bayonet-type bulbs are fitted, ensure that the live contact(s) bear firmly against the bulb contact.
d) Always ensure that the new bulb is of the correct rating and that it is completely clean before fitting it.
2 Some switch illumination/pilot bulbs are integral with their switches, and cannot be renewed separately.

Vanity mirror lights

3 Carefully prise the mirror unit from the sunvisor **(see illustration)**.
4 Prise the festoon type bulb from the bulbholder contacts **(see illustration)**.
5 Refitting is a reversal of removal. Insert the top edge of the mirror unit first.

Rear courtesy/reading lights

6 Using a small flat-bladed screwdriver,

9.3 Prise the mirror assembly from the sunvisor . . .

carefully prise the lens from place **(see illustration)**.
7 Depress the retaining clips and pull down the front edge of the light unit **(see illustration)**.
8 Disconnect the bulbholder connector, remove the reflector and pull the festoon type bulb from the holder **(see illustration)**.
9 Refitting is a reversal of removal.

Front courtesy/reading lights

10 Carefully prise the lenses from the cover **(see illustration)**.
11 Fold down the cover behind the interior mirror, then press the clips outwards and remove the lens/cover assembly **(see illustration)**.
12 Remove the bulb from the bulbholder.
13 Refitting is a reversal of removal.

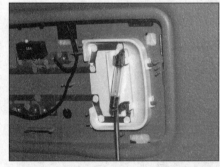

9.4 . . . and remove the festoon bulb

9.6 Prise the rear courtesy/reading light lens from position

9.7 Depress the clips and pull down the front edge of the light unit

9.8 Remove the reflector

9.10 Prise the front courtesy/reading light lenses from place

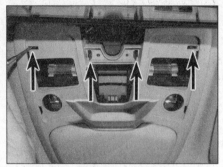

9.11 Release the clips (arrowed) and remove the cover

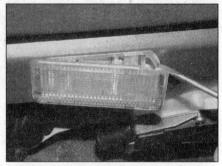

9.14 Prise the right-hand end of the lens from the glovebox aperture

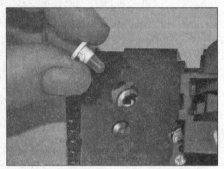

9.18 The heater control panel bulb is integral with the holder

9.26 The lighting switch illumination bulbs are integral with the holder

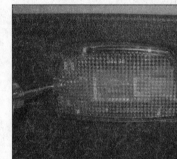

9.32 Carefully prise the luggage compartment light unit from place

Glovebox light

14 Carefully prise the light unit from the underside of the facia **(see illustration)**.
15 Pull the festoon bulb from the contacts.
16 Refitting is a reversal of removal.

Heater control/switch panel illumination bulbs

17 Remove the heater control panel as described in Chapter 3.
18 Rotate the bulbholder anti-clockwise and pull it from the rear of the panel **(see illustration)**. The bulbs are integral with the holder.
19 Note that the bulbs for the lower row of switches cannot be renewed.
20 Refitting is a reversal of removal.

Door edge marker light bulb

21 Prise the lower edge of the light lens (where fitted) from the door.

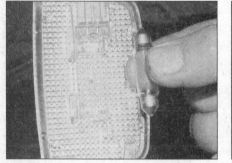

9.36 Pull the festoon bulb from place

22 Withdraw the unit from the door, twist the lens from the bulbholder and pull out the wedge-base bulb.
23 Refitting is a reversal of removal.

Automatic transmission selector panel illumination bulb

24 The selector panel is illuminated by LEDs. If faulty the entire panel must be renewed.

Lighting switch illumination bulbs

25 Remove the switch as described in Section 4.
26 Rotate the bulbholder(s) anti-clockwise, and remove it from the rear of the unit **(see illustration)**.
27 Refitting is a reversal of removal.

Instrument panel bulbs

28 It is only possible to renew the illumination

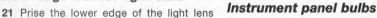
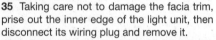

9.40 Rotate the bulbholder anti-clockwise, and pull it from the transponder

bulbs on vehicles manufactured up to and including 2003 model year. After this date, the panel is illuminated by LEDs, which cannot be renewed independently of the instrument panel.
29 Remove the instrument panel completely as described in Section 5.
30 Rotate the bulbholder anti-clockwise and pull it from the rear of the panel. Pull the bulb from the holder.
31 Refitting is a reversal of removal.

Luggage area illumination bulb

32 Carefully prise the light unit from position **(see illustration)**.
33 Remove the bulb from the holder.
34 Refitting is a reversal of removal.

Footwell lights

35 Taking care not to damage the facia trim, prise out the inner edge of the light unit, then disconnect its wiring plug and remove it.
36 Pull the festoon bulb from the contacts **(see illustration)**.
37 Refitting is a reversal of removal.

Ignition switch illumination

38 Undo the three bolts securing the lower steering column shroud, and detach it from the upper shroud.
39 Disconnect the transponder wiring plug, depress the clip and slide the transponder from the ignition switch **(see illustration 4.8)**.
40 Rotate the bulbholder anti-clockwise and remove it from the transponder. The bulb is integral with the holder **(see illustration)**.
41 Refitting is a reversal of removal.

10.2 Undo the bumper side guide screws (arrowed)

10.3a Undo the screw on the outer side of the headlight . . .

10.3b . . . and the remaining headlight screws (arrowed)

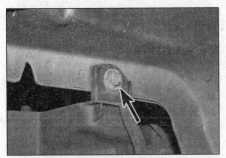

10.7a The lower air baffle is secured by one bolt each side (arrowed – viewed through the wheel arch) . . .

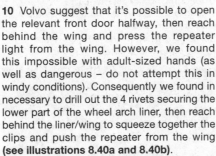

10.7b . . . and a clip each side at the front (arrowed – shown with the bumper removed for clarity)

10.8 Undo the 3 bolts (arrowed) and remove the foglight

10 Exterior light units – removal and refitting

Caution: Ensure the ignition is turned off before proceeding.

Headlight

1 Remove the front bumper as described in Chapter 11.
2 Mark the fitted positions of the bumper side guides, then undo the screws **(see illustration)**. Pull the guide outwards slightly for access to the rearmost headlight retaining screw.
3 Remove the 4 headlight retaining screws **(see illustrations)**.
4 Disconnect the wiring plug as the headlight is removed.
5 Refitting is a reversal of removal. Have the headlight beam alignment checked on completion (see Section 11).

Front foglight

6 Apply the handbrake, chock the rear wheels, then jack up the front of the car and support it securely on axle stands.
7 Undo the bolts/release the clips and remove the air baffle assembly from behind the front bumper **(see illustrations)**.
8 Disconnect the foglight wiring plug, then undo the three Torx bolts and remove the foglight **(see illustration)**.
9 Refitting is a reversal of removal.

Direction indicator side repeater

10 Volvo suggest that it's possible to open the relevant front door halfway, then reach behind the wing and press the repeater light from the wing. However, we found this impossible with adult-sized hands (as well as dangerous – do not attempt this in windy conditions). Consequently we found in necessary to drill out the 4 rivets securing the lower part of the wheel arch liner, then reach behind the liner/wing to squeeze together the clips and push the repeater from the wing **(see illustrations 8.40a and 8.40b)**.
11 Disconnect the bulbholder wiring plug.
12 Refitting is a reversal of removal.

Rear light clusters

13 From within the luggage compartment, rotate the retaining catch anti-clockwise to the vertical position, then fold down the access panel behind the rear light cluster **(see illustration 8.44)**.
14 Disconnected the rear light cluster wiring plugs(s).
15 Undo the four nuts and remove the cluster from the vehicle **(see illustration)**.
16 Refitting is a reversal of removal.

High-level brake light

17 Removal of the high-level brake light on these models involves partial removal of the rear headlining. In order to remove and refit the headlining without damage, considerable skill and experience is required, and therefore is best entrusted to a Volvo dealer or automotive upholstery specialist. Note that the bulbs in the high-level brake light are actually LEDs (light-emitting diodes), and these cannot be renewed separately.

Number plate light

18 Undo the Torx bolt securing the relevant light unit to the boot lid **(see illustration 8.49)**.
19 Carefully prise/slide out the light unit **(see illustration 8.50)**.
20 Rotate the bulbholder anti-clockwise and pull it from the light unit.
21 Refitting is a reversal of removal.

11 Headlight beam alignment – checking and adjusting

1 Beam alignment should be carried out by a Volvo dealer or other specialist heaving the necessary optical alignment equipment.
2 For reference, the headlights can be adjusted by means of the vertical and

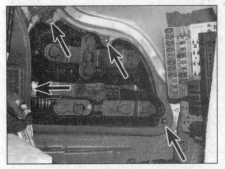

10.15 Undo the 4 nuts (arrowed) and remove the rear light cluster

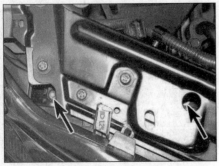

11.2a Headlight beam alignment adjustment screws (arrowed) – early models . . .

11.2b . . . and later models (arrowed)

horizontal adjuster controls at the top of the headlight unit (see illustrations).

3 Some models are equipped with an electrically-operated headlight beam adjustment system which is controlled through the switch on the facia. On these models, ensure that the switch is set to the off position before adjusting the headlight aim.

12 Headlight beam control motor – removal and refitting

Removal

1 Although not essential, this operation is much easier (especially refitting) if the headlight unit is removed as described in Section 10.

2 If not already done, disconnect the wiring

12.4 Rotate the motor (see text) to release the bayonet fitting . . .

13.2 Undo the bolt (arrowed) and remove the horn

connector at the beam control motor on the rear of the headlight unit.

3 Remove the plastic bulb cover/peel away the rubber cap adjacent to the motor.

4 Turn the motor clockwise (right-hand side) or anti-clockwise (left-hand side) to release the motor bayonet fitting attachment (see illustration).

5 Angle the motor downwards so the motor shaft comes out of the top of the slot in the rear of the headlight reflector. Remove the motor (see illustration).

Refitting

6 Turn the beam height control adjuster on the motor anti-clockwise as far as it will go to extend the motor shaft fully.

7 Lightly lubricate the end of the motor shaft with medium grease.

8 Working through the bulb aperture in the rear of the headlight. Hold the headlight

12.5 . . . then angle the motor downwards to disengage the shaft

14.2 Disconnect the hose and wiring plug from the washer pump

reflector, while engaging the motor shaft with the slot in the back of the reflector.

9 Turn the motor anti-clockwise to lock the bayonet attachment.

10 Reconnect the wiring connectors and check the operation of the motor.

11 Refit the cover to the rear of the headlight.

12 Have the beam adjustment basic setting checked and if necessary adjusted by a dealer or specialist.

13 Horn – renewal

1 Remove the front bumper as described in Chapter 11.

2 Unbolt the horn from its bracket and remove it (see illustration). Disconnect the wiring plug as the horn is removed.

3 Refitting is a reversal of removal.

14 Washer system components – removal and refitting

Windscreen washer pump

Removal

1 Remove the washer reservoir as described in this Section.

2 Note their fitted locations, then pull the hose(s) from the motor, and disconnect the motor wiring plug (see illustration).

3 Place a container under the reservoir, and be prepared for spillage.

4 Grip the washer pump and pull it out of the reservoir.

Refitting

5 Refitting is a reversal of removal. Coat the rubber grommet in soap solution to aid refitting.

Washer reservoir

Removal

6 From within the engine compartment, undo the retaining screw, then remove the washer fluid reservoir filler neck by pulling it up and out of the tank. Separate the hoses from the filler neck – yellow valve for the front windscreen washer and white valve for the rear screen washer (where fitted).

7 Remove the front bumper as described in Chapter 11.

8 Mark the fitted position of the bumper guide on the driver's side, then undo the bolts and remove the guide from the vehicle (see illustration 10.2).

9 Disconnect the wiring plugs from the level sensor and pump(s) on the reservoir, then undo the bolts, and lower the reservoir from position (see illustration).

14.9 Undo the 2 bolts (arrowed) and remove the washer reservoir

14.11 Prise the plastic grommet from the lower edge of the bonnet

14.13 Squeeze together the jet retaining clips (arrowed – shown with the jet removed for clarity)

Refitting

10 Refitting is a reversal of removal.

Washer jets

Removal

11 Open the bonnet, and prise out the plastic grommets (where fitted) at the lower edge of the bonnet **(see illustration)**.
12 Disconnect the jet wiring plug (where applicable) and disconnect the washer hose.
13 Squeeze together the two retaining clips on the underside of the jet using pliers, and push the jet from the bonnet **(see illustration)**.

Refitting

14 Push the jet into its location until the side catches spring out to lock. Reconnect the fluid hose and wiring plug (where applicable)
15 Adjust the jet nozzles using a pin so that liquid is sprayed onto the centre of the glass.

Washer fluid level sensor

16 Refer to Section 6.

Non-return check valve

Removal

17 To prevent washer fluid running back into the reservoir, a non-return valve is fitted into the supply hose to each washer jet. Open the bonnet, prise out the plastic rivets and release the washer hose from the retaining clips.
18 Carefully pull the hoses from the non-return valve, noting the direction of flow marking on the valve.
19 It should only be possible to blow through the valve in one direction. If faulty, the valve must be renewed.

Refitting

20 Refitting is a reversal of removal.

15 Wiper arms – removal and refitting

Removal

1 Lift up or prise off the cover (where applicable) then slacken the nut at the base of the wiper arm **(see illustration)**.
2 Press the front wiper arms down, and tap

them gently to break the bond between the arm and spindle – use tape to protect the arm. Using a rocking motion, pull the arms off the splines. If necessary, use a puller to remove the arms **(see illustration)**.

Refitting

3 Switch the relevant wiper on, then switch it off again to ensure that the motor and linkage are parked. Position the windscreen wiper arms so that the middle of the wiper blade is 50 mm from the top edge of the cowl panel.

16 Windscreen wiper motor and linkage – removal and refitting

Removal

1 Switch the wipers on, then off again

15.1 Lift up the cover and undo the wiper spindle nut (arrowed)

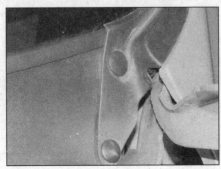

16.3 Prise out the corner trim panel plastic clips

to ensure that the motor and linkage are parked.
2 Remove the windscreen wiper arms as described in Section 15.
3 Open the bonnet, prise out the plastic clips then remove the plastic trim panels at the front lower corners of the windscreen – the panels are hooked under the bottom edge of the screen **(see illustration)**.
4 Push in the centre pins, then lever out the four plastic rivets securing the scuttle trim panel **(see illustration)**. Remove the trim panel – the upper edge of the panel slides out from the trim at the base of the windscreen. **Note:** *The centre pins are easily lost – try to catch them as they are pushed through the rivets.*
5 Disconnect the wiper motor wiring plug, then undo the bolts and remove the linkage/ frame **(see illustration)**.
6 Mark the position of the motor crank arm

15.2 If necessary, use a puller to remove the arm from the spindle

16.4 Scuttle trim panel plastic expansion rivets (right-hand side ones arrowed)

16.5 Undo the 2 bolts (arrowed) and remove the wiper linkage and motor assembly

17.2 Undo the bolts (arrowed) and detach the headlight wiper motor

relative to the frame, undo the nut and remove the crank arm from the motor.

7 Undo the three motor retaining bolts and remove the motor from the frame. The frame and linkage arms are an assembly, and cannot be individually renewed.

Refitting

8 Refit the motor to the frame, and secure with the three mounting bolts.

9 If a new motor is being fitted, temporarily reconnect the wiring connectors at the car, switch on the motor then switch it off again to ensure that it is parked.

10 Position the crank arm on the motor, with the marks made on removal aligned. Prevent the crank arm from turning by holding it with a spanner, then refit and tighten the nut.

11 Alternatively, if a new frame and linkage are being fitted, set the motor to the park position as described previously then, when connecting the crank arm to the motor, position it so that it is parallel with the linkage arm directly above.

12 The assembled components can now be refitted using a reversal of removal.

17 Headlight wiper motor – renewal

1 Remove the headlight as described in Section 10.

2 Undo the two bolts and remove the motor **(see illustration)**.

3 Refitting is a reversal of removal. Take care not to trap the washer hose when installing the motor. Before refitting the wiper arm, switch the motor on and off so that it is in the park position.

18 Audio units – removal and refitting

Facia-mounted audio units

1 Remove the climate control panel as described in Chapter 3.

Up to and including 2004 model year

2 Undo the two screws at the lower edge of

the audio unit, and lower it from the centre panel and manoeuvre it rearwards. Before it's disconnected, if the CD/radio mechanism is being renewed, the old unit must be reset as follows: Hold the unit as it was installed (15° to 20° from the horizontal), then turn on the ignition, and disconnect the green connector from the unit for 5 seconds **(see illustrations)**. Reconnect the unit, which has now been reset. Wait until no further noise is heard from the unit, then unplug it and withdraw it from the vehicle.

From 2005 model year

3 Release the 4 clips and press the audio unit from the mounting **(see illustration)**. Note that if a new Volvo audio unit has been fitted, suitable software will need to be downloaded from Volvo. Entrust this task to a Volvo dealer or suitably-equipped specialist.

All models

4 Refitting is a reversal of removal.

CD autochanger

5 Open the boot lid, and open the access panel on the left-hand side of the luggage compartment.

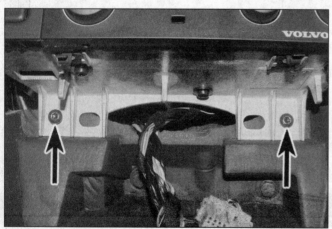

18.2a Undo the 2 screws (arrowed) under the facia-mounted audio unit

18.2b Unplug the green connector (arrowed) from the rear of the unit

6 Undo the screws securing the changer bracket to the vehicle body, then unhook the bracket and lift it up.

7 Disconnect the wiring plugs, then undo the screws securing the bracket to the changer.

8 Refitting is a reversal of removal.

Audio amplifier

9 Remove the driver's seat as described in Chapter 11.

10 Undo the two retaining screws, and disconnect the wiring plugs as the amplifier is withdrawn **(see illustration)**.

11 Refitting is the reversal of removal.

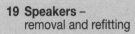

19 Speakers –
removal and refitting

Facia speaker

1 Carefully prise up the speaker/display unit grille on the top of the facia **(see illustrations)**.

2 Undo the screws and lift the speaker/display unit up **(see illustration)**. Disconnect the wiring and remove the speaker.

3 Refitting is a reversal of removal, making sure the speaker is correctly located.

Door speaker

4 Remove the door trim panel as described in Chapter 11.

5 Drill out the rivets securing the speaker to the door frame **(see illustration)**.

6 Remove the speaker and disconnect the wiring connector.

7 To remove the tweeter, release the retaining clips **(see illustration)**.

8 Refitting is a reversal of removal.

Parcel shelf speaker

9 Remove the parcel shelf as described in Chapter 11.

10 Disconnect the speaker wiring plug.

11 Undo the two screws at the front of the speakers, then lift the speaker from position **(see illustration)**.

12 Refitting is a reversal of removal.

18.3 Release the 2 clips each side and press the audio unit from the mounting

18.10 Audio amplifier retaining screws (arrowed)

19.1a Prise up the speaker grille from the facia . . .

19.1b . . . or the speaker/display unit surround trim

19.2 Facia speaker screws (arrowed)

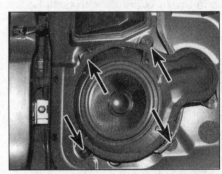

19.5 Drill out the speaker rivets (arrowed – front door speaker shown)

19.7 Release the clips and remove the tweeter

19.11 Undo the 2 screws (arrowed) and remove the speaker

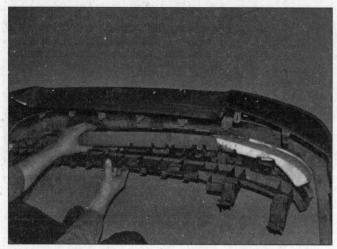

20.2 Unclip the inner section of the rear bumper . . .

20.3 . . . then prise out the clips (arrowed) and remove the aerial

20 Radio aerial and amplifier – removal and refitting

Removal

Bumper-mounted aerial

1 The aerial is fitted behind the rear bumper. Remove the bumper and luggage compartment right-hand side trim panel as described in Chapter 11.
2 Disconnect the aerial wiring plug, then release the clips and remove the inner section of the bumper **(see illustration)**.
3 Release the 2 clips and remove the aerial **(see illustration)**.

Bumper aerial amplifier

4 The amplifier is fitted behind the right-hand side luggage compartment trim panel. Remove the panel as described in Chapter 11.
5 Undo the single retaining screw, and remove the amplifier. Disconnect the wiring plug as the amplifier is removed.

Rear windscreen aerial

6 The main aerial may be a wire filament incorporated into the rear window glass. Remove the left-hand C-pillar trim as described in Chapter 11. The aerial works in conjunction with a signal booster located behind the trim panel adjacent to the rear window.

Refitting

7 Refitting is a reversal of removal.

21 Anti-theft alarm and immobiliser system – general information

Note: *This information is applicable only to the systems fitted by Volvo as original equipment.*

All models are equipped with an anti-theft alarm, and most are also equipped with an ignition immobiliser.

Immobiliser

The electronic immobiliser is automatically activated when the ignition key is removed from the ignition switch. When activated, it cuts the ignition circuit, preventing the engine from being started.

The system is disarmed when the ignition key is inserted into the ignition switch, as follows. The head of the ignition key contains a transponder microchip, and the ignition lock contains a reader coil. When the key enters the lock, the reader coil recognises the signal from the microchip, and de-activates the immobiliser. It is essential that the key tag showing the key number is not lost (this will be supplied with the car when new). Any duplicate keys will have to be obtained from a Volvo dealer, who will need the key number to supply a duplicate – any keys cut elsewhere will work the door locks, but will not contain the transponder chip necessary to de-activate the immobiliser and allow the engine to be started.

The immobiliser reader coil can be removed from the ignition switch, after removing the column lower shroud. However, it is unclear at the time of writing whether a new reader coil can be matched to a particular key or control unit.

Any problems or work involving the immobiliser system should be entrusted to a Volvo dealer or specialist, as dedicated electronic equipment is required to diagnose faults, or to 'match' the various components.

Alarm

An anti-theft alarm system is fitted as standard equipment. The alarm has switches on all the doors, the boot lid, the bonnet and ignition switch. If the boot lid, bonnet or any of the doors are opened or the ignition switch is switched on whilst the alarm is set, the alarm horn will sound and the hazard warning lights will flash. The alarm also has an immobiliser function which makes the ignition inoperable whilst the alarm is triggered.

The alarm system may be upgraded with various options, to give greater security:
a) *The glass breakage sensor detects the sound of glass breaking, such as when a side or rear window is attacked by a thief trying to gain entry. If this is not fitted, and the doors are not opened, the standard alarm will not sound.*
b) *The movement sensor system detects movement inside the car – if access has been gained without the alarm sounding, this sensor should trigger the alarm. The system consists of an emitter and a sensor – the emitter sends out a high-frequency wave signal, which is detected by the sensor. If the wave pattern is distorted or interrupted, the alarm will be triggered.*
c) *The inclination sensor detects movement of the vehicle body, and in particular, any change in attitude resulting from it being jacked up. The sensor often takes the form of a mercury switch, or it may be a ball-bearing and saucer type. Once the alarm is set and the position of the switch has been noted, any attempt to rock the car, or to jack it up, will result in the alarm sounding.*
d) *The backup battery is perhaps the most useful of any of the alarm options. One of the most common methods of disabling an alarm is to disconnect the vehicle battery. If a backup battery is fitted, the alarm will still sound even after being tampered with in this way.*

Signals from the alarm system switches and contacts which are integral with the door, bonnet and boot lid locks are sent to a central control unit inside the car once the system is set. The control unit monitors the signals and activates the alarm if any of the signal loops are broken, or if an attempt is made to start the car (or to hot-wire the ignition).

The status of the system is displayed by means of a flashing LED located in the centre of the facia.

Should the alarm system become faulty, bear in mind the following points:

a) As with other electrical equipment, many faults are caused by poor connections or bad earths.

b) Check the operation of all the door, bonnet and boot lid switches, and the operation of all interior lights.

c) The alarm system may behave oddly if the vehicle battery is in poor condition, or if its terminals are loose.

d) If the system is operating correctly, but gives too many false alarms, a Volvo dealer or specialist may be able to reduce the sensitivity of some of the system sensors (where fitted).

e) Ultimately, the vehicle may have to be taken to a Volvo dealer or a suitably-equipped garage for examination. They will have access to a special diagnostic tester which will quickly trace any fault present in the system.

22 Supplemental Restraint System (SRS) – general information and precautions

General information

A supplemental restraint system is fitted in various forms as standard or optional equipment depending on model and territory.

The main system component is a driver's airbag, which is designed to prevent serious chest and head injuries to the driver during an accident. Similar airbags for the front seat passenger, side airbags (built into the side of the front seats), and side curtain airbags are also standard fitment. Side impact crash sensors are located on the B and C-pillars of the vehicle, with a frontal sensor incorporated into the SRS module located under the centre console. The module incorporates a deceleration sensor, and a microprocessor ECM, to monitor the severity of the impact and

trigger the airbag where necessary. The airbag is inflated by a gas generator, which forces the bag out of the module cover in the centre of the steering wheel, or out of a cover on the passenger's side of the facia/seat cover/headlining. A contact reel behind the steering wheel at the top of the steering column ensures that a good electrical connection is maintained with the airbag at all times, as the steering wheel is turned in each direction.

In addition to the airbag units, the supplemental restraint system also incorporates pyrotechnical seat belt tensioners operated by gas cartridges in the belt inertia reel assembly. The pyrotechnical units are also triggered by the crash sensor, in conjunction with the air bags, to tighten the seat belts and provide additional collision protection.

All models also incorporate a side impact protection system (SIPS) as standard equipment. In its basic form, the SIPS system is essentially an integral part of the vehicle structure in which strengthening agents are used to distribute side impacts through the bodywork. This is done by reinforcing the lower areas of the doors and door pillars, and providing strengthening bars in the seats and centre console. In this way, side impacts are absorbed by the body structure as a whole, giving exceptional impact strength.

Precautions

⚠️ **Warning: Any attempt to dismantle the airbag module, SIPS bag, crash sensors, contact reel, seat belt tensioners or any associated wiring or components without this equipment, and the specialist knowledge needed to use it correctly, could result in severe personal injury and/or malfunction of the system.**

• **Before carrying out any work on the SRS components, disconnect the battery and wait for at least 5 minutes for any residual electrical energy to dissipate before proceeding.**

• **Handle the airbag unit with extreme care as a precaution against personal injury, and always hold it with the cover facing away from the body. If in doubt concerning any proposed work involving the airbag unit or its control circuitry, consult a Volvo dealer.**

• **Note that the airbag(s) must not be subjected to temperatures in excess of 90°C. When the airbag is removed, ensure that it is stored the correct way up to prevent possible inflation.**

• **Do not allow any solvents or cleaning agents to contact the airbag assemblies. They must be cleaned using only a damp cloth.**

• **The airbag(s) and control unit are both sensitive to impact. If either is dropped or damaged they should be renewed.**

• **Disconnect the airbag control unit wiring plug prior to using arc-welding equipment on the vehicle.**

23 Supplemental Restraint System (SRS) – component renewal

Note: Before proceeding, refer to the warnings in Section 22.

Driver's airbag

Removal

1 Disconnect the battery negative lead (see Chapter 5A), and wait 10 minutes before proceeding.

2 Insert a flat-bladed screwdriver in through the holes in the rear of the steering wheel, lift up the screwdriver handle and release the spring clip each side **(see illustrations)**. Turn the steering wheel 90° in each direction to gain access to the holes.

3 Return the wheel to the straight-ahead position.

4 Lift the airbag module off the steering wheel, disconnect the wiring connector(s) from the

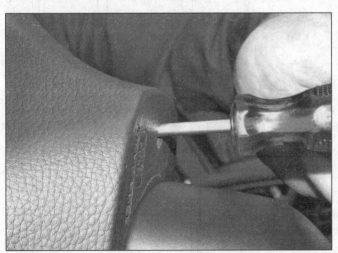

23.2a Insert a screwdriver into the rear of the steering wheel . . .

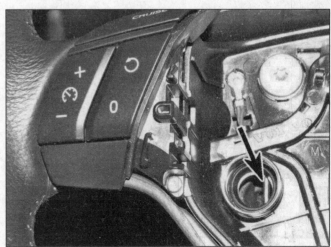

23.2b . . . then lift the screwdriver handle to release the clip (arrowed)

23.4a Lift the airbag from place . . .

23.4b . . . then squeeze the sides of the clips together and disconnect the wiring connectors

23.5a Remove the airbag contact unit locking screw from the storage position (arrowed) . . .

23.5b . . . and insert it into the hole (arrowed) to lock the contact unit

rear of the unit and remove it from the vehicle (see illustrations).

⚠️ **Warning: Position the airbag unit in a safe place, with the mechanism facing downwards as a precaution against accidental operation. Do not attempt to open or repair the airbag unit, or apply any electrical current to it. Do not use any airbag which is visibly damaged or which has been tampered with.**

5 Undo the contact unit locking screw from the steering wheel, then insert it into the contact unit plug to lock it in position (see

illustrations). Once it has been locked, no attempt should be made to turn the steering wheel, or the contact reel will be damaged.

Refitting

6 Unlock the contact reel by removing the screw. Store the screw in the lower part of the steering wheel, returning it to its original location.

7 Rest the airbag unit on the bottom edge of the steering wheel hub and reconnect the wiring connector. Swing the airbag unit up into position, checking carefully that the wiring is not pinched.

8 Press the airbag into place, ensuring the clips fully engage.

9 Make sure that no-one is inside the car. Switch on the ignition, then reconnect the battery negative lead. Switch the ignition off, then on again, and check that the SRS warning light comes on, then goes out within 7 seconds.

Driver's airbag contact reel

Removal

10 Remove the airbag unit as described above, and the steering wheel as described in Chapter 10.

11 Taking care not to rotate the contact unit, undo the four retaining screws and remove it from the steering column switch assembly. Disconnect the wiring plug (see illustration).

Refitting

12 If a new contact unit is being fitted, cut the cable-tie which is fitted to prevent the unit accidentally rotating.

13 A new reel should be supplied in the centralised position – if not, or there is a chance the unit is not centralised, proceed as follows. Turn the reel gently clockwise as far as it will go, then turn it back anti-clockwise two turns. Continue turning until the lug on the reel is at the 1 o'clock position. On later models, a yellow mark must also be visible in the contact unit window (see illustration). Lock the reel in this position by screwing in the locking screw located in the plastic retaining strip.

14 Fit the unit to the steering column switch assembly and securely tighten its retaining screws.

15 Refit the steering wheel as described in Chapter 10, and the airbag unit as described above.

Passenger's airbag

Removal

16 Disconnect the battery negative lead

23.11 Undo the screws (arrowed) and remove the airbag contact unit

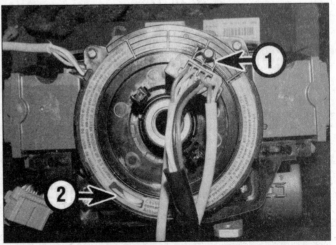

23.13 The lug (1) must be at the 1 o'clock position, and the yellow mark (2) must be visible in the contact unit window

23.18 Undo the screw (arrowed) and remove the vent tube from the underside of the facia

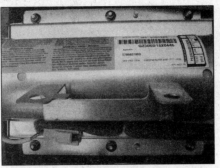

23.19 Undo the 6 nuts and remove the passenger's airbag

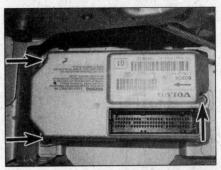

23.25 The airbag control unit is secured by 3 screws (arrowed)

(see Chapter 5A), and wait 10 minutes before proceeding.

17 Remove the complete facia as described in Chapter 11.

18 Undo the retaining screw, then unclip and remove the air vent duct from the underside of the facia **(see illustration)**.

19 Undo the 6 retaining nuts, and remove the airbag from the facia **(see illustration)**.

Refitting

20 Refitting is a reversal of removal.

21 On completion, make sure that no-one is inside the car. Switch on the ignition, then reconnect the battery negative lead. Switch the ignition off, then on again, and check that the SRS warning light comes on, then goes out within 7 seconds.

Airbag control unit

Removal

22 Disconnect the battery negative lead as described in Chapter 5A. Wait at least 10 minutes before proceeding, to allow and residual electrical energy to dissipate.

23 Remove the centre console as described in Chapter 11.

24 Lift up the rubber cover (where fitted), then release the locking catch and disconnect the sensor wiring plug.

25 Note its fitted location, undo the 3 screws and remove the module **(see illustration)**.

Refitting

26 Refitting is a reversal of removal, ensuring the module is fitted with the arrow on its top surface facing forwards.

27 On completion, make sure that no-one is inside the car. Switch on the ignition, then reconnect the battery negative lead. Switch the ignition off, then on again, and check that the SRS warning light comes on, then goes out within 7 seconds. **Note:** *If a new control unit has been fitted, suitable software will need to be downloaded and installed from Volvo. Entrust this task to a Volvo dealer or suitably-equipped specialist.*

Side airbags

28 The side airbag units are built into the front seats, and their removal requires that the seat fabric be removed. This is not

23.31a B-pillar crash sensor (arrowed)

considered to be a DIY operation, and should be referred to a Volvo dealer or upholstery specialist.

Side crash sensors

Removal

29 The side crash sensors are fitted to vehicles B-pillar (between the driver's and passenger's doors), and to the C-pillar.

30 Remove the B-pillar trim or rear seat side cushion (as applicable) as described in Chapter 11.

31 Release the clips and disconnect the wiring plug from the sensor **(see illustrations)**.

32 Undo the two retaining screws and remove the sensor.

Refitting

33 Refit the sensor(s) to the pillar(s) and tighten the retaining screws to the specified torque. Reconnect the wiring plug.

24.2 Parking assistance module (arrowed)

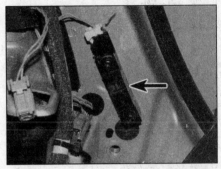

23.31b C-pillar crash sensor (arrowed)

34 The remainder of refitting is a reversal of removal.

Side curtain airbag

35 In order to remove the side curtain air bag(s), the headlining must be removed. This is not considered a DIY operation, and should be entrusted to a Volvo dealer or upholstery specialist.

24 Parking assistance system – removal and refitting

Control module

1 The parking assistance module (PAM) is located behind the luggage compartment right-hand (vehicles up to and including 2004 model year), or left-hand (vehicles from 2005 model year) side trim panel. Remove the panel as described in Chapter 11.

2 The module is secured in place using a Velcro mounting **(see illustration)**. Release the Velco, remove the module and disconnect the wiring plugs.

3 Refitting is a reversal of removal.

Sensors

4 The sensors are set into the rear bumper. Remove the rear bumper as described in Chapter 11.

5 Disconnect the wiring plug from each sensor.

6 Spread the retaining clips and pull the sensor from the inside of the bumper.

7 Refitting is a reversal of removal.

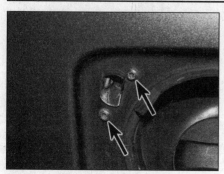

25.2 Open the fuel filler flap and undo the 2 bolts (arrowed)

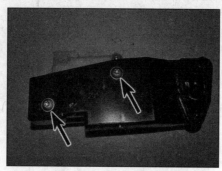

25.3 The filler flap motor is secured to the bracket by 2 bolts (arrowed)

25 Fuel filler flap release motor – removal and refitting

Removal

1 Remove the right-hand luggage compartment side panel trim as described in Chapter 11.
2 Open the fuel filler flap and remove the 2 Torx bolts (see illustration).
3 Disconnect the motor wiring plug, then if required, undo the 2 Torx bolts and detach the motor from the bracket (see illustration).

Refitting

4 Refitting is the reversal of removal.

Volvo S60 wiring diagrams   Diagram 1

Warning: This vehicle is fitted with a supplemental restraint system (SRS) consisting of a combination of driver (and passenger) airbag(s), side impact protection airbags and seatbelt pre-tensioners. The use of electrical test equipment on any SRS wiring systems may cause the seatbelt pre-tensioners to abruptly retract and the airbags to explosively deploy, resulting in potentially severe personal injury. Extreme care should be taken to correctly identify any circuits to be tested to avoid choosing any of the SRS wiring in error.
For further information see airbag system precautions in body electrical systems chapter.
Note: The SRS wiring harness can normally be identified by yellow and/or orange harness or harness connectors.

Key to symbols

Fusible link		Ganged switch		Connecting wires	
Fuse		Single switch		Wire splice, soldered connection or connectorised junction	
Bulb		Relay		Alternative layout depending on model / year (diesel / petrol)	
Heating element		K — Graphical representation of a component for which no additional data is provided (i.e. electronic assembly)		Y/G — Wire colour (yellow with green stripe)	
M — Electric motor		Earth point		Diode	
Outline indicates the item is part of a larger assembly		E1 — Earth point with reference (see earth locations on this page)		Light emitting diode	
2 ⊗ 1 — Outline indicates the item is an indiviual part and not part of an assembly. Number indicates pin number		89 — Item reference; refering to key at top of diagram page		parking heater E:H — Chain dash line indicates item specific to a particular varient	
				Light sensitive diode	

Key to circuits

Diagram 1	Information on wiring diagrams
Diagram 2	Power distribution system; early 2005 models
Diagram 3	Power distribution system; 2005/6 models
Diagram 4	Power distribution system; 2007/8 models
Diagram 5	Starting and charging, engine cooling fan, indicators and hazard warning, wing mirror lights
Diagram 6	Headlights, sidelights, fog lights, driving lights, brakelights, numberplate lights and reversing lights
Diagram 7	Headlight levelling, interior lighting
Diagram 8	Windscreen wipers / washers, headlight pressure washers, headlight wiper / washers, heated door mirrors and rear window, rain sensor
Diagram 9	Central locking, powered sun roof, powered door mirrors
Diagram 10	Powered windows, typical climate control system
Diagram 11	Powered seats, seat heaters
Diagram 12	CAN bus topograhpy and diagnostic connector, seat belt warning, trailer connector
Diagram 13	Instruments
Diagram 14	Fuse details

Key to earth points

E1	Left MacPherson strut (inner wing)
E2	Left MacPherson strut (inner wing)
E3	Left hand A post
E4	Left hand A post
E5	Left hand side, front seat riser
E6	Upper windscreen member
E7	Left hand side, rear seat riser

E15	Right MacPherson strut (inner wing)
E14	Right hand side A post
E13	Right hand side A post
E12	Right hand side, front seat riser
E11	Right hand side, rear seat riser
E10	Right hand D post
E9,E10	Boot space

Wire colours

B	Black	P	Purple	
G	Green	R	Red	
K	Pink	S	Grey	
Lg	Light green	U	Blue	
N	Brown	W	White	
O	Orange	Y	Yellow	

Key to items

1 Battery
2 Ignition switch
3 Engine compartment fuse box
  a) main fuse links
  b) starter relay
  c) wiper speed relay
  d) intermittent wipe relay

e) fuel system relay
f) climate control system relay
g) glow pulgs relay
h) engine management relay
j) headlight washer relay
4 Passenger compartment fuse box
5 Battery mounted fuse box

Diagram 2

7 Central electronics module
  a) Fuses 3,5-10,17-23,31-32,34
  b) Fuses 1-2,11,13-16,26-30,33
8 Rear electronics module
  a) Fuses 1-38

H33801

Power distribution system

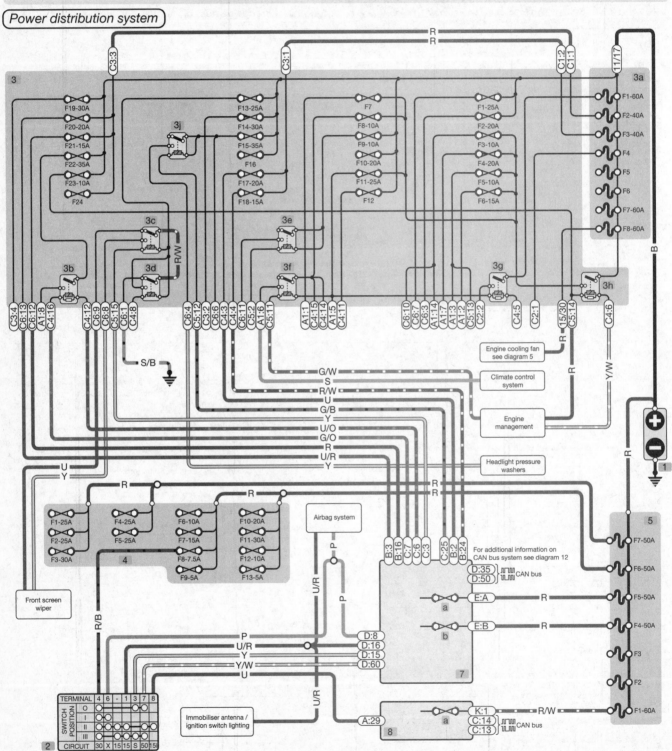

Wire colours

B	Black	P	Purple
G	Green	R	Red
K	Pink	S	Grey
Lg	Light green	U	Blue
N	Brown	W	White
O	Orange	Y	Yellow

Key to items

1 Battery
2 Ignition switch
3 Engine compartment fuse box
  a) main fuse links
  b) starter relay
  c) wiper speed relay
  d) intermittent wipe relay

  f) climate control system relay
  g) glow pulgs relay
  h) engine management relay
  j) headlight washer relay
4 Passenger compartment fuse box
5 Battery mounted fuse box

Diagram 3

7 Central electronics module
  a) Fuses 3,5-10,17-23,31-32,34
  b) Fuses 1-2,11,13-16,26-30,33
8 Rear electronics module
  a) Fuses 1-38

H33802

Power distribution system 2005/6

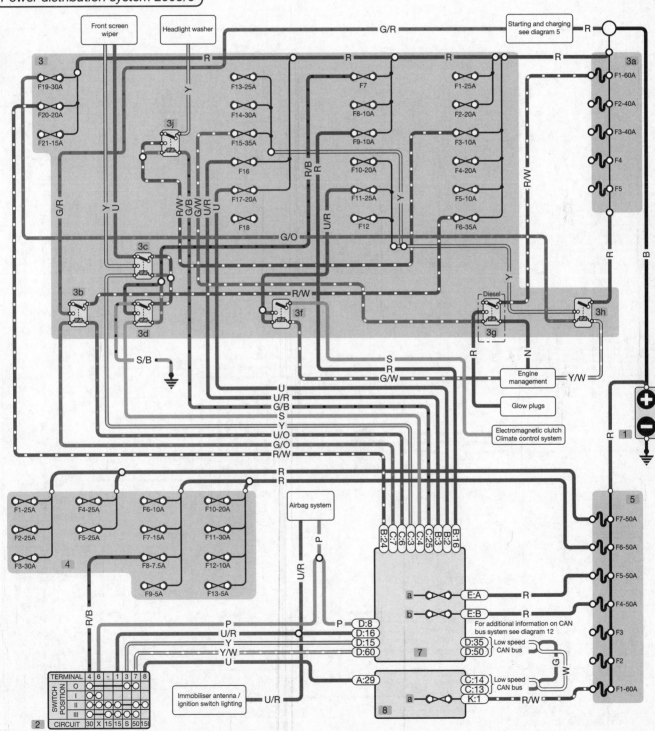

Wire colours

B	Black	P	Purple
G	Green	R	Red
K	Pink	S	Grey
Lg	Light green	U	Blue
N	Brown	W	White
O	Orange	Y	Yellow

Key to items

1 Battery
2 Ignition switch
3 Engine compartment fuse box
 a) main fuse links
 b) starter relay
 c) wiper speed relay
 d) intermittent wipe relay

f) climate control system relay
g) glow pulgs relay
h) engine management relay
 j) headlight washer relay
4 Passenger compartment fuse box
5 Battery mounted fuse box
6 Main fuse (diesel)

Diagram 4

7 Central electronics module
 a) Fuses 3,5-10,17-23,31-32,34
 b) Fuses 1-2,11,13-16,26-30,33
8 Rear electronics module
 a) Fuses 1-38

H33803

Power distribution system 2007/8

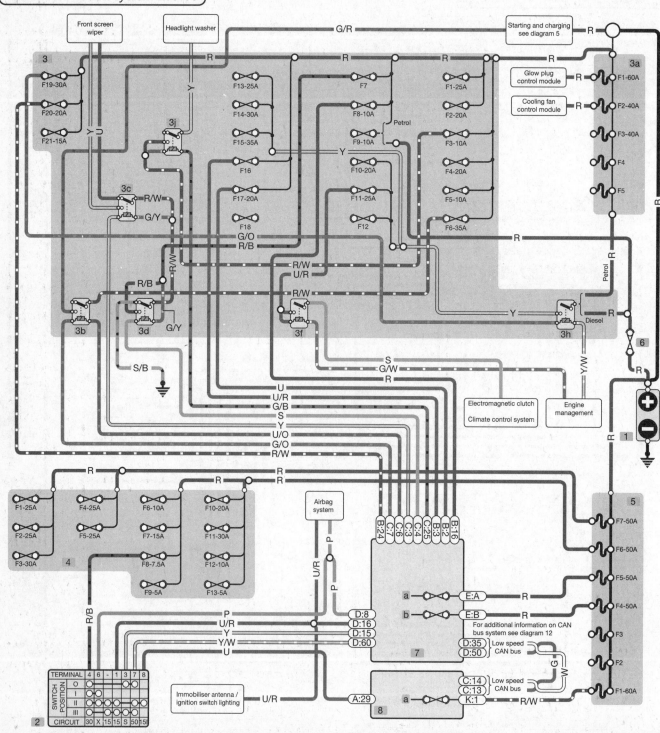

Wire colours

B	Black	P	Purple
G	Green	R	Red
K	Pink	S	Grey
Lg	Light green	U	Blue
N	Brown	W	White
O	Orange	Y	Yellow

Key to items

3 Engine compartment fuse box
   a) main fuses
4 Passenger compartment fuse box
5 Battery mounted fuse box
7 Central electronics module
8 Rear electronics module
10 Starter motor
11 Alternator
12 Engine control module
13 Fan control module
14 Cooling fan

15 Front power outlet
16 Rear power outlet
17 Luggage compartment
   power outlet
18 Steering wheel module
19 Rotary joint
20 Horn switches
21 Horn
22 Hazard warning switch
23 Front left indicator
24 Front right indicator

25 Rear LH light cluster
   a) indicator
26 Rear RH light cluster
   a) indicator
27 LH door module
28 RH door module
29 Upper electronics module
30 RH door mirror
   a) light
31 LH door mirror
   a) light

Diagram 5

H33804

Power supply outline

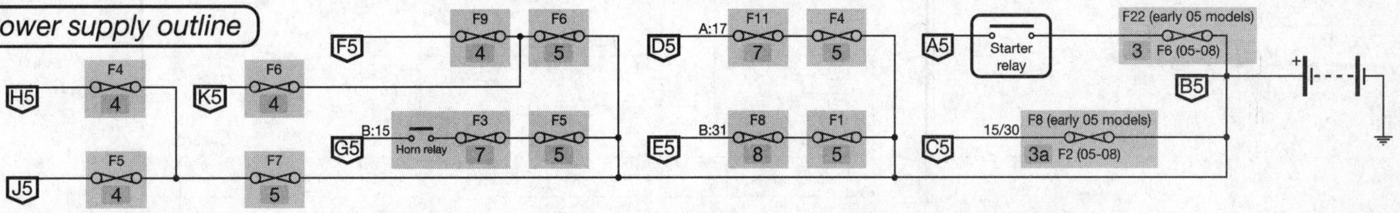

Starting and charging

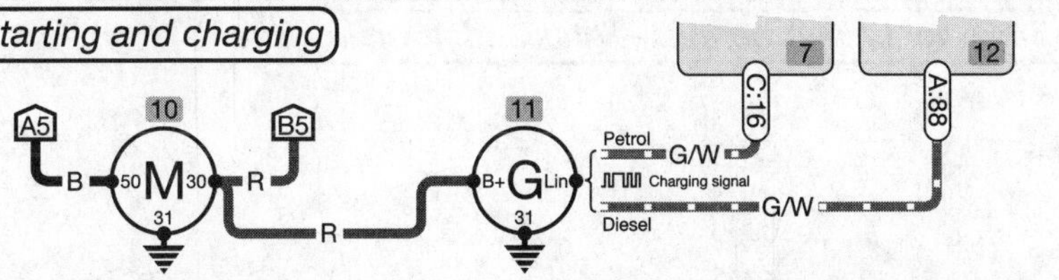

Engine cooling fan

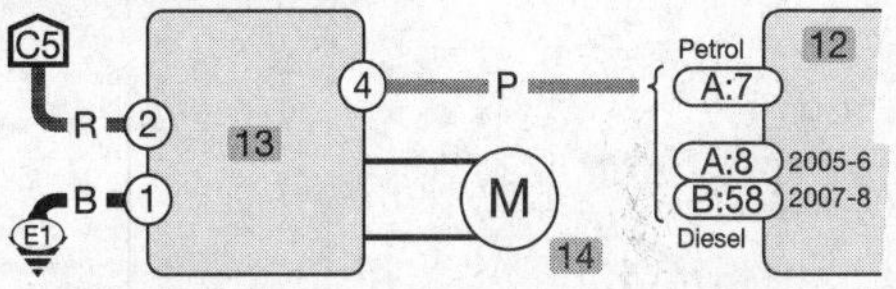

Power outlets

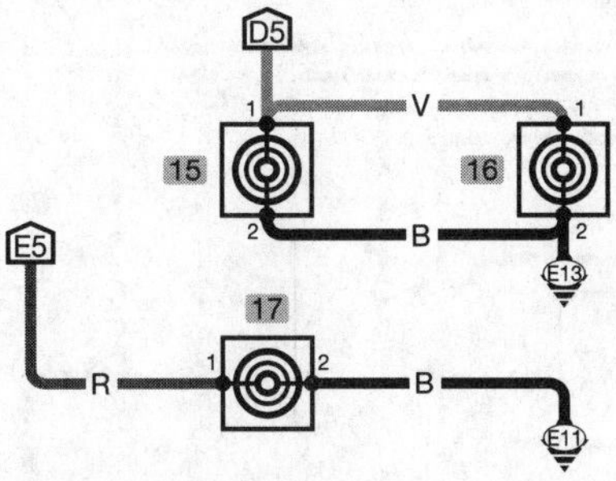

Horn

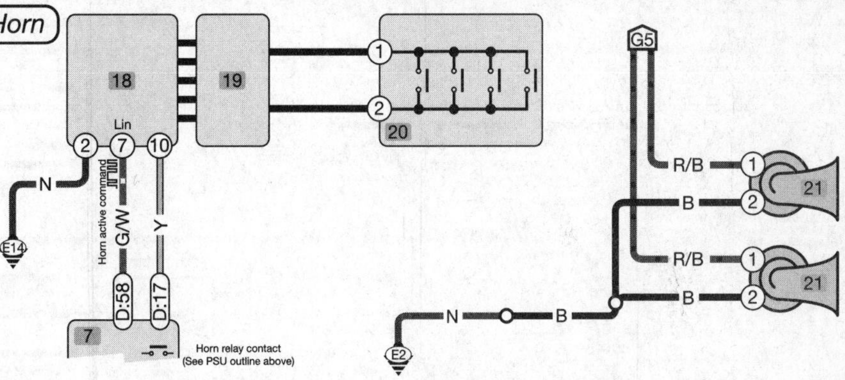

Indicators and hazard warning

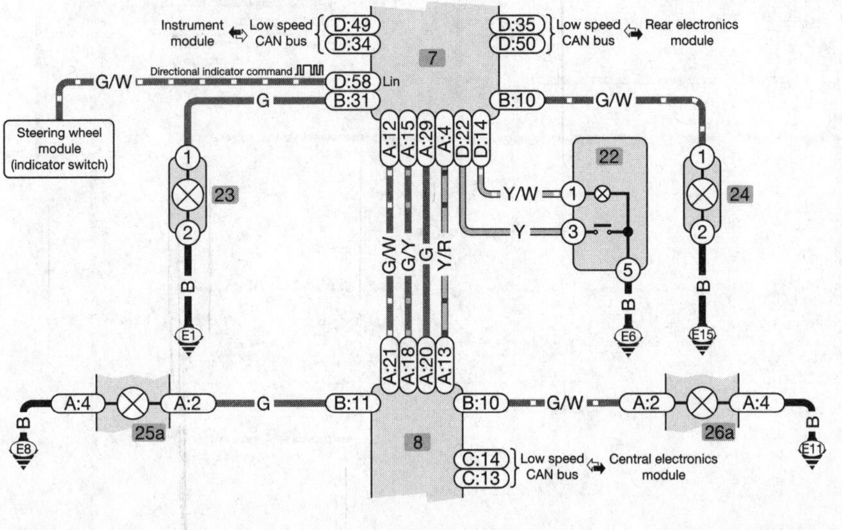

Door mirror lights

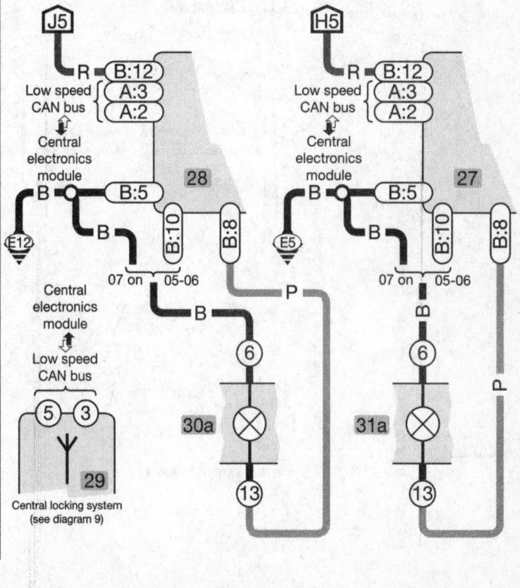

Diagram 6

Wire colours

B	Black	P	Purple	
G	Green	R	Red	
K	Pink	S	Grey	
Lg	Light green	U	Blue	
N	Brown	W	White	
O	Orange	Y	Yellow	

Key to items

4 Passenger compartment fuse box
5 Battery mounted fuse box
7 Central electronics module
8 Rear electronics module
18 Steering wheel module
25 Rear LH light cluster
  b) parking light
  c) reversing light
  d) fog light
  e) tail light 1
  f) tail light 2
  g) brake light

26 Rear RH light cluster
  b) parking light
  c) reversing light
  d) fog light
  e) tail light 1
  f) tail light 2
  g) brake light
35 Light switch module
36 RH side marker light
37 LH side marker light
40 Brake switch
41 High level brake light

42 Front left fog lamp
43 Front right fog lamp
44 Headlamp assembly LH
  a) mainbeam unit
  b) dipbeam unit
  c) sidelight
  d) driving lamp
  e) xenon ECU
45 Headlamp assembly RH
  (as above)
46 Number plate lights
47 Reversing switch

H33805

Power supply outline

See diagrams 2,3 & 4 for enhanced power distribution information

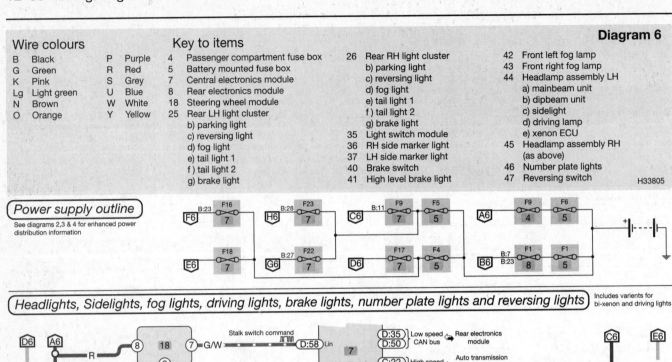

Headlights, Sidelights, fog lights, driving lights, brake lights, number plate lights and reversing lights

Includes varients for bi-xenon and driving lights

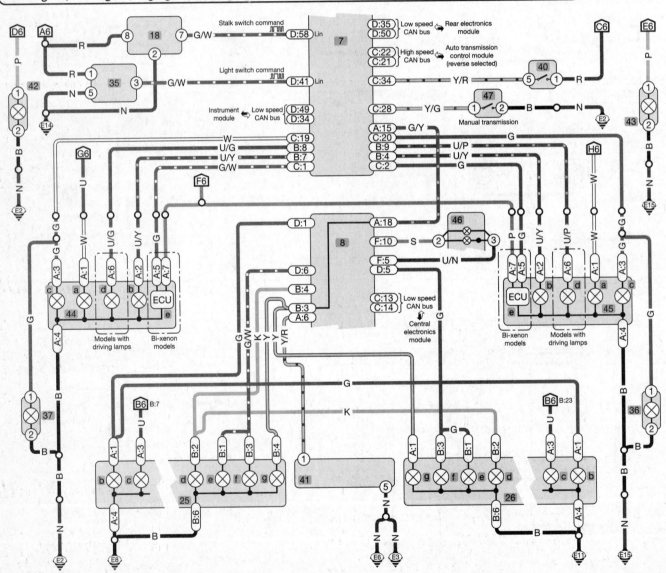

Wire colours

B	Black	P	Purple
G	Green	R	Red
K	Pink	S	Grey
Lg	Light green	U	Blue
N	Brown	W	White
O	Orange	Y	Yellow

Key to items

4 Passenger compartment fuse box
5 Battery mounted fuse box
7 Central electronics module
8 Rear electronics module
27 LH door module
28 RH door module
29 Upper electronics module
35 Light switch module
50 Headlight levelling potentiometer
51 Rear LH body angle sensor
52 LH headlight tilt motor
53 RH headlight tilt motor
54 RH front courtesy light
55 LH front courtesy light
56 Ignition key illumination
57 Glovebox light
58 LH boot light
59 RH boot light
60 Rear reading light
61 LH vanity mirror light
62 RH vanity mirror light
63 Dome light switch
64 RH front door switch
65 LH front door switch
66 RH rear door switch
67 LH rear door lock
68 Boot lid lock unit switch

Diagram 7

H33806

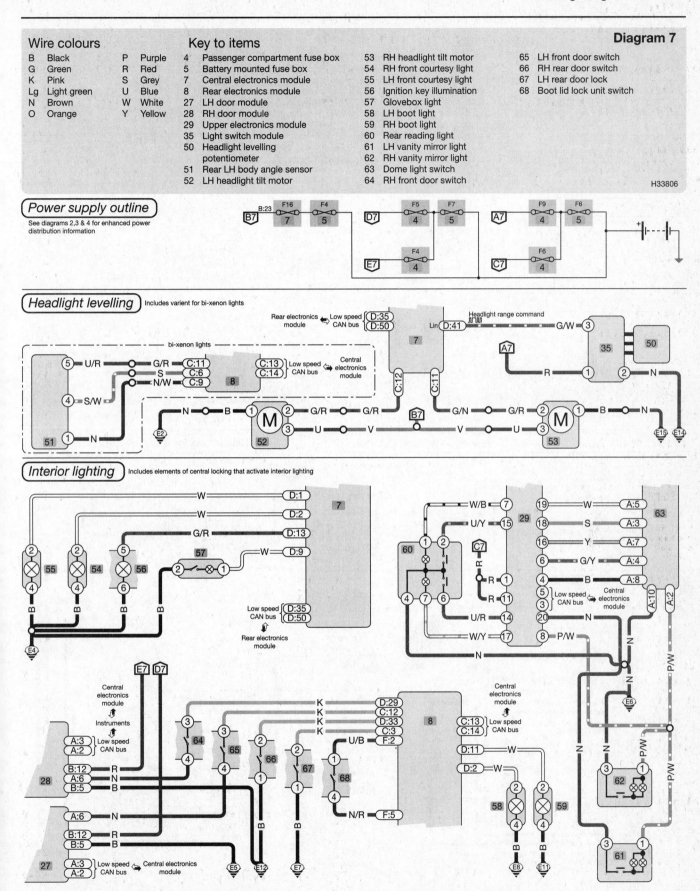

Power supply outline

See diagrams 2,3 & 4 for enhanced power distribution information

Headlight levelling

Includes varient for bi-xenon lights

Interior lighting

Includes elements of central locking that activate interior lighting

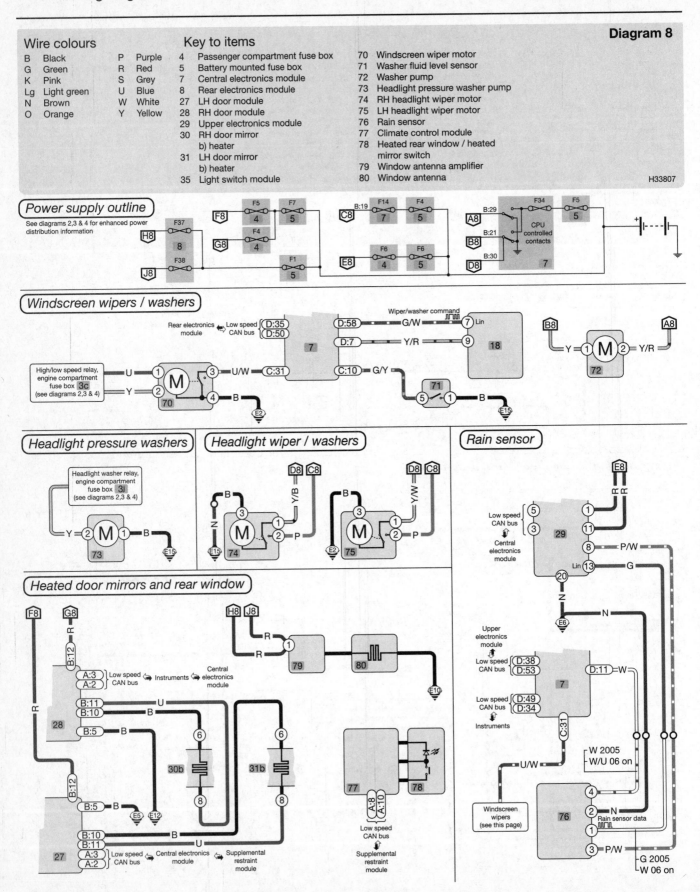

Diagram 8

Wire colours

B	Black	P	Purple
G	Green	R	Red
K	Pink	S	Grey
Lg	Light green	U	Blue
N	Brown	W	White
O	Orange	Y	Yellow

Key to items

4 Passenger compartment fuse box
5 Battery mounted fuse box
7 Central electronics module
8 Rear electronics module
27 LH door module
28 RH door module
29 Upper electronics module
30 RH door mirror
    b) heater
31 LH door mirror
    b) heater
35 Light switch module

70 Windscreen wiper motor
71 Washer fluid level sensor
72 Washer pump
73 Headlight pressure washer pump
74 RH headlight wiper motor
75 LH headlight wiper motor
76 Rain sensor
77 Climate control module
78 Heated rear window / heated
    mirror switch
79 Window antenna amplifier
80 Window antenna

H33807

Power supply outline

See diagrams 2,3 & 4 for enhanced power distribution information

Windscreen wipers / washers

Headlight pressure washers

Headlight wiper / washers

Rain sensor

Heated door mirrors and rear window

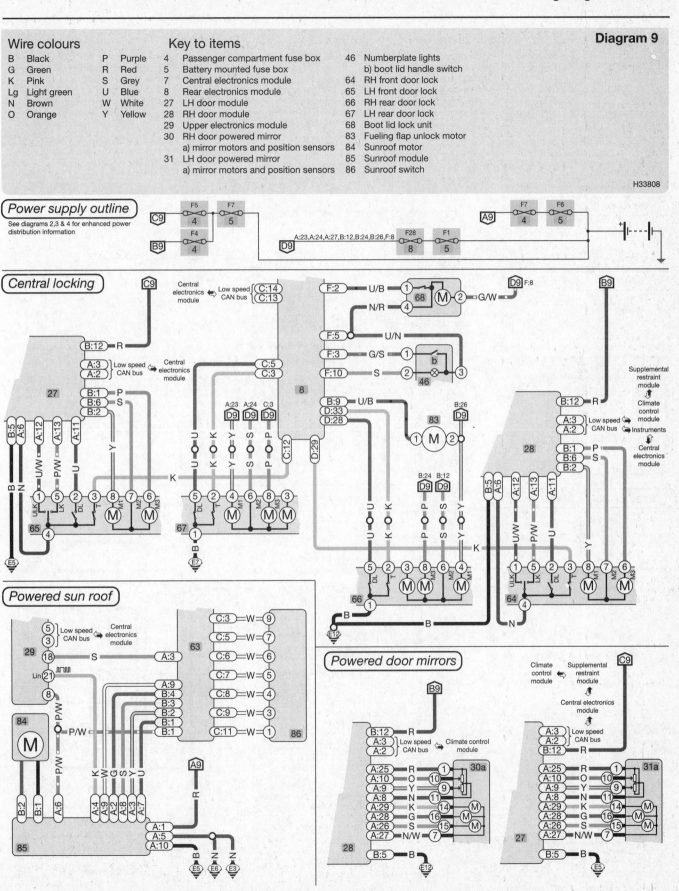

Wire colours

B	Black	P	Purple
G	Green	R	Red
K	Pink	S	Grey
Lg	Light green	U	Blue
N	Brown	W	White
O	Orange	Y	Yellow

Key to items

4	Passenger compartment fuse box	46	Numberplate lights
5	Battery mounted fuse box		b) boot lid handle switch
7	Central electronics module	64	RH front door lock
8	Rear electronics module	65	LH front door lock
27	LH door module	66	RH rear door lock
28	RH door module	67	LH rear door lock
29	Upper electronics module	68	Boot lid lock unit
30	RH door powered mirror	83	Fueling flap unlock motor
	a) mirror motors and position sensors	84	Sunroof motor
31	LH door powered mirror	85	Sunroof module
	a) mirror motors and position sensors	86	Sunroof switch

Diagram 9

H33808

Power supply outline

See diagrams 2,3 & 4 for enhanced power distribution information

Central locking

Powered sun roof

Powered door mirrors

Wire colours

B Black
G Green
K Pink
Lg Light green
N Brown
O Orange

P Purple
R Red
S Grey
U Blue
W White
Y Yellow

Key to items

4 Passenger compartment fuse box
5 Battery mounted fuse box
7 Central electronics module
8 Rear electronics module
12 Engine control module
27 LH door module
28 RH door module
29 Upper electronics module
31 LH door mirror
  c) external air temperature sensor
77 Climate control module
88 LH front power window motor

89 RH front power window motor
90 LH rear power window switch
91 RH rear power window switch
92 LH rear power window motor
93 RH rear power window motor
94 Fan control module
95 Passenger compartment fan
96 Coolant temperature sensor
97 Pressure sensor
98 Damper motor LH
99 Damper motor RH
100 Damper motor de-frost

101 Damper motor re-circulation
102 Damper motor floor vent
103 Air quality sensor
104 Solar sensor / twilight sensor
105 Evaporator temperature sensor

Diagram 10

H33809

Power supply outline

See diagrams 2,3 & 4 for enhanced power distribution information

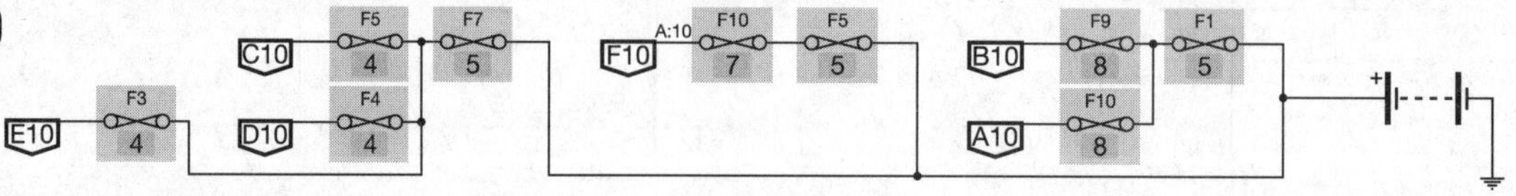

Powered windows

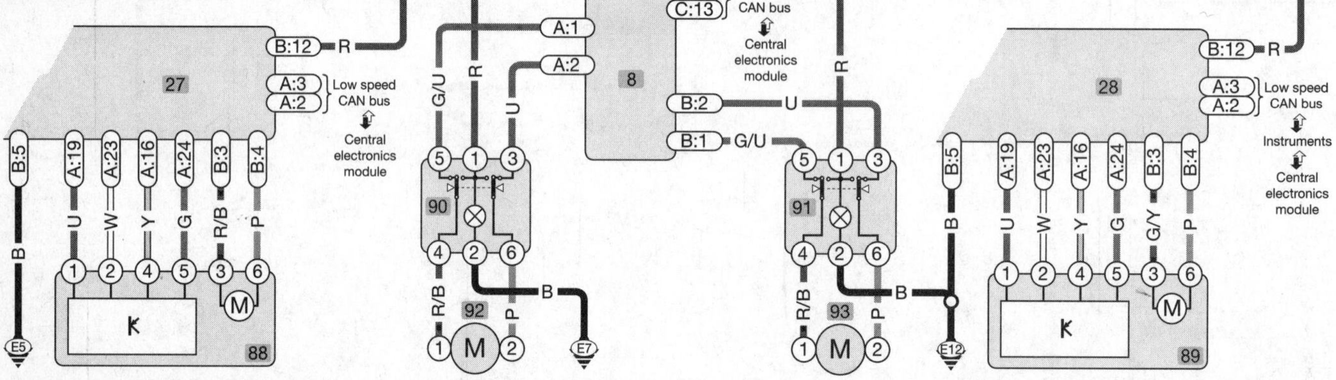

Typical climate control system

2005 model shown

ß = Diesel
* = non turbo petrol models
ECC = electronic climate control

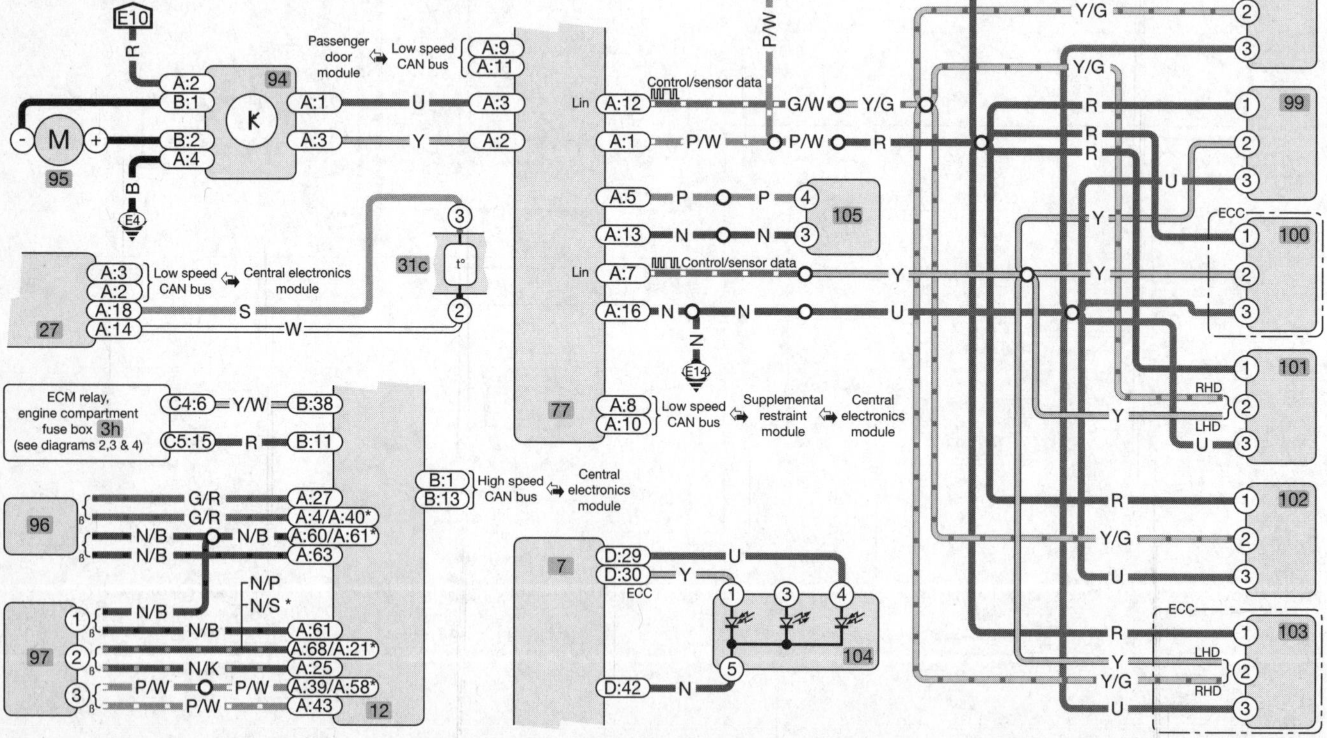

Wire colours

B	Black	P	Purple
G	Green	R	Red
K	Pink	S	Grey
Lg	Light green	U	Blue
N	Brown	W	White
O	Orange	Y	Yellow

Key to items

4 Passenger compartment fuse box
5 Battery mounted fuse box
7 Central electronics module
77 Climate control module
108 Drivers seat switch unit
　a) back rest tilt control
　b) seat slide control
　c) seat raise/lower control
　d) seat front tilt control
　e) operate control

109 Passenger seat switch unit
　a) seat front tilt control
　b) seat raise/lower control
　c) seat slide control
　d) back rest tilt control
110 Powered seat module
111 Drivers seat motor backrest angle
112 Drivers seat slide motor
113 Drivers seat raise/lower motor
114 Drivers seat front tilt motor
115 Passenger seat front tilt motor
116 Passenger seat raise/lower motor

117 Passenger seat slide motor
118 Passenger seat backrest angle motor
119 LH seat heater module
120 RH seat heater module
121 Drivers seat heater switch
122 Passenger seat heater switch
123 RH backrest heater
124 RH seat heater
125 RH seat temperature sensor
126 LH backrest heater
127 LH seat heater
128 LH seat temperature sensor

Diagram 11

H33810

Power supply outline

See diagrams 2,3 & 4 for enhanced power distribution information

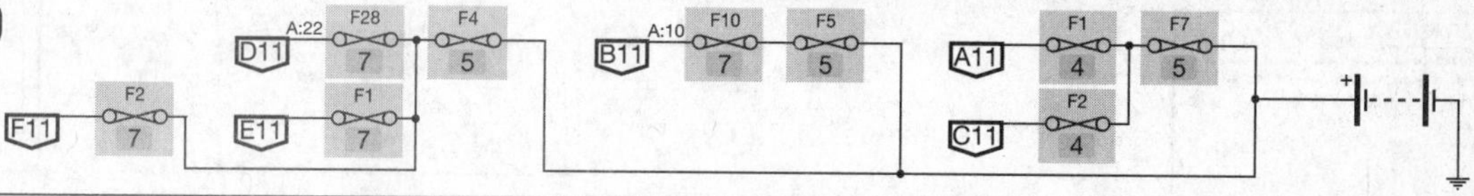

Powered seats

* = 2008

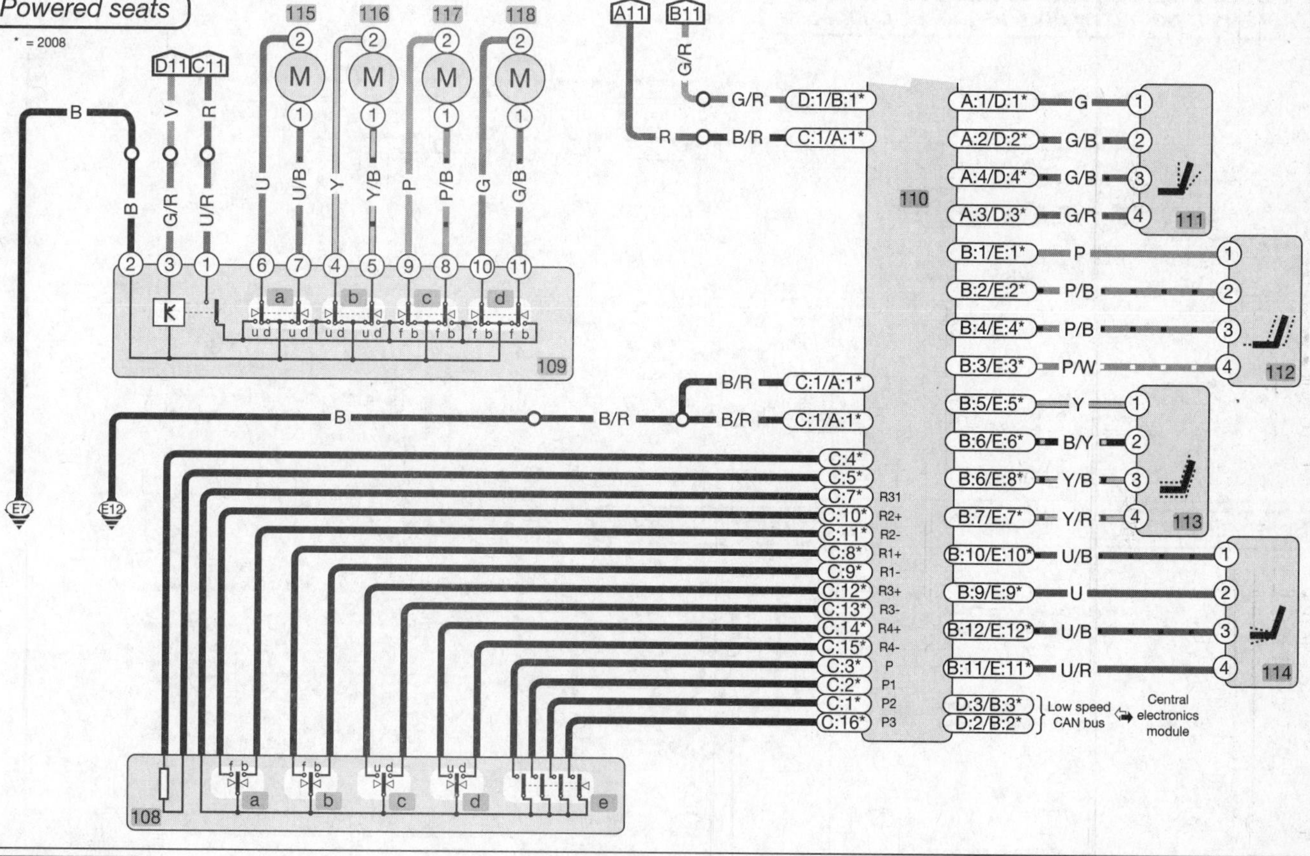

Seat heaters

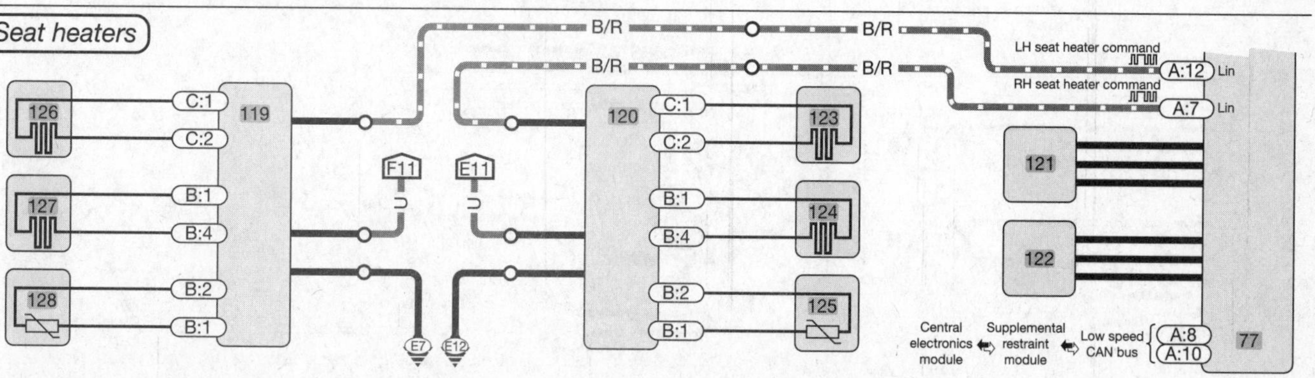

LH seat heater command
RH seat heater command

Central electronics module

Supplemental restraint module

Low speed CAN bus

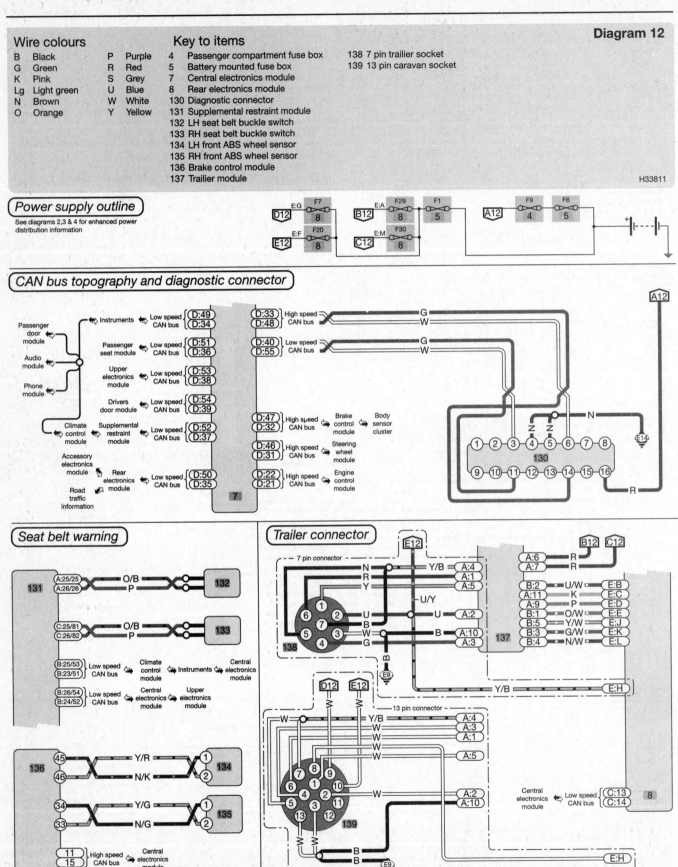

Wire colours

B	Black	P	Purple
G	Green	R	Red
K	Pink	S	Grey
Lg	Light green	U	Blue
N	Brown	W	White
O	Orange	Y	Yellow

Key to items

4 Passenger compartment fuse box
5 Battery mounted fuse box
7 Central electronics module
8 Rear electronics module
130 Diagnostic connector
131 Supplemental restraint module
132 LH seat belt buckle switch
133 RH seat belt buckle switch
134 LH front ABS wheel sensor
135 RH front ABS wheel sensor
136 Brake control module
137 Trailer module

138 7 pin trailer socket
139 13 pin caravan socket

Diagram 12

H33811

Power supply outline
See diagrams 2, 3 & 4 for enhanced power distribution information

CAN bus topography and diagnostic connector

Seat belt warning

Trailer connector

Wire colours

B	Black	P	Purple	
G	Green	R	Red	
K	Pink	S	Grey	
Lg	Light green	U	Blue	
N	Brown	W	White	
O	Orange	Y	Yellow	

Key to items

4 Passenger compartment fuse box
5 Battery mounted fuse box
7 Central electronics module
12 Engine control module
28 RH door module
31 LH door mirror
   c) external air temperature sensor
134 LH front ABS wheel sensor
135 RH front ABS wheel sensor
136 Brake control module
143 Coolant temperature sensr

144 Oil pressure sensor
145 Oil level sensor
146 Coolant level sensor
147 Brake fluid level sensor
148 Washer fluid level sensor
149 Parking brake switch
150 Impulse sensor
151 Instruments module
152 Fuel pump
   a) Injector side fuel level sensor
   b) Pump side fuel level sensor

Diagram 13

H33812

Power supply outline

See diagrams 2,3 & 4 for enhanced power distribution information

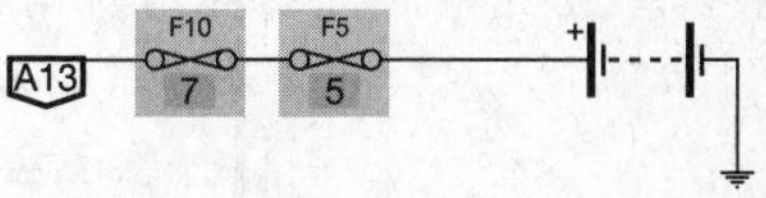

A13   F10 7   F5 5   +

Instruments

Module power supplies have been detailed in previous diagrams

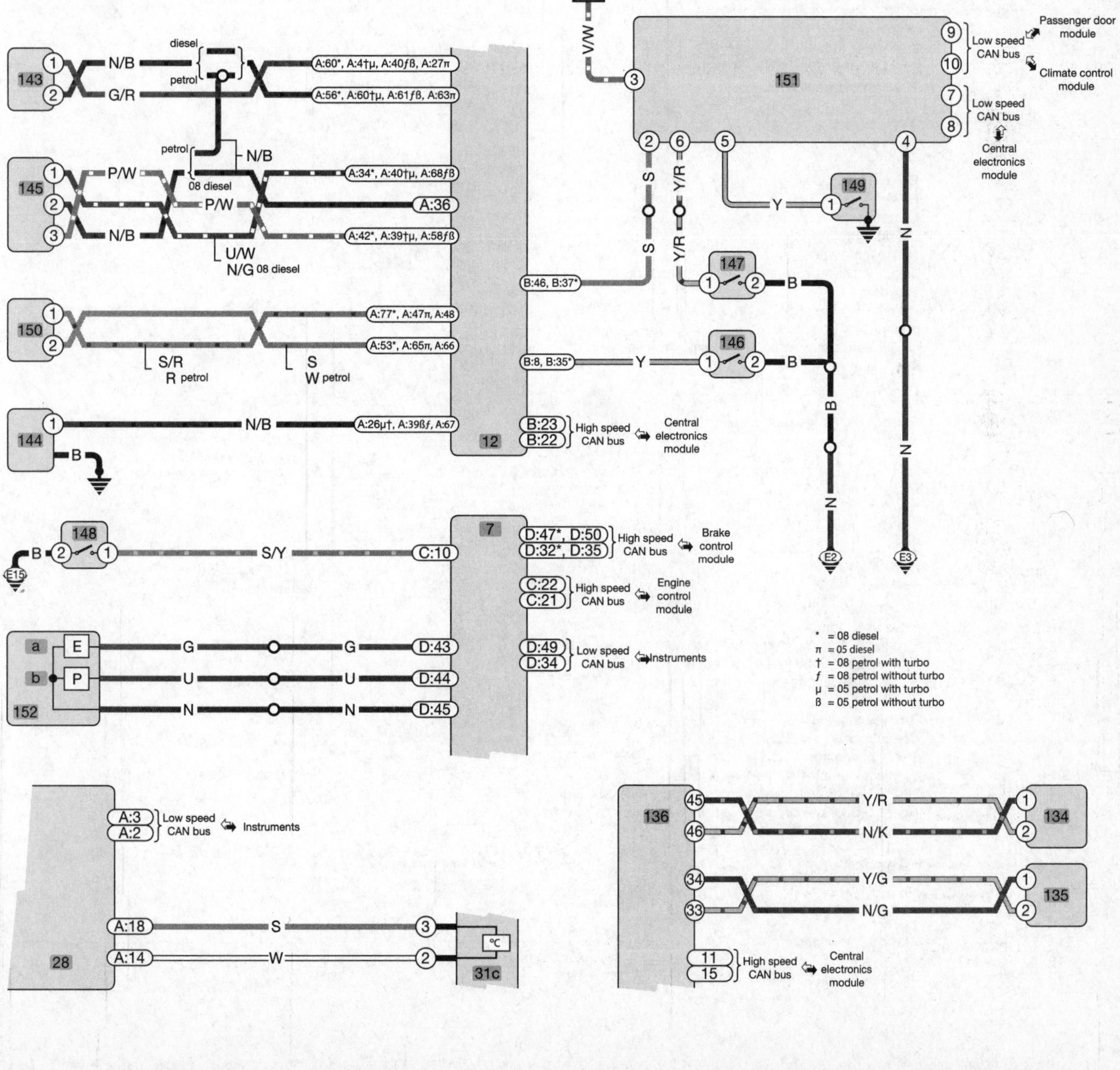

A13
V/W

151

9 ⎤ Low speed Passenger door module
10 ⎦ CAN bus   Climate control module
7 ⎤ Low speed
8 ⎦ CAN bus   Central electronics module

143
1 N/B diesel A:60*, A:4†µ, A:40ƒß, A:27π
2 G/R petrol A:56*, A:60†µ, A:61ƒß, A:63π

petrol N/B

145
1 P/W   A:34*, A:40†µ, A:68ƒß
2 P/W 08 diesel A:36
3 N/B   A:42*, A:39†µ, A:58ƒß
   U/W
   N/G 08 diesel

150
1   A:77*, A:47π, A:48
2   A:53*, A:65π, A:66
   S/R   S
   R petrol W petrol

144
1 N/B A:26µ†, A:39ßƒ, A:67
   B

148
2 1 S/Y C:10

a E G G D:43
b P U U D:44
152 N N D:45

28
A:3 ⎤ Low speed Instruments
A:2 ⎦ CAN bus

A:18 S 3
A:14 W 2 31c °C

12
B:46, B:37*
B:8, B:35* Y
B:23 ⎤ High speed Central electronics module
B:22 ⎦ CAN bus

7
D:47*, D:50 ⎤ High speed Brake control module
D:32*, D:35 ⎦ CAN bus
C:22 ⎤ High speed Engine control module
C:21 ⎦ CAN bus
D:49 ⎤ Low speed Instruments
D:34 ⎦ CAN bus

147
1 2 B
146
1 2 B

149
1

2 S S
6 Y/R
5
4

* = 08 diesel
π = 05 diesel
† = 08 petrol with turbo
ƒ = 08 petrol without turbo
µ = 05 petrol with turbo
ß = 05 petrol without turbo

136
45 Y/R 1 134
46 N/K 2
34 Y/G 1 135
33 N/G 2
11 ⎤ High speed Central electronics module
15 ⎦ CAN bus

Typical fuse details (based on 2005 model)

Diagram 14

Engine compartment fuse box 3

Link	Rating	Function
F1	25A	Optional parking heater
F2	20A	Optional auxiliary lamps
F3	10A	Throttle
F4	20A	Oxygen sensors, ECM (diesel), HP valve (diesel)
F5	10A	Crankcase vent heater
F6	15A	Mass air flow ensor, ECM, injectors (petrol)
F7	-	-
F8	10A	Accelerator pedal sensor, AC compressor, fan module
F9	-	-
F10	-	-
F11	20A	Ignition coils (petrol), relay coils
F12	-	-
F13	25A	Windscreen wipers
F14	30A	ABS
F15	35A	Headlamp high pressure washer
F16	-	-
F17	20A	LH dipped beam
F18	15A	Front parking lamps
F19	30A	ABS
F20	20A	RH dipped beam
F21	15A	Fuel pump
F22	35A	Starter motor
F23	10A	ECM supply, engine relay coil

Passenger compartment fuse box (end of dash board) 4

Fuse	Rating	Function
F1	25A	Powered seat LH
F2	25A	Powered seat RH
F3	30A	Climate control system fan
F4	25A	RH door module
F5	25A	LH door module
F6	10A	Lighting, ceiling light, upper electronics module
F7	15A	Sunroof
F8	7.5A	Ignition switch, SRS system, ECM, optional PACOS, immobiliser
F9	5A	OBDII, light switch module, steering angle sensor, steering wheel module
F10	20A	Audio
F11	30A	Amplifier
F12	10A	Road traffic information display
F13	5A	Telephone
F14	-	-
.		
.		
F38	-	-

Luggage compartment (REM) fuse box 8

Fuse	Rating	Function
F1	10A	Reversing lamps
F2	15A	Parking lamps, fog lamps, luggage compartment lighting, number plate lighting, LED's in brake lighting
F3	20A	Accessories (accessory electronics module)
F4	-	-
F5	10A	Rear electronics module(REM)
F6	7.5A	CD auto changer, TV, RTI
F7	15A	Trailer connector
F8	15A	Luggage compartment power socket
F9	20A	Rear RH door powered window, powered window lock
F10	20A	Rear LH door powered window, powered window lock
F11	-	-
F12	-	-
F13	15	Diesel filter heater
F14	-	-
F15	-	-
F16	-	-
F17	5A	Audio accessories
F18	-	-
F19	15A	Foldable head restraint

Luggage compartment fuse box (continued)

Fuse	Rating	Function
F20	20A	Trailer connector
F21	-	-
F22	-	-
F23	7.5A	All wheel drive (AWD)
F24	15A	Four-C SUM
F25	-	-
F26	6A	Parking assistance
F27	30A	Main fuse for trailer connector, Four-C, parking assistance, AWD
F28	15A	Central locking system
F29	25A	Trailer lighting left side
F30	25A	Trailer lighting right side
F31	40A	Main fuse (F37, F38)
F32	-	-
.		
.		
F36	-	-
F37	20A	Heated rear window
F38	20A	Heated rear window

Passenger compartment (CEM) fuse box (under dash board) 7

Fuse	Rating	Function
F1	15A	Seat heater, RHS
F2	15A	Seat heater, LHS
F3	15A	Horn
F4	-	-
F5	-	-
F6	-	-
F7	-	-
F8	5A	Siren
F9	5A	Brake lamp switch feed
F10	10A	Instruments, climate control, powered driving seat
F11	15A	Front and rear power outlets
F12	-	-
F13	-	-
F14	15A	Headlamp wipers
F15	5A	ABS, STC/DSTC
F16	10A	Power steering, xenon headlamps, headlamp levelling
F17	7.5A	Fog lamp front left
F18	7.5A	Fog lamp front right
F19	-	-
F20	-	-
F21	10A	Transmission control module
F22	10A	Main beam left
F23	10A	Main beam right
F24	-	-
F25	-	-
F26	-	-
F27	-	-
F28	5A	Power passenger seat, audio
F29	-	-
F30	5A	BLIS
F31	-	-
F32	-	-
F33	20A	Vacuum pump
F34	15A	Washer pump
F35	-	-
F36	-	-

Typical fuse box details (based on 2005 model)

Diagram 15

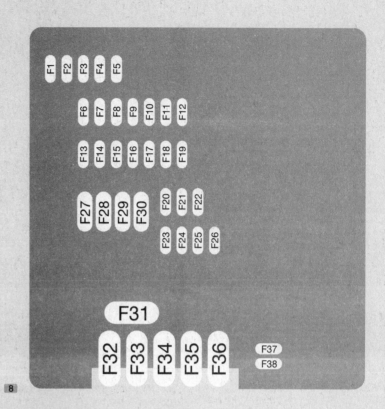

Dimensions and weights

Note: *All figures are approximate, and may vary according to model. Refer to manufacturer's data for exact figures.*

Dimensions

Overall length (depending on model)	4580 mm
Overall width.	1800 mm
Overall height	1430 mm
Wheelbase	2720 mm

Weights

Kerb weight	Refer to identification plate on the left-hand front inner wing
Maximum roof rack load	100 kg
Maximum trailer weight (braked)	1600 kg

Fuel economy

Although depreciation is still the biggest part of the cost of motoring for most car owners, the cost of fuel is more immediately noticeable. These pages give some tips on how to get the best fuel economy.

Working it out

Manufacturer's figures

Car manufacturers are required by law to provide fuel consumption information on all new vehicles sold. These 'official' figures are obtained by simulating various driving conditions on a rolling road or a test track. Real life conditions are different, so the fuel consumption actually achieved may not bear much resemblance to the quoted figures.

How to calculate it

Many cars now have trip computers which will

display fuel consumption, both instantaneous and average. Refer to the owner's handbook for details of how to use these.

To calculate consumption yourself (and maybe to check that the trip computer is accurate), proceed as follows.

1. Fill up with fuel and note the mileage, or zero the trip recorder.
2. Drive as usual until you need to fill up again.
3. Note the amount of fuel required to refill the tank, and the mileage covered since the previous fill-up.
4. Divide the mileage by the amount of fuel used to obtain the consumption figure.

For example:

Mileage at first fill-up (a) = 27,903
Mileage at second fill-up (b) = 28,346
Mileage covered (b - a) = 443
Fuel required at second fill-up = 48.6 litres

The half-completed changeover to metric units in the UK means that we buy our fuel in litres, measure distances in miles and talk about fuel consumption in miles per gallon. There are two ways round this: the first is to convert the litres to gallons before doing the calculation (by dividing by 4.546, or see Table 1). So in the example:

48.6 litres ÷ 4.546 = 10.69 gallons
443 miles ÷ 10.69 gallons = 41.4 mpg

The second way is to calculate the consumption in miles per litre, then multiply that figure by 4.546 (or see Table 2).

So in the example, fuel consumption is:

443 miles ÷ 48.6 litres = 9.1 mpl
9.1 mpl x 4.546 = 41.4 mpg

The rest of Europe expresses fuel consumption in litres of fuel required to travel 100 km (l/100 km). For interest, the conversions are given in Table 3. In practice it doesn't matter what units you use, provided you know what your normal consumption is and can spot if it's getting better or worse.

Table 1: conversion of litres to Imperial gallons

litres	1	2	3	4	5	10	20	30	40	50	60	70
gallons	0.22	0.44	0.66	0.88	1.10	2.24	4.49	6.73	8.98	11.22	13.47	15.71

Table 2: conversion of miles per litre to miles per gallon

miles per litre	5	6	7	8	9	10	11	12	13	14
miles per gallon	23	27	32	36	41	46	50	55	59	64

Table 3: conversion of litres per 100 km to miles per gallon

litres per 100 km	4	4.5	5	5.5	6	6.5	7	8	9	10
miles per gallon	71	63	56	51	47	43	40	35	31	28

Maintenance

A well-maintained car uses less fuel and creates less pollution. In particular:

Filters

Change air and fuel filters at the specified intervals.

Oil

Use a good quality oil of the lowest viscosity specified by the vehicle manufacturer (see *Lubricants and fluids*). Check the level often and be careful not to overfill.

Spark plugs

When applicable, renew at the specified intervals.

Tyres

Check tyre pressures regularly. Under-inflated tyres have an increased rolling resistance. It is generally safe to use the higher pressures specified for full load conditions even when not fully laden, but keep an eye on the centre band of tread for signs of wear due to over-inflation.

When buying new tyres, consider the 'fuel saving' models which most manufacturers include in their ranges.

Driving style

Acceleration

Acceleration uses more fuel than driving at a steady speed. The best technique with modern cars is to accelerate reasonably briskly to the desired speed, changing up through the gears as soon as possible without making the engine labour.

Air conditioning

Air conditioning absorbs quite a bit of energy from the engine – typically 3 kW (4 hp) or so. The effect on fuel consumption is at its worst in slow traffic. Switch it off when not required.

Anticipation

Drive smoothly and try to read the traffic flow so as to avoid unnecessary acceleration and braking.

Automatic transmission

When accelerating in an automatic, avoid depressing the throttle so far as to make the transmission hold onto lower gears at higher speeds. Don't use the 'Sport' setting, if applicable.

When stationary with the engine running, select 'N' or 'P'. When moving, keep your left foot away from the brake.

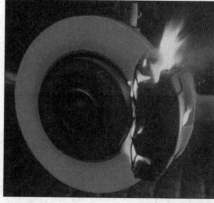

Braking

Braking converts the car's energy of motion into heat – essentially, it is wasted. Obviously some braking is always going to be necessary, but with good anticipation it is surprising how much can be avoided, especially on routes that you know well.

Carshare

Consider sharing lifts to work or to the shops. Even once a week will make a difference.

Electrical loads

Electricity is 'fuel' too; the alternator which charges the battery does so by converting some of the engine's energy of motion into electrical energy. The more electrical accessories are in use, the greater the load on the alternator. Switch off big consumers like the heated rear window when not required.

Freewheeling

Freewheeling (coasting) in neutral with the engine switched off is dangerous. The effort required to operate power-assisted brakes and steering increases when the engine is not running, with a potential lack of control in emergency situations.

In any case, modern fuel injection systems automatically cut off the engine's fuel supply on the overrun (moving and in gear, but with the accelerator pedal released).

Gadgets

Bolt-on devices claiming to save fuel have been around for nearly as long as the motor car itself. Those which worked were rapidly adopted as standard equipment by the vehicle manufacturers. Others worked only in certain situations, or saved fuel only at the expense of unacceptable effects on performance, driveability or the life of engine components.

The most effective fuel saving gadget is the driver's right foot.

Journey planning

Combine (eg) a trip to the supermarket with a visit to the recycling centre and the DIY store, rather than making separate journeys.

When possible choose a travelling time outside rush hours.

Load

The more heavily a car is laden, the greater the energy required to accelerate it to a given speed. Remove heavy items which you don't need to carry.

One load which is often overlooked is the contents of the fuel tank. A tankful of fuel (55 litres / 12 gallons) weighs 45 kg (100 lb) or so. Just half filling it may be worthwhile.

Lost?

At the risk of stating the obvious, if you're going somewhere new, have details of the route to hand. There's not much point in achieving record mpg if you also go miles out of your way.

Parking

If possible, carry out any reversing or turning manoeuvres when you arrive at a parking space so that you can drive straight out when you leave. Manoeuvering when the engine is cold uses a lot more fuel.

Driving around looking for free on-street parking may cost more in fuel than buying a car park ticket.

Premium fuel

Most major oil companies (and some supermarkets) have premium grades of fuel which are several pence a litre dearer than the standard grades. Reports vary, but the consensus seems to be that if these fuels improve economy at all, they do not do so by enough to justify their extra cost.

Roof rack

When loading a roof rack, try to produce a wedge shape with the narrow end at the front. Any cover should be securely fastened – if it flaps it's creating turbulence and absorbing energy.

Remove roof racks and boxes when not in use – they increase air resistance and can create a surprising amount of noise.

Short journeys

The engine is at its least efficient, and wear is highest, during the first few miles after a cold start. Consider walking, cycling or using public transport.

Speed

The engine is at its most efficient when running at a steady speed and load at the rpm where it develops maximum torque. (You can find this figure in the car's handbook.) For most cars this corresponds to between 55 and 65 mph in top gear.

Above the optimum cruising speed, fuel consumption starts to rise quite sharply. A car travelling at 80 mph will typically be using 30% more fuel than at 60 mph.

Supermarket fuel

It may be cheap but is it any good? In the UK all supermarket fuel must meet the relevant British Standard. The major oil companies will say that their branded fuels have better additive packages which may stop carbon and other deposits building up. A reasonable compromise might be to use one tank of branded fuel to three or four from the supermarket.

Switch off when stationary

Switch off the engine if you look like being stationary for more than 30 seconds or so. This is good for the environment as well as for your pocket. Be aware though that frequent restarts are hard on the battery and the starter motor.

Windows

Driving with the windows open increases air turbulence around the vehicle. Closing the windows promotes smooth airflow and

reduced resistance. The faster you go, the more significant this is.

And finally . . .

Driving techniques associated with good fuel economy tend to involve moderate acceleration and low top speeds. Be considerate to the needs of other road users who may need to make brisker progress; even if you do not agree with them this is not an excuse to be obstructive.

Safety must always take precedence over economy, whether it is a question of accelerating hard to complete an overtaking manoeuvre, killing your speed when confronted with a potential hazard or switching the lights on when it starts to get dark.

Conversion factors

Length (distance)

Inches (in)	x 25.4	= Millimetres (mm)	x 0.0394	= Inches (in)
Feet (ft)	x 0.305	= Metres (m)	x 3.281	= Feet (ft)
Miles	x 1.609	= Kilometres (km)	x 0.621	= Miles

Volume (capacity)

Cubic inches (cu in; in³)	x 16.387	= Cubic centimetres (cc; cm³)	x 0.061	= Cubic inches (cu in; in³)
Imperial pints (Imp pt)	x 0.568	= Litres (l)	x 1.76	= Imperial pints (Imp pt)
Imperial quarts (Imp qt)	x 1.137	= Litres (l)	x 0.88	= Imperial quarts (Imp qt)
Imperial quarts (Imp qt)	x 1.201	= US quarts (US qt)	x 0.833	= Imperial quarts (Imp qt)
US quarts (US qt)	x 0.946	= Litres (l)	x 1.057	= US quarts (US qt)
Imperial gallons (Imp gal)	x 4.546	= Litres (l)	x 0.22	= Imperial gallons (Imp gal)
Imperial gallons (Imp gal)	x 1.201	= US gallons (US gal)	x 0.833	= Imperial gallons (Imp gal)
US gallons (US gal)	x 3.785	= Litres (l)	x 0.264	= US gallons (US gal)

Mass (weight)

Ounces (oz)	x 28.35	= Grams (g)	x 0.035	= Ounces (oz)
Pounds (lb)	x 0.454	= Kilograms (kg)	x 2.205	= Pounds (lb)

Force

Ounces-force (ozf; oz)	x 0.278	= Newtons (N)	x 3.6	= Ounces-force (ozf; oz)
Pounds-force (lbf; lb)	x 4.448	= Newtons (N)	x 0.225	= Pounds-force (lbf; lb)
Newtons (N)	x 0.1	= Kilograms-force (kgf; kg)	x 9.81	= Newtons (N)

Pressure

Pounds-force per square inch (psi; lbf/in²; lb/in²)	x 0.070	= Kilograms-force per square centimetre (kgf/cm²; kg/cm²)	x 14.223	= Pounds-force per square inch (psi; lbf/in²; lb/in²)
Pounds-force per square inch (psi; lbf/in²; lb/in²)	x 0.068	= Atmospheres (atm)	x 14.696	= Pounds-force per square inch (psi; lbf/in²; lb/in²)
Pounds-force per square inch (psi; lbf/in²; lb/in²)	x 0.069	= Bars	x 14.5	= Pounds-force per square inch (psi; lbf/in²; lb/in²)
Pounds-force per square inch (psi; lbf/in²; lb/in²)	x 6.895	= Kilopascals (kPa)	x 0.145	= Pounds-force per square inch (psi; lbf/in²; lb/in²)
Kilopascals (kPa)	x 0.01	= Kilograms-force per square centimetre (kgf/cm²; kg/cm²)	x 98.1	= Kilopascals (kPa)
Millibar (mbar)	x 100	= Pascals (Pa)	x 0.01	= Millibar (mbar)
Millibar (mbar)	x 0.0145	= Pounds-force per square inch (psi; lbf/in²; lb/in²)	x 68.947	= Millibar (mbar)
Millibar (mbar)	x 0.75	= Millimetres of mercury (mmHg)	x 1.333	= Millibar (mbar)
Millibar (mbar)	x 0.401	= Inches of water (inH₂O)	x 2.491	= Millibar (mbar)
Millimetres of mercury (mmHg)	x 0.535	= Inches of water (inH₂O)	x 1.868	= Millimetres of mercury (mmHg)
Inches of water (inH₂O)	x 0.036	= Pounds-force per square inch (psi; lbf/in²; lb/in²)	x 27.68	= Inches of water (inH₂O)

Torque (moment of force)

Pounds-force inches (lbf in; lb in)	x 1.152	= Kilograms-force centimetre (kgf cm; kg cm)	x 0.868	= Pounds-force inches (lbf in; lb in)
Pounds-force inches (lbf in; lb in)	x 0.113	= Newton metres (Nm)	x 8.85	= Pounds-force inches (lbf in; lb in)
Pounds-force inches (lbf in; lb in)	x 0.083	= Pounds-force feet (lbf ft; lb ft)	x 12	= Pounds-force inches (lbf in; lb in)
Pounds-force feet (lbf ft; lb ft)	x 0.138	= Kilograms-force metres (kgf m; kg m)	x 7.233	= Pounds-force feet (lbf ft; lb ft)
Pounds-force feet (lbf ft; lb ft)	x 1.356	= Newton metres (Nm)	x 0.738	= Pounds-force feet (lbf ft; lb ft)
Newton metres (Nm)	x 0.102	= Kilograms-force metres (kgf m; kg m)	x 9.804	= Newton metres (Nm)

Power

Horsepower (hp)	x 745.7	= Watts (W)	x 0.0013	= Horsepower (hp)

Velocity (speed)

Miles per hour (miles/hr; mph)	x 1.609	= Kilometres per hour (km/hr; kph)	x 0.621	= Miles per hour (miles/hr; mph)

Fuel consumption*

Miles per gallon, Imperial (mpg)	x 0.354	= Kilometres per litre (km/l)	x 2.825	= Miles per gallon, Imperial (mpg)
Miles per gallon, US (mpg)	x 0.425	= Kilometres per litre (km/l)	x 2.352	= Miles per gallon, US (mpg)

Temperature

Degrees Fahrenheit = (°C x 1.8) + 32   Degrees Celsius (Degrees Centigrade; °C) = (°F - 32) x 0.56

It is common practice to convert from miles per gallon (mpg) to litres/100 kilometres (l/100km), where mpg x l/100 km = 282

Spare parts are available from many sources, including maker's appointed garages, accessory shops, and motor factors. To be sure of obtaining the correct parts, it may sometimes be necessary to quote the vehicle identification number. If possible, it can also be useful to take the old parts along for positive identification. Items such as starter motors and alternators may be available under a service exchange scheme – any parts returned should always be clean.

Our advice regarding spare part sources is as follows:

Officially-appointed garages

This is the best source of parts which are peculiar to your car, and are not otherwise generally available (eg, badges, interior trim, certain body panels, etc). It is also the only place at which you should buy parts if the vehicle is still under warranty.

Accessory shops

These are very good places to buy materials and components needed for the maintenance of your car (oil, air and fuel filters, spark plugs, light bulbs, drivebelts, oils and greases, brake pads, touch-up paint, etc). Parts like this sold by a reputable shop are of the same standard as those used by the car manufacturer.

Motor factors

Good factors will stock all the more important components which wear out comparatively quickly and can sometimes supply individual components needed for the overhaul of a larger assembly. They may also handle work such as cylinder block reboring, crankshaft regrinding and balancing, etc.

Tyre and exhaust specialists

These outlets may be independent or members of a local or national chain. They

frequently offer competitive prices when compared with a main dealer or local garage, but it will pay to obtain several quotes before making a decision. Also ask what 'extras' may be added to the quote – for instance, fitting a new valve and balancing the wheel are both often charged on top of the price of a new tyre.

Other sources

Beware of parts of materials obtained from market stalls, car boot sales or similar outlets. Such items are not always sub-standard, but there is little chance of compensation if they do prove unsatisfactory. In the case of safety-critical components such as brake pads there is the risk not only of financial loss but also of an accident causing injury or death.

Second-hand components or assemblies obtained from a car breaker can be a good buy in some circumstances, but this sort of purchase is best made by the experienced DIY mechanic.

Vehicle identification numbers

Modifications are a continuing and unpublicised process in vehicle manufacture, quite apart from major model changes. Spare parts manuals and lists are compiled upon a numerical basis, the individual vehicle identification numbers being essential to correct identification of the component concerned.

When ordering spare parts, always give as much information as possible. Quote the vehicle type and year, vehicle identification

number (VIN), and engine number, as appropriate.

The vehicle identification number (VIN) appears on a metal plate attached to the right-hand front inner wing, left-hand front inner wing, or on the drivers door aperture pillar (see illustrations). The model plate also gives vehicle loading details, engine type, and various trim and colour codes. The VIN also appears on a plastic tag attached to

the passenger side of the facia panel, visible through the windscreen, and at the top of the engine compartment bulkhead.

The engine number is stamped on the right-hand end of the cylinder block (see illustration).

The transmission identification numbers are located on a plate attached to the top of the transmission casing, or cast into the casing itself.

The VIN plate is mounting on the inner wing in the engine compartment . . .

. . . on a plate on the facia (visible through the windscreen) . . .

. . . and on the op of the engine compartment bulkhead (arrowed)

The engine number is stamped on the right-hand end of the cylinder block (arrowed)

Whenever servicing, repair or overhaul work is carried out on the car or its components, observe the following procedures and instructions. This will assist in carrying out the operation efficiently and to a professional standard of workmanship.

Joint mating faces and gaskets

When separating components at their mating faces, never insert screwdrivers or similar implements into the joint between the faces in order to prise them apart. This can cause severe damage which results in oil leaks, coolant leaks, etc upon reassembly. Separation is usually achieved by tapping along the joint with a soft-faced hammer in order to break the seal. However, note that this method may not be suitable where dowels are used for component location.

Where a gasket is used between the mating faces of two components, a new one must be fitted on reassembly; fit it dry unless otherwise stated in the repair procedure. Make sure that the mating faces are clean and dry, with all traces of old gasket removed. When cleaning a joint face, use a tool which is unlikely to score or damage the face, and remove any burrs or nicks with an oilstone or fine file.

Make sure that tapped holes are cleaned with a pipe cleaner, and keep them free of jointing compound, if this is being used, unless specifically instructed otherwise.

Ensure that all orifices, channels or pipes are clear, and blow through them, preferably using compressed air.

Oil seals

Oil seals can be removed by levering them out with a wide flat-bladed screwdriver or similar implement. Alternatively, a number of self-tapping screws may be screwed into the seal, and these used as a purchase for pliers or some similar device in order to pull the seal free.

Whenever an oil seal is removed from its working location, either individually or as part of an assembly, it should be renewed.

The very fine sealing lip of the seal is easily damaged, and will not seal if the surface it contacts is not completely clean and free from scratches, nicks or grooves. If the original sealing surface of the component cannot be restored, and the manufacturer has not made provision for slight relocation of the seal relative to the sealing surface, the component should be renewed.

Protect the lips of the seal from any surface which may damage them in the course of fitting. Use tape or a conical sleeve where possible. Lubricate the seal lips with oil before fitting and, on dual-lipped seals, fill the space between the lips with grease.

Unless otherwise stated, oil seals must be fitted with their sealing lips toward the lubricant to be sealed.

Use a tubular drift or block of wood of the appropriate size to install the seal and, if the seal housing is shouldered, drive the seal down to the shoulder. If the seal housing is unshouldered, the seal should be fitted with its face flush with the housing top face (unless otherwise instructed).

Screw threads and fastenings

Seized nuts, bolts and screws are quite a common occurrence where corrosion has set in, and the use of penetrating oil or releasing fluid will often overcome this problem if the offending item is soaked for a while before attempting to release it. The use of an impact driver may also provide a means of releasing such stubborn fastening devices, when used in conjunction with the appropriate screwdriver bit or socket. If none of these methods works, it may be necessary to resort to the careful application of heat, or the use of a hacksaw or nut splitter device.

Studs are usually removed by locking two nuts together on the threaded part, and then using a spanner on the lower nut to unscrew the stud. Studs or bolts which have broken off below the surface of the component in which they are mounted can sometimes be removed using a stud extractor. Always ensure that a blind tapped hole is completely free from oil, grease, water or other fluid before installing the bolt or stud. Failure to do this could cause the housing to crack due to the hydraulic action of the bolt or stud as it is screwed in.

When tightening a castellated nut to accept a split pin, tighten the nut to the specified torque, where applicable, and then tighten further to the next split pin hole. Never slacken the nut to align the split pin hole, unless stated in the repair procedure.

When checking or retightening a nut or bolt to a specified torque setting, slacken the nut or bolt by a quarter of a turn, and then retighten to the specified setting. However, this should not be attempted where angular tightening has been used.

For some screw fastenings, notably cylinder head bolts or nuts, torque wrench settings are no longer specified for the latter stages of tightening, "angle-tightening" being called up instead. Typically, a fairly low torque wrench setting will be applied to the bolts/nuts in the correct sequence, followed by one or more stages of tightening through specified angles.

Locknuts, locktabs and washers

Any fastening which will rotate against a component or housing during tightening should always have a washer between it and the relevant component or housing.

Spring or split washers should always be renewed when they are used to lock a critical component such as a big-end bearing retaining bolt or nut. Locktabs which are folded over to retain a nut or bolt should always be renewed.

Self-locking nuts can be re-used in non-critical areas, providing resistance can be felt when the locking portion passes over the bolt or stud thread. However, it should be noted that self-locking stiffnuts tend to lose their effectiveness after long periods of use, and should then be renewed as a matter of course.

Split pins must always be replaced with new ones of the correct size for the hole.

When thread-locking compound is found on the threads of a fastener which is to be re-used, it should be cleaned off with a wire brush and solvent, and fresh compound applied on reassembly.

Special tools

Some repair procedures in this manual entail the use of special tools such as a press, two or three-legged pullers, spring compressors, etc. Wherever possible, suitable readily-available alternatives to the manufacturer's special tools are described, and are shown in use. In some instances, where no alternative is possible, it has been necessary to resort to the use of a manufacturer's tool, and this has been done for reasons of safety as well as the efficient completion of the repair operation. Unless you are highly-skilled and have a thorough understanding of the procedures described, never attempt to bypass the use of any special tool when the procedure described specifies its use. Not only is there a very great risk of personal injury, but expensive damage could be caused to the components involved.

Environmental considerations

When disposing of used engine oil, brake fluid, antifreeze, etc, give due consideration to any detrimental environmental effects. Do not, for instance, pour any of the above liquids down drains into the general sewage system, or onto the ground to soak away. Many local council refuse tips provide a facility for waste oil disposal, as do some garages. If none of these facilities are available, consult your local Environmental Health Department, or the National Rivers Authority, for further advice.

With the universal tightening-up of legislation regarding the emission of environmentally-harmful substances from motor vehicles, most vehicles have tamperproof devices fitted to the main adjustment points of the fuel system. These devices are primarily designed to prevent unqualified persons from adjusting the fuel/air mixture, with the chance of a consequent increase in toxic emissions. If such devices are found during servicing or overhaul, they should, wherever possible, be renewed or refitted in accordance with the manufacturer's requirements or current legislation.

Note: It is antisocial and illegal to dump oil down the drain. To find the location of your local oil recycling bank, call this number free.

OIL CARE
FOLLOW THE CODE
OIL BANK LINE
0800 66 33 66
www.oilbankline.org.uk

The jack supplied with the vehicle tool kit should **only** be used for changing the roadwheels in an emergency – see *Wheel changing* at the front of this book. When carrying out any other kind of work, raise the vehicle using a heavy-duty hydraulic (or 'trolley') jack, and always supplement the jack with axle stands positioned under the vehicle jacking points. If the roadwheels do not have to be removed, consider using wheel ramps – if wished, these can be placed under the wheels once the vehicle has been raised using a hydraulic jack, and the vehicle lowered onto the ramps so that it is resting on its wheels.

Only ever jack the vehicle up on a solid, level surface. If there is even a slight slope, take great care that the vehicle cannot move as the wheels are lifted off the ground. Jacking up on an uneven or gravelled surface is not recommended, as the weight of the vehicle will not be evenly distributed, and the jack may slip as the vehicle is raised.

As far as possible, do not leave the vehicle unattended once it has been raised, particularly if children are playing nearby.

Before jacking up the front of the car, ensure that the handbrake is firmly applied. When jacking up the rear of the car, place wooden chocks in front of the front wheels, and engage first gear (or P).

The jack supplied with the vehicle locates in the sill flanges, at the points marked on each side of the car **(see illustration)**. Ensure that the jack head is correctly engaged before attempting to raise the vehicle.

When using a hydraulic jack or axle stands, the jack head or axle stand head may be placed under one of the four jacking points inboard of the door sills **(see illustration)**. When jacking or supporting the vehicle at these points, always use a block of wood between the jack head or axle stand, and the vehicle body. It is also considered good practice to use a large block of wood when supporting under other areas, to spread the load over a wider area, and reduce the risk of damage to the underside of the car (it also helps to prevent the underbody coating from being damaged by the jack or axle stand). **Do not** jack the vehicle under any other part of the sill, engine sump, floor pan, subframe, or directly under any of the steering or suspension components.

Never work under, around, or near a raised vehicle, unless it is adequately supported on stands. Do not rely on a jack alone, as even a hydraulic jack could fail under load. Makeshift methods should not be used to lift and support the car during servicing work.

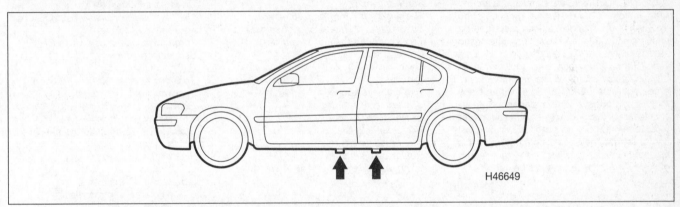

H46649

The jack supplied with the vehicle engages with jacking points inboard of the sill flanges (arrowed)

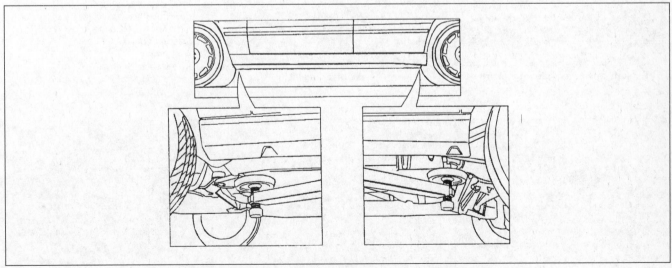

Jacking points for use with a workshop (trolley) hydraulic jack

Introduction

A selection of good tools is a fundamental requirement for anyone contemplating the maintenance and repair of a motor vehicle. For the owner who does not possess any, their purchase will prove a considerable expense, offsetting some of the savings made by doing-it-yourself. However, provided that the tools purchased meet the relevant national safety standards and are of good quality, they will last for many years and prove an extremely worthwhile investment.

To help the average owner to decide which tools are needed to carry out the various tasks detailed in this manual, we have compiled three lists of tools under the following headings: *Maintenance and minor repair, Repair and overhaul*, and *Special*. Newcomers to practical mechanics should start off with the *Maintenance and minor repair* tool kit, and confine themselves to the simpler jobs around the vehicle. Then, as confidence and experience grow, more difficult tasks can be undertaken, with extra tools being purchased as, and when, they are needed. In this way, a *Maintenance and minor repair* tool kit can be built up into a *Repair and overhaul* tool kit over a considerable period of time, without any major cash outlays. The experienced do-it-yourselfer will have a tool kit good enough for most repair and overhaul procedures, and will add tools from the *Special* category when it is felt that the expense is justified by the amount of use to which these tools will be put.

Maintenance and minor repair tool kit

The tools given in this list should be considered as a minimum requirement if routine maintenance, servicing and minor repair operations are to be undertaken. We recommend the purchase of combination spanners (ring one end, open-ended the other); although more expensive than open-ended ones, they do give the advantages of both types of spanner.

☐ *Combination spanners:*
   Metric - 8 to 19 mm inclusive
☐ *Adjustable spanner - 35 mm jaw (approx.)*
☐ *Spark plug spanner (with rubber insert) - petrol models*
☐ *Spark plug gap adjustment tool - petrol models*
☐ *Set of feeler gauges*
☐ *Brake bleed nipple spanner*
☐ *Screwdrivers:*
   Flat blade - 100 mm long x 6 mm dia
   Cross blade - 100 mm long x 6 mm dia
   Torx - various sizes (not all vehicles)
☐ *Combination pliers*
☐ *Hacksaw (junior)*
☐ *Tyre pump*
☐ *Tyre pressure gauge*
☐ *Oil can*
☐ *Oil filter removal tool*
☐ *Fine emery cloth*
☐ *Wire brush (small)*
☐ *Funnel (medium size)*
☐ *Sump drain plug key (not all vehicles)*

Repair and overhaul tool kit

These tools are virtually essential for anyone undertaking any major repairs to a motor vehicle, and are additional to those given in the *Maintenance and minor repair* list. Included in this list is a comprehensive set of sockets. Although these are expensive, they will be found invaluable as they are so versatile - particularly if various drives are included in the set. We recommend the half-inch square-drive type, as this can be used with most proprietary torque wrenches.

The tools in this list will sometimes need to be supplemented by tools from the *Special* list:

☐ *Sockets (or box spanners) to cover range in previous list (including Torx sockets)*
☐ *Reversible ratchet drive (for use with sockets)*
☐ *Extension piece, 250 mm (for use with sockets)*
☐ *Universal joint (for use with sockets)*
☐ *Flexible handle or sliding T "breaker bar" (for use with sockets)*
☐ *Torque wrench (for use with sockets)*
☐ *Self-locking grips*
☐ *Ball pein hammer*
☐ *Soft-faced mallet (plastic or rubber)*
☐ *Screwdrivers:*
   Flat blade - long & sturdy, short (chubby), and narrow (electrician's) types
   Cross blade – long & sturdy, and short (chubby) types
☐ *Pliers:*
   Long-nosed
   Side cutters (electrician's)
   Circlip (internal and external)
☐ *Cold chisel - 25 mm*
☐ *Scriber*
☐ *Scraper*
☐ *Centre-punch*
☐ *Pin punch*
☐ *Hacksaw*
☐ *Brake hose clamp*
☐ *Brake/clutch bleeding kit*
☐ *Selection of twist drills*
☐ *Steel rule/straight-edge*
☐ *Allen keys (inc. splined/Torx type)*
☐ *Selection of files*
☐ *Wire brush*
☐ *Axle stands*
☐ *Jack (strong trolley or hydraulic type)*
☐ *Light with extension lead*
☐ *Universal electrical multi-meter*

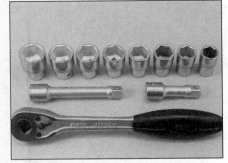

Sockets and reversible ratchet drive

Brake bleeding kit

Torx key, socket and bit

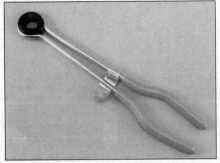

Hose clamp

Angular-tightening gauge

Special tools

The tools in this list are those which are not used regularly, are expensive to buy, or which need to be used in accordance with their manufacturers' instructions. Unless relatively difficult mechanical jobs are undertaken frequently, it will not be economic to buy many of these tools. Where this is the case, you could consider clubbing together with friends (or joining a motorists' club) to make a joint purchase, or borrowing the tools against a deposit from a local garage or tool hire specialist. It is worth noting that many of the larger DIY superstores now carry a large range of special tools for hire at modest rates.

The following list contains only those tools and instruments freely available to the public, and not those special tools produced by the vehicle manufacturer specifically for its dealer network. You will find occasional references to these manufacturers' special tools in the text of this manual. Generally, an alternative method of doing the job without the vehicle manufacturers' special tool is given. However, sometimes there is no alternative to using them. Where this is the case and the relevant tool cannot be bought or borrowed, you will have to entrust the work to a dealer.

- [ ] Angular-tightening gauge
- [ ] Valve spring compressor
- [ ] Valve grinding tool
- [ ] Piston ring compressor
- [ ] Piston ring removal/installation tool
- [ ] Cylinder bore hone
- [ ] Balljoint separator
- [ ] Coil spring compressors (where applicable)
- [ ] Two/three-legged hub and bearing puller
- [ ] Impact screwdriver
- [ ] Micrometer and/or vernier calipers
- [ ] Dial gauge
- [ ] Stroboscopic timing light
- [ ] Dwell angle meter/tachometer
- [ ] Fault code reader
- [ ] Cylinder compression gauge
- [ ] Hand-operated vacuum pump and gauge
- [ ] Clutch plate alignment set
- [ ] Brake shoe steady spring cup removal tool
- [ ] Bush and bearing removal/installation set
- [ ] Stud extractors
- [ ] Tap and die set
- [ ] Lifting tackle
- [ ] Trolley jack

Buying tools

Reputable motor accessory shops and superstores often offer excellent quality tools at discount prices, so it pays to shop around.

Remember, you don't have to buy the most expensive items on the shelf, but it is always advisable to steer clear of the very cheap tools. Beware of 'bargains' offered on market stalls or at car boot sales. There are plenty of good tools around at reasonable prices, but always aim to purchase items which meet the relevant national safety standards. If in doubt, ask the proprietor or manager of the shop for advice before making a purchase.

Care and maintenance of tools

Having purchased a reasonable tool kit, it is necessary to keep the tools in a clean and serviceable condition. After use, always wipe off any dirt, grease and metal particles using a clean, dry cloth, before putting the tools away. Never leave them lying around after they have been used. A simple tool rack on the garage or workshop wall for items such as screwdrivers and pliers is a good idea. Store all normal spanners and sockets in a metal box. Any measuring instruments, gauges, meters, etc, must be carefully stored where they cannot be damaged or become rusty.

Take a little care when tools are used. Hammer heads inevitably become marked, and screwdrivers lose the keen edge on their blades from time to time. A little timely attention with emery cloth or a file will soon restore items like this to a good finish.

Working facilities

Not to be forgotten when discussing tools is the workshop itself. If anything more than routine maintenance is to be carried out, a suitable working area becomes essential.

It is appreciated that many an owner-mechanic is forced by circumstances to remove an engine or similar item without the benefit of a garage or workshop. Having done this, any repairs should always be done under the cover of a roof.

Wherever possible, any dismantling should be done on a clean, flat workbench or table at a suitable working height.

Any workbench needs a vice; one with a jaw opening of 100 mm is suitable for most jobs. As mentioned previously, some clean dry storage space is also required for tools, as well as for any lubricants, cleaning fluids, touch-up paints etc, which become necessary.

Another item which may be required, and which has a much more general usage, is an electric drill with a chuck capacity of at least 8 mm. This, together with a good range of twist drills, is virtually essential for fitting accessories.

Last, but not least, always keep a supply of old newspapers and clean, lint-free rags available, and try to keep any working area as clean as possible.

Micrometers

Dial test indicator ("dial gauge")

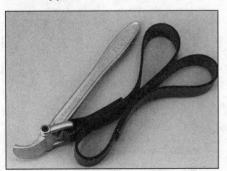

Strap wrench

Compression tester

Fault code reader

This is a guide to getting your vehicle through the MOT test. Obviously it will not be possible to examine the vehicle to the same standard as the professional MOT tester. However, working through the following checks will enable you to identify any problem areas before submitting the vehicle for the test.

It has only been possible to summarise the test requirements here, based on the regulations in force at the time of printing. Test standards are becoming increasingly stringent, although there are some exemptions for older vehicles.

An assistant will be needed to help carry out some of these checks.

The checks have been sub-divided into four categories, as follows:

1 Checks carried out **FROM THE DRIVER'S SEAT**

2 Checks carried out **WITH THE VEHICLE ON THE GROUND**

3 Checks carried out **WITH THE VEHICLE RAISED AND THE WHEELS FREE TO TURN**

4 Checks carried out on **YOUR VEHICLE'S EXHAUST EMISSION SYSTEM**

---

1 Checks carried out **FROM THE DRIVER'S SEAT**

Handbrake

☐ Test the operation of the handbrake. Excessive travel (too many clicks) indicates incorrect brake or cable adjustment.
☐ Check that the handbrake cannot be released by tapping the lever sideways. Check the security of the lever mountings.

☐ Check that the brake pedal is secure and in good condition. Check also for signs of fluid leaks on the pedal, floor or carpets, which would indicate failed seals in the brake master cylinder.
☐ Check the servo unit (when applicable) by operating the brake pedal several times, then keeping the pedal depressed and starting the engine. As the engine starts, the pedal will move down slightly. If not, the vacuum hose or the servo itself may be faulty.

Steering wheel and column

☐ Examine the steering wheel for fractures or looseness of the hub, spokes or rim.
☐ Move the steering wheel from side to side and then up and down. Check that the steering wheel is not loose on the column, indicating wear or a loose retaining nut. Continue moving the steering wheel as before, but also turn it slightly from left to right.
☐ Check that the steering wheel is not loose on the column, and that there is no abnormal

Footbrake

☐ Depress the brake pedal and check that it does not creep down to the floor, indicating a master cylinder fault. Release the pedal, wait a few seconds, then depress it again. If the pedal travels nearly to the floor before firm resistance is felt, brake adjustment or repair is necessary. If the pedal feels spongy, there is air in the hydraulic system which must be removed by bleeding.

movement of the steering wheel, indicating wear in the column support bearings or couplings.

Windscreen, mirrors and sunvisor

☐ The windscreen must be free of cracks or other significant damage within the driver's field of view. (Small stone chips are acceptable.) Rear view mirrors must be secure, intact, and capable of being adjusted.

290mm

☐ The driver's sunvisor must be capable of being stored in the "up" position.

Seat belts and seats

Note: *The following checks are applicable to all seat belts, front and rear.*

☐ Examine the webbing of all the belts (including rear belts if fitted) for cuts, serious fraying or deterioration. Fasten and unfasten each belt to check the buckles. If applicable, check the retracting mechanism. Check the security of all seat belt mountings accessible from inside the vehicle.

☐ Seat belts with pre-tensioners, once activated, have a "flag" or similar showing on the seat belt stalk. This, in itself, is not a reason for test failure.

☐ The front seats themselves must be securely attached and the backrests must lock in the upright position.

Doors

☐ Both front doors must be able to be opened and closed from outside and inside, and must latch securely when closed.

2 Checks carried out WITH THE VEHICLE ON THE GROUND

Vehicle identification

☐ Number plates must be in good condition, secure and legible, with letters and numbers correctly spaced – spacing at (A) should be at least twice that at (B).

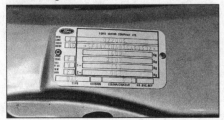

☐ The VIN plate and/or homologation plate must be legible.

Electrical equipment

☐ Switch on the ignition and check the operation of the horn.

☐ Check the windscreen washers and wipers, examining the wiper blades; renew damaged or perished blades. Also check the operation of the stop-lights.

☐ Check the operation of the sidelights and number plate lights. The lenses and reflectors must be secure, clean and undamaged.

☐ Check the operation and alignment of the headlights. The headlight reflectors must not be tarnished and the lenses must be undamaged.

☐ Switch on the ignition and check the operation of the direction indicators (including the instrument panel tell-tale) and the hazard warning lights. Operation of the sidelights and stop-lights must not affect the indicators - if it does, the cause is usually a bad earth at the rear light cluster.

☐ Check the operation of the rear foglight(s), including the warning light on the instrument panel or in the switch.

☐ The ABS warning light must illuminate in accordance with the manufacturers' design. For most vehicles, the ABS warning light should illuminate when the ignition is switched on, and (if the system is operating properly) extinguish after a few seconds. Refer to the owner's handbook.

Footbrake

☐ Examine the master cylinder, brake pipes and servo unit for leaks, loose mountings, corrosion or other damage.

☐ The fluid reservoir must be secure and the fluid level must be between the upper (A) and lower (B) markings.

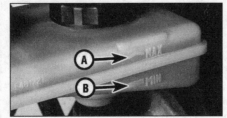

☐ Inspect both front brake flexible hoses for cracks or deterioration of the rubber. Turn the steering from lock to lock, and ensure that the hoses do not contact the wheel, tyre, or any part of the steering or suspension mechanism. With the brake pedal firmly depressed, check the hoses for bulges or leaks under pressure.

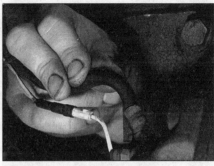

Steering and suspension

☐ Have your assistant turn the steering wheel from side to side slightly, up to the point where the steering gear just begins to transmit this movement to the roadwheels. Check for excessive free play between the steering wheel and the steering gear, indicating wear or insecurity of the steering column joints, the column-to-steering gear coupling, or the steering gear itself.

☐ Have your assistant turn the steering wheel more vigorously in each direction, so that the roadwheels just begin to turn. As this is done, examine all the steering joints, linkages, fittings and attachments. Renew any component that shows signs of wear or damage. On vehicles with power steering, check the security and condition of the steering pump, drivebelt and hoses.

☐ Check that the vehicle is standing level, and at approximately the correct ride height.

Shock absorbers

☐ Depress each corner of the vehicle in turn, then release it. The vehicle should rise and then settle in its normal position. If the vehicle continues to rise and fall, the shock absorber is defective. A shock absorber which has seized will also cause the vehicle to fail.

Exhaust system

☐ Start the engine. With your assistant holding a rag over the tailpipe, check the entire system for leaks. Repair or renew leaking sections.

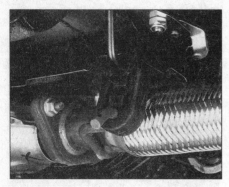

3 Checks carried out
WITH THE VEHICLE RAISED AND THE WHEELS FREE TO TURN

Jack up the front and rear of the vehicle, and securely support it on axle stands. Position the stands clear of the suspension assemblies. Ensure that the wheels are clear of the ground and that the steering can be turned from lock to lock.

Steering mechanism

☐ Have your assistant turn the steering from lock to lock. Check that the steering turns smoothly, and that no part of the steering mechanism, including a wheel or tyre, fouls any brake hose or pipe or any part of the body structure.

☐ Examine the steering rack rubber gaiters for damage or insecurity of the retaining clips. If power steering is fitted, check for signs of damage or leakage of the fluid hoses, pipes or connections. Also check for excessive stiffness or binding of the steering, a missing split pin or locking device, or severe corrosion of the body structure within 30 cm of any steering component attachment point.

Front and rear suspension and wheel bearings

☐ Starting at the front right-hand side, grasp the roadwheel at the 3 o'clock and 9 o'clock positions and rock gently but firmly. Check for free play or insecurity at the wheel bearings, suspension balljoints, or suspension mountings, pivots and attachments.

☐ Now grasp the wheel at the 12 o'clock and 6 o'clock positions and repeat the previous inspection. Spin the wheel, and check for roughness or tightness of the front wheel bearing.

☐ If excess free play is suspected at a component pivot point, this can be confirmed by using a large screwdriver or similar tool and levering between the mounting and the component attachment. This will confirm whether the wear is in the pivot bush, its retaining bolt, or in the mounting itself (the bolt holes can often become elongated).

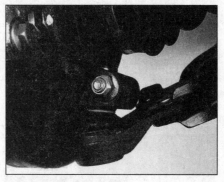

☐ Carry out all the above checks at the other front wheel, and then at both rear wheels.

Springs and shock absorbers

☐ Examine the suspension struts (when applicable) for serious fluid leakage, corrosion, or damage to the casing. Also check the security of the mounting points.

☐ If coil springs are fitted, check that the spring ends locate in their seats, and that the spring is not corroded, cracked or broken.

☐ If leaf springs are fitted, check that all leaves are intact, that the axle is securely attached to each spring, and that there is no deterioration of the spring eye mountings, bushes, and shackles.

☐ The same general checks apply to vehicles fitted with other suspension types, such as torsion bars, hydraulic displacer units, etc. Ensure that all mountings and attachments are secure, that there are no signs of excessive wear, corrosion or damage, and (on hydraulic types) that there are no fluid leaks or damaged pipes.

☐ Inspect the shock absorbers for signs of serious fluid leakage. Check for wear of the mounting bushes or attachments, or damage to the body of the unit.

Driveshafts
(fwd vehicles only)

☐ Rotate each front wheel in turn and inspect the constant velocity joint gaiters for splits or damage. Also check that each driveshaft is straight and undamaged.

Braking system

☐ If possible without dismantling, check brake pad wear and disc condition. Ensure that the friction lining material has not worn excessively, (A) and that the discs are not fractured, pitted, scored or badly worn (B).

☐ Examine all the rigid brake pipes underneath the vehicle, and the flexible hose(s) at the rear. Look for corrosion, chafing or insecurity of the pipes, and for signs of bulging under pressure, chafing, splits or deterioration of the flexible hoses.

☐ Look for signs of fluid leaks at the brake calipers or on the brake backplates. Repair or renew leaking components.

☐ Slowly spin each wheel, while your assistant depresses and releases the footbrake. Ensure that each brake is operating and does not bind when the pedal is released.

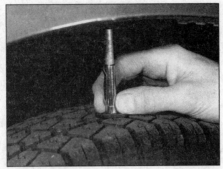

□ Examine the handbrake mechanism, checking for frayed or broken cables, excessive corrosion, or wear or insecurity of the linkage. Check that the mechanism works on each relevant wheel, and releases fully, without binding.

□ It is not possible to test brake efficiency without special equipment, but a road test can be carried out later to check that the vehicle pulls up in a straight line.

Fuel and exhaust systems

□ Inspect the fuel tank (including the filler cap), fuel pipes, hoses and unions. All components must be secure and free from leaks.

□ Examine the exhaust system over its entire length, checking for any damaged, broken or missing mountings, security of the retaining clamps and rust or corrosion.

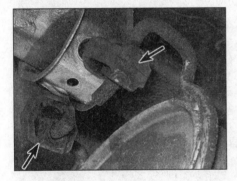

Wheels and tyres

□ Examine the sidewalls and tread area of each tyre in turn. Check for cuts, tears, lumps, bulges, separation of the tread, and exposure of the ply or cord due to wear or damage. Check that the tyre bead is correctly seated on the wheel rim, that the valve is sound and properly seated, and that the wheel is not distorted or damaged.

□ Check that the tyres are of the correct size for the vehicle, that they are of the same size

and type on each axle, and that the pressures are correct.

□ Check the tyre tread depth. The legal minimum at the time of writing is 1.6 mm over at least three-quarters of the tread width. Abnormal tread wear may indicate incorrect front wheel alignment.

Body corrosion

□ Check the condition of the entire vehicle structure for signs of corrosion in load-bearing areas. (These include chassis box sections, side sills, cross-members, pillars, and all suspension, steering, braking system and seat belt mountings and anchorages.) Any corrosion which has seriously reduced the thickness of a load-bearing area is likely to cause the vehicle to fail. In this case professional repairs are likely to be needed.

□ Damage or corrosion which causes sharp or otherwise dangerous edges to be exposed will also cause the vehicle to fail.

4 Checks carried out on YOUR VEHICLE'S EXHAUST EMISSION SYSTEM

Petrol models

□ The engine should be warmed up, and running well (ignition system in good order, air filter element clean, etc).

□ Before testing, run the engine at around 2500 rpm for 20 seconds. Let the engine drop to idle, and watch for smoke from the exhaust. If the idle speed is too high, or if dense blue or black smoke emerges for more than 5 seconds, the vehicle will fail. Typically, blue smoke signifies oil burning (engine wear); black smoke means unburnt fuel (dirty air cleaner element, or other fuel system fault).

□ An exhaust gas analyser for measuring carbon monoxide (CO) and hydrocarbons (HC) is now needed. If one cannot be hired or borrowed, have a local garage perform the check.

CO emissions (mixture)

□ The MOT tester has access to the CO limits for all vehicles. The CO level is measured at idle speed, and at 'fast idle' (2500 to 3000 rpm). The following limits are given as a general guide:

At idle speed – Less than 0.5% CO
At 'fast idle' – Less than 0.3% CO
Lambda reading – 0.97 to 1.03

□ If the CO level is too high, this may point to poor maintenance, a fuel injection system problem, faulty lambda (oxygen) sensor or catalytic converter. Try an injector cleaning treatment, and check the vehicle's ECU for fault codes.

HC emissions

□ The MOT tester has access to HC limits for all vehicles. The HC level is measured at 'fast idle' (2500 to 3000 rpm). The following limits are given as a general guide:

At 'fast idle' – Less then 200 ppm

□ Excessive HC emissions are typically caused by oil being burnt (worn engine), or by a blocked crankcase ventilation system ('breather'). If the engine oil is old and thin, an oil change may help. If the engine is running badly, check the vehicle's ECU for fault codes.

Diesel models

□ The only emission test for diesel engines is measuring exhaust smoke density, using a calibrated smoke meter. The test involves accelerating the engine at least 3 times to its maximum unloaded speed.

Note: *On engines with a timing belt, it is VITAL that the belt is in good condition before the test is carried out.*

□ With the engine warmed up, it is first purged by running at around 2500 rpm for 20 seconds. A governor check is then carried out, by slowly accelerating the engine to its maximum speed. After this, the smoke meter is connected, and the engine is accelerated quickly to maximum speed three times. If the smoke density is less than the limits given below, the vehicle will pass:

Non-turbo vehicles: 2.5m-1
Turbocharged vehicles: 3.0m-1

□ If excess smoke is produced, try fitting a new air cleaner element, or using an injector cleaning treatment. If the engine is running badly, where applicable, check the vehicle's ECU for fault codes. Also check the vehicle's EGR system, where applicable. At high mileages, the injectors may require professional attention.

Engine

- [ ] Engine fails to rotate when attempting to start
- [ ] Engine rotates, but will not start
- [ ] Engine difficult to start when cold
- [ ] Engine difficult to start when hot
- [ ] Starter motor noisy or excessively-rough in engagement
- [ ] Engine starts, but stops immediately
- [ ] Engine idles erratically
- [ ] Engine misfires at idle speed
- [ ] Engine misfires throughout the driving speed range
- [ ] Engine hesitates on acceleration
- [ ] Engine stalls
- [ ] Engine lacks power
- [ ] Engine backfires
- [ ] Oil pressure warning light illuminated with engine running
- [ ] Engine runs-on after switching off
- [ ] Engine noises

Cooling system

- [ ] Overheating
- [ ] Overcooling
- [ ] External coolant leakage
- [ ] Internal coolant leakage
- [ ] Corrosion

Fuel and exhaust systems

- [ ] Excessive fuel consumption
- [ ] Fuel leakage and/or fuel odour
- [ ] Excessive noise or fumes from exhaust system

Clutch

- [ ] Pedal travels to floor – no pressure or very little resistance
- [ ] Clutch fails to disengage (unable to select gears)
- [ ] Clutch slips (engine speed increases, with no increase in vehicle speed)
- [ ] Judder as clutch is engaged
- [ ] Noise when depressing or releasing clutch pedal

Manual transmission

- [ ] Noisy in neutral with engine running
- [ ] Noisy in one particular gear
- [ ] Difficulty engaging gears
- [ ] Jumps out of gear
- [ ] Vibration
- [ ] Lubricant leaks

Automatic transmission

- [ ] Fluid leakage
- [ ] Transmission fluid brown, or has burned smell
- [ ] General gear selection problems
- [ ] Transmission will not downshift (kickdown) with accelerator pedal fully depressed
- [ ] Engine will not start in any gear, or starts in gears other than Park or Neutral
- [ ] Transmission slips, shifts roughly, is noisy, or has no drive in forward or reverse gears

Driveshafts

- [ ] Vibration when accelerating or decelerating
- [ ] Clicking or knocking noise on turns (at slow speed on full-lock)

Braking system

- [ ] Vehicle pulls to one side under braking
- [ ] Noise (grinding or high-pitched squeal) when brakes applied
- [ ] Excessive brake pedal travel
- [ ] Brake pedal feels spongy when depressed
- [ ] Excessive brake pedal effort required to stop vehicle
- [ ] Judder felt through brake pedal or steering wheel when braking
- [ ] Brakes binding
- [ ] Rear wheels locking under normal braking

Suspension and steering

- [ ] Vehicle pulls to one side
- [ ] Wheel wobble and vibration
- [ ] Excessive pitching and/or rolling around corners, or during braking
- [ ] Wandering or general instability
- [ ] Excessively-stiff steering
- [ ] Excessive play in steering
- [ ] Lack of power assistance
- [ ] Tyre wear excessive

Electrical system

- [ ] Battery will not hold a charge for more than a few days
- [ ] Ignition/no-charge warning light remains illuminated with engine running
- [ ] Ignition/no-charge warning light fails to come on
- [ ] Lights inoperative
- [ ] Instrument readings inaccurate or erratic
- [ ] Horn inoperative, or unsatisfactory in operation
- [ ] Windscreen wipers inoperative, or unsatisfactory in operation
- [ ] Windscreen washers inoperative, or unsatisfactory in operation
- [ ] Electric windows inoperative, or unsatisfactory in operation
- [ ] Central locking system inoperative, or unsatisfactory in operation

Introduction

The vehicle owner who does his or her own maintenance according to the recommended service schedules should not have to use this section of the manual very often. Modern component reliability is such that, provided those items subject to wear or deterioration are inspected or renewed at the specified intervals, sudden failure is comparatively rare. Faults do not usually just happen as a result of sudden failure, but develop over a period of time. Major mechanical failures in particular are usually preceded by characteristic symptoms over hundreds or even thousands of miles. Those components which do occasionally fail without warning are often small and easily carried in the vehicle.

With any fault finding, the first step is to decide where to begin investigations. Sometimes this is obvious, but on other occasions, a little detective work will be necessary. The owner who makes half a dozen haphazard adjustments or replacements may be successful in curing a fault (or its symptoms), but will be none the wiser if the fault recurs, and ultimately may have spent more time and money than was necessary. A calm and logical approach will be found to be more satisfactory in the long run. Always take into account any warning signs or abnormalities that may have been noticed in the period preceding the fault – power loss, high or low gauge readings, unusual smells,

etc – and remember that failure of components such as fuses or spark plugs may only be pointers to some underlying fault.

The pages which follow provide an easy-reference guide to the more common problems which may occur during the operation of the vehicle. These problems and their possible causes are grouped under headings denoting various components or systems, such as Engine, Cooling system, etc. The general Chapter which deals with the problem is also shown in brackets; refer to the relevant part of that Chapter for system-specific information. Whatever the fault, certain basic principles apply. These are as follows:

Verify the fault. This is simply a matter of

being sure that you know what the symptoms are before starting work. This is particularly important if you are investigating a fault for someone else, who may not have described it very accurately.

Don't overlook the obvious. For example, if the vehicle won't start, is there fuel in the tank? (Don't take anyone else's word on this particular point, and don't trust the fuel gauge either). If an electrical fault is indicated, look for loose or broken wires before digging out the test gear.

Cure the disease, not the symptom. Substituting a flat battery with a fully-charged one will get you off the hard shoulder, but if the underlying cause is not attended to, the new battery will go the same way. Similarly, changing oil-fouled spark plugs for a new set will get you moving again, but remember that the reason for the fouling (if it wasn't simply an incorrect grade of plug) will have to be established and corrected.

Don't take anything for granted. Particularly, don't forget that a 'new' component may itself be defective (especially if it's been rattling around in the boot for months), and don't leave components out of a fault diagnosis sequence just because they are new or recently-fitted. When you do finally diagnose a difficult fault, you'll probably realise that all the evidence was there from the start.

Consider what work, if any, has recently been carried out. Many faults arise through careless or hurried work. For instance, if any work has been performed under the bonnet, could some of the wiring have been dislodged or incorrectly routed, or a hose trapped? Have all the fasteners been properly tightened? Were new, genuine parts and new gaskets used? There is often a certain amount of detective work to be done in this case, as an apparently-unrelated task can have far-reaching consequences.

Diesel fault diagnosis

The majority of starting problems on small diesel engines are electrical in origin. The mechanic who is familiar with petrol engines but less so with diesel may be inclined to view the diesel's injectors and pump in the same light as the spark plugs and distributor, but this is generally a mistake.

When investigating complaints of difficult starting for someone else, make sure that the correct starting procedure is understood and is being followed. Some drivers are unaware of the significance of the preheating warning light – many modern engines are sufficiently forgiving for this not to matter in mild weather, but with the onset of winter, problems begin.

As a rule of thumb, if the engine is difficult to start but runs well when it has finally got going, the problem is electrical (battery, starter motor or preheating system). If poor performance is combined with difficult starting, the problem is likely to be in the fuel system. The low-pressure (supply) side of the fuel system should be checked before suspecting the injectors and high-pressure pump. The most common fuel supply problem is air getting into the system, and any pipe from the fuel tank forwards must be scrutinised if air leakage is suspected. Normally the pump is the last item to suspect, since unless it has been tampered with, there is no reason for it to be at fault.

Engine

Engine fails to rotate when attempting to start

- [ ] Battery terminal connections loose or corroded *(see Weekly checks)*
- [ ] Battery discharged or faulty (Chapter 5A)
- [ ] Broken, loose or disconnected wiring in the starting circuit (Chapter 5A)
- [ ] Defective starter solenoid or ignition switch (Chapter 5A or 12)
- [ ] Defective starter motor (Chapter 5A)
- [ ] Starter pinion or flywheel ring gear teeth loose or broken (Chapter 2A, 2B or 5A)
- [ ] Engine earth strap broken or disconnected (Chapter 5A or 12)
- [ ] Engine suffering 'hydraulic lock' (eg, from water ingested after traversing flooded roads, or from a serious internal coolant leak) – consult a Volvo dealer or specialist for advice
- [ ] Automatic transmission not in position P or N (Chapter 7B)

Engine rotates, but will not start

- [ ] Fuel tank empty
- [ ] Battery discharged (engine rotates slowly) (Chapter 5A)
- [ ] Battery terminal connections loose or corroded *(see Weekly checks)*
- [ ] Ignition components damp or damaged – petrol models (Chapter 1A or 5B)
- [ ] Immobiliser fault, or 'uncoded' ignition key being used (Chapter 12 or Roadside repairs)
- [ ] Crankshaft sensor fault (Chapter 4A or 4B)
- [ ] Broken, loose or disconnected wiring in the ignition circuit – petrol models (Chapter 1A or 5B)
- [ ] Worn, faulty or incorrectly-gapped spark plugs – petrol models (Chapter 1A)
- [ ] Preheating system faulty – diesel models (Chapter 5A)
- [ ] Fuel injection system fault (Chapter 4A or 4B)
- [ ] Air in fuel system – diesel models (Chapter 4B)
- [ ] Major mechanical failure (eg, timing belt snapped) (Chapter 2A or 2B)

Engine difficult to start when cold

- [ ] Battery discharged (Chapter 5A)
- [ ] Battery terminal connections loose or corroded *(see Weekly checks)*
- [ ] Worn, faulty or incorrectly-gapped spark plugs – petrol models (Chapter 1A)

- [ ] Other ignition system fault – petrol models (Chapter 1A or 5B)
- [ ] Preheating system faulty – diesel models (Chapter 5A)
- [ ] Fuel injection system fault (Chapter 4A or 4B)
- [ ] Wrong grade of engine oil used (Weekly checks, Chapter 1A or 1B)
- [ ] Low cylinder compression (Chapter 2A or 2B)

Engine difficult to start when hot

- [ ] Air filter element dirty or clogged (Chapter 1A or 1B)
- [ ] Fuel injection system fault (Chapter 4A or 4B)
- [ ] Low cylinder compression (Chapter 2A or 2B)

Starter motor noisy or excessively-rough in engagement

- [ ] Starter pinion or flywheel ring gear teeth loose or broken (Chapter 2A, 2B or 5A)
- [ ] Starter motor mounting bolts loose or missing (Chapter 5A)
- [ ] Starter motor internal components worn or damaged (Chapter 5A)

Engine starts, but stops immediately

- [ ] Loose or faulty electrical connections in the ignition circuit – petrol models (Chapter 1A or 5B)
- [ ] Vacuum leak at the throttle body or inlet manifold – petrol models (Chapter 4A)
- [ ] Blocked injectors/fuel injection system fault (Chapter 4A or 4B)
- [ ] Air in fuel, possibly due to loose fuel line connection – diesel models (Chapter 4B)

Engine idles erratically

- [ ] Air filter element clogged (Chapter 1A or 1B)
- [ ] Vacuum leak at the throttle body, inlet manifold or associated hoses – petrol models (Chapter 4A)
- [ ] Worn, faulty or incorrectly-gapped spark plugs – petrol models (Chapter 1A)
- [ ] Valve clearances incorrect – petrol models only (Chapter 2A)
- [ ] Uneven or low cylinder compression (Chapter 2A or 2B)
- [ ] Camshaft lobes worn (Chapter 2A or 2B)
- [ ] Timing belt incorrectly fitted (Chapter 2A or 2B)
- [ ] Blocked injectors/fuel injection system fault (Chapter 4A or 4B)
- [ ] Air in fuel, possibly due to loose fuel line connection – diesel models (Chapter 4B)

Engine (continued)

Engine misfires at idle speed

- ☐ Worn, faulty or incorrectly-gapped spark plugs – petrol models (Chapter 1A)
- ☐ Vacuum leak at the throttle body, inlet manifold or associated hoses – petrol models (Chapter 4A)
- ☐ Blocked injectors/fuel injection system fault (Chapter 4A or 4B)
- ☐ Faulty injector(s) – diesel models (Chapter 4B)
- ☐ Uneven or low cylinder compression (Chapter 2A or 2B)
- ☐ Disconnected, leaking, or perished crankcase ventilation hoses (Chapter 4C)

Engine misfires throughout the driving speed range

- ☐ Fuel filter choked (Chapter 1A or 1B)
- ☐ Fuel pump faulty, or delivery pressure low – petrol models (Chapter 4A)
- ☐ Fuel tank vent blocked, or fuel pipes restricted (Chapter 4A or 4B)
- ☐ Vacuum leak at the throttle body, inlet manifold or associated hoses – petrol models (Chapter 4A)
- ☐ Worn, faulty or incorrectly-gapped spark plugs – petrol models (Chapter 1A)
- ☐ Faulty injector(s) – diesel models (Chapter 4B)
- ☐ Faulty ignition coil – petrol models (Chapter 5A)
- ☐ Uneven or low cylinder compression (Chapter 2A or 2B)
- ☐ Blocked injector/fuel injection system fault (Chapter 4A or 4B)
- ☐ Blocked catalytic converter (Chapter 4A or 4B)
- ☐ Engine overheating – petrol models (Chapter 3)
- ☐ Fuel tank level low – diesel models (Chapter 4B)

Engine hesitates on acceleration

- ☐ Worn, faulty or incorrectly-gapped spark plugs – petrol models (Chapter 1A)
- ☐ Vacuum leak at the throttle body, inlet manifold or associated hoses – petrol models (Chapter 4A)
- ☐ Blocked injectors/fuel injection system fault (Chapter 4A or 4B)
- ☐ Faulty injector(s) – diesel models (Chapter 4B)
- ☐ Faulty clutch pedal switch (Chapter 6)

Engine stalls

- ☐ Vacuum leak at the throttle body, inlet manifold or associated hoses – petrol models (Chapter 4A)
- ☐ Fuel filter choked (Chapter 1A or 1B)
- ☐ Fuel pump faulty, or delivery pressure low – petrol models (Chapter 4A)
- ☐ Fuel tank vent blocked, or fuel pipes restricted (Chapter 4A or 4B)
- ☐ Blocked injectors/fuel injection system fault (Chapter 4A or 4B)
- ☐ Faulty injector(s) – diesel models (Chapter 4B)

Engine lacks power

- ☐ Air filter element blocked (Chapter 1A or 1B)
- ☐ Fuel filter choked (Chapter 1A or 1B)
- ☐ Fuel pipes blocked or restricted (Chapter 4A or 4B)
- ☐ Valve clearances incorrect – some petrol models only (Chapter 2A)
- ☐ Worn, faulty or incorrectly-gapped spark plugs – petrol models (Chapter 1A)
- ☐ Engine overheating – petrol models (Chapter 4A)
- ☐ Fuel tank level low – diesel models (Chapter 4B)
- ☐ Accelerator position sensor faulty (Chapter 4A or 4B)
- ☐ Vacuum leak at the throttle body, inlet manifold or associated hoses – petrol models (Chapter 4A)
- ☐ Blocked injectors/fuel injection system fault (Chapter 4A or 4B)
- ☐ Faulty injector(s) – diesel models (Chapter 4B)
- ☐ Timing belt incorrectly fitted (Chapter 2A or 2B)
- ☐ Fuel pump faulty, or delivery pressure low – petrol models (Chapter 4A)
- ☐ Uneven or low cylinder compression (Chapter 2A or 2B)

- ☐ Blocked catalytic converter (Chapter 4A or 4B)
- ☐ Brakes binding (Chapter 1A, 1B or 9)
- ☐ Clutch slipping (Chapter 6)

Engine backfires

- ☐ Timing belt incorrectly fitted (Chapter 2A or 2B)
- ☐ Vacuum leak at the throttle body, inlet manifold or associated hoses – petrol models (Chapter 4A)
- ☐ Blocked injectors/fuel injection system fault (Chapter 4A or 4B)
- ☐ Blocked catalytic converter (Chapter 4A or 4B)
- ☐ Ignition coil unit faulty – petrol models (Chapter 5B)

Oil pressure warning light illuminated with engine running

- ☐ Low oil level, or incorrect oil grade (see Weekly checks)
- ☐ Faulty oil pressure sensor, or wiring damaged (Chapter 12)
- ☐ Worn engine bearings and/or oil pump (Chapter 2A, 2B or 2C)
- ☐ High engine operating temperature (Chapter 3)
- ☐ Oil pump pressure relief valve defective (Chapter 2A or 2B)
- ☐ Oil pump pick-up strainer clogged (Chapter 2A or 2B)

Engine runs-on after switching off

- ☐ Excessive carbon build-up in engine (Chapter 2A or 2B)
- ☐ High engine operating temperature (Chapter 3)
- ☐ Fuel injection system fault (Chapter 4A or 4B)

Engine noises

Pre-ignition (pinking) or knocking during acceleration or under load

- ☐ Ignition timing incorrect/ignition system fault – petrol models (Chapter 1A or 5B)
- ☐ Incorrect grade of spark plug – petrol models (Chapter 1A)
- ☐ Incorrect grade of fuel (Chapter 4)
- ☐ Knock sensor faulty – petrol models (Chapter 4A)
- ☐ Vacuum leak at the throttle body, inlet manifold or associated hoses – petrol models (Chapter 4A)
- ☐ Excessive carbon build-up in engine (Chapter 2A, 2B or 2C)
- ☐ Blocked injector/fuel injection system fault (Chapter 4A or 4B)
- ☐ Faulty injector(s) – diesel models (Chapter 4B)

Whistling or wheezing noises

- ☐ Leaking inlet manifold or throttle body gasket – petrol models (Chapter 4A)
- ☐ Leaking exhaust manifold gasket or pipe-to-manifold joint (Chapter 4A or 4B)
- ☐ Leaking vacuum hose (Chapter 4A, 4B, 5B or 9)
- ☐ Blowing cylinder head gasket (Chapter 2A or 2B)
- ☐ Partially blocked or leaking crankcase ventilation system (Chapter 4C)

Tapping or rattling noises

- ☐ Valve clearances incorrect – some petrol models (Chapter 2A)
- ☐ Worn valve gear or camshaft (Chapter 2A or 2B)
- ☐ Ancillary component fault (coolant pump, alternator, etc) (Chapter 3, 5A, etc)

Knocking or thumping noises

- ☐ Worn big-end bearings (regular heavy knocking, perhaps less under load) (Chapter 2C)
- ☐ Worn main bearings (rumbling and knocking, perhaps worsening under load) (Chapter 2C)
- ☐ Piston slap – most noticeable when cold, caused by piston/bore wear (Chapter 2C)
- ☐ Ancillary component fault (coolant pump, alternator, etc) (Chapter 3, 5A, etc)
- ☐ Engine mountings worn or defective (Chapter 2A or 2B)
- ☐ Front suspension or steering components worn (Chapter 10)

Cooling system

Overheating

- [ ] Insufficient coolant in system (see Weekly checks)
- [ ] Thermostat faulty (Chapter 3)
- [ ] Radiator core blocked, or grille restricted (Chapter 3)
- [ ] Cooling fan faulty, or control module fault (Chapter 3)
- [ ] Inaccurate coolant temperature sender (Chapter 3)
- [ ] Airlock in cooling system (Chapter 3)
- [ ] Expansion tank pressure cap faulty (Chapter 3)
- [ ] Engine management system fault (Chapter 4A or 4B)

Overcooling

- [ ] Thermostat faulty (Chapter 3)
- [ ] Inaccurate coolant temperature sender (Chapter 3)
- [ ] Cooling fan faulty (Chapter 3)
- [ ] Engine management system fault (Chapter 4A or 4B)

External coolant leakage

- [ ] Deteriorated or damaged hoses or hose clips (Chapter 1A or 1B)
- [ ] Radiator core or heater matrix leaking (Chapter 3)
- [ ] Expansion tank pressure cap faulty (Chapter 1A or 1B)
- [ ] Coolant pump internal seal leaking (Chapter 3)
- [ ] Coolant pump gasket leaking (Chapter 3)
- [ ] Boiling due to overheating (Chapter 3)
- [ ] Cylinder block core plug leaking (Chapter 2C)

Internal coolant leakage

- [ ] Leaking cylinder head gasket (Chapter 2A or 2B)
- [ ] Cracked cylinder head or cylinder block (Chapter 2)

Corrosion

- [ ] Infrequent draining and flushing (Chapter 1A or 1B)
- [ ] Incorrect coolant mixture or inappropriate coolant type (see Weekly checks)

Fuel and exhaust systems

Excessive fuel consumption

- [ ] Air filter element dirty or clogged (Chapter 1A or 1B)
- [ ] Fuel injection system fault (Chapter 4A or 4B)
- [ ] Engine management system fault (Chapter 4A or 4B)
- [ ] Crankcase ventilation system blocked (Chapter 4C)
- [ ] Tyres under-inflated (see Weekly checks)
- [ ] Brakes binding (Chapter 1A, 1B or 9)
- [ ] Fuel leak, causing apparent high consumption (Chapter 1A, 1B, 4A or 4B)

Fuel leakage and/or fuel odour

- [ ] Damaged or corroded fuel tank, pipes or connections (Chapter 4A or 4B)
- [ ] Evaporative emissions system fault – petrol models (Chapter 4C)

Excessive noise or fumes from exhaust system

- [ ] Leaking exhaust system or manifold joints (Chapter 1A, 1B, 4A or 4B)
- [ ] Leaking, corroded or damaged silencers or pipe (Chapter 1A, 1B, 4A or 4B)
- [ ] Broken mountings causing body or suspension contact (Chapter 1A or 1B)

Clutch

Pedal travels to floor – no pressure or very little resistance

- [ ] Air in hydraulic system/faulty master or slave cylinder (Chapter 6)
- [ ] Faulty hydraulic release system (Chapter 6)
- [ ] Clutch pedal return spring detached or broken (Chapter 6)
- [ ] Broken clutch release bearing or fork (Chapter 6)
- [ ] Broken diaphragm spring in clutch pressure plate (Chapter 6)

Clutch fails to disengage (unable to select gears)

- [ ] Air in hydraulic system/faulty master or slave cylinder (Chapter 6)
- [ ] Faulty hydraulic release system (Chapter 6)
- [ ] Clutch disc sticking on transmission input shaft splines (Chapter 6)
- [ ] Clutch disc sticking to flywheel or pressure plate (Chapter 6)
- [ ] Faulty pressure plate assembly (Chapter 6)
- [ ] Clutch release mechanism worn or incorrectly assembled (Chapter 6)

Clutch slips (engine speed increases, with no increase in vehicle speed)

- [ ] Faulty hydraulic release system (Chapter 6)
- [ ] Clutch disc linings excessively worn (Chapter 6)
- [ ] Clutch disc linings contaminated with oil or grease (Chapter 6)
- [ ] Faulty pressure plate or weak diaphragm spring (Chapter 6)

Judder as clutch is engaged

- [ ] Clutch disc linings contaminated with oil or grease (Chapter 6)
- [ ] Clutch disc linings excessively worn (Chapter 6)
- [ ] Faulty or distorted pressure plate or diaphragm spring (Chapter 6).
- [ ] Worn or loose engine or transmission mountings (Chapter 2A or 2B)
- [ ] Clutch disc hub or transmission input shaft splines worn (Chapter 6)

Noise when depressing or releasing clutch pedal

- [ ] Worn clutch release bearing (Chapter 6)
- [ ] Worn or dry clutch pedal bushes (Chapter 6)
- [ ] Worn or dry clutch master cylinder piston (Chapter 6)
- [ ] Faulty pressure plate assembly (Chapter 6)
- [ ] Pressure plate diaphragm spring broken (Chapter 6)
- [ ] Broken clutch disc cushioning springs (Chapter 6)

Manual transmission

Noisy in neutral with engine running

- [ ] Lack of oil (Chapter 1A or 1B)
- [ ] Input shaft bearings worn (noise apparent with clutch pedal released, but not when depressed) (Chapter 7A)*
- [ ] Clutch release bearing worn (noise apparent with clutch pedal depressed, possibly less when released) (Chapter 6)

Noisy in one particular gear

- [ ] Worn, damaged or chipped gear teeth (Chapter 7A)*

Difficulty engaging gears

- [ ] Clutch fault (Chapter 6)
- [ ] Worn or damaged gearchange cables (Chapter 7A)
- [ ] Lack of oil (Chapter 7A)
- [ ] Worn synchroniser units (Chapter 7A)*

Jumps out of gear

- [ ] Worn or damaged gearchange cables (Chapter 7A)
- [ ] Worn synchroniser units (Chapter 7A)*
- [ ] Worn selector forks (Chapter 7A)*

Vibration

- [ ] Lack of oil (Chapter 7A)
- [ ] Worn bearings (Chapter 7A)*

Lubricant leaks

- [ ] Leaking driveshaft or selector shaft oil seal (Chapter 7A)
- [ ] Leaking housing joint (Chapter 7A)*
- [ ] Leaking input shaft oil seal (Chapter 7A)*

Although the corrective action necessary to remedy the symptoms described is beyond the scope of the home mechanic, the above information should be helpful in isolating the cause of the condition, so that the owner can communicate clearly with a professional mechanic.

Automatic transmission

Note: *Due to the complexity of the automatic transmission, it is difficult for the home mechanic to properly diagnose and service this unit. For problems other than the following, the vehicle should be taken to a dealer service department or automatic transmission specialist. Do not be too hasty in removing the transmission if a fault is suspected, as most of the testing is carried out with the unit still fitted. Remember that, besides the sensors specific to the transmission, many of the engine management system sensors described in Chapter 4 are essential to the correct operation of the transmission.*

Fluid leakage

- [ ] Automatic transmission fluid is usually dark red in colour. Fluid leaks should not be confused with engine oil, which can easily be blown onto the transmission by airflow.
- [ ] To determine the source of a leak, first remove all built-up dirt and grime from the transmission housing and surrounding areas using a degreasing agent, or by steam-cleaning. Drive the vehicle at low speed, so airflow will not blow the leak far from its source. Raise and support the vehicle, and determine where the leak is coming from. The following are common areas of leakage:
  - a) Fluid pan
  - b) Dipstick tube (Chapter 1A)
  - c) Transmission-to-fluid cooler unions (Chapter 7B)

Transmission fluid brown, or has burned smell

- [ ] Transmission fluid level low (Chapter 1)

General gear selection problems

- [ ] Chapter 7B deals with checking the selector cable on automatic transmissions. The following are common problems which may be caused by a faulty cable or sensor:

a) Engine starting in gears other than Park or Neutral.
b) Indicator panel indicating a gear other than the one actually being used.
c) Vehicle moves when in Park or Neutral.
d) Poor gear shift quality or erratic gear changes.

Transmission will not downshift (kickdown) with accelerator pedal fully depressed

- [ ] Low transmission fluid level (Chapter 1)
- [ ] Engine management system fault (Chapter 4)
- [ ] Faulty transmission sensor or wiring (Chapter 7B)
- [ ] Faulty selector cable (Chapter 7B)

Engine will not start in any gear, or starts in gears other than Park or Neutral

- [ ] Faulty transmission sensor or wiring (Chapter 7B)
- [ ] Engine management system fault (Chapter 4)
- [ ] Faulty selector cable (Chapter 7B)

Transmission slips, shifts roughly, is noisy, or has no drive in forward or reverse gears

- [ ] Transmission fluid level low (Chapter 1)
- [ ] Faulty transmission sensor or wiring (Chapter 7B)
- [ ] Engine management system fault (Chapter 4)

Note: *There are many probable causes for the above problems, but diagnosing and correcting them is considered beyond the scope of this manual. Having checked the fluid level and all the wiring as far as possible, a dealer or transmission specialist should be consulted if the problem persists.*

Driveshafts

Vibration when accelerating or decelerating

- [ ] Worn inner constant velocity joint (Chapter 8)
- [ ] Bent or distorted driveshaft (Chapter 8)
- [ ] Worn intermediate bearing (Chapter 8)

Clicking or knocking noise on turns (at slow speed on full-lock)

- [ ] Worn outer constant velocity joint (Chapter 8)
- [ ] Lack of constant velocity joint lubricant, possibly due to damaged gaiter (Chapter 8)
- [ ] Worn intermediate bearing (Chapter 8)

Braking system

Note: *Before assuming that a brake problem exists, make sure that the tyres are in good condition and correctly inflated, that the front wheel alignment is correct, and that the vehicle is not loaded with weight in an unequal manner. Apart from checking the condition of all pipe and hose connections, any faults occurring on the anti-lock braking system should be referred to a Volvo dealer or specialist for diagnosis.*

Vehicle pulls to one side under braking

- [ ] Worn, defective, damaged or contaminated brake pads on one side (Chapter 1A, 1B or 9)
- [ ] Seized or partially-seized brake caliper piston (Chapter 1A, 1B or 9)
- [ ] A mixture of brake pad lining materials fitted between sides (Chapter 1A, 1B or 9)
- [ ] Brake caliper mounting bolts loose (Chapter 9)
- [ ] Worn or damaged steering or suspension components (Chapter 1A, 1B or 10)

Noise (grinding or high-pitched squeal) when brakes applied

- [ ] Brake pad friction lining material worn down to metal backing (Chapter 1A, 1B or 9)
- [ ] Excessive corrosion of brake disc (may be apparent after the vehicle has been standing for some time (Chapter 1A, 1B or 9)
- [ ] Foreign object (stone chipping, etc) trapped between brake disc and shield (Chapter 1A, 1B or 9)

Excessive brake pedal travel

- [ ] Faulty master cylinder (Chapter 9)
- [ ] Air in hydraulic system (Chapter 1A, 1B, 6 or 9)
- [ ] Faulty vacuum servo unit (Chapter 9)

Brake pedal feels spongy when depressed

- [ ] Air in hydraulic system (Chapter 1A, 1B, 6 or 9)
- [ ] Deteriorated flexible rubber brake hoses (Chapter 1A, 1B or 9)
- [ ] Master cylinder mounting nuts loose (Chapter 9)
- [ ] Faulty master cylinder (Chapter 9)

Excessive brake pedal effort required to stop vehicle

- [ ] Faulty vacuum servo unit (Chapter 9)
- [ ] Faulty vacuum pump – diesel models (Chapter 9)
- [ ] Disconnected, damaged or insecure brake servo vacuum hose (Chapter 9)
- [ ] Primary or secondary hydraulic circuit failure (Chapter 9)
- [ ] Seized brake caliper piston (Chapter 9)
- [ ] Brake pads incorrectly fitted (Chapter 9)
- [ ] Incorrect grade of brake pads fitted (Chapter 9)
- [ ] Brake pad linings contaminated (Chapter 1A, 1B or 9)

Judder felt through brake pedal or steering wheel when braking

Note: *Under heavy braking on models equipped with ABS, vibration may be felt through the brake pedal. This is a normal feature of ABS operation, and does not constitute a fault*

- [ ] Excessive run-out or distortion of discs (Chapter 1A, 1B or 9)
- [ ] Brake pad linings worn (Chapter 1A, 1B or 9)
- [ ] Brake caliper mounting bolts loose (Chapter 9)
- [ ] Wear in suspension or steering components or mountings (Chapter 1A, 1B or 10)
- [ ] Front wheels out of balance *(see Weekly checks)*

Brakes binding

- [ ] Seized brake caliper piston (Chapter 9)
- [ ] Incorrectly-adjusted handbrake mechanism (Chapter 9)
- [ ] Faulty master cylinder (Chapter 9)

Rear wheels locking under normal braking

- [ ] Rear brake pad linings contaminated or damaged (Chapter 1 or 9)
- [ ] Rear brake discs warped (Chapter 1A, 1B or 9)

Suspension and steering

Note: *Before diagnosing suspension or steering faults, be sure that the trouble is not due to incorrect tyre pressures, mixtures of tyre types, or binding brakes.*

Vehicle pulls to one side

☐ Defective tyre *(see Weekly checks)*
☐ Excessive wear in suspension or steering components (Chapter 1A, 1B or 10)
☐ Incorrect front wheel alignment (Chapter 10)
☐ Accident damage to steering or suspension components (Chapter 1A or 1B)

Wheel wobble and vibration

☐ Front wheels out of balance (vibration felt mainly through the steering wheel) *(see Weekly checks)*
☐ Rear wheels out of balance (vibration felt throughout the vehicle) *(see Weekly checks)*
☐ Roadwheels damaged or distorted *(see Weekly checks)*
☐ Faulty or damaged tyre *(see Weekly checks)*
☐ Worn steering or suspension joints, bushes or components (Chapter 1A, 1B or 10)
☐ Wheel bolts loose (Chapter 1A or 1B)

Excessive pitching and/or rolling around corners, or during braking

☐ Defective shock absorbers (Chapter 1A, 1B or 10)
☐ Broken or weak spring and/or suspension component (Chapter 1A, 1B or 10)
☐ Worn or damaged anti-roll bar or mountings (Chapter 1A, 1B or 10)

Wandering or general instability

☐ Incorrect front wheel alignment (Chapter 10)
☐ Worn steering or suspension joints, bushes or components (Chapter 1A, 1B or 10)
☐ Roadwheels out of balance *(see Weekly checks)*
☐ Faulty or damaged tyre *(see Weekly checks)*
☐ Wheel bolts loose (Chapter 1A or 1B)
☐ Defective shock absorbers (Chapter 1A, 1B or 10)

Excessively-stiff steering

☐ Seized steering linkage balljoint or suspension balljoint (Chapter 1A, 1B or 10)

☐ Broken or incorrectly-adjusted auxiliary drivebelt (Chapter 1A or 1B)
☐ Incorrect front wheel alignment (Chapter 10)
☐ Steering rack damaged (Chapter 10)

Excessive play in steering

☐ Worn steering column/intermediate shaft joints (Chapter 10)
☐ Worn track rod balljoints (Chapter 1A, 1B or 10)
☐ Worn steering rack (Chapter 10)
☐ Worn steering or suspension joints, bushes or components (Chapter 1A, 1B or 10)

Lack of power assistance

☐ Broken or incorrectly-adjusted auxiliary drivebelt (Chapter 1A or 1B)
☐ Incorrect power steering fluid level *(see Weekly checks)*
☐ Restriction in power steering fluid hoses (Chapter 1A or 1B)
☐ Faulty power steering pump (Chapter 10)
☐ Faulty steering rack (Chapter 10)

Tyre wear excessive

Tyres worn on inside or outside edges

☐ Tyres under-inflated (wear on both edges) *(see Weekly checks)*
☐ Incorrect camber or castor angles (wear on one edge only) (Chapter 10)
☐ Worn steering or suspension joints, bushes or components (Chapter 1A, 1B or 10)
☐ Excessively-hard cornering or braking
☐ Accident damage

Tyre treads exhibit feathered edges

☐ Incorrect toe-setting (Chapter 10)

Tyres worn in centre of tread

☐ Tyres over-inflated *(see Weekly checks)*

Tyres worn on inside and outside edges

☐ Tyres under-inflated *(see Weekly checks)*

Tyres worn unevenly

☐ Tyres/wheels out of balance *(see Weekly checks)*
☐ Excessive wheel or tyre run-out
☐ Worn shock absorbers (Chapter 1A, 1B or 10)
☐ Faulty tyre *(see Weekly checks)*

Electrical system

Note: *For problems associated with the starting system, refer to the faults listed under 'Engine' earlier in this Section.*

Battery will not hold a charge for more than a few days

☐ Battery defective internally (Chapter 5A)
☐ Battery terminal connections loose or corroded *(see Weekly checks)*
☐ Auxiliary drivebelt worn or incorrectly adjusted (Chapter 1A or 1B)
☐ Alternator not charging at correct output (Chapter 5A)
☐ Alternator or voltage regulator faulty (Chapter 5A)
☐ Short-circuit causing continual battery drain (Chapter 5A or 12)

Ignition/no-charge warning light remains illuminated with engine running

☐ Auxiliary drivebelt broken, worn, or incorrectly adjusted (Chapter 1A or 1B)
☐ Internal fault in alternator or voltage regulator (Chapter 5A)
☐ Broken, disconnected, or loose wiring in charging circuit (Chapter 5A or 12)

Ignition/no-charge warning light fails to come on

☐ Warning light bulb blown (Chapter 12)
☐ Broken, disconnected, or loose wiring in warning light circuit (Chapter 5A or 12)
☐ Alternator faulty (Chapter 5A)

Electrical system (continued)

Lights inoperative

- ☐ Bulb blown (Chapter 12)
- ☐ Corrosion of bulb or bulbholder contacts (Chapter 12)
- ☐ Blown fuse (Chapter 12)
- ☐ Faulty relay (Chapter 12)
- ☐ Broken, loose, or disconnected wiring (Chapter 12)
- ☐ Faulty switch (Chapter 12)

Instrument readings inaccurate or erratic

Fuel or temperature gauges give no reading

- ☐ Faulty gauge sender unit (Chapter 3, 4A or 4B)
- ☐ Wiring open-circuit (Chapter 12)
- ☐ Faulty instrument cluster (Chapter 12)

Fuel or temperature gauges give continuous maximum reading

- ☐ Faulty gauge sender unit (Chapter 3, 4A or 4B)
- ☐ Wiring short-circuit (Chapter 12)
- ☐ Faulty instrument cluster (Chapter 12)

Horn inoperative, or unsatisfactory in operation

Horn operates all the time

- ☐ Horn push either earthed or stuck down (Chapter 12)
- ☐ Horn cable-to-horn push earthed (Chapter 12)

Horn fails to operate

- ☐ Blown fuse (Chapter 12)
- ☐ Cable or connections loose, broken or disconnected (Chapter 12)
- ☐ Faulty horn (Chapter 12)

Horn emits intermittent or unsatisfactory sound

- ☐ Cable connections loose (Chapter 12)
- ☐ Horn mountings loose (Chapter 12)
- ☐ Faulty horn (Chapter 12)

Windscreen wipers inoperative, or unsatisfactory in operation

Wipers fail to operate, or operate very slowly

- ☐ Wiper blades stuck to screen, or linkage seized or binding (Chapter 12)
- ☐ Blown fuse (Chapter 12)
- ☐ Battery discharged (Chapter 5A)
- ☐ Cable or connections loose, broken or disconnected (Chapter 12)
- ☐ Faulty wiper motor (Chapter 12)

Wiper blades sweep over too large or too small an area of the glass

- ☐ Wiper blades incorrectly fitted, or wrong size used (see Weekly checks)
- ☐ Wiper arms incorrectly positioned on spindles (Chapter 12)
- ☐ Excessive wear of wiper linkage (Chapter 12)
- ☐ Wiper motor or linkage mountings loose or insecure (Chapter 12)

Wiper blades fail to clean the glass effectively

- ☐ Wiper blade rubbers dirty, worn or perished (see Weekly checks)
- ☐ Wiper blades incorrectly fitted, or wrong size used (see Weekly checks)
- ☐ Wiper arm tension springs broken, or arm pivots seized (Chapter 12)
- ☐ Insufficient windscreen washer additive to adequately remove road film (see Weekly checks)

Windscreen washers inoperative, or unsatisfactory in operation

One or more washer jets inoperative

- ☐ Blocked washer jet
- ☐ Disconnected, kinked or restricted fluid hose (Chapter 12)
- ☐ Insufficient fluid in washer reservoir (see Weekly checks)

Washer pump fails to operate

- ☐ Broken or disconnected wiring or connections (Chapter 12)
- ☐ Blown fuse (Chapter 12)
- ☐ Faulty washer switch (Chapter 12)
- ☐ Faulty washer pump (Chapter 12)

Washer pump runs for some time before fluid is emitted from jets

- ☐ Faulty one-way valve in fluid supply hose (Chapter 12)

Electric windows inoperative, or unsatisfactory in operation

Window glass will only move in one direction

- ☐ Faulty switch (Chapter 12)

Window glass slow to move

- ☐ Battery discharged (Chapter 5A)
- ☐ Regulator seized or damaged, or in need of lubrication (Chapter 11)
- ☐ Door internal components or trim fouling regulator (Chapter 11)
- ☐ Faulty motor (Chapter 11)

Window glass fails to move

- ☐ Blown fuse (Chapter 12)
- ☐ Faulty relay (Chapter 12)
- ☐ Broken or disconnected wiring or connections (Chapter 12)
- ☐ Faulty motor (Chapter 11)
- ☐ Faulty control module (Chapter 11)

Central locking system inoperative, or unsatisfactory in operation

Complete system failure

- ☐ Remote handset battery discharged, where applicable
- ☐ Blown fuse (Chapter 12)
- ☐ Defective control module (Chapter 12)
- ☐ Broken or disconnected wiring or connections (Chapter 12)
- ☐ Faulty motor (Chapter 11)

Latch locks but will not unlock, or unlocks but will not lock

- ☐ Remote handset battery discharged, where applicable
- ☐ Faulty master switch (Chapter 12)
- ☐ Broken or disconnected latch operating rods or levers (Chapter 11)
- ☐ Faulty control module (Chapter 12)
- ☐ Faulty motor (Chapter 11)

One solenoid/motor fails to operate

- ☐ Broken or disconnected wiring or connections (Chapter 12)
- ☐ Faulty operating assembly (Chapter 11)
- ☐ Broken, binding or disconnected latch operating rods or levers (Chapter 11)
- ☐ Fault in door latch (Chapter 11)

Note: *References throughout this index are in the form* "**Chapter number**" • "**Page number**". *So, for example, 2C•15 refers to page 15 of Chapter 2C.*

Note: References throughout this index are in the form "Chapter number" • "Page number". So, for example, 2C•15 refers to page 15 of Chapter 2C.

Note: *References throughout this index are in the form "**Chapter number**" • "**Page number**". So, for example, 2C•15 refers to page 15 of Chapter 2C.*

Haynes Manuals – The Complete UK Car List

Title	Book No.
ALFA ROMEO Alfasud/Sprint (74 - 88) up to F *	0292
Alfa Romeo Alfetta (73 - 87) up to E *	0531
AUDI 80, 90 & Coupe Petrol (79 - Nov 88) up to F	0605
Audi 80, 90 & Coupe Petrol (Oct 86 - 90) D to H	1491
Audi 100 & 200 Petrol (Oct 82 - 90) up to H	0907
Audi 100 & A6 Petrol & Diesel (May 91 - May 97) H to P	3504
Audi A3 Petrol & Diesel (96 - May 03) P to 03	4253
Audi A4 Petrol & Diesel (95 - 00) M to X	3575
Audi A4 Petrol & Diesel (01 - 04) X to 54	4609
AUSTIN A35 & A40 (56 - 67) up to F *	0118
Austin/MG/Rover Maestro 1.3 & 1.6 Petrol (83 - 95) up to M	0922
Austin/MG Metro (80 - May 90) up to G	0718
Austin/Rover Montego 1.3 & 1.6 Petrol (84 - 94) A to L	1066
Austin/MG/Rover Montego 2.0 Petrol (84 - 95) A to M	1067
Mini (59 - 69) up to H *	0527
Mini (69 - 01) up to X	0646
Austin/Rover 2.0 litre Diesel Engine (86 - 93) C to L	1857
Austin Healey 100/6 & 3000 (56 - 68) up to G *	0049
BEDFORD CF Petrol (69 - 87) up to E	0163
Bedford/Vauxhall Rascal & Suzuki Supercarry (86 - Oct 94) C to M	3015
BMW 316, 320 & 320i (4-cyl) (75 - Feb 83) up to Y *	0276
BMW 320, 320i, 323i & 325i (6-cyl) (Oct 77 - Sept 87) up to E	0815
BMW 3- & 5-Series Petrol (81 - 91) up to J	1948
BMW 3-Series Petrol (Apr 91 - 99) H to V	3210
BMW 3-Series Petrol (Sept 98 - 03) S to 53	4067
BMW 520i & 525e (Oct 81 - June 88) up to E	1560
BMW 525, 528 & 528i (73 - Sept 81) up to X *	0632
BMW 5-Series 6-cyl Petrol (April 96 - Aug 03) N to 03	4151
BMW 1500, 1502, 1600, 1602, 2000 & 2002 (59 - 77) up to S *	0240
CHRYSLER PT Cruiser Petrol (00 - 03) W to 53	4058
CITROËN 2CV, Ami & Dyane (67 - 90) up to H	0196
Citroën AX Petrol & Diesel (87 - 97) D to P	3014
Citroën Berlingo & Peugeot Partner Petrol & Diesel (96 - 05) P to 55	4281
Citroën BX Petrol (83 - 94) A to L	0908
Citroën C15 Van Petrol & Diesel (89 - Oct 98) F to S	3509
Citroën C3 Petrol & Diesel (02 - 05) 51 to 05	4197
Citroën CX Petrol (75 - 88) up to F	0528
Citroën Saxo Petrol & Diesel (96 - 04) N to 54	3506
Citroën Visa Petrol (79 - 88) up to F	0620
Citroën Xantia Petrol & Diesel (93 - 01) K to Y	3082
Citroën XM Petrol & Diesel (89 - 00) G to X	3451
Citroën Xsara Petrol & Diesel (97 - Sept 00) R to W	3751
Citroën Xsara Picasso Petrol & Diesel (00 - 02) W to 52	3944
Citroën ZX Diesel (91 - 98) J to S	1922
Citroën ZX Petrol (91 - 98) H to S	1881
Citroën 1.7 & 1.9 litre Diesel Engine (84 - 96) A to N	1379
FIAT 126 (73 - 87) up to E *	0305
Fiat 500 (57 - 73) up to M *	0090
Fiat Bravo & Brava Petrol (95 - 00) N to W	3572
Fiat Cinquecento (93 - 98) K to R	3501
Fiat Panda (81 - 95) up to M	0793
Fiat Punto Petrol & Diesel (94 - Oct 99) L to V	3251
Fiat Punto Petrol (Oct 99 - July 03) V to 03	4066
Fiat Regata Petrol (84 - 88) A to F	1167
Fiat Tipo Petrol (88 - 91) E to J	1625
Fiat Uno Petrol (83 - 95) up to M	0923
Fiat X1/9 (74 - 89) up to G *	0273
FORD Anglia (59 - 68) up to G *	0001
Ford Capri II (& III) 1.6 & 2.0 (74 - 87) up to E *	0283
Ford Capri II (& III) 2.8 & 3.0 V6 (74 - 87) up to E	1309

Title	Book No.
Ford Cortina Mk I & Corsair 1500 ('62 - '66) up to D*	0214
Ford Cortina Mk III 1300 & 1600 (70 - 76) up to P *	0070
Ford Escort Mk I 1100 & 1300 (68 - 74) up to N *	0171
Ford Escort Mk I Mexico, RS 1600 & RS 2000 (70 - 74) up to N *	0139
Ford Escort Mk II Mexico, RS 1800 & RS 2000 (75 - 80) up to W *	0735
Ford Escort (75 - Aug 80) up to V *	0280
Ford Escort Petrol (Sept 80 - Sept 90) up to H	0686
Ford Escort & Orion Petrol (Sept 90 - 00) H to X	1737
Ford Escort & Orion Diesel (Sept 90 - 00) H to X	4081
Ford Fiesta (76 - Aug 83) up to Y	0334
Ford Fiesta Petrol (Aug 83 - Feb 89) A to F	1030
Ford Fiesta Petrol (Feb 89 - Oct 95) F to N	1595
Ford Fiesta Petrol & Diesel (Oct 95 - Mar 02) N to 02	3397
Ford Fiesta Petrol & Diesel (Apr 02 - 05) 02 to 54	4170
Ford Focus Petrol & Diesel (98 - 01) S to Y	3759
Ford Focus Petrol & Diesel (Oct 01 - 05) 51 to 05	4167
Ford Galaxy Petrol & Diesel (95 - Aug 00) M to W	3984
Ford Granada Petrol (Sept 77 - Feb 85) up to B *	0481
Ford Granada & Scorpio Petrol (Mar 85 - 94) B to M	1245
Ford Ka (96 - 02) P to 52	3570
Ford Mondeo Petrol (93 - Sept 00) K to X	1923
Ford Mondeo Petrol & Diesel (Oct 00 - Jul 03) X to 03	3990
Ford Mondeo Petrol & Diesel (July 03 - 07) 03 to 56	4619
Ford Mondeo Diesel (93 - 96) L to N	3465
Ford Orion Petrol (83 - Sept 90) up to H	1009
Ford Sierra 4-cyl Petrol (82 - 93) up to K	0903
Ford Sierra V6 Petrol (82 - 91) up to J	0904
Ford Transit Petrol (Mk 2) (78 - Jan 86) up to C	0719
Ford Transit Petrol (Mk 3) (Feb 86 - 89) C to G	1468
Ford Transit Diesel (Feb 86 - 99) C to T	3019
Ford 1.6 & 1.8 litre Diesel Engine (84 - 96) A to N	1172
Ford 2.1, 2.3 & 2.5 litre Diesel Engine (77 - 90) up to H	1606
FREIGHT ROVER Sherpa Petrol (74 - 87) up to E	0463
HILLMAN Avenger (70 - 82) up to Y	0037
Hillman Imp (63 - 76) up to R *	0022
HONDA Civic (Feb 84 - Oct 87) A to E	1226
Honda Civic (Nov 91 - 96) J to N	3199
Honda Civic Petrol (Mar 95 - 00) M to X	4050
Honda Civic Petrol & Diesel (01 - 05) X to 55	4611
Honda Jazz (01 - Feb 08) 51 - 57	4735
HYUNDAI Pony (85 - 94) C to M	3398
JAGUAR E Type (61 - 72) up to L *	0140
Jaguar MkI & II, 240 & 340 (55 - 69) up to H *	0098
Jaguar XJ6, XJ & Sovereign; Daimler Sovereign (68 - Oct 86) up to D	0242
Jaguar XJ6 & Sovereign (Oct 86 - Sept 94) D to M	3261
Jaguar XJ12, XJS & Sovereign; Daimler Double Six (72 - 88) up to F	0478
JEEP Cherokee Petrol (93 - 96) K to N	1943
LADA 1200, 1300, 1500 & 1600 (74 - 91) up to J	0413
Lada Samara (87 - 91) D to J	1610
LAND ROVER 90, 110 & Defender Diesel (83 - 07) up to 56	3017
Land Rover Discovery Petrol & Diesel (89 - 98) G to S	3016
Land Rover Discovery Diesel (Nov 98 - Jul 04) S to 04	4606
Land Rover Freelander Petrol & Diesel (97 - Sept 03) R to 53	3929
Land Rover Freelander Petrol & Diesel (Oct 03 - Oct 06) 53 to 56	4623
Land Rover Series IIA & III Diesel (58 - 85) up to C	0529
Land Rover Series II, IIA & III 4-cyl Petrol (58 - 85) up to C	0314

Title	Book No.
MAZDA 323 (Mar 81 - Oct 89) up to G	1608
Mazda 323 (Oct 89 - 98) G to R	3455
Mazda 626 (May 83 - Sept 87) up to E	0929
Mazda B1600, B1800 & B2000 Pick-up Petrol (72 - 88) up to F	0267
Mazda RX-7 (79 - 85) up to C *	0460
MERCEDES-BENZ 190, 190E & 190D Petrol & Diesel (83 - 93) A to L	3450
Mercedes-Benz 200D, 240D, 240TD, 300D & 300TD 123 Series Diesel (Oct 76 - 85)	1114
Mercedes-Benz 250 & 280 (68 - 72) up to L *	0346
Mercedes-Benz 250 & 280 123 Series Petrol (Oct 76 - 84) up to B *	0677
Mercedes-Benz 124 Series Petrol & Diesel (85 - Aug 93) C to K	3253
Mercedes-Benz C-Class Petrol & Diesel (93 - Aug 00) L to W	3511
MG A (55 - 62) *	0475
MGB (62 - 80) up to W	0111
MG Midget & Austin-Healey Sprite (58 - 80) up to W *	0265
MINI Petrol (July 01 - 05) Y to 05	4273
MITSUBISHI Shogun & L200 Pick-Ups Petrol (83 - 94) up to M	1944
MORRIS Ital 1.3 (80 - 84) up to B	0705
Morris Minor 1000 (56 - 71) up to K	0024
NISSAN Almera Petrol (95 - Feb 00) N to V	4053
Nissan Almera & Tino Petrol (Feb 00 - 07) V to 56	4612
Nissan Bluebird (May 84 - Mar 86) A to C	1223
Nissan Bluebird Petrol (Mar 86 - 90) C to H	1473
Nissan Cherry (Sept 82 - 86) up to D	1031
Nissan Micra (83 - Jan 93) up to K	0931
Nissan Micra (93 - 02) K to 52	3254
Nissan Primera Petrol (90 - Aug 99) H to T	1851
Nissan Stanza (82 - 86) up to D	0824
Nissan Sunny Petrol (May 82 - Oct 86) up to D	0895
Nissan Sunny Petrol (Oct 86 - Mar 91) D to H	1378
Nissan Sunny Petrol (Apr 91 - 95) H to N	3219
OPEL Ascona & Manta (B Series) (Sept 75 - 88) up to F *	0316
Opel Ascona Petrol (81 - 88)	3215
Opel Astra Petrol (Oct 91 - Feb 98)	3156
Opel Corsa Petrol (83 - Mar 93)	3160
Opel Corsa Petrol (Mar 93 - 97)	3159
Opel Kadett Petrol (Nov 79 - Oct 84) up to B	0634
Opel Kadett Petrol (Oct 84 - Oct 91)	3196
Opel Omega & Senator Petrol (Nov 86 - 94)	3157
Opel Rekord Petrol (Feb 78 - Oct 86) up to D	0543
Opel Vectra Petrol (Oct 88 - Oct 95)	3158
PEUGEOT 106 Petrol & Diesel (91 - 04) J to 53	1882
Peugeot 205 Petrol (83 - 97) A to P	0932
Peugeot 206 Petrol & Diesel (98 - 01) S to X	3757
Peugeot 206 Petrol & Diesel (02 - 06) 51 to 06	4613
Peugeot 306 Petrol & Diesel (93 - 02) K to 02	3073
Peugeot 307 Petrol & Diesel (01 - 04) Y to 54	4147
Peugeot 309 Petrol (86 - 93) C to K	1266
Peugeot 405 Petrol (88 - 97) E to P	1559
Peugeot 405 Diesel (88 - 97) E to P	3198
Peugeot 406 Petrol & Diesel (96 - Mar 99) N to T	3394
Peugeot 406 Petrol & Diesel (Mar 99 - 02) T to 52	3982
Peugeot 505 Petrol (79 - 89) up to G	0762
Peugeot 1.7/1.8 & 1.9 litre Diesel Engine (82 - 96) up to N	0950
Peugeot 2.0, 2.1, 2.3 & 2.5 litre Diesel Engines (74 - 90) up to H	1607
PORSCHE 911 (65 - 85) up to C	0264

* Classic reprint

Title	Book No.
Porsche 924 & 924 Turbo (76 - 85) up to C	0397
PROTON (89 - 97) F to P	3255
RANGE ROVER V8 Petrol (70 - Oct 92) up to K	0606
RELIANT Robin & Kitten (73 - 83) up to A *	0436
RENAULT 4 (61 - 86) up to D *	0072
Renault 5 Petrol (Feb 85 - 96) B to N	1219
Renault 9 & 11 Petrol (82 - 89) up to F	0822
Renault 18 Petrol (79 - 86) up to D	0598
Renault 19 Petrol (89 - 96) F to N	1646
Renault 19 Diesel (89 - 96) F to N	1946
Renault 21 Petrol (86 - 94) C to M	1397
Renault 25 Petrol & Diesel (84 - 92) B to K	1228
Renault Clio Petrol (91 - May 98) H to R	1853
Renault Clio Diesel (91 - June 96) H to N	3031
Renault Clio Petrol & Diesel (May 98 - May 01) R to Y	3906
Renault Clio Petrol & Diesel (June '01 - '05) Y to 55	4168
Renault Espace Petrol & Diesel (85 - 96) C to N	3197
Renault Laguna Petrol & Diesel (94 - 00) L to W	3252
Renault Laguna Petrol & Diesel (Feb 01 - Feb 05) X to 54	4283
Renault Mégane & Scénic Petrol & Diesel (96 - 99) N to T	3395
Renault Mégane & Scénic Petrol & Diesel (Apr 99 - 02) T to 52	3916
Renault Megane Petrol & Diesel (Oct 02 - 05) 52 to 55	4284
Renault Scenic Petrol & Diesel (Sept 03 - 06) 53 to 06	4297
ROVER 213 & 216 (84 - 89) A to G	1116
Rover 214 & 414 Petrol (89 - 96) G to N	1689
Rover 216 & 416 Petrol (89 - 96) G to N	1830
Rover 211, 214, 216, 218 & 220 Petrol & Diesel (Dec 95 - 99) N to V	3399
Rover 25 & MG ZR Petrol & Diesel (Oct 99 - 04) V to 54	4145
Rover 414, 416 & 420 Petrol & Diesel (May 95 - 98) M to R	3453
Rover 45 / MG ZS Petrol & Diesel (99 - 05) V to 55	4384
Rover 618, 620 & 623 Petrol (93 - 97) K to P	3257
Rover 75 / MG ZT Petrol & Diesel (99 - 06) S to 06	4292
Rover 820, 825 & 827 Petrol (86 - 95) D to N	1380
Rover 3500 (76 - 87) up to E *	0365
Rover Metro, 111 & 114 Petrol (May 90 - 98) G to S	1711
SAAB 95 & 96 (66 - 76) up to R *	0198
Saab 90, 99 & 900 (79 - Oct 93) up to L	0765
Saab 900 (Oct 93 - 98) L to R	3512
Saab 9000 (4-cyl) (85 - 98) C to S	1686
Saab 9-3 Petrol & Diesel (98 - Aug 02) R to 02	4614
Saab 9-5 4-cyl Petrol (97 - 04) R to 54	4156
SEAT Ibiza & Cordoba Petrol & Diesel (Oct 93 - Oct 99) L to V	3571
Seat Ibiza & Malaga Petrol (85 - 92) B to K	1609
SKODA Estelle (77 - 89) up to G	0604
Skoda Fabia Petrol & Diesel (00 - 06) W to 06	4376
Skoda Favorit (89 - 96) F to N	1801
Skoda Felicia Petrol & Diesel (95 - 01) M to X	3505
Skoda Octavia Petrol & Diesel (98 - Apr 04) R to 04	4285
SUBARU 1600 & 1800 (Nov 79 - 90) up to H *	0995
SUNBEAM Alpine, Rapier & H120 (67 - 74) up to N *	0051
SUZUKI SJ Series, Samurai & Vitara (4-cyl) Petrol (82 - 97) up to P	1942
Suzuki Supercarry & Bedford/Vauxhall Rascal (86 - Oct 94) C to M	3015
TALBOT Alpine, Solara, Minx & Rapier (75 - 86) up to D	0337

Title	Book No.
Talbot Horizon Petrol (78 - 86) up to D	0473
Talbot Samba (82 - 86) up to D	0823
TOYOTA Avensis Petrol (98 - Jan 03) R to 52	4264
Toyota Carina E Petrol (May 92 - 97) J to P	3256
Toyota Corolla (80 - 85) up to C	0683
Toyota Corolla (Sept 83 - Sept 87) A to E	1024
Toyota Corolla (Sept 87 - Aug 92) E to K	1683
Toyota Corolla Petrol (Aug 92 - 97) K to P	3259
Toyota Corolla Petrol (July 97 - Feb 02) P to 51	4286
Toyota Hi-Ace & Hi-Lux Petrol (69 - Oct 83) up to A	0304
Toyota Yaris Petrol (99 - 05) T to 05	4265
TRIUMPH GT6 & Vitesse (62 - 74) up to N *	0112
Triumph Herald (59 - 71) up to K *	0010
Triumph Spitfire (62 - 81) up to X	0113
Triumph Stag (70 - 78) up to T *	0441
Triumph TR2, TR3, TR3A, TR4 & TR4A (52 - 67) up to F *	0028
Triumph TR5 & 6 (67 - 75) up to P *	0031
Triumph TR7 (75 - 82) up to Y *	0322
VAUXHALL Astra Petrol (80 - Oct 84) up to B	0635
Vauxhall Astra & Belmont Petrol (Oct 84 - Oct 91) B to J	1136
Vauxhall Astra Petrol (Oct 91 - Feb 98) J to R	1832
Vauxhall/Opel Astra & Zafira Petrol (Feb 98 - Apr 04) R to 04	3758
Vauxhall/Opel Astra & Zafira Diesel (Feb 98 - Apr 04) R to 04	3797
Vauxhall/Opel Astra Petrol (04 - 07) 04 - 07	4732
Vauxhall/Opel Astra Diesel (04 - 07) 04 - 07	4733
Vauxhall/Opel Calibra (90 - 98) G to S	3502
Vauxhall Carlton Petrol (Oct 78 - Oct 86) up to D	0480
Vauxhall Carlton & Senator Petrol (Nov 86 - 94) D to L	1469
Vauxhall Cavalier Petrol (81 - Oct 88) up to F	0812
Vauxhall Cavalier Petrol (Oct 88 - 95) F to N	1570
Vauxhall Chevette (75 - 84) up to B	0285
Vauxhall/Opel Corsa Diesel (Mar 93 - Oct 00) K to X	4087
Vauxhall Corsa Petrol (Mar 93 - 97) K to R	1985
Vauxhall/Opel Corsa Petrol (Apr 97 - Oct 00) P to X	3921
Vauxhall/Opel Corsa Petrol & Diesel (Oct 00 - Sept 03) X to 53	4079
Vauxhall/Opel Corsa Petrol & Diesel (Oct 03 - Aug 06) 53 to 06	4617
Vauxhall/Opel Frontera Petrol & Diesel (91 - Sept 98) J to S	3454
Vauxhall Nova Petrol (83 - 93) up to K	0909
Vauxhall/Opel Omega Petrol (94 - 99) L to T	3510
Vauxhall/Opel Vectra Petrol & Diesel (95 - Feb 99) N to S	3396
Vauxhall/Opel Vectra Petrol & Diesel (Mar 99 - May 02) T to 02	3930
Vauxhall/Opel Vectra Petrol & Diesel (June 02 - Sept 05) 02 to 55	4618
Vauxhall/Opel 1.5, 1.6 & 1.7 litre Diesel Engine (82 - 96) up to N	1222
VW 411 & 412 (68 - 75) up to P *	0091
VW Beetle 1200 (54 - 77) up to S	0036
VW Beetle 1300 & 1500 (65 - 75) up to P	0039
VW 1302 & 1302S (70 - 72) up to L *	0110
VW Beetle 1303, 1303S & GT (72 - 75) up to P	0159
VW Beetle Petrol & Diesel (Apr 99 - 01) T to 51	3798
VW Golf & Jetta Mk 1 Petrol 1.1 & 1.3 (74 - 84) up to A	0716
VW Golf, Jetta & Scirocco Mk 1 Petrol 1.5, 1.6 & 1.8 (74 - 84) up to A	0726

Title	Book No.
VW Golf & Jetta Mk 1 Diesel (78 - 84) up to A	0451
VW Golf & Jetta Mk 2 Petrol (Mar 84 - Feb 92) A to J	1081
VW Golf & Vento Petrol & Diesel (Feb 92 - Mar 98) J to R	3097
VW Golf & Bora Petrol & Diesel (April 98 - 00) R to X	3727
VW Golf & Bora 4-cyl Petrol & Diesel (01 - 03) X to 53	4169
VW Golf & Jetta Petrol & Diesel (04 - 07) 53 to 07	4610
VW LT Petrol Vans & Light Trucks (76 - 87) up to E	0637
VW Passat & Santana Petrol (Sept 81 - May 88) up to E	0814
VW Passat 4-cyl Petrol & Diesel (May 88 - 96) E to P	3498
VW Passat 4-cyl Petrol & Diesel (Dec 96 - Nov 00) P to X	3917
VW Passat Petrol & Diesel (Dec 00 - May 05) X to 05	4279
VW Polo & Derby (76 - Jan 82) up to X	0335
VW Polo (82 - Oct 90) up to H	0813
VW Polo Petrol (Nov 90 - Aug 94) H to L	3245
VW Polo Hatchback Petrol & Diesel (94 - 99) M to S	3500
VW Polo Hatchback Petrol (00 - Jan 02) V to 51	4150
VW Polo Petrol & Diesel (02 - May 05) 51 to 05	4608
VW Scirocco (82 - 90) up to H *	1224
VW Transporter 1600 (68 - 79) up to V	0082
VW Transporter 1700, 1800 & 2000 (72 - 79) up to V *	0226
VW Transporter (air-cooled) Petrol (79 - 82) up to Y *	0638
VW Transporter (water-cooled) Petrol (82 - 90) up to H	3452
VW Type 3 (63 - 73) up to M *	0084
VOLVO 120 & 130 Series (& P1800) (61 - 73) up to M *	0203
Volvo 142, 144 & 145 (66 - 74) up to N *	0129
Volvo 240 Series Petrol (74 - 93) up to K	0270
Volvo 262, 264 & 260/265 (75 - 85) up to C *	0400
Volvo 340, 343, 345 & 360 (76 - 91) up to J	0715
Volvo 440, 460 & 480 Petrol (87 - 97) D to P	1691
Volvo 740 & 760 Petrol (82 - 91) up to J	1258
Volvo 850 Petrol (92 - 96) J to P	3260
Volvo 940 petrol (90 - 98) H to R	3249
Volvo S40 & V40 Petrol (96 - Mar 04) N to 04	3569
Volvo S40 & V50 Petrol & Diesel (Mar 04 - Jun 07) 04 to 07	4731
Volvo S70, V70 & C70 Petrol (96 - 99) P to V	3573
Volvo V70 / S80 Petrol & Diesel (98 - 05) S to 55	4263

AUTOMOTIVE TECHBOOKS

Title	Book No.
Automotive Electrical and Electronic Systems Manual	3049
Automotive Gearbox Overhaul Manual	3473
Automotive Service Summaries Manual	3475
Automotive Timing Belts Manual – Austin/Rover	3549
Automotive Timing Belts Manual – Ford	3474
Automotive Timing Belts Manual – Peugeot/Citroën	3568
Automotive Timing Belts Manual – Vauxhall/Opel	3577

DIY MANUAL SERIES

Title	Book No.
The Haynes Air Conditioning Manual	4192
The Haynes Car Electrical Systems Manual	4251
The Haynes Manual on Bodywork	4198
The Haynes Manual on Brakes	4178
The Haynes Manual on Carburettors	4177
The Haynes Manual on Diesel Engines	4174
The Haynes Manual on Engine Management	4199
The Haynes Manual on Fault Codes	4175
The Haynes Manual on Practical Electrical Systems	4267
The Haynes Manual on Small Engines	4250
The Haynes Manual on Welding	4176

* Classic reprint

CL23.12/07

Preserving Our Motoring Heritage

< The Model J Duesenberg Derham Tourster. Only eight of these magnificent cars were ever built – this is the only example to be found outside the United States of America

Almost every car you've ever loved, loathed or desired is gathered under one roof at the Haynes Motor Museum. Over 300 immaculately presented cars and motorbikes represent every aspect of our motoring heritage, from elegant reminders of bygone days, such as the superb Model J Duesenberg to curiosities like the bug-eyed BMW Isetta. There are also many old friends and flames. Perhaps you remember the 1959 Ford Popular that you did your courting in? The magnificent 'Red Collection' is a spectacle of classic sports cars including AC, Alfa Romeo, Austin Healey, Ferrari, Lamborghini, Maserati, MG, Riley, Porsche and Triumph.

A Perfect Day Out

Each and every vehicle at the Haynes Motor Museum has played its part in the history and culture of Motoring. Today, they make a wonderful spectacle and a great day out for all the family. Bring the kids, bring Mum and Dad, but above all bring your camera to capture those golden memories for ever. You will also find an impressive array of motoring memorabilia, a comfortable 70 seat video cinema and one of the most extensive transport book shops in Britain. The Pit Stop Cafe serves everything from a cup of tea to wholesome, home-made meals or, if you prefer, you can enjoy the large picnic area nestled in the beautiful rural surroundings of Somerset.

> John Haynes O.B.E., Founder and Chairman of the museum at the wheel of a Haynes Light 12.

< Graham Hill's Lola Cosworth Formula 1 car next to a 1934 Riley Sports.

The Museum is situated on the A359 Yeovil to Frome road at Sparkford, just off the A303 in Somerset. It is about 40 miles south of Bristol, and 25 minutes drive from the M5 intersection at Taunton.
Open 9.30am - 5.30pm (10.00am - 4.00pm Winter) 7 days a week, *except Christmas Day, Boxing Day and New Years Day*
Special rates available for schools, coach parties and outings Charitable Trust No. 292048